FROM NICAEA TO CHALCEDON

Frances M. Young

FROM NICAEA
TO CHALCEDON

A Guide to the Literature and
its Background

FORTRESS PRESS   PHILADELPHIA

Library of Congress Cataloging in Publication Data

Young, Frances M. (Frances Margaret)
  From Nicaea to Chalcedon.

  Bibliography: p.
  Includes index.
    1. Church history—Primitive and early church,
ca. 30–600.   2. Fathers of the church— Biography.
3. Christian literature, Early—History and criticism.
4. Theology, Doctrinal—History—Early church, ca. 30–600.
I. Title.
BR205.Y68   1983   270.2   83–1760
ISBN 0–8006–0711–2

K357D83   Printed in the United Kingdom   1–711

Contents

Contents

Preface

The period from Nicaea to Chalcedon is one of the most significant in the formation of the doctrine of the church. Yet the average student of Christian doctrine rarely gets to grips with the background or the literature of the period, let alone the theological argumentation to be found in the texts. It seems that those who use a standard text-book like that of J. N. D. Kelly, need a companion to provide background material, an introduction to the characters involved in the disputes, to the literary sources and the critical questions which they pose; the subject-matter of the traditional patrology needs more discursive presentation and the interpretative issues discussed by patristic scholars require communication to a wider audience. To provide this kind of material is the purpose of this guide book. It presents a series of essays on a number of significant literary figures, laymen, bishops and heretics of the fourth and fifth centuries, essays which offer biographical, literary-critical and theological information. Some are chosen for their importance in the history of doctrine, some because new material has thrown light upon their work, some because they will broaden the reader's understanding of the culture and history of the period or of live issues in the church at the time.

I hope in this way to have bridged several different approaches: the historian tends to see but a collection of warring prelates and hard-headed politicians, the biographer often borders on the hagiographical, the churchman is only interested in whether they were orthodox or not, the patristic scholar is immersed in critical questions, tracing fragments, establishing texts, and the historian of doctrine tends to flatten the characters into ciphers for particular doctrinal standpoints. Of course I exaggerate – but here is offered an attempt to bring together the fruits of these many different approaches and so put them all in a different perspective.

The guide is also intended to help the student with bibliography, though I have avoided duplicating the lists already available in the larger Patrologies. A number of standard works and articles are referred to in the Notes, but they are not listed elsewhere. Two bibliographical lists, selected on quite different principles have been provided. Bibliography A lists only works in English – for there are now so many undergraduates overawed by the suggestion that they should tackle books in foreign languages, that it seemed vital to meet their needs. Bibliography B is intended for the more advanced student, to update Quasten at least for those Fathers included in the book; it lists those publications in English, French and German which have appeared since 1960. The original collection of material was drawn up by my research student, Mrs Judith Lieu, whose assistance has been invaluable. I must express here my gratitude for her methodical search of catalogues, bibliographies and indexes in the Bodleian library. I have subsequently checked up on practically every item listed. There may well be some significant items that have slipped through the net, but the budding research student should be able to make a start here and expand the bibliography further for himself.

I am very grateful for the advice and support of Professor Maurice Wiles, who has read the whole in typescript and made a number of valuable comments. The errors which remain are mine. Experts on each subject treated will no doubt easily detect shortcomings. All I can do is offer the excuse that only the finest scholars can encompass more than a very small area in depth. I have endeavoured to learn from the experts as far as possible.

I am grateful for hours of practical assistance with proofs and indexing from Alan Morrison, Duncan Rayner and Deborah Ford, and for the diligence of Jean Cunningham of SCM Press in preparing an exceedingly complex typescript for the printer.

Frances M. Young

Abbreviations

Chapter One

The Birth of Church History and its Sequel

I. Eusebius of Caesarea

Eusebius sums up an age of transition. His works reflect the church's movement from being a persecuted minority to being the dominant faith of the Roman empire, in terms of influence if not yet numbers. It was perhaps the perfect moment for 'the father of church history' to take up his pen. It was the end of one era, the start of another.

It is natural to think of Eusebius as belonging to the fourth century; for its early decades saw the production of all his literary output. Besides he was involved in the deliberations of Nicaea and subsequent events. In many ways, however, Eusebius reflects the problems and presuppositions of the third century. In all his work an apologetic purpose can be discerned, and in spite of moving eagerly with political developments, he was not open in his theological thinking to the new demands and difficulties of the Arian controversy.

However, this in itself makes him a more interesting figure. We can be pretty sure that he spoke for a solid mass of conservative churchmen, facing with dread and uncertainty the apparent innovations to their faith, yet welcoming with sincere idealism the conversion of the emperor and the triumph of the church. In the pages of his works we meet popular Origenism, the faith of the ordinary educated Christian, not very sophisticated or profound, and surprisingly literal-minded in its approach to scripture and doctrine. In his actions we may see compromise, but if so it was probably born out of a genuine desire for the preservation of the traditional faith and the unity of the church.

1. Life

Surprisingly little is known of Eusebius' life. He seems to have been born in the early 260s, probably in Palestinian Caesarea, which remained his home throughout his life. Caesarea had been Origen's base for the last twenty years of his life, and it was probably on this account that the city attracted Eusebius' teacher, Pamphilus, an eager collector of Origen's works. The early career of Eusebius is particularly obscure, apart from his acknowledged devotion to Pamphilus, whose name he took, Εὐσέβιος ὁ Παμφίλου.[1] The house of Pamphilus became a school boasting a remarkable library where he and Eusebius worked in collaboration with one another. Eventually they produced a joint defence of the great scholar to whom they both owed so much. If Eusebius' quotations are anything to go by, the library must have been a comprehensive collection, not only of Christian literature, but of most literature in the Greek language, especially philosophical works. Under Pamphilus, Caesarea also became a centre for the correction of manuscripts, and it was from Eusebius that Constantine later ordered fifty copies of the scriptures for his new churches in Constantinople.[2]

Eusebius grew up in a time of peace. The Decian persecution had faded into the past. The church was expanding throughout the empire. He was probably already forty when renewed persecution hit the church with the edict of Diocletian in AD 303. For ten years he lived through Rome's final bitter onslaught on Christianity, and it is from his pen that we have detailed eyewitness accounts of the effects of persecution in Egypt and Palestine. He apparently toured these areas, and could report many incidents first hand. In 307, Pamphilus was imprisoned, and eventually died as a martyr. Exactly how Eusebius survived we do not know, but the later accusation that he offered sacrifice to save his life was probably unfounded. It is a remarkable fact that a good deal of Eusebius' literary work seems to date from the persecution period. He and other Christians openly visited those suffering for their faith in prison or in the mines, apparently unmolested; in fact the joint *Defence of Origen* dates from the time of Pamphilus' imprisonment. In spite of the fact that the library housed many copies and versions of the scriptures – the first target of the authorities – it was not destroyed. We can only conclude that the persecution was carried out somewhat sporadically and unsystematically.

In 313, the persecution ceased and Eusebius became bishop of Caesarea. This position he held for the rest of his life. He must have been nearly seventy when he was elected bishop of Antioch after the deposition of Eustathius. Wisely he refused the honour, ostensibly on grounds of careful adherence to canon law as established at Nicaea,[3] but perhaps also on account of devotion to his library.

But if he remained bishop of Caesarea, this did not mean that he lived peacefully in an ecclesiastical backwater. His later years as bishop are better known to us, as he became involved in the politics of the newly-established official church, and stormy years they were. At one time his orthodoxy was impugned, and his acquiescence at Nicaea apparently caused him some embarrassment. However, in spite of the doctrinal conclusions of Nicaea, Eusebius' admiration for Constantine was augmented rather than diminished, and Constantine seems to have recognized the distinction and usefulness of so accomplished a Christian scholar. Immediately after the Council, Constantine celebrated the twentieth anniversary of his succession, and Eusebius delivered a panegyric in his honour, a task he was to fulfil again at the thirtieth anniversary. Immediately before the latter, he took a prominent part in the councils of Antioch and Tyre, proceedings which dealt with the 'ultra-Nicene' bishops, Eustathius and Athanasius. As a result of this confrontation with the young upstart of Alexandria, not to mention other manoeuvres during his episcopacy, Eusebius has continually faced charges of semi-Arianism, or of trimming his sails to fit the political wind. The justice of these charges will be considered later, but in fairness to Eusebius, we should remember that already at the time of Nicaea, he had probably reached sixty, and the council of Tyre was ten years later. He was an old man, profoundly thankful for the triumph of the church and a little out of his depth in the rapidly moving controversies and developments of the new era. It is hardly surprising that an aged and respected bishop with an essentially conservative outlook should find the intense singlemindedness of the young Athanasius distinctly uncongenial, even offensive. All Eusebius wanted was peace in the church for the triumphant celebration of Constantine's Tricennalia. He lived on to see out Constantine's reign, and died about AD 340, having spanned a significant turning-point in Christian history.

2. The *Ecclesiastical History* and earlier historical writings

One consequence of our meagre knowledge of Eusebius' life is difficulty in the matter of dating his writings, a question to which much scholarly work has been devoted. The matter is complicated by the successive editions and redactions through which his work seems to have passed. The general order of composition can be established by cross-references, and the dating of certain sections is fixed fairly generally by allusions to the contemporary situation. But his works are massive, and must have been assembled over considerable periods of time.

The *Ecclesiastical History*[4] clearly went through several editions. Most generally accepted is the theory of E. Schwartz that the first edition consisting of eight books appeared in approximately 312; that Book IX was added in 315 and Book X in 317; and that a final edition appeared about the time of Nicaea, when the character of the references to the Emperor Licinius was changed to conform with his downfall. The addition of the final books remains undisputed, but more recent investigators have tended to put the date of the first edition, consisting of only seven books, as early as 303,[5] and now the case has been put for considerable revision of these earlier sections in later editions.[6] Whatever the original date of publication, it seems highly likely that much of the work was conceived and accomplished before persecution broke out, and then was subsequently brought up to date on several different occasions.

Prior to the *Ecclesiastical History*, Eusebius composed the *Chronicle*. The Greek original is no longer extant, though the work survives in an Armenian translation. The first part of this composition is a continuous prose narrative of the histories of various nations, consisting largely of excerpts from accounts accessible to Eusebius, but with some attempt at cross-reference; the second part, known as the *Chronological Tables*, is a note-form summary in parallel columns, a tabulated conspectus which brings into line the different systems of dating and displays the parallel development of the major peoples of the ancient Near Eastern and Mediterranean areas. The idea of such a table seems to have been Eusebius' own,[7] and its subsequent popularity is evidenced by the Latin version produced by Jerome, who took the opportunity of bringing the *Tables* on down to his own day, and also made various additions elsewhere.

Chronological schemes had been attempted before, by Julius Africanus, for example; but these had been constructed in the interests of apologetic and eschatology, to show that Moses and the prophets lived before Plato by whom they were plagiarized, or to fit everything from creation to incarnation into 5500 years, on the assumption that after 6000 years would come the Millennium, the Great Sabbath. Eusebius was dependent on his predecessors for his material – in fact it has been noted that he tends to be more reliable when dependent on documentary evidence for the past than when recounting events of his own day – but he abandoned these dogmatic preconceptions. He calculated on the basis of biblical information 5199 years between Adam and Abraham, and brought Moses' date considerably nearer the fall of Troy.

Nevertheless, Eusebius cannot be entirely absolved of the charge of distortion for the sake of propaganda. He was in any case uninterested in Millenarianism, and the priority of Jewish to Greek philosophy he was to prove in a different way. His own interest is revealed in the fact that by the time of Augustus the parallel columns were reduced to two: only imperial and Christian chronology now mattered. Yet living in Palestine, Eusebius must have been all too aware of the neighbouring Persian empire, and other works show that he knew of Christian missions outside Roman boundaries. It is hard not to conclude that Eusebius' *Chronological Tables* were deliberately framed to fit one of his favourite apologetic themes – namely the providential coincidence of the incarnation and the establishment of world peace under Augustus. This is not the only case where later apologetic arguments have been traced in this early work.

In his prologue to the *Ecclesiastical History*, Eusebius states that it is an amplification of the information collected in the latter part of the *Chronological Tables*.[8] There is evidence that the *Tables* originally ended in 303 and like the *History* went through successive editions.[9] It seems then that the *Ecclesiastical History* arose naturally out of the *Chronicle* as Eusebius' next major project. It is this background which enables us to understand the somewhat strange divisions of material in the *Ecclesiastical History*. The work has evolved out of chronography; and so chronological rather than logical sequence is followed. The imperial succession provides the framework of the history, and information about Christian leaders like Justin Martyr and Origen is divided up and put in three different sections under the reigns of three different emperors. Eusebius states in his preface that his purpose is to trace the lines of succession from the holy apostles, the names and dates of the heretics, the calamities which have overtaken the Jews since their conspiracy against the Saviour, and the persecutions and heroic martyrdoms suffered for the faith. These other subjects also tend to impose a framework, and the various episcopates interlock with the imperial reigns. The result is an apparent confusion of order and subject, which is somewhat bewildering to the reader.

Eusebius was first and foremost a scholar, not of the clear-thinking philosophical type (he hardly had the ability), but one who

loved to sort evidence and amass information. As a historian, he
was not very imaginative – rather a chronicler; but from our point
of view, his chief asset is his love of documents, of quoting the
actual texts to demonstrate what he was recording. Attention is
drawn to the nature of his work by the fact that a modern selection
of texts illustrating church history is entitled *A New Eusebius*.[10]
Without Eusebius, our knowledge of the early church would be
considerably impoverished.[11] It may well be that his repertoire was
limited to the literary works and dossiers of letters contained in his
library;[12] to some extent, we can correct and amplify his information from other works available to us. However, this is not always
the case, and then his inadequacies become tantalizing: what
exactly did Paul of Samosata teach and why was he condemned?
Eusebius preserves details of his immoral life and anti-ecclesias-
tical conduct, but never fully explains his heretical doctrines. On
the other hand, he provides us with our only fragments of Papias'
writings, in spite of his somewhat derogatory opinion of his
intelligence; and we owe to him the survival of very early
martyrologies, and extracts from such important figures as Melito
of Sardis and Dionysius of Alexandria. Besides this, he lists the
works of the more important ecclesiastical authors, and provides a
chronological scheme, which, though needing some modification,
remains indispensable as a guide to reconstructing the general
sequence of events in church history from New Testament times to
his own day.

Eusebius is chiefly known for his work on church history; yet
here, as well as in his theology, he has been the butt of criticism. He
has been accused of deliberate distortion of facts and mutilation of
documents;[13] the tendentious character of his work has been
stressed; his lack of judgment and insight, his disregard for social
and political factors, have often been remarked. In particular, the
value of his accounts of the events of his own time has been the
subject of much dispute. Books VIII–X of the *Ecclesiastical History*,
and the associated pamphlet, the *Martyrs of Palestine*, are concerned with the progress of the persecution years. The *Martyrs of
Palestine* exists in two recensions, a longer version only extant in
Syriac, and a shorter Greek version, appended in four manuscripts
to Book VIII of the *Ecclesiastical History*. Eusebius claims to have
been an eyewitness of many of the events described, and for the
effect of persecution on the Christian population they are invaluable contemporary documents. But when it comes to detail,
reconstruction of the chronology of the persecution from Eusebius'
account is extremely difficult,[14] and inscriptions cast doubt on the

reliability of Eusebius' transmission of contemporary rescripts.[15] The whole account is influenced by Eusebius' point of view: Licinius, for example, is blackened after being hailed as a hero, and the actions of Maximin are distorted to comply with Eusebius' vicious judgment on his character as persecutor. Eusebius' honesty has been impugned; he deliberately rewrote imperial history to suit his own purposes, it has been claimed.

Perhaps, however, his qualities as a historian should be judged in the light of contemporary norms, rather than by the exacting standards of today. The thing that makes Eusebius dull and difficult to follow is the very methodology which distinguishes his work from pagan historical writing. History was a literary form, 'a rhetorical work with a maximum of invented speeches and a minimum of authentic documents'.[16] Eusebius, although an educated man, did not attempt to follow the traditional path of Thucydides and Livy. Of course Eusebius was not working entirely in a vacuum. In various ways the works of pagan historians and philosophers anticipated his interests. Disciples of Aristotle wrote histories based on 'successions', showing how one master followed another in a particular subject (e.g. Aristoxenus' *History of Music*); and Diogenes Laertius in his *Life and Opinions of the Philosophers* mixes biography with explanations of doctrines, lists schools and heads of schools, and discusses *haireseis* (divergent groups). So Eusebius' lists of bishops had pagan precedents, as did his discussion of heretical sects.[17] Furthermore Eusebius' overall understanding of history was framed as a reaction to what his pagan predecessors had made of it all: fate and fortune had been their preoccupation, freewill and providence is Eusebius' answer.[18] However, in his reliance on documentary evidence, in his refusal to produce creative writing, he was inventing a new kind of historical presentation. He himself claims to have been 'the first to venture on such a project and to set out on what is indeed a lonely and untrodden way',[19] and for this reason he begs the pardon of his readers for his deficiencies. He had no precedent to follow, because this history was not a study of human politics or military strategy; it was not written to please or exhort. It was intended to convince of the truth of Christian claims, and thus introduced the methods of a controversialist into historical composition. Its purpose was apologetic; and so evidence is piled up to prove points, and an erudition is displayed which is not found in pagan historical writing. Perhaps, as Momigliano suggests, Eusebius paved the way for the development of modern historical methodology, based on careful documentation.

Eusebius relied on evidence because he was an advocate seeking to establish truth and convince his readers of it; he had no intention of being impartial, and since his truth was theological truth, his work was bound to be tendentious. His work was that of a Christian theologian presenting events as a history of salvation; in this respect, he followed in the tradition of Jewish historical writing, as found in scripture, and to some extent in Josephus. It is not surprising that, having developed his theory of the historical process, he should see events in the light of his conclusions. He was presenting the triumph of orthodoxy against heresy, of Christianity over idolatry; he was bearing witness to the judgment of God and the providential activity of the divine Logos, as discerned in the events of history. Inevitably, distasteful facts were suppressed, like the pervasiveness of millenarian beliefs in the second century; inevitably awkward facts were distorted, like the refusal to attribute persecution to the 'good emperor', Marcus Aurelius. Judgments were bound to be passed and revised in the light of his Christian prejudices, as in the case of Licinius. Eusebius was certainly not an objective historian in the modern sense; he was a propagandist. Yet his search for facts and his desire to present evidence was in itself ahead of his time. Eusebius set a precedent and evolved a pattern which was to become standard for writing ecclesiastical history. Most of his successors made no attempt to replace his work, but rather continued it and brought it up to date – surely a testimony to their estimate of his achievement.

3. Apologetic works

Before 303, Eusebius had mapped out the framework of his thought in the *Chronicle*, the *General Elementary Instruction* (which is no longer extant), and possibly the first draft of his *Ecclesiastical History*. The next few years, the years of persecution, were in fact almost more active than ever from a literary point of view: new editions and versions were in preparation, and new works conceived. The *Defence of Origen*, the *Life of Pamphilus*, the massive answer to Porphyry's great work *Against the Christians*, none of them extant but all referred to in other works, seem to date from this period. The *Praeparatio evangelica* and its accompanying *Demonstratio evangelica*, seem to date from post-persecution days, though some passages suggest that persecution was still in progress, or at least might be expected again in the near future.[20] Whatever the date of the complete works, many of the ideas had already been worked out earlier. Not only do we find theories once sketched in the *Ecclesiastical History*, now developed and proved in greater detail in these later volumes, but much of the *Demonstratio* we can see is based on the extant *Prophetic Eclogues*,[21] a collection of Old Testament texts fulfilled in Christ, which had apparently been excerpted from the *General Elementary Instruction*. In fact, the more one reads Eusebius, the more one is struck by his ability constantly to re-state the same arguments and re-use the same material in a new context. Early sketches are taken up and developed in greater detail, then forcefully summarized in popular rhetorical works. The culmination of the process is seen in the *Theophania*, written late in life and declaring in final form the proofs of the superiority of Christianity which had concerned Eusebius throughout his life. We even find the familiar Eusebian arguments in his panegyric delivered at Constantine's Tricennalia.

The historian was at heart an apologist, and his apologetic interests are given their full scope in the *Praeparatio* and *Demonstratio*. The character of these works is similar to that of his historical writings, relying heavily on extracts from the wealth of material in his library. One could imagine him reproducing his card-index with connecting sentences; yet in his day such convenient aids were far from available, and his labours were inevitably considerable: checking references in a roll cannot have been easy, and the non-scriptural writings were unlikely to be in codex-form. The *Praeparatio evangelica* and its companion volume are massive works reflecting massive research, not just in Christian archives, but in the bulk of Greek prose literature. The central themes of traditional apology are given support from the very words of the opposition, the anti-Christian Porphyry being cited with remarkable frequency and at great length. Eusebius' method, though invaluable to posterity, is not conducive to readability. He is more of an editor or compiler than an author; to a greater extent even than in the *Ecclesiastical History*, he seems dominated by his vast resources of material. Yet scholars interested in tracing the lost works of pagan philosophers and historians cannot be too grateful to Eusebius.[22]

The impression given by these works is that Eusebius was setting out to confirm the church's position, rather than discover new ideas and insights. He prefers to reproduce the thoughts and statements of others. Yet it has been argued that Eusebius has given apologetic a new and original historical perspective. This is based upon the frequency with which Eusebius presents the primitive religion of the Hebrews (by which he means biblical patriarchs) as the perfect ideal restored in Christianity.[23] In the light of this, it is claimed, we can stand back and see beneath the mass of detail an

overall vision of the religious history of mankind,[24] inspired partly
by Porphyry's theory that a purer and simpler worship of the
heavenly bodies preceded the development of bloody sacrifices and
the deification of heroes and natural forces, partly by the traditional
Christian explanation of idolatry and polytheism as the seductive
activity of evil demons. This overall picture may be summarized as
follows: At the time of the Fall, man had turned from the true God
to worship the material. At first, they had worshipped the stars,
which were at least heavenly bodies, but then they had gone on
lowering their sights, worshipping the elements, natural forces and
finally their own famous ancestors, as gods. The evil demons had
made the most of man's freewill and encouraged his downfall with
seductive temptations. Thus polytheism had evolved. Meanwhile,
the Logos had undertaken the salvation of mankind, and revealed
the true religion to Abraham and his successors; but their descen-
dants had lost the vision, and Moses was chosen to establish a legal
set-up which would preserve the essential features of the true
religion in symbols, in a materialist form which weak and sinful
men could grasp. So we find polytheism and Judaism, both
materialistic, both the result of human folly and ignorance, but one
deriving from a divine attempt to save mankind from the worst
excesses. Then, at a carefully prepared moment in history, and in
fulfilment of the prophecies given to the Jews, the Logos came
himself in the flesh to reveal again the true religion and re-establish
purity and faith among all nations. Thus Christianity came into
being, not as an innovation, but as a return to the primitive religion
which was alone pure and true. Basically Christianity for Eusebius
is a revelation of the right way to worship the one true God, and in
this respect is distinguishable from all other religions of man.

It is hardly Eusebius' main purpose to present this history, and he
never quite succeeds in bringing it out with perfect consistency;
the status of the primitive astral religion varies, as well as his
estimate of Moses' role. Ideas of this kind, however, certainly seem
to underlie his material; and to spell them out helps to make sense
of his apologetic works. Into the scheme Eusebius incorporated the
classic apologetic weapons,[25] in particular the old accusation that
all Greek knowledge, religion and philosophy had been plagiarized
from the barbarians. He acknowledges, like so many Christians
before him, that Plato had discovered the truth, though he got it
from Moses. He repeats traditional arguments against astrology
and belief in fate; he uses standard attacks to expose the error of
each school of philosophy. He explains the source of oracles, and
their cessation at the time of Christ, in terms of the battle between

the Logos and the evil demons. He incorporates the long-standing Christian argumentation from the evidence of prophecy and its fulfilment. No available stone is left unturned in the endeavour, on the one hand to discredit paganism in both crude and more sophisticated forms, and on the other hand to answer the standard charges against Christianity, that Christians abandoned their ancestral religion for a new superstition, and that they fell between two stools in being neither Jew nor Greek.[26] Yet through all the mass of documentation and argumentation, it is possible to discern an understanding of providence in human history which has convinced Eusebius of the truth of Christianity. What impresses him most, and has contributed to the scheme already outlined, is (i) the fulfilment of prophecy, (ii) the miraculous success of Christianity and (iii) the evidence of providential coincidence. To each of these arguments Eusebius constantly returns, and it is worthwhile to look briefly at each theme.

(i) In the *Eclogae propheticae* and the *Demonstratio*, the argument from prophecy is used with force. Jesus Christ was the only man who fulfilled the prediction of another prophet like Moses, the only one to establish a new covenant and set up a new law. He alone was the fulfilment of the prophecies.[27] Eusebius draws on traditional Christian proof-texts, and for him the Old Testament scriptures are divinely-inspired oracles which, being fulfilled in Christ, constitute proof of the Christian claims. 'The new scriptures shall prove the old, and the gospels set their seal on the prophetic evidence.'[28]

However, in Eusebius' estimate of Moses, we find all the ambiguity of the relationship between Christianity and Judaism. Without Moses, there would have been no record of the ideal religion of the patriarchs; without Moses, there would have been no prophecies. Moses was indispensable – and yet he was the originator of Judaism. The Jews to whom the scriptures belonged were the implacable enemies of Christianity; their charges had to be met. Besides, Christians, while accepting the scriptures, refused in certain crucial respects to obey their directives. Eusebius appreciated the force of these facts, and in the *Demonstratio* he set out to account for them.

By way of explanation, he utilizes the estimate of the Jewish law traditional since St Paul. The legal system, the polity, established by Moses had a pedagogical purpose; it was not the whole truth about God and his worship; it was a prophetic symbol, and when the truth came, the symbol had to be done away with. Besides this, Eusebius produced a number of very practical objections to the

suggestion that Gentiles as well as Jews were to obey the law; all
nations, for example, could not travel to Jerusalem to perform
sacrifice.[29] Moses was a law-giver for the Jews; Jesus Christ was
like Moses, in that he too was a lawgiver, but his law was superior;
it was universal and replaced the Mosaic code which was now
obsolete.

The replacement of the law, however, was not to detract from the
scriptures as a book of prophecy. The Mosaic writings were
divinely inspired and had the truth enshrined in them; they were to
be carefully distinguished from other oracles and prophetic
writings, whose source was the demons.[30] The Jews had failed to
see the truth when it had been unveiled in Christ; therefore their
nation and polity was destroyed by the Romans under the providence of God. In fact this had been predicted in veiled terms in their
own prophecies. Clinging to the materialist symbol, they failed to
discern spiritual reality and made permanent what was intended to
be an interim measure. Christianity was the revelation of the
reality behind the symbol.

Thus the argument from prophecy, already used to good effect in
the *Ecclesiastical History*, as well as the *Eclogae propheticae*,
could still stand, and clearly Eusebius found it a forceful one.

(ii) The miraculous success of Christianity was another compelling fact in Eusebius' eyes. The argument becomes more and more
forceful with the progress of political developments; but already
before the triumph of Constantine it was being utilized. The rapid
spread of the gospel to all lands and nations, the conversion of
mankind from 'devilish polytheism in all its forms', were already
being described with enthusiasm in the *Ecclesiastical History*.[31]
Still more does Eusebius wax eloquent in his later works, when his
readers could be encouraged to step on the band-waggon of the
triumphant church with its magnificent imperially supported new
buildings and multitudinous congregations. Yet it is the miraculous success of the gospel in its early days which remains one of
Eusebius' chief weapons against pagan scoffers. If Christianity was
a massive hoax perpetrated by the disciples of a false magician, how
could it have survived as a pure philosophy of life requiring
abstemious and sacrificial behaviour from its adherents? How
could illiterate, Syriac-speaking rustics have pulled off such a hoax
on the sophisticated Graeco-Roman world? Why should people be
prepared to die for something they knew to be false? Eusebius is
perhaps at his most forceful in developing these particular arguments,[32] and he recognizes this by reproducing them in the *Laus
Constantini* and again in the *Theophania*.

(iii) The evidence of providential coincidence was for Eusebius the most powerful argument of all. One of the features of Eusebius' concept of historical development is his identification of Christianity with civilization and peace. Idolatrous mankind is depicted as savage and barbarous; and the establishment of civilized peace under Augustus is not merely coincidental with the incarnation, but almost consequent upon it. Two great powers sprang up together to give peace to all,[33] the Roman empire and the Christian church; this miracle is attributed to the work of providence providing conditions for the rapid spread of Christian missions, and the overthrow of polytheism.

But what then of the persecutions? If the peace of Rome and the peace of the church are to be almost identified, how is the conflict between the church and the empire to be explained? Eusebius seems to have tried various methods of accounting for this. In the *Ecclesiastical History* the earlier persecutions are attributed to 'bad emperors', or to the misleading of 'good emperors' by wicked advisers. God allowed occasional confrontations in order to prove that the church did not owe its success to the connivance of the secular power. God permitted persecution so that the glorious deeds of the martyrs might shine forth as yet another proof of the power of Christianity, overcoming even death. It seems that along these lines, before the outbreak of Diocletian's persecution, Eusebius had come to terms with the empire and outlined the historical perspectives he was to develop later. Then the bitter onslaught came. How was he to face it and justify it?

Eusebius begins his account of the great persecution[34] by a description of the peace and success of the church in the years immediately preceding it. These were the early years of his life. He had not experienced the days of suppression; he saw the authorities tolerating large congregations and great church buildings. On looking back, however, he decided that outward success must have sapped the spiritual strength of the church; abuse and disagreement, hypocrisy and worldliness had taken over. So God fulfilled the warnings of the prophets, and in his own time Eusebius saw churches in ruins, scriptures in flames, bishops in hiding and the faithful in prison. This was God's judgment on the church, purifying and chastening it. Later he reverts to old theories of 'bad emperors', as the persecution inexplicably drags on; and eventually he sees confirmation of this in the terrible misfortunes which overtook the persecuting princes, and the success of the Christian sympathizer, Constantine.[35] Finally he comes to see the sequence of events as a demonstration of divine judgment in history, preparing the way for the glorious climax in Constantine's victory and the establishment of peace on earth.[36] His long-standing views on providence had been vindicated by the political events of his own lifetime. The unity of church and empire was fully realized. What greater proof could there be of the truth of Christianity?

4. Political writings

Constantine was the most convincing proof in Eusebius' eyes; it was the fact which clinched his apologetic argument, an argument whose development had begun long before. Now perhaps we can understand Eusebius' attitude to the emperor. We can hardly wonder that in panegyrics like the *Laus Constantini* he comes close to blind adulation and Constantine's personal faults are ignored. Not only is this consistent with the conventional form of panegyric, but it was inevitable in view of the significance of Constantine as confirmation of Eusebius' religious convictions. Eusebius may be criticized for short-sightedness in his unqualified surrender to imperial glory, but nevertheless it is utterly comprehensible in the light of his understanding of divine activity in history.

It is also comprehensible in the light of contemporary culture. Eusebius foreshadowed the imperial theology of the Byzantine empire in his descriptions of Constantine's role. In his panegyrics, the empire on earth is seen as an imitation of God's sovereign rule in heaven. Imperial epithets are used of God and divine epithets of the emperor. Monarchy alone ensures peace; democracy means anarchy. So there is one God and one emperor under God.[37] Close parallels have been traced between such views and the theory of kingship developed by Hellenistic philosophy, as found in Plutarch and Diotogenes;[38] and similar vocabulary is found in pagan panegyrics.[39] Eusebius has taken up and Christianized the theory of kingship found in popular philosophy of his day. Constantine has become the ideal 'philosopher-king',[40] who has the right to rule others because he has learned to govern his own unruly passions; he is depicted as ascribing all his success to God, refusing excess flattery, caring nothing for his gorgeous apparel, for the paraphernalia of his office, for the sheer power of his position. His humility, generosity and piety are stressed, and direct communication with the Logos is attributed to him. Thus he becomes the example and teacher of his subjects, as well as their ruler; like a radiant sun, he illuminates the most distant subjects of his empire. When Constantine feasts the bishops, it is like feasting in the kingdom of God. Eusebius comes dangerously near to seeing in Constantine a new manifestation of the Logos on earth. In adopting the language of the imperial cult, Eusebius oscillates between exaggerating the specifically Christian aims of the emperor, and suppressing distinctively Christian themes in the interest of achieving religious unity and consensus in the empire – in other words, he readily became a spokesman for what seems to have been Constantine's general religious policy.[41] Eusebius' attitudes were not unrealistic at the time, and as yet the dangers of the subservience of the church to its political masters was not apparent.

This discussion assumes that the collection of works concerned with Constantine is genuine, but in fact it has been the subject of much controversy. It begins with what is known as the *Vita Constantini*,[42] which is in fact not a 'Life' in the biographical sense, but an encomium written after the death of Constantine to celebrate his achievements. Historically speaking, the work is unfair and dishonest, suppressing uncomfortable facts and exaggerating the emperor's Christian virtue. However, the author states that he is only concerned to present 'those royal and noble actions which are pleasing to God, the Sovereign of all',[43] because it would be disgraceful if the evil deeds of a Nero should be given fine rhetorical treatment, while Constantine's goodness were passed over in silence. In other words, he is writing in the traditions of imperial panegyric, and there is no pretence at objectivity or exhaustive biographical treatment. He is to give an account only of circumstances which have reference to Constantine's religious character.[44] It is hardly fair to condemn the author as a dishonest historian on the basis of the omissions and distortions of this particular work, though to our tastes, it is a work of sickening flattery. To this encomium are appended a speech by Constantine (*Ad Coetum sanctorum*), the panegyric which Eusebius offered to the emperor on the occasion of the Tricennalia, and a treatise dedicated to the emperor describing the great new church he built over the Lord's sepulchre in Jerusalem. (The latter two works are together known as the *Laus Constantini*.)[45]

But was Eusebius the author of the *Vita Constantini*? Are *authentic* documents preserved within the encomium and appended to it, or not? Recent investigations suggest that the answer to both these questions should be in the affirmative, in spite of difficulties and a long history of doubt.[46] A. H. M. Jones has noted that a papyrus (PLond. 878) is a contemporary copy of the edict quoted in *Vita Constantini* ii.27–28.[47] There can be no doubt about the authenticity of this document, and the implication is that the rest are also genuine. Jones further remarks that he finds it 'difficult to believe that a later forger would have troubled to search out the original of old documents and copy them *in extenso'*, so adding weight to the accumulation of arguments against posthumous forgery of the entire *Vita*, though later revision is still not out of the question. It is noticeable that some passages of the *Vita* are closely paralleled in the *Ecclesiastical History* and the *Laus*; we have already remarked on Eusebius' propensity for re-using material.

As we have seen, the emphasis of Eusebius' writings on the emperor is very much in line with his most important ideas. Constantine has come as the final proof of God's activity in history, judging the wicked and overcoming evil and idolatry in all its forms. Constantine has come to ensure peace in the world and in the church. The consonance of this with Eusebius' views on providence may explain his exaggerated description of Constantine's measures against idolatry, and his glossing over the nature and seriousness of the doctrinal disputes in the church. It is interesting that concerns similar to those of Eusebius are reflected in Constantine's speech – and if this is not genuine, they can be found in many of his rescripts: the desire for peace in the church, the assertion of the superiority and truth of Christianity, the arguments against polytheism and philosophy, the justification of the incarnation. Eusebius was prepared to make himself the mouthpiece of the imperial policy,[48] to respond to Constantine's attempts at *rapprochement* between pagan and Christian, to give Constantine a special place in relation to the Supreme God even at the expense of playing down distinctively Christian ideas, not simply because he was an abject time-server, but because Constantine's advent confirmed his theology and his philosophy of history.

All this serves as a reminder that during the years of the Arian struggle, there were other issues at stake which seemed far more important. For Constantine and Eusebius, the primary issue was Christianity's claim to be the truth in the face of the pagan majority. It was this fact which made the unity of the church so vitally important to both. Internal squabbles undermined their overall purposes. The actions and compromises of both are explained by this background. It is far from surprising that Eusebius' accommodating attitudes commended themselves more to the emperor than Athanasius' intransigence. The bishop of Caesarea stood for inclusiveness; the bishop of Alexandria for exclusiveness.

5. Eusebius' christology

The part played by Eusebius in the Arian controversy and the proceedings at Nicaea has been the subject of much discussion by historians and theologians alike. The teaching of Arius and his opponents will be examined in the next chapter. Eusebius' christological position cannot be exactly identified with that of either side in the dispute. He thought in terms of one transcendent Supreme God, who mediated himself to the world through the Logos. Perhaps somewhat naively, he thought of this Being as divine, but not in the same ultimate sense as the God from whom he derived his being; besides, the ultimate source of all things was not divided or reduced by the generation of the Logos, who was the 'perfect creation of a perfect Creator'.[49] To this extent, Eusebius was Arian in tendency, though he certainly did not subscribe to the Arian conclusion that the Logos was a mutable creature. Eusebius was convinced of his perfection, his changelessness, even in the context of the incarnation, and this belief had the same quasi-docetic results in some of Eusebius' statements as appear in anti-Arian exegesis;[50] the Logos himself did not suffer on the cross, but only his body. However, Eusebius could see nothing wrong in believing in a hierarchy of divine beings; a radical distinction between divine and non-divine did not appear on his map of the universe.

Nevertheless, he did believe in a *de facto* distinction between the one Supreme God to whom worship should be offered, and all other inferior spiritual beings, whether angels or demons, who should not receive worship.[51] Where was the Logos to fit into the monotheism versus polytheism debate? It is at this point that Eusebius is shown up as an amateur when it comes to theology and philosophy. He follows traditional Origenist patterns and fails to see the problems involved. There is a fundamental contradiction between his monotheism and his christology. 'Even the only-begotten of God and the first-born of the whole world, the beginning of all, commands us to believe his Father alone true God, and to worship only him.'[52] Yet the Logos is also to receive worship, for he is God's vice-gerent, his image and his instrument, a second Lord.[53] Eusebius goes to a great deal of trouble to prove that there is only one God, and so there can only be one Logos; but one God plus one divine Word, on the face of it, makes two divine beings, both of whom are to receive worship. One feels that Eusebius can easily be charged with ditheism, especially in the rhetorical and loose expressions of the *Theophania*.

Perhaps Eusebius is a little confused and self-contradictory in his assertion of the uniqueness of God, while defending the divinity of the Word and his right to receive worship. But his position is comprehensible in terms of the Neoplatonic/Origenist heritage on which he drew. Already the second-century Neopythagorean Numenius had spoken of a second God, and Eusebius is responsible for preserving the vast majority of Numenius' fragments.[54] In both cases the need for a secondary divine being arose from the classic problem of the Platonic–Pythagorean tradition, the need for some ontological connection between the One and the Many. Like Origen, Eusebius cast the Logos in this mediatorial role: God is the One who utterly transcends the Many; the Logos is both One and Many, being the image of God and at the same time pervading all things. He is the Neoplatonic World-Soul,[55] the instrument through which God created and sustains the world, and the mediator who reveals and displays providential love in his direction of the world and its history. Thus the Logos could in no sense be identified with God; to admit that he was 'of one substance with the Father' was to undermine both God's uniqueness and the mediatory position of the Logos. The Logos 'was necessary because the uncreated and immutable substance of Almighty God could not be changed into the form of a man'.[56] So close did Eusebius come to denying his own belief in the changelessness of the Logos. No wonder he found the language of the Arians more in line with his conservative thinking. As far as he was concerned, the Logos must remain an intermediary link between God himself and the beings he had created.

One reason for Eusebius' failure to appreciate the position of the anti-Arians was his soteriological outlook. Eusebius was an intellectual Christian. 'We have been delivered by the grace and beneficence of Almighty God, by the ineffable power of our Saviour's *teaching* in the gospel, and by *sound reasoning*'; 'we have received these proofs after subjecting them to the tests and enquiries of a critical judgment.'[57] Such sentences have at times been regarded as witnessing to Eusebius' conversion, though he may well have been born and brought up a Christian. Nevertheless, they do make the point that his faith was the reasoned faith of an intellectual who found the Christian account of things more convincing than that of its rival religious philosophies. He was not driven by deep religious passions. As von Campenhausen suggests, monotheism and morality was the heart of the gospel for Eusebius.[58] The work of Christ was that of teacher and revealer pointing the way to the true religion and overcoming ignorance and idolatry. It is true that Eusebius uses and interprets the imagery of sacrifice to explain Christ's death, which he sees as a triumph over the opposing powers of evil. He even describes salvation as deification, using Athanasius' word θεοποίησις.[59] But always the conventional images are expounded in such a way as to account for the death of Christ within Eusebius' understanding of his revelatory function; the providential oversight and progressive education of wandering mankind involved conquering the powers of evil, destroying false religion, and cleansing men of their sins and weaknesses.[60] For Eusebius the important result of the coming of the Lord remained fundamentally the establishment of the true religion, the revelation of the true God over against the error and vice of idolatry. This is particularly apparent if we contrast the main emphasis of the argument of the *Theophania* with that of Athanasius in the *Contra gentes* and *De incarnatione*, even though the similarities are so striking.[61] Unlike Athanasius, Eusebius did not argue from Christ's revelatory and redeeming work to his essential, undiluted divinity; in fact this would undercut the ability of the Logos to act as an intermediary. A second Lord might become incarnate, whereas this was inconceivable for the transcendent First Cause. An image can reveal without being identical with the original; a deputy can act with the delegated powers of his superior. Eusebius' position was far from unreasonable within the terms of his own understanding of Christian salvation, just as it was acceptable within the terms of contemporary thought. It simply belonged to third-century Neoplatonism, to the world which produced Origen and Porphyry, to a hierarchical understanding of the spiritual world.[62] Now Arius had raised new questions and forced upon the church a more sophisticated and critical statement of its claims. Was Christ really divine? or only semi-divine? How is divinity to be defined? In what sense if any at all, is the Logos to be regarded as God? Eusebius failed to grasp the importance of the issues. Arius spoke a language he understood; his opponents seemed to confuse his carefully conceived hierarchical scheme. So he championed Arius, and if modern reconstructions of events are right, he found himself excommunicated at a synod in Antioch in 324.

The hints and silences in the accounts of the proceedings at Nicaea are particularly tantalizing. Eusebius describes the occasion in the *Vita Constantini*, and in a letter to his church at Caesarea gives a tendentious account of how agreement was reached on the creed.[63] From these accounts it might be concluded that Eusebius himself gave the opening address; then later he produced the traditional baptismal creed of this church as a possible compromise document and accepted the addition of certain terms, with which he found it hard to agree, only when they had been carefully expounded to his satisfaction by the emperor. But the course of events seems to have been somewhat compressed and distorted in these accounts. It takes a fair stretch of the critical imagination to see the Nicene creed as a revised version of the Caesarean creed quoted by Eusebius,[64] and it is far more likely, especially in view of his recent condemnation at Antioch, that Eusebius produced his creed in reply to attacks from the anti-Arian faction. It undoubtedly represented the traditional faith of the church and cleared his name, but it had no relevance to the theological matter in dispute.

Eusebius eventually signed the new creed, with its *homoousion*, presumably in deference to the emperor's wishes and for the sake of peace in the church; but in his letter to his church, his embarrassment is evident. Does this mean that Eusebius sacrificed principle to political expediency?

Such a judgment is probably unfair. The christological section of the *Demonstratio evangelica* suggests that Eusebius disliked 'substance' terminology, because of the danger of its being understood in a materialist sense.[65] His analogies concentrate on the fragrance emanating from an object, or a ray of light issuing from its source; and even these he describes as earthly images, illustrations far transcended by theology which is not connected with anything physical. The Son was begotten unspeakably and unthinkably.[66] He certainly accepted that the Logos was derived from the Father in a unique sense, though insisting that the manner of it surpassed human understanding. So, in spite of his distrust of the terminology produced, Eusebius was prepared to be accommodating, if only others would make concessions too. If we compare the *Demonstratio* with his later dogmatic treatises, it is clear that the signing of the Nicene creed made no basic change to his christology; yet his reservations were no more dishonest than those of many who today subscribe to the Thirty-Nine Articles. Nevertheless, his change of attitude invited comment and criticism.

In the old days of controversy, it is hardly surprising that some condemned Eusebius, others tried to defend the 'father of church history' from the charge of heresy. Clearly Eusebius' position was neither on one side nor the other, and like Constantine himself, in some bewilderment, he acted primarily in the interests of church unity. What then of the sequel to Nicaea? Was Eusebius similarly motivated in his subsequent actions?

Nicaea produced a formula; the problem now was its interpretation.[67] It had been a compromise which even extremists whose agreement was fundamentally impossible, had been induced to sign. Cracks had been papered over, but soon revealed themselves again. Eustathius seems to have been the first to attack Eusebius for distorting the meaning of the Nicene creed; Athanasius was uncompromising, defying the wishes of the emperor himself. From Eusebius' point of view, both were wantonly disrupting the peace of the church for which he had been prepared to make considerable concessions. The rights and wrongs of the case brought up at Tyre are far from clear. If Athanasius' works seem to prove that all the charges were trumped up, nevertheless his own followers were equally unscrupulous, and we cannot doubt that there was suppression and distortion of the evidence on both sides. No compromise was possible, and the only way of ensuring peaceful and successful celebrations for the thirtieth year of Constantine's reign was to remove the most intransigent customer. If it were not for Athanasius, the dream of church unity might be realized, and this was fundamental to Eusebius' political theory and historical philosophy. So Athanasius was condemned at Tyre. In the case of Marcellus, Eusebius took up his pen, replying to Marcellus' attack on his own theology.[68] The main thing that this work reveals, however, is Eusebius' continuing failure to appreciate the issues and his basic inadequacy when it came to doctrinal questions; long quotations from Marcellus are left to speak for themselves with little real attempt at refutation. It was all too obvious to Eusebius that Marcellus' theology was wrong and dangerous, and that his own position represented the 'theology of the church'. This only goes to prove Eusebius' essential conservatism and short-sightedness. The other work of his old age, the *Theophania*, shows that throughout his life Eusebius was more concerned with upholding the true religion against polytheism than in refining his somewhat confused and anachronistic understanding of the relationship between God and the Logos. His heart lay in the defence of a united church, and the promulgation of the truth of Christianity, whose success he regarded as the goal of the historical process.

6. Exegetical works

It is remarkable that a self-confessed disciple of Origen should be so concerned with the objectivity of events on the plane of history. Does this concern have a marked effect on his exegesis? After all, for Eusebius the importance of Abraham, as the one to whom the true religion had originally been revealed, rested on the fact that he was a historical figure, maybe idealized, but certainly more than symbolic. We possess little of Eusebius' exegetical work, though he was renowned in his day as a student of the Bible. Considerable fragments of a *Commentary on the Psalms* and a *Commentary on Isaiah* had been found in the Catenae, but there was little else of significance before the discovery of an almost complete copy of the latter in a manuscript in Florence.[69] This has now been published in the GCS series, and on the whole confirms previous conclusions regarding Eusebius' Old Testament exegesis which had been based on his treatment of Old Testament texts in the *Prophetic Eclogues* and the *Demonstratio evangelica*. Here several features are striking: firstly, his constant discussion of Greek versions other than the LXX, and occasional reference to Hebrew; secondly, his understanding of the *literal* meaning of a prophecy as its fulfilment in a later historical event. On the whole Eusebius did not revel in the allegorical tradition, though he regularly used allegory to interpret numbers, animals and natural phenomena. Occasionally in the *Demonstratio* he offers two interpretations, literal and figurative; an example is provided by the prophecies of peace at the coming of Emmanuel: literally they refer to the peace of the empire at the time of the incarnation, figuratively to the peace of the individual soul who receives 'God with us'.[70] More often Eusebius distinguished between direct and veiled predictions. The latter notion permitted a rather arbitrary application of texts to future events through use of allegorical methods, but generally speaking his interpretations keep to this concrete historical approach rather than seeking spiritual and psychological insights. For Eusebius, unlike Origen, Old Testament history was a living reality, and in his *Onomasticon*[71] we can see him working it out on the ground, so to speak, by providing an alphabetically arranged handbook to biblical sites with potted histories and geographical details. Again, for Eusebius the New Testament was the authentic record of the historical Jesus, and he faced seriously the discrepancies between the gospels, seeking to explain them in *Gospel Questions and Solutions*,[72] assuming that a historical explanation could be found. For a pupil of Origen, Eusebius was surprisingly literal-minded; and yet Origen had anticipated his critical and textual interests.

So Eusebius inherited Origen's critical spirit rather than his bent for allegorical exegesis. He was also heir to the intellectualist approach of Origen, which saw Christianity as the truth, but was open-minded towards the culture and learning of the pagan world. He owed most to Origen in his philosophy, which remained second-hand and amateurish. From Origen came his concept of the universe as the home of a hierarchy of spiritual beings, and his understanding of the Logos as the intermediary between the transcendent God and his multifarious creation. From Origen came his avoidance of crude millenarian beliefs and his concentration on the moral education of mankind by the Logos. The chief difference was that, whereas Origen emphasized the progress of the individual soul, Eusebius saw this education as a long-term evolutionary process worked out in the course of history.

Thus the concrete historical reality of the Christian church was of far greater significance to Eusebius than to his theological master; and he it was who became the first ecclesiastical historian. He also became the first theoretician of Byzantine Caesaro-papism. He had his faults, his tendency to suppress awkward information, his over-enthusiastic response to Constantine; but his main shortcoming was sheer mediocrity and conservatism in theology. At least he pioneered the writing of church history, and others were able to follow where he had led.

II. Eusebius' Successors

Subsequent attempts to write church history all indicate the dominating influence of Eusebius' work. When Rufinus of Aquileia introduced church history to the Latin world, he basically used the *Ecclesiastical History* of Eusebius together with the now lost continuation added by Gelasius, a later bishop of Caesarea. For the next century and a half, Greek historians of the church did not attempt to replace the work of Eusebius,[73] but rather chose to take up the story where he left off. Four of those who assumed his mantle deserve attention, Socrates, Sozomen, Philostorgius and Theodoret.

1. Socrates

Though he was the most important ecclesiastical historian of the succeeding period, little is known of Socrates apart from what we can glean from his work. He was apparently a citizen of Constantinople by birth, and may never have left the city, though descriptions of local customs elsewhere suggest that he perhaps travelled a good deal. His exact dates cannot be determined. His *Ecclesiastical History* ends in 439, and allusions to at least one revision of the work suggest that he lived for some time after that date. He was probably old enough to have some memory of about the last forty years he describes. He was a layman, a lawyer by profession. Interestingly enough, the final year of his history corresponds to the date of the publication of the Theodosian Code, and the work is dedicated to a man named Theodore. Was this the Theodore who was one of the nine law commissioners who supervised the Code's compilation? Perhaps Socrates was commissioned to produce a historical survey to aid the commissioners in their selection of ecclesiastical legislation.[74] The controversies of the previous century clearly complicated their task, since it was necessary to reject the legislation of Arian emperors. Socrates begins with the reign of Constantine and the Arian controversy, a fact which lends support to this hypothesis.

On the other hand, Socrates consciously and deliberately began where Eusebius left off, feeling it necessary to explain the overlap at the beginning. He regarded Eusebius' treatment of Constantine's reign and the rise of Arianism as inadequate, pointing out that in the *Life of Constantine*, Eusebius was 'more intent on the rhetorical finish of his composition and the praises of the emperor than on an accurate statement of facts'.[75] So his first book deals with the reign of Constantine and imperial reigns mark off the limits of each subsequent book.

Whatever the occasion or purpose of Socrates' history, its model was Eusebius; and like Eusebius, Socrates was an admirer of Origen.[76] Origen is his court of appeal when making theological judgments, and the opponents of Origen, like Theophilus of Alexandria, come in for sharp criticism. Socrates took up this pro-Origenist stance at a time when it was not easy or respectable to do so. As in the case of Eusebius, this reverence for Origen produced a Christian humanism of a scholarly and critical kind, coupled in Socrates' case with a remarkably tolerant spirit. This was also fostered by his espousal of the Academy's position of 'methodical doubt' whereby various opinions were marshalled alongside each other and the inadequacy of human knowledge demonstrated. Socrates hated most the heretics who arrogantly claimed to know the whole truth, accusing them of 'sophistry' and love of dispute. He was not given to reverence for contentious bishops either.

So Socrates' attitudes were very different from those of Eusebius at a number of points:

(i) Where Eusebius was anxious to camouflage disputes in the church, Socrates regards these as the material for history. He concludes his work by praying that the church everywhere may live in peace, and adds the comment: 'as long as peace continues, those who desire to write histories will find no materials for their purpose.' Elsewhere he claims that he would have been silent if the church had remained undisturbed by divisions.[77]

(ii) Eusebius was intolerant of heresy and schism, but Socrates praises imperial tolerance towards heretics,[78] and openly expresses admiration for the Novatian sect, whose strict standards certainly appeared attractive compared with the worldly ecclesiastics of orthodoxy. He can even be charitable towards contemporary

Arians, especially those who held Origen and Plato in esteem. However, for all his tolerance and lack of enmity, he writes from the standpoint of post-Arian orthodoxy, and subscribes to the theory that heresies, once divorced from the orthodox church, inevitably subdivide into multifarious sects.[79] He disclaims any attempt to analyse or understand the philosophical and theological issues at stake in doctrinal disputes. He simply adopts the view that disorder is bad, heresy is bad and lack of charity is bad.

(iii) Eusebius wrote with enthusiasm and respect of the heroes, scholars and leaders of the church. Socrates is almost cynical about ecclesiastics and ecclesiastical politics. The subject of his work is the 'contentious disputes of bishops and their insidious designs against one another'; for 'the bishops are accustomed to do this in all cases, accusing and pronouncing impious those they depose, but not explaining their warrant for so doing'.[80] He deliberately refrains from using honorific titles for the bishops, like 'most dear to God' or 'most holy'.[81] Socrates is not afraid to criticize: in telling the story of John Chrysostom, he does not attempt to hide the faults of the recently reinstated saint. He is prepared to examine and assess Nestorius' views for himself rather than join automatically in the witch-hunt. On the whole he makes realistic assessments of the characters involved, and is not disposed to hagiography. He recognizes that ambition and jealousy now affect high ecclesiastical politics.[82]

(iv) Eusebius welcomed with enthusiasm the new link between church and state, regarding it as providential. Socrates, just over a century later, is less enthusiastic, recognizing its ambiguous character. When Socrates reflected on how the affairs of state were closely interwoven with ecclesiastical history, he produced the theory that church and state were somehow linked in a kind of cosmic sympathy (an idea with Neoplatonic roots).[83] The result was that dissensions in the church produced dissensions in the state, and *vice versa*. Likewise peace and prosperity in either church or state would mean peace and prosperity for the other. The emperors had a key role in church history 'because from the time they began to profess the Christian religion, the affairs of the church depended on them, so that even the greatest synods have been and still are convened by their appointment'.[84] Socrates believed that it was the emperor's task to foster harmony in both political and ecclesiastical spheres. This he did through his piety (εὐσέβεια), through the power of his prayers, through his virtue and orthodoxy. In the past, state patronage had not always enhanced the unity of the church; Socrates explained the problems in terms of 'bad emperors', rather as Eusebius had explained the persecutions. By contrast, the current emperor, Theodosius II, deserved a eulogy[85] – for peace and prosperity were now established. So for all his scepticism, Socrates could be as unrealistic as Eusebius: his work ends with a premature and over-enthusiastic assessment of the situation, written a few years before the Council of Chalcedon and the subsequent Monophysite schism.

(v) Where Eusebius was anxious to show the workings of providence in history, Socrates disclaims any attempt to analyse the mysterious reasons for the providences and judgments of God, virtually claiming that an objective account of the disputes in the church is his sole purpose.[86] About the cause of a hailstorm, popularly ascribed to divine vengeance for the deposition of John Chrysostom, he professes agnosticism. Yet he has not entirely abandoned the idea of providence; he seems to understand it as channelled through the emperor, as long as he has the necessary piety. Thus Socrates did recognize as an act of God the subjugation of Theodosius II's enemies; and thunderbolts and plagues, fulfilling a prophecy in Ezekiel, deterred recent barbarian ravages – for God rewarded the meekness of Theodosius. (Modern historians would call it weakness!)

Socrates' aims and interests in writing his history were therefore not always very close to those of Eusebius. The apologetic interest is less obvious (though Downey has traced several apologetic motifs); and within the limits imposed by his culture, Socrates the lawyer seems to have attempted to give a tolerant and unbiassed account of the events of that stormy century. The methods of Eusebius he did adopt, examining and quoting original documents to support and amplify his account, thus preserving many invaluable texts. He speaks of the laborious task of sifting documents, testing evidence, and of enquiring of a variety of witnesses whose accounts inevitably conflicted.[87] He recognizes that facts can be suppressed or distorted by partiality and prejudice. He tries to distinguish between hearsay and genuine information. But at times, Socrates falls uncritically into reproducing popular estimates of people and events which are not always consistent with his efforts at considered judgment. It is Philostorgius and the pagan historians who tell us how Constantine murdered his son Crispus, a fact suppressed by all orthodox Christian writers, including Socrates. Furthermore, he was certainly limited in the achievement of his ideals by the source material available to him.

What source material did Socrates use? He began with the works of Eusebius and Rufinus; on a number of occasions he acknowledges his debt to the latter, or deliberately corrects his errors.[88] He accepted these histories not uncritically, and used alongside records of conciliar decisions, letters and other documents he had available. Some light is thrown on his methods by the Introduction to Book II, which explains why he revised his first two books. He first wrote them following Rufinus; then he came across the writings of Athanasius and other contemporaries of the events he was describing, and these he assumed to be more accurate than later conjectures. For this reason he made his revision in the light of this new material. But the problem is that Athanasius' apologetic writings and dossiers of documents are themselves tendentious, putting only his side of the case. Socrates did not confine himself to 'orthodox' sources, as is shown by his use of Sabinus, a Macedonian heretic who made a collection of conciliar acts.[89] Yet he was bound to view the events of the last century from the current 'official' view, and he is critical of Sabinus for his tendentious remarks and selection of material. He could not entirely divorce himself from contemporary prejudices. Furthermore, he was unable to appreciate the real issues involved and was thus blind to the sort of considerations which gave each group its theological and political impetus. His descriptions of the battle between Eusebius of Caesarea and Athanasius is concerned not with the issues, nor even with the personalities, but rather with retrieving Eusebius' reputation as orthodox in spite of his opposition to the one who defended the Nicene creed single-handed for such a long period; so he generalizes the situation, affirming that they and others at this time were engaged in a 'contest in the dark', neither party understanding distinctly the reasons for the dispute, each writing *as if* they were adversaries![90] Socrates' inability to face and clarify the issues reduces his overall value to those now trying to appreciate what was involved in the disputes. Besides, in detail he sometimes failed to make accurate reconstructions and telescoped events or characters, confusing Maximin and Maximian, for example.

Compared with other historians of his day, however, Socrates' achievement was considerable. Sozomen, Philostorgius and Theodoret more consciously and deliberately represented a point of view than Socrates. They, like Socrates, wrote histories which began where Eusebius left off, and covered approximately the same period. Inevitably their chief matter was the long Arian conflict, and this was bound to give their work a different character from that of Eusebius. It was no longer possible to present a picture of a single successful institution, ironing out or suppressing differences in belief and practice. Now the historian could not help belonging to a party. For Sozomen, far more than for Socrates, the subject and purpose of his history was to tell the story of the gradual but triumphant progress of orthodoxy against political and ecclesiastical odds. Eusebius' apologetic search for the providential hand of God in events is again at the centre. The same is true for Philostorgius, but he was an ardent follower of the neo-Arian, Eunomius, and therefore his interpretation of the course of events is exactly opposite to that of Sozomen. For him, history is now progressing to its dreadful climax, as truth is suppressed and God's true prophets and servants persecuted. It is surprising that his 'heretical' history survived long enough to be epitomized by the tenth-century librarian, Photius, though we can only regret its loss in our attempts to understand the disputes of the fourth-century. We have enough in Photius' précis and other surviving fragments to see how recrimination and distortion of fact were the weapons used on every side. Personal slanders were the natural accompaniment of doctrinal disputes, and to advance a plausible charge of adultery sufficient to condemn the beliefs of the opposition. For Philostorgius, if not for the orthodox historians, the scandalous charges advanced against Athanasius were true.[91] On both sides, the heroes of the faith were regarded as spotless in virtue and inspired with miraculous powers. Their enemies were the enemies of God, dogged by a hostile providence. Such is the picture presented by Philostorgius and Sozomen, though from opposite sides of the fence. By contrast, it is refreshing to meet the amused anticlericalism and tolerance of Socrates. The mere fact that he was prepared to read Nestorius for himself rather than regurgitate malicious gossip says a great deal for his insight and critical ability in such a period.

2. Philostorgius

Unlike Socrates, Philostorgius consciously and deliberately set out to disclose in the course of history the providential designs of God. Miracles and portents figure largely in his presentation. Those who are sympathetic to the 'true faith' prosper; disaster attends those rulers who persecute the Eunomians. Illness is a sign of divine punishment; earthquake a scourge of divine wrath. This pattern is truly in the tradition of Eusebius' work, though it is worked out somewhat more crudely, and with an apocalyptic and astrological flavour that Eusebius would certainly have repudiated. The sack of Rome is no brief incident of the past for Philostorgius, but a sign of the approaching end of the world, foreshadowed by the appearance of the comet in 389.[92] Recent events are described in vivid apocalyptic imagery: famine, pestilence, ravages of wild beasts and barbarians, water and fire pouring from heaven, hailstorms and snow, gales and earthquakes, all reveal the anger of God. The disastrous reign of Theodosius II is heralded by an eclipse of the sun and the appearance of a meteor. The scourges of the divine wrath descended upon the earth. It seems that Philostorgius intended to create the impression that the empire was entering its last days, and Photius' summary does not entirely obscure this.

What kind of man was Philostorgius? He was a Cappadocian, who went to Constantinople at the age of twenty. He came from an Arian family, and in the capital soon attached himself to Eunomius, who clearly made a deep impression on him. Unlike Socrates, Philostorgius *is* inclined to hagiography, and most of the honours go to Eunomius who is acclaimed for his intelligence and virtue, his grace and dignity – even his lisp and his skin disease adding to his elegance and majesty![93]

Philostorgius had great powers of description and was remarkably sensitive to natural beauty as well as uncommon wonders.[94] The capital city made a powerful impression on him and he revels in the account of its foundation and splendid buildings. He appears to have enjoyed travel and describes the wonders of the Holy Land at first hand. He had a geographical curiosity which allows us some insight into current conceptions of the world, like the speculation that the great rivers of the world (including the Nile!) all flowed from Paradise which was located somewhere in the East. Philostorgius was fascinated by strange phenomena of all kinds,[95] comets and visions and portents, prodigies from heaven, abnormalities like giants and dwarfs and weird grotesque creatures. He was a cultured layman according to the educational standards of the time, and it is instructive to see the importance granted to astrology and the miraculous in the sophisticated society of this period. Credulity was more common than scepticism. Philostorgius explicitly rejects a rationalist explanation of madness in favour of demon possession.[96]

Philostorgius, like Eusebius, was concerned in the debate with pagans. He tells us that he wrote a work against Porphyry on behalf of the Christians, and he is concerned to show that Christians do not worship martyrs nor the image of Constantine.[97] Contemporary pagans attributed the disasters of Theodosius' reign to the abandonment of the old gods. Philostorgius, as we have seen, produces a somewhat different interpretation. Indeed, he directs a good deal of his history to polemic against the heathen. He tells with enthusiasm of Christian missions outside the Roman empire in the reign of Constantius, and groans at the indignities inflicted on Christians under Julian, taking the same attitude towards him and his policies as any of the so-called orthodox writers.

Philostorgius' *Church History* was probably written in the early 430s, that is, a little earlier than the work of Socrates. It was ostensibly a continuation of Eusebius, a history and apology for the 'true church' as it confronted paganism and false orthodoxy. The great events for Philostorgius were those which affected the Eunomian church,[98] an emphasis which distorts the overall picture. Photius was not completely wide of the mark when he described the work as not so much a history as a panegyric of the heretics. Philostorgius does not mention a single bishop of the great centres of the church, Antioch, Constantinople, Rome or Alexandria (apart from his *bête noire*, Athanasius). All who oppose Eunomius tend to be bracketed together, whether homoousian or homoiousian, even Arians![99] Every other party did at least agree that the reality of the Godhead is ultimately shrouded in mystery, whereas Eunomius insisted that theology can be exactly exposed to the full light of knowledge. Philostorgius therefore praises Eusebius as historian while accusing him of erroneous opinions in matters relating to religion, because he considered the deity as unintelligible and incomprehensible.[100] Arius himself is castigated for the absurd error of affirming that God cannot be known or comprehended or conceived by the human mind. Eunomius alone purified the doctrines of the faith obscured by the passage of time, and then held to them consistently.

Yet Philostorgius was not merely a narrow sectarian. He shows admiration for the wisdom and literary style of Eunomius' chief opponents, Basil of Caesarea and Gregory Nyssen. He had some competence in literary criticism and a breadth of interest in secular events and the natural world which is hardly paralleled among the orthodox historians. Furthermore it is clear that he used sources, particularly Arian sources, which are no longer available to us. We can only regret that more 'unorthodox' literature has not survived.

One surprising feature of Philostorgius' work is his indifference to the monastic movement. His heroes are renowned for sanctity and miraculous powers, but there appears to be no mention of the ascetic ideals which gripped Christian leaders in this period. Some have seen ascetic features in the glowing description of Theophilus, his ideal missionary traveller, but Philostorgius is in fact more interested in his doctrines and miracles.

3. Sozomen

Socrates, in his more comprehensive and balanced survey of the history of the Eastern Church, gives some attention to the origins, ideals and literature of monasticism,[101] and notices the influence of the monks in the events he is describing. It is Sozomen, however, who gives great emphasis to ascetic characters. Sozomen's work sometimes gives the impression of being a gossip column rather than serious history. It is full of anecdotes and biographical details. He clearly delights in describing the ascetic feats and consequent miracles of his heroes. One of his purposes is to present monasticism as the true philosophy, and in each period he devotes chapters to the lives of contemporary ascetics, martyrs and saints. He uses a great deal of biographical and hagiographical sources and surveys the celebrated monks of Egypt, Palestine, Syria and Persia, those who introduced monasticism to Asia Minor and Europe. Furthermore, the testimony of a monk like Antony is sufficient in his mind to allay all doubts about the legitimacy of Athanasius' succession to the Alexandrian see, and the destruction of heresy is ultimately attributed to popular admiration for the ascetics, who were faithful to the Nicene faith.[102]

In his Preface, Sozomen tells us some of the things which influenced his decision to write a history. He is impressed by the miraculous change made by the advent of Christianity, by the destruction of the ancient cults of the nations and the impressive witness of Christian martyrs. He felt drawn to give an account of these events from the beginning, but was deterred by the work of his predecessors, particularly Eusebius, and chose instead simply to summarize events up to the deposition of Licinius and begin a full narration at that point. His summary is no longer extant.

Sozomen goes on to list his aims and methods. He claims to follow in the tradition of seeking not only oral testimony but records of earlier events, laws, proceedings of synods, epistles. The bulk of the material he found so great that he decided to summarize the contents of documents rather than quote verbatim. Compared with Socrates, he reproduces very few actual texts. He mentions the existence of collections of documents made by the partisans of each sect to support their own viewpoint, and claims to have sought historical accuracy and truth in spite of all obstacles. Nevertheless, truth for him is the demonstrable fact, proved by history, that the doctrine of the catholic church is the most genuine, having survived all attacks through the providential guidance of God. He proposes to survey not merely events connected with the church in the Roman empire, but also the church among the Persians and barbarians; nor will he confine his account to church politics, since, as we have seen, the character and deeds of the monks are both relevant to ecclesiastical history and important to record. In fact, he begins his history with Constantine's triumph, the prosperity of the church and the virtue of the monks, denying the Arian controversy priority of place in his opening book.

In certain respects Sozomen is the true successor of Eusebius, since the tracing of God's providence in history is his primary purpose. He writes from the point of view of a largely intolerant orthodoxy seeing its triumph as the triumph of God. Fulfilled prophecy and miracle attest the truth of God's activity in events. Christianity is the true and universal religion. The enforcement of doctrinal conformity (though not uniformity in practice[103]) is proper for orthodox rulers, if not for those who supported the Arians: thus Valens is treated as a cruel oppressor while Constantine and Theodosius the Great are glorified for efforts to suppress paganism and heresy. Theodosius' weak but orthodox successors are given excessive flattery. Sozomen thus reflects the same attitude as his predecessors, idealizing the emperor because his pious orthodoxy was thought to ensure the safety of church and state. His dedicatory preface shows that he wrote his history to attract the emperor's literary patronage, and submitted it to the palace for revision.

As a historian, Sozomen leaves much to be desired. He is far less successful than Socrates in carrying out his aims, and really makes no attempt at objective judgment. He lacks critical ability and accepts statements in his sources at their face-value. He sometimes presents several different views, as when he gives five different accounts of the death of Arius! He thus gives the appearance of being fair, while attempting no analysis or sifting of the evidence available. Besides, he does not follow his predecessors in acknowledging his most important sources. Much of his work runs closely parallel to that of Socrates, and it is clear that he used Socrates' history at least as a guide-book and directory to sources, without acknowledging his debt. He has added a great deal of supplementary material, some of it based on additional sources and documents, though much of it is anecdotal material and fuller narratives. He is more prepared to make use of rumour and popular speculations, without critical assessment of their value, especially reporting current views as to the divine mercy or wrath to be seen in a particular event. He is utterly uncritical as far as the miraculous is concerned. He is too quick to blacken or whitewash, giving even Constantius the benefit of the doubt, sure that he really upheld the Nicene faith under a different slogan.[104] Did Sozomen really fail to see any difference between *homoousios* and *homoiousios*? It is hard ✕ to believe of an educated man of that period, even if he does protest his lack of dialectical ability. He falls easily into flattery and seeks to defend heroes like John Chrysostom from criticisms such as those adduced by Socrates.

It seems that Sozomen left his work unfinished. In the dedication to the emperor, he mentions his intention to continue to Theodosius' seventeenth consulship (i.e. 439, the year in which Socrates concluded his work), but the ninth book breaks off abruptly in 425. It is possible that imperial censors were responsible, but probably the most satisfactory explanation is that he died before completion of the work.[105] Perhaps he undertook the project late in life after an active career as a lawyer. His exact dates are difficult to determine, but he was clearly a contemporary of Socrates. He originated from Palestine and seems to have travelled widely before settling in Constantinople. He gives us more information about the Syrian and Western church than Socrates. His style is superior to that of Socrates, who specifically aims at simplicity and tends to be dull. Sozomen certainly had descriptive powers, and was not afraid to write in a style to please an educated public.

4. Theodoret

Far from being merely a historian, Theodoret was bishop of Cyrrhus near Antioch and one of the leaders of the so-called Antiochene school during the christological controversies of the fifth century. He wrote dogmatic and exegetical treatises, as well as apologetic and history; a good deal of his correspondence is extant.[106] For the moment, we will only discuss that part of his work which is related to Eusebius' interests.

The *Ecclesiastical History* of Theodoret differs from that of the others we have been considering precisely because it was written by a bishop who was deeply involved in the controversies of his own time. The book is extremely partisan, the heretics being consistently blackened and dubbed 'Ariomaniacs', afflicted with the 'Arian plague'. At times one feels that he is deliberately correcting the assessments of Socrates, and camouflaging the faults of 'good' bishops and emperors. Typical is his embarrassment at the story of Chrysostom's conflict with the empress:[107] neither side could be criticized, so the imperial names are concealed to avoid the difficulty. Thus the story is skated over and the causes of

Chrysostom's exile and disfavour suppressed. It is a good thing Theodoret is not our only source, or we should be left guessing about the course of events. Throughout, Theodoret's narrative is more compressed than that of the other historians, and he does not waste words explaining his purpose and method. Even more than Socrates, he sometimes simply strings documents together with brief comments.

The work of Theodoret draws particular attention to the problem of the interrelationship between the various historians of the period. There seems to be little doubt that he knew Socrates and Sozomen, and possibly Rufinus and Philostorgius. It used to be thought that he was largely a plagiarist, producing a clerical account of matters inadequately treated by uncomprehending laymen. More recently, however, attention has been drawn to the fact that Theodoret produces different documents from Socrates on a number of occasions, and that his wording suggests independent use of the same sources. Theodoret's one comment on his purpose is to the effect that he is attempting 'to record in writing events in ecclesiastical history hitherto omitted'. Omitted by whom? It is true that he only specifically refers to Eusebius, but he adds, 'I shall begin my history from the period at which his terminates.' Is this what he means by the events hitherto omitted? One suspects rather that he is alluding to the work of his contemporaries and indicating that he intends to fill in details they overlooked and correct their presentation where it was at fault. A comparison between his first book and that of Socrates confirms this impression. Where Socrates referred to collections of letters made by Alexander and Arius and quoted selected examples, Theodoret makes brief reference to a letter reproduced by Socrates and then himself quotes another.[108] Although elsewhere he makes the same selection as Socrates,[109] Theodoret does seem to have refrained from slavish copying and done his own research.

Theodoret's chief importance is in the additional documentary sources that he reproduces. His assessment of the course of the Arian controversy has no independent value; for him, the Arian heresy was simply explicable as a work of the devil, inspired by jealousy at the sight of the church prosperous, peaceful and successful under Constantine: Satan was 'unable to bear the sight of the church sailing on with favourable winds' and 'eager to sink the vessel steered by the Creator and Lord of the universe'.[110] As Christians, the Greeks had given up worshipping the creature instead of the Creator, so, not daring to declare open war on God, the evil one insidiously set about reducing the Creator to a creature, by playing on the ambition of Arius and instigating his heresy. Like Eusebius, Theodoret saw history as the triumph of the true church against enemies, external or internal, in league with the evil powers.

Also like Eusebius, Theodoret refrained from offering any account of the controversies in which he himself was involved. Both had reason for feeling some embarrassment about the situation. Eusebius favoured Arius, who had been condemned; Theodoret had favoured Nestorius and continued to oppose the victorious party after Nestorius' condemnation. In the events of their own time, each came under fire for upholding truth as they saw it; each felt the unity of the church threatened. Each avoided raising the issues in their historical works. Theodoret's history concludes at the death of Theodore of Mopsuestia, whose teaching had profoundly influenced the author himself, and also stimulated the Nestorian view. The consequent disruption of the church is concealed and the work ends with a list of bishops of the great cities during the period covered, thus drawing together the lists of contemporary bishops which punctuated the narrative throughout. Such a finale reminds us that his interest in presenting the church as a successful, God-directed institution was greater than that of the lay historians. On the other hand, the work seems to date from the 440s when there was a lull in the conflict, and Theodoret may have been trying to encourage unity by reminding all sides of their common war against the Arians.

Like Eusebius, Theodoret was an apologist as well as an historian.[111] His *Graecarum affectionum curatio* (*Cure for Pagan Maladies*) was the last attempt at a comprehensive work of apology. In an age when Christianity was dominant, the need for apologies in the old tradition gradually died out. The question is whether Theodoret's work was purely a literary activity or whether it really spoke to the conditions of the time.

As suggested by its subtitle: *The Truth of the Gospel proved from Greek Philosophy*, the work has much in common with Eusebius' *Praeparatio evangelica*. It cannot be denied that Theodoret owed a great deal to the apologetic tradition and the contributions of his predecessors; he used not only their arguments and themes, but also their citations from pagan literature. Clement's *Stromateis* and Eusebius' *Praeparatio* are particularly important in this regard. The extent of his dependence has led to low estimates of his originality and of the relevance of the work when the empire had been Christian for a century.

There is no doubt that this is to underestimate Theodoret's achievement. For all its dependence on Eusebius' *Praeparatio*, in many ways it is a superior work. Often more careful and exact references to the sources are given, which suggests independent checking and an erudition of his own. Furthermore, where Eusebius had simply provided a framework of topics and strung together long quotations with brief introductory comments in a diffuse and repetitive sort of way, Theodoret constructed a careful argument into which the much briefer quotations are fully integrated. Besides this, it has been shown that Theodoret adapted the traditional material and arguments for his own purposes, and moulded it to fit contemporary issues. His intended audience was cultivated and educated, steeped in the literature and traditions of the Graeco-Roman heritage, scornful of the barbarous origins of Christianity and the crudity of its holy books, suspicious of its novel and irrational tendencies and scandalized by the veneration of the dead in the martyr-cult and the excesses of the extreme ascetics. They were the sort who had comparatively recently supported the pagan revival under Julian the Apostate, and attributed imperial disasters to the rejection of the ancient traditional gods. We should not forget that Augustine's *City of God* was approximately contemporary with this work. Paganism still had its attractions and its adherents, especially among the upper classes with a literary education. Antioch still remembered the prowess of the pagan sophist, Libanius, the tolerant but unconverted teacher of so many Christian leaders, including John Chrysostom. To such people, faith was inadequate as a source of knowledge, creation out of nothing was philosophically absurd, and Christian, especially monastic, ideals were a mockery compared with a life of culture and virtue. Theodoret set out to undermine their false preconceptions about Christianity and to show it consistent with, and indeed superior to, the best traditions of Greek philosophy. He diagnosed and prescribed for the illnesses of the soul which was unable to overcome its inherent distaste for the truth of the gospel.

Theodoret's most original contribution was his organization of the material to meet contemporary criticisms. Each book is devoted to a particular topic and skilfully compares and contrasts Christian and pagan views. Books II–XI cover traditional topics: the First Principle and origins of the universe, angels and spiritual beings, matter and cosmogony, concepts of human nature, providence, sacrifices and cults, veneration of the martyrs, laws and customs, true and false prophecies, and the prospect of final judgment. In each case, however much he is indebted to earlier apologists, Theodoret gives his own carefully worked out and coherent exposition of the issue, maybe not making any brilliant contribution, but with clarity and relative brevity. The prominence

ence of his discussion of the martyr-cult, which is given a whole book, reflects his awareness of the particular issues which were causing scandal in his own time. Besides this, the traditional material and arguments are given a particular bent and emphasis by being put within a certain framework: Book I meets the philosopher's dislike of being asked to rely on faith rather than reason, and the last book, XII, deals with the practical outworkings of faith in Christian virtue. It is in these two areas that Theodoret comes closest to originality and proves that he was not merely writing an anachronistic work based only on traditional material. He updated the traditional arguments and faced current issues in the confrontation between Christian and pagan values. It is not for nothing that his work has been regarded as the last and most beautiful apology for Christianity.

Apart from this major treatise, Theodoret produced other works of an apologetic nature, in particular the *Ten Discourses on Providence*.[112] They were most probably delivered to the cultured Greek congregation of Antioch, sometime between 431 and 435. Unlike most sermons, they are reasoned arguments, lectures rather than homilies on scriptural texts. They indicate the need to confirm fashionable Christians in their faith, but also to convince fringe members of congregations in an age of official Christianity. They reflect the same qualities as the *Curatio*, in that they are heavily dependent on the many previous discussions of the theme, both pagan and Christian, while being a brilliantly clear restatement of the arguments. Theodoret also claims to have written an apologetic work against the Jews,[113] another concern he shared with Eusebius. A possible fragment of this lost work has been the subject of much dispute; it has even been suggested that no such treatise ever existed, the references to anti-Jewish as well as anti- pagan writing being in fact allusions to the *Curatio*.[114]

So amongst other interests, Theodoret shared the chief preoccupations of Eusebius, namely apologetic and history. In both activities he drew on the work of others, but made his own modifications to fit the temper of the times or the truth as he saw it. His history may reveal a lack of sympathy for freethinkers, but his apologetic work shows him a man of culture, an impression confirmed by his correspondence. Like others in this period, he had a somewhat schizophrenic mentality, open to the richness of the Graeco-Roman literary heritage, but closed to speculation and deviation in matters of belief.

III. Tales of the Monks

When Eusebius wrote his *Martyrs of Palestine* he entered a long-standing tradition – that of collecting *Acts* of the martyrs, transcripts of trials, and biographical accounts of the heroes of the faith.[115] During Eusebius' lifetime, however, persecution ceased and martyrdom became a thing of the past. Others became the 'athletes' of Christ, carrying on the war against the powers of evil; the monks in the deserts replaced the martyrs as the heroes and saints of the faith.[116] Sozomen's interest in these characters, then, was in a sense a continuation of one of Eusebius' themes, and Theodoret's *Historia religiosa* did not fall outside the major preoccupations of his great predecessor. The Syrian ascetics he described had taken up the martyr's mantle. Most of the works to be considered in this section can be regarded as belonging to an established literary genre.

Yet the monastic movement did stimulate its own literary tradition, which itself contributed to stimulating the movement. The first major contribution was Athanasius' *Life of Antony*, which will be discussed more fully in the following chapter. This publicized the ideals of ascetic withdrawal throughout the Christian world, and by using a literary and philosophical dress, ensured that the illiterate Copts became the models of life even for the educated and sophisticated. The deserts of Egypt became the goal of pilgrims and the subject of a flourishing literature: in Greek, the *History of the Monks in Egypt* and the *Lausiac History* of Palladius; in Latin, the works of Jerome, Rufinus and John Cassian. Later the various collections of *Apophthegmata patrum* were assembled and took literary form; and meanwhile, Theodoret produced his account of the rather different asceticism of Syria. It is the Greek material of this type which we shall examine here.

1. The *Lausiac History* and *Historia monachorum*

Two rather similar accounts of the early monks in Egypt achieved great popularity in the Middle Ages, that of Rufinus and the *Lausiac History* of Palladius. Modern researches have revealed that both of these works have a very complicated textual history. A Greek text which corresponds to the bulk of Rufinus' Latin work is now recognized as original and known as the *Historia monachorum in Aegypto*.[117] The authorship of this work is a matter of much speculation; the only known fact is that it was by a monk connected with Rufinus' community on the Mount of

Olives. This could explain Rufinus' use of the material in his Latin account. The Greek original, which was probably written about the year 400, describes a visit to the great monastic centres of Egypt made by a party of seven pilgrims in 394–5. The work is very similar in content to that of Palladius – indeed at points they report the same anecdotes – but this work is arranged in the form of a travelogue, describing one after another the ascetic centres passed on a journey northwards along the Nile, thus giving a striking picture of the surge of monastic life in Egypt at this time.

The *Lausiac History* purports to be autobiographical, and to describe what Palladius learned of the ascetic movement from his own visit to the great centres of Egypt. What he describes belongs almost exactly to the same period, that is the 390s, though his work was written some years later, round about 420. In the case of this work too, critical problems have beset the investigator. The textual confusion was the first difficulty. The work was so popular that it exists in many different versions: Latin, Syriac, Armenian, Coptic, Ethiopic, Arabic and Old Sogdian. Besides this, the Greek manuscripts contain a number of different redactions: material was inserted, rearranged and rewritten at will. Credit for sorting all this out goes to Dom Cuthbert Butler,[118] who showed that of the two basic text-types, the longer recension was a combination of Palladius' *Lausiac History* with the *Historia monachorum*, whereas the shorter version represents the original. Controversy has pursued his work, however, particularly since R. Draguet insisted that he gave too little attention to an important manuscript in Oxford.[119] However, for practical purposes, Butler's text has provided a reasonably reliable working base.

The second difficulty is the relationship between this material and other parallel texts. Did Palladius make use of the *Historia monachorum*? Did Sozomen use these two works as sources for the monastic chapters of his history, or did all three use a common source? What is the relationship between these works and the extant Coptic records of the early saints? The answers to these questions are still debated, but it looks as though the *Historia monachorum* and Palladius are independent witnesses which largely confirm each other; that Sozomen did use both these texts as sources (Socrates after all knew and referred to Palladius' work);[120] and that for the most part extant Coptic versions of the same lives and anecdotes are dependent on the *Lausiac History* rather than *vice versa*.

However, the continuing discussion of these questions is related to the third difficulty, namely the question of historical reliability.

The nineteenth-century rationalist tendency to dismiss all material containing miraculous elements gave way to attacks of a literary-critical kind. Discussion has focused on three areas: the question of the autobiographical framework, the picture of Pachomius' foundations at Tabennesi, and the account of John of Lycopolis. The basic charge made is that Palladius' material was drawn from earlier written sources and then artificially strung together by the provision of a fictitious autobiographical framework. Bousset argued this thesis,[121] and found confirmation of his view when Nau published his *Histoire de S. Pachome*, some hitherto unpublished Greek material together with a translation of a Syriac version: the chapters in the *Lausiac History* were clearly dependent on this material. Then Peeters[122] discovered that a Coptic Life of John of Lycopolis had used both the *Historia monachorum* and the *Lausiac History* as sources and, when they contradicted each other, preferred the former; this preference, Peeters argued, was based on local knowledge, and he proceeded to show that most of Palladius' narrative is exactly what one would expect if he was 'writing up' an imaginary visit to the famous hermit. Furthermore, the supposed date of Palladius' visit cannot be integrated with the autobiographical material offered in Palladius' book. In fact, the difficulty of reconstructing a chronologically coherent account of Palladius' movements gives plausibility to the charges advanced, quite apart from the fact that considerable evidence has been produced which seems to indicate that some parts of the work are based on literary sources rather than being the reminiscences of an eyewitness.[123]

However, the case for Palladius' trustworthiness has not gone by default. Halkin,[124] who collected together and edited all the Greek lives of Pachomius, argued that the dependence claimed by Bousset went the other way: Palladius was the original. Others have shown important weaknesses in Peeters' arguments.[125] Derwas Chitty, the author of the classic book on Egyptian and Palestinian monasticism, *The Desert a City*, is not alone in regarding Palladius as a more sober and reliable source than the *Historia monachorum*, whose author appears extremely gullible.[126] Certainly partial use of sources should not undermine all Palladius' claims, nor should overall estimates of the work be based on problematic details. A case in point is the tale of Potamiaena. Her martyrdom is described by Eusebius,[127] who dates it to the persecution in 202–3; Palladius puts it in the time of Diocletian's co-emperor, Maximian, that is, about a hundred years later. But granted the discrepancy, the fact that Palladius tells the story at all is a point of some interest.

Potamiaena was not one of his edifying ascetics, and to that extent she does not really fit into his work; yet Palladius devoted a section to recounting the tale. He told the story because he had heard it from Isidore, who had heard it from Antony – in other words, he passed it on as one of the good stories circulating orally in the desert community. This is a clue to the character of the book. What Palladius provides is a somewhat haphazard collection of tales, based partly on hearsay, partly on sources, partly on his own experience. It reflects the traditions and legends floating around the monastic communities to which he himself belonged for a dozen or so years. Prophecy, miracles and extraordinary ascetic feats were the stuff of the tradition, part of the atmosphere built into that particular outlook and style of life. The prevalence of marvellous stories is no reason for doubting Palladius' good faith, since it faithfully reflects the attitude of mind which he shared with his subjects. And the structure of the book may not be so haphazard after all; for Buck[128] has shown that it is best understood as autobiographical, each item being placed according to the context in which Palladius received the information. To treat the book thus can help to resolve some of the chronological puzzles. So, making some allowance for a tendency to exaggeration and idealization, there seems little reason to dispute eyewitness statements and descriptions given by Palladius himself; and even the chronological haziness may be best attributed to the inconsistencies of an old man's memory, retracing events of thirty or forty years earlier.

So it seems most likely that Palladius was a contemporary observer of much that he describes, and that his work must be regarded as a most important source for the study of the early monastic movement, its ideals and its mentality. It is not a work of ascetic theory, nor a defence of monasticism against its critics, but a collection of anecdotes intended to edify the reader. The failures and weaknesses of some are not concealed behind the achievements of the greatest; for it all provides useful material for example or warning. As a manual of spiritual edification, the work drew its authority from the fact that its author spoke of his own encounters with the holy men.[129]

What was it that Palladius admired in these ascetics? Theoretically he was primarily interested in the suppression of passion; but he was also quick to criticize spiritual pride: 'Drinking wine within reason is better by far than drinking water in arrogance.' Questions of diet are a constant preoccupation; but his heroes are also remarkably well versed in the scriptures, and live a life of quiet industry and prayer. There are tales of tempting demons and

ministering angels, of miraculous cures and prophecies fulfilled.
But the dominating note is the conquest of bodily weakness. His
heroes try to deny the need for sleep and undergo in the open the
fierce midday sun and the cold air of midnight. They are preoccupied with suppressing sexual passions: Palladius reports that near
the time of his death, Evagrius said: 'This is the third year that I
have not been tormented by carnal desires', and he comments,
'this, after a life of such toil and labours and continual prayer'. Yet
some of the strangest stories betray a genuine awareness of the
spiritual aim of physical mortification:

> Early one morning when (Macarius) was sitting in his cell, a gnat
> stung him on the foot. Feeling the pain, he killed it with his
> hands and it was gorged with his blood. *He accused himself of
> acting out of revenge*, and he condemned himself to sit naked in
> the marsh of Scete out in the great desert for a period of six
> months. Here the mosquitoes lacerate even the hides of the wild
> swine just as wasps do. Soon he was bitten all over his body, and
> he became so swollen that some thought he had elephantiasis.
> When he returned to his cell after six months he was recognized
> as Macarius only by his voice.[130]

Palladius' aim was to convince the imperial chamberlain, Lausus,
to whom the work is dedicated (hence *Lausiac History*), that it is
possible to rise above physical needs and self-regard. That is why he
responded to his request that he should record the stories of the
fathers, those he had seen and others he had heard about, through
his own life and travels in the great monastic centres.

What information can we glean about the author of this work?
Some details of his life remain in dispute. When did he spend three
years in Jerusalem? Did he make a journey to the borders of India?
How did he visit John of Lycopolis and return to Asia Minor in time
to be consecrated bishop of Helenopolis within a space of six to
twelve months? However, for all the difficulties, it is possible to
reconstruct a fairly clear picture from his writings.

Palladius was a Galatian, born in the early 360s. He went to Egypt
(perhaps after three years at Jerusalem) in order to see the saints for
himself, beginning in Alexandria in 388. There he approached
Isidore, an old man of seventy who had accompanied Athanasius to
Rome fifty years before. Isidore refused to take on the training of
Palladius, and passed him on to Dorotheus, a solitary who had lived
for sixty years in a cave five miles from the city. After three years,
Palladius had to abandon his apprenticeship there owing to a
breakdown in health; he describes Dorotheus' life as squalid and

harsh – perhaps as an excuse for his failure, but one suspects that he did not feel a great respect for extreme asceticism. When he enquired why Dorotheus subjected his body to such extreme tests, he received the reply, 'It kills me, I will kill it.' Undeterred, however, Palladius went on to visit the mountain of Nitria, close to 'the great desert which stretches as far as Ethiopia and the Mazicae and Mauretania'. Here there were some five thousand anchorites. After a year with the most notorious of these, he passed on to the innermost desert and to Cellia, where he attached himself to Evagrius Ponticus. Evagrius was the writer of many ascetical treatises which had a profound influence on Eastern devotion and spirituality, but his strongly Origenist theology made him a controversial figure; he was later condemned and most of his writings were consigned to oblivion. Others were deeply influenced by him, however, and so his ideas were widely disseminated. Palladius' own work is permeated with Evagrius' teaching, though it is expressed in his assumptions and vocabulary, in his descriptions of the monks' life-style, rather than in theoretical exposition.[131] The rest of Palladius' career arose from his involvement with the Origenist party.[132] After further travels in Egypt (he claims that he visited the Pachomian monasteries and that John of Lycopolis prophesied his future involvement in ecclesiastical politics – but these are sections where his dependence on sources has been canvassed), he left for Palestine – on medical advice, he states, but it was just about the time when Egypt became too hot for known Origenists. In Palestine, he was in close contact with the Origenists based on the Mount of Olives – Rufinus and Melania. He went to Constantinople and was consecrated bishop of Helenopolis by John Chrysostom. Thus he became embroiled in the controversy over John's behaviour, was himself charged with Origenism at the Synod of the Oak in 403, and even travelled to Rome in his efforts to plead the cause of 'the blessed John'. In exile, he composed a Platonic Dialogue, the *Dialogus de vita sancti Joannis Chrysostomi*, a work to which further reference will be made in Chapter 4. He spent his exile in Egypt, so again had ample chance to glean information from the famous monastic centres. The *Lausiac History* was written around 420 after he had returned to Asia Minor, a move made possible by the rehabilitation of John's memory. According to Socrates,[133] Palladius became Bishop of Aspouna, and he tells us himself that when he composed the *Lausiac History* he had been a monk for thirty-three years, a bishop for twenty, and he was fifty-six years old. The date of his death is unknown.

There is another work attributed to Palladius, the *De gentibus Indiae et Bragmanibus*. Its authenticity has been defended by Coleman-Norton,[134] and the recent appearance of new editions of the text indicate a resurgent interest in the work.[135] The author claims to have travelled to the borders of India, a journey which does not fit into any other information we have about our Palladius, but it cannot be decisively ruled out, especially as there are stylistic connections. The actual information about India is in fact all second-hand; the author got it from another traveller, a Theban called Scholasticus, and rounds off with a commentary on Arrian's *Anabasis*. An interest in the ascetic practices of the Brahmins is not out of character with what we know of Palladius from the *Lausiac History*.

2. Collections of Sayings

The *Lausiac History* and the *Historia monachorum* are literary works, similar to Athanasius' *Life of Antony* in that they were written by cultured Greek visitors. Though less overlaid with philosophical ideals, they too reflect the interests and style of their authors – not to mention their propensity for gossip and idealization. The same sort of thing could be said of the Latin literature of Rufinus, Jerome and Cassian: all had visited the desert and experienced it at first hand, yet all were to some extent outside admirers. Some of the famous ascetics were themselves Greek-speaking immigrants and scholars, like Evagrius Ponticus and a little later Arsenius, but many were uneducated Copts who knew no Greek and were often illiterate. The stylized material of the *Apophthegmata patrum* enables us to some extent to lift the curtain of polish and culture and take a peep at the bald simplicity of the oral traditions. The collections are admittedly later in date, and the critical questions surrounding them are desperately complex; yet here can be traced something like the sources that must have provided Palladius and others with a good deal of their material. Although some of Palladius' heroes were figures of obscurity, many were the leaders of early monasticism, like Amoun and Pachomius, or characters so famous that their sayings were handed down and can be found in the *Apophthegmata*, people like Pambo, Macarius the Great and Macarius the Alexandrian, Moses the Ethiopian and Paul the Simple. For the most part, the *Apophthegmata* complement Palladius' information, rather than overlapping it; and the larger collections of anecdotes and sayings tend to come from the great figures of the next generation. One-seventh of the collection is attributed to Poemen, and even though it is possible that more than one Poemen has been confused, it is plausible that Poemen's associates, the generation which retreated from the old centre at Scetis after barbarian devastation (407–8), were responsible for the nucleus of the collections.[136] On the other hand, parts of the Alphabetic collection seem dependent on a small collection made by Abba Esaias at Gaza in the mid-fifth century; this survives in Syriac and begins: 'My brethren, what I saw and heard with the Old Men, these things I relate to you, taking away nothing and adding nothing.' The anecdotes are then related as told to Esaias. Esaias also originated from Scetis, and this may be a more reliable clue to the origins of the written collections.[137]

The immensity of the problems confronting the investigator must not be minimized. The variety of texts, collections and versions makes the field a highly complicated one in which conclusions are inevitably tentative. The nature of the literature is such that precise dating is impossible. Edifying sayings and anecdotes were added or re-arranged, attributed to different fathers, expanded or given a new context. Each monastery seems to have had its own *Gerontikon* or *Paterikon*, with which collections from elsewhere might be integrated. Oral and written material seems to have co-existed, and each affected the other. Much of the material exists only in the manuscripts, and critical texts are lacking even for the published material. Most of the material is now accessible through the French translations published by the monks of Solesmes; but a good deal of the original text which they translated remains unpublished.[138]

Generally speaking, the collections can be classified into two main types – the Alphabetic and the Systematic – according to the pattern adopted for arranging the individual pericopae. The Latin version, a translation made in the mid-sixth century by Pelagius the deacon and John the subdeacon, is the best known example of the topical or systematic arrangement, whereby the material is classified under headings of the twenty or so monastic virtues: 'of quiet', 'of patience', 'that a monk might not possess anything', 'that nothing ought to be done for show', 'of humility', and so on.[139] A number of unpublished Greek manuscripts have the same arrangement.[140] The best known Greek text, however, belongs to the other main type in which the arrangement is made alphabetically, according to the name of the particular ascetic of which the anecdote is told, or the saying reported.[141] Anonymous *logia* do not appear at the end of the text as promised in the Preface, but the deficiency has been partially made up by the publication of some material from the Codex Coislinianus 126.[142] (Unfortunately the text is incomplete since publication was interrupted by the First World War.) Other unpublished material of the Alphabetic-Anonymous type is to be found in manuscripts which are probably to be regarded as superior and more complete.[143] Within the two basic types of collection, there are considerable variations in content and order; and the situation is further complicated by the existence of other Latin collections as well as Syriac, Coptic and Armenian versions.

The most comprehensive survey of all this material is that of W. Bousset.[144] He concluded that the alphabetic collection dated from around AD 530, though it is clearly based on an earlier less systematic collection dating probably from the second half of the fifth century. The topically arranged collection was in turn dependent on the alphabeticon. However, these conclusions were based on the published texts alone, and they have been questioned by the more recent studies of J. C. Guy, who suggests on the basis of the evidence of the Greek manuscripts, that the relationship is more complex, the two types deriving independently from earlier less systematic collections. Within each type, a history of development, of scribal additions and rearrangements can be traced. Guy based this study on the Greek evidence only, and Derwas Chitty doubts his conclusions:[145] the Latin version is based on an earlier stage in the development than any of the Greek manuscripts, and this, he believes, is demonstrably dependent on the Alphabeticon. So the critical questions are far from being resolved. Whether or not further investigation will call in question the other generally accepted conclusion, namely that the written collections in Greek antedate those extant in Coptic, remains to be seen. Protagonists for the priority of the Coptic material have not been lacking.

In spite of the problems, can anything be said about the nature and value of the material we have? Basically we have anthologies of wise sayings or 'oracles' from the most famous Egyptian solitaries, and anecdotes concerning their miraculous feats. As in the case of Palladius, the rationalist dismissal of this material as totally legendary has met with a reaction in the twentieth century, and many have stressed the value of the material as a source for understanding the spirit and history of the monastic communities. However, methods of comparative assessment or 'form criticism' need to be more fully developed. This is the merit of J. C. Guy's[146] proposed analysis into (i) primary material consisting of charismatic or prophetic words of the spirit-filled 'abba' for a specific occasion; (ii) secondary, literary apophthegms of more general application; and (iii) edifying episodes, miracle-stories and biographical anecdotes which became associated with the sayings-collections. Guy regards it as highly likely that the processes of oral transmission and written collection co-existed over a long period of time, each developing and being adapted to the needs of the communities, and each affecting the other. Something of this process can still be seen at work in the textual transmission of the material as available to us, modifications and additions being clearly in evidence.

In Guy's view, the basis of the spiritual education in the desert was the charismatic word;[147] the saying of the experienced ascetic was full of the Spirit, and able to effect action in the disciple. So a dialogue between master and pupil is a form which frequently appears. The *Apophthegmata* instil obedience, but it is not obedience to a set of rules; it is obedience in the context of a relationship between the 'elder' who is the model, and the disciple who imitates.

> A brother asked Abba Poemen, 'Some brothers live with me; do you want me to be in charge of them?' The old man said to him, 'No just work first and foremost, and if they want to live like you, they will see to it themselves.' The brother said to him, 'But it is they themselves, Father, who want me to be in charge of them.' The old man said to him, 'No, be their example, not their legislator.'[148]

Such a story throws much light on the character of *Apophthegmata* themselves, the repetition of precept and example took the place of learning rules. Occasionally quite contradictory advice can be found if individual pericopae are compared.

The *Apophthegmata* originated in an unliterary, indeed occasionally anti-literary, milieu, a milieu in which books, writing and dogma took second place to attitudes and way of life. Whatever the authenticity of the individual pericopae, the contents give a graphic impressionist picture of life in the Egyptian deserts, the excesses and graces of the heroes of the faith. It is instructive to remember how influential was this literature in shaping the ideals of Christian piety for many centuries. Inevitably some anecdotes strike the modern reader as bizarre, and the obsession with sexual temptations now seems psychologically inevitable in the situation to which these fanatics subjected themselves; yet there are also pearls of perennial wisdom and scenes with a delightfully natural and human touch. A brother goes away from the community hoping to overcome his anger if there is no one around to arouse him; his jug of water falls over three times, and in a great rage he breaks it. Back he goes to the community having learned the need for struggle, patience, and above all, help from God, in *all* places.[149] Most of the vivid pictures lose their effect when reduced to bald summaries. To read the texts themselves is to come away with a moving impression of the patience and gentleness, the wisdom and humility, the hospitality and sincerity of the characters depicted. A superficial estimate of the anchorite's ideal might suggest that his outlook was self-centred – a search for personal salvation ignoring the welfare of society; but the *Apophthegmata* reveal a genuine desire to eradicate the self and in humility put first the good of others. Particularly attractive is the story of Abba John: he and others were travelling by night and the guide lost the way. Rather than upset and shame the guide, John pretended to be unwell and unable to proceed before morning.[150] Typical is the saying of Antony:

> Who sits in solitude and is quiet has escaped three wars: hearing, speaking, seeing; yet against one thing shall he continually battle: that is, his own heart.[151]

But there is also the anonymous logion:

> If you see a young man ascending to heaven by his own will, catch him by his feet and throw him down to the earth, for it is not expedient for him.[152]

In the literature concerned with Egyptian monasticism, we find pictures drawn at two different levels. In the more literary works, a philosophic ideal overlays the material, an ideal which could and did attract the sophisticated and educated, the Cappadocians and Augustines of the time. Yet even here, lying behind the literary presentation, it is possible to discern the picture given in the collections of *Apophthegmata*. Greek-speaking, educated ascetics measure themselves by the harsh simplicity of illiterate and enthusiastic Copts, retreating from the social and political dominance of the Graeco-Roman civilization. One of the most famous ascetics was Arsenius, who had been tutor to the princes, Arcadius and Honorius:

> One day Abba Arsenius consulted an old Egyptian monk about his own thoughts. Someone noticed this and said to him, 'Abba Arsenius, how is it that you, with such good Latin and Greek education, ask this peasant about your thoughts?' He replied, 'I have indeed been taught Latin and Greek, but I do not even know the alphabet of this peasant.'[153]

Perhaps there is a little evidence of tension between Greek and Copt, educated and illiterate, in the *Apophthegmata*. There are differing estimates of the value of books, and anecdotes like the story told of Evagrius:

> One day at the Cells, there was an assembly about some matter or other and Abba Evagrius held forth. Then the priest said to him, 'Abba, we know that if you were living in your own country you would probably be a bishop and a great leader; but at present you are here as a stranger.' He was filled with compunction, but was not at all upset and bending his head he replied, 'I have spoken once and will not answer, twice but I will proceed no further' (Job 40.5).[154]

Another anecdote shows the embarrassment on the other side. An old man was shocked to find Arsenius lying on a bed with a pillow; he was ill and was tended by a priest. The priest questioned the man, who agreed that as a shepherd he had lived a hard life and he was actually more comfortable in his cell. The priest said:

> You see this Abba Arsenius. When he was in the world he was the father of the emperor, surrounded by thousands of slaves. . . . Beneath him were spread rich coverings. While you were in the world as a shepherd you did not enjoy even the comforts you now have, but he no longer enjoys the delicate life he led in the world. So you are comforted while he is afflicted.

The old man saw the point and begged for forgiveness.[155] The number of characters in the *Apophthegmata* who belonged to the wider world is an impressive testimony to the common life that was achieved; though the Origenist controversy must have fuelled the tensions. By and large the stories show men expressing their faith in humility, chastity and the struggle against demonic temptations, a struggle which they knew they experienced directly, even if now we might attribute it to over-heated imaginations. On the whole, extremes of asceticism gave way to moderation and common sense: 'we have not been taught to kill our bodies, but to kill our passions', said Abba Poemen to Abba Isaac.[156] And some of the demand for patience arose from very human situations:

> Another day when a council was being held in Scetis, the fathers treated Moses (the Ethiopian) with contempt in order to test him, saying, 'Why does this black man come among us?' When he heard this he kept silence. When the council was dismissed, they said to him, 'Abba, did that not grieve you at all?' He said to them, 'I was grieved, but I kept silence.'[157]

One suspects that such incidents of racial prejudice were not always mere pretence.

All this material, together with the more literary works mentioned earlier and such material as the *Lives* and *Rule* of Pachomius, is a vast area of study with many fascinations. The problem of the manuscript traditions, the relationship between the various sources, the question of the reliability of each pericope, the effects of turning oral material into literary material and of translation from one language to another – all these problems make the study of this literature, in general terms at least, somewhat analogous to study of the gospels. Whatever the detailed solutions to the critical problems, these documents provide us with virtually our only source-material for the origins and character of Egyptian and Palestinian monasticism, a movement which had an enormous influence on the wider church scene in the period with which we are dealing. In general terms we cannot doubt that the impression they create is a reliable reflection of the ethos that developed in the desert communities.

3. The monks of Syria

With Theodoret's *Historia religiosa*[158] we move from Egypt, the cradle and 'holy land' of the monastic movement, to the rather different atmosphere of Syria. Syrian asceticism had a character and history of its own, and almost certainly had independent roots.[159] Radical discipleship, taking literally the demand to forsake all and follow Christ, seems to have been characteristic of primitive Syrian Christianity, including the universal requirement of chastity after baptism; and the early Christian monks seem to have assimilated to their Christian discipleship a local ascetic tradition whereby individuals abandoned civilized life and reverted to the natural life of wild beasts, eating uncooked the natural produce of the earth, and wandering through the wilderness. In its developed form, Syrian asceticism went to strange extremes, so that ancient and modern critics alike have written deprecatingly of the way in which the holy men of Syria and Mesopotamia vied with each other in ascetic exercises. To pray and sing hymns continually while deliberately subjecting the body to unheard-of discomforts seems to have been the main object in view. The ascetics lived in permanent darkness in caves or tombs, or on high mountain tops unprotected from the extremes of the climate. Not content with simple food and clothing, they fasted completely for ever-increasing periods, and clad themselves in iron so that they were bent continually to the ground, or their skin was chafed till the blood ran. The culmination was Symeon Stylites' thirty-odd years on a sixty-foot pillar, an example which subsequently produced a 'pillar-saint' tradition in the early Byzantine period. We seem a long way from the saying of the *Apophthegmata* against doing things for show, or the wise reply of Abba Poemen to the question how one should fast:

> I would have it so that every day one should deny oneself a little in eating, so as not to be satisfied . . . (for) all these things did the great old men try out and they found that it is good to eat a little every day, and on certain days a little less.[160]

Theodoret had close personal connections with the monks of the Syrian provinces and the Euphrates region (for details, see ch. 5.VII); and whatever our reaction, it is clear that he regarded the Syrian ascetics with veneration. His rhetorical prologue compares them with the heroes of the theatre and the games, describing them as athletes or gladiators who take on the whole armour of God to struggle against unseen enemies. Yet he will not write 'encomia' exalting their spiritual prowess as individuals; for their exploits are charismata, mysterious workings of the Holy Spirit, demonstrating 'philosophy' – ἀπάθεια (passionlessness) in a body subject to passion (παθητός), zeal for incorporeal nature and heavenly citizenship. The monks live the lives of angels, for they imitate while in the body the life of non-bodily beings. Theodoret's work is clearly intended to edify, and he claims to write a record for posterity; but was there some other purpose?

Theodoret refers to his *Historia religiosa* in his *Ecclesiastical History*, and by relating it in various ways to his other writings, as well as considering internal evidence, it is possible to date the work fairly definitely to around 444. At this time Theodoret had been bishop of Cyrrhus for twenty years, and during the extended, though not unruffled, lull in the christological battle with Alexandria, had devoted himself to composing scriptural commentaries. As we shall see later, Theodoret's literary activity was very wide-ranging – he seems to have tried out more or less every ecclesiastical genre from apologetics to history, to exegesis, to anti-heretical tracts. It is possible that he had no greater motive than to contribute to the growing literature of spiritual edification through telling the deeds of the saints.

However, the distinguished scholar P. Peeters, in a study of the *Lives* of St. Symeon,[161] advanced the view that Theodoret wrote under immediate pressures, his purpose being to rehabilitate his reputation among the monks of Syria; he was tarred with the

Nestorian brush, was at loggerheads with John of Antioch over the Formulary of Reunion and was getting a cold reception among the ascetics. So he wrote the *Historia religiosa* to prove his championship of the Syrian ascetics against the Egyptian monks who flocked to Cyril's support. This view has met with some trenchant criticisms. Richard[162] showed that relations with John of Antioch had long since been restored, and that there are no signs of the conflict Peeters imagined in the period when the *Historia religiosa* was written. It is true that some of his letters show him trying to ensure the monks' support when renewed conflict broke out; but, Canivet argues,[163] these letters are not so much concerned with his personal position as the need to involve the monks in ecclesiastical affairs and to guarantee their orthodoxy. It is significant that impeccable orthodoxy is the mark of every one of the characters portrayed in the *Historia religiosa*; but Theodoret's aim was to keep the potentially autonomous monastic communities under episcopal authority and in line with the episcopate on doctrinal issues. Self-defence was not among his intentions.

Apologetic for the ascetic movement, however, may well have been an important purpose, though Theodoret probably had a number of somewhat mixed motives. As Canivet observes, we have considerable evidence that in this period cultivated and civilized people, especially pagans, despised the monks as ignorant rustics or hypocrites undermining society. There are also traces of criticism directed particularly against the ascetic practices of the Syrians which were unfavourably compared with those of the heroes of Palestine and Egypt. Although Theodoret never makes this apologetic purpose explicit, never directly answering criticisms, his choice of irreproachable examples and his presentation of the anchorites as the prototypes of the Christian life, as the heroes of a new kind of epic, as the champions in a new kind of conflict, as the incarnation of a new type of humanity – all this suggests that he is offering a reply to detractors. He says he means to avoid panegyric and write an *historia*: but history in the ancient world meant presenting moral examples, and his collection of 'lives' is in the fashionable tradition of 'Lives of the Sages'. The true philosophy is presented by means of a series of biographical portraits. Theodoret's title was *Philotheos historia*, perhaps an echo of Galen's *Philosophos historia*.

This background accounts for the somewhat different form of Theodoret's work compared with those considered earlier. Theodoret does not offer a rather diffuse collections of sayings and anecdotes, nor an autobiographical account of his travels, but a series of 'Lives of the Saints'. The work consists of 30 biographies (mostly of outstanding individuals, though nos. 22, 24 and 29 combine two together), with a prologue and a concluding essay, 'On Love', which was probably written a few years later. All Theodoret's characters were founders of monasteries or great individual exponents of the anchorite life, and all are presented as faultless models of the monastic ideal in one form or another. Theodoret gives some hints about the intended arrangement – generally speaking, it follows a chronological and geographical scheme. Thus Theodoret begins with those who had died before his time, and goes on to contemporaries including several he had known in his youth – Aphraat, Peter, Zeno, Macedonius. A third of the book deals with monks still alive at the time of writing; in the case of Symeon Stylites, who lived until 459, the part referring to his death is clearly a later interpolation.[164] Men are in the majority, but the final three are holy women. A few of the 'Lives' are brief notices, but in many cases the Life gives some account of the origin of the subject, his methods of asceticism, and a number of anecdotes, each one being a literary piece potentially independent of the entire work. This is particularly true of the 'Life of Symeon', the relationship of Theodoret's Life with other early Lives being in this case a critical question of some complexity.

This bring us to the question of sources. Theodoret, anxious to provide guarantees of the extraordinary things he relates, affirms that he has seen some facts with his own eyes, and what he has not seen himself, he has heard from those who had been witnesses. This seems to exclude written sources, and Canivet[165] argues that that is the case. Theodoret reports the popular legends which had grown up around such early figures as James of Nisibis. He frequently tells us where he got his information from, where possible naming a reliable witness like his pious mother or Acacius of Beroea. Even the 'Life of Symeon' distinguishes between what Theodoret had himself seen and what he had heard from others. Canivet is disposed to take Theodoret's word for it. Yet the 'Life of Symeon' is far more of a 'Saint's Day Sermon' or exhortation to pilgrims than the other Lives; it follows the pattern of a panegyric, tends towards the rhetorical in style, and compares its hero with Old Testament prophets. Thus it bears more of the marks that came to characterize the hagiographical tradition, and lacks the spontaneity of other pieces where Theodoret claims personal acquaintance. Furthermore, it presents an apology for 'Stylitism' which closely resembles that of the Syriac Life written in 474; so far from the Syriac being dependent on Theodoret, as Delahaye suggested,[166] the most likely explanation is that of Festugière, namely that both drew on the 'official' apologetic legend composed by the attendant monks.[167] Theodoret himself speaks of other accounts already existing in the saint's lifetime. That Theodoret's account is a patchwork, partially drawing on source-material and partially on his personal experience, seems most likely; but clearly the critical questions surrounding this part of Theodoret's work remain complex.

Without Theodoret's *Historia religiosa*, our knowledge of Syrian monasticism would be seriously depleted. Many of the characters he describes would be unknown, and the spread of the movement in the late fourth and early fifth centuries would be obscure. Yet there is a sense in which Theodoret has attempted to 'domesticate' the wilder elements of the movement he describes.[168] Extreme ascetic practices are reported, but Theodoret tends to avoid dwelling on them, approves of ecclesiastics who tried to moderate them and hastens to characterize the 'angelic life' of his characters. In what respects did they live the life of angels? Most obviously in their virginity – for immortal beings do not need to propagate the species; but more importantly in their perpetual worship – the work of angels is to dance in heaven and sing to the glory of the Creator. Chanting psalms and singing hymns, contemplating the divine beauty through reading the scriptures – these were the principal activities for the sake of which the monk abandoned the world and sought to eliminate all distractions. Physical needs were neglected for the sake of continual prayer and prostration. True, there is an element of deliberate mortification of the flesh which implies a rejection of the body as an alien element; dualism was never far away in the Orient, and Theodoret here no doubt reflects the mentality of those he describes. He himself, however, appears very sympathetic to marriage in his other writings, and like most of the Fathers, definitely opposed the extreme dualism of Manicheans and others. Even the ideal of ἀπάθεια (passionlessness) which figures so prominently in the *Historia religiosa*, he elsewhere recognizes to be an attribute of God alone, unattainable for created beings. On the whole, even in this work, Theodoret favours moderation, serenity, gentleness and meekness, so much so that there is sometimes a certain incongruity between his factual reports of the ascetics and his generalizing descriptions. Part of this taming process he achieved by 'Hellenizing' his characters, depicting them according to the philosophical and heroic models of the genre he had chosen; thus Theodoret attributes to his new-style philosophers the cardinal Greek virtues: σωφροσύνη, δικαιοσύνη,

ἀνδρεία and σοφία (temperance, justice, courage and wisdom) –
though in his conclusion, he sees their highest motivation in terms
of Christian virtue, ἀγάπη (love). What really impresses Theodoret
about the ascetics is that they surpass the normal capabilities of
human nature – they represent the new humanity constituted in
Christ. His heroes have undertaken a campaign against evil and
paganism, a combat with the devil who is overcome by their
exorcisms and cures, a race in which they will win an imperishable
crown; for they are the imitators of God's prophets, indeed the
imitators of Christ himself. This gives them παρρησία (freedom to
speak familiarly) before God, and authority among men.

For another role performed by the angels is the protection of
nations and individuals. So the ascetics were angels on earth with
power and authority in the world of affairs. Although their ideal
was to avoid human contact and converse with God (Symeon's
column got higher and higher to avoid the crowds), it is clear that
the holy men, so far from merely providing an edifying example,
actually played a positive role in the half-Christian society of the
dying Roman empire.[169] They were sought out by the populace for
cures to diseases of the flesh as well as social and political ills, for
judicial decisions and advice of all sorts. In these pages we not only
read of Symeon Stylites on his pillar dispensing justice, comfort and
spiritual assistance to all comers regularly at the ninth hour, and
then returning to prayer at sunset until the ninth hour of the
following day – but we also see how natural Theodoret regards it
that his pleasure-loving young mother should have sought a cure
from Peter the Galatian when suffering from an eye-complaint, and
that his childless parents should have turned for help to Macedonius the 'barley-eater'. Furthermore, we find anecdotes in which
holy men stood up to heretic emperors, and acted as '*patroni*' for
citizens subject to imperial displeasure. Their extraordinary feats
set them apart as holy, and their holiness gave them a freedom of
speech in the courts of earth and heaven which was denied to
others. So their intercessory powers were highly valued, and
illiterate rustics acquired a prestige which made them a new social
élite. The outstanding ascetic, of whatever social class, surpassed
human limitations and belonged to the angelic world. This was
Theodoret's justification of what was already a social fact: the
extraordinary impact of 'wild vagrants in skins . . . [who] disquieted
the Greco-Roman world by their histrionic gestures',[170] and the
consequent shift in power and influence that took place in the
society and culture of the late Roman empire.

Theodoret's picture of the monks living an 'angelic life' picks up a motif already found in the *Historia monachorum*. In the prologue to that work, we also find the monks depicted as new prophets, true servants of God, not preoccupied with food and clothing but with continuous prayer and hymn-singing, awaiting the return of Christ in the desert. Syrian asceticism may have had its own characteristics and its own roots, yet the similarities run deep. In Egypt and Syria alike, the anchorites were sought out for cures, and consulted like the oracles of the classical world. And in all the monastic literature the monks have taken the offensive against the powers of evil;[171] they have marched into the desert to meet the demons on their own territory; they have tackled them through healing and exorcism; they have captured their citadels, the tombs; and they continue the struggle to the end, outwitting their most dangerous weapons – temptations and evil thoughts. Thus the monks followed Christ with a faith capable of moving mountains. Is it any wonder that miracles and prodigies flourished, that the wild beasts were tamed, and heaven anticipated on earth?

IV. Conclusion

In this chapter we have moved from the atmosphere of the third century when the church was a persecuted minority still seeking intellectual and social acceptability, to the very different ethos of the early Byzantine period with its popular devotion to relics, martyrs, saints and holy men. Yet there is a religious and literary tradition which spans the centuries. Theodoret shares the interests and the culture of Eusebius in more than one respect; for if in the realm of philosophical theology, Eusebius had hardly moved with the times, in other ways he anticipated the attitudes and outlook of the Christian empire and the imperial church of the Byzantine world. The church was now in a position to review its past; and while popular Christianity developed the cult of its dead heroes, the cultured produced literary works most of which were concerned to glorify the triumph of the one true catholic and orthodox church. In this atmosphere both hagiography and church history flowered.

Chapter Two

Athanasius and some Fellow-Alexandrians of the Fourth Century[1]

The history and theology of the fourth century is dominated by the figure of Athanasius, who as Patriarch of Alexandria forged a remarkable link with Rome and the West, publicized Egypt's monastic movement and won over the monks themselves to catholic orthodoxy, and against all odds courageously upheld the faith of Nicaea through skilful politics and theological acumen. Athanasius became a legendary figure, to some extent even in his own lifetime. Part of the aim in this chapter is critically to examine that legend, while providing an interpretation of his overall theological position.

A contrasting figure is found in Athanasius' contemporary and fellow-Alexandrian, Didymus the Blind. Posterity has relegated him to relative obscurity, and he was not a prominent public figure in his own day. Yet he too was a legend in his own lifetime, a scholar whose fame drew the educated Christian public from afar. Current interest in Didymus has been stimulated by new discoveries which have given us direct access to many lost writings.

First, however, another Alexandrian takes the stage. The local priest Arius has given his name to one of the bitterest disputes in the history of the early church. The Arian controversy rumbled on from Nicaea (325) to Constantinople (381), and for the church at large it had wide political and theological implications. On the one hand it stimulated the discussions which led to the formulation of the trinitarian dogma and ultimately the Chalcedonian definition, on the other hand it shattered the unity of the church just as it acquired peace, power and influence in the empire, and it even exacerbated the unhappy state of the Catholic West when it fell a century later before the barbarian invaders – for the barbarians were converts to the Arian version of Christianity. Arianism certainly caused havoc, and Arius came to be regarded as the arch-heretic. His opponents believed that his ideas were deliberately framed to deceive the unwary and corrupt the gospel. But how far was their estimate of Arius just? It is by no means clear that what he actually taught deserved the vilification it has received from his own day to the present, and he was after all merely the trigger which set off the conflagration. The main protagonists were the leading bishops of the East, and the issues became more subtle as the controversy developed. Arius' views need to be distinguished from the sophisticated philosophies of the later Arian sophists, Aetius and Eunomius. To many of his own contemporaries he certainly did not appear in the same light as he did in retrospect; for it is quite clear that at first many found his position more in line with traditional Christianity than that of his opponents. The ambivalent reaction of Eusebius of Caesarea we have already noted. Can we get behind the slanted traditional picture, and reassess Arius' position?

I. Arius

Here is not the place for a history of the controversy with all its complicated political ramifications, but a sketch of Arius' career will provide the background for our discussion. Arius was a native of Libya, but Alexandria had become his place of residence. At the time when his views became controversial, probably but not certainly around 318[2], he was serving as a priest in the city, and apparently his preaching attracted a large following. It is reported that before this he had connections with the Meletians, a group of schismatics who had split with bishop Peter at the time of the Great Persecution. However, he had been reconciled with bishop Achillas, and ordained presbyter; Alexander, Achillas' successor in the episcopal seat, apparently held him in high esteem.[3] Socrates claims that Arius spoke out because of a sermon preached by Alexander which seemed to him to be dangerously Sabellian.[4] However, the evidence suggests that it is unlikely that Alexander was instrumental in initiating the controversy, even if he unconsciously stimulated it – rather he was reluctantly drawn in when it became apparent that Arius' views were causing considerable disruption in the Church. According to Rufinus, Alexander was a 'gentle and quiet' man,[5] and there is evidence that he went out of

his way to secure a fair hearing for Arius: this is reflected in
Sozomen's account of his wavering between the opposing views
expressed by his clergy,[6] and contemporary charges of irresolution
and excessive forbearance.

At this point, then, we can reconstruct a picture of a gentle and
tolerant bishop gradually forced to move against a popular preacher
whose controversial views were finding increasing support among
considerable sections of the community. The spread of Arius' ideas
amongst the working classes was stimulated by the composition of
popular songs 'for the sea, for the mill, and for the road', suitably
set to music.[7] A synod of Egyptian bishops eventually excommunicated Arius, who then toured the major Eastern sees
building up support for himself.[8] Eusebius of Nicomedia became
his most persistent and influential advocate, and Eusebius of
Caesarea allowed him to preach.

It is from this period that our earliest evidence of Arius's views
comes. Epiphanius preserves several letters written by Arius, and
reports that in his day seventy letters from Alexander to episcopal
colleagues in the East were extant.[9] The first of Arius' letters[10] that
we know is an appeal to Eusebius of Nicomedia, written before he
left Egypt, complaining that he has been excommunicated because
he says that the Son had a beginning, whereas God is without
beginning. Arius contrasts his position with that of Alexander who
persecutes him for refusing to preach the eternal generation of the
Son. The second letter of Arius is addressed to Alexander,[11] and is
usually attributed to his time at Nicomedia.[12] It is an ἔκθεσις
πίστεως, a public letter outlining his position. He claims that he is
setting out the faith of their forefathers, but then gives the
impression that he basically argued from propositions of a strictly
monotheistic character: God alone is ingenerate ($\dot{\alpha}\gamma\dot{\epsilon}\nu(\nu)\eta\tau o\varsigma$),[13]
alone eternal, alone without beginning, alone true, alone has
immortality, alone is wise, alone good, alone sovereign. The Son is
not coeternal with the Father, but God is before all things, being
Monad and Beginning of all. Arius appeals to Alexander by
suggesting that this is no different from the faith he learned from
him, his bishop, and claims that his condemnation of Sabellian and
Adoptionist errors is equal to Alexander's. The representation of
Alexander's views is rather different from that given in his earlier
appeal to Eusebius, but this is surely no more than should be
expected in the circumstances. The first was written in the heat of
anger at his excommunication, the second is an appeal to sink their
differences and recognize their common ground. On the other side,
two of Alexander's letters to episcopal colleagues, preserved by

Socrates and Theodoret, show that once convinced of Arius' error and intransigence, the bishop remained firm in his condemnation. The first[14] contains a useful summary of Arius' teaching, which confirms the impression gained from Arius' own extant writings; the second[15] warns a number of bishops outside Egypt about Arius and his followers, accusing them of hiding their corrupting doctrine with all too persuasive and tricky discourses, and attacking some of the standard Arian assertions.

The subsequent history is well known. Constantine was moved to intervene and, at the first Ecumenical Council at Nicaea, the majority condemned Arius and accepted the Nicene creed. However, the embarrassment of Eusebius of Caesarea, an embarrassment quite evident in his explanatory letter to his home church,[16] indicates that even at the time misgivings were felt. Conflict was bound to break out again. Few refused to accept Arius when Constantine recalled him from exile and sought his reinstatement as priest. During these negotiations, Constantine obtained from Arius a confession of faith, a letter which simply produced a creed, written in straightforward biblical phrases and avoiding all controversial language. Socrates and Sozomen[17] who preserve this letter, differ as to whether it was required before Arius' recall or before the Council of Tyre in 335. Only a year after that Council, Arius died, but his doctrines survived to disrupt the church for many more decades.

Arius has been dismissed as of small literary importance.[18] It is true that he wrote little beside the letters already referred to, but his use of verse forms may not be unimportant in the history of hymnography. Some of the popular songs already referred to may have been incorporated in the one literary work we know of, the *Thalia* (Banquet). This survives only in quotations made by opponents for the purpose of refuting the views expressed; the text must have disappeared very early since no one quotes more than the standard Arian formulae after Athanasius and Marcellus of Ancyra. Reconstruction of the work has proved virtually impossible, since Athanasius, our main source, makes few direct quotations, collects random examples out of context, frequently paraphrases, and his citations are vague enough to cast doubt on whether his source is always the *Thalia*. Athanasius scorns the *Thalia* as an imitation of the dissolute drinking-songs of the Egyptian Sotades and accuses Arius of 'dancing and joking in his blasphemies against the Saviour',[19] but it may not be fair to trust his biassed judgment. The quotations seem to indicate that the work was indeed written in verse – the opening seven lines suggest the presence of an acrostic poem – but the metrical form has been difficult to establish. Some have resorted to the suggestion that the work was not wholly in metrical form, but possibly contained some formal argument and exegesis.[20] It was apparently during his stay with Eusebius of Nicomedia that Arius put his heresy on paper in this rather unusual fashion, though this interpretation of the evidence has been challenged.[21]

In spite of vast extant literature from Arius' opponents, our knowledge of Arius' original teaching, its sources and inspiration, is limited. The fifth-century historians give the impression that he was a superb dialectician and was misled by his own logical powers.[22] From this, the conclusion has sometimes been drawn that Arius was simply trying to work out the logical consequences of his philosophical presuppositions. He began with the proposition that the essential attribute of God is that his being is underived (ἀγέν(ν)ητος); the Son was begotten (γεννητός), and this derivative state means that he differs essentially from true God. Therefore, he must be a creature, though, as traditional phrases indicated, he was the first and greatest of God's creatures, through whom the rest of creation was formed. Since he was a creature he was fallible and passible; furthermore, being other than the Father, he could not know him perfectly and accurately. It was these corollaries which showed up the extreme to which Arius' logic had taken him. Alexander reports that Arians were even willing to admit that, though in fact sinless, the Word of God could have fallen like the devil. The orthodox, then, soon came to recognize that Arius' theories struck at the heart of the Christian gospel of redemption and revelation through the very Word of God himself, and reduced the Lord they worshipped to the level of a demi-god or demon. Thus a widespread estimate of Arius is that he was moved more by logic than by faith, that his monotheism was more philosophical than scriptural and that, as his contemporaries said, it was no better than paganism. As Pollard put it, Arius transformed the 'living God of the Bible' into the 'Absolute of the philosophical schools'.[23] If that estimate is fair, then Arius undoubtedly was the 'arch-heretic' which tradition has made him out to be.

However, more and more objections have been raised against this estimate of Arius' theological position. That Arius was moved more by cosmological or logical considerations that any sense of salvation in Christ is open to question; for a Saviour who realistically faced and conquered genuine temptations to which, being τρεπτός (changeable), he might have succumbed but over which he nevertheless triumphed κατὰ χάριν (by grace), has some soteriological advantages over a divine being who triumphs willy-nilly.[24] Following up this possibility has produced some startling results; for it has been suggested that examination of the thrust of the arguments used by Arius' opponents confirms the hints found in the extant fragments that whatever the form in which they are expressed, Arius' views basically *arose* out of such soteriological considerations.[25] The nub of the argument between Arius and his opponents concerned the nature of sonship, the Arians insisting that the Son was Son by grace and obedience on the grounds that our salvation depended upon his identity with us. 'Christ's limitations are exactly ours (willing, choosing, striving, suffering, advancing) and likewise Christ's benefits and glories are exactly ours . . . . what the Arians are proclaiming is not a demotion of the Son, but a promotion of believers to full and equal status as Sons.'[26] The issues were not trinitarian as the textbooks suggest, but soteriological, ethical and christological.

This somewhat revolutionary suggestion may well have gone too far in rejecting standard estimates of Arius; but there are other reasons for questioning the traditional characterization of Arianism as a pagan or philosophical distortion of Christian truth. There are a number of evident facts which do not accord well with that judgment: (i) His position could be presented as thoroughly scriptural – at Nicaea his opponents were forced to adopt the non-scriptural, philosophical term *homoousios* (of the same substance) in order to exclude his views.[27] He proved during his career that he had no difficulty in accepting creeds couched in traditional scriptural language. (ii) The argument with Arius revolved around certain key texts of scripture, and often his opponents had to produce very forced exegesis to counter his position. Recent studies have therefore taken very seriously the possibility that Arius' views had their starting-point in scripture. Boulerand[28] notes that Theodoret says that Arius had been put in charge of scriptural exposition; and that Hilary states that Arius' principal doctrine, that there is only one God, he got from Moses. The character of Arius' teaching presupposes, not any current philosophical monotheism, but an exegetical debate within Christian circles about the status of the Logos. Arius adopted a literalist interpretation of those texts which attributed progress and human weakness to the Son of God, and found this confirmed by John 14.28: My Father is greater than I. He accepted the traditional view that Wisdom in Proverbs 8 is identical with the Logos, and on the basis of v. 22 concluded that the Logos was God's creature.

Of course Arius used certain philosophical terms, like Monad and ἀγέν(ν)ητος. But then so did everyone else. Studies of the philosophy of Arius have converged to show that Arius himself, unlike the later Arian Sophists Aetius and Eunomius, is unlikely to have imported philosophical considerations into his theology; rather he inherited them through the Christian tradition itself. Barnard[29] has demonstrated important connections between the thought of Arius and that of the earlier apologist, Athenagoras; and Stead[30] has suggested that 'Arius draws upon a Platonic tradition evolving within the church rather than representing a violent incursion of alien philosophy'. That Arius had fundamentally conservative intentions now seems highly probable; that he forged various fluid ideas into a system with 'remorseless logic'[31] is more debatable. The complex question of his antecendents becomes more and more crucial in estimating his contribution.

There has been considerable controversy over what those antecedents were. A less than respectable background was suggested by Arius' ancient opponents, and some investigators have accepted that their accusations had some basis in fact. Alexander's encyclical accuses Arius of resurrecting the heresies of Ebion, Artemas, Paul of Samosata and Lucian, his successor; if this can be accepted as evidence, it suggests that Arius' ideas were ultimately derived from the notorious Paul, heretical bishop of Antioch, through a continuing adoptionist tradition there. The evidence is good that Arius received his theological education in the school of Lucian of Antioch; he appeals to Eusebius of Nicomedia as a 'fellow-Lucianist', and Lucian's pupils who included a number of bishops around the Eastern Mediterranean apparently united in Arius' defence when opposition became evident. The connection between Lucian and Paul of Samosata, however, is hard to establish on the meagre evidence we have; we know little of Paul's actual position and virtually nothing of Lucian's teaching.[32] That Lucian was a revered martyr, and a textual critic who probably made an important contribution to establishing the Byzantine text of the New Testament, is the sum total of our knowledge. Arius' literalism in scriptural interpretation may well be one of the features inherited from his Antiochene connection: but whether Arianism had its doctrinal roots in Antioch is less certain. The fact is that links can be traced between Arius' views and those of earlier Alexandrians, even if a continuous or coherent tradition cannot be established. Arius' doctrine of God has affinities with Athenagoras and Clement, his subordinationism belongs to the Origenist tradition, his theological method is anticipated in Dionysius of Alexandria, and his biblical literalism may be connected with bishop Peter.[33] Arius was guilty not so much of demoting the Son as exalting the Father; for, as Stead has shown, he taught a hierarchical Trinity of the Origenist type, a fact obscured by Athanasius for his own polemic purposes but confirmed by the reaction of Eusebius of Caesarea. Athanasius emphasized the fact that Arius ranked the Logos among the creatures; whereas Arius' main concern was probably to avoid attributing physical processes like emanation or generation to God, a traditional point developed earlier against the Gnostics. Arius therefore expressed coherently what many Christians had long since assumed.

Sozomen tells us that Arius originated these disputations 'under a pretext of piety and of seeking a complete discovery of God'. These phrases suggest that Arius may have been an original thinker with honest intentions, though the hint is masked by the charge of pretext. Alexander's reference to Arius' persuasive and tricky discourses no doubt reflects the fact that Arius' account of Christian belief was attractive, probably because of its literalism, its clarity and its simplicity. Indeed, the popularity of his biblical solution to the tension between monotheism and faith in Christ is beyond dispute; and there is no reason to doubt Arius' sincerity or genuine Christian intention. Though his opponents attributed his popularity to deception, it is more likely that it was a response to one who was enthusiastic in his pursuit of the true meaning of the Christian confession.

Yet perhaps this estimate is attributing too much initiative to Arius. It is not impossible that he was simply a die-hard conservative who was not afraid to challenge what he considered the innovations of his bishop, and who attracted a following merely on the grounds that he voiced what so many others felt about dangerous theological developments. Those who opposed Arianism found it difficult to find a formula which would effectively exclude his line of interpretation, simply because he had a serious claim to be voicing tradition; he genuinely believed that he was setting forth 'our faith from our forefathers'. Like Eusebius, he was concerned about 'monotheism and morality'.[34] If this estimate is right, the Arius was not himself the arch-heretic of tradition, nor even much of an enquirer; rather he was a reactionary, a rather literal-minded conservative who appealed to scripture and tradition as the basis of his faith.

II. Athanasius

1. The Legend

It was Alexander's successor, Athanasius, who bore the brunt of the controversy into which his predecessor had been drawn. In his early years he served Alexander as deacon and personal secretary, and in this capacity he was present at Nicaea. Of the two, Athanasius undoubtedly had the stronger personality, and posterity has given him credit for inspiring Alexander's determined opposition to Arius; Gregory of Nazianzus represents him as taking a stand against the Arian 'plague' at the actual Council, even though he was not yet a bishop.[35] In fact it is hardly likely that a young deacon would have had any opportunity of contributing to the discussions of such a venerable collection of episcopal dignitaries, and even if he influenced his own bishop, Alexander's part in the proceedings does not appear to have been crucial; he was certainly not responsible for introducing the key Nicene formulation.

The enhanced role of Athanasius at Nicaea is one feature of the 'legend of Athanasius' which rapidly developed. This 'good tradition' has affected all the main sources, for Athanasius' own apologetic works were a primary source for the historians. Thus the classic picture is of a steadfast saint and theologian who almost single-handed defended the Nicene formula through the reigns of Arian emperors, and finally engineered a reconciliation among anti-Arian parties in the East. A typical reconstruction of the troubled but triumphant life depicted in the sources would run something like this:

Athanasius was still only in his thirties when he succeeded Alexander as bishop in 328. The seat he inherited proved to be a somewhat uncomfortable one. Constantine's aim at Nicaea had been to establish unity in the church, but the *homoousion* formula was received with considerable misgivings by the majority of Eastern bishops, and when it became politically expedient, few refused to accept Arius and his associates into communion with the church. Athanasius was the only really influential figure who remained obstinate. Charges of murder and black magic secured his deposition at the scarcely impartial Synod of Tyre (335), and appeal to Constantine merely induced the conspirators to produce the simpler but more disturbing charge that Athanasius had interfered with the sailing of corn-ships from Alexandria to the capital. This accusation aggravated any suspicions the emperor already harboured that the bishop was becoming too powerful in Egypt, and gave him an opportunity of removing the one obstacle to the restoration of peace in the church. Athanasius was sent into exile at Trier.

This was merely the beginning of Athanasius' troubles. After Constantine's death in 337, Athanasius returned home, but the Eastern empire was now under Constantius, an Arian sympathizer, and the Eastern bishops were, on the whole, prepared to toe the imperial line. In 339, Athanasius fled again to the West, where the Pope and Constans were in sympathy with him. It is said that Athanasius introduced the new monasticism to the Western church during his exiles, as well as building up formidable support for his own position. From 340, the Western and Eastern halves of empire and church were divided by the Arian doctrines, a tragic situation exemplified in the irreconcilable split at the Council of Sardica in 343.

After the death of Gregory, the usurper of Athanasius' see, Constantius gave way to pressure from Constans and Athanasius was reinstated (346); but once his advocate had been murdered, his position was far from secure. Athanasius' career shows how it was becoming increasingly difficult for a far-flung and diverse community like the church to maintain independence from the political power of its most illustrious lay member. The presence of Constantius, now sole emperor, coerced even a Western Council (Milan 355) to depose Athanasius, and in 356 the imperial soldiers arrived at his church door. George the Cappadocian, who superseded Athanasius amid scenes of plunder and violence, was intensely unpopular with the people of Alexandria who stood by their deposed bishop throughout his third exile. This time Athanasius did not flee abroad, but stayed concealed amongst the loyal monks of Egypt, sometimes even within the city of Alexandria itself. Many were the legends told of how Athanasius eluded the imperial detectives during this period, sometimes escaping very narrowly; as the 'invisible patriarch', he successfully adminstered the church of the faithful who protected him, kept him informed of the situation, and distributed the apologetic pamphlets which he wrote in hiding. Twice more under Julian the Apostate and Valens the Arian, Athanasius spent short periods of exile concealed in this fashion by his local supporters. It was during Athanasius' episcopacy that a close alliance was forged between the archbishop of the city and the monks of the countryside, an alliance which proved a powerful political force in the following century. In the wider sphere, Athanasius attained such respect that he was appealed to as an authority by Basil of Caesarea; and he made a genuine ecumenical attempt to bring together the various anti-Arian parties in the later years of his life, notably in his *Tomus ad Antiochenos*, a conciliar letter addressed to the split church in Antioch.

Athanasius died in 373, an aged but triumphant upholder of his convictions. During his forty-five years as bishop, he had only two extended periods of relatively peaceful residence in his seat, from 346 to 356, and the last seven years of his life. He had lived as a martyr for the sake of truth.

Alongside this 'good tradition', however, there are traces of a less favourable estimate of Athanasius current among his contemporaries.[36] Certainly he must have been a politician capable of subtle manoeuvres; the first seems to have been in his own election, which was definitely contested, may have been illegal, and looks as though it was enforced. There seems to have been a pitiless streak in his character – that he resorted to violence to achieve his own ends is implied by a good deal of evidence. When he succeeded Alexander, he inherited a volatile local situation. The surprising strength of the Meletian party in Egypt has often been overlooked through preoccupation with the Arian problem, but there is evidence to suggest that thirty-five out of sixty-five Egyptian bishops were Meletians. Athanasius managed to antagonize this group rather than facilitate their reconciliation according to the provisions of Nicaea, and it was evidence supplied by the Meletians which made Athanasius vulnerable to attack at the Council of Tyre. That he did not scruple to use force in his dealings with this group can hardly be doubted, and his deposition at Tyre was based, not on doctrinal considerations, but upon his misconduct in Egypt. Rusch is certainly right in suggesting that the hostile reports of Philostorgius, the evidence of the papyri, and the criticisms that Gregory Nazianzen felt that he had to answer in his panegyric, must be admitted as evidence in the search for the 'historical Athanasius'.

Besides this, the idea that Athanasius' influence dominated the Eastern church from 345 to 373 has been subjected to searching criticism by J. M. Leroux.[37] According to his interpretation of the evidence, Athanasius was out of touch: he went on fighting the old battle against Arius when everyone else was struggling with the much subtler issues raised by Aetius and Eunomius; he had no idea of the real situation in Antioch, Basil only appealed to him because he had influence in the West, and the *Tomus ad Antiochenos* was addressed only to the quarrelsome ultra-Nicenes. Thus, in Egypt alone did Athanasius have the ascendency attributed to him, and even here he had had to defend himself; his apologetic works were a means of justifying his dubious career to his own flock and were not widely disseminated elsewhere. Ecclesiastical politics in the East mostly passed him by.

This 'deflation' of Athanasius probably goes to far; some elements in the good tradition are certainly right. By the end of his life, Athanasius had forged a remarkable alliance with the Coptic monks and had won complete ascendency over Egypt. It was on the power-base he had established that successors like Theophilus and Cyril were to challenge the authority of Constantinople and of the emperor himself. If his local position was so shaky to start with, his political skills must have been the more considerable.[38] Furthermore, he did obstinately hold out for a particular theological position, and with the backing of the West, upheld it whatever the cost. Why was it that he was unable to compromise? What was the driving force behind his single-mindedness?

We are in the fortunate position of having plenty of material in which to find the answer to these questions. In spite of his turbulent career, Athanasius' literary output was enormous, and most of it is concerned with the bitter controversies in which he was involved. His own writings not merely provide the bulk of our information about the stormy events of his life and the various charges brought against him; but they also allow us to see the force of his argumentation, the clarity and consistency of his theological thinking, and the sincerity of his belief that he was safeguarding the truth of scripture, the tradition of the church, and the faith for which the martyrs had died during his early years. We can here detect the presuppositions of his faith, and so appreciate why it was that the refutation of Arianism was for him a matter of life and death, for which he would face all difficulties and every form of persecution.

2. The *De Incarnatione*

Some development can be traced in Athanasius' thought as far as details and means of expression are concerned, but the central core of his position was never touched. His earliest writings are in fact the key to his life and his dogmatic argumentation. Yet it is usually assumed that the *Contra gentes* and the *De incarnatione*, two volumes of a single apologetic work, were

written before the outbreak of the Arian controversy. The grounds
on which this dating rests lie in the absence of any reference to
Arius in these works, but this argument is not necessarily
conclusive, since there is no reference to Arius in the *Festal
Letters* of 329–335;[39] surely a warning would be more appropriate
in a pastoral letter than in a work intended to interest non-
believers? Supporters of such an early date suggest that Athanasius, as yet barely in his twenties, wrote the work as a theological
essay not intended for publication. The shorter and longer
versions of the work evidenced in the textual traditions are
explained as two different drafts, both found among Athanasius'
papers at the end of his life.[40] If this is correct, Athanasius had laid
the foundations of his mature faith at a remarkably early age. A
later date seems on the face of it much more likely. Furthermore,
the relationship between these volumes and Eusebius'
Theophania is less puzzling if they are assigned to Athanasius'
first exile at Trier.[41] The *Theophania* undoubtedly appeared in the
early 330s. It is hardly likely that the aged and respected scholar
and historian, Eusebius, would have drawn from the apologetic
work of a young deacon scarcely out of his teens. Either the
similarities must be attributed to a common apologetic tradition
and a common cultural and religious milieu,[42] or else we must
accept a much later date for Athanasius' work. That Athanasius
made use of Eusebius' work is made all the more probable by the
parallel connections between their exegesis of the Psalms;
Rondeau[43] has shown that here Athanasius uses the historical and
philological erudition of Eusebius, but has a quite different
theological perspective. So Athanasius is likely to have used
Eusebius' apologetic work similarly, plundering it for material
but correcting it theologically so as to present overall a somewhat
different outlook. There are indications that this was Athanasius'
intention. Eusebius attributes evidential value to Christ's death
and resurrection, while Athanasius emphasizes the soteriological
aspects, stressing Christ's identification with men in his death
and resurrection. Furthermore, some expressions seem to contain
veiled criticism of the inadequate understanding of the Arians,
with whom Eusebius was sympathetic, as in the reference to 'the
true Son of God who is the Power and the Wisdom and the Word of
the Father'.[44] Where Eusebius and Arius had a fundamentally
cosmological approach, Athanasius began with the saving act of
the incarnation.

Most probably, then, it was in exile at Trier that Athanasius
proceeded, not merely to assemble well-worn arguments against

paganism, but to present systematically what the Christian gospel really meant. Here we find set out the basic presuppositions that lay behind his long life of conflict and controversy. The *Contra gentes*,[45] the first volume, follows many of the classic Jewish and Christian arguments against polytheism and idol-worship. The traditional religio-philosophical problems of the origin of evil and the existence of the soul appear. Theism is proved by the argument from design. The possibility of natural theology is admitted, though regarded as remote. Yet, even here, we can detect the characteristics of Athanasius' thought which appear more obviously in the *De incarnatione*. There we see that the truth of salvation in Christ is the only thing that really matters, as far as Athanasius is concerned. What then is his understanding of salvation in Christ?

Each of these volumes begins with an account of man's original state and his fall from grace. The two differing accounts highlight the two primary concerns of Athanasius' soteriology, human irrationality and human mortality, both alike caused by the same disaster. For man, along with the rest of creation, was called into existence out of τὰ οὐκ ὄντα (non-being). But God chose to endow man with his own image, with a share in the rational being of the Logos himself, so that he might enjoy, at least in a partial way, the eternal life of God himself. However, man forfeited his share in the Logos by disobedience. The incarnation, Athanasius argues, was the only solution to the consequences:

(i) *Man's irrationality*

In the *Contra gentes* (2–5) man who originally had *theōria* (vision) of God and all that was good, turned to 'things nearer to himself', the material rather than the spiritual; he became corrupted by selfish desires and worshipped the creature instead of the Creator. This theme is taken up in the *De incarnatione* (11–16); men could not be λογικοί once they had lost the Logos of God; they were reduced to the level of beasts, and worshipped idols in bestial form; indeed idolatry is the proof of man's irrationality. Men might have learned of God by contemplating the harmony and order of the universe he created, or by listening to the prophets and wise men he sent, or by living according to the law which he gave to the Jews but intended for all nations. But even so, men could not have regained full knowledge of God without their share in the Logos. Ultimately, the only solution was to renew God's image in men, and this was accomplished by the Logos himself dwelling in a man; he came and taught men at their own level and revealed God through direct contact with them. True revelation of God was a prime necessity for salvation.

(ii) *Man's mortality (De incarnatione 6–10)*

God had given man a share in the Logos; he had also given men freewill. So he tried to safeguard his gift by making it conditional upon man's obedience to a particular law. If that law was broken, man would be turned out of paradise and left to inevitable submergence under the forces of death and corruption; he would return to the nothingness from which he came. Man disobeyed, and forfeited the principle of life, the Logos.

For Athanasius, this left God in an intolerable position. It was unthinkable that God should go back on his word; man having transgressed must die; God could not falsify himself. But it was not worthy of God's goodness that his work should perish, especially in the case of beings which had been endowed with the nature of the Logos himself; it would have been better never to have created them. This has been described as the 'divine dilemma';[46] somehow God's integrity had to be salvaged while the demands of his love were met.

The answer was the incarnation. The Logos took a human body capable of dying; when the Logos died the death owed by all humanity, the debt to God's honour was paid and death itself was overcome. Man's corrupt nature was re-created when the body of the Logos was raised and clothed in incorruptibility. The indwelling Logos restored the lost image of God to mankind, and God was reconciled to himself.

Athanasius has frequently been accused of being so concerned with death that he neglects the seriousness of sin and the need of salvation from guilt.[47] Certainly his emphasis in the *De incarnatione* is on death, but it must be remembered that death is the direct outcome of man's disobedience to God's express command. Athanasius shows a predominant interest in death because it was the curse of sin, the mark of the loss of that nature which man had possessed. If it had been a case of a mere trespass, he says,[48] repentance could have solved the problem; but man's situation was worse than that, for the result of sin had been a corruption of nature and a loss of grace which only the re-creating power of the Logos could restore. Creation and re-creation were both performed by the same Logos of God.

Re-creation is Athanasius' main understanding of salvation in Christ. Man would have lived ὡς θεός (as God), if it had not been for the Fall. Scripture says, 'Ye are all gods and sons of the Most

High.'[49] Here are the seeds of Athanasius' doctrine of θεοποίησις (deification), first hinted at towards the end of the *De incarnatione*, where he sums up his position in a much quoted sentence: αὐτὸς γὰρ ἐνηνθρώπησεν, ἵνα ἡμεῖς θεοποιηθῶμεν (He became man, that we might become god).[50]

3. *Against the Arians*

Salvation in Christ, understood in terms of revelation and re-creation, is the faith that Athanasius was prepared to defend to the uttermost. Everything else he came to stand for is merely a corollary of this central fact of his religious consciousness. His lifelong fight against the Arians was entirely motivated by soteriological concerns. Never again did he give a full account of his position, but behind all his arguments against his opponents this twin understanding of salvation can be detected. In the course of the long and diffuse polemic of the *Orationes contra Arianos*, his two major concerns constantly recur as the basis of argument. Revelation and re-creation involved the restoration to men of the true Logos of God; so right from the start Athanasius' soteriology implied that God alone could be the source of salvation, that God alone could take the initiative and deal with man's sorry plight. This conviction spurred him in defence of the essential Godhead of the Logos; the Logos is not a creature but is of one substance with the Father (ὁμοούσιος τῷ πατρί), because only so is our salvation fully realized and guaranteed: that was Athanasius' central argument.

The three *Orations against the Arians*[51] constitute Athanasius' most important dogmatic work. The work became the anti-Arian classic, and the argumentation developed here was later followed very closely by others, for example, by Cyril in his *Thesaurus de sancta et consubstantiali Trinitate*.[52] The first book opens with a defence of the Nicene doctrine against the Arian position and the rest deals with the favourite Arian proof-texts. At first sight it appears as though the urgency of Athanasius' argumentation leads him to disregard literary form; for his presentation seems ill-arranged and repetitious to the point of boredom. Kannengiesser, however, is developing a thesis to explain this,[53] namely that the work consists of an original nucleus to which further material was added later. How convincing will prove his development of the thesis, namely that the third book stands entirely apart and may not even be by Athanasius (as is certainly true of *Oration IV*), remains to be seen. The work as a whole has been regarded as the principal source for understanding Athanasius' theology, and if Kannengiesser is right, a great deal of revision will have to take place. For the moment we will assume that the *Orations I–III* can be used together and that they do provide material for understanding Athanasius' impressively consistent position.

Arius maintained that the Logos, while different from all other creatures, including angels and heavenly beings, was even so a creature and not essentially God himself. That at least was what Athanasius understood him to mean and obviously this doctrine compromised his whole understanding of salvation. True revelation of God was not possible if the Logos was not God. So in the *Contra Arianos* he constantly returns to this theme. Johannine texts like 'No one knows the Father except the Son', 'I and the Father are one', and many others are quoted over and over again. Heb. 1.3 where Christ is described as the radiance of God's glory and the very stamp of his nature is a favourite text, expounded in such a way as to highlight the unity of Father and Son in their revelatory activity. Likewise, the re-creation of human nature could only be accomplished by God himself. Only if the Lord of life himself submitted to death, could death be overcome for all mankind; he became the first-born of the dead by his resurrection. At this point, however, Athanasius' emphases have changed a little since the *De Incarnatione*. He concentrates more on our redemption from sin and the curse, on Christ's bearing our sins and weaknesses. He seems to have become more aware of the depths of evil and suffering from which Christ freed mankind. But this does not weaken the argument: a mere creature could no more cleanse mankind from the depths of sin than raise him to new life; the Logos must be God.[54] Besides this, Athanasius' characteristic idea of θεοποίησις or υἱοποίησις (deification or filiation) is far more prominent than in the *De Incarnatione*. The Logos took a body, so that in it we might be renewed and deified;[55] by being σύσσωμοι with him (i.e. sharing in a common body), we are transformed into perfect man, we ascend to heaven, and this is to be made divine.[56] Only if the Logos is himself God could he accomplish this for us.

This raises some of the difficulties of Athanasius' position.

(i) In what sense do we become divine? In fact, Athanasius himself is concerned to elucidate this. We never become θεοί (gods) or sons of God in the same sense as the Logos is θεός and son of God: he is Son in nature and truth, we are sons by appointment and grace.[57] Insistence on this difference was important since Arius appeared to teach that the Logos was son in the same limited sense as we are. Athanasius instinctively felt that this jeopardized our sonship; there could be no adoption without the true Son in whom we participate by the Spirit; if there is divinization through the

Logos, it must be because he is by nature and substance true God of true God.[58] As an argument this position may not have much validity, but religiously it has some force, and it is consistent with Athanasius' total soteriological picture.

(ii) Did the Logos dwell in an individual man, or in collective humanity, a sort of Platonic idea of Man?[59] Athanasius certainly did not have the sort of interest in the concrete and historical situation of Christ's earthly life which a modern investigator has. Details of Christ's life appear in his writings only because of their soteriological significance: he wept and was afraid in Gethsemane in order to prove that he had really taken a human body and really bore our weaknesses.[60] Besides, there are many passages which seem to suggest that the incarnation automatically sanctified human nature as a whole. On the other hand, in some passages, he certainly does not describe an automatic transformation; it depends on the individual's participation in the Logos through the Spirit, on being 'created in him'. This may not seem far from the Pauline conception that Christians are 'in Christ' and die and rise with him, crucifying the old self and accepting new life; but even the language of participation has Platonic overtones, and the most satisfactory understanding of Athanasius' viewpoint is in terms of such philosophical presuppositions – by this time they were common currency in intellectual circles, so that their use implies no great philosophical sophistication. The humanity of Christ in Athanasius' thought is certainly not quite ordinary humanity, if only because its relation to our humanity is different from that of any other man.

(iii) Does not Athanasius' account of the incarnation seem docetic? On many occasions, Athanasius' exegesis is virtually docetic and seems to us forced and unnatural. All is subordinated to the purpose of showing that the Logos in himself had all the attributes of divinity, e.g. impassibility, omniscience, etc. The texts implying weakness or ignorance he explains as merely referring to the incarnation-situation. At one point, Athanasius even goes so far as to say τὰ ἡμῶν ἐμιμήσατο – he imitated our characteristics.[61] Arius' explanation of such texts – that the Logos was fallible and a mere creature – had to be refuted at all costs.

Besides this, the weight of the evidence supports those who argue that Athanasius did not think that Christ had a human soul; he was Apollinarian before Apollinarius.[62] But this does not necessarily mean that Athanasius was crypto-docetic in his outlook. Again an explanation can be found in current philosophy. To Platonists, human existence was the soul's experience of being trapped in the flesh and succumbing to its temptations. If Athanasius understood human life in this way, then in general terms his view of the incarnation was perfectly legitimate. The Logos had the experience of being human because he, like us, was trapped in flesh and, like us, was tempted by it; but the subject of the experience being the Logos, he did not in the process succumb to sin, because of his very nature. This was no docetic charade, but a real experience of the conditions of human life, the only difference being that he could have no guilt or sinfulness. In fact, docetism would have entirely undermined Athanasius' soteriology; only if the Logos assumed real human flesh could he have any relationship with us.[63] Nevertheless, changeless involvement in the human condition was not easy to conceive, and Athanasius' position led him into the sort of forced exegesis we have referred to.

Athanasius himself does not seem to have reflected on these problems at all. They simply fell outside his perspective. Current assumptions about man's dual nature (soul and body) may appear in his work, but he had no great interest in anthropological analysis for its own sake, and still less an interest in developing a philosophical theology. If we think through what he has to say in his own terms, then the problems of his theology become less pressing. Athanasius' fundamental ideas all derive from his radical distinction between the Creator and everything created out of nothing. Man's intelligence and permanence depended upon his relationship with the Creator, and the incarnation was the means of establishing that relationship at a more secure level. Christ had to share humanity's creatureliness, just as he had to share the divinity of the Creator, so that Creator and creature could be united in him. θεοποίησις (deification) could never obliterate the ontological distinction between God and his creatures, but the humanity of the Logos made participation in God possible through incorporation in him. The question of the human soul of Christ did not appear within Athanasius' horizon; yet docetism would have destroyed his soteriology.[64] The conjunction of Creator and creature in the incarnation, a conjunction which overcame the inherent passibility and destructibility of the creature – this it was that dominated Athanasius' thought.

The *Orationes contra Arianos* were probably not written earlier than Athanasius' third exile among the monks in Egypt, though the question of date has also been reopened by Kannegiesser's literary analysis – he would put the original nucleus as early as 340.[65] Certainly the argumentation is grounded in the soteriology expounded in the *De Incarnatione*, though its presentation implies some development in outlook and considerable reflection on its application to Arianism. Some interval between the apologetic treatises and this extended work of polemic seems likely; but how long depends on detailed critical examination of the relationship between this work and Athanasius' other writings.

4. Apologies, letters and other writings

The third exile seems to have been Athanasius' most productive period. It was at this time that he assembled a number of pamphlets in defence of his own position, including the *Apologia contra Arianos*, the *Apologia ad Constantium imperatorem*, the *Apologia de fuga*, and the Epistle *De Synodis Arimini et Seleuciae*.[66] Many of these were attempts to justify his own actions, as well as to account for the implacable stance he took against the Arians. Also at this time he wrote the *Historia Arianorum ad monachos*; this was an appeal to the Egyptian monks which was intended to be privately circulated, for the reader is instructed to return the document when read. Many of these apologetic works take the form of dossiers of relevant documents, like letters and quotations from conciliar proceedings; this makes them most valuable for reconstructing the history of events during these troubled years, and indeed Athanasius' own biography. Yet their objective appearance is deceptive to the extent that the documents were carefully selected to support Athanasius' case. At other periods in his life, Athanasius wrote letters of defence or explanation which are of similar historical interest. The encyclical of 339 is the earliest of his polemical writings, an appeal to his colleagues as the usurper Gregory took over his see. Another encyclical to the bishops of Egypt in 356 warns them of the heretics, and gives an account of Arius' death. The Epistle *De decretis Nicaenae Synodi* (350–51), defends the Nicene formula, and gives some account of the proceedings which produced it. The Epistle *De sententia Dionysii* defends the orthodoxy of one of his predecessors in the episcopal seat at Alexandria whose views had proved susceptible of an Arian interpretation.

Important as these works are from a historical point of view and as evidence that the fundamentals of Athanasius' position remained consistent throughout his life, more interesting for doctrinal studies are some other letters from a later part of his life which reveal him applying the principles for which he had always stood to fresh controversies. Four *Letters to bishop Serapion*,[67] dating again from the third exile, use the arguments already traced in relation to the Logos in order to establish the essential divinity of the Holy Spirit. Since our salvation depends on a relationship with God which is grounded in participation in the Spirit, the Spirit must be *homoousios* with God; he cannot be a creature. He is of the Holy Triad; he is the vital activity and gift whereby the Logos sanctifies and enlightens. These letters were occasioned by Serapion writing to Athanasius about certain persons who had given up the Arian account of the Logos, but understood the Holy Spirit in Arian terms as one of the ministering spirits who differed from the angels only in degree. It is hardly surprising that Athanasius was quick to see that the same principles applied.

The christological problem of the relation between Godhead and manhood in Jesus Christ also became more explicit towards the end of Athanasius' life. The *Letters to Epictetus, Adelphius and Maximus*[68] attempt to deal with this problem. Athanasius yet more emphatically insists that the Logos must have become truly human, because it was man that needed saving; but his basic position remained unchanged. The Logos, being divine, could not suffer or be weak; but his body wept and suffered and died, and since it was the body of the Logos, the Logos, who was not 'outside it', could be said to be involved in the suffering of his own flesh. He admits it is a paradox that the impassible, divine Logos shared in the passion; but had he not been impassible and unchangeable his victory over the weaknesses of the flesh would not have been achieved. It is noticeable that, as ever, soteriological considerations direct Athanasius' argumentation.

Debate over Athanasius' christology has centred on the issue of the human soul of Jesus. As we have already noticed, it is highly unlikely that Athanasius thought of the Incarnate Logos as having assumed a human soul.[69] The anti-Apollinarian literature attributed to him is certainly not genuine, and his authentic writings do not make any use of the idea. It has been argued, however, that at the end of his life Athanasius came to recognize the need to assert the presence of a human soul in the Saviour; appeal is made in particular to a phrase in the *Tomus as Antiochenos* which Athanasius wrote on behalf of the Council of Alexandria in 362. It was apparently at this council that Athanasius first met the question, and he accepted the force of the soteriological argument that 'the salvation effected in the Word himself was a salvation not of body only, but also of soul'; therefore 'it was not possible, when the Lord became man for us, that his body should be without intelligence'.[70] If there was any way of winning Athanasius' support, appeal to soteriological principles was it. But Athanasius may not have interpreted the words οὐ σῶμα ἄψυχον οὐδ' ἀναίσθητον οὐδ' ἀνόητον εἶχεν (the Saviour had 'not a body

without a soul nor without sense or intelligence') as an assertion
that the Saviour had a *human* soul; he probably envisaged a body
animated and made intelligent by the presence of the Logos.[71] This
would have been all his soteriology required, even for the salvation
of the soul. In fact, Athanasius never made any constructive use of
the idea of Christ's human consciousness, even subsequent to this
council. The Logos took a body, human flesh; the Logos remained
the subject of all the incarnate experiences, triumphing over the
sins and weaknesses of his humanity. The body was his temple; it
was impersonal – τὸ ἀνθρώπινον; it was the instrument by which he
effected the sanctification of human nature. Only because the
Logos is by nature unchangeable, is the triumph over temptation
and sin ensured. A fallible human soul, which could have explained
the fears and ignorance of the human Jesus, had no place in
Athanasius' view of the matter. His thought remained within the
soteriological framework with which he began. Salvation, understood as revelation and re-creation, depended on the unchangeable,
invincible power of the Logos taking human nature and triumphing
over its weakness and sin.

In other ways too the *Tomus ad Antiochenos* presents us with
interpretative problems. To what extent did it achieve the reconciliation of the majority of anti-Arian factions? Many have presented this as an ecumenical achievement: summoned on
Athanasius' initiative, the Council of Alexandria in 362 produced
the *Tome*, a document which took its stand simply on the Nicene
Creed, refusing to get into endless controversy over vocabulary
when the intention of the disputants was the same. Athanasius'
success in effecting a reconciliation in the church at this council
was rewarded by his fourth exile; for the occupant of the imperial
throne was Julian the Apostate and the last thing this pagan
revivalist wanted was a peaceful church attracting new converts.
So here at the end of his life, it is said, Athanasius appears as not
uncompromising, except where the heart of his convictions were
attacked. He was prepared to be flexible. This flexibility and
moderation can also be seen in the fact that Athanasius hardly uses
the word *homoousios* in his *Orations against the Arians* or any of
his works of defence; he hesitated to over-employ this word
because he knew how controversial it was and how readily it lent
itself to a number of different interpretations. The *Orations* are full
of intended periphrases expressing the same idea, and his reticence
was probably the result of his 'fine theological tact'.[72]

We have already noted some of the difficulties with this view.
The Antiochene schism was not healed by the *Tome*, and it is

possible that the document never intended to address itself to the
fundamental split in the Antiochene church – nothing is said about
bishop Meletius, who though no Arian, led the majority church.
The Synod at Alexandria is likely to have been a local reunion of
exiled bishops, and did not have the universal character ascribed to
it.[73] In any case, Julian was already trying to get rid of Athanasius
before the Synod met.[74] Athanasius' avoidance of the word
homoousios is easily exaggerated, and certainly need not reflect
'tact' towards other parties: he himself may have only gradually
recognized its usefulness; certainly he knew that many agreed with
the Arian criticism that the term was not scriptural, so that the case
against Arius had to be proved by other means. The Nicene Council
had not yet achieved the general respect and recognition which it
had a generation later, and a simple appeal to its formulae would
convince no one. Athanasius' flexibility may well have been
overestimated, along with the extent of his authority and influence
outside Egypt.

Some of the criticisms need to be taken seriously: the Council
seems to have been a small gathering of ultra-Nicenes, and the
Tome is only concerned with the local situation in Antioch, not
with terms for the reconciliation of all parties in the East. Yet in the
reaction against the accepted view, the pendulum has swung too
far. There are strong indications that Athanasius did have the
followers of Meletius in mind when he urged reunion and tolerance;[75] and the *Tome* itself clearly indicates that he did adopt a
noncommittal attitude towards use of the word *hypostasis*
(another word for substance) and that he did appeal to those united
in spirit to sink verbal differences for the sake of peace. Athanasius'
intransigence can be exaggerated as much as his saintliness; and
Julian's repeated, and increasingly wrathful, letters ordering his
departure from Alexandria indicate that the emperor thought he
was a force to be reckoned with in the wider sphere of ecclesiastical
politics.

Whatever the actual situation in his lifetime, Athanasius very
rapidly acquired legendary status as the one who defended Nicene
orthodoxy pretty well single-handed through the years of Arian
ascendency. Many dogmatic works of the period came to be
attributed to him, like the twelve books *De Trinitate* and the
Athanasian Creed, both of which originated in the West. Some
anti-Apollinarian treatises bear his name, but it is now generally
agreed that they are not the work of Athanasius; they differ from his
authentic work in language and style, and were probably written
after his death.[76] The genuine work of Athanasius, as we have

indicated, was Apollinarian in tendency, though the issues had not yet been so explicitly raised as to demand a response. In fact, many Apollinarian tracts were circulated in the fifth century under Athanasius' name, and some of the characteristic teminology of Cyril of Alexandria seems to have originated from these pseudonymous pamphlets, which for Cyril had the authority of his great predecessor.[77]

5. Pastor and teacher

The Athanasius legend presents him as a fine leader motivated by honesty, faith and charity. It might be nearer the truth to say that he was vehement to the point of violence, and that his 'charity' was the face of an astute politician out to achieve his own ends. There is little doubt that Athanasius had a tendency to see things in black and white; you were either for him or against him. Yet clearly Athanasius was a leader capable of inspiring deep loyalty – otherwise his legend could never have developed. As pastor and ascetic he came to enjoy the love and respect of Egypt, including the extreme ascetics of the desert. Some extant material is not primarily concerned with the controversial issues of the day, but reflects these other aspects of his activities. We may suspect underlying political motives; but taken at face-value, they throw interesting light on the fundamentally Christian aims of Athanasius' life.

(i) As a pastor, he never neglected his episcopal duties, in so far as he was able to carry them out. Almost every year, often in the most difficult of circumstances, he followed the custom of writing to the Egyptian churches announcing the date of Easter. Apart from a few fragments, all these epistles were lost until a Syriac version of thirteen *Festal Letters* dating from 329 to 348 turned up in a desert monastery early last century.[78] In these letters, Athanasius occasionally deals with pastoral problems, like the influence of evildoers or heretics, or which books are to be regarded as Holy Scripture (incidentally, the 39th letter which deals with this question is particularly interesting, since it contains the first list of New Testament books which exactly corresponds with the twenty-seven later canonized); but his aim is to inspire his flock to keep the Christian Passover by fasting and then feasting in a spirit of true worship and purity. His letters are full of scriptural quotations, traditional typology and simple piety. They make up, to some extent, for the loss of his sermons.

(ii) Jerome tells us that Athanasius frequently wrote on virginity.[79] The authenticity of the *De Virginitate* is still debated, but some authentic fragments of other treatises have appeared comparatively recently in Coptic, Syriac and Armenian.[80] Athanasius' most significant contribution to ascetical literature, however, was his *Life of Antony*. The spread of the monastic ideal owed much to this work. Two Latin translations appeared almost immediately, and we also know of Syriac, Armenian and Arabic versions. Its widespread influence is attested by many of the Fathers; for example, Gregory of Nazianzus, John Chrysostom, Jerome; it was a factor in Augustine's conversion.[81] In the immediate future, Athanasius' reputation rested on his contribution to monastic literature, as much as his defence of Nicene orthodoxy.

The *Life of Antony*[82] was almost certainly written in exile soon after Antony's death in 356.[83] It has been suggested that one of its purposes was to foster Athanasius' good relations with the monks of Egypt, and, like the *Historia Arianorum ad monachos*, it was intended for private circulation. Internal evidence indicates, however, that it was destined for a readership overseas, apparently monks who wished to vie with the Egyptians; so it looks as though the recipients were to be Athanasius' contacts in the West. According to the Prologue, Athanasius had been personally acquainted with Antony, had seen him many times and even acted as his attendant; but his *Life* is an idealized picture intended as a pattern of discipline, a curious blend of traditional and legendary material with Athanasius' own philosophical and ecclesiastical ideals. Miraculous cures, exorcisms, supernatural visions and graphically depicted battles with the devil give a predominantly mythological flavour; but Athanasius is at pains to state that Anthony never had dealings with Meletians, Manichaeans or Arians, that he observed the rule of the church and submitted to the clergy,[84] that he strove for virtue and ἀπάθεια (freedom from passion) – for likeness to the divine.[85] The work seems to have been modelled on some literary Life, like that of Plotinus or Apollonius, and according to literary convention long discourses, to monks, to pagans, punctuate the work; yet Antony's lack of culture and illiteracy is also stressed, so as to highlight his remarkable wisdom.[86] The work was to have an appeal to educated and non-educated alike, to the extremes of those attracted to monasticism, the illiterate Copts and the philosophically inclined.

It has been claimed that the *Vita Antonii* reflects a different theology and a different asceticism from Athanasius' other works. Up to a point this is undoubtedly true; the work has a very different tone. The predominance of the devil and the demons is the most obvious example; they hardly appear elsewhere in Athanasius' writings. But this contrast can be exaggerated. The *De incarnatione* celebrates Christ's victory over the powers of death and sin rather than the devil; but the devil appears in the Long Recension, and the theme is one of victory. For Antony, too, the theme is victory over the powers of evil. Christ has cut the sinews of the devils; their power is destroyed since Christ overcame death, dispelled ignorance and freed mankind from idolatry, magic and astrology. To display one's belief in this by brandishing the weapon of prayer and uplifting the sign of the cross, disarms them completely. With these weapons, the devils' own territory, the tombs and the desert, can be invaded with success. In the accounts of visions, miracles and temptations, we are given a lively picture of the victorious Christ working through Antony to overcome evil and confuse the wordly-wise. Victory is attributed to God; Antony, the ideal ascetic, is the instrument of God's saving activity: 'This was Antony's first triumph over the devil – or rather the first triumph of the Saviour in Antony.'[87] The power of the divine Logos is displayed as effecting salvation through victory over human sin and mortality. Antony becomes the instrument of the Logos, as the humanity of Christ had been the Logos' instrument in the incarnation. The ascetic is represented, not as retiring into solitariness simply for the salvation of his own soul, but as marching into the desert to engage the devils in battle, and so make a positive contribution to the salvation of the world by participating in the Logos' saving work. Philosophical ideals of striving for mastery over the passions, the subjection of the physical to the spiritual, the achievement of likeness to the divine – these ideals as well as the naive psychology of the ascetics are assimilated to the Christian ideal of θεοποίησις[88] which was so important to Athanasius' soteriology.

Athanasius was a controversial figure throughout most of his life. He has been described as 'wily, brutal and unscrupulous'.[89] He certainly inspired hatred as well as blind loyalty. His complicity in the scandals discussed at Tyre cannot be entirely ruled out, in spite of the special pleading of his defensive works and the orthodox historians. He was a bit of a tyrant, and violent acts were committed in his name. The many Eastern bishops who, whether really Arian in sympathy or not, regarded him as a trouble-maker best got out of the way, probably had some reason for so thinking. Yet he rapidly became the hero of orthodoxy, a saint within a generation. It was in fact less than ten years after his death that Gregory of Nazianzus delivered a glowing panegyric on Athanasius at Constantinople:[90] He was the pillar of the church; he cleansed the temple in imitation of Christ, not with whips but with persuasive argument. Later Athanasius became known as the 'Father of Orthodoxy'. He deserved this title not merely for his stubborn resistance to every attack on his person and the principles for which he stood, but also because in fact the orthodox tradition owes an enormous debt to his theological writings. In the later christological battles, all sides accepted Athanasius as authoritative; he alone of the Eastern Fathers had an immediate, direct and lasting influence on the West. So he is honoured still as the hero of the church's struggle against Arianism. His arguments met with success, even though in many respects his ideas had a certain novelty, because he appealed to the Christian experience of salvation in Christ. 'He became human that we might be deified; he revealed himself in a body so that we might perceive the Mind of the unseen Father; and he endured shame from men that we might inherit immortality.'[91] This was Athanasius' starting-point, and from here he argued that revelation and θεοποίησις depended upon the Son sharing the essential nature of the Godhead. Arianism simply did not account for his understanding of the Christian gospel. The consequences of Athanasius' argument have been crucial for the development of Christian theology.

III. Didymus the Blind

1. Life

Conflict and turmoil were the marks of Athanasius' life. For his younger contemporary, Didymus, life was very different. So few were the events of his long and peaceful existence that a biographical sketch is hardly possible. The predominant impression of Didymus found in contemporary sources, is of an aged and revered teacher in the Origenist tradition, highly respected in ecclesiastical circles around the Mediterranean for his outstanding erudition and prodigious memory. His reputation was enhanced by his simple asceticism and by the fact that his remarkable learning had been acquired in spite of his being afflicted with blindness from childhood.

This impression of Didymus' life and character comes from the peaceful years at the end of the fourth century when the heat had passed out of the Arian controversy. The picture is drawn from a number of his disciples. Palladius in his *Lausiac History*[92] includes Didymus among the famous monks he visited in Egypt. Origen's translator and apologist, Rufinus, was Didymus' pupil; in fact, he spent a total of eight years at Didymus' feet,[93] obtained a treatise on

the death of infants from his master,[94] and drew on Didymus'
commentary on Origen's *De principiis* when he made his Latin
translation of the work.[95] Jerome, the great biblical scholar from
the West, acknowledges his debt to Didymus in the preface to many
of his commentaries,[96] and apparently made a point of going to
Alexandria in order to meet him and get him to clarify certain of his
perplexities.[97] It was at Jerome's request that Didymus wrote his
Commentary on Zechariah,[98] and it was Jerome who ensured an
abiding reputation for Didymus in the West by translating his
treatise on the Holy Spirit. After so many expressions of respect,
Jerome's later condemnation of Origen, and with him, his late
disciple, Didymus, was particularly abhorrent to the loyal
Rufinus.[99]

Didymus' reputation was world-wide, but he himself was an
Alexandrian by birth and he never ventured far from the city. At the
age of four, before he had started school or learned to read, he lost
his sight. He was obviously a scholar from birth, for despite this
handicap, he succeeded in attaining competence in all the subjects
that constituted higher education in his day: our sources list
dialectic, geometry, arithmetic, astronomy, music, poetry,
rhetoric, and philosophy, including Aristotle's syllogisms and
Plato's eloquence.[100] Sozomen tell us that he taught himself by
feeling letters that had been carved on a tablet,[101] but his greatest
asset seems to have been a memory which retained everything that
was read to him. Rufinus gives the impression that he deliberately
cultivated this ability by quietly recalling and ruminating on what
he had heard during the long hours when sighted people needed to
sleep.[102] The wide range of accomplishments attributed to Didymus is not obviously reflected in his extant writings,[103] though
the vast quantity of quotations, in particular from biblical and
Christian sources, but also from pagan literature, bears witness to
his remarkable powers of memory and the breadth of his literary
knowledge. Anecdotes concentrate on the contrast, so impressive
to his contemporaries, between his physical blindness and his
mental perspicacity. For example, Antony, the founder of monasticism, is said to have visited him and told him not to grieve over the
loss of his sight, which even ants and flies possess, but to rejoice in
having the vision of angels, the ability to discern God.[104] Jerome
regularly calls him Didymus the Seeing, rather than Didymus the
Blind.

Didymus lived until 398, by which time he was eight-five. It is
hard to realize that when Athanasius held the Council of Alexandria in 362, Didymus was nearly fifty. Didymus had lived all

through the years of turmoil, but they seem to have affected the course of his life remarkably little. This is somewhat surprising. Didymus remained faithful to the Nicene position all his life. Indeed Socrates ranks him as the Alexandrian counterpart to Basil of Caesarea and Gregory of Nazianzus – a bulwark against Arianism raised up by God's providence.[105] Furthermore, at an early age his erudition was recognized and Athanasius appointed him head of the Church School.[106] It has usually been assumed that this meant he was head of the Catechetical School, the Christian University which had flourished in the past under Clement and Origen;[107] but the continuous existence of such an institution has been questioned,[108] and Didymus' immunity from Arian persecution suggests that he was not an obviously public figure. In fact, we know little of the conditions of his teaching. He may have given official lectures in Alexandria, but we may surmise that any official activities must have ceased during the years of Arian ascendency at least. He spent most of his life as a monk, and his custom may well have been to give less formal instruction in the privacy of his anchorite cell.

Rufinus puts great store on having heard Didymus teach in person by word of mouth.[109] But Didymus also produced a vast collection of written works for which he was well-known outside Egypt, perhaps especially in the West.[110] Unfortunately, little of Didymus' work survived his condemnation as an Origenist in 553. In the sixteenth century, all that was known was the *De Spiritu Sancto* in Jerome's Latin version, and a Latin text of the *Commentary on the Catholic Epistles*. Since then, the Greek texts of several dogmatic works have been traced among the works of other more respectable Fathers of the church. The most important of these is the treatise *De Trinitate* which Mingarelli recognized as Didymus' work in the eighteenth century. There are cross-references to the authentic treatise *On the Holy Spirit* which seem to establish the attribution. Recent work has re-opened the question;[111] but even though Didymus' authorship of this treatise can no longer be regarded as absolutely assured it will be assumed here that it was Didymus' work. Also plausibly attributed to Didymus is a work *Against the Manichees*. More contentious is the view that Didymus was the author of Books IV and V of Basil's *Contra Eunomium*,[112] and of the important little treatise *Adversus Arium et Sabellium* attributed to Gregory of Nyssa.[113] The latter is the earliest work in which the formula 'one *ousia* and three *hypostases*' appears; was Didymus the architect of this brilliant solution to the contentions of the East?

2. Biblical commentaries

Didymus was best known in his own day as a biblical commentator, and extensive quotations from his commentaries, particularly the *Commentary on the Psalms*, have been identified in the Catenae. But our knowledge of Didymus' exegetical work is being dramatically increased as a result of the chance discovery of a considerable number of papyri in a munitions dump at Tura during the Second World War. The first text to be published was the *Commentary on Zechariah* which appeared in the *Sources Chrétiennes* series in 1962, to be followed a good many years later by the *Commentary on Genesis*. Meanwhile, the *Commentary on Job*, the *Commentary on the Psalms* and the *Commentary on Ecclesiastes* have been gradually appearing in a somewhat cumbersome typescript form in the series *Papyrologische Texte und Abhandlungen*.[114]

The publication of this material is so recent that scholarly discussion of its significance has not yet advanced very far. First impressions suggested that it did not make a great deal of difference to what we already knew.[115] It had long been clear that scripture was Didymus' chief inspiration. His dogmatic treatises are saturated with unnecessarily long quotations from scripture, by which he is led into rambling digressions. The *De Trinitate* fits this characterization, for it is mainly a vast collection of scripture proofs, arranged by topics. The bulk of Didymus' work was scriptural commentary – we already knew that he had written commentaries on Genesis, Exodus, Leviticus, Job, the Psalms, Proverbs, Ecclesiastes, Song of Songs, Isaiah, Jeremiah, Daniel, Hosea, Zechariah, and the whole of the New Testament except Mark and some of the shorter Pauline Epistles. Didymus, we knew, regarded speculation as sophistry and searching the scriptures as the way of wisdom.[116]

We knew too that Didymus was an Origenist who used the allegorical method in his commentaries, and this also is generally confirmed by the new discoveries. Origen in expounding his method distinguished three senses of scripture, but in practice his exegetical work is based on a distinction between the literal meaning and one or more allegorical meanings. First impressions of Didymus' techniques, based on the new information provided by the *Commentary on Zechariah*, suggested that he was content with distinguishing two senses, though he had a range of descriptions of the 'higher meaning', like ἀναγωγή, ἀλληγορία, θεωϹία, τροπολογία, διανοία; this meaning was reached by interpreting symbolically, mystically or spiritually.[117] As for Origen, so for Didymus, everything was potentially a symbol, especially numbers and descriptive passages. Thus, in the Zechariah commentary, elaborate sums are supposed to elucidate the mystical significance of the date on which Zechariah had his vision;[118] the man on the horse is the Saviour made man; the mountains are the two Testaments, which are described as cloud-covered because they are fertile and rich in thoughts of God and the incarnation; the vision occurs at night, since there is plenty of obscurity in the enigmatic and profound prophecies of the two Testaments.[119] As in Origen, so in Didymus references to God's anger or other anthropomorphic traits are allegorized away: God is immutable, beyond change and emotion, but he seeks the repentance and education of sinful men by means of chastisement.[120] Allegorical interpretation is popularly regarded as a way of importing into the scriptural text a philosophy alien to it; at points, Didymus seemed to extract such speculative meanings, and to differ in no very significant ways from his great master, Origen.

Closer study of Didymus' commentaries, however, has suggested that more precise definition of his methodology might well advance our entire understanding of the Alexandrian allegorical tradition. Debate has centred on definition of his technical terms; is it true that he makes no attempt to distinguish ἀλληγορία and ἀναγωγή? It seemed at first that it might be possible to restrict ἀναγωγη to christological, as distinct from general philosophical or mystical, meanings.[121] Didymus' allegory seems modified more than Origen's by a sense of scriptural unity, of the primacy of christological understanding, and the importance of ecclesiastical rather that heretical interpretations. Over and over again interpretation is offered simply in the form of collections of texts from elsewhere in scripture, often, it is true, texts with only allusive or verbal connections with the passage under discussion; yet the guiding principle is that scripture points to God in Christ. So, for example, in Zechariah 3, the high priest, Joshua, stands accused by Satan, but vindicated by God; and to Didymus, the passage is a description of Jesus, the great high priest after the order of Melchisedek, who freed mankind by bearing their sins on the cross and overcoming the power of the devil.

The most satisfactory account of Didymus' procedure, however, concentrates on the structure of his hermeneutics, and concludes that the distinctions he makes are not based on theological content, but on interpretative principles.[122] This it is which may prove significant for future estimates of the whole allegorical tradition.

Many have dismissed allegory as highly speculative and little related to the text. Yet it is clear that Didymus, in his exegetical practice, pays close attention to the text to be explained, and works according to carefully established principles of interpretation. First he examines what the text actually says, its logic and structure; then he enquires into its historical or factual reference in the external world. Then he is in the position to ask whether the text can be understood as figurative discourse, consistently working according to traditional 'figures' like Jerusalem = Church, to probe possible deeper meanings. Finally he may enquire whether it may signify some other order of reality, whether it has a reference to the spiritual world. Didymus is thus careful to distinguish between the 'wording' and the 'reference' of the text at both literal and spiritual levels, and it is along these lines that the distinction between ἀναγωγη and ἀλληορία is to be understood, ἀλληγορία leading to the recognition of a figurative sense in the language, ἀναγογή to the reality to which the figurative language refers. Didymus assumes a *consistency* of reference, so that when the same word appears in different texts, it still carries the same connotations. In this way he can trace the divine intention throughout scripture and bring it into dynamic relation with contemporary Christian life.

3. Contribution to doctrine

Didymus was a man of the Bible. He was Origenist in his method of exposition. The extent of Didymus' dependence on Origen was discussed as early as Jerome. The work that could have told us most, his commentary on Origen's *De Principiis*, is unfortunately lost. We gather from Jerome[123] that it was a defence of Origen against current attacks, in which Didymus gave an interpretation of Origen's trinitarian doctrine which conformed with later orthodoxy, but accepted uncritically what became his most controversial doctrines like the pre-existence of souls and the ἀποκατάστασις (the universal restoration of all things to the original state of perfection). In his extant works, there are only hints that he accepted the latter doctrine,[124] though he clearly believed the former.[125] But Didymus was not the slavish follower of a great man of the past. He found inspiration in Origen and defended him on points where current debate had not yet fixed the rules, but he was far from unaware of the contemporary theological climate. Jerome had to admit, even in his anti-Origen phase, that Didymus was certainly orthodox in the matter of the Trinity. In fact, Didymus was an intelligent contributor to contemporary debate.

Intelligent, but not brilliantly original, Didymus seems to have absorbed ideas from many sources and presented them with ample documentation in formulae that would be easily assimilated. He may not have invented the formula 'one *ousia* in three *hypostases*',[126] but he hammered it home with pages and pages of scriptural proofs. His argumentation against the Arians and the Macedonians, who applied Arian arguments to the Holy Spirit rather than the Logos, follows the pattern developed by his predecessors and contemporaries, but it was Didymus who amassed the material and produced scholarly monographs on the divinity of the Holy Spirit and the nature of the Trinity. His dogmatic works reveal a mind averse to philosophical speculation, desiring only to press home relevant biblical passages and express the traditional faith of the church in the formulae which now appeared to be the only adequate expression of that faith. To open the pages of the *De Trinitate* is to find an essentially pious man, concentrating on the ἰσοτιμία (equality of honour), the fact that the three *hypostases* are worshipped as one saving God.[127]

Didymus' most interesting contribution to contemporary debate was in the field of christology. The bitter controversies of the fifth century were still in the future, but already the question of whether the Logos assumed a soul as well as flesh in the incarnation had come into the open. In Didymus' works, there are no explicit references to Apollinarius, but he constantly uses anti-Apollinarian formulae, stressing that the Saviour did not assume a body without a soul and a mind.[128] The debates which interested him more directly were with the Arians and Manichaeans, and the interesting thing is that he has realized the relevance of this assertion to these other problems. Both of these opponents were docetic, the latter explicitly so, regarding the body of Christ as a fantasy, the former effectively so, by denying that the body had a human soul.[129] He reproaches the Arians on the same grounds as Athanasius had, accusing them of attributing human characteristics to the Divine Logos instead of to his flesh; but, unlike Athanasius, he recognizes that their exegesis is possible because it rests on the presupposition that the indwelling Logos replaced the soul in the Saviour's body.[130] Neither soul-less flesh, nor Divinity needs food or sleep, he says; therefore the ineffable incarnation was not without soul.[131] The weaknesses and passions of Jesus Christ which are described in scripture, should be attributed to his fallible human soul. He maintained all the consequences of being made man; he was entirely like us; he assumed not merely bodily pains and weaknesses, but also psychological tensions and mental suffering.[132] The difference between the soul of Jesus and that of other men was a difference in quality, not nature: he remained sinless in spite of temptation and the possibility of succumbing to it. Didymus assigns to the soul of Jesus a genuinely positive role in the incarnation. The Saviour's human soul was fallible, but in fact by remaining sinless, it conformed perfectly with the intention of its Creator. So, not needing salvation itself, it became the instrument of our salvation. It seems most likely that at this point Didymus was indebted to Origen, according to whom the Logos united himself with humanity through the medium of the one soul that had remained sinless.[133] Following this line of thought, Didymus saw its relevance to contemporary discussions, and made a constructive contribution by assimilating this idea to the soteriological tradition so well represented by Athanasius.[134] It was because the Logos had assumed human nature in its totality, that the whole man, body, soul and mind, was saved in him.

In the struggle with the Arians, Athanasius found himself playing a lonely political role; he found himself forced to defend his obstinacy, and his writings were motivated by the necessity of clarifying his doctrinal position and confuting his opponents. Didymus, on the other hand, was first and foremost a learned recluse who kept out of the political fires. His reputation rested on solid scholarship and his ability as a teacher. He revelled in learning for its own sake. His knowledge was encyclopedic. Socrates remarks that anyone who wants to get an idea of Didymus' vast erudition will discover it by consulting the enormous volumes he produced.[135] In the *De Trinitate*, apart from the range of scriptural quotations, references can be found to the Iliad and Odyssey, Orpheus, Pindar, Diagoras of Melos, Sophocles, Euripides, Plato the Comedian, Aratos, Hermes Trismegistus and the Sybillines. Plato, Aristotle and Porphyry are mentioned, though Didymus' philosophical views are mainly eclectic and secondhand.[136] It was the easy mastery of such a range of material which impressed his pupils so much. His qualities as a teacher are also to some extent reflected in his written works. Being blind, he relied on secretaries to produce his manuscripts, and it seems probable that the written text is largely based on teaching material. Mingarelli, who discovered the *De Trinitate* in the eighteenth century, certainly thought that large parts of this treatise were originally prepared as lectures.[137] Didymus repudiates the attempt to produce polished literary work,[138] and his style is diffuse and repetitious as if he were pressing home his points to a class.[139] He documents his arguments with detailed quotations. He digresses onto interesting side-issues, clarifying minor points *en passant*. He concentrates on easily memorable formulae. He summarizes his arguments, outlines his chain of reasoning, lists all his points.[140] He had the ability of a good teacher to absorb ideas from others and present them in a form that others would find easy to assimilate.

Didymus was a scholar and a teacher; but for all his academic attainments, he was essentially a pious monk and a conservative churchman. His scholarship was entirely devoted to the elucidation of scripture and the doctrines of the church. In these areas of speciality, he displayed little originality, though he undoubtedly contributed to the consolidation of the orthodox position. His main source-book, his real inspiration, was the Bible, and in the long term, it was as an exegete that he had an abiding influence. The discovery of the *Commentary on Zechariah* revealed the extent to which mediaeval allegory unconsciously followed Didymus through the medium of Jerome, who did not hesitate to draw from Didymus' work when composing his own influential commentary.[141] It is good to see recent discoveries and research rehabilitating the memory of a simple, scholarly churchman, whose subsequent condemnation, for speculations not his own, was most unfortunate. Didymus did not base his faith on philosophical theory, but on his study of scripture and his experience of worship.

Chapter Three

The Cappadocians

The political eclipse of Arianism came with the appointment of Theodosius to the Eastern throne. By this time, AD 379, the defenders of orthodoxy were recognized in three bishops from the province of Cappadocia. It is true that Basil, the great bishop of Caesarea, had not survived to see this triumphant day, but his friend, Gregory Nazianzen, and his brother, Gregory Nyssen, were consciously carrying on his work and perpetuating his influence. In days of persecution, these three had stood by Nicene orthodoxy; now in days of peace, their work was to provide the theological basis for the lasting definition of Eastern trinitarianism.

This important contribution, however, by no means exhausts their interest and significance. One striking feature of their writings is the wealth of their religious language and imagery, their comprehensive acceptance of biblical, devotional and doctrinal traditions. But these traditions were not fossilized, and each of the three had a very personal contribution to make, not only to the development of doctrine, but also to various aspects of the Christian life. Perhaps the most fascinating aspect of their work is the evidence it provides concerning two areas of tension in the contemporary church: first the tension between faith and culture, that is, the pagan culture of the Graeco-Roman world with which the new official religion had to come to terms; and, secondly, the tension produced by the rise and dominance of the monastic ideal. In both cases, it was only because men like the Cappadocian fathers found a balance between extremes, that the church did not sell itself to the world, or withdraw from the world into the desert. Yet this balance was hardly intentional; it arose out of circumstances, out of the inconsistencies of ingrained attitudes, as the consequences of each individual's character.

I. Biographical

The lives of the three Cappadocians were closely interlinked,[1] and so was their work. All three came from well-established Christian families. Of a family of nine, Basil, Gregory and Peter became bishops; their grandparents had been martyrs, their mother and sister were saints. Their friend, Gregory, was the son of the bishop of Nazianzus, a recent convert, won by his Christian wife. So they grew up under the influence of strongly committed parents and none of the three experienced the psychological stimulus of conversion to the faith. They all speak with the conviction of a faith into which they had been born, a faith whose images, expressions, vocabulary and attitudes were second nature to them.

Yet their experience was not narrow and sectarian. Their families were Christian, but they also belonged to the higher classes of Cappadocia; they were rich enough and proud enough to provide their sons with a first-class classical education. Basil's younger brother was less fortunate in this respect, but the elder son studied in Caesarea, the capital of Cappadocia, in Constantinople and finally Athens, the leading university of the world. In Caesarea he had already been acquainted with Gregory from Nazianzus, and now, in Athens, the friendship blossomed into intimacy. Gregory's educational career had in fact been very similar, though while Basil was at Constantinople, he and his brother Caesarius had visited the famous centres of Christian learning, Palestinian Caesarea and Alexandria, both, of course, famed for their connection with Origen. Athens, however, was Gregory's enthusiasm. He spent most of his twenties there, unable to tear himself from the pursuit of learning. Reluctantly, he followed Basil back to Cappadocia in about 357, unable to bear the old haunts without his friend.

The friendship seems to have meant more to Gregory than to Basil; Gregory clung to a more forceful *alter ego*, and was hurt when Basil appeared to let him down. The story of their love and their quarrels is woven into the course of Gregory's vacillating career. Rarely did the friends enjoy again the community of life and interests which their student days had provided.

In their correspondence, Gregory refers to an agreement they had made while at Athens to share a 'life of philosophy' together.[2] But for Basil, this must have been mere student idealism. On his return to Caesarea, he found himself the centre of admiring attention, and quickly proved a success as a rhetorician. There is little doubt he enjoyed his reputation and riches. But if Basil was to dominate others, he himself seems to have found a dominating influence in his sister, Macrina, who had already dedicated herself to an ascetic life.[3] He soon gave up his career, received baptism and set out on a long journey through Egypt, Palestine, Syria and Mesopotamia to visit the monks and solitaries of the deserts. He returned to found a coenobitic monastery and to become the major influence in the organization of monastic communities in Asia Minor.

Now Basil looked for the support of his friend. He wrote and urged Gregory to join him in his retreat in Pontus. Gregory, too, had received baptism, which in this period implied a resolution to give up worldly ambitions. But he was reluctant to commit himself to the ascetic life. His ageing parents, in need of help and support, provided an excuse. He visited Basil for a short time, but returned. His letters reveal an ambivalence between sincere idealism, and joking parodies of Basil's over-enthusiasm.[4] Several times he returned to Pontus, but never for long. He and Basil compiled the *Philocalia*, a collection of extracts from Origen; Basil probably discussed early versions of his *Rules* for monastic organization with his friend.[5] But Gregory's position with regard to monasticism remained ambiguous – he saw it as fine in theory but not so good in practice.

Yet Gregory was sufficiently held by the ideal to resent it when others forced him to renounce the ascetic life. The future will show that the less he was free to retire from the world, the more he felt the urge to do so. Basil, on the other hand, appeared to throw himself into ecclesiastical politics with a certain unscrupulousness, as if conscious that the monastery was too small a stage for his abilities. Gregory became more and more sensitive to his friend's apparent disloyalty to their ideals.

The first blow to Gregory's ever-frustrated intentions was his ordination (which both then and later was not part of the monastic vocation in the Eastern church). His father compelled him to accept the priesthood and help with the running of his diocese. Gregory fled to Pontus, but soon realized he had no alternative but to accept his new status.[6] Already Basil had been active outside the walls of his monastery and moved in episcopal circles. In 359, both Dianius, the bishop of Caesarea, and Gregory's father had been misled into signing the creed of Rimini, little realizing the significant difference between *homoousios* and *homoiousios*. Each had renounced his error under the influence of Basil and Gregory, respectively. Now, the new bishop of Caesarea, Eusebius, who was a theological novice, persuaded Basil to become his assistant; so he, too, was ordained priest. For a spell he returned to his monastery when relations with Eusebius became strained; but his friend, Gregory, was instrumental in effecting a reconciliation between the two and Basil returned to his duties. He was needed to defend the church in the last period of Arian ascendency, under Valens.[7]

We know very little of the early career of Gregory, Basil's younger brother. He himself affirms that he owed his education to Basil,[8] and certainly he never benefited, as Basil had, from travel to the educational centres of the time. Yet, wherever he received his education, he is scarcely inferior to the other two in the rhetorical skills admired in that period, and his philosophical ability is superior to that of his brother and his friend. He seems to have been destined for the priesthood, and was ordained early as a lector. But a letter from Gregory Nazianzen reveals that he had suddenly thrown over his ecclesiastical career, and turned rhetor.[9] It seems that during his 'worldly' period he married a Christian called Theosebeia;[10] there is no evidence that he ever lived as a withdrawn ascetic, in spite of Basil's entreaties that he should join him at Pontus.[11] His rhetorical career did not last long, however, whether through disillusionment, the effect of Gregory's letter, or the influence of his family background; quite apart from anything else, Macrina seems to have been a formidable sister, and Gregory was susceptible to dreams induced by his repressed guilt.[12] He soon abandoned worldly pursuits.

In 370, Eusebius died. Basil was his obvious successor. The stuff of politics, however, is ambition, competing groups and frantic lobbying. Basil realized that the church was not immune from such pressures and his election was by no means secure. He was not above entering the arena on its own terms. Unfortunately he misjudged the sensibilities of his friend and nearly sacrificed his support by feigning ill-health in order to secure Gregory's immediate presence. The disillusioned Gregory could see nothing but self-seeking ambition in Basil's activities. Nevertheless, his father realized the value of securing Basil's election as metropolitan of Cappadocia and the quarrel was patched up. Basil was indebted to the aged bishop of Nazianzus for his influential support.[13]

But trouble did not end with his election. Politics makes enemies. Basil was envied his abilities and suspected of pride. To add to his difficulties, the Arian emperor, Valens, divided the province of Cappadocia into two, ostensibly for administrative reasons. Since ecclesiastical provinces conventionally followed those of the empire, a potential rival to Basil was created in the new capital of Tyana, whose bishop, Anthimus, did not hesitate to take the opportunity of declaring himself metropolitan of Cappadocia Secunda. Basil entered a power struggle and tried to consolidate his own position by appointing people he could trust to newly-created sees. Gregory of Nazianzus found himself consecrated bishop of a strategically important crossroads, Sasima, with customs inspectors and innkeepers as virtually his only parishioners. He felt insulted and a mere pawn in the hands of Basil's ambition. The fourth century was a time of reluctant bishops, but none more so than Gregory.[14] Meanwhile another new bishop appeared in the country town of Nyssa, namely Gregory, Basil's younger brother.

Basil was not altogether fortunate in his choice of support. His friend never took up his episcopacy at Sasima, and his brother proved tactless and incompetent in ecclesiastical affairs,[15] succumbing eventually to Arian plots and being deposed for misappropriating church funds. Severe strain was put on Basil's relationship with both Gregories by the politics of his episcopacy. On the one side, Basil's patience was much tried by their weaknesses; on the other, his friend resented Basil's betrayal of their youthful ideals, and his brother, one suspects, suffered from an inferiority complex. Yet both looked back with respect after Basil's premature death and their own rise to influential positions.

Basil's achievements as bishop were enormous.[16] At a purely practical level, he established charitable institutions, hospitals and schools; he organized monasteries and brought administrative skill to the running of the diocese. He provided strong moral leadership in a time of laxity, basing his ideas on a return to the simple life of the primitive church. In the troubled days of an Arian emperor, he remained a fortress of Nicene orthodoxy which the imperial power dared not directly touch. His personal confrontation with Valens became legendary. His vast correspondence with the leading Nicene theologians is a testimony to his indefatigable energy in the service of truth as he understood it. His dogmatic treatises confronted the Anomoian Eunomius, and took up the more recent debate concerning the divinity of the Holy Spirit. Furthermore, he reformed the liturgy of his cathedral and was formidable in preaching and exegesis. It was not without reason that he became known as Basil the Great.

Basil died in 379, just before the triumph of Nicene orthodoxy
was assured. He was only forty-nine, but his health had been ruined
by over-enthusiastic asceticism. For Gregory of Nazianzus, this
was the last of a number of deeply felt bereavements. In the early
370s, he had found himself delivering funeral orations for his
brother, his sister and his father,[17] whose death was soon followed
by that of his mother. Gregory refused to succeed his father, and
after administering the diocese for a while, he retired to a
monastery in Seleucia, as he had so long desired. It was here,
confined himself to a sick-bed, that he heard of Basil's death.

But Gregory was not to lie in Seleucia for long. Representatives
arrived from the tiny community of faithful Nicene Christians in
Constantinople. The capital city was a hotbed of religious differences, and the home town of vacillating courtiers who followed
the creed of the current emperor. Consequently the churches had
been in the hands of the Arians for most of the previous fifty years.
With the appointment of Theodosius, the hour had come for the
Nicenes to establish their position, and in Gregory Nazianzen they
thought they had found the required leader. In vain, Gregory
pleaded his devotion to ascetic retirement. He gave way to what
appeared to be a call to duty, protesting that he had no ambition for
high places in the church or in the world.[18] Perhaps he protests too
much; the compliment to his abilities must have been sweet after
the insult of Sasima.

And in fact Gregory was a resounding success. His brilliant
oratory attracted crowds to the tiny chapel of the Resurrection. His
Five Theological Orations[19] brought disarray in the enemy camp.
He suffered from Arian violence and hostile plots, but the Nicene
forces steadily grew. His reputation was somewhat diminished by
his unfortunate support for a scheming adventurer, the philosopher
Maximus, who ingratiated himself with Gregory and then had
himself secretly consecrated archbishop. Doubts about Gregory's
judgment, however, were soon dissipated; the Emperor Theodosius
arrived, routed the Arians and installed him in the cathedral as
potential archbishop.

Meanwhile for Gregory of Nyssa, long since restored to his see,
Basil's death had been rapidly followed by that of his sister Macrina.
These events led him consciously to adopt the mantle of his lost
brother, and he entered a period of vast literary activity. He
defended his brother's works in specially written apologies; he
carried on the debate with Eunomius; he pursued the defence of the
Holy Spirit. Gregory did not follow Basil slavishly; he was prepared
to correct and develop.[20] Yet Basil's *Rules* lie behind the *De*

Instituto Christiano, and his *Hexaemeron* inspired the *De Opificio Hominis*. (Indeed, so closely did the two become associated in their discussion of man's origins that in the various manuscript traditions, each has assigned to him some homilies on the creation of man, which are clearly intended to supplement the nine homilies on the *Hexaemeron*; the authorship of these homilies remains disputed: Sources Chrétiennes published them as Basil's, and Jaeger's new edition of Gregory includes them in a supplement.) In 381, Basil's shadow lay over the Council of Constantinople; as his brother, defender and representative, Gregory achieved prominence, and his theology seems to have had more than a little influence on the council's deliberations.[21] So the man who had once given the impression of being a bad administrator and a tactless negotiator, suddenly came to wield considerable influence.

At this council, called by Theodosius to seal the triumph of the Nicene position, the two Gregories came together as the foremost defenders of the truth; but while one was to continue to enjoy the favour of the imperial court and the esteem of the orthodox world, the other was to retire into obscurity. The council began by confirming Gregory Nazianzen's election to Constantinople, and he became chairman. But he soon withdrew in disgust at the political wrangling of the assembled bishops, and in his absence, the delayed Egyptian delegation arrived and began to sow doubts about the legality of his election. According to the Nicene canons, bishops could not be transferred from one see to another, and Gregory had been consecrated to Sasima. The one thing Gregory feared was accusations of ambition and self-seeking; so he let his case go by default. He offered his resignation and returned home, intending once more to live an ascetic life. He actually found himself forced to sort out the affairs of the diocese, since no successor to his father had yet been appointed. Finally a successor was installed, and Gregory retired to nurse his ill-health and his hurt feelings, finding solace in the composition of poetry. He died about 390.

The other Gregory, however, had been named as one of the pillars of orthodoxy; the bishop of humble little Nyssa was one of three appointed to regulate the ecclesiastical affairs of Asia Minor, and in succeeding years he found himself travelling around the East arranging elections and fulfilling imperial missions. Declining influence and personal differences with Basil's successor marred his final years, but the quality of his literary productions did not suffer. The last mention we have of him is his attendance at a synod in Constantinople in 394.

The lives of these three men are relatively well known to us because of the fact that they all left valuable collections of correspondence.[22] Indeed, very precise and detailed reconstructions can be produced of certain episodes in their careers. Only thirty letters have reached us from the pen of Gregory Nyssen, but the others were extremely prolific. Basil's correspondence runs to a collection of 365 Epistles, though some are addressed to him rather than being his own composition. Some of the letters cannot be dated, but those that can cover the course of his career, 1–46 coming from the early period and 47–291 from his episcopal years. These letters provide a rich supply of information about the church in this period, as well as Basil's own life and interests. Doctrinal and administrative problems are discussed as well as personal matters. The letters are written with the elegance of style customary in the period, though they were not intended for publication.

Gregory Nazianzen was apparently the first Greek author to publish a collection of his own epistles,[23] at the request of a young admirer, who also asked for advice on epistolary composition. Gregory suggested that letters should be short, clear, simple and charming, citing Basil's letters as models of the art of letter writing.[24] 244 of Gregory's survive, some of them being early correspondence, including several to his friend Basil, but many being the conscious literary creations of his last years. Gregory's *Letters* and *Poems* go together. A few letters deal with doctrinal issues, the letters to Cledonius being important statements of the case against Apollinarius (the first of these was in fact officially adopted by the Council of Chalcedon); and 38 of the poems were occasioned by the necessity of opposing heretics in their own terms – for Apollinarians, like Arians, had resorted to poetic propaganda. But the vast majority of letters and poems are personal and autobiographical, and they reveal most clearly the tensions of conflicting ideals in the course of his life.[25]

II. Withdrawal and Involvement

Already, in tracing the lives of the three Cappadocian Fathers, we have seen illustration of the two areas of tension mentioned earlier. The tensions produced by the monastic ideal are most clearly illustrated by the tragic indecisiveness of Gregory Nazianzen. Gregory was sensitive, introspective, over-enthusiastic, unsure of himself, easily slighted and easily depressed. His inadequacies aggravated the situation. Yet his problems were not simply of his own making. They reflect tension in contemporary attitudes. In his

career has been traced the personal outworking of the conflict
between philosophy and rhetoric, a conflict inherent in the classical
tradition since Socrates and the Sophists.[26] Be that as it may, the
impact of the monastic movement among Christians aggravated the
conflict of ideals – the conflict between withdrawal for contemplation and duty to the community, leadership, success. It was in this
century that potential Christian leaders first had to weigh the rival
claims of the active and contemplative life, to balance the demands
of duty to the church against the desire for personal salvation
reached only, according to the ideals of the time, by withdrawal from
the world. The most remarkable figures of this period and succeeding generations sought to combine the two. Within decades, John
Chrysostom would try to be an ascetic while Patriarch of Constantinople, only to find the seat too hot for a hair shirt. Gregory never
resolved this tension satisfactorily, though his experience did produce an influential discussion of the qualities and dedication
requisite for ordination to the priesthood, a discussion that presented responsible service as not only a perfectly valid way of
obedience to God, but indeed a more arduous one.[27] Yet, however
much he saw practical virtue as a possible path towards the preliminary purification required, for Gregory the goal remained θεωρία –
contemplation.

Basil was not similarly troubled in spirit by the tension. On the
face of it, we have here a consistent character, a man who renounced
the world and devoted himself to the service of the church. Yet his
ideals and his achievements were not really reconcilable. The rule of
obedience was perhaps his most original contribution to the development of coenobitic monasticism;[28] yet Basil was obedient to
none. He was domineering as a bishop, and insensitive to the
scruples of his friend and his brother. Humility and self-denial were
required of the brethren in his communities; yet Basil was ambitious
for his see and jealous of his authority. That he was accused of pride
and haughtiness is clear from Gregory's defence of his character in
his panegyric: 'What they term pride', says Gregory, 'is, I fancy, the
firmness and steadfastness and stability of his character.'[29] Yet
Gregory himself never ceased to regard his consecration as bishop of
Sasima as an act of tyranny on Basil's part.[30] It was no doubt for the
good of the church that a character like Basil failed to put his own
theory into practice. However, in his life and his writings, Basil
provides a revealing illustration of the difficulty of living in accordance with the conscious ideology of the period when responsibilities
made their own inescapable demands, demands only too suited to
the character and temperament with which he had been endowed.

In their own way, each of the three Cappadocians balanced contemplation and withdrawal with confrontation and involvement. An account of Gregory Nyssen's political manoeuvring makes strange reading alongside his mystical writings. No doubt human weaknesses, ambition, inconsistency, played their part in this apparent ambivalence. But, in fact, scripture provided models for living with this tension. To both Gregories, the great figures of the Bible, like Moses and Paul, appeared as mediators, whose mystical experience of God was transmitted to the people.[31] So their ideal was to aim at balance, and in the long term, the development of this ideal was of more significance than the personal tensions from which it evolved.

III. Christianity and Contemporary Culture

When pagan culture and Christian tradition are put in the scales, we find a similar unstable but significant balance. The balance is hardly surprising when one remembers that their theological lineage goes directly back to Origen,[32] whose devotion to the text of scripture was counterbalanced by an acceptance of the Greek philosophical tradition. Nevertheless, it is interesting to witness the conscious and unconscious interplay of two traditions in the minds of these three great men, an interplay that was the inevitable result of their family background and education, and yet could only be achieved by inconsistency in their attitudes.

When Basil was baptized and renounced the world, he at the same time renounced pagan culture. In accordance with Christian traditions, he denounced the philosophers. The same conventional polemic appears in the works of both Gregories. Dabbling in philosophy was the source of heresy. Grudging recognition might be given to Plato, but only if his dependence on Moses was stressed. In theory only the Bible pointed the way to truth.[33]

Yet the value of pagan education could not be denied by its beneficiaries. Basil claims to have given up cultural pursuits,[34] but writes *An Address to Young Men on How They Might Derive Benefit from Greek Literature*.[35] He accepts that training in pagan literature is a useful preparation for the difficulty of scriptural exegesis. Where there is an affinity with Christian values the two traditions should be set side by side; the fruit of the soul is truth, but 'external wisdom' (that is, non-Christian wisdom) may adorn it. His main concern, however, is the moral content of the literature, and he warns that the soul must be watched in case pleasure in the poet's words leads the reader to accept the more evil sort of influence like those who take poisons with honey. The reader is to take what is appropriate and useful, and guard against what is harmful; so Basil collects examples of virtue and good philosophy from Hesiod, Homer, Plato and many others. He recognizes that the classical tradition provided the only method of education, and recommends its acceptance at least as a *'praeparatio evangelica'*.

In his Homilies on the *Hexaemeron*,[36] Basil draws on the best of contemporary science; he considers the solutions of other philosophies to intellectual problems concerning the nature and origin of the universe; he argues the validity of the Christian doctrine of creation as a viable solution to these problems. The methods and questions of the philosophers are his presuppositions, and their examples, their illustrations, their suggestions provide much of his material. He presents his hearers with a complete Christian philosophy, not just ethics but cosmogony and physics. Yet here more than anywhere the tensions and contradictions are apparent. Basil is preaching to a congregation; he is the official representative of the orthodox church. He has to reflect the traditional attitudes.[37] So he expresses contempt for the philosophers and scientists who busy themselves in vain with unanswerable questions, and produce solutions which are the arrogant demonstrations of human reason. Their mutual contradictions prove their folly. Their elaborately clever systems distract them from the one truth worth knowing. Christians do not need any information which is not provided by scripture, and they should avoid 'busy-bodying' curiosity about the universe, the shape of the earth, the number of the heavens. Scripture alone suffices. Yet even as he mocks the philosophers, he displays his own up-to-date knowledge of astronomy. There is a real sense in which the bishop tied to orthodox tradition breathes the Greek spirit of enquiry; the monk renouncing the world appreciates the natural order. By careful assimilation, Basil has in fact achieved a remarkable synthesis between biblical teaching and selected elements of the profane systems.[38]

But what exactly *was* Basil's own point of view? It is possible that he modified his own views over the years: classical allusions are far more frequent in his early letters than in those of the episcopate. Be that as it may, quite clearly Basil was capable of adapting his style and his approach to his audience, quoting only the Bible in his ascetical works, but being freer in his use of quotations and allusions in other literary genres.[39] Even so, many of his compositions show a remarkably unselfconscious marriage of cultures, which is perhaps especially well evidenced in the collocation of biblical and Hellenic motifs in his letters of consolation.[40]

Basil's rather grudging recognition provides a contrast to the enthusiasm of his friend, Gregory. It was Julian's attempt to deny education to Christians which roused Gregory more than anything. He asserts that he has given up all other worldly things, riches, nobility, fame, etc., but 'words' – that is, literature, culture, argument – these he cannot renounce. His *Orations against Julian*[41] were composed after Julian's death, and were probably never actually delivered. They are unattractive pieces of invective, but of interest here because we can see how Gregory attacks the claim that the Greek language, mathematics, poetry, etc., belongs to paganism. No race or religion has an exclusive claim to culture, for culture has been derived from many sources. Julian's edict and Gregory's intense reaction to it bear witness to the contemporary tension in the church. Julian had taken the Christians at their word: if nothing is required beyond orthodox faith, if the wisdom of the world is vanquished by God's foolishness, if literature and philosophy are superfluous beside the scriptures, then it is inconsistent for Christians to be professional teachers of rhetoric. Therefore they were to be excluded from this profession. By this edict, Julian aimed to turn the schools into centres of pagan propaganda. If the pagan reaction had been stronger and more lasting than it proved to be, the church could have found itself deprived of educated leaders within a generation. Gregory may have criticized Gregory of Nyssa for adopting the profession of rhetor, but he knew that the church could not afford to lose the only intellectual tools available for the education of theologians and the development of apologetic argument.

But Gregory's anger was not merely academic; his emotions and personality were involved. In spite of some conventional polemic against literature and philosophy, he of all men could not disclaim the classical heritage. Athens, not Palestine, had held him in his twenties. In his epistles and poems, we see his real feelings, his genuine devotion to literature, philosophy and rhetoric. These he regarded as the auxiliaries of Christian doctrine. In him, more than in any other of the Fathers, accord between Hellenism and Christianity was realized, concludes Fleury.[42] In his panegyrics on Caesarius, Athanasius and Basil[43], he particularly stresses the fact that they were men of culture, men who had enjoyed a comprehensive education. Gregory was prepared to admit that Christianity owed much to 'external wisdom', since, for him, classical culture was an ancient and treasured heritage, a legacy to all men; indeed, culture was the foundation of human, as distinct from bestial, life. Pagan philosophy was only false because it tended to be distracted

by beautiful discourse and inessential vanities; philosophy Christianized, however, related human *logos* to the divine *Logos*, producing practical virtue and contemplation, and so leading to the
truth.[44]

In fact, the extant works of all three Cappadocians reveal how
much they had assimilated contemporary culture and philosophy.
The roots of their education remained alive, even where they are
unwilling to admit it. Rhetoric and philosophy are renounced for
their own sake, but become the handmaid of theology. Modern
studies have revealed the very considerable range of literature
known to them all – at least from school text-books and probably
often first-hand. Quotations and allusions are there, even though
they are not acknowledged.[45] But more than this, the spirit and
methods of contemporary intellectual pursuits remain alive in
their ecclesiastical works. Yet undoubtedly, of the three, Gregory
Nazianzen was most deliberately a man of literature. His
Orations[46] are fine examples of contemporary rhetoric, used not
slavishly but intelligently, to express Christian ideas and senti-
ments. They are speeches on themes rather than homilies on texts.
That we find their style burdensome is not relevant; they suited the
taste of the day. In his *Poems*, he consciously imitated the classics
of the past, inspired by a desire to create a parallel Christian
literature. That most of his verses lack the quality of originality and
inspiration is the fault of the contemporary 'classicism', the effect
of exclusive interest in a golden age long past, an attitude which had
afflicted the educational tradition of many centuries and would
continue to do so for many more to come. While such an
atmosphere lasted, his poems were respected and in fact his
personal 'confessions' show signs of genuine inspiration at times,
even though this is cramped by the traditional literary form in
which he felt obliged to express himself.[47]

The bulk of Gregory Nyssen's work[48] consists of anti-heretical,
dogmatic, exegetical and ascetical treatises – in other words, he did
not on the face of it utilize contemporary literary forms as much as
the other Gregory. Yet he had once embarked on a career as rhetor,
and rhetorical norms pervade his work, especially his homilies. His
panegyrics on saints and martyrs, and the three funeral orations
delivered at Constantinople, are notable examples of his adaptation
of pagan oratorical techniques to Christian use; and his *De
infantibus praemature abreptis* (On Infants' Early Deaths) is an
elaborate rhetorical exercise which conforms to the rules of
Isocrates.[49] However much Gregory sneers at Eunomius for being a
mere rhetor who enjoys playing with words for effect, he is himself

tarred with the same brush. As for his charges that Eunomius makes too much use of pagan philosophy and Aristotelian logic, there is in fact 'not a little of these elements to be found in him'.[50] He uses the *Categories* to refute his opponent, and is now widely regarded as one of the greatest philosophical minds of the early church. His *Dialogue on the Soul and the Resurrection* is a Christian *Phaedo*, a literary account of a conversation with his sister Macrina on the eve of her death, Macrina becoming Gregory's mouthpiece as Socrates had been Plato's. Both this and many of his other works reveal that Gregory knew the Platonic dialogues and was able to make a constructive adaptation of Plato's reasoning. It is also clear that Gregory knew the works of the Neoplatonists, Plotinus, Porphyry and Iamblichus, as well as the traditions of the contemporary Platonic school at Athens.[51] It is not at all clear where and how he acquired his philosophical education, but he certainly had it. In fact, so wholeheartedly did he accept the approach and attitude of contemporary philosophy that one critic has suggested that he was really a born philosopher reluctantly forced into the straitjacket of orthodoxy by his domineering family.[52] This estimate hardly does justice to the complexities of Gregory's character and thought, but it does highlight the extent of his largely unacknowledged debt to the pagan philosophical tradition. So important are the philosophical elements in Gregory's theological thought that they will be treated more fully at a later point in this chapter.

Over the centuries the church had adapted itself and its message to the contemporary situation, partly consciously, partly unconsciously. It is not surprising that men see the Christian tradition with the cultural spectacles of their own time. Yet at the same time, the church had always distinguished itself not merely from other religions, but from the world, its ideals and purposes, its wealth and its wisdom. This double-edged tradition affected the stance of the Cappadocians. The church was now beginning to take over the world, not merely in political terms, but in the sphere of philosophy and culture. The ambivalent attitude expressed in the writings of the Cappadocians reflects the emergence of a Christianized culture. This new culture is dependent on the pagan culture of the past, but it has to be distinguished from it. It must disown its inheritance, while embracing its newly-acquired riches. It must renounce the world and its wisdom, but to win the world, it had to talk its language. For all its superficial inconsistency, this attitude served the needs of the day.

IV. Basil and the Ascetic Movement

A striking contrast to Basil's *Hexaemeron* is provided by his *Ascetica*. A desire to return to the simplicity of the primitive church in Jerusalem determines the flavour and tone of his ascetic teaching. It is true that his ideals are affected by contemporary presuppositions about the soul and the body; it is also true that the ethical teaching of Hellenistic philosophers has influenced his maxims; nevertheless, scripture provides his means of expression. For him, scripture was the only rule; his own *Rules* are merely systematic aids for those seeking spiritual perfection.[53]

The *Ascetica* attributed to Basil constitute a collection of thirteen writings, some undoubtedly inauthentic. The collection has a long history of use in the Eastern church, and so has been preserved in a number of textual traditions and versions; inevitably then, study of these documents has been fraught with prior critical questions, and no serious student of the material can get far without consulting the major works of Gribomont and Rudberg.[54] Their conclusions have won fairly general acceptance.

It appears probable that Basil's first ascetic treatise was the work known as the *Moralia*; Gribomont is not alone in suggesting that it was composed about 360 while Basil was at his monastery in Pontus. Yet the character of this work suggests that it could be a pastoral work belonging to the years of his episcopate.[55] It consists basically of lists of scriptural citations, the author merely providing links and headings. Who was the collection made for? What was its purpose? Since chs. 70–79 are concerned with the proper duties of ministers of the word, married people, parents, slaves, soldiers and magistrates, it was hardly intended only for monks. Gribomont[56] suggested that the ascetic movement in Basil's eyes was a movement of reform in the church. Basil was here setting out the evangelical basis of the movement, emphasizing continence rather than condemnation of marriage and riches, overcoming the fears of extremism aroused by such groups as the Messalians. He was looking for New Testament norms in a situation where ascetic propaganda was causing dissension. But it could be that it was, as Lèbe suggests, no more than a handy synthesis of the moral teaching Basil had been giving as priest and bishop, drawn up during his later years. Whatever its original intention, the treatise certainly appears to be authentic, and the theoretical basis of much of Basil's ascetic teaching. What is notable is its entirely scriptural content.

If we assume that the *Moralia* was the first work, the second seems to have been the work known as the *Little Asceticon*. This does not survive in its original form in Greek, but Rufinus' translation and a Syriac version appear to be good witnesses. It consisted of answers to practical questions, the questions presupposing a somewhat Messalian atmosphere, the answers deliberately counselling restraint. At this stage Basil seems to have been much under the influence of Eustathius of Sebaste, which perhaps explains Sozomen's comment that some attributed the ascetic treatises to Eustathius rather than Basil. Basil's own ideas were more fully developed as later versions appeared.

Probably dating from his episcopate are the two works known as the *Shorter Rules* and the *Longer Rules*, though not exactly in the form found in the later collections. These editions seem to come from a sixth-century redactor. Basically, however, they collect genuine Basilian pieces, and Basil himself may have initiated the formation of an ascetic corpus by combining an early version with the *Moralia*. In the works which became known as the *Rules*, Basil seems to be trying to regulate and reform ascetic communities under his episcopal jurisdiction, or at least to be providing a compendium of his teaching for the use of monks. Yet they do not really establish a monastic rule in the sense of a legalistic code of practice. Rather they trace out an ascetical way of life on the basis of the New Testament,[57] very much as his earlier treatises did. Basil had been evolving monastic 'regulations' ever since his letter to Gregory on the monastic life, and these documents appear to be the culmination of the process, a synthesis of his teachings for the use of monks. The *Longer Rules* discuss the fundamental principles of monasticism in fifty-five sections; the *Shorter Rules* take the form of question and answer, providing brief applications (313 of them) to the details of daily life.

The most refreshing aspect of Basil's ascetic teaching, apart from the profoundly scriptural basis of it, is his recognition of the need for community, for a society in which alone true Christian virtue can be expressed. Having explored the various ascetic traditions of Syria and Palestine, he recognized the dangers and eccentricities involved in an individualistic search for personal purity in isolation from others; he adopted the communal ideas of Pachomius. But this was not merely a response to practical problems. The strong escapist currents of contemporary soteriology were tempered in Basil's thought by an unusually profound insight into the nature of New Testament ethics. He saw that it was impossible to practise the law of love in solitude. The solitary neglected to feed the hungry and clothe the naked. He therefore failed to obey the commands of God, and total obedience is the radical demand of Christ. The Christian virtues of humility, obedience and love can only be worked out in the context of a community serving the needs of society.

Thus the most important source of Basil's teaching was the Acts' account of the primitive Christian community. Undoubtedly his family background, the writings of Origen, the examples of Antony, Pachomius and other famous ascetics, the outlook of contemporary philosophy, Christian tradition and probably the ascetic teaching of Eustathius, all made large contributions to the total picture. Basil's asceticism bears the characteristic marks of the period: celibacy and withdrawal from worldly pursuits, the search for union with God through meditation and prayer, refusal of all but the barest necessities of life, these are inevitably the basic features of his teaching. Yet certain characteristics undoubtedly drew inspiration from the teaching of Jesus and the example of his first disciples. All things were to be held in common and to be used for the benefit of the sick and the needy. The monastery was to be situated within reach of suffering humanity, and provide a hospital and schools. The monk was to engage in manual work for the maintenance of the community and its welfare services. Thus Basil sought to resuscitate and perpetuate the fervour of the early church in his monastic communities.

In fact, Basil's organization would inevitably tend to breed subservience rather than imaginative ventures in the service of others. Obedience and humility were notably lacking amongst the individualistic ascetics of the desert, who accepted the authority of none but the Lord. For Basil, the community was necessary not only to nurture love, but also to provide a specific context in which obedience and humility could be fostered. For this reason, the monk had to discipline himself to unquestioning obedience to his superior, and to calm acceptance of the judgment and criticism of his fellow-monks. No doubt this required a greater self-sacrifice than merely giving up worldly goods and ambitions, but it meant that 'institutionalization' was inevitable, and the primitive fervour Basil sought to re-create would be dampened by the discipline of routine, by the deliberate destruction of emotion, by authoritarianism.

Nevertheless, for Basil, the monk was the authentic Christian who set out to live Christianity in its fullness. In theory, Basil could not tolerate a dual morality: every Christian is called to utter obedience to every precept in the gospels. But in practice, he saw monasteries as providing the conditions in which this ideal could flourish and be perfected. The spirit of self-sacrificial love for others is at least the mainspring of Basil's teaching, whether or not it could be realized most effectively in the monastic conditions which he envisaged.

V. The Dogmatic Debates

All three Cappadocians were involved in the dogmatic controversies of their time, and a considerable amount of the published work of Basil and his brother was directly concerned with these issues. Eunomius was the contemporary promulgator of extreme Arian views, and during 363–365 Basil wrote a treatise against his recently published *Apologia*. The first three books of the *Contra Eunomium* are genuine, the other two, probably the work of Didymus the Blind, being erroneously added on to the end.[58] Book I argues that ἀγεννησία (ingenerateness) is *not* the essential characteristic of the deity; Book II defends the *homoousion* of the Logos, and Book III applies the argument to defence of the divinity of the Holy Spirit also. This was followed by a treatise specifically on the Holy Spirit,[59] written about 375 and used a few years later by St Ambrose when he composed his *De Spiritu Sancto*. In these works, Basil laid the foundations on which the two Gregories based their definitive exposition of trinitarian theology, even though he himself was chary of using the *homoousion* of the Holy Spirit, a point on which Gregory Nazianzen upbraids him.

Discussion about the Holy Spirit raised serious questions about the relationship between tradition and innovation. Could doctrine develop? After all, scripture did not provide clear teaching on the divine nature of the Spirit. Gregory Nazianzen admitted that the Spirit's divinity was only becoming clear in the life of the church, and that therefore doctrine was not a static entity revealed once for all. Revelation was progressive, and still continuing. The Old Testament revealed the Father, the New Testament revealed the Son. There were stages of illumination depending upon the capacity of the recipients. The disciples were not yet ready for a full revelation of the Spirit's divinity (John 16.12).[60] Basil had not been so daring; he maintained the over-riding importance of scripture and tradition, and therefore had to find a way of arguing that the divinity of the Holy Spirit was an apostolic doctrine. A distinction between *kerygma* and *dogma* became his way of handling the problem. The publicly proclaimed teaching of the church, enshrined in the creed, was *kerygma*; *dogma* was the secret and mystical tradition reserved for the initiates. The exact implications of this have been the subject of some discussion. Did Basil adopt the Origenist idea of advanced secret doctrines for an élite, an idea deliberately dropped by Gregory Nazianzen?[61] That he uses that kind of language cannot be denied; yet the élite was almost certainly *all* the baptized. What Basil referred to, and this can be documented by examining his arguments, was the theological implication of the sacraments and the church's customs, those aspects of the church's life taught only to catechumens.[62] In practical terms, those who submitted to baptism in this period were an élite, and the 'mysteries' of the faith were reserved by the *disciplina arcani* from public promulgation. This explains Basil's reserve in public preaching concerning the Holy Spirit, when he was prepared to acknowledge his divinity in private correspondence. It was the liturgy which provided the data on which such a doctrine was based. So the concept of *dogma* made it possible for Basil to disclaim any charges of innovation when he argued that the divine nature of the Holy Spirit was implied by the doxology, baptism, sanctification, and so on. He could circumvent the traditional accusations against heretics, that they took pride in intellectualism and philosophy, were avid for originality and prestige, and failed to accept the authority of the sacred text and the tradition of the church,[63] because what he called *dogma* was as apostolic in origin as the *kerygma*, or at least, so far as he and his contemporaries knew. Scripture and tradition remained the bulwark against newfangled doctrines, even as doctrinal advances were made.

Eunomius' reply to Basil inspired his brother Gregory to his defence. A literary debate ensued during the course of which Gregory composed at least four treatises against his opponent. The order of these books became confused in the manuscript tradition, but has now been restored in the new critical edition of W. Jaeger.[64] Gregory also defended the divinity of the Holy Spirit in several small treatises, one of which appears among Basil's correspondence, an indication of the confused state in which Gregory's works have survived. Another treatise *Quod non sint tres dii* clarifies his trinitarian theology, and probably dates from the end of his career.

In these controversial writings, we find many of the standard polemical ploys. The heretic is accused of being unbiblical and impious; of using sophistry and syllogisms to trample on the being of God. The debate with Eunomius became a personal feud, pamphlet following counter-pamphlet, slanders and misrepresentations being the tricks of the trade. Yet in the midst of what may seem uncharitable and offensive argument, the fundamentals of trinitarian orthodoxy were finally fashioned. These treatises present the peak of anti-Arian argumentation and are therefore of great importance in the history of dogma.

The heart of Eunomius' position consists in his insistence that God is knowable – indeed, completely comprehensible because he is simple unity. With respect to the Being (*ousia*) by which he is one, God is not separated or divided into more, nor is he 'becoming sometimes one and sometimes another, nor changing from being what he is, or split from one *ousia* into a threefold *hypostasis*: for he is always and absolutely one, remaining uniformly and unchangeably God.'[65]

There are some ways in which Gregory of Nyssa undoubtedly shares Eunomius' definition of divinity,[66] in spite of the scorn with which he quotes his words. The whole basis of Gregory's trinitarian doctrine is the idea that God is incomposite, homogeneous, unchangeable and indivisible, attributes all of which Eunomius accepted. From any other source, Gregory might have recognized something of his own position being voiced. What Eunomius is denying in the quoted words is a caricature of Cappadocian trinitarianism, not the somewhat sophisticated position which had in fact been developed.

What then is the essential difference between the two protagonists? Eunomius concludes that this definition of God as simple unity can only be safeguarded by isolating the Supreme and Absolute One from the second and third, which came after and are therefore inferior and derivative. Thus ἀγεννησία becomes for him the essentially divine attribute which guarantees God's simplicity and uniqueness. Gregory on the other hand, uses the very same definition of God in order to argue that a plurality or hierarchy of separated beings is impossible: one infinite cannot be greater or less than another. There may be 'three subjects', Gregory argues, but their infinity means that they are indistinguishable alongside one another. To speak of 'large' and 'small', or 'before' and 'after' introduces compositeness into the single unity of the undivided divine substance. There is existence and non-existence; there cannot be degrees of Being or priorities of Being; one cannot be more or less existent than another.

The drive of Gregory's argument, then, is against the possibility of a 'hierarchy of Being'. Eunomius' very desire to separate God in his absoluteness from the created order led him into a 'hierarchical' position; since he wanted to continue using scriptural language of his derivative Logos, he could not avoid producing 'a new God springing up from nothing'.[67] Eunomius was trying to establish an absolute distinction between God and his creation; Gregory already accepted this as fundamental, but his God was a trinitarian God.

For Gregory, Father and Son express not so much different Beings as an eternal relationship within one divine Being; for without the Son, the Father has neither existence nor name.[68] Yet he is sensitive to the charge of 'tritheism'. Undoubtedly this is due to the fact that he defines the *ousia* which Father, Son and Spirit share, in a generic sense, and his favourite analogy is the universal human *ousia* shared by particular men, e.g. Peter, James and John.[69] Furthermore, in speaking of generation, Gregory points out that even among men and animals the production of a son does not divide or diminish the substance of a father.[70] No matter how much he protests their common eternity, common activity and common will, it is difficult to call a theology based on such a definition of their common nature, monotheistic. Yet his definition of divine substance, as we have seen, resolves this difficulty for him. If divine substance is in principle indivisible, incomposite and undifferentiated, if number is inapplicable to divine simplicity so that one and one and one cannot be added together to make three, if each is infinite so that they cannot exist alongside each other but only in each other, then the oneness of God is by definition ensured. If divine substance is in principle unchangeable, then the mutual relationships within the Godhead are eternal and non-hierarchical. Polytheism and Judaism are alike avoided, and the fundamental distinction between God and creation safeguarded.[71]

Such a conception has its difficulties, of course. The transcendence of God had once made his relationship with the world problematical and the Logos had filled the role of mediator. Now the Logos shared the transcendence of the divine Being. Christological difficulties were bound to ensue. Inevitably the exegesis of gospel texts entered the debate with Eunomius, as it had between Arius and Athanasius, and Gregory adopts the same sort of solution as his predecessor. Yet, more than Athanasius, he was forced to face the problem of docetism by the heresy of Apollinarius, and his *Antirrheticus adversus Apollinarem* is his reply to the heretic's *Demonstration of the Divine Incarnation*.[72] As the problems raised by Arius were, for the majority, resolved in trinitarian terms, the scene of debate was shifting and new problems emerging.

Meanwhile, the trinitarian debate involved the parties in some other interesting theological issues, one being the question of theological language and its basis.[73] Eunomius wanted to claim that all descriptions of the Logos were analogical; he was Son of God metaphorically, not literally. Gregory of course accepts the analogical character of titles like 'stone', 'door', 'way', 'shepherd', etc., but tries to distinguish between these and other names which have the function of defining his nature. 'Son' and 'only-begotten God' must be taken in a more literal sense. The principle on which he makes this distinction is that images used of his relationship with men are analogical, whereas names expressing his relationship with God are essential.[74]

Yet it was Gregory who insisted on God's incomprehensibility. How then could he justify the attempt to define God or express his essential Being? Gregory admits that all names are inadequate and humanly contrived expressions, but he goes on to argue that they are not arbitrary, for they are grounded in the prior existence and activity of God. Though he has to accommodate himself to the limitations of human perception, God cannot be a party to deception; so the names revealed in scripture have sufficient grounding in reality to form a basis for theological construction. They have to be critically tested; for so wide is the gulf between Creator and creature, finite and Infinite, that they are misleading as well as applicable. They also have to be multiplied, for no one epithet can express or define the totality of the infinite God; and their status has to be determined in accordance with the principle mentioned earlier, the distinction between those that apply to God absolutely and those that have a relative reference. However, critically evaluated, the variety of attributes indicated by the names derived from scripture can provide a positive theological language without endangering the transcendent unity of God's nature.

There is always, nevertheless, a 'difference of unlikeness'. Eunomius' arrogant claim to define and delimit the Being of God will not do: 'the infinity of God exceeds all the significance and comprehension that names can furnish.'[75] For all the detail of his trinitarian discussions, Gregory stands ultimately before a mystery, and this is where his dogmatic theology and his so-called mysticism coalesce.

VI. Gregory the Theologian

Unlike his fellow-Cappadocians, Gregory Nazianzen left no treatises dealing with the controversial issues of the day. Yet 'the theologian' is the title by which he has been honoured down the centuries. It is perhaps on his ability to communicate, his 'popularization', his clarity and ease of expression that his reputation rests. For him, preaching and theology were integrated; his *Five Theological Orations*[76] were a brilliant summary for the city congregation of what was becoming the accepted trinitarian orthodoxy. These statements were the height of Gregory's achievement.

In the theology of Gregory Nazianzen, the Trinity is absolutely central. His technical vocabulary is drawn from the background of doctrinal controversy; his work lacks startling originality. But this does not detract from his achievement. Where Basil had been a bit chary of openly asserting the divinity of the Holy Spirit, in spite of the general drift of his argumentation, Gregory did not hesitate to take the lead.[77] His work was one of consolidation. He was conscious of finding the 'mean' between heretical extremes, and at the same time of affirming a theology of positive significance.[78]

A study of the doctrinal controversies of the fourth and fifth centuries may leave one with a sense of frustration. Were the debates really significant? Were the contenders not hair-splitting in a matter that is beyond human knowledge? Standing back from the debates, we may be tempted to wonder how so much unnecessary passion could have been expended on relatively technical issues. It is when we sense the *religious* significance of the issues that we begin to appreciate why emotions were roused. Athanasius, as we have seen, was driven by the urgency of his sense of salvation in Christ: Arian simplification just could not contain the depths of that experience. Gregory was likewise driven by the pressures of his religious consciousness. For him, the cold technicality of logical argumentation detracted from his sense of mystery in the divine. The Arians, he felt, were too rational by half. An adequate theology had to do justice to his experience of awe and mystery in the universe, in ascetic contemplation, in the liturgy and in scripture. Gregory knew that men can know nothing of God, except what God has chosen to reveal in limited human terms. So he is often hesitant and plainly aware of the complexity of the problems he is discussing. He exhorts his congregations to cling to the essentials, and particularly to the sure foundation of the cross of Christ.[79]

Gregory's theology shared the apophatic, negative stress we have already observed in the argumentation of Gregory Nyssen. God is incorporeal, ingenerate, unchangeable, incorruptible and incomprehensible. We can only understand *that* he is, not *what* he is. Yet, for Gregory, this is not the end of discussion. For God has come to meet us, and our faith is not vain. The Trinity expresses both the mystery of God's nature, and of his loving outreach towards his creation. The Trinity is the object of Gregory's devotion, and the ground of his faith and his life. Knowledge of the Trinity comes through scripture and tradition, and through the continuing revelation of the Spirit in the church. For all his rhetorical tricks, Gregory had an outstanding ability to draw on the vast range of imagery and symbolism, the expression of faith and worship, originating in the Bible and developing in the life of the church. Rationalist tools, like Origen's theodicy, he converted into urgent appeals and dire warnings for his sinful and unrepentant congregations, by drawing on the prophetic writings of the Old Testament.[80] His God is not just the God of the philosophers or dogmaticians, but the God of Abraham, Isaac and Jacob, acting in the events of his own time. His entire approach is saturated with biblical imagery and typological symbolism, centring on the cross of Christ and brought alive for the Christian of his own day: 'Yesterday, the lamb was slain and the door-posts anointed, and Egypt bewailed her first-born, and the Destroyer passed us over. . . . To-day, we have escaped from Egypt, and from Pharaoh, and there is none to hinder us from keeping the feast to the Lord our God. . . . Yesterday, I was crucified with him; today I am glorified with him . . . yesterday, I was buried with him; today, I rise with him. . . .'[81] Of all the Fathers, Gregory makes most use of the idea of Christ's sacrifice, not as part of a doctrinal system or a consistent theory of atonement, but as an emotive affirmation of faith in his preaching and personal devotion. Here, too, we find a refusal to oversimplify. The popular view that the devil received Christ as the ransomprice, he dismisses as outrageous. But how could the offering be made to God? It was not from slavery to God that man needed redemption; nor does God need or delight in sacrifice. The Father accepted it, he concludes, 'because of the economy', the need to sanctify mankind by the humanity of God, to overcome the tyrant, and draw us to himself by the mediation of his Son.[82] The distinctive message of Christianity is expressed not in logical systems, but in evocative images.

Gregory is true to nearly every aspect of Christian thought about salvation in the East. He was able to express the faith in the pictorial and rhetorical language that appealed to his contemporaries. In all this, he was able to impart a sense of the depth, the complexity, the mystery of the Christian conception of God and of his relation with the world; thus he outshone those who indulged in the niceties of technical debate, and became revered as the theologian *par excellence.*

VII.   Gregory of Nyssa and Neoplatonic Mysticism

It is widely accepted that modern studies, largely initiated by
Daniélou, have established Gregory Nyssen's originality and
genuine philosophical ability, and have rediscovered the fundamental importance of his mysticism for his theological thought.[83] That
Gregory was no mere eclectic compiler of ideas but a Christian
Neoplatonist who expressed his mystical experience through
scriptural symbols allegorically interpreted, has become the standard judgment. Yet some recent studies have called this consensus
in question – for after all, the validity of this estimate does depend
upon the definition of philosopher or mystic which is operative.
Thus, G. C. Stead has asserted that Gregory is not a philosopher in
the sense that he engages with philosophical questions, only in the
sense that as a theologian, he draws eclectically from philosophy in
order to systematize his theological insights;[84] and Mühlenberg's
study of Gregory's thought on God's infinity has inspired a reassessment of the so-called mystical work, the *Life of Moses*, which
suggests that theological controversies of the time had a formative
influence, and that while the symbolic language of the mysteries is
used, this arises out of the need to deal with cognitive problems, not
out of any kind of 'mystical experience'.[85] Certainly there is a risk
that a later mystical schema similar to that of Dionysius the
Areopagite has been anachronistically read into the text.

Nevertheless the influence of Plotinus has been established, and
one is probably justified in asking whether the pendulum has not
swung too far. Philosophy in Gregory's day was not 'rational thought
without presuppositions', but a way of life.[86] Besides, the bias of
ancient culture was veneration of the past. The philosophical
schools of the Hellenistic world were interpreters of the wisdom of
earlier great thinkers. In the schools, this tended to become bound by
tradition and scholasticism, but in Plotinus, Gregory had a predecessor who was no mere commentator tied to the mainstream of the
Platonic tradition. Rather, in certain key passages in the Platonic
dialogues, he found the foundations of true philosophy, opinions
which accorded with his own. 'It must be the opinion of anyone who
studies the *Enneads* that Plotinus' major motive for philosophizing
is to rationalize his own intuitions and experiences. Plotinus is a
Platonist because Plato enables him to achieve this with the most
success.'[87]

Much the same can be said of Gregory, though for him Plotinus
himself, along with scripture and the traditions of the church, has

become a major source of his expression and understanding. His dependence on Plotinus he does not acknowledge, but there can be no doubt that Gregory knew the major Platonic dialogues and the *Enneads* at first hand. His work does not reflect simply a general cultural atmosphere. Yet he is neither a slavish imitator, nor a collector of quotations. The imagery, the vocabulary, the thought-world of Plato and Plotinus become the expression of his Christian experience, and are wedded to the imagery, vocabulary and thought-world of Christian traditions, scripture and liturgy. Nor is this a shot-gun wedding, superficial and artificial. Gregory was not 'scared of being anything but orthodox'.[88] Rather his religious experience was expressed in a subtle amalgam of scriptural and philosophical symbols. The integration of Plato's image of the cave in *Republic* VII with the grotto at Bethlehem is a case in point: as Daniélou points out,[89] the combination indicates that God descends into the shadows of the cave to bring illumination, rather than man having to find his own way of ascent. The Christian gospel transforms the essentially Platonic motif.

Whether because of mystical experience or because of other pressures like the Origenist controversy and the debate with Eunomius, it is clear that in certain respects Gregory breaks with traditional Platonic presuppositions. One was the universal presupposition that perfection is static, an ultimate to be reached by philosophical ascent. All change from what is perfect, they imagined, must be for the worse. Much of the Platonist tradition, therefore, including Origen, envisaged a fall and return, and the good as the changeless perfection lost. But Gregory saw perfection in terms of constant progress. There is no limit to virtue; so perfection cannot be grasped or possessed. The race goes on for ever; the ascent is never-ending. To gain a vision of God, it is necessary to follow him. There is no danger of the soul becoming satiated and therefore being distracted from the pursuit of God, for every summit reached is a revelation of greater heights above. For participation in God only produces more intense desire: this truly is the vision of God, never to be satisfied in the desire to see him.[90]

This notion of perpetual progress is grounded in Gregory's most fundamental theological perceptions: man's mutability, making possible constant change and progress, and God's incomprehensibility, ensuring that never can he be wholly grasped; true knowledge of God is the seeing which consists in not seeing. The incomprehensibility of God is grounded in his infinity, and this positive use of the idea of infinity is also important.[91] Infinity had for long implied indefiniteness, formlessness, in the Greek philosophical tradition. It was distasteful to a culture whose idea of the good and the beautiful was based on symmetry, proportion and mathematical categories. Goodness meant limit. The Platonic forms were finite beings. But already for Plotinus the One transcended the forms in being formless and 'beyond being'.[92] The apophatic theology of Philo and Clement of Alexandria had toyed with the idea of God's infinity. Now positive affirmation of God's infinity appears in Christian writers, anxious to assert that his goodness, power and love have no limit; and, in Gregory's case, that man's eternal progress towards the divine is likewise limitless. The soul enters a 'luminous darkness', in which it can know nothing of an infinite and incomprehensible God, but yet senses his presence in a union of mystical love. This experience is not cyclic, lost and found over and over again, but a perpetual discovery of deeper and deeper riches, a never-ending process of 'becoming'. For God remains ever inaccessible, and yet intimately near.

For one concept where Platonist and biblical traditions coalesced was in the understanding of man's soul as an image of the divine. For Plotinus and Gregory the ascent begins with purification from fleshly desires, and the turning of the soul inward upon itself, to find knowledge of God in its own purity. Gregory uses Plotinus' language and imagery to describe this process. Yet subtle differences have been stressed,[93] perhaps overstressed. It is true that Gregory insists on the goodness of creation, and, perhaps a bit reluctantly, the importance of the body as a constitutive part of human nature. But for Plotinus also, the ultimate source of everything is the transcendent One. The beauty and harmony of the universe reveals its divinity, and leads the soul to contemplation of the intelligible. In spite of his identification of matter with evil, Plotinus was also opposed to the Gnostics, and like the Christians defined evil as non-being. For both, a dualist doctrine was no ultimate solution. Besides this, both stress the moral content of the process of purification, and the stripping away of distracting sense-perceptions. Furthermore, recent studies have stressed that Plotinus' mysticism is really 'theistic' : the soul is not absorbed into the One so as to lose its identity.[94] The One remains transcendent, as God does for Gregory, and if Plotinus can be described as a mystic, Gregory can too.[95]

Yet there is a distinctively Christian colouring to Gregory's philosophy. Platonic imagery is filled out with biblical symbols, and phrases inherited from the exegesis of the Platonist Jew, Philo. Allegorical exegesis of the *Life of Moses* and the *Song of Songs* forms the vehicle for describing the ladder of ascent. Furthermore, the process is essentially sacramental, being expressed in the death and resurrection symbolism of baptism, and the spiritual feeding of the eucharist. Above all, it is christological. An individual can progress towards God and the experience of contact with him, because mankind as a whole has ascended in Christ. By being in Christ, man is resurrected and his double (body-soul) constitution is unified.

Perhaps most significant, however, are differences in their understanding of God. Both Gregory and Plotinus have a radically apophatic theology. Nothing can be known of God, or of the 'One'. Yet there is some truth in the oversimplified generalization that Plotinus' soul has to search for God, while Gregory's God has searched for his soul. Furthermore, Plotinus' soul, like the whole universe, is ultimately derived from the One by a process of spontaneous activity, the overflow of its abundant life; but Gregory's soul is created by God, as a conscious act of will and of love. For Gregory there is a gulf fixed between the self-existent Trinity and all its creatures, bridged only by the grace which makes man in its own image and recreates that lost image through the incarnation.[96] Gregory's dogmatic theology and his philosophy are ultimately inseparable. Both are expressions of his understanding and experience of the Christian gospel of salvation in Christ.

VIII. Preachers and Teachers of the Church

The Cappadocian Fathers were cultured leaders of the church, steeped in the traditions of developing Christian apologetic and theology, and immersed in the moral, liturgical and mystical life of the Christian community. Basil is said to have reformed the liturgy of his cathedral at Caesarea,[97] and his *De Spiritu Sancto* defends certain innovations. There can be no doubt that he made contributions in this field. It is probable that the *Liturgy of St Basil*, still employed in the Orthodox Church on a number of important occasions, did originate from Basil himself, though his contribution is likely to have been that of reviser and enlarger of an older liturgy, rather than that of creator of an entirely new rite.[98]

A considerable amount of the work of these three men is in the form of homilies or sermons, and here we can see them fulfilling the role of pastors, teachers and leaders. Apart from his *Letters* and *Poems*, all we have from Gregory Nazianzen is a collection of 45 *Orations*, clearly a selection of his best speeches or sermons. As we have already seen, they follow the style and pattern of contemporary rhetorical practice, and are not exegetical sermons; however, many were delivered on a specific occasion and deal with particular urgent problems. His attempt to avoid ordination occasioned an apology and explanation which became a classic exposition of the responsibilities of the priesthood.[99] A terrible hailstorm destroyed the crops of his father's parishioners; so Gregory delivered an urgent call for repentance in the face of God's chastisement.[100] The *Theological Orations* answered the need of the hour in Constantinople. Of the large number of panegyrics, conventionally brilliant eulogies of great men, many were occasioned by the relevant 'saint's day', or were delivered as funeral orations. The liturgical sermons on Christmas and Easter are fine expressions of the essential Christian gospel in the dress of rhetoric and scriptural typology. For all his faults, Gregory knew the pastoral needs of his people; he knew how to rise to the occasion; and he was clearly influenced by the liturgical pattern of the Christian year.

A number of Basil's occasional sermons[101] have survived also, some for feast-days, some concerned with Christian duties such as fasting, vices like anger, avarice, drunkenness and jealousy, virtues like humility. A few deal with the problem of evil and God's providence, one occasioned by a period of drought and famine. The devices of contemporary rhetoric were his means of expression, but evidently his pastoral and moral concerns overrode any desire simply to give pleasure to his hearers.

Gregory Nyssen has also left a variety of homilies and orations, sermons for feast-days, some moral and dogmatic homilies, panegyrics on saints, and three funeral orations delivered in Constantinople, one on the emperor's daughter, and one on the emperor's wife – a clear testimony to his reputation as an orator. Indeed, his style is generally considered more affected, more studiously rhetorical, than the style of his fellow-Cappadocians.

However, Basil and his brother also preached exegetically. Series of sermons following through a biblical book are characteristic. Basil's commentary on the creation-story in Genesis, the *Hexaemeron*, takes the form of nine homilies, and there are thirteen genuine homilies on the Psalms. Gregory's eight homilies on Ecclesiastes, fifteen homilies on the Song of Songs, and eight homilies on the Beatitudes are among his most important mystical works.

Basil wrote no formal commentaries, but his exegetical methods are evident in the homilies and other writings. He inclines to a literal method of exposition, rarely turning to allegory, frequently using scriptural texts to support his rigorous moral demands. By contrast, his brother inclined to a 'spiritual' interpretation, following Origen, for example, in his allegorical exegesis of the Song of Songs. However, Gregory felt constrained to write an *Explicatio apologetica in Hexaemeron* to correct misunderstanding of Basil's work, and also to complete it with a treatise on the creation of man, the *De Opificio*.[102] It is remarkable that in these works he follows Basil's example and avoids figurative allegory. The *De Opificio* is an important statement of Gregory's anthropology, especially man's creation in the image of God and its implications. Gregory is somewhat torn between the dualistic analysis of man current at the time, and the affirmation that man is the crown and perfection of God's creation; but on the whole the idea that man's enjoyment of the world is part of God's creative purpose is allowed to predominate.

The treatise *De Vita Moysis* is perhaps the best example of Gregory's exegetical methods, as well as a fine expression of his mystical theology. It falls into two parts, the first summarizing the historical life of Moses as depicted in Exodus and Numbers, the second using this as the symbol of the soul's ascent to God through purification, withdrawal, darkness and ecstasy. Here the allegorical method clearly becomes paramount.

Gregory's ascetical works are also important. The *De Virginitate* was his earliest work, written before he became bishop of Nyssa; already asceticism is seen as the way of mystical ascent, and Gregory regrets his marriage which debars him from the beauty of virginity. The complete *De Instituto Christiano* has recently been rediscovered, and has been shown to be the culmination of Gregory's ascetic thought, being even later than the *Life of Moses*.[103] Other important treatises include the *De Perfectione* and the *Vita Macrinae*, a biography of his sister which offers an ideal for the imitation of the would-be ascetic.

Gregory was by far the most prolific writer of the three. Apart from the many works already mentioned, attention must be drawn to the *Oratio Catechetica Magna*,[104] a significant attempt to write a comprehensive account of Christian theology. It was intended for Christian teachers, to assist them in catechesis of converts. The work covers the doctrine of the Trinity, the drama of redemption in Christ, reversing the fall and tricking the devil out of his possession of mankind, and then finally the means of receiving the benefits of this redemption, the sacraments and faith of the church. Distaste for the notorious 'fish-hook' device for catching the devil, should not blind us to the importance of this constructive outline of the developed faith of the fourth-century church.

The importance of the Cappadocians is therefore not confined to the history of dogma. To appreciate the life of the fourth-century church in its tensions, its spiritual richness, its vitality and its doctrinal struggles, it is to their writings that we must turn. The twentieth-century reader will not find everything to his taste, but he will have the fascination of exploring a wide-ranging culture which is both different from, and continuous with, his own Christian heritage.

Chapter Four

The Temper of the Times: Some Contrasting Characters of the Late Fourth Century

I. Introduction

In studying the Cappadocians, we have already observed that their significance in the life of the church at that time went far beyond their contribution to the development of doctrine. It is very easy for the student of doctrine to isolate his study from the on-going life and history of the church, thus distorting his understanding of the context of theological discourse. The aim of this chapter is to widen the perspective still further.

Although they are but a selection of the authors listed in a Patrology, none of the figures that appear here have much place in the typical History of Doctrine; and the particular controversy which dominated the period also tends to be bypassed. Yet for those who lived through it, the Origenist controversy was just as vital and all-consuming as any other major theological conflict; and in many ways these characters and these events were to have a profound effect upon the subsequent development of the Christian *mores*. Cyril contributed to the development of the liturgical practices of Jerusalem, and so influenced the world-wide liturgical life of the church through returning pilgrims. Epiphanius' encyclopedias were widely read for centuries to come, and John Chrysostom became perhaps the most influential of all the Fathers through the extensive copying and circulation of his published homilies. The popular mind and devotion of the Byzantine church owed its formation more to these men than to great philosophical theologians; and the effect of the Origenist controversy was to deepen suspicion of theological exploration, to enhance conservatism and to encourage unadventurous preservation of a rigidified tradition.

None of the figures that appear here have much place in the story of Nicaea and Chalcedon; yet they all illustrate important aspects of the life of the church as it was experienced in this formative period. Cyril's career provides interesting comment on the difficulties created by the Arian controversy for simple, sincere, conservative bishops who tried to keep out the fray. Epiphanius represents the fanatical, slogan-shouting mind which could not distinguish central from peripheral matters or think through fundamental theological issues. Chrysostom, the over-upright ascetic who could not compromise with political realities, was caught in the highly political cross-fire of the church of this period, and in his losing battle to maintain the moral values of the biblical tradition highlights the increasing social pressures which forced the church to forfeit its innocence. By contrast, Nemesius and Synesius got away with quiet, literary pursuits in local backwaters, endeavouring to preserve the classical traditions of the philosophical life and standing for ancient humanist ideals in an increasingly intolerant age. But they too point to social pressures on the church: certainly Synesius was unsure how far he was really a Christian, even though thrust onto the bishop's throne because of his social class and his local standing in the community, and this may have been true of Nemesius too.

Thus the lives, thoughts and literary remains of these five characters are of fundamental importance for understanding the period with which we are concerned.

II. Cyril of Jerusalem

The catechetical lectures of Cyril of Jerusalem are rightly well-known and readily accessible to students.[1] Interest has largely centred upon the information they provide for the study of fourth-century liturgy. Yet this by no means exhausts their importance.

Cyril's career provides an interesting contrast to the impression created by the lectures. Although they were delivered in the mid-fourth century when the world was in a turmoil over the issues raised by Arianism, the catechumens were given no explicit guidance on the issues, but simply instructed in the traditional faith. The meagre information we have about Cyril's life, however, shows that no bishop in this period could escape the vicissitudes of church politics. For one reason or another, he was exiled and restored three times.

The chief authorities on which any reconstruction must be based are the historians, Socrates, Sozomen, Rufinus and Theodoret, with some comments by Epiphanius and Jerome. Their evidence is not entirely compatible,[2] especially over the question of Cyril's doctrinal position. Jerome[3] gives an account of how Cyril obtained the episcopate, turning the whole incident into a nasty piece of Arian politics; it is true that Jerome had personal reasons for being malicious, but his allegations cannot be wholly dismissed. Rufinus[4] indicates that Cyril varied in his allegiance. Certainly there are hints that he had Arian associates, though later he joined the homoiousians and eventually was involved in the Council of Constantinople in 381. The Council's letter to the Pope speaks of him with respect, mentioning his many struggles against the Arians;[5] but others hint that he renounced his former opinions in order to join the orthodox ranks.[6] Whatever Cyril's position, all this indicates clearly the tendency in this period to blacken or whitewash a leading figure simply by putting a label on him. At the time, which party represented 'orthodoxy' was not by any means obvious. In all probability Cyril found himself caught in the crosscurrents of contemporary ecclesiastical politics without being doctrinally committed to any particular party. His own position is likely to have been Origenist in lineage, and his thought, subordinationist yet not truly Arian, seems to have affinities with that of Eusebius of Caesarea;[7] that is, he began as an anti-Nicene conservative, strongly opposed to Marcellus of Ancyra, not to mention Athanasius of Alexandria. In fact, his catechetical lectures reveal total dedication to the traditional faith – a fact which has been used to prove his essential orthodoxy. It seems likely that it was not so much doctrinal issues, but matters of personal rivalry and church order which determined his position at various stages in his career.[8]

It was certainly not over doctrine that his dispute with Acacius originated. Acacius, bishop of Caesarea, was Cyril's canonical superior who had consecrated him in 350; by the orthodox historians he is regarded as a leading Arian, and his subsequent opposition to Cyril is attributed to this cause. But the real issue over which he and Cyril quarrelled was a matter of church property. The church at Jerusalem had been the recipient of many rich gifts and dedications, especially from the imperial household; it was also the haven of pilgrims and ascetics. In the mid-50s, famine caused much distress, especially among the 'saints'. Cyril sold church treasures, according to Sozomen in order to feed the hungry.[9] Scandal ensued when someone noticed an actress wearing a robe he had himself dedicated to the church. For two years, Cyril resisted Acacius' summons to account for his actions, but was eventually deposed in his absence in 357. Two years later his case came up at Seleucia in an atmosphere hostile to Acacius; but Cyril's reinstatement was short-lived. Constantius, for one reason or another,[10] came round to Acacius' view and sent Cyril into exile. Underlying the bitterness may have been the threat posed for Caesarea by the rising influence of the see of Jerusalem as it became a centre of pilgrimage. Certainly this became an issue towards the end of the century, and in 451, at Chalcedon, Jerusalem became a patriarchate.

Subsequently, like many others, Cyril found his position subject to imperial whims. He was able to return under Julian the Apostate, but when Valens reverted to Constantius' policy in 367, Cyril found himself banished for the remaining eleven years of his reign. His banishment under these circumstances turned him into an anti-Arian hero, especially since he now associated himself with the neo-Nicenes, and after Valens' death joined in the movement which culminated in the Council of 381. Six years later he died.

Hardly a hint of these troublesome times appears in the *Catechetical Orations*. True, it is highly probable that they were delivered during one of Cyril's first Lents as a bishop, if not while he was still a presbyter; most of the events just described were still in the future. Yet the controversy over Athanasius and his reinstatement in 346 meant that the Eastern Church could not forget the storms induced by Arius. It was in an unsettled atmosphere that Cyril addressed the candidates for baptism. He does so with cool authority, indicating no party position in the current debates. His hearers are warned about heretics, but those actually named are the Gnostics and Manichees,[11] not the Arians. They are warned against false teachings, and some of these include identifiable doctrines of contemporaries, like Marcellus[12] or indeed the Arian faction;[13] but when Cyril reaches the stage in his exposition of the faith which obliges him to speak of the Son's generation from the Father, he advises his flock to profess ignorance on matters too high even for angels. The ordinary Christian is told to ignore party strife, and probably that is exactly what Cyril himself tried to do. The chanting mobs of Alexandria were perhaps not as typical of church life in this period as we might have supposed.

Cyril produces a straightforward statement of Christian belief immune from the controversies of the time. New and old covenant must not be divided. God the Creator is One, but also Trinity; the Trinity is not three gods, not three different grades of divinity, nor coalesced into a Sabellian One. This is clearly stated in a lecture on the Holy Spirit[14] which anticipates the position still to be hammered out in controversy with the Macedonians; likewise Cyril anticipates the approach of Leo's *Tome* in his simple summary of the incarnate state: 'Christ was twofold. . . . As man, he ate . . ., as God, he made five loaves feed five thousand men. As man he truly died, and as God . . . he raised to life his body.'[15] These anticipations are not due to any brilliance or profundity in his theology. Cyril states the traditional faith and disregards those issues which aroused the current difficulties in exposition of that faith.

Simplified and uncontroversial as we find his position, might it therefore be possible perhaps to discern in these lectures a 'popular' Christianity, uninvolved in the professional sophistications of the clerics? Unfortunately this is a claim difficult to make; the Christian belief of the populace remains elusive. In the first place, the audience that heard these lectures must have been at least literate, sufficiently cosmopolitan to use Greek rather than the local vernacular, and probably quite well educated. This outline of Christian belief requires considerable ability to follow arguments and to think in verbal rather than pictorial terms. It utilizes many of the standard apologetic ploys and presumes the need to equip the convert with intellectual weapons to confront the sceptic. Furthermore, any person who sought baptism in this period was virtually a 'semi-professional', often on the point of taking monastic vows. If one seeks to unearth the probably only half-formed belief of the nominally Christian populace rather than that of an élite, it is hardly to be found here. Even the sophisticated crowds that flocked to hear John Chrysostom were less select than Cyril's dedicated audience.

Yet one thing we do find recommended here is a more practical and less rarefied Christian life-style than that in the ascetic treatises of the period. Cyril follows St Paul in his advice on chastity and marriage, even allowing a second marriage.[16] Bodily needs are not to be despised. True, self-indulgence and luxury are to be avoided, but meat is not taboo, nor are riches accursed. To suggest such things belongs to the heretics. God is the source of all and to be worshipped as such; his gifts are to be put to good use.[17] On the clause 'Maker of heaven and earth', Cyril waxes eloquent on the marvels of creation, evoking a sense of wonder and worship worthy of Job and the Psalms, both of which he here quotes.[18] The extreme otherworldliness so often attributed to this period of monastic upsurge was certainly tempered by the continued use of the biblical traditions once employed to uphold the goodness of creation against the Gnostics.

The lectures that we have consist of a Procatechesis, welcoming the candidates to preparation for baptism during Lent, and indicating their responsibilities; five lectures on the faith arranged by topic, leading up to the recitation of the creed which candidates then had to commit to memory; and thirteen expounding the credal formulae. The Jerusalem creed itself is not quoted, but can be reconstructed on the basis of the lectures.[19] How exactly the eighteen pre-baptismal lectures fitted into the forty days of Lent has been the subject of some discussion; Telfer's suggestion[20] that these Greek lectures more or less alternated with lectures in the local vernacular has some attractions, but there is no direct evidence to prove it. In the days after Easter there followed further gatherings for the exposition of the sacraments to which the neophytes had just been admitted, and the final words of the final pre-Easter lecture anticipate these further lectures to come. Most manuscripts then contain five *Mystagogical Catecheses* which fulfil this role.

However, there has been considerable controversy over the date and authorship of the *Mystagogical Catecheses*. Strong grounds can be adduced for attributing them to Cyril's successor as bishop of Jerusalem, namely John,[21] whom we shall meet again as a key figure in the Origenist controversy. There are four basic arguments favouring this view.

First, there is the manuscript evidence. Some manuscripts do not contain the *Mystagogical Catecheses* at all, which suggests they may not have originally been associated with the pre-Easter set. In one manuscript, they are actually ascribed to John, and in three others, Cyril and John are mentioned as authors of the whole collection. On the other hand, five manuscripts treat the *Mystagogical Catecheses* as continuous with the rest, and the whole is attributed to Cyril.[22] F. L. Cross[23] explained this by suggesting that Cyril used the same text year after year, and his successor John inherited it. Although it is possible that such a theory could be right in general terms, it falls to the ground with respect to the specific text which we have extant, in view of the number of circumstantial details which point to a single occasion.[24] The usual assumption that Cyril spoke *extempore* (though after an established plan perhaps) fits better with the text, at any rate that of the pre-baptismal set of lectures which were clearly taken down by stenographers as delivered during one particular Lent; indeed, it is possible to date them fairly definitely to 348 or 350 (the latter date is the year in which Cyril was consecrated, but there are some reasons for thinking that he may have lectured on behalf of his predecessor while still a priest).

Secondly there is the literary evidence. There are references to the pre-baptismal set in fifth-century literature, whereas the *Mystagogical Catecheses* are not mentioned until the second half of the sixth century. Even after that people like Photius fail to allude to the *Mystagogical Catecheses*, even though specifically referring to Cyril's *Catechetical Lectures*.

Thirdly, there is the internal evidence. The description of the lectures to come which appears in the final lecture before Easter, does not exactly fit what we actually find in the post-Easter set. Furthermore, there are some inconsistencies between the two groups of lectures: the baptismal symbolism of Romans 6 forms the subject of the Second Mystagogical Catechesis, thus being treated as esoteric teaching for the initiated, but in the Procatechesis Cyril clearly expects the candidates to be already familiar with it. In addition to this, the character of the two sets is somewhat different: the *Mystagogical Catecheses* do not appear to have been taken down as spoken; the style is terser, on the whole, and lacks the direct address and circumstantial details of the earlier set.

Finally, there are the liturgical arguments. The practices described in the *Mystagogical Catecheses* seem to belong to the late fourth century, rather than the date presumed by the Lent lectures.

Such arguments appeared to carry so much cumulative weight, that most investigators were accepting John's authorship, or expressing the view that certainty was impossible. However, a couple of articles have now defended the ascription of these lectures to Cyril, while assigning them to a much later date than the pre-baptismal set. C. Beukers[25] has argued that the final catechesis must belong to a year between 383 and 386, though his evidence need not necessarily point to that conclusion; and E. Yarnold[26] has put a strong case for Cyrilline authorship, suggesting that the character of the *Mystagogical Catecheses* and the doubt about their authorship is explained if we suppose that they were the outline notes on the basis of which Cyril was accustomed to lecture, expanding as he went along.

> Because of the *disciplina arcani* these notes would not be intended for publication, and would probably bear no author's name. . . . The ascription to John may have been a conjecture based on the fact that the MS was found in Jerusalem after Cyril's

death. The dual ascription to Cyril and John would have a similar explanation. The MS may have been the work of Cyril, come into John's possession, and been used by him in his own preaching.

Yarnold's arguments against John's authorship, and for the continuity of style, theology and spirituality, appear very strong, assuming as he does that the *Mystagogical Catecheses* bear the marks of a period thirty or forty years later than the pre-Lent set.

The dating of the *Mystagogical Catecheses* is crucial to the historian of liturgy as they are one of the richest and earliest sources he possesses. One problem which has arisen is how to relate the evidence they provide to that found in the *Peregrinatio Etheriae*,[27] the account in Latin of a lady's pilgrimage to the Holy Places, in which the practices of the Jerusalem church are described in some detail. Both texts seem to belong to the 380s, and yet at certain crucial points they do not appear to be compatible. Probably the difficulties have been exaggerated. The 'tourist' does not always get every item of information absolutely accurate, after all,[28] and in any case many think the *Peregrinatio* should be dated twenty or more years later. Besides, liturgical developments were clearly proceeding at a pace in this particular half-century. Specialists have in fact attributed several significant innovations to none other than Cyril himself. Certainly, some interesting changes took place during his episcopate. In the *Catechetical Lectures*, there is no trace of the elaborate Holy Week celebrations characteristic of Jerusalem at the end of the century and described with enthusiasm in the *Peregrinatio Etheriae*. Yet interest in the local sites is apparent in the lectures, and Cyril and his hearers were assembled in the beautiful new buildings provided by Constantine for Christian worship in the holy city. Already Jerusalem was the goal of pilgrimages and an attraction to the devout. The conditions for the development of a commemorative cycle already existed, and by the end of Cyril's episcopacy, the pattern had been established. The same sort of situation is apparent in the matter of the daily round of Offices; a complete cycle is described by Etheria, though observances of this kind are not mentioned to the catechumens about forty years earlier. It seems very likely that Cyril was responsible both for introducing monastic observances to the 'secular' church at Jerusalem and for the pattern of Holy Week celebration.[29] The practices of the Jerusalem church were clearly recommended to churches elsewhere by returning pilgrims, and thus Cyril had a remarkable influence on the world-wide church.

But did Cyril also make innovations in the eucharistic celebration? The peculiar features of the rite described in the *Mystagogical Catecheses* when compared with other evidence of the period, are clear.[30] We have here the first evidence for the consecration and conversion of the elements by invocation of the Holy Spirit (the Epiclesis); the first evidence for the use of liturgical vestments, for the carrying of lights, and for other significant details like the symbolic handwashing and the use of the Lord's Prayer after the eucharist prayer.[31] Such features appear elsewhere towards the end of the century, presumably spread by returning pilgrims, and are most likely to have been gradually introduced at Jerusalem as her rites were suitably elaborated for use in her lavishly reconstructed basilica, a process which must have taken place in the main during Cyril's episcopate. Part of this process may have included an increase in what was regarded as subject to the *disciplina arcani*, a possibility which would account for some of the inconsistencies between the main body of the *Catechetical Lectures* and the five *Mystagogical Catecheses*.

Whatever their date and whatever Cyril's liturgical contributions, the *Mystagogical Catecheses* are not just descriptions of ritual acts. The comments on their meaning are integrated into a fascinating theological whole. The author presents the sacraments as a means by which the believer is transformed into Christ. Baptism is understood as a dying and rising with Christ; 'Christ was really crucified, really buried and truly rose ... in order that partaking in the imitation of his sufferings, in truth we might gain salvation.' Chrism means that we have become 'Christs', anointed with the Holy Spirit. By partaking of the eucharistic food, which becomes the body and blood of Christ by the invocation of the Holy Spirit, the Christian is made of the same body and the same blood with him; 'thus we become "Christ-bearers", because his body and blood are diffused through our members'. This is how we become 'sharers in the divine nature' (II Peter 1.4).[32] The idea of salvation is one of what we might call 'Christification' conveyed in and through the mystery-sacraments.

Apart from the *Catechetical Lectures*, very little survives from Cyril's pen or pulpit. One item of interest is a letter to the Emperor Constantius.[33] The authenticity of this letter has been questioned on the grounds that the word *homoousios* occurs in the final blessing: there is MS evidence, however, that the final phrases were a later addition to the text, and in other respects the letter fits

Cyril's style and the situation of 351 so well that its basic trust-worthiness is to be accepted.

The letter's purpose is to describe the appearance of a cross of light in the sky above Golgotha, witnessed by the whole population of the city.[34] Cyril regards this as proof that Constantius' piety towards God ensures imperial victory. He makes no reference to Constantine's decisive vision of the cross, though there are clear parallels suggesting that both phenomena may have been parhelia.

Cyril does refer to the discovery of the wood of the cross itself during Constantine's reign. That Cyril was, like so many of his contemporaries, affected by increasing interest in the holy sites and their relics is clear. The special position of Jerusalem is not ignored in his lectures. A legend about Cyril[35] arises from this special position. When under Julian the Jews were permitted to rebuild the temple, a prophecy of their failure was attributed to Cyril, which was then immediately fulfilled by the earthquake. The point of the story seems to be that in Jerusalem the high priest of the New Covenant inherits the prophetic powers attributed to the old high priest in John 11.51. Hearsay seems to be the only basis on which the story rests, since the supposed prophecy is almost exactly a quotation from the lectures[36] and in that context has no bearing on the temple incident. However, the lectures were delivered a decade or so earlier, and those disposed to look for prophecy are rarely deterred by inappropriate contexts. The very existence of the story, like so much of our information about Cyril, is indicative of the atmosphere of the period.

The only other extant work is a *Sermon on the Paralytic*.[37] By contrast with the dogmatic interests of the *Catecheses*, this sermon is firmly within the Alexandrian tradition of mystical allegory, a fact which might arouse doubts about its authorship. On the other hand, there is nothing improbable about it. There were close links between Egyptian and Palestinian Christianity, and Origen himself had eventually settled in Palestinian Caesarea. Without wanting to suggest that Cyril was an 'Origenist', Stephenson[38] has convincingly shown that certain passages in the *Catechetical Orations* are entirely compatible with the evidence of the sermon, and that Cyril embraced the view that scripture could be given a 'contemplative exegesis (ἐξήγησις θεω-ρητική) leading to a higher knowledge (γνῶσις), as well as the more literal sense normally expounded in the lectures. Indeed, the Sermon can provide an important key to understanding some aspects of Cyril's thought. The secrecy surrounding the imparting of enlightenment to those seeking baptism is itself consonant with the esoteric leanings of the Alexandrian tradition.

It was Cyril's successor who was to be embroiled in controversy as a defender of Origen, and the close links between the ecclesiastics and monks of Egypt and Palestine become entirely evident in the story of that conflict. It was Epiphanius who would provoke it.

III. Epiphanius of Salamis

The work of Epiphanius is best known because it has proved a quarry for material needed by the textual critic of the New Testament and the historian of the early church. What scholarly work there is, is primarily concerned to trace Epiphanius' sources and estimate the reliability of his evidence about the many important heretical movements which he describes; very little has treated Epiphanius as interesting in himself. This is not very surprising, but there are features of his life and work which illustrate well the atmosphere within the church in this period.

Few would claim that Epiphanius was an original thinker or an attractive personality; yet in some ways it is precisely his intolerant fanaticism which is interesting. The mere fact that he largely relies on shouting formulae rather than careful argument is a useful reminder that trinitarian orthodoxy won the church over not through abstruse philosophical reasoning or the careful sustained explication of works like the great Cappadocian treatises, but by constant unquestioning affirmation in the life of the church, backed by political strength and scornful prejudice against all possible alternatives. As a scholar reputed to be master of five languages, as an upholder of the one true faith of the holy catholic church, Epiphanius bears comparison with Eusebius, and yet the differences are marked: for where Eusebius looked for truth, Epiphanius hunted out error, believing that κακοπιστία (bad belief) is worse than ἀπιστία (lack of belief).[39]

1. The *Ancoratus*

It is clear that for Epiphanius Christianity had become a set of dogmas to be upheld in every paradoxical particular with no concessions to deviant interpretations. There are some things, he thought, about which enquiry should not be made.[40] Scripture speaks the truth in everything; heresy is false because it does not receive the Holy Spirit according to the traditions of the fathers of

the holy catholic church of God.[41] 'Search the scriptures . . . and the
Spirit itself . . . will reveal to you the knowledge of the word of the
Son of God, so that you may not wander from the truth and lose
your own soul.'[42] For that is the penalty for unorthodox speculation. 'Heresies and their founders are the gates of Hades.'[43]

These remarks are to be found in the *Ancoratus*. Epiphanius'
most important work was, of course, the *Panarion* or *Haereses*;[44]
but before he turned to that major encyclopedia of heretical sects,
Epiphanius had written in 374 this shorter treatise which throws
considerable light on his own position. The work is called the
Ancoratus (᾽Αγκυρωτός), the well-anchored man, because in it he
sets out to reply to several Christians who had written from Syedra
in Pamphylia asking him about the true faith, and particularly to a
certain Palladius who described with some concern the dangers
confronting one tossed in the storms of heresy. It is here that we can
see how Epiphanius establishes the true faith, not so much by
argument as by formulaic confessions, scriptural allusions or
quotations, together with heated denial of herctical suggestions.
His Greek is direct and straightforward; indeed his works were very
popular, partly perhaps because they were written in 'elevated
koinē' rather than in the artificial literary style then current.[45] But
he was also popular, one suspects, because in his work the familiar
ecclesiastical language is simply reproduced. It is not just that he
depends on current orthodox apologetic, as when he denies such
classic errors as the idea that the Father has two Sons, or on current
orthodox exegesis in dealing, for example, with awkward subordinationist texts like Proverbs 8.22; nor is it simply that he
appeals to the classic trinitarian proofs, like the threefold *Sanctus*
and God's plural address at creation, 'Let *us* make man in our
image.' The fact is that he is so moulded by ecclesiastical style that
he actually writes in credal patterns. Not only does he quote two
actual creeds at the end of his work, one of which has caused
considerable discussion because of its remarkable similarity to the
creed adopted at Constantinople seven years later,[46] but the
structure and content of his phraseology echoes the familiar style of
the classic confessional definitions, particularly in its piling up of
participial clauses: the holy Word himself . . . becoming man in
truth and being God in truth, not changing his nature, not altering
his Godhead, begotten in flesh, the enfleshed Word, the Word
become flesh. . . .[47] We seem to have direct access to the current
ecclesiastical jargon and formulaic ways of confession and preaching. Over and over again, as a substitute for thought or careful
explanation there appears a battery of mixed scriptural and extra-

scriptural catch-phrases, nominatives stretching over pages: Christ is 'the only-begotten, the perfect, the uncreated, the immutable, the unchangeable, the unknowable, the unseen, become man among us . . . the one who though rich became poor for us . . . one Lord, King, Christ, Son of God, seated in heaven on the right hand of the Father . . .' and so on.[48] Scripture and tradition provide Epiphanius with his tools.

But for Epiphanius, the truth can only be properly maintained by avoiding error. The *Ancoratus* contains a number of anti-heretical digressions, and already we find a bitter attack on Origen and his followers, revealing the particular prejudice which was to give Epiphanius his not very honourable place in the events of early Byzantine history. Again, already in the *Ancoratus*, he lists eighty heresies, and it is interesting that we find here roughly the scheme of heretical sects which provides the pattern of his later work. After Moses up to the incarnation there were eleven heresies; after the incarnation, sixty more. Before the Mosaic law there were five heresies and the four sects of the Greeks; so that counting their 'mothers' the total number of heresies is eighty. Such is the first outline of Epiphanius' scheme, with the enumeration of the sects by name.

2. The *Panarion*

It is in fact the case that the work *Against the Heresies* developed out of this preliminary sketch in the *Ancoratus*. This time Epiphanius was approached by Acacius and Paul, archimandrites of Chalcis and Beroea in Coele-Syria, with a request to clarify the eighty heresies listed in his first work. Epiphanius replied that he had been in process of doing exactly that when their letter arrived; from his comments it is possible to date the work as completed in approximately 377. His largest work is thus devoted to the description and rebuttal of false doctrines – he wanted to provide antidotes to the poisons of heresy and entitled it the 'Medicine-chest' – *Panarion*.

The medical image is not, however, the one sustained throughout this vast compendium. Epiphanius was clearly fascinated by catalogues and genealogies: a list of Roman emperors, and a list of all the nations descended from Shem, Ham and Japheth appear in the *Ancoratus*, as well as the catalogue of heresies. More lists appear in the concluding section of the *Panarion*, entitled περὶ πίστεως (*On Faith*). This interest is explicitly acknowledged in the opening paragraphs of the *Panarion*, where Epiphanius makes it clear that what he is seeking to do is to map out a genealogy of heresy. He also uses the analogy of biological classification: he wants to trace the genera and species. He is making an attempt to devise a family tree, to systematize the rise and proliferation of heresy within a world context. This image is sometimes lost in the course of this enormous work, but it is noticeable that there are references to the derivation of one group of heretics from another: Basileides and Satornilus derived their teachings from Menander who followed Simon Magus, from whom the 'false-named *Gnosis*' took its roots. The genealogical scheme, however, most clearly affects the first volume of the first book of the total work. (Epiphanius himself divided it into seven τόμοι – volumes – arranged in three βιβλία – books.[49]) For, as already hinted in the *Ancoratus*, Epiphanius does not restrict heresy to Christian deviations: heresy, which means division, is essentially the break-down of mankind's unity, and its parentage can be traced right back to the origins of history.[50]

The first volume of Epiphanius' work, therefore, indulges in a wandering and partly repetitive survey of world history, largely drawn from the Bible though with scraps of Greek history fed into the biblical outline, and punctuated by lists of names, genealogies and enumerations of generations. Now and again Epiphanius supplies reflections on the significance of it all. In the beginning there was no heresy. There was true faith: Adam, was neither an idolator nor circumcised, but in a sense held the faith of the holy catholic church of God which existed from the beginning and was later to be revealed again. Because of Adam's sin, there appeared the opposite of true faith – adultery, rebellion, idolatry. Piety and impiety, faith and unfaith co-existed, with the great biblical figures like Abel, Enoch, Methuselah and Noah representing the former which was the image of Christianity;[51] Abraham in particular is presented as the type of the Christian, prefiguring in his departure from his father's house the call of the first disciples.[52] Several times in the text Epiphanius stresses that there was as yet no heresy, no variety of opinions, nor any device other than adultery or idolatry, that is, the opposite of the true worship and faith of the holy, catholic church; and he seems at this stage to identify the origins of heresy with the scattering of mankind after the tower of Babel. Yet, somewhat inconsistently, Epiphanius imposes on this early history his first four heresies: Barbarism, he attributes to the period between Adam and Noah, Scythian superstition, to the period between Noah and the tower of Babel; thereafter, with the development of magic and astrology, arose Hellenism, and with the circumcision of Abraham, came Judaism. The subsequent story is concerned with the fragmentation of these four great divisions into smaller sects: Hellenism produced four, the Stoics, the Platonists, the Pythagoreans and the Epicureans; Samaritanism split off from Judaism and then produced four sects of its own; and Judaism produced seven pre-Christian heresies. Thus prior to the coming of Christ, there were twenty heresies altogether, as Epiphanius has already indicated in his outline in the *Ancoratus*.

The inconsistencies in the application of the word heresy and in the assessment of Abraham's role alert us to the artificiality of the scheme. Comparison with the summaries found in the *Ancoratus* and even more significantly the prefatory letter to Acacius and Paul, provides further confirmation.[53] Of a number of variations in the order of the heresies as they appear in the text and in each of the summary lists, the most significant is the position of Samaritanism. In the summaries it is treated as one of the five 'mothers of heresy', and in the *Ancoratus* is even carelessly placed 'before the Law'; in the text, however, the Samaritan schism is placed after the description of the sects of Hellenism.[54] Since other variations are attributable to the fact that in his text Epiphanius faithfully follows the order of his sources,[55] it is tempting to suggest in this case that the actual course of the history which he is presenting affected his order. But the real reason is that Epiphanius' framework was controlled by his exegesis of two particular biblical texts.

The text which directs his presentation in the first volume of the *Panarion* he quotes from Paul as follows: in Christ Jesus, there is neither barbarian, nor Scythian, Greek nor Jew, but new creation. This is in fact a somewhat mixed memory of Galatians 3.28; 6.15 and Colossians 3.11; but it gives him *four* great divisions of mankind from which all subsequent heresies stemmed. That he can only enumerate further splintering in Judaism and Hellenism simply reinforces the artificiality of his analysis.

The text which determines the overall scheme is eventually divulged to us in the concluding essay *On Faith*. Epiphanius quotes from the Song of Songs (Cant. 6.7): 'There are sixty queens, and eighty concubines and maidens without number; but my dove, my perfect one, is only one.' The one dove is, of course, the holy catholic church; and the concubines are the heresies. Now we understand why somehow or other Epiphanius has to press his heresies into the number eighty, urging his readers not to worry about the fact that different names and subsequent sectarian splits apparently upset his calculations. There must be seventy-five sects and five 'mothers of heresies' in order to reach the correct number. Then with evident delight, Epiphanius goes on to explain also the sixty queens and maidens without number, for this is an excuse to produce more of his beloved lists and generation counts. The queens are the faithful in each generation before Christ, those like Enoch, Methuselah, Lamech and Noah described in the first volume, and there were sixty generations of them, ten from Adam to Noah, ten from Noah to Abraham and then following Matthew's genealogical table, fourteen from Abraham to David, fourteen from David to the captivity, fourteen from the captivity to Christ. The total sixty-two does not worry Epiphanius, for scripture provides several examples where seventy serves for seventy-two. Then the maidens without number are the countless philosophers and false teachers: he lists fourty-four Greek philosophers from Thales to Epicurus, reports that there were supposed to be seventy-two philosophers in India, including the Brahmins, and mentions the Magi and the mystery-religions. It is surely apparent that without the controlling power of the Canticles text, Epiphanius could have included many more religious and philosophical sects in his catalogue of heresies: indeed his mention of the Peripatetics in the letter to Acacius and Paul suggests a certain embarrassment at describing only four heresies of Hellenism. The word αἵρεσιϛ, from which we get our word 'heresy', was the classical designation for different philosophical sects, and Hellenism had in fact produced many more schools of philosophy. But Epiphanius had to produce the number eighty, and this is not the only expedient he adopted in order to do so. Some distinct groups are conflated, some heresies appear to have been created out of minor allusions (e.g. the Melchizedekians)[56] or out of small incidents in Epiphanius' life (e.g. the Antidikomarianitae, a group to whom he wrote defending the perpetual virginity of Mary). It never seems to have entered his head that *future* heresies might be expected and that would finally undermine his attempt to show the fulfilment of his guiding prophecy.

Epiphanius' work was not only directed by theoretical applications of prophecy. His choice of targets, particularly in the later parts of the work, was undoubtedly guided by his fanatical animosities. He had no power of distinguishing between major and minor distortions of truth; schism and heresy was all the same to him. Homoiousians were no nearer salvation than Manichees, Novatians no more Christian than Gnostics. All heresies, even the defunct, were capable of generating further error, and many of the sects he describes, like the Montanists, the Novatians, Marcionites and others, did in fact still exist. So Epiphanius' work was no mere historical survey. For the early centuries he relied on older sources:

from Dositheus to Noetus he seems to have followed Hippolytus' *Syntagma* extremely closely (in fact, the *Panarion* has been described as a new edition of Hippolytus, brought up to date and augmented);[57] he quotes extensively from Irenaeus and from a number of lost heretical works, so preserving the Greek text of many interesting documents – hence his value for modern scholars, in spite of his inaccuracy and lack of critical sense.[58] But for him this compendium was no mere academic exercise, a fact well-illustrated by the events of his life. As a young monk in Egypt he had been subject to gnostic attempts to entrap him, and he had acquired an aversion to followers of Origen which was never to leave him. In the end his fanatical zeal against the greatest of Greek theologians was to cause untold disruption and tragedy in the church.

3. Life

Epiphanius was born about 315. He grew up in Palestine and his native tongue was Syriac; he learned Greek at school, though unlike most of the great Christian writers of this period he seems to have been unacquainted with the classical *paideia*. Sozomen says he was educated by the Egyptian monks, and certainly as a young man he spent some time in Egypt where he acquired Coptic. (Jerome, in fact, calls him πεντάγλωττος, five-tongued,[59] but his knowledge of Latin seems to have been pretty slight and the few Hebrew words he mentions in his writings are probably the only basis of the claim that he had a fifth language.) He was an enthusiastic ascetic who on his return from Egypt founded his own monastery near his birth-place, Eleutheropolis near Gaza. He maintained close Palestinian contacts even after 367 when he was elected bishop of Constantia in Cyprus, a position he held until his death thirty-six years later.

It was during the first ten years of his episcopate that Epiphanius wrote those works already discussed, and one interesting feature of the *Panarion* is that it reveals his estimate of the current warring factions of the 360s and 370s: the seventy-second heresy he details is that of Marcellus, and the seventy-third that of the semi-Arians or Homoiousians – clearly Epiphanius' sympathies lay with the former who did at least accept the *homoousion*. Epiphanius, then, was an extremely ardent upholder of the Nicene formula; yet he did not participate in the Council of Constantinople in 381 which re-established the Nicene faith. The reason is typical of him: In the 360s a series of misunderstandings produced two anti-Arian bishops of Antioch, Paulinus and Meletius, a factor contributing to the confusion and division in the anti-Arian ranks. Epiphanius, together with Athanasius and Rome, supported Paulinus, but Basil of Caesarea and many others in the East favoured Meletius. In 381, most were prepared to compromise in settling the dispute in favour of Meletius' successor, but Epiphanius cut the council in order to accompany Paulinus to Rome and protest.

4. Other works

In the early 390s Epiphanius composed two more treatises, this time concerned with biblical problems, though going far beyond mere exegesis. Both of them largely survive in translations, *On Weights and Measures* in Syriac, and *On the Twelve Gems* in a number of fragments of which the most complete is the Georgian. *On Weights and Measures*[60] is a most inadequate title for what is almost a biblical encyclopedia, though the matter he keeps reverting to in the central section of the book is the question of the correct equivalents for the units of measure and weight used in the Bible. Epiphanius begins by explaining the conventional signs in the biblical text, the obelus, asterisk and signs of punctuation; he then gives an introduction to the various Greek translations available, telling at some length the story of the seventy-two translators of the Septuagint, dating the version of Aquila and Symmachus, and even, in spite of his anti-Origenism, describing the *Hexapla*. By now he is about a quarter of his way through the book, and he begins to list weights and measures, but his digressions take up most of the space and some are quite astounding: because the *modius* = twenty-two *xestai*, he finds occasion to list the twenty-two works of creation, the twenty-two generations from Adam to Jacob, the twenty-two letters of the Hebrew alphabet and the twenty-two books of the Old Testament. On another occasion, he meditates upon the number four – there were four books in the Ark (Genesis–Numbers), four rivers out of Eden, four quarters of the world, four seasons of the year, four watches of the night, and four spiritual creatures (Ezek. 1.5) with four faces, man, lion, ox and eagle, which represent the four gospels, Matthew, Mark, Luke and John. The last quarter of the book turns from weights and measures to geographical matters, listing and commenting upon the names of biblical places. Since Epiphanius was born and brought up in Palestine, this might have been interesting; but he seems largely dependent not on personal knowledge, but on earlier encyclopedias like Eusebius' *Onomasticon*.

The *De Gemmis*[61] is ostensibly an elaborate exegetical exercise dealing with the twelve stones of Aaron's breastplate (Exod. 28); but in reality, it was probably intended to provide a Christian counter-blast to the pagan quasi-scientific and mystical interpretation of precious stones. First, drawing on current literature, he gives a description of each gem with an account of where it is found and what medicinal properties it has; then he embarks on symbolical and allegorical expositions of the association of each gem with the particular name of one of the twelve patriarchs, a technique which enables him to wander in a disorderly fashion over a good deal of exegetical and theological ground.

The discursive writings of this conservative fanatic were widely read in the Christian world, an indication of their popularity being the many oriental versions of his writings. His reputation for learning was such that odd works like the *Physiologus*, the principal source of mediaeval bestiaries, came to be attributed to him. However, apart from the treatises mentioned, little else remains that is authentic. There are a few genuine letters scattered about in various collections, but most of the homilies and exeget-ical fragments attributed to him are regarded as spurious. Frag-ments exist of works against images to which the Iconoclasts appealed in the later controversies; the authenticity of these fragments has been defended by K. Holl,[62] who claims that they represent three separate works on the topic. That Epiphanius did have strong views on this subject is clear from an incident he describes in a letter which has survived in Jerome's Latin transla-tion: journeying in Palestine, he went into a village church to pray and there found an embroidered curtain bearing an image either of Christ or of one of the saints. He tore it asunder and advised the custodians to use it as a winding sheet for some poor person.

5. The Origenist controversy

This incident occurred during the fateful trip to Palestine in 394 when the Origenist controversy flared up – in fact it is described in an important letter written to John of Jerusalem at the height of their quarrel. The animosities had long been germinating. From very early in his career Epiphanius clearly regarded the teaching of Origen as the cause of Arianism and many other errors. The monasteries in Egypt were already divided into Origenist and anti-Origenist camps when he was there as a young man. In the *Panarion*, long before any public controversy, he detailed his charges against the Origenist heresy: Origen said that the only-begotten Son cannot *see* the Father, nor the Spirit the Son, nor can the angels see the Spirit, nor men the angels; the Son is not of the *ousia* of the Father – he is altogether other (in other words, created), but called Son by grace. Origen spoke of the pre-existence of souls as angels, of their incarnation in flesh as punishment for sin; he said Adam lost the image of God and the 'coats of skin' God made for Adam and Eve (Gen. 3) were their bodies. Origen denied the resurrection of the dead. Origen allegorized Paradise and treated all scripture as riddles and parables, claiming it was hard for human beings to understand. Charges covering the same ground occur nearly twenty years later in the letter to John. The anti-Origenist groups in Egypt became known as the Anthropomorphites, and it is quite clear that they stood for a crudely literalist understanding of theological statements and of the Bible, feeling deep misgivings about the spiritualizing tendencies of Origenism. Epiphanius voiced their anti-intellectualism, and saw theological speculation as the cause of everything that was damaging the church in his time.

The story of the controversy has often been told and can be found in detail elsewhere.[63] Epiphanius preached an anti-Origenist sermon in the church at Jerusalem which provoked the bishop, Cyril's successor John. He then enlisted the support of his old friend Jerome, and between them they created great difficulties in the diocese over which John was supposed to have jurisdiction. The famous quarrel between Rufinus and Jerome, the heads of rival Latin monasteries in the Holy Land, soon reached a peak of literary blast and counterblast. Jerome had been an admirer of Origen, but he was not the only actor in the drama who changed sides. In 399, the bishop of Alexandria, Theophilus, to whom John had once appealed for support, also became a turn-coat and started persecution of the Origenist monks in Egypt. Personality and expediency seem to have played a larger role in this controversy than conviction, though Epiphanius was characteristically consistent in his position throughout. As a result of persecution in Egypt, four of these monks, the so-called Tall Brothers, fled to Palestine, and then travelled on to Constantinople seeking support and spreading the controversy. Their arrival in Constantinople gave Theophilus a chance to lay schemes for the downfall of John Chrysostom, and Epiphanius, now in his eighties but still burning with anti-Origenist zeal, obeyed the summons to a council in Constantinople. However, he then realized he was being used as a tool by Theophilus and hurried home, only to die at sea on the way. By now it was 403, and the controversy he had initiated had gone its way for ten years. Its tragic outcome was soon to be realized.

IV. John Chrysostom

1. The Origenist controversy

The bitterest fruit of the Origenist controversy was the tragic end of John Chrysostom. It is ironical that one so little influenced by the great theologian of the third century was the most important victim of the campaign. Indeed, it is clear that political factors and other personal motives were ultimately far more important. However, the occasion was provided by the current theological battle.

The most important source for understanding the events associated with Chrysostom's fall is the *Dialogue* written in his defence by Palladius.[64] The value of this is that it clearly comes from someone intimately involved in the events. Maybe it is partisan and very hostile to all considered the enemies of John; yet at the same time the criticisms which it answers give some indication of the hostility he aroused and the reasons why. Socrates' evidence is less direct but more impartial.[65] It is instructive, by the way, to see the high proportion of their histories that both Socrates and Sozomen devoted to these events – a clear indication of the importance attached to them at the time. For the participants, the period between Arianism and Nestorianism was not devoid of serious controversy over issues of real importance to the development of the church.

It is impossible here to record all the detail with which we are presented in the accounts. The essential movements seem to be as follows. The Tall Brothers, accused of Origenism and hounded through Palestine by Theophilus, arrived in Constantinople and appealed to Chrysostom. Chrysostom did not receive them to communion, but out of charity and respect for their ascetic holiness, he allowed them hospitality while he communicated with Alexandria about their persecution. Theophilus refused to negotiate and demanded their expulsion. Meanwhile they appealed to the emperor, who was induced to summon Theophilus to answer charges against his conduct in the affair. Thus, Theophilus came to the capital.

Theophilus realized that somehow the tables had to be turned. He rejected conciliatory gestures from Chrysostom, and set about an attack on him rather than his own defence. Clearly he was able to play upon a large element of resentment against the archbishop. He collected a group of bishops at the Oak near Chalcedon, formed a Synod, and summoned Chrysostom to answer charges. Chrysostom demanded a fair hearing before a less hostile council, but since Theophilus had by now the support of the court, his deposition was guaranteed (403). Most accounts stress the extreme wickedness of Theophilus as an agent of the devil, arriving with massive bribes and sheer insolence to carry out a well-laid plot. For all the tendency to blacken the opposition, it is hard to dismiss such charges totally.

Chrysostom was soon vindicated when disaster recalled the empress to her fear of divine displeasure. Theophilus made a precipitate departure. But the scenario was not yet complete. Our fanatical prophet could not resist criticism of the empress' *hybris* when she had her statue erected and dedicated with much pomp a few months later. The resultant imperial hostility was soon played upon by the agents of Theophilus, and amidst massacre, riot and arson, John and his followers were driven from the city at Easter (404). Chrysostom spent several years in exile in Armenia, but his continuing influence through correspondence riled the court, and he died in 407 while being conveyed to a more remote locality.

What were the real charges against Chrysostom, and did they have any basis? His two chief accusers were two deacons that he expelled, according to his defenders, for murder and fornication. Most of the charges were comparatively trivial, though they add up to severe treatment of his clergy, misuse of church property, an unfortunately sarcastic, almost libellous, tongue towards those who expected respect, and refusal to practise the traditions of hospitality. We can deduce that Chrysostom's ascetic ideals made him a somewhat arrogant and self-righteous critic of clerical lapses, and induced him to withdraw from the luxurious entertainments expected of him; that his concern for the poor and his personal habits could easily be misrepresented by the suspicious; and that his rigorous standards caused considerable unpopularity. Chrysostom was not blessed with tact or diplomacy, it seems. This impression is confirmed by Palladius' treatment of critical rumours: he defends Chrysostom for eating alone and for failing to provide hospitality, denies his tyrannical deposition of sixteen Asian bishops, and tried to put his arrogant self-assertion into a better light.

One suspects, however, that underlying all the machinations was Theophilus' suspicion of the rising power of the upstart see of Constantinople. That ecclesiastical power struggle had already begun when Alexandria contested the consecration of Gregory Nazianzen in 381; it was to continue in the christological battle between Cyril and Nestorius; but here we have the classic case of a dispute over non-issues for the sake of weakening the church in the capital. Theophilus had opposed Chrysostom's election; now he took his revenge, and his power to do so was almost certainly enhanced, not only by Chrysostom's own personality, but also by current uncertainties about canon law. In the course of the events and afterwards the validity of appeal to the canons of previous councils was contested, often on the grounds that the councils in question had been of an Arian character; and besides this, the status of the see of Constantinople was probably uncertain – a primacy of honour was accorded in 381, but perhaps not jurisdiction. Theophilus seems to have proceeded as if the bishop of Constantinople had no metropolitan status but was himself under the jurisdiction of Heracleia whose bishop presided at the Synod of the Oak;[66] and he also made use of the resentment of the Asian bishops deposed by Chrysostom a few years earlier (401). Whether or not Chrysostom had any canonical jurisdiction in Asia, the fact that appeal had been made to him probably justified his actions; but it was easily turned into charges of power-seeking and tyranny.

Ultimately, however, responsibility lay with the court. Theophilus would have been powerless if Chrysostom had not offended those in high places. It is not for nothing that his contemporaries compared him with the prophets of the Old Testament. His fearless denunciations were perhaps deliberately reminiscent of Old Testament models. He is said to have likened Eudoxia to Jezebel and Herodias, and the charge is far from improbable. Arcadius was too weak to accept criticism, or to resist the competing influence of other powerful ecclesiastical figures. So Chrysostom became a martyr, and was indeed honoured as such by Arcadius' son, Theodosius II, when he brought back his relics to the capital with much pomp and celebration. His career provides illuminating comment on relations between church and state in this period.

2. Chrysostom and Christian morals

The whole unfortunate episode is also a reminder that the conduct of church leaders was as much an issue at this time as their theological beliefs. Here the accusations centred on behaviour, treatment of people and use of church property. The appeal from Asia had been concerned with charges against clerics of giving and receiving bribes to obtain ecclesiastical office. The standards expected of churchmen presented a real problem in a period in which the church acquired great treasures, and ecclesiastical office had become an attractive public career with power, influence, riches and patronage. The church was caught in a sociological dilemma. Once her members had been the 'elect', a small minority of the saved with very high standards of conduct, and a tradition of opposition to the *status quo*. Now the church was part of the establishment, dedicated to upholding the prosperity of the empire under God. Socrates bears witness to the fact that the old rigorist sect of the Novatians had not only survived but was attractive to his generation, and the monastic movement is powerful testimony to the fact that many saw a serious lowering of standards as the church accommodated itself to a new role in the secular world. The preaching career of Chrysostom provides further comment on the situation. His life was a campaign for the purity of Christian life in the world as well as in the ascetic's cell and at every level of the church hierarchy. Sadly but understandably, he reaped his reward, and his acts recoiled upon him.

As a young man, Chrysostom had embraced the monastic life. He had been educated to take his place in the world; for he was the most eloquent pupil of the famous sophist, Libanius, destined according to Sozomen[67] to be his successor if he had not been stolen by the Christians. At the age of eighteen he became dissatisfied with worldly ideals, was baptized and became a lector. He experimented with an ascetic home-life in response to the wishes of his widowed mother, but later, possibly after her death, retired to the mountains and caves. There he permanently damaged his health with excessive mortifications of the flesh. When he retreated, he found himself forced into ecclesiastical orders, eventually to be 'kidnapped' and consecrated bishop of the capital city. Already as a priest in Antioch, his fame as a pulpit orator was world-wide; and as the author of many books, he appears in Jerome's *De viris illustribus* which dates from 392, six years before Chrysostom was translated to Constantinople.

Retreat from the caves did not mean retreat from his ideals. There have been some who have suggested that Chrysostom softened his standards when he became involved in pastoral work, and certainly there is a difference in atmosphere between his negative descriptions of marriage in the early work *De virginitate* and his more positive preaching to his largely married congregations. But the change was not so much a relaxing of standards as a deeper realization of the demands of Christian perfection. Like so many of his contemporaries, Chrysostom began by understanding Christian perfection in terms of the philosophic ideals of detachment and otherworldliness; but then, like Basil, he realized that to be like God meant love and generosity towards other men.[68]

Yet in enlarging his views, Chrysostom did not alter his fundamental position. To love meant to be involved; but it also meant detachment from the selfish passions associated with sex, with the possession of riches and with worldly success.

Even so, Christian perfection was to be the aim of all believers, whether or not they withdrew from the battle and distraction of city life. As early as his treatises on monasticism,[69] written while still young and enthusiastic about the ascetic ideal, Chrysostom refused to admit a double standard: there was no difference between the monk and the man of the world apart from the fact that one took a wife and the other did not.[70] In his works on virginity,[71] it is clear that idealization of chasitity did not mean total disparagement of marriage – that was to despise God's good creation and was the way of the heretic; it was because marriage was good that virginity was the greater attainment.[72] He always admitted that in some ways life was really easier for the monk: he battled in a less demanding arena than those who stayed in the world; he suffered less from distractions, from temptations and the demands made by others; he more readily found peace and philosophy.[73] In the *De Sacerdote*,[74] a revealing dialogue indicating his high estimate of the responsibilities of the priesthood and certainly his best-known work, Chrisostom confesses to having deceived his friend Basil and deliberately evaded the challenges and temptations of ordination (though whether the incident is historical is a matter of dispute).[75] He retreated to find solitude, to find purity and holiness. This work on the priesthood, probably composed soon after his ordination, contrasts the active and contemplative lives, and Chrysostom shows no doubt about which he now felt was superior at least for those great enough to cope with the demands. Throughout his subsequent life, his constant problem was living and preaching his puritanical ideals as the standard for all Christians in the world. Simplicity, purity, holiness, an independence of worldly goods and concerns, concern rather for the poor and the kingdom of heaven – such are the recurring themes of Chrysostom's exhortations, and the examples to which he appeals are the monks and ascetics. If he expected such behaviour from lay people, still more did he expect it of the clergy. His demanding standards are evident in his tirade against the practice of consecrated virgins housekeeping for ascetic or celibate priests:[76] the mere possibility of scandal, let alone the reality of it was enough to cause him disquiet. We can well believe that he was intolerant of clerical lapses as well as being a scathing critic of extravagance and worldliness.

The flavour of Chrysostom's moral teaching can readily be sampled by reading the short treatise *On Vainglory and the Education of Children*. In the eighteenth and nineteenth centuries, this little work was rejected as spurious (it does not appear in Migne's *Patrologia*); but it was rehabilitated by the work of S. Haidacher (1907), and is now generally regarded as a genuine and illuminating document.[77] The integrity of the work has been questioned, but in fact the conjunction of these two topics is very significant.[78] Chrysostom begins by deploring the fact that κενοδο-ξία (vainglory) has even invaded the church, and after a sophistical proof that men deceive themselves by seeking honour from others, he turns to the question of inculcating true values into the young. Interestingly enough, he repudiates any attempt to advise parents to educate their offspring for monasticism;[79] rather he wishes to establish high moral standards within the conditions of the world. His demands are rigorous – no theatre or amusements, biblical stories instead of fables, no young women; yet at the same time, he admits the need for lightheartedness, for an appreciation of beauty, and for genuine relationships resting on respect even for a younger brother or indeed servants. Gold and silver may be condemned as unnecessary for life; but Chrysostom's ideals are far from wholly negative.

In fact, for all the reports of his harshness and excessive zeal for temperance, in spite of repeated condemnations of pomp and extravagance, of luxurious eating and drinking, of games and the theatre, of ornate dress and make-up, Chrysostom does show appreciation of the good things of life. It was not riches in themselves that Chrysostom blamed, but rapacity and arrogance. Wine and wealth should not be despised; they are God's good gifts. 'Wine was given by God, not that we might be drunk, but that we might be sober, that we might enjoy ourselves, not that we might suffer pain.'[80] 'God made you a rich man, why make yourself poor? God made you rich so that you could help those in need'; though Chrysostom adds that an important motive for doing so is 'that you may have release from your sins through generosity to others'.[81] Even a wife is a blessing; for she can 'gently soothe her husband when he comes home harassed from business'.[82] To despise good things was to fall into the heresy of the Manichees.

3. The goodness of God

Indeed, the goodness and bounty of God, his mercy and φιλανθρωπία (love for man) is a constant theme of Chrysostom's preaching. He was adored by the populace because he chastised the Pharisaical with his wit and condemned the prosperous and insensitive, while offering the poor and the sinner the mercy of a kind and loving Father. The tension between his rigorous standards and his open acceptance of the penitent was already noted by Socrates. Throughout his account of John's life, Socrates had emphasized the excessive harshness with which he tried to root out evil in the church, and at the end he commented:

> Indeed it is most inexplicable to me, how with a zeal so ardent for the practice of self-control and blamelessness of life, he should in his sermons appear to teach a loose view of temperance. For . . . he did not scruple to say, 'Approach although you may have repented a thousand times'. For this doctrine, many even of his friends censored him.[83]

Yet it was this which more than anything else fired Chrysostom in his exhortations. His most frequent theme is an appeal to ἐλεημοσύνη, a word which has roughly the same double sense as the English 'charity'.[84] In most cases, his appeal is a practical call to almsgiving. In a society of extreme poverty and excessive riches, Chrysostom constantly urged his hearers to practise generosity, to relieve suffering, to recognize Christ among the poor. 'The rich man is not the man who owns a lot, but the man who gives a lot.'[85] Riches, like fresh air, sun and water, should be held in common.[86] But this was no socialist programme, nor was it simply a call to good works to earn treasure in heaven rather than on earth. For ἐλεημοσύνη meant more than charitable donations. On one occasion he pictured ἐλεημοσύνη as a dove interceding on our behalf at the judgment, taking us under his wings and saving us from punishment. She it was who saved mankind; for if God had not had mercy on us (ἠλέησεν ἡμᾶς), all would have been lost. She reconciled us while we were still enemies; she brought about myriads of good things; she persuaded the Son of God to become a slave and empty himself. 'Let us, beloved, strive after her through whom we are saved,' Chrysostom continues. 'Let us love her, let us value her more than money . . .' God prizes her more than sacrifice. Nothing is more characteristic of a Christian than π᾽λεημοσύνη. But it does not stem from us first; for God had already shown his mercy towards us.[87]

This mythical personification is a characteristic trick of sophistry, but for Chrysostom's age it was an effective way of making his appeal. More important than the style is the nature of the appeal. Philanthropic works are grounded in God's own 'philanthropy'; for φιλανθρωπία means literally 'love of man'. The classic studies of

Chrysostom invariably enquire how far his thought was Pelagian; but surely that is an unjustifiable question. The paradox of divine grace and human freedom would not become a controversial issue until four years after his death. Chrysostom was well aware that in the achievement of salvation neither God's grace nor human effort was sufficient without the other. Thus he often coupled both emphases: In willing lies everything, with grace from above;[88] virtue comes neither wholly from God nor simply from ourselves. . . . The grace of the Spirit leads us.[89] Augustine as well as Pelagius found passages in Chrysostom to support his case.[90] Certainly, judged by later standards, much of Chrysostom's exhortations appear Pelagian, and he undoubtedly urged his hearers to make considerable moral effort; yet few were more conscious of the fact that it was God's love which was the motive of all Christian action. He certainly preaches a doctrine of merit at times, but he also glories in the salvation gratuitously given by God, and is not wholly insensitive to Paul's doctrine of justification by grace through faith.[91] On Romans 1.17, for example, Chrysostom points out that it is 'not your own righteousness, but that of God. . . . For you do not achieve it by toilings and labour, but you can receive it as a gift from above, contributing one thing only, namely "believing".'[92] Further, it is because of God's love displayed in the incarnation that there are constant opportunities for repentance, at least until the final judgment. Repentance can always heal our failings, and true repentance involves not only recognition and confession of our sins with humility, prayers and tears, but also much ἐλεημοσύνη, renunciation of anger, evil and all kinds of sin, conversion of brethren from their wanderings and bearing all things with gentleness.[93] The answer to Socrates' perplexities is that Chrysostom preached no cheap forgiveness, but a gracious though demanding God who calls on men to respond with true Christian holiness, a message not unlike that of John Wesley.

Chrysostom the preacher was well aware that men generally respond to concrete pictures rather than abstract conceptions. God is graphically presented as Father, Judge or King; his anger appears in disaster, his love when men turn in repentance. A mixture of fear, respect and somewhat subservient love is the attitude with which he should be approached; yet the marvellous thing about being in Christ is that it gives men παρρησία (freedom of speech) before God.[94] This freedom, this possibility of standing before God with the self-confidence almost of a trusted confidant, is a frequent theme in Chrysostom. Thus, in many ways the God of Chrysostom is highly anthropomorphic; and the language used of the incarnate

Son is understandably even more personal – he is our brother and companion, our leader and advocate, our guide and priest. Salvation is expressed in parables of personal relationships. Indeed, if we try to analyse in logical or literal terms the ways in which Chrysostom preaches salvation, we are bound to find a fundamental inconsistency between two approaches: on the one hand, he stresses the activity of God's love in dealing with evil and overcoming the devil, on the other hand, he emphasizes the grace of our High Priest winning round an offended Father by his sacrifice. Neither view is presented as a 'theory of atonement': both are pictorial ways of presenting the significance of the cross. Chrysostom does not seek to integrate these graphic pictures into any theological system. Only when it comes to helping his congregations to sort out the issues raised by contemporary battles with heresy, does he use the more technical formulae concerning God's nature; and even here, he avoids the abstruse to a remarkable extent. His first sermon against the followers of Eunomius[95] is a typical example. After a topical reference to the absence of bishop Flavian, he turns to the lovely hymn to love in I Corinthians 13. Love is the essential characteristic of the Christian life, and it surpasses knowledge. Scripture shows this in many places and further insists that God is greater than human comprehension can conceive. 'I know God is everywhere, and wholly present everywhere, but how, I know not; I know he is without beginning, derivation or end, but how, I know not.' God's judgments are inscrutable and his ways indiscernible. We can only know in part. Scriptural allusion and quotation abounds; and far from proceeding with abstract argument, Chrysostom creates a sense of wonder and of worship, honouring a God beyond our deepest imaginings. The mystical flights and metaphysical arguments of Gregory of Nyssa seem to lie behind much of what Chrysostom says; but he turns it into a simple but profound faith for his mixed congregation of city dwellers. The blasphemous arrogance of the heretics contrasts with his call to humility and the repeated exhortations to prayer found in the subsequent homilies of this series.

4. Chrysostom's christology

As in theology, so in christology Chrysostom's approach is fundamentally practical. Having accepted the Nicene *homoousion*, he is obliged to comment on scriptural texts which seem to imply a quite different understanding of Jesus Christ. He resorts to distinguishing between his titles, functions and attributes κατ' ἀνθρωπότητα and those κατὰ θεότητα, the human and the divine, a fundamentally

Antiochene position, though not yet the subject of controversy. That Chrysostom should adopt Antiochene procedures is not at all surprising in view of the fact that his theological teacher was Diodore, who may be regarded as the father of the Antiochene school.[96] Yet for Chrysostom the procedure is not just a theoretical convenience. It has highly practical effects. For it allows him a thoroughly realistic exegesis of Jesus the man, the pioneer, overcoming temptation and leading his brethren to glory; but there are times when it leads him into paradox. How can Christ sit as Judge and stand as suppliant-priest at the same time? Chrysostom first remarks on his eternal intercession for us, and later in the same sermon insists that his priesthood is not eternal but only a function of the incarnation; he only needed to make one sacrifice and then for the future he can take his throne. His priesthood refers to his ἀνθρωπότης, though when speaking of his manhood it is manhood θεότητα ἔχουσα (having godhead) that is referred to, and the persons should not be divided.[97] Chrysostom is already, though perhaps rather naively, wrestling at a practical and exegetical level with the theological difficulties which became central in the ensuing controversies. He is also struggling with the terminology: on Philippians 2.5–11, he comments,

> Remaining what he was, he took that which he was not. . . . Let us not confuse or divide the natures. There is one God, one Christ, the Son of God; when I say one, I mean ἕνωσις (union), not σύγχυσις (confusion); one nature did not change into the other, but was united with it.[98]

Chrysostom refused to hazard an answer to the question, How?[99] It was an ineffable, indefinable union.[100]

5. Sacramental doctrine

In dogmatics, Chrysostom popularized rather than contributed; in liturgy, however, composition and innovation has been attributed to him by tradition. It is difficult to ascertain his precise contributions and the liturgy which bears his name certainly comes from a much later date. Nevertheless, his comprehensive works provide many details illuminating the worship and liturgy of his time and his teaching on baptism and eucharist provides important evidence for late fourth-century practice and theology.

In this connection, Harkins' English translation of his *Baptismal Instructions* is of particular importance.[101] Here we have brought together for the first time in easily accessible form catechetical homilies from various partly overlapping collections. The com-

plete collection of Chrysostom's works produced by Montfaucon
(and reprinted in Migne) contains only two homilies delivered to
candidates for baptism, but others were found and published by
Papadopoulos-Kerameus in Russia in 1909, and more still, discovered at the Stavronikita monastery on Mount Athos, were
published in the Sources Chrétiennes series by A. Wenger in
1957.[102]

A striking feature of these homilies is the vivid sense that the
baptized are transferring from one side to the other in a real conflict
between God and the devil. They are now soldiers of Christ, and
faith is a contract made with God through the Spirit. The newly
enlisted must expect ambush and attack from the enemy; he must
be alert and thoroughly renounce his old ways. He is warned against
worldliness and the specific manifestations of it which constantly
appalled Chrysostom – luxury and gluttony, expensive adornment
and makeup, the theatre and circus, oaths and superstitions. The
moral demands of the Christian life figure far more than the need
for correct dogmatic affirmations. These homilies provide excellent examples of Chrysostom's primary concerns, and of his
preaching techniques, his superb mastery of scriptural phraseology,
of typology and of image and parable.

But more to our purpose here, the discourses now available
provide liturgical evidence on a par with the *Mystagogical Catecheses* of Cyril of Jerusalem, and more reliably dated; for it is pretty
clear that they come from Chrysostom's Antiochene period and
almost certainly from the years 388–90. Quite apart from containing fairly detailed evidence concerning the actual rites
practised at the time, these homilies confirm the stark realism
which had already been noticed elsewhere as a feature of Chrysostom's attitude towards the sacraments. Baptism is not a simple
washing away of sin, but a melting down and remoulding;[103] thus
Chrysostom emphasizes the genuine re-creation involved – the
cross, the death and resurrection – is more than symbolic. The
eucharistic elements are not just consecrated bread and wine
symbolizing the body and blood of Christ; for 'the devil flees at the
sight of one returning from the Master's table with mouth and
tongue stained with his precious blood.'[104] That the eucharistic
bread and wine actually constitute the body and blood of Christ
slain on the altar, a fearful and holy sacrifice, Chrysostom often
emphasized. On one occasion,[105] he set himself to elucidate the
paradox that there is one Christ who died once for all, and yet
countless and repeated celebrations of the eucharist; the mere fact
that this posed a problem is indicative of Chrysostom's usual

assumption that in the elements Christ is actually present and what is offered is a real sacrifice. However, once faced with the explicit problem of the relationship between the cross and the eucharist, Chrysostom affirms the fact that what is offered is the same, not a different sacrifice, and not even a repetition of the original sacrifice; indeed, he has to resort to the explanation that 'we celebrate a memorial of a sacrifice', and even though the word *anamnēsis* has a stronger force than its English equivalent and carries with it the notion of realistic representation, nevertheless one cannot help feeling that this explanation is tamer than his very forceful language elsewhere. Chrysostom's language comes alive when one feels the pulse of devotion and the energy of his Christian life-style; exact theological definitions pale before his vivid pictures and lively exhortations.

6. Chrysostom's sermons and their hearers

More than anywhere else in patristic literature, in reading the homilies of Chrysostom one feels in touch with the semi-Christian populace, so thoroughly human and alive, responsive to striking image and parable, appreciative of clever speaking and yet titillated by the unsophisticated amusements of early Byzantine city life. They are a fickle crowd, lost without leadership, easily led astray, capable of riot and arson, but also of respect and hero-worship. Historians of social and cultural conditions in this period turn primarily to Chrysostom, who provides some of the richest source material.[106] His sermons are full of delightful touches and revealing asides: beware of pickpockets while you are engrossed in the sermon!

A number of occasional sermons have survived which are specifically linked with incidents in Chrysostom's career. His first sermon after ordination and sermons preached before and after his first brief exile are of personal interest. Others are linked with public incidents, like the two sermons delivered in Constantinople on the occasion of Eutropius' fall from power. But the best-known group, and the ones which better than any others give a graphic picture of the Antiochene populace and Chrysostom's relationship with it, are the twenty-one discourses *De statuis*. It was these which established the young priest's reputation. The story is told not only by the church historians but also by Libanius: in 387, at the news of extra taxes, the citizens of Antioch ran riot, and amongst other damage, smashed the imperial statues. When they came to their senses, they rushed to the church in fear of reprisals for such an insult to the imperial family. Bishop Flavian set out on an exhausting mission of appeal to the emperor, and while they awaited news, Chrysostom comforted and harangued the people from the pulpit day after day, urging them to repent, to amend their ways and to trust in God. He castigates them for their discontent at the penalties exacted by the royal commissioners. Finally he gives a moving account of Flavian's successful audience with the emperor. Chrysostom rose to the occasion and dealt with the issues of the moment; in such sermons one appreciates most his qualities as preacher and pastor.

Chrysostom's extant works are largely sermons, sermons for specific occasions, sermons for liturgical feasts, panegyrical sermons on saints and martyrs, sermons on themes – against the theatre, or for charity; but the majority of those surviving are exegetical sets covering Genesis and the Psalms, some of Isaiah, Matthew and John, Acts and all the Pauline epistles (which for Chrysostom included Hebrews). It is not exactly clear how these running commentaries in homily-form were produced and published. The comparative lack of topical reference led Baur[107] to the view that, unlike other homilies which were taken down by stenographers as they were delivered, the exegetical sermons were composed and published by Chrysostom himself as a sort of literary commentary in homiletic form. Yet this conclusion is not satisfactory for all the material. Enough topical reference is found to date many of the sequences, or at least to decide whether they belong to the Antioch or Constantinople period of Chrysostom's work. The individual sermons tend to fall into exegetical and exhortatory sections, the latter stressing Chrysostom's favourite moral themes and certainly having a basis in his regular preaching rather than in literary activity. In the case of the Genesis homilies, we seem to have two editions of the first eight, and the double text is usually explained by attributing one to stenographers and the other to Chrysostom's issuing a more official and literary version; a certain roughness in the text, and asides referring to immediate distractions like the sacristan lighting the lamps, are features characteristic of one version more than the other. Perhaps this case provides the clue to the relationship between Chrysostom's regular preaching on a biblical book, and the written form in which the exegetical homilies mostly survive.

For the modern reader, the most disturbing aspect of Chrysostom's sermons is their chaotic form. On the whole they fall into an exegetical first half, followed by a long exhortation on one of his favourite themes, the latter bearing precious little relation to the former. Sometimes he ranges over several topics in long irrelevant

digressions. His themes are repeated over and over again: in his
ninety homilies on Matthew, for example, it is reckoned that he
spoke on almsgiving forty times, poverty thirteen times, avarice
more than thirty times and wealth wrongly acquired or used, about
twenty times.[108] It seems that he received criticism for such things
in his own time, since he insists that he preaches daily on
almsgiving and love of one's neighbour because the congregation
shows little sign of having learned the lesson,[109] and justifies his
habit of ranging over many topics in one sermon by saying that, like
a doctor, he does not imagine the same medicine is suitable for all
his patients.[110] With such comments, we can hardly regard these
exegetical collections as purely literary creations divorced from
Chrysostom's regular preaching task.

For the study of the biblical text and of exegetical methods in use
at this date in Antioch and also Constantinople, these homilies
have no rival. Like others in the Antiochene tradition of exegesis,
Chrysostom repudiates allegorical flights of fancy and treats the
text as straightforwardly as possible. His main aim is to indicate
and elucidate the meaning of the text for his congregation, noting
where the stops should come, explaining difficult words or phrases,
bringing out the sense by reference to the context or other usages
elsewhere. He does not shrink from accepting that much of the Old
Testament refers to mundane and even immoral matters and is to
be taken as history, not symbol, as literal (though interim)
commandments, not spiritual directives in veiled form; indeed he
regards it as a universal law of scripture that it supplies the
interpretation if an allegory is intended, so as to prevent the
uncontrolled passion of those bent on allegorizing from penetrating
everywhere without system or principle.[111] Yet to see prophecies of
the New Testament in the Old was not to allegorize but to
recognize the voice of God: the Psalms could prove the divinity of
Christ, because messianic references are embedded in the text,
veiled until the fulfilment was revealed. Chrysostom's perspective
is that of a fourth-century churchman regarding the scriptural text
as divine oracles, miraculously delivered to men in spite of their
barbarity, in spite of the poverty of the writer's intellect – after all,
Paul was a mere tent-maker![112] All the more remarkable, then, is
Chrysostom's sensitive appreciation of the Pauline epistles as
'occasional' writings reflecting Paul's efforts to deal with pastoral
problems; the way in which he tries to understand the particular
difficulties, his constant attempts to interpret the mind of the
writer, to show what Paul's aim and intention was in the given
situation, is noticeable. Appeal to Paul's purpose even provides the

criterion for deciding between conflicting interpretations: that which is in harmony with the apostle's thought takes precedence over mere attention to words. In summaries, Chrysostom seeks to trace the thread of Paul's argument. Of course, the problems of his time intrude; wherever christological texts appear, the dangerous heresies which threaten Chrysostom's congregation easily become the subject of his exegesis; but Paul is made to teach a post-Nicene theology because he wrote the words of the Spirit, which have a cutting edge like a sharp two-edged sword.[113] In his day, Chrysostom could hardly have approached dogmatic matters in any other way. When it comes to texts on the Christian life and the call to Christian discipleship, then he is able to speak with deep passion and with quite remarkable insight into the challenge of the gospel sayings and the depth of Paul's faith in God's saving mercy.

Chrysostom studies are complicated by considerable critical problems, due in large part to his exceptional reputation as orator, saint and martyr. In the first place a multitude of spurious writings has been attributed to him and copied in manuscript collections of his works; then his name accompanies enormous numbers of fragments in catenae and florilegia. The task of distinguishing the authentic is by no means complete. The abundant manuscript tradition is itself an *embarras de richesses* (Baur counted nearly two thousand MSS, and more recent researches suggest that the total number will prove to be in the region of three to four thousand); besides, there are many ancient translations of his works which also frequently pose problems of authenticity. The result is that a complete critical text of his works is not yet available.[114]

In the course of this survey, many of the more important authentic works of Chrysostom have been mentioned, though for a comprehensive list, the *Clavis Patrum Graecorum*[115] should be consulted. Some can be dated exactly, others are difficult to place; but most can be assigned to particular periods of his life. Many of the literary treatises seem to be early, certainly those on monasticism, virginity and the priesthood; the homilies span the years of his priesthood and episcopate, those on Acts, Colossians, Thessalonians and Hebrews clearly belonging to Constantinople. After his exile Chrysostom's literary activity changed again, and it is largely through correspondence that he had continuing influence. About 236 letters are extant, showing a concern for over one hundred different persons. Through his correspondence, Chrysostom supported missionary endeavours, and attempted to present his own case to Pope Innocent. His correspondence is therefore far from devoid of interest.

He wrote most intimately to the rich deaconess, Olympias,[116] who had been associated with him in generous charitable works in Constantinople, and whose conduct in the affair of the 'Tall Brothers' Palladius had to defend along with Chrysostom's own. In these letters, Chrysostom is of course affected by the rhetorical conventions in which he had been so well trained. Yet at the same time a personal flavour pervades them, and the austere ascetic reveals his human sensibility. He is not averse to giving dramatic descriptions of his own physical sufferings; implicitly he confesses his lack of ἀπάθεια (passionlessness). Yet the impressive thing is that the focus is away from his personal hardships, grim though they were, to concern for Olympias. Her 'loss of heart' (ἀθυμία) he regards as a deeply serious matter. Suffering can become a 'great treasure' if faced in the right way. His words have all the more force because the experience of rejection, illness and physical hardship is his as well. The thought of the letters is particularly remarkable for its subtle blend of Stoic and Christian motifs. Like the Stoic, Chrysostom sees physical suffering as merely external, and encourages Olympias to be like a rock in the tempest or an impregnable citadel. However, biblical figures, particularly Job and Paul, provide his examples, and the chief encouragement is the abuse and rejection suffered by Christ himself. The attitude recommended goes beyond Stoic ἀπάθεια to glorifying and praising God in the midst of tribulation, remembering his φιλανθρωπία, his love and care for mankind.

Most biographies of Chrysostom have difficulty in avoiding a hagiographical appearance, and the more one reads his works, the more admiration one feels for the quality of his preaching. If his style and methods of sermon construction fail to appeal to our taste, they were nevertheless the most effective method of communication in his time; it is no wonder that his great collections of exegetical sermons were carefully preserved and regularly read in the Greek-speaking church. His brilliant use of sophistical conventions with flexibility and originality is hardly matched elsewhere;[117] nor is his remarkable grasp of the Christian message as it spoke to his own day. He tried to recall a corrupt and officially Christian society to the standards preached in the gospels, his most frequent theme revolving around the social questions of wealth and property.

In spite of the fact that he unavoidably speaks the language of the past and his works read as topical for an age long gone, his vivid imagery, together with his love and understanding of the Bible and of the erring hearts of men, gives his work an abiding quality and relevance. Christianity is not simply a set of disputed doctrines, but a way of life, and Chrysostom never lets this be forgotten.

V. Nemesius of Emesa

Nemesius too was concerned about ethics and God's providence, but he was an altogether different character from Chrysostom. We have absolutely no information about Nemesius apart from what we can glean from his book *On the Nature of Man*, but the character of this work is enough to indicate how different was his approach and personality.

1. The identity of Nemesius

On the Nature of Man is the impersonal work of a scholar exploring the great questions of man's fundamental constitution, purpose, faculties and potential, an exploration carried out by means of the then conventional scholarly methods and probably drawing all its material from standard text-books of the time. In fact, a common estimate of Nemesius' achievement is that his work is a totally unoriginal compendium of the received scientific knowledge of antiquity – though for Nemesius himself, of course, such an estimate would not be uncomplimentary, since he belonged to a period in which the ancients were to be respected and innovation was despised. In view of this, the overall perspective given to the discussion by his own understanding and purpose is in itself a remarkable indication of thoughtful handling of the knowledge received from his sources, however conventional his methods. Occasional inconsistencies betray his dependence on others, but surprisingly few on the whole. His discussion is often a salutary reminder of the complexity of the questions and he never concludes an argument by dogmatizing. He has difficulty in integrating the polarities of his thought, at times, but even the greatest thinkers are not entirely consistent.

The character of the work has meant that the question of Nemesius' sources has been the primary matter discussed by scholars. For he has been regarded as of interest not for his own thought – for everything was plagiarized – but rather for preserving the thought of more distinguished contributors to Hellenistic science. It is clear that Nemesius drew a great deal on Galen, whose views he often explicitly discusses, though not always simply agreeing with him. More speculative is the ultimate attribution of many of his ideas to Posidonius, who is never mentioned. On the basis of Jaeger's studies, there was wide acceptance that Posidonius' ideas played an important part in Nemesius' work;[118] but that was in the period when classicists all accepted that Posidonius, the Stoic who in the first century B C adopted many Platonic ideas, was an original contributor to the development of Hellenistic philosophy in general and Middle Platonism in particular. Recently the very limited extent of our knowledge of Posidonius has become more widely recognized,[119] and this must in itself reopen the question of Nemesius' sources. In fact, his immediate sources are probably largely untraceable; for when Nemesius puts forward the views of older authorities like Plato and Aristotle, he usually seems to be quoting handbooks or commentaries rather than working from personal acquaintance with the texts. The views which have been attributed to Posidonius were probably part of the received wisdom of school philosophy in Nemesius' time, and certainly some were commonplace in the more recent thinking of a Neoplatonist like Iamblichus – the unity and sympathy of all parts of the universe, for example. If it is true that only in Nemesius do we find the integration of the two ideas that the universe has a graduated ascending order of being, and that man provides the link between the physical and spiritual worlds,[120] it is hazardous to assume that this connection originated centuries earlier in the work of Posidonius and Nemesius alone has preserved it. His use of Galen and, in some sections, his dependence on Origen's (largely lost) *Commentary on Genesis*, is more assured, though here again the conclusions are reached to a pretty fair extent by skilled deduction rather than concrete evidence.[121]

There are other teasing questions posed by this work. Who exactly was the obscure scholar who wrote it? At what date was it produced? It is first quoted in the seventh century and was used extensively by John of Damascus in the eighth, but otherwise there is no information apart from the manuscripts themselves. Several manuscripts, together with the seventh-century citations, attribute the work to Nemesius of Emesa, but others treat all or part of it as the work of Gregory of Nyssa, and John Damascene gives no indication of the author. The most natural assumption is that the otherwise unknown name, Nemesius of Emesa, does represent the author; but who was he? and when did he live? Presumably 'of Emesa' means that he was bishop of that Syrian city. Gregory of Nazianzus knew a Nemesius who was provincial governor of Cappadocia between 383 and 389.[122] He was not a Christian, but then most of this treatise is not explicitly Christian, and since

Gregory urges his acquaintance to make a serious study of Christianity, conversion is not out of the question. An ex-provincial governor could well have become a bishop soon after his baptism.[123] It is impossible to confirm such a speculation, but the date at least seems to fit the evidence of the treatise itself. The views of Apollinarius and Eunomius are discussed as if they are contemporaries, and the work reveals a rather circumspect approach to Origen. The name of Origen is mentioned only three times; on the first occasion his views are criticized and on the third a rather derogatory story about him, no doubt in popular circulation at the time, is used as an illustration. On the second occasion a very brief statement of Origen's account of memory is offered among other accounts and without comment (Jaeger saw reason to attribute this to the Neoplatonist philosopher of the same name rather than to the Christian Origen). In other words, when Origen's name is mentioned, it is never as an appeal to a respected authority; and yet there are many passages which are probably indebted to Origen's *Commentary on Genesis*, and Nemesius' thought seems to follow a mildly Origenist line on a number of occasions.[124] We may conclude that it had become foolhardy to reveal strongly Origenist sympathies, but formal condemnation had not yet taken place. Thus a date round about 395–400 seems most likely.

Can we glean any more about the author from his work? The large amount of anatomical and physiological information in the treatise strongly suggests that the author had studied medicine and knew the works of Galen and probably some other medical texts first-hand. This does not necessarily mean he was a professional physician. Caesarius, Gregory Nazianzen's brother, is the usual parallel cited: he studied medical science as part of a gentleman's liberal education, and on the basis of his knowledge gave medical advice in the imperial household; yet Gregory explicitly tells us that he was not a professional practitioner and never took the Hippocratic oath.[125] If Nemesius is correctly identified as Gregory's correspondent, then he was a trained lawyer rather than a physician.

So all we can say with any confidence is that Nemesius was the sort of person who could have written a work like this. So what is the treatise like? What was its purpose? What are its contents?

2. The work's purpose

Nemesius begins with an overall summary of his subject. He proposes to treat the nature of man, and there is a general consensus that man is composed of soul and body. The trouble is that there are widely differing views about the nature of the soul and its relationship with the body, and it is therefore these matters which are to occupy his attention in the first place. In the course of the first summary chapter, Nemesius refers to the following authorities: Plotinus, Apollinarius, Aristotle, Plato, Moses and Paul. The discussion moves from a review of other people's philosophical conclusions to a presentation of man's 'dual nature' – his links both with irrational animals and spiritual beings, his potential for good or evil – and concludes with ethical exhortation. Thus the introductory chapter reveals something of Nemesius' method and his purpose, and provides an overall perspective of understanding of his subject. Ultimately his concern is with moral questions, and his address is to the cultured and educated in general. His method is that of contemporary philosophical treatises, listing authorities, acknowledging different conclusions, arguing for the most reasonable position; but his purpose is to lead beyond the standard pagan discussions to a Christian viewpoint. So this treatise has often been described as a work of apologetic, but it is not by any means a conventional apologetic work; for it is far from dominated by specifically Christian themes. Rather it is a contribution to a philosophical discussion which was going on among Christian and pagan intellectuals alike, and Nemesius is still free to explore the possibility of various answers about the origin and nature of the soul, the extent of human freewill, the proper ethical ideal, and so on. What he succeeds in doing is to produce a rational account of man which integrates certain Christian standpoints into the prevailing scientific knowledge of antiquity, producing a coherent and attractive philosophical position which would have its own apologetic force.

Nemesius' second long section confirms these conclusions about the nature and purpose of his work. Here he turns to discussion of the soul, and again begins with a review of various philosophical approaches. Democritus, Epicurus and the Stoics are said to affirm that the soul is corporeal; but various different views of its material essence have been proposed. As these proposals are listed and the discussion proceeds to other possibilities, the following names are added to the list of those whose views are considered: Critias, Hippon, Heraclitus, Pythagoras, Dicaearchus, the Manichees, Ammonius the master of Plotinus, Numenius the Pythagorean, Xenocrates, Cleanthes, Chrysippus, the characters in Plato's *Phaedo*, Galen, Aristotle, Eunomius, and Apollinarius – several of these are discussed more than once. Anyone who recognizes these names will immediately notice that there is no sense in which a chronological history of philosophy is being offered. Rather the arrangement is topical: different kinds of views on the soul are reviewed, and the sources span nearly a thousand years from the pre-Socratic philosophers to contemporary Christian thinkers. (Is it chance that they all happen to be heretics?) All are treated to the same courteous discussion, but the conclusion is eventually reached that 'the soul is not body, nor harmony, nor temperament, nor any other quality,' but rather it is 'incorporeal being', which survives separation from the body. In a final few sentences Nemesius adds that while the proofs of Plato and others are difficult and obscure, except for the trained philosopher, for the Christian, the teaching of holy scripture is quite sufficient anyway; but for those who do not accept the scriptures, there are good reasons for adopting his conclusion. In other words, he seeks to reach a reasonable consensus with his pagan contemporaries on the nature of man.

Clearly it is impossible to review the whole of this lengthy treatise in such detail. The contents of the third chapter on the union of soul and body will be discussed later in another connection, and the reader must be left to study for himself[126] the bulk of this text with its fascinating details concerning how the ancients thought the human body works, its composition out of the classic four elements, its digestive and respiratory systems, its senses, how sense-perception is related to knowledge and thought, what the different parts of the brain do, and so on. Suffice it here to comment upon a few particular emphases which permeate this work.

3. Man is a unity

The most striking thing about Nemesius' presentation of man's nature is the fact that his overall picture is far from dualistic. Man can be analysed into a being composed of soul and body, and clearly soul and body are separable, as in death; and yet man alive is a psychosomatic whole in which body and soul are intimately united. 'A living creature is composed of soul and body; the body is not a living creature by itself, nor is the soul, but soul and body together.'[127] The soul is the driving force (ἐνέργεια) of muscular movement: 'Whatever movement takes place by the operation of nerves and muscles involves the intervention of soul, and is accomplished by an act of will.'[128] Soul also provides the ἐνέργεια in respiration: panting and sobbing accompany moments of great grief, and soul keeps respiration going during sleep, since it is essential for human life. So the physical and the 'psychic' are intimately woven together: τὸ ψυχικὸν συνεπλάκη τῷ φυσικῷ.[129]

Quite how this intimate union is achieved Nemesius is less able to understand, since it is not paralleled by other cases of mixing or union in the physical world. The soul has its own independent existence – in fact Nemesius is close to embracing an Origenist view of the soul's pre-existence –[130] and it is incorporeal. Being incorporeal it cannot suffer change by its association with the body, and yet it has established its presence in every part of the body. It preserves its own identity of being and yet modifies whatever it indwells without itself being transformed. Soul is not located in body and yet it is bound by habit to the body.[131] The intimate weaving together of τὰ ψυχικά and τὰ φυσικά is attributed to the providence of the Creator.[132] The Christian doctrine of the resurrection of the body becomes a natural corollary of the anthropological position adopted by Nemesius, though Nemesius makes little use of it,[133] and has somewhat of a tendency to oscillate between this insistence on the unity of body and soul, and an acceptance of the soul's independence.

However, his basic picture of man's unitary being is intimately related to his views on ethics and providence. In the early part of his work, as we have seen, Nemesius treats man as the link between the physical and spiritual realms; man thus finds himself on the border between rational and irrational, and capable of following carnal pleasures or the direction of reason.[134] Now if Nemesius had imagined a great dichotomy between these two worlds, he would have been led into a strongly dualist view of man as a spiritual being trapped in flesh and seeking purification of the soul by escape from it, a view more or less presupposed by a good deal of the current ascetic enthusiasm. Nemesius, however, rejoices in man as crown and lord of the animal creation, for whose sake all else was created,[135] and he recognizes that there is a 'this-worldly' morality. A living creature cannot avoid 'passion' (which is in any case a highly ambiguous term);[136] man needs to distinguish between good and bad passions,[137] rather than attempting to eliminate them altogether. Deeds of virtue are themselves performed κατὰ πάθος (with emotion). So the ethical aim must be to find the Aristotelian 'mean' with regard to the passions.[138] The worthy man can face grief with proper moderation of passion (μετριοπαθής), not overwhelmed by emotion but battling for mastery over it.[139]

Yet Nemesius also presents a higher ideal: in the face of grievous circumstances, 'the contemplative will be entirely unmoved (ἀπαθής), seeing that he has severed himself from present things and cleaves to God,'[140] God being depicted as above all mutability.[141] Has he betrayed his basic position? At first sight we do seem to have an inconsistency, and Nemesius himself fails to draw the threads very closely together. He makes the ancient distinction between the contemplative and the active life,[142] and he recognizes that there are two kinds of 'good' for humanity: one kind applies to the soul and body together, or to put it another way, to the soul as it makes use of the body, and the virtues are a good example of this; the other concerns the proper functions of the soul alone without involving the body, godliness (εὐσέβεια) or philosophic contemplation (ἡ τῶν ὄντων θεωρία) being the classic expression of this alternative.[143] These two ethical standards run parallel with the oscillation between his profound recognition of the soul's union with the body in man as we know him, and his insistence that the soul is an independent entity. Yet there are hints that he had a more coherent picture underlying his various comments, and that his 'purer' ideal did not imply a dualist position. He adopts the view that the soul has both rational and irrational faculties, so the passions are movements of the irrational soul.[144] And even the spiritual realm cannot be regarded as beyond emotion, since there are pleasures of the soul just as there are pleasures of the body.[145] The contemplative life may be purer than the active life, but contemplation is itself a form of activity, though it takes place in stillness. (Similarly, God is unmoved, and yet is also the Mover.)[146] Nemesius, not with total clarity but certainly with courage, seems to be feeling his way towards the idea of sublimation of the passions rather than their suppression or denial. He refuses to oversimplify the questions of 'passion' and 'pleasure', any more than the nature and faculties of soul. In doing this he was following in the wake of important discussions deriving from Plato and Aristotle which the tendencies of Neoplatonic teaching and the ascetic movement in Christianity were in danger of submerging.

This interpretation of Nemesius' position makes sense of his discussion of freewill. Because man is physically composed of the various elements which make up the material universe, he is mutable; because man is endowed with reason and can deliberate about courses of action, he has freewill. It is by exercising his power of choice and using his reason that man can tame and direct his passions, and even, through contemplation of God, remain immutable (ἄτρεπτος).[147] Man's badness is not inherent in his physical nature, but is simply the result of his habits, his wrong choices.[148] Man's noblest purpose is fulfilled when he makes the right choices, and above all when he chooses the purest pleasure of the soul – the activity of contemplation. The Platonic intellectual ideal is thus married to a Christian view of creation, and no blame can be attached to the Creator for the human plight. Man's glory is that he is a μιχρὸς χόσμος – a mini-universe – in which the physical and spiritual are bound together according to the purposes of the Creator.[149] Thus man epitomizes the unity of all creation. There is no radical dichotomy between the physical and the spiritual, the corporeal and the incorporeal, for in man they are wedded together, forming part of an ordered hierarchy of created being, a chain in which man provides the crucial link. 'We may see herein', says Nemesius,

> the best proof that the whole universe is the creation of one God,[150] . . . God created both an intelligible and a phenomenal order, and required some one creature to link these two together in such wise that the entire universe should form one agreeable unity, unbroken by internal incoherences. For this reason, then, man was made a living creature such as should combine together the intelligible and phenomenal natures.[151]

Thus in Nemesius' work, because of his interest in the unity of creation, we find the integration of the two traditional themes: man as the link between physical and spiritual, and the creation as consisting of ascending orders of being. That this comes from a source is probable, though apparently it is unique to Nemesius amongst extant philosophical writings.[152]

4. Ethical and theological implications

Towards the end of his work, Nemesius drifts away from the central theme, the nature of man. His consideration of ethics naturally leads him on to a discussion of freewill, fate and providence. A doctrine of fate removes all ethical incentive; yet man's freedom is circumscribed by circumstances; and God's providence over all his unified creation is the only doctrine which satisfies Nemesius' analysis both morally and scientifically. Just as his unitary view of man's nature is never completely undermined by his contemplative ideal of man, so his occasional admissions that God transcends the mutability of his creation do not detract from his insistence that God's providence oversees the smallest details. For God the Creator cannot be profaned by intimate knowledge of and loving care for his own creatures.[153] The brilliant design and utter goodness of creation is the basis for his understanding of man, his nature and his purpose. It was not unnatural for him to turn to the new theme of providence, for that provides the overall context for all his earlier discussions. It is a pity that his discussion tails off with every sign of incompleteness. Perhaps Nemesius died before completing his task.

Ethics and providence were classic talking points in ancient philosophy. So was the nature of the soul and the composition of the physical universe. What is it then that gives Nemesius' work a specifically Christian colouring?

Of course, Nemesius adopts views on creation, providence, freewill, and so on, which are consonant with Christian views, but interestingly enough, he often fails to press elements which are specifically and uniquely Christian: for example, he assumes *creatio ex nihilo*, for he mentions it twice in passing, but this particular contentious subject is not specifically debated. Nemesius seeks a consensus with pagan philosophy rather than looking for conflict or being defensive about controversial points. For the most part it is incidental hints which point to the Christian motivation of Nemesius' overall discussion – the casual introduction of references to Hebrew ideas (probably picked up from his source, Origen), or to the scriptures, to Moses or Paul, or the occasional quotation of a text. There are only three passages which have a strong Christian colouring, and one of these is probably the least happy section of Nemesius' work. He is trying to indicate the characteristic and distinguishing marks of man as distinct from other creatures, and he begins by stating that there are two choice prerogatives which man shares with no other creature: firstly through repentance he can gain forgiveness, and secondly his mortal body can be immortalized[154] – in other words, he turns to the credal affirmations of the forgiveness of sins and the resurrection of the body to provide his distinguishing characteristics, though he explores neither very deeply. Alongside this he adopts the pagan clichés that laughter is a peculiarity of the human animal and that man's ability to learn and practise arts and sciences is also a distinguishing mark of the human species. This is one of the less well-integrated sections of Nemesius' work and the Christian motifs seem to be dragged in and rather baldly stated. However, the point of the remarks is to distinguish man both from irrational animals and from spiritual, angelic beings, with both of whom man has a kinship; so within Nemesius' overall account of man's position, it has a certain relevance and importance.

A little earlier in his introductory summary, Nemesius has given an account of the Fall, and here an important and characteristically Christian theme apparently fitted neatly into his argument. Man, the link between two worlds, was created neither mortal nor immortal: his destiny depended upon the exercise of this choice, whether he should give himself up to his bodily passions or put the good of his soul first. Man was to be kept in ignorance of his potential until he achieved perfection; so he was forbidden to eat of the Tree of Knowledge. He disobeyed and so became the slave of his bodily needs, losing his chance of a higher life.[155] Such is Nemesius' account: however, for the bulk of his work, Nemesius writes as if the Fall had never happened, as if man's potentialities were the same. It is hardly surprising therefore that he has been accused (slightly anachronistically) of Pelagianism. As for most of the Eastern Fathers, the theme of man's freewill and moral potential was so important to him that he failed to grasp the seriousness of the Fall in the intense way that someone like Augustine perceived it.

Did he then take no account of redemption in Christ? Again it is there in hints and no doubt if pressed, Nemesius would have stated that Christ reversed the Fall and therefore man had regained his original potentialities. But these characteristic Christian themes are not central to Nemesius' study, and the one passage[156] where he deals with the incarnation is the most unexpected feature of his work. For where many Christians were solving their christological problem by appeal to the soul-body analogy, Nemesius virtually reverses the argument and illustrates his soul-body problem by appeal to the analogy of the Incarnate Word.

As we have noticed, Nemesius is at a loss to find a suitable analogy for elucidating the mysterious union of soul and body in human nature. Physical analogies imply either mixture, and therefore the transformation of the two entities into a third, or juxtaposition, which is not a real union. Neither will satisfy Nemesius in the case of the union of soul and body. The soul cannot be changed by association with the body or it would cease to be soul. The union must be without confusion (καὶ ἥνωται τοίνυν καὶ ἀσυγχύτως ἥνωται τῷ σώματι ἡ ψυχή). There is genuine union, since there is a community of feeling (συμπάθεια) throughout the whole living creature – it is one thing. As an incorporeal entity, the soul has located itself in every part of the body, as if giving up its independent existence, and yet without doing so. It makes important changes to the body without being in any way changed itself (τρέπουσα, but not τρεπομένη). It is not confined by the body – it is in a sense part of the universal mind – so it is not related to the body by location (ἐν τόπῳ) but by 'a habitual relation of presence there' (ἐν σχέσει), (and here Nemesius introduces a very surprising religious analogy) 'even as God is said to be in us'. The soul is bound to the body by habit, or by inclination (τῇ πρός τι ῥοπῇ) or by disposition (τῇ διαθέσει). Soul cannot be 'located' and when we say it is 'there', we mean its activity is there. To parallel this kind of relation with God's presence is not surprising; what is surprising is that Nemesius can give no more definite account of the soul-body union in which he so strongly believes.

Now many of the terms Nemesius has used in this discussion are remarkably close to the kind of language which was to become so prominent in the ensuing christological debates. Indeed, quite quickly, Nemesius picks up the christological theme, drawing attention to the parallel. The union of the divine Word with his manhood can be described in the same sort of way: 'For he continued thus in union without confusion and without being circumscribed' (ἐνωθεὶς ἔμεινεν ἀσύγχυτος καὶ ἀπερίληπτος). Having introduced the parallel, however, Nemesius tries to draw out a distinction, namely that the soul does somehow seem to suffer with the body, whereas the Word does not share in human infirmities, while sharing with humanity his own Godhead; indeed he thinks that the language he has been using applies more precisely to the incarnation than it does to the soul-body union. Yet it is difficult for him to specify exactly where the distinction lies in view of his earlier insistence that the soul suffers no change by association with the body; and furthermore, he goes on to quote a passage from Porphyry, which Porphyry intended to elucidate the soul-body union, but Nemesius uses it specifically in order to indicate that the Christian doctrine of the union of God and man is not absurd or incredible. Whether Nemesius likes it or not, his analogies undoubtedly reduce the uniqueness of the incarnation. Because the soul is incorporeal, its union with the body must be without confusion or impairment of the superior, spiritual being; the union takes place because the soul can pervade the body throughout, without being invaded or changed itself. Neither the incarnation, nor the presence of God in man can he describe in fundamentally different terms.

In the succeeding chapter, it will be important to recall this brief contribution of Nemesius to the christological discussion. Quite clearly he holds an 'Antiochene' view of the union of the immutable Word-God with the whole (body+soul) Man; yet this cannot involve for Nemesius a dualist doctrine of 'Two Sons'. Nemesius is at a loss to give an adequate account of the soul-body union, yet the union of soul and body is so close as to produce one living creature, man; even if he, or indeed other Antiochenes were at a loss to give a satisfactory account of the union of Word and Man in Christ, this did not necessarily mean that they envisaged anything other than a real union in one individual. This was not a union by mere divine grace (εὐδοκία) but by nature (φύσις), as Nemesius indicates in a strong aside directed against 'the opinion of certain men of note'. Nemesius may have been alluding here to extreme views expressed by Theodore of Mopsuestia – indeed, in this section, Nemesius gives the impression of being briefly sidetracked by a contemporary controversy; for he fails to draw any distinctly Christian conclusions about the nature of man from his excursion into christological discussion.

Nemesius had his problems. Some of his conclusions, pieced together from his various sources, are held together in uncomfortable tension. But at least he tried to wrestle with the complexity of the questions in a relatively broad context and with a relatively broad outlook. He refused to dogmatize; he did not condemn but argued. It was because of people like Nemesius that dogmatic Christianity did not submerge the intellectual heritage of the Graeco-Roman world. Nemesius brought all his pagan philosophy into the church and moulded together an understanding of man which stands out against the ascetic currents of the period for its humanity and its optimism.

VI. Synesius of Cyrene

From the amount of space devoted to Synesius of Cyrene in the typical church history, it might appear that he was a figure of considerable unimportance. As a representative of the particular period in which he lived, however, his significance is greater.[157] A glance at the bibliographies would quickly reveal the fact that Synesius catches the interest of classicists, Byzantinists and historians of late antiquity, and the reason for this becomes apparent as soon as one begins to study his career.

Synesius was a well-educated, prominent, upper-class member of his local community who ended up as a bishop. This would not be so surprising if it were not for his lack of Christian convictions and his life as a 'pagan'. In an earlier period of scholarship, many enthusiastic books were written on this cultured Hellene, and much ink expended on the question when he was converted.[158] Yet there is no trace in his very personal works of any crisis or change in his faith; he did not go through the spiritual turmoils of his contemporary, Augustine of Hippo. He seems to have slipped quietly into the church, and not really committed himself until the episcopal honours were thrust upon him. Even then, there is no obvious break in his thinking or his circle. He complains of a change in his way of life, and amongst his correspondence there are epistles of an ecclesiastical character; but Christianity certainly did not appear to him to represent a fundamental change in his values or beliefs, not even a glorious culmination of them.

What we know of Synesius comes largely from his extant works. These include a number of small treatises, some hymns and a collection of letters.[159] Difficulties with dating his birth, death and most of the events of his life lie in lack of specific evidence. None of his letters can be dated later than 413, and he does not appear to have heard of the ghastly lynching by Christian fanatics of his heroine Hypatia, which took place in 415.[160] So the end of his life can be established with some probability, and clearly he did not survive long as a bishop, since it was already about 410 when Theophilus consecrated him. How old he was at either of these dates is a matter of considerable dispute; his birth has been dated as early as 360 and as late as 375.[161]

The firmest date in his career is his visit to Constantinople which lasted three years from 399 to 402.[162] He was chosen by his fellow-citizens of the Pentapolis to represent them before the emperor. This area of Libya was in financial ruin, and Synesius eventually obtained some remission of taxes. It is significant that his fellow-citizens turned to him to act as their ambassador in this way, since it throws light on their election of him as bishop; it was determined more by their faith in him as a politician and local leader, than as pastor and theologian. It was as *patronus* rather than as spiritual father that he helped his flock, in particular defending the people against the cruel prefect, Andronicus, whose excommunication by Synesius is said to be the first recorded.[163] One of the things he dreaded about becoming a bishop was being overwhelmed by the enormous burden of arbitration in local disputes and of correspondence on behalf of individuals seeking the righting of wrongs or personal advancement. He had already done much of this kind, but without detriment to his philosophy.[164] Most of his life was clearly spent as the local squire. His pursuits were gentlemanly, a devotion to literature (his works are almost a mosaic of allusions to classical authors, especially Plato, Plutarch and Homer),[165] and to the chase (he was a connoisseur of arms, dogs and horses).[166] He was an intensely patriotic 'Tory'; the solution to the military and economic problems of the empire and his own province lay for him in a citizen-army fully committed to the defence of its property, rather than professional parasites, with no personal motivation to anything but plundering the produce of the area. His commitment to this view was put to the test several times in his life, when barbarian tribes were ranging over the countryside and Synesius found himself taking a personal lead in organizing local defence.[167] His ideal was philosophy, or quiet retirement from public life to cultivate contemplation and the arts; but true to the classical Greek spirit of loyalty to the city, he responded repeatedly to calls on his sense of duty.[168] His consecration as a bishop was simply the culmination of a lifetime of public service.

Apart from this, we know that Synesius went to Alexandria for his higher education and studied with the remarkable daughter of Theon, Hypatia; that he visited Athens and was definitely of the view that Alexandria had outstripped the more ancient centre of learning;[169] and that he married sometime after his return from Constantinople, a marriage solemnized by the patriarch, Theophilus, who later consecrated him as bishop.[170] His close connections with Alexandria are further shown by his correspondence.

The correspondence of Synesius seems to range in date from about 395 to the end of his life. The order in the standard editions is certainly not chronological, and in many cases it is doubtful whether the chronological order can be reconstructed. From these letters, many of them lively and personal pieces, even though written in accordance with the rhetorical conventions of the day and with an eye on publication, we can glean not only personal information but also vivid impressions of the life and society of the times. Synesius had about forty correspondents, to some of whom only one or two letters survive. Most frequently appear letters to Euoptius, his brother, to Herculian and Olympias, two fellow-students in Alexandria, and to Pylaemenes and Troilus, a well-known rhetorician, both of whom he met in Constantinople.[171] In these he reveals considerable narrative powers, humour and intimacy. One of the most discussed, *Epistle* 4,[172] is a superb account of a disastrous sea-voyage along the coast from Alexandria to Cyrene. Everything goes wrong, and when the vessel is caught in a storm further from land than it might have been, the crowning touch comes when at dusk the captain and half the crew abandon the tiller and ropes to prostrate themselves and read their sacred rolls: they are Jews and the Sabbath has begun! The letter is written with somewhat donnish humour, savouring the slight exaggeration of an escapade after it is over, with plenty of literary quotes and allusions. However, it is also interesting from other points of view. It was clearly written in Synesius' pagan days, and is full of current popular superstitions,[173] quite apart from the vivid picture of the cosmopolitan sea-faring community of Alexandria.

Scattered amongst such gems of private correspondence are several letters to Theophilus referring difficult ecclesiastical matters for his judgment, as well as a number which reveal Synesius' state of mind as he considered his possible consecration. But perhaps most interesting are the seven letters to Hypatia. Hypatia, according to Socrates (vii.15), was the most outstanding philosopher of her time, who pursued the Platonism of Plotinus and attracted pupils from afar. The daughter of an eminent mathematician, she incurred no hint of slander, even though she was constantly in masculine society. Synesius' letters indicate the degree of philosophic friendship and devotion she elicited from her pupils, and even in the sad days of his episcopacy, when everything seemed against him and his three sons had died, it was to the pagan, Hypatia, that he turned for comfort.[174] Earlier in his life, he appeals to her judgment before publishing some of his works.[175]

Synesius' treatises show a wide range of literary skills, and a variety of interests. The *De regno* is the speech addressed to Arcadius on behalf of his fellow-citizens; the *De providentia* an allegorical retelling of the myth of Osiris and Typhos which provides allusive comment on the current political and moral situation at the court in Constantinople. After his return,[176] he composed a humorous sophistic speech *In Praise of Baldness*, a deliberate counterweight to the treatise of Dio Chrysostom in praise of hair; a more serious work on *Dreams*, which with the *Hymns* gives us most of our insight into his philosophical and theological position; and the *Dion*, a fascinating comment on his way of life and the relationship between philosophical and sophistic ideals. A couple of Orations on the political situation in the Pentapolis,[177] and some fragments of homilies, complete the list of his extant works, apart from the interesting description of the 'astrolabe' which he sent to Paeonius with the instrument itself. Exactly what this, or indeed what the hydroscope was which he asked Hypatia to send him in *Epistle* 15, has been the subject of much inconclusive discussion. Here it is sufficient to comment that he almost invites comparison with Jefferson, the all-round eighteenth-century gentleman who combined literary pursuits with a practical and inventive interest: Synesius even constructed a machine to hurl long-distance missiles at the enemy.[178]

From the above survey, it should be apparent that Synesius' life and works are likely to provide contrasts and insights in relation to several themes raised in earlier chapters. (i) Like Eusebius, he addressed the emperor: how do their approaches compare? (ii) Unlike Gregory Nazianzen, he achieved a balance between rhetoric and philosophy: how did he reach his position of relaxed and active humanism? (iii) He hovers between Christianity and Hellenism, finding no need for commitment and discerning no essential opposition between the two: why did he not feel the same conflicts as the Cappadocians? Each of these themes is worth pursuing further.

(i) The traditions of panegyric had an effect upon Eusebius' attitude to Constantine which we can only regard as unpalatable (even if understandable in the circumstances). By contrast, Synesius' speech is openly critical of the situation of Arcadius' court, so much so that there was a time when scholars believed it could not be the actual words he spoke in the presence of the emperor, a view successfully demolished by Lacombrade.[179] Synesius' speech, no less than Eusebius', draws on longstanding traditions and conventions, but he uses them to present a picture of the ideal king, with implied condemnation of Arcadius' present style and policies. His indebtedness to Dio Chrysostom's *Orations on Kingship*[180] is very considerable, but it is not slavish. What he does, in effect, is to enter current debates at court about certain policy matters, in particular voicing the position of Aurelian against the infiltration of Goths to high places; but he does this in the guise of exhorting the young emperor to emulate the philosopher-king who first rules over his own passions (chs. 6 and 22), the shepherd-king (chs. 5–6) whose concern for and leadership of his flock is personal, open and direct, the father-king, whose presence is the image of God on earth, whose calling is to imitate the divine, especially in his goodness and providential care for his people (chs. 4–5). Synesius concludes from this ideal that Arcadius should abandon his isolated and protected luxury, open himself to suppliants, ban the foreigners and lead a citizen-army in defence of the state – a somewhat unrealistic and anachronistic plea in the conditions of the early Byzantine world. Yet clearly Synesius, so far from being a subservient flatterer like Eusebius, is a bold and open critic. The difference lies partly in the different historical contexts, but is also attributable to Synesius' very real veneration for the classical ideals of Homer and Plato.

(ii) This desire to reinvigorate contemporary society with the ideals of the past also explains the fact that he admits no division between philosophy and rhetoric. According to *Epistle* 154, Synesius wrote the *Dion* in the face of personal charges that he was faithless to philosophy because he professed grace and harmony of style and enjoyed literature. Synesius retorts with an attack on contemporary philosophers who refused to take any pleasure in beauty and harmony of speech or life. 'I know I am a man, and neither a god that I should be adamant in the face of every pleasure, nor a brute that I should take delight in the pleasures of the body.' What passionate attachment is more free from passion, he asks, than a life spent in literature? Included in his attacks are certain 'foreign philosophers' who are particularly extreme in their asceticism, take no part in public life and become unsociable in their haste to release themselves from nature. In spite of opinions to the contrary,[181] it seems impossible, considering the period in which Synesius was writing, not to identify this as a criticism of the excesses of Christian monks. Synesius in this treatise stands for the Hellenic 'mean' in contrast with all current extremism. In Kingsley's novel *Hypatia*, he is aptly described by Raphael as 'the only Christian from whom he had ever heard a hearty laugh'.[182]

If he professes philosophy but refuses to subscribe to fashionable extremist ideals, much the same is true of the sophistic way of life. The lawyer and rhetorician, growing fat and prosperous on the rewards of his services, or composing elegant speeches with no content, were equally to be criticized. In his letters, Synesius begs his friends to withdraw from ambitious careers and devote themselves to philosophy. This does not mean a lack of patriotism or a total withdrawal from public service: for philosophy should be the crown of rhetoric, and no other science will be able to govern affairs as well as this philosophy. Synesius regrets that in his day circumstances afforded no room for the philosopher to control the state. He idealizes the philosopher-king.[183] Dio Chrysostom provides his model, because even as a philosopher he retained his sophistry, his linguistic elegance and his political influence with Trajan.

Synesius, the self-styled philosopher, both enjoyed sophistic exercises (the *Encomium on Baldness* is a classic of this type), and involved himself in public life. He anachronistically believed that the philosopher had a contribution to make to society. Even though he bitterly regrets his loss of leisure when faced with the episcopacy, he liked to think of himself as a philosopher-priest.[184]

(iii) Synesius' theology is particularly fascinating. Apart from the *Hymns* and the treatise on *Dreams*, there is little direct discussion of theological or even philosophical matters, but his unguarded allusions give us some important clues. Even his *Encomium on Baldness* has theological comments: baldness is related to the divine . . . a shrine to the God through whom we have wisdom; whereas hair has lack of reason, brute tendencies and all that is opposed to God – it is an excrescence of imperfect matter.[185] In the political works, we find the old monotheistic idealism of the

empire, with a general belief in God's providential favour when
men behave themselves. His theism has precious little to differentiate it from that of popular Christianity, though there is no
hint of specific Christian beliefs and much use of pagan myths, at
least in their literary forms. The *Dion*, which certainly has no claim
to be regarded as a Christian work, reveals that in spite of the
criticisms noted, Synesius shared with pagan and Christian philosophers the ideal of freedom from passion and contemplation of
the divine. In his treatise on *Dreams*, he shows more tendencies of a
pagan Neoplatonic nature, a fascination with the possibility of
divination and prediction, theoretically based on a doctrine of the
sympathy of the whole universe which is one organism. He argues
for the importance of dreams as a way of ascent to God for the soul,
provided the imaginative faculty is tempered by philosophical
discrimination. But the *Hymns* indicate how little difference he
saw between his lifelong philosophic theism and his Christianity.
Whether he uses Christian or pagan imagery and devotional
language, or a mixture of the two, his piety is much the same. There
is no abrupt transition in style or content or atmosphere. Whether
addressing God as 'Master of the thunderbolt, higher than the gods'
as in pagan hymns to Zeus, or as 'Source of the Son, Form of the
Father', or 'God, the glorious Son of the eternal God', the same basic
spirituality is present, and when the Neoplatonic Trinity becomes
a Christian Trinity is by no means clear.[186]

If put to the test, Synesius would have been condemned for 'that
eclectic farrago of his which he calls philosophic Christanity'.[187]
There does not seem to have been any clear break in his thinking,
but rather an evolution; perhaps even that was not a linear
development, since the *Hymns* all seem to date from approximately the same time, whether using philosophic or Christian
phraseology.[188] Synesius never seems to have acquired the usual
Christian temper of 'exclusiveness'. Most of the Fathers, for all that
they embraced classical education, felt the need to carry on the
tradition that Christianity was different, distinctive and incapable
of syncretistic compromise; in theory, if not in practice, paganism
must be confronted, not taken into partnership. As a bishop,
Synesius acquired the ecclesiastical habit of objecting to deviations
from orthodoxy and proper moral standards, and he had a healthy
respect for his office as a priest of God.[189] But this was continuous
with his patriotism: even in the early philosophical work *De
providentia*, he says of the Arian Goths that they bring innovations
into 'our religion', clearly identifying himself with official
orthodoxy in spite of his largely pagan outlook. The Roman empire

had always been a 'divine institution' which owed its success and stability to the gods or God, and to that extent deviation and anti-social conduct were alike politically intolerable. Theologically, Synesius himself required the possibility of honest dissent, but divisiveness he could not countenance.

Before he took up his ecclesiastical duties, Synesius made it clear exactly where he stood:

> For my own part, I can never persuade myself that the soul is of more recent origin than the body. Never would I admit that the world and the parts which make it up must perish. The resurrection, which is an object of common belief, is nothing for me but a sacred and mysterious allegory. . . . The philosophic mind, albeit the discerner of truth, admits the employment of falsehood, . . . the false may be beneficial to the populace, and the truth injurious to those not strong enough to gaze steadfastly on the radiance of real being. . . . I can take over the holy office on condition that I may prosecute philosophy at home, and spread legends abroad. . . .[190]

For Synesius, the real distinction was not between Christianity and paganism, but between philosophy and popular myths. His con-version to philosophy was arguably the most significant turning point in his life.[191] Perhaps he was nearer the mark than other Christians could admit, either because they were bred in the old exclusiveness or because their attitudes were moulded by a radical conversion experience. Such was not Synesius' way. To state whether one thinks Synesius was really a Christian or not, says more about one's own understanding of Christianity than about Synesius himself.

Chapter Five

The Literature of Christological Controversy

I. Introduction: Eustathius

The problems of christology were a direct result of the Arian controversy and its outcome at Nicaea. Two different ways of meeting the Arian position produced two different christological traditions which came into conflict. The tensions between these two types of christology have left a continuing mark on subsequent church history, for Monophysite and Nestorian churches survive in the Middle East to this day, and in the West, Chalcedon has proved less a solution than the classic definition of a problem which constantly demands further elucidation.

Nicaea changed the whole theological landscape. God's transcendent Being, immutable and impassible, eternal and underivative, was an assumption which went unquestioned by all parties. Prior to Arius most theologians presupposed a hierarchy of Being whereby this transcendent unoriginate God was linked on the ladder of existence with his creation through the mediating Logos: in Platonic terms, the One-Many or Indefinite Dyad provided the link between the Many and the ultimate One.[1] As a result of the Arian controversy, the hierarchy was destroyed and a radical distinction was established between the Creator and everything which derived its being from his creative activity; or, to put it another way, the question was pressed on which side of the fundamental divide between the self-existent and the contingently existent was the Logos to be found. The Arian answer was perfectly clear and unequivocal. So was the opposing Nicene answer, but it was not for that reason any more satisfactory. One way or another, the Platonic hierarchal scheme had to be abandoned. New questions changed the ground of debate.

Arius insisted that the Being of the Logos was derivative and contingent and therefore mutable. He supported his contention by appeal to scriptural texts which attributed weakness or fallibility to Jesus Christ, that is, the Logos. The basic presupposition with which he worked was that the Logos was the subject of all the human experiences of Jesus.

The Nicene formula insisted that the Being of the Logos was not derivative, but in every respect of the same transcendent nature as the self-existent God. The supporters of such a claim were inevitably confronted with extreme difficulties in dealing with the mediatorial activity of the Logos in creation and incarnation. The Logos could no longer belong to both sides of the divide and provide the link between Creator and creature. Being immutable and impassible, he could not become involved in the world of 'becoming' and change and destruction. How then were the opponents of Arius to account for those texts which ascribe weakness and fallibility, and indeed passion and death, to the incarnate Logos? The christological problem was bound to become the next major issue.

We have already explored the answer given by Athanasius. The Logos himself did not experience weakness, suffering and death in his essential Being; it was the flesh he took which was subject to these human limitations. It might look as though Athanasius was 'dividing the Christ', but in fact, as we have seen, his solution was ultimately nearer to docetism. The Logos remained the subject of the incarnation, but the incarnation became less then fully real: 'he imitated our condition.'[2] There is a sense in which the heresy of Apollinarius can be seen as the logical extreme of Athanasius' position; and the fully developed Alexandrian christology found in the works of Cyril is its mature outcome. In this christological tradition, the Logos is seen as existing in two states, a pre-existent eternal transcendent state, and a voluntarily accepted incarnate state in which he allows himself fleshly experience, even though in his essential nature he is incapable of development, addition or change. The Logos remains the essential subject; the flesh is 'impersonal humanity' and the reality of the human nature of Jesus Christ is in constant danger of being submerged.

Another approach to the problem emerged during the fourth century, and produced a theological tradition associated with Antioch. This may have had roots in earlier Antiochene trends, in the christology of Paul of Samosata, for example; but there are some grounds for the view that it only developed as a response to the christological problems posed by Arianism. The alternative way of answering Arius was to assert that the transcendent Logos could not in reality be the subject of the incarnate experiences and to attribute weakness, fallibility and passion to 'the Man' he assumed. The difference between these two kinds of thought, Alexandrian and Antiochene, is often expressed in the formulae *Word-Flesh Christology* and *Word-Man Christology*. These terms are useful up to a point, but the two sides tended to use overlapping terminology and not stick to a consistent set of terms. It is perhaps better, therefore, to see the distinction as two different answers to the question, 'Who was the subject of the incarnate experiences of Jesus Christ?[3] For the Alexandrians the subject remained the Word, who though transcendent accommodated himself to the conditions of human nature; for the Antiochenes, the corollary of Nicaea was that the Word could not possibly be regarded as the immediate subject of the incarnate experiences without a blasphemous denigration of his essential divinity. Naturally this produced a dualistic christology in which the unity of the Christ as the Word incarnate was dangerously undermined. Neither christological tradition was without its difficulties.

The fact that these patterns of approach to the christological problem emerged explicitly out of the new theological demands of the post-Nicene situation is suggested by the case of Eustathius of Antioch. Various vague accounts of Eustathius' deposition leave the historian guessing to some extent, but the consistent witness of the sources is that he was violently opposed to Arianism, and unable to compromise in the period of *rapprochement* after Nicaea.[4] Many fragments of his writings have survived because over a century later Theodoret of Cyrrhus was able to appeal to Eustathius as a hero of the anti-Arian struggle accepted by both sides in the later christological debate. Eustathius was at loggerheads with Eusebius of Caesarea, and suffered the same fate as that other uncompromising anti-Arian Athanasius. It is hardly surprising that his vehement defence of Nicaea was widely interpreted as Sabellian, and Antioch lost its bishop, as Alexandria did some years later, in the reaction against the Nicene position.

Traditionally, then, Eustathius' error was regarded as trinitarian rather then christological. In this century, however, the idea has gained currency that Eustathius stands in a continuous Syrian tradition providing the link between later Antiochenes like Theodore of Mopsuestia and the earlier heretic Paul of Samosata.[5] His trinitarian ideas, it is said, tend in a Sabellian direction, the Logos being treated as divine 'energy' rather than as a 'person', and his christology is exaggeratedly dualistic to the point of adoptionism; furthermore, his only complete surviving work is a homily on the Witch of Endor directed against Origen's allegorical exegesis, another feature which anticipates views characteristic of the Antiochenes.

Careful editing and examination of the fragments, however, has suggested that this judgment is only partially true.[6] Eustathius' trinitarian views seem perfectly in line with those of his orthodox contemporaries (Athanasius, for example), and he does not criticize or repudiate allegorical method as such. Certainly some of his christological formulae foreshadow those of the later Antiochenes, but dualistic statements predominate among the fragments because a high proportion were preserved in Dyophysite collections (florilegia). Besides they are drawn largely from his anti-Arian writings, and elsewhere he often affirms the unity of the Saviour. It was the Arian controversy which turned Eustathius into an 'Antiochene'.

'Why do they think it important to show that Christ assumed a body without a soul?' he asks.[7] This was a perceptive question for so early a stage in the discussion. Like Didymus later, he saw that the presence of a human soul in the Christ would avoid the difficulties of attributing creaturely weakness and fallibility to the divine Logos. The Logos, he insisted, remained impassible and omnipresent; but the Man he assumed, the temple he built for himself, was born, was crucified, was raised, and glorified. Athanasius in a sense 'divided the natures' to counter Arius, but Eustathius came much closer to treating the Man rather than the Logos as Christ's personal subject, so avoiding the docetic tendencies of Athanasius' approach. 'Not in appearance and supposition but in very reality God was clothed with a whole man, assuming him perfectly.'[8] To insist on the integrity of Christ's humanity was one way of meeting the Arian challenge.

Athanasius and Eustathius, then, were the classic defenders of Nicaea; bishop of Antioch and bishop of Alexandria, they shared the distinction of being deposed for their resolute opposition to Arianism. Almost incidentally, they mapped out two different christological approaches as part of their response to the Arian challenge, each of which was to develop into a distinctive christological tradition in the succeeding period. The extreme forms of each christology were condemned, possibly through exaggerated misinterpretations by the opposing side. In the persons of Cyril and Nestorius, the two traditions came into open and damaging conflict, from which neither side emerged the victor. Meanwhile in the generation after Nicaea, the two ways of approach were represented by Apollinarius of Laodicea and Diodore of Tarsus.

II. Apollinarius and Diodore

1. Apollinarius and the Alexandrian tradition

It can be misleading to identify the two types of christology with geographical locations. In a later period, Syriac Christianity was divided between Nestorian and Monophysite groups, and Antioch had its Monophysite bishops just as did Alexandria. Even in the Nestorian controversy when Antioch and the Oriental bishops seem solidly identified with the 'two natures' christology, Cyril had his supporters in the city and among Syriac-speaking bishops and monks. In fact, Syria was the scene of the first round in the conflict, for the Laodicea with which Apollinarius is connected was a Syrian sea-port not far from Antioch; Antioch was where Jerome heard Apollinarius lecture in 373; and it was in Antioch that Apollinarius took the step of consecrating Vitalis, so initiating the Apollinarian schism.

It is natural to associate Apollinarius with Alexandria, however, for his father originated from there, settling in Laodicea as a teacher; and all our sources testify to Apollinarius' friendship with Athanasius. This seems to have been initiated in 346 when Athanasius was returning to Alexandria from one of his periods of exile; the bishop of Laodicea, having refused to receive him to communion himself, excommunicated Apollinarius for doing so. From then on Apollinarius seems to have headed a separated group of loyal Nicenes in Laodicea, and was eventually consecrated their bishop. His lasting friendship with Athanasius is a well-attested fact. There was an extensive correspondence between the two, and Athanasius seems to have consulted Apollinarius on theological points, apparently even submitting to him the draft of his *Epistle to Epictetus* for comment.[9] As far as Athanasius was concerned, Apollinarius was a staunch supporter of Nicene orthodoxy, and for most of his life that remained Apollinarius' reputation.

It is also natural to associate Apollinarius with Alexandria because of the close links between his theological stance and what became the typical Alexandrian christology. After his views had been condemned a number of Apollinarian treatises were circulated under others' names, that of Athanasius being one of the most important. Cyril of Alexandria quite unwittingly took much of his christological vocabulary and theology from these works, thinking that they came from his authoritative predecessor. A notable example is the confession of faith addressed to the Emperor Jovian.[10] One of Apollinarius' followers, Polemon, quoted this letter as from his master, so confirming the impression given by its style and contents that its superscription is fraudulent. This confession follows a somewhat credal pattern (its title suggests that it was an exposition of the Nicene Creed), affirming that the same one is pre-existent and incarnate, and describing the Son of God as the one begotten before all ages, and at the end of the ages born according to the flesh from Mary for our salvation. This double γέννησις (one Greek word serves for begetting and giving birth), and the unity of subject in the Nicene creed, were both to become typical of Cyril's standpoint. So were statements like 'the same one is Son of God κατὰ πνεῦμα (according to the Spirit) and Son of Man κατὰ σάρκα' (according to the flesh), or 'one Son has not two natures but one'. Most notorious, however, is the catch-phrase μία φύσις τοῦ Θεοῦ Λόγου σεσαρκωμένη (one enfleshed nature of the God-Word), which was to become a slogan for Cyril's party. It is hardly surprising that the Antiochenes at first took Cyril's position to be Apollinarian. Later it will be worth considering in what ways Cyril's christology differed from that of Apollinarius. Both of them claimed to be upholding the teaching of Athanasius.[11]

Reconstructing what Apollinarius actually taught is a very complicated process, even though study has been facilitated by Lietzmann's careful edition of the fragments. As already noted, the Apollinarians secured the survival of a number of works under false names. Inevitably there is some doubt as to which may be confidently attributed to Apollinarius himself; two pseudo-Athanasian pieces, the *Quod unus sit Christus* and the *De Incarnatione Dei Verbi*, Lietzmann attributed to his followers. Besides this there are a considerable number of fragments, mostly preserved in anti-Apollinarian works like Gregory Nyssen's systematic refutation of Apollinarius' *Apodeixis*; sometimes it is hard to decide whether a purported fragment is a quotation or a comment on the character of his teaching, especially when contradictory statements are found elsewhere. Apart from this we are dependent upon reports, and given the possibility that both his friends and his enemies may have misrepresented his teaching, it is no wonder that there are a number of unsettled issues of interpretation. It can be stated without too much fear of contradiction that Apollinarius thought of the incarnation as the Logos taking the place of the human mind in Jesus Christ, but the corollaries of this theory, precisely how and why it was worked out, whether this was the central feature of his theology – all these matters raise more difficulties.

2. Problems of interpretation

The first problem concerns the situation out of which Apollinarius' teaching arose. In spite of his well-known opposition to Arianism, there is a basic christological similarity in that both assumed that the Logos replaced the human soul in the Christ. Did Apollinarius get his ideas from his opponents? The little treatise *Kata meros pistis* (The faith in detail) is largely concerned with trinitarian questions, but there are several paragraphs which discuss the incarnation. Here Apollinarius is not only opposed to those who attach human things to the deity as if they belonged to him, things like progress, sufferings, attaining to glory and so on (clearly the Arians are in view here), but he also criticizes those who divide human things from the Godhead, emphasizing in his treatment the uniting of Godhead with flesh.[12] He states that 'if anyone calls him Son of God as being filled with deity, not as being begotten from divinity, he denies the Logos . . . and destroys knowledge of God.'[13] He outlines a view of the σάρκωσις (enfleshment) of the Logos which involves God living on earth while remaining the same, filling everything and at the same time 'being mixed (συγκεκράμενος) with flesh'.[14] Whoever he is criticizing does not agree with this idea of God being made flesh but instead attaches a man to God.[15] He can hardly now be referring to Arius. What he has in mind appears to be the so-called Antiochene christology, for again in the *De Unione* he warns against denying the Godhead by speaking of the 'whole man'.[16] When we notice that in his *First Letter to Dionysius*[17] he expresses concern about contemporary followers of Paul of Samosata, and that he certainly wrote a treatise against Diodore, the suspicion grows that one factor in his thinking was profound opposition to the kind of christological development found in Eustathius and actively propagated in his own generation by Diodore.

This view certainly seems to make better sense than the extraordinary idea that he poached his main idea from the Arian opposition. What is much more likely is that he and the Arians shared presuppositions which were very widespread, and Apollinarius made them explicit under quite different pressures. However, it may be that the influence of his opposition to the Antiochenes has been exaggerated. There are reasons for thinking that the two sides did not come into direct conflict until after Apollinarius' condemnation, and we have yet to discuss at what point Diodore's christological views had developed and become notorious. Might some other situation have stimulated Apollinarius' thinking?

In an interesting study by Mühlenberg, Apollinarius' thought has been set against a quite different background.[18] Beginning from the *Apodeixis*, he argues that Apollinarius' prime concern was to contrast Christ, the θεὸς ἔνσαρκος (God enfleshed) with the ἄνθρωπος ἔνθεος (man inspired) or divine man through whom knowledge of God was mediated in the philosophical tradition. From this philosophical tradition Apollinarius accepted that God was νοῦς (Mind), and that salvation was knowledge of God; from the Christian tradition he accepted that knowledge of God came through the incarnation. Thus he developed further the 'revelation' aspect of Athanasius' soteriology. His emphasis on the fact that the divine mind was enfleshed arose from his sense that what Christianity had to offer was truth, direct and genuine knowledge of God. Inevitably he reacted to christologies of the Antiochene type as a betrayal of Christianity to Jews and pagans. For him Jesus was to be absolutely identified with God. To compromise that identification by introducing a human mind was to undermine the distinct truth which Christianity claimed. When worked out in detail with its attendant criticisms of other expositions of Apollinarius' whole standpoint, this interpretation of Apollinarius' theology has not proved entirely convincing, but there are enough hints in the fragments to suggest that this motive may have played some part in Apollinarius' thinking.

Nevertheless we can hardly doubt that the Arian controversy provided the main context within which Apollinarius' basic ideas arose. His views were in many ways a natural development from the basic principles and assumptions of Athanasius' theology. Athanasius had argued that only God could save, and this is a frequent refrain of Apollinarius'.[19] Athanasius had argued that only one who was truly Son of God could reveal God to man, and Apollinarius shared that viewpoint: 'The very man who speaks to us the things of the Father is God the Creator of the ages.'[20] Athanasius had insisted that redemption depended on the Logos being ἄτρεπτος (immutable); likewise Apollinarius argues that it is only because the Logos is ἄτρεπτος and ἀπαθής (impassible) that the fallibility and passibility of humanity is overcome and salvation achieved. Athanasius never seems to have faced the question whether Christ had a human soul or mind; in Apollinarius' time, however, this question was gradually coming into the open, the christological implications of Arius' views being increasingly recognized. Apollinarius assumed that every mind was an αὐτοκράτωρ, a self-moving, self-governing will, and he came to the conclusion that two such entities could not exist in one person.[21] Apollinarius also assumed that the human mind was τρέπτος, changeable, fallible and liable to sin, and he found a mixture of the ἄτρεπτος and the τρέπτος impossible to conceive. They would be bound to conflict with one another.[22]

Given these assumptions, it is hardly surprising that he interpreted Athanasius' teaching as implying a denial of a human mind or soul in the Christ. Salvation depended upon the incarnation of the unchangeable power of divinity. 'The human race is not saved by the assumption of a mind and a whole man, but by the taking of flesh . . . An ἄτρεπτος νοῦς (immutable Mind) was needed which would not fail through weaknes of understanding.'[23] Maybe opposition to the developing Antiochene christology helped to focus his thinking, but his basic understanding was long since framed. Interestingly wnough the evidence suggests that Apollinarius not merely accepted but approved of both the *Tomus ad Antiochenos* and Athanasius' later christological writings, a fact which both confirms the view that these writings were directed not against Apollinarius but others, and enhances the possibility that Athanasius himself did not interpret the christological language of these documents as affirmations of the presence of a *human* mind or soul in the Christ.[24] Even Apollinarius could say that the Saviour did not have a σῶμα ἄψυχον (a body without soul) or ἀναίσθετον (without sense) or ἀνόητον (without mind), in the same breath asserting that he did not assume a human mind;[25] for he thought of the Logos as providing the body's intelligence and vitality.

The second problem of interpretation concerns Apollinarius' anthropology. Rufinus suggested that Apollinarius began by teaching that Christ 'assumed only a body and not a soul at all', but that in the course of controversy he shifted his ground and 'said that he did possess a soul, but only on its animating and not its rational side, and that to supply the place of a rational soul there was the Word of God.'[26] It will be recalled from the section on Nemesius that contemporary Platonism commonly recognized a distinction between the rational and irrational parts of the soul; Nemesius, however, mentions Plotinus and Apollinarius as protagonists of the view that the soul and the mind are two different things, man being composed of three elements, body, soul and mind. Others like Theodoret[27] set out to disprove the 'trichotomist' view of man as a way of confuting Apollinarius. The evidence is therefore quite strong that Apollinarius' anthropology did not follow the usual dualism of soul and flesh.

To complicate things further the fragments contradict one
another. Some imply a dichotomist soul-flesh or spirit-flesh
position, others the more controversial trichotomist analysis. The
fact of the matter seems to be that a specific anthropological theory
is not central to Apollinarius' thought. He basically thinks of man
as a νοῦς ἔνσαρκος (a mind enfleshed) or as a composite of πνεῦμα and
σάρξ (spirit and flesh)[28] deriving his various different sets of
terminology from the language of St Paul. Paul himself, while most
often seeming dualistic almost to the point of Gnosticism, can
also speak in what appear to be trichotomist terms. Apollinarius
adopts the apostle's language. A man is a νοῦς ἔνσαρκος, the
Logos is also νοῦς ἔνσαρκος. That is what it meant for him to be in the
likeness of man. 'Because of this he was man; for man is a νοῦς ἐν
σαρκί (mind in flesh) according to Paul.' 'Paul calls the last (Adam)
life-giving Spirit.' 'The Christ having God as spirit, that is, mind,
together with soul and body, is reasonably called the "man from
heaven".' 'If man is composed of three and the Lord is man, the Lord
is of three, spirit, soul and body, but he is "heavenly man and living
Spirit".'[29] Precise anthropological terms were not Apollinarius'
prime concern; his main interest was to contrast his view of the θεὸς
ἔνσαρκος (God enfleshed) with the more generally acceptable idea of
an ἄνθρωπος ἔνθεος (man inspired). Even Jews and pagans could
stomach the latter, but it was inadequate because it would imply a
human mind enlightened by wisdom (as is the case with other
men), and so the arrival of Christ would not be an ἐπιδημία θεοῦ
(God's stay on earth) but the birth of a man.[30]

So we turn to a third problem. Paul speaks of a 'heavenly man'
and Apollinarius, as we have just seen, adopts his terminology. His
ancient critics represent him as having taught that the Logos' flesh
pre-existed from the beginning, and much effort was expended in
confuting this view. However, modern studies of Apollinarius,
notably those of Raven and Prestige,[31] have asserted that at this
point Apollinarius has been misrepresented; this was a view held
by some of his more extreme followers, but not by Apollinarius
himself. Gregory of Nyssa misinterpreted what he wrote.

Now it is true that Apollinarius took the virgin birth very
seriously and frequently spoke of the Son of God receiving flesh
from Mary. He also specifically denies the heavenly origin of the
flesh.[32] Yet he did apparently make a good deal of the 'man from
heaven' in the *Apodeixis*, contrasting him with the man from
earth, and he seems to speak of the man Christ pre-existing as life-
giving Spirit.[33] There are hints that he may have thought of God
having always been in some sense 'enfleshed': thus he is reported to

have said 'God having been ἔνσαρκος (enfleshed) before the ages, afterwards was born through a woman.'[34] One thing he insists on is that the Trinity is three, not four, by implication attributing to his opponents the view that the Trinity was expanded into four by the assumption of the glorified Man. Perhaps then his view of God's changelessness led him to posit the eternal union of Logos and flesh. A passage from the *First Letter to Dionysius*, however, suggests that the only thing Apollinarius really cared about was the union, and he was not disposed to examine too closely its corollaries: 'we are not afraid of the false charges of those who divide the Lord into two *prosōpa* (persons),' he says; 'if they blaspheme us pretending that in maintaining the evangelical and apostolic unity we say the flesh comes from heaven (we are not afraid), since we read the holy scriptures describing the one from heaven, as Son of Man.' (He alludes to John 3.13.) 'Nor when we say the Son of God was born of a woman can we be blamed for saying that the Word is from earth and not from heaven. We say both, the whole is from heaven through the Godhead and the whole is from woman through the flesh; we do not know division of the one *prosōpon*, nor do we separate the earthly from the heavenly nor the heavenly from the earthly.'[35]

3. The union of Christ

Whatever the problems or implications, the union is Apollinarius' chief concern, and what gives this over-riding importance in his eyes is its soteriological implications. It is not just that Apollinarius has adopted Athanasius' perception that salvation depends upon God remaining ἄτρεπτος (immutable) so as to free man from his sin and mortality; he has reflected upon the problem of mediation. A mediator stands in the middle. The pre-Arian view saw the Logos as standing in the middle by being a link in the chain of Being; but for Apollinarius he is mediator in the sense of being the mean between God and man. The mean between a horse and a donkey is a mule; between white and black is grey, between winter and summer is spring. The mean between God and man is Christ. He is neither wholly man nor wholly God, but a mixture of God and man. He is God by the enfleshed spirit and man by the flesh assumed by God.[36] Thus he is mediator as the one who unites man and God, and it is this new creation, the divine mixture, God and flesh perfected in one nature,[37] that brings θεοποίησις (divinization) and salvation to mankind. Apollinarius is far from being chary of explaining the union in terms of μῖξις (mixture) or σύγκρασις (combination); for him the union is an organic or biological union exactly analogous to the composition of man out of flesh and spirit.[38] The virgin birth is important precisely because it produces a biological freak; there is no male sperm charged with vivifying power – instead there is the descent of the Spirit. So the 'one nature' did not mean for Apollinarius that the Logos took on a new condition of existence (as it would for Cyril), but it meant that Christ is a unique kind of being combining God and man. That is why 'eternal enfleshment' is an idea not wholly foreign to the tendencies of his thought. Nor is it strange to find the idea of the flesh being *homoousios* (of one substance) with God: 'Flesh did not become an addition to the Godhead by grace, but it is συνουσιωμένη (united in *ousia*) with the Godhead and σύμφυτος (innate, natural) to it.' 'His flesh gives us life because it is συνουσιωμένη with the Godhead.'[39] (This union of *ousia* was what offended Diodore more than anything else; his treatise against Apollinarius is called *Contra Synousiastes*). This concept of union may also help to explain Apollinarius' anthropological confusion. For in this unique individual, the Logos is not just the Mind, he is also the life-giving principle – the πνεῦμα ζωοποιοῦν. So whether Apollinarius uses dichotomist or trichotomist language depends upon whether he is thinking of the moral issues at stake (and therefore treating the Logos as νοῦς, Mind), or whether he is concentrating his attention on the imparting of divine life and immortality to man. Far from clearly distinguishing spirit, mind and soul, his only interest really was to establish the organic unity of this unique mediator. This 'compound unity' which he posited meant that Apollinarius did in a sense recognize the two natures (as Theodoret could show in his florilegia) and that for him, unlike the later Eutychians, the flesh was not transformed into divinity,[40] but was united with divinity to form a unique *tertium quid*.

We have noticed several points where Apollinarius' views seem to be derived from scripture; yet Raven and Mühlenberg have each regarded his christology as the culmination of the Hellenic tradition of Christian theology. Broad generalizations of this kind should be treated with caution. If Raven thought the Monophysite type of theology was Hellenic, and regarded the Antiochene 'two natures' christology as representing the more realistic biblical tradition native to Syria, Wigram[41] reversed the assessment, regarding the Dyophysite position as belonging to Greek intellectualism and attributing Monophysitism to the simple Syrian ascetic. Yet there is no doubt that Apollinarius' teaching was highly sophisticated, and Apollinarius himself was a highly cultured intellectual who had received a thoroughly Greek educa-

tion. We should never forget that he and his father remained
schoolteachers though becoming clerics, and that the few details of
his life that we have are connected with his love of the classics. The
first incident that we know anything about was when the two
Apollinarii, father and son, were excluded from communion and
sent to do penance for attending the recital of a hymn in honour of
Dionysus. The incident arose because of their friendship with
Epiphanius the Sophist whose lectures they both attended. Some
thirty years later (AD 360), when the Emperor Julian forbade
Christians to teach pagan literature in schools, the two Apollinarii
published a re-written Bible for school use in the form of Homeric
epics, Euripidean tragedies, comedies like those of Menander,
Pindaric lyrics and Platonic dialogues. All this has been lost; some
have argued that Apollinarius was the author of an extant paraphrase of the Psalms in hexameters, but its authenticity has been
seriously undermined by the most recent critical examination.[42]

One way or another Apollinarius had proved a notable defender
of the faith, against Julian, against Arius. He also wrote thirty books
against Porphyry and many commentaries on scripture. He was a
powerful and respected academic. It was not only Athanasius who
had consulted him; Basil as a young man wrote to enquire about the
meaning of *homoousios* – a correspondence whose authenticity
was doubted in the light of Basil's later embarrassed denials, but has
now been successfully defended by Prestige and de Riedmatten.[43]
Although most attention has inevitably been given to Apollinarius'
christology, his trinitarian views, as expressed in the *Kata meros
pistis* and the Basil correspondence, are not without interest.
Apollinarius succeeds in upholding the *homoousion*, the Trinity as
a whole being the one holy God to whom worship is due, while at
the same time preserving some of the traditional subordinationism
as a defence against Sabellianism. The Son is God because he has
'the Father's Deity naturally' (τὴν πατρικὴν θεότητα φυσικῶς);[44] 'we
say the Trinity is one God, not as knowing one by a combination of
three but thus – what the Father is as source and origin (ἀρχικῶς τε
καὶ γεννητικῶς), this the Son is as image and offspring (εἰκὼν καὶ
γέννημα) of the Father.' He is not the Father's brother.[45] The
Cappadocians were to develop trinitarian thinking away from these
subordinationist tendencies, while almost representing the
homoiousion tradition which Apollinarius repudiated in this
passage.[46]

How was it then that this respected leader of the faithful Nicenes
in Laodicea came to be condemned for heresy? This is the historical
puzzle raised by the career of Apollinarius. He is supposed to have

taught his dangerous doctrines for thirty years without meeting any opposition. He was eventually excluded by the Council of Constantinople (381), though in somewhat ambiguous terms. Prior to that, in the late 370s he had been condemned by the Roman pope and by a local synod at Antioch. As already noted, the idea that earlier in the 360s his condemnation was implied by the *Tomus ad Antiochenos*, or that Athanasius criticized him in the *Epistle to Epictetus*, now seems very unlikely. In the 370s Jerome attended his lectures in Antioch – he was still respected by the wider church. About the same time, however, Epiphanius found dangerous views being expressed in Antioch, at this stage associating them with Vitalis. A few years later he wrote very strongly against Apollinarius in the *Adversus haereses*. Most people, however, were still much more worried by the Arian ascendency and the tragic split among the anti-Arians in Antioch, where the Eustathian party had the support of Rome while the more moderate party was favoured by the majority of Eastern bishops. (Jerome, when in Antioch, was most perplexed as to which party he ought to communicate with.) Basil expressed concern about Apollinarius' activities about this time, but he was less worried by his doctrinal position than by his formation of yet another schismatical group in the Syrian capital. Even after his condemnation Apollinarius was accorded great respect by his critics for his life and his scholarship, and clearly he enjoyed the support of many Nicenes almost until the Nicene cause emerged triumphant. Apart from Epiphanius' criticisms, it was not until after 381 that energetic refutations of his doctrine were produced by the two Gregories of Cappadocia, Gregory Nazianzen in his letters to Cledonius, and Gregory Nyssen in his *Antirrheticus*, a point-by-point refutation of Apollinarius' *Apodeixis*.

4. Diodore of Tarsus

Another critic of Apollinarius, Diodore of Tarsus, was more local and more directly involved to the extent that he may have provided some of the grist for Apollinarius' mill. They must have been close contemporaries, Apollinarius probably being somewhat the older man; for Diodore became bishop of Tarsus just as Apollinarius was being rejected, and Apollinarius seems then to have been well into his sixties. Though sharply divided in their christology, in other ways they had a number of similarities. Both seem to have been well educated in the classics, for Diodore apparently studied at Athens as a young man. Like Apollinarius, he used his learning to confute paganism – both apparently wrote lengthy tomes against

Porphyry, and Diodore is said to have written on many other philosophical topics, astronomy, providence, first principles, the elements, and so on. Both were involved in the struggle against Julian; for if Apollinarius foiled him with his massive literary productions, the sources attribute heroic acts to Diodore when Julian settled on Antioch and began his programme of re-establishing pagan rites. Julian himself confessed that he found Diodore a great thorn in his side:

> Diodore, a charlatan priest of the Nazarene ... is clearly a sharp-witted sophist of that rustic creed. ... For he sailed to Athens to the detriment of the public welfare, rashly taking to philosophy and literature, and arming his tongue with rhetorical devices against the heavenly gods.

Julian went on to suggest that Diodore's pitifully wasted condition was a sign not of his philosophic habits (referring to his asceticism), but of the punishment of the gods.[47] It is difficult to reconcile such reports with Jerome's somewhat disparaging remarks suggesting that Diodore was an inferior imitator of Eusebius of Emesa and 'unacquainted with literature'.[48]

So Diodore, like Apollinarius, seems to have been advanced in secular learning and to have confronted paganism. Both also confronted heresy, Arianism and Sabellianism being enemies they had in common – indeed, Diodore's trinitarian teaching seems to have had a remarkable similarity to that of Apollinarius with its tendency towards subordinationism.[49] Both also made a distinctive contribution to the musical life of the Christian community; for Apollinarius' sacred songs became popular for festivals and were even sung by men at their work and women at the loom, while Diodore introduced the practice of antiphonal psalm-singing, dividing the choir into two groups.[50] Both were steeped in the scriptures and both produced biblical commentaries characterized by economy of explanation and lack of speculative allegory.[51]

It was Diodore, however, who acquired the greater reputation in this particular area. Most of Diodore's life was spent in a monastery near Antioch, and there he exercised a profound influence on two outstanding figures of the next generation, John Chrysostom and Theodore of Mopsuestia. The most important thing Diodore seems to have done was to lay the foundations of biblical exegesis which enabled one pupil to develop his great work of scriptural commentary, becoming known as 'The Interpreter', and the other to earn his great name for exegetical preaching.

Some fragments of Diodore's commentaries have been preserved in the Catenae, but the work of collecting, editing and publishing them has not yet been effectively carried out. There is continuing debate about the authenticity of the available material, and considerable confusion between extracts attributed to Diodore and extracts attributed to Theodore. The general lines of Diodore's approach seem fairly clear, however; he insisted primarily on the 'historical' dimension of the text, and rejected excessive allegorizing. His main concern was elucidation of the actual words and sentences of scripture, providing etymologies, trying to discern the 'scriptural' sense of words by comparing texts, looking at the context and sequences of thought, paraphrasing to bring out the meaning. His detractors found his work prosaic and unexciting. However, he did not abandon the traditional view that the Old Testament had a prophetic sense, that an action or event might be a 'type' pointing beyond itself to fulfilment in Christ. What he repudiated was the elaborate and artificial interpretation of every verbal detail according to imaginative allegorical symbols. What he emphasized was the importance of taking the factual reference of the text seriously. Altogether Diodore does not seem to have gone far beyond the commonsense practice of many exegetes in this period, and parallels to his methods and comments can be traced in many contemporaries not associated with the Antiochene tradition, people like Eusebius of Caesarea, Eusebius of Emesa, Epiphanius, Basil, occasionally even Gregory of Nyssa though he stood nearer to the Origenist approach. Diodore's successors, especially Theodore, were to develop some of his ideas to extremes; but Diodore himself seems to have concentrated primarily on refining the techniques of explication without calling in question too many traditional assumptions about the christological reference of the whole of scripture. However, in view of the state of the evidence, no assessment can be regarded as entirely authoritative.

Indeed, if the fragmentary character of Apollinarius' work makes reconstruction of his teaching difficult, how much more is this so in the case of Diodore. Of his huge output very little remains, and concerning the reliability of the surviving dogmatic fragments serious doubts have been raised because mostly they come from hostile sources. Fragments in Latin and a few in Greek can be found in the literature of later christological controversy, but nearly all of what has survived has been preserved by Syrian Monophysite writers in their native Syriac. All this material appears to derive ultimately from collections of quotations (florilegia) drawn up by the opponents of the Antiochene theology at the time of the

Nestorian controversy. For the later Monophysites used Cyril's now lost work, *Contra Diodorum et Theodorum*; and Cyril seems not to have consulted the original works of his opponents himself, but to have based his work on previously prepared florilegia. These, it has been suggested, originally came from Apollinarians who had tampered with the material to blacken Diodore's name.[52] The basis of that final claim seems little more than speculation, and most recent discussions have assumed the authenticity of the fragments, if only because the terminology used has not been adapted to conform with the later formulae of the Antiochene school – in other words, Diodore's christology as portrayed in the fragments is distinctive and therefore not likely to have been falsified.[53] Yet doubts remain; obviously selection will have lifted his more controversial remarks out of context, and a complete picture of the basic shape and motives of his theological position is unlikely to be obtainable. Furthermore, the majority of the extracts are drawn from his work *Against the Synousiasts*, so that they are likely to reflect strong reaction against Apollinarius and not necessarily give a balanced view of Diodore's own theology. Access to the extant fragments is less straightforward than is the case for Apollinarius, but they have been collected and published in periodical articles, the Syriac being supplied with French or German translation.[54]

5. Diodore's christology

The difficulties posed by lack of evidence used to be resolved by the assumption that Diodore was an important representative of the Antiochene school; his doctrine, like his exegesis, was associated with that of his pupil Theodore, though regarded as probably less extreme since his other famous pupil, John Chrysostom, was clearly nearer to the orthodox mainstream. So no one questioned the fact that he was instrumental in developing the Word-Man or 'two natures' christology which Antiochene theologians so determinedly defended in the ensuing christological controversies. A fragment of Cyril complains that having abandoned the Macedonian heresy, Diodore consorted with the orthodox until he fell into another sickness, saying and writing that the one born of the holy virgin from the seed of David was a different Son from the Word of the Father.[55] This summary of his position was taken as typical, and while the question how far he was a 'Nestorian before Nestorius' was repeatedly debated, the generally Antiochene bent of his christological thinking went unchallenged. It was assumed that he must have been the most important of those described by Apollinarius as followers of Paul of Samosata, who divided the

Christ and taught 'two Sons'. Grillmeier's suggestion[56] that he actually started out from a Word-Flesh type of christology was therefore an innovation which stimulated some strong replies.[57]

Diodore's terminology, argues Grillmeier, is predominantly of the Word-Flesh type. Like Athanasius, he not merely attributes Jesus' increase in age and wisdom to the flesh, not the Logos, but even understands this increase not as human progress but as the gradual imparting of wisdom to the flesh by the Godhead. Never does the human soul of Jesus play a positive role in his christological formulations, nor is it the central point in his debate with Apollinarius, where he is chiefly concerned with the theological dangers of Apollinarius' fusion of Word and flesh into one unique entity. Only gradually did his thinking shift from the Word-Flesh pattern which, Grillmeier suggests, he got from Eusebius of Emesa, a key link in the history of christology. Even when Apollinarianism drove him to modify his thinking, the soul never became a 'theological factor', a positive element in his christological thinking.

It must be admitted that Diodore does speak of the Logos taking flesh rather than 'a man'. Even Cyril accuses Diodore of trying to get away with his Nestorianism by deceptively speaking of 'soulless flesh'.[58] Theodore's formula 'the Man assumed' is never found in the fragments of Diodore, and it is proper that we should be warned against assuming that Diodore was the source of all his pupil's ideas. Yet the fragments we have do assert a christological dualism which Grillmeier, according to his critics, has only succeeded in obscuring. Over-concentration on the Word-Flesh/Word-Man formulae can result in imposing a preconceived framework on the material and so distort the interpreter's perception. The terminology should not be regarded as decisive: representatives of both sides in the christological controversies continued to use 'flesh' and 'man' interchangeably, asserting that this was scriptural usage. Nor is the use or absence of a 'human soul' in a christology an infallible guide to the basic christological principles in operation: Didymus of Alexandria, for example, affirmed the soul but did not develop an Antiochene dualism.[59] Soul or no soul, what makes Diodore's christology Antiochene is his refusal to make the Logos the direct subject of the incarnate experiences. 'The one who is the seed of David', 'the one born of Mary', he it is who suffers and dies and is raised, not the Logos.[60] The Logos did not submit to two γεννήσεις (meaning 'begetting' and 'birth'), one before the ages from God and one from the virgin; rather he built himself a temple in Mary's womb. He was not *mixed* with flesh; for the one who was begotten from the Father before all ages did not receive change or suffering. He was not changed into flesh, he was not crucified, he did not eat or drink or grow tired, but remained incorporeal and undefiled, never departing from his Father's likeness.[61] According to Diodore, 'the likeness of the Father' must be distinguished from 'the likeness of a servant'. Paul speaks not of the God-Word becoming a child from Mary, but of the Man born of Mary being sent for our salvation. The one born of Mary, being really a man, could not have existed before the heaven and the earth; if he did, he was not man. If he was from Abraham, how could he be before Abraham? If he was son of David, how could he be before the ages?[62] Given statements of this kind, it is not surprising that a Monophysite excerpter could parallel Diodore's remarks with those of Leo the blasphemer (meaning the Pope whose *Tome* was canonized at Chalcedon).[63] Diodore did teach a 'two natures' christology with a strongly dualistic basis. Only καταχρηστικῶς (by improper usage) could the son of David be identified with the Son of God.[64] Naturally enough, Diodore's opponents accused him of preaching 'two Sons'; and his reply avoided the point. He asserted that he did not say two sons of David, for he did not say that the God-Word became Son of David; nor did he say two Sons of God, for he did not say two came from God's *ousia*, but that the God-Word dwelt in the seed of David.[65] Diodore failed to see that what worried his critics was precisely that refusal to identify the Son of God with the son of David which suggested two different sons in a loose collocation.

So, on the basis of the surviving fragments, Grillmeier's critics undoubtedly appear to have the stronger case, especially when it is recognized that one important fragment in which Diodore appears to assert the unity of Christ is in fact an attempt to summarize Apollinarian teaching. If at first sight it looked as though Diodore accepted the body-soul analogy as a christological paradigm and affirmed a unity of subject, the same one being from God and in the manger, on the cross and in heaven, such an interpretation cannot be maintained in the light of another fragment where Diodore subjects the body-soul analogy to searching criticism and asserts clearly that '*they* confess that the same one is of God before the ages and of David in the last times . . . *they* confess that the same one is impassible and passible . . .'. In both passages[66] Diodore is stating the Apollinarian position in order to highlight their error. He could not see how any identification could be made between the divine and human subjects.

There is nothing quite like paucity of evidence for producing new theories and lively debates, and when that evidence is clearly slanted and is drawn almost entirely from one work related to one controversy, the potential for producing reconstructions with quite different emphases is greatly enhanced. Of course, Grillmeier admits that Diodore develops a christology of 'distinction' or 'division', but he puts his emphasis on the fact that this is built onto a Word-Flesh framework. What his critics do not seem to have fully grasped is the fact that Grillmeier's main point concerns the background and development of Diodore's ideas rather than their eventual shape. What he is arguing is that Diodore did not start out with a ready-made Word-Man framework inherited from some long-standing Antiochéne tradition. He repudiated Paul of Samosata; direct influence from Eustathius is unlikely in view of the fact that Diodore did not belong to the Eustathian party nor regarded the soul as an important issue. So Grillmeier makes much of the link with Eusebius of Emesa which Jerome mentions, and on this basis posits a development from Logos-Sarx roots. If Grillmeier is right, it reduces the likelihood that Apollinarius developed his views in conscious opposition to Diodore, and there are certainly indications that they did not come into direct doctrinal conflict with one another until the 380s, that is, after Apollinarius had been condemned; thus, while their positions may have hardened because of their reaction to one another, this reaction did not create their differing christologies.

Why then did Diodore develop a christological duality? Grillmeier suggests that the debate with Julian was instrumental. Julian credits Diodore with having invented the divinity of Christ, and elsewhere accuses some who distinguish Jesus Christ from the Logos of evading the issue. 'Was Diodore driven to work out two subjects for christological sayings by the attacks of the pagan emperor?' asks Grillmeier. Certainly the starting-point of Diodore's theology seems to be the need to preserve 'the Godness of God' in the person of the Logos. To identify a man with God incarnate was nothing other than blasphemous, and certainly laid the Christians open to ridicule from philosophers. The God-Word simply could not accept change or suffering, since he was incorporeal, infinite, and in every way shared the divinity of the Father; Diodore complains of the injury done to the Word by putting him in composition with the body.[67] But could it not be that Diodore inherited this concern for the unalterable divinity of the Logos from the debate with the Arians, which was by no means over at the time when his theology must have been developing? His process of reasoning could well have followed the same pattern as that of Eustathius, even though he did not adopt the notion of the human soul as a way of explicitly working out the problems. By implication if not terminology, he made the man descended from David and born of Mary the subject of those incarnate experiences which he could not attribute to the Logos. He had taken a parallel if not identical step, and the Arian controversy is sufficient to account for it. Apollinarius certainly seems to have reacted against a christology which was remarkably similar to that found in the fragments of Diodore, a fact which suggests that Apollinarius himself did not stimulate the development of this line of argument. It arose primarily, it would seem, in the continuing struggle with Arianism.

We can find further confirmation of this. Undoubtedly in many respects Diodore anticipated the 'two natures' christology of Theodore and the later Antiochenes, and this includes treating the union between divine and human in Christ as one not of nature but of grace. There was one Son of God by nature, affirmed Diodore, and the Man from Mary, though by nature from David, was from God by grace; he shared the one Sonship, one glory, one immortality and one worship, by grace. Like his successors Diodore had to defend himself from the charge that he regarded the one from David's seed as no different from the prophets; the prophets, he explained, enjoyed only particular grace in moderate quantities, whereas he had it permanently and was entirely filled with the glory and wisdom of the God-Word.[68] However, even at this point, where Diodore so clearly anticipates the later Antiochenes, his thinking can be seen to be related to earlier opponents of Arius. Like Athanasius, he attributes weakness, mutability, and so on, to the flesh, and to the God-Word things like miracles, exceptional powers, superhuman knowledge; and among the achievements of the Godhead he appears to have reckoned the conquest of temptation.[69] In other words, where the later Antiochenes insisted on the moral victory of the Man, Diodore seems to have followed the older view that only one who was immutable by nature could have remained immutable in the face of temptation. Similarly he treats the progress of the Saviour as the gradual revelation of the Logos, rather than the advancement of human maturity.[70] His thought still moves along the lines of the anti-Arian arguments developed by Athanasius, and thus what offended Diodore about Apollinarian teaching was not its denial of a human soul or mind in the Christ, but its blending of flesh and Word into one entity so compromising the utter divinity of the Logos. Indeed, there is a sense in which each of these antagonists was developing different aspects of Athanasius' answer to Arius.

There is a good deal to be said therefore for accepting Grillmeier's argument that Diodore did not start out with a ready-made Word-Man christology. Yet the surviving fragments, most of which come from his work against Apollinarius, do suggest that, whatever the roots of his theology, it had developed along the lines which in many ways foreshadow the ideas, if not the terminology, of the later Antiochenes, and over and over again in his debate with Apollinarius arguments later used in christological conflicts were anticipated.

Diodore and Apollinarius had a good deal in common, even in the doctrinal area. They shared opposition to Arianism, had similar trinitarian views, appealed to scripture and acted in loyal devotion to Nicene orthodoxy. They even used christological language which to a considerable extent overlapped.[71] But each was associated with a different anti-Arian group in Antioch, and each approached the christological question in a totally different way. So it happened that at the time when Apollinarius was losing the support of the catholic church, Diodore rose to prominence; elected bishop of Tarsus in 378, he was present at the Council of Constantinople three years later and, together with Gregory of Nyssa and one or two others, he was officially designated an exponent of orthodoxy. Both Diodore and Apollinarius lived until the early 390s; but if Diodore, unlike Apollinarius, died in the peace of the church, his teaching became highly controversial within half a century and was eventually condemned. So by a curious irony, the two opponents came to share the same fate, and though both had lived as defenders of the faith, most of their writings are lost in obscurity.

III. Theodore of Mopsuestia

Now is the time for me to say, 'Sing unto the Lord a new song, for he has done marvellous things.' Indeed a new song is required for new things, as we are dealing with the New Testament which God established for the human race through the Economy of our Lord Jesus Christ, when he abolished all old things and showed new things in their place. Every man who is in Christ is a new creature; old things are passed away and all things are become new . . . . He gave us this new covenant which is fit for those who are renewed; and because of this covenant we receive the knowledge of these mysteries so that we should put off the old man and put on the new man who is renewed after the image of him who

created him, where there is neither Jew nor Greek, bond nor
free, but Christ is all and in all. This will take place in reality
in the next world . . . Because it was necessary that the faith in
the truth of the future gifts should remain in us, . . . these
awe-inspiring mysteries were confided to us in order that
through them as through symbols we might gradually approach our future hope . . .[72]

These were the words with which Theodore greeted prospec-
tive Christians in his catechetical lectures. In true Pauline
fashion, and indeed in Pauline language, he confronted them
with the *newness* of the gospel and the exhortation to conform
their lives to the promise of incorruptibility in Christ. What a
striking appreciation of the eschatological dimension of New
Testament thought, an appreciation which considerably
modifies, if it does not quite remove, the current Platonic
emphasis on escape from the world below to the world of
spiritual realities in heaven! While at times retaining the
language of earthly and heavenly, of time and eternity,
Theodore also points to successive stages in the creative
purposes of God, of a new creation anticipated in Christ and
awaiting its final consummation.

Those doctrines recognized as characteristic of Theodore are
closely related to this perception. His sense of God's purposes
unfolding in history reinforced his insistence on literal exegesis
of scripture; the writings of the Old Testament addressed
themselves primarily to their own contemporary situation,
while the New Testament proclaims a new saving act of God
and points forward to the consummation of his purposes in the
future. Allegorical method was to be eschewed, if only because
it destroyed this perspective and undermined the newness of the
gospel by finding Christ everywhere in the Old Testament. Also
clearly linked with his eschatological perspective is Theodore's
so-called doctrine of the two ages; he criticized the current
tendency to see man as primarily a spiritual being trapped in
flesh by the Fall, and explored the Pauline contrast between
man-in-Adam and man-in-Christ, creation and new creation,
two καταστάσεις (states). Such thinking is again the basis of his
characteristic emphasis on the genuine and complete manhood of
Christ. The 'man assumed' has a crucial place in the shape of
Theodore's christology, because for Theodore salvation depends
upon a Christ who is the first fruits of this new creation.

Given these characteristic doctrines, it is hardly surprising that some recent work displays a tendency to adulate Theodore as a much misunderstood forerunner of modern theology and exegesis.[73] But this estimate will not altogether do. Theodore was still a child of his time; current debates and current presuppositions inevitably coloured his thinking. The features congenial to modern thought are easily exaggerated, and factors of supreme importance to him are sometimes glossed over or disregarded. Yet Theodore's rehabilitation was due, and the narrowly defined debate as to whether he was a heretic or not is in danger of missing the more interesting aspects of his contribution. Like Origen he was a man of outstanding influence and importance, with a particularly interesting place in the history of theology; like Origen he was condemned in the sixth century by an edict of Justinian I, having been a contentious figure since his own day. The supreme allegorist and allegorism's prime critic were both victims of Byzantine politics, and both alike deserved reassessment. That reassessment has been facilitated by modern scholarship, by its collection and critical examination of alleged fragments, by its rediscovery, translation and interpretation of lost works.

What then do we know of this remarkable figure? The only fact about Theodore's life of any interest to Socrates and Sozomen was his early association with John Chrysostom.[74] They were fellow-students under Libanius, and together gave up secular pursuits for an ascetic life, concentrating on biblical studies under Diodore. When Theodore, attracted by marriage and a legal career, abandoned the monastery, Chrysostom wrote two eloquent letters which succeeded in persuading him against his intentions.[75] It is evident that Theodore, though still under twenty, had won Chrysostom's admiration and respect for the intensity of his commitment to study and for the joy with which he practised ascetic self-discipline. Further details of his life are shrouded in mist, but it seems likely that he stayed on as Diodore's pupil until Diodore left to become bishop of Tarsus in 378. Probably about 383 he was ordained priest in Antioch, and he was consecrated bishop of Mopsuestia in 392. There he is reputed to have been an active evangelist who turned many from the errors of idolatry and paganism, as well as establishing the truth against Arian and other heretics. His defenders later spoke of him expounding scripture 'in all the churches of the East',[76] but this probably refers to the widespread influence of his scriptural commentaries rather than extensive travels. Theodore died in 428.

So on the whole Theodore's life was uneventful. When he died he was held in great respect, especially in those regions under the influence of the Patriarchate of Antioch. Within three years, however, the Nestorian controversy had broken out. Theodore's name was associated with that of Nestorius, and so were Theodore's doctrines. The Antiochenes steadfastly refused to countenance his condemnation even when they compromised over the case of Nestorius; but for the Monophysites his work was always to be suspect, once they had identified him and Diodore as the true originators of Nestorianism. His eventual condemnation meant the disappearance of most of his works, apart from quotation and misquotation in controversial writings and histories. Yet for a century they had enjoyed wide dissemination among the Dyophysites, and particularly the Nestorians in Syria. Prior to Chalcedon – indeed, in the early stages of the christological battle – Syriac translations of the revered works of Theodore 'the Interpreter' had been produced, and it is to Syriac sources that we now look for a considerable amount of our information about Theodore and his work. Four treatises have been known in Syriac versions in modern times: his *Disputation with the Macedonians* (published 1913),[77] his *De Incarnatione* (lost before publication – one of the less generally known tragedies of the First World War), his *Catechetical Homilies* (published 1932)[78] and his *Commentary on John* (published 1940).[79] Syriac catalogues of the thirteenth and fourteenth centuries give us an idea of the quantity of works once available.

Theodore's output seems to have been largely commentaries on scripture and dogmatic works. He seems to have commented on almost all the books of the Bible, but prior to the publication of the Syriac version of the *Commentary on John*, only two exegetical works survived in their entirety, the complete Greek text of his *Commentary on the Minor Prophets*, and a Latin version of the *Commentary on the Ten Minor Epistles of St Paul*[80] which escaped destruction by being attributed to Ambrose. Otherwise the character of his commentaries can only be assessed from descriptions and quotations, though from the catenae quite extensive Greek fragments of his *Commentaries on Genesis, on the Psalms* and *on the Gospel of John* have been gleaned.[81] The most important of his dogmatic works were those against Apollinarius and Eunomius, and above all his *De Incarnatione*. Of these we now have only a collection of fragments from various sources: the *Acta Conciliorum* quoting the documents on the basis of which Theodore was condemned; the *Defence of the Three Chapters* written in Latin by Facundus; and the treatise of Leontius of Byzantium *Against the Nestorians and the Eutychians*. The authenticity and accuracy of these fragments has been seriously questioned, particu-

larly by Richard and Devreesse,[82] who brought charges of deliberate falsification against the compilers of hostile florilegia (collections of extracts). Discrepancies between the Greek fragments
and various Syriac discoveries provided evidence of tampering with
the tradition at some point. A spirited defence of the integrity of the
Greek fragments by F. A. Sullivan[83] reopened the question; he
argued that absolute confidence in the word for word accuracy of
the Syriac translator was misplaced, and serious modification or
interpolation of the Greek text was unproven. Not all have been
convinced, however;[84] there is at least substantial evidence that
the compiler did not shrink from deliberate suppression of the
context, so putting Theodore's views in the blackest possible
light.[85] The question of context is what makes the Syriac evidence
so indispensable, for the Syriac version of the *Catechetical
Homilies* provides us with our only complete dogmatic work in
which suspicious statements can be seen in a total context and
therefore in better perspective. However, the continuing critical
problems mean that the student of Theodore is hampered by lack of
a convenient and reliable collection of extant texts; Migne is
hopelessly out of date and in need of critical revision, and the more
recently discovered material in the catenae and in Syriac are
scattered about in learned articles and oriental collections.

As we have noticed, the churches of the East honoured Theodore
as 'the interpreter'; and there are indeed good reasons for seeing
interpretation of scripture as his main interest, as well as the basis
of much of his characteristic theology. How then did Theodore
interpret? What methods did he use? What presuppositions can we
discern underlying his work?

1. Interpretation of scripture

Theodore's commentaries are brief and largely confined to the
basics of scriptural exegesis. Where appropriate he discusses
problems of translation and text, within the limitations of available
techniques and his lack of Hebrew. He discusses the meanings of
words and phrases, especially those distinctive and characteristic
of biblical usage. He notes where metaphorical expressions are
used, for he knows that it is nonsense to take some phrases literally.
Frequently he makes use of summaries and paraphrases to bring out
the gist of the argument in the text before him, and he regularly
writes historical and circumstantial introductions to fill in and
explain the background. The result, it must be admitted, is often
dull. Where recent work commends his historico-critical sense,
earlier scholars commented upon the dry, pedestrian character of

his commentaries compared with the imaginative insights of allegorical and mystical exegesis.[86]

It is reported that Theodore wrote a book *On Allegory and History* and the universal comment of ancient witnesses was that Theodore avoided allegory and concentrated on historical interpretation – indeed, he was accused of interpreting the Old Testament like the Jews. The church in general found his attitude problematical not simply because of the deeply engrained influence of allegory against which the Antiochene standpoint was a healthy reaction, but because of the long tradition of christological interpretation of the Old Testament which went right back to the New Testament itself. Theodore's early work was the most startling. He himself almost admits that he over-played his hand in the *Commentary on the Psalms*.[87] For most commentators the fact that verses from Psalms 22 and 69 appear on the lips of Jesus in the gospel accounts of the passion was enough to establish their prophetic character; and an extension of the principle meant that large areas of the Psalter were traditionally interpreted as direct prophecy of the Messiah. For Theodore, however, the only direct prophecy to be found was Psalm 16.10, 'Thou wilt not abandon my soul to Hades, Nor let thy holy one see corruption.'[88] Occasionally by prophetic inspiration the psalmist spoke in the person of the Messiah, Psalms 2 and 8 being examples; but most of the traditional messianic psalms were to be given quite different interpretations. How was Theodore led to conclusions so extreme for his age?

Some of the basic principles along which Theodore worked were exemplary. Texts were not to be lifted out of context. Arbitrary shifts of subject were not plausible. So to take individual verses from the Psalms as messianic prophecies when the rest of the psalm did not fit had to be disallowed. That immediately excluded a number of the traditional christological texts; in the Septuagint version, the subject of Psalm 22 mentions his 'transgressions', and therefore he cannot be identified with Christ. Another principle was that passages in the Old Testament belonged to one specific historical context, usually contemporary with the prophet or writer; thus David sang, 'My 'God, my God, why hast thou forsaken me?' as a lament over Absalom. Certainly Christ took over David's lament on the cross, but its primary meaning was to be referred to the original event in David's life. Unfortunately in the case of the Psalter, Theodore was unable to rid himself of the tradition that David was the author of the entire collection; and that being the case the good directions he followed led him into some strange alleys. Solomon is clearly the subject of Psalm 72; so it must have been composed prophetically by David in Solomon's person. If this explanation worked in this case, there was no reason why it should not work in the case of other historical difficulties. Certain Psalms undoubtedly referred to the disasters under the Maccabees and not to events which occurred in David's lifetime; so David was again prophesying. Each psalm Theodore attributed in its entirety to a particular situation, unearthing the most plausible context. Rarely was this the events of the life and death of the Christ.

If Theodore's principles produced some aberrations in the case of the Psalms, they proved more reasonable when he turned to the Minor Prophets. Here he insisted that each prophet was preaching a message for the people of his own day. He sketched the situation, the doom overhanging the people in pre-exilic times, the judgment that came upon them, the hopes of restoration held out to them; he set the later prophets correctly in the context of the Return and its problems. The circumstances of the prophets were Theodore's preoccupation, for therein lay the key to understanding their message. If the prophetic words appeared to point to Christ, it was because they were shadows, glimmerings of the providential care of God for his people which reached its fullness in Christ. Zechariah cannot have had a vision of the Son of God; for God was not known as Father and Son until the New Testament.

It is this last argument which reveals Theodore's basic reasoning and accounts for the oddities in his exegesis. Theodore had not rejected the current idea that prophecy was inspired prediction. He accepted that the prophets and supremely David, predicted events which occurred centuries later in the history of Israel. So why could he not accept that the prophets of the Old Testament predicted Christ? Fundamentally it was because such a notion flattened out the difference between the Old and New Testaments; it undermined the Christian claim to new revelation in Christ. Before the time of Christ, nothing was clear; what indications there were, were merely shadows, vague prefigurations. It was the need to preserve the distinctiveness of the New Testament which stimulated Theodore's radical criticism of the traditional christological understanding of the Old Testament, thus producing results scandalous in contemporaries' eyes – he even asserted that the Song of Songs was Solomon's love poem and had nothing to do with the marriage of Christ and the Church. Yet he did recognize that the same God was God of both Testaments, and that both Testaments pointed in the same direction. So he admitted some of the classic 'types', though only if he could recognize a genuine correspondence

(μίμησις – imitation), an Old Testament situation closely para-
lleling a New Testament situation.[89] Thus the sprinkling of blood
which marked the end of Israelite slavery in Egypt was a prophetic
image of deliverance from sin and death through the blood of
Christ; and the historical Jonah prefigured the historical Jesus, the
extraordinary events of his life signifying by μίμησις Christ's
rejection, resurrection and conversion of the Gentiles. Such prefigurations Theodore could acknowledge as long as neither the
factuality of the original events was undermined, nor the newness
of the New Testament compromised. This was the kind of thing
meant by Paul in the 'allegory' of Sarah and Hagar (Gal. 4);[90] it was
abusing the apostle's words, Theodore insisted, to take ἀλληγορούμ-
ενα as justifying the fables and fantasies of allegorical interpretation. There are two different covenants (or Testaments) though
they have a certain rapport which is discerned in the 'types'.

If the New Testament was to be seen as radically different, was
the commentator to approach its interpretation along quite different lines? Certainly there is a difference apparent in Theodore's
New Testament commentaries, but there are also similarities.
There is the same historical awareness: Theodore takes the
chronology and historical detail of John's gospel very seriously
indeed, and goes to considerable trouble to indicate the historical
circumstances of Paul's epistles. The method of commentary
remains similar, concentrating on the background situation, problems in the text, explication of obscurities, and elucidation of the
argument of the sequence of the narrative. The key difference is
that for Theodore the New Testament, unlike the Old Testament,
contains the truth and the whole truth in the matter of Christian
doctrine. In other words Paul and the author of John's gospel
actually taught the theology of Theodore and his orthodox contemporaries. So dogmatic concerns play a very important part in his
efforts to interpret – in fact, he stated it as a principle that
commentators should concentrate on problem texts, particularly
those twisted by the heretics.[91]

The effect of this presupposition is considerable. Theodore
cannot help distorting the meaning of Johannine texts as he labours
to distinguish things said of the Logos from those said of the 'Man
Assumed'. In his concern to establish the truth as far as the
controversial issues of the day were concerned, he fails to present
the subtle unity and irony of the Johannine portrait of Christ. This,
together with the fact that his generally over-literal bent blinds him
to the symbolic overtones of this, the 'spiritual gospel', renders this
commentary probably his least successful. With the writings of

Paul Theodore shows a greater affinity and depth of appreciation (indeed there are passages in the *Commentary on John* which can only be described as Pauline exegesis of the Johannine text, the high-priestly prayer of John 17 being a particularly striking example).[92] As already observed, his religious perception focused like Paul's upon the newness of the gospel, the end of the old order, the creation of a new mankind in Christ, the gift of the Holy Spirit, the foretaste of the age to come in the grace received through baptism and eucharist. Yet the dogmatic interest is not absent from his commentaries on the Pauline epistles; a major purpose of New Testament interpretation is the establishment of orthodox doctrine and the confusion of the heretics.[93] It is this standpoint which sharply distinguishes Theodore's approach from that of modern critical scholarship. For all his sense of history, Theodore had no awareness of doctrinal development. Anachronistic interpretation of the Old Testament in terms of Christ he discerned and criticized; but it was inconceivable to him that the New Testament writers did not share his basic theological assumptions.

Yet the interrelationship between theology and exegesis is never entirely straightforward. For all that has just been said, one important element in Theodore's thought seems to lie in his readiness to disregard certain presuppositions of contemporary Platonism – the basic context in which Christian theology was operating at this time; and this readiness seems to have been induced, partially at least, by his reading of the Bible. The extent to which he abandons metaphysical terms in favour of biblical images is probably rather exaggerated by Rowan Greer,[94] but we have already observed this happening in the case of his eschatology, and this is not the only area of his theology affected. Theodore's anthropology is significantly different from that of, say, Gregory of Nyssa, not to mention Apollinarius; and as R. A. Norris has shown,[95] the difference lies not in his supposed Aristotelianism, but in the degree to which Platonic assumptions are modified, or at any rate balanced, by certain biblical insights, by his over-riding concern with morality, and by the understanding of salvation consequent upon his perception that man's rationality consists in his mutability, his freedom of choice. For Theodore's primary interest centred on the *will* of man, rather than his intellect, on the soul's involvement in practical moral action within the created order, rather than its contemplative transcendence of the flesh and the material world. Man was created to perform a certain function in the universe, as the keystone of the whole; so Adam's fall had cosmic consequences. The new age depended on the re-creation of

man, rather than his translation to a co-existent spiritual realm.
Man's resurrection meant the restoration of the cosmos and
established a bond of harmony for the whole creation.[96] There
remain many tensions and inconsistencies in Theodore's thought,
for many of the current Platonic commonplaces he took for granted
alongside his fresh understanding.[97] Thus the two states are
characterized in rather Platonic terms as mortal and immortal,
mutable and immutable, passible and impassible. Furthermore,
Theodore oscillates between regarding man's present mutable state
as providential and necessary for man to exercise his will, and
accepting the tradition of Christian Platonism that mortality is the
tragic result of a fall from perfection. Yet his moral interest
remained predominant, and needless to say, markedly affected
Theodore's christology.

2. Christology

Apart from scriptural exegesis, christology was clearly the matter
of most concern to Theodore. He not only wrote specific treatises
against what he regarded as misguided christological theories, but
he composed a massive treatise on the subject of the incarnation.
We are told[98] that the *De Incarnatione* contained fifteen books and
showed by the clearest reasoning and the testimony of scripture
that just as the Lord Jesus possessed deity in its fullness, so he
possessed humanity in its fullness. It also discussed what full
humanity means, arguing that man consists of two substances,
soul and body, and that his spirit and the senses are inborn faculties
of the soul rather than different substances. The fourteenth book, we
are told, dealt with the divine nature; and the fifteenth clinched the
whole dissertation with citations from the Fathers. It is unfortunate that all the access we have to this work is through fragments,
often deliberately quoted to show that Theodore's views were
heretical.

The general characteristics of Theodore's christology have been
frequently described. His emphasis was upon the two distinct
natures of Christ. In the face of Apollinarianism, Theodore asserted
that the Man Assumed was a complete man, perfect in everything
which belongs to human nature and composed of a mortal body and
a rational soul. In the face of Neo-Arianism, Theodore asserted that
the Son was true God of true God, consubstantial with the Father.
How much this dual stress arose out of the controversial background is a matter of debate. What has caught people's interest of
recent years has been Theodore's highly realistic emphasis on the
genuine human experience of Jesus, and many, like Norris, would

argue that this is no mere response to Apollinarius but a deeply ingrained aspect of his total thought. Similarly it can be argued that his emphasis on the transcendence of the Logos is no mere safeguard in the face of contemporary conflicts, but an essential element in his religious consciousness. If God is to be God his divine nature cannot be compromised. Theodore regards as utterly foolish those who imagine that there is a natural kinship between God and Man.[99] There is a great chasm between the eternal and the contingent.[100] That God transcended time and space, passion, limitation and change was no mere theological axiom, but a central element in Theodore's understanding of God's otherness. Yet this very transcendence implied immanence, for the uncircumscribed must be everywhere. Schooled by Nicaea, Theodore was bound to attribute the same universality to the divine Logos. The Logos could not move from place to place,[101] nor 'become' flesh, except $\kappa\alpha\tau\grave{\alpha}$ $\tau\grave{o}$ $\delta o\kappa\epsilon\tilde{\iota}\nu$[102] – he meant 'metaphorically' rather than 'docetically' because he continued: 'In appearance, not in the sense that he did not take real flesh, but in the sense that he did not *become* flesh.' For Theodore truer expressions are to be found in the phrases 'he tabernacled among us' or 'he assumed flesh' – 'flesh' being a term which he explicitly takes to mean human nature in its entirety.[103] So the incarnation could not imply any change in the essential Godhead any more than it could undermine the autonomy of the manhood.

It is hardly surprising that the standard criticism of Theodore's christology has been that in his concern to avoid compromising either the divinity or the humanity of the Christ, he failed to give an adequate account of the unity. He was himself offended by language of 'two Sons',[104] but he nevertheless insisted in effect on two subjects.[105] A number of comments may help to put this dualism into better perspective.

(i) Within the basic framework of Theodore's thought, both God and man were each required to perform their own appropriate action in order that salvation could be achieved: on the one hand, an act of God's creative grace was required to re-fashion man and to bring the new state or age into being; on the other hand, since man's will was the seat of sin, man had to achieve his perfection by exercising that will in obedience to God. God could not play man's part, any more than man could play God's part. The two have to co-operate while acting independently. In spite of certain tales of Theodore's association with Pelagians, really his thought does not belong to either side in that contemporary Western dispute.[106]

(ii) Current anthropology operated with a dualism of body and soul in which the mode of unity remained a puzzle, though its actuality could not be denied. If Nemesius could speak of the soul dwelling in the body by habit, inclination or disposition and take it that this was a sufficient account of man's basic unity,[107] it is not surprising that Theodore should regard terminology not dissimilar as adequate for expressing the unity of Christ. The God-Word united the Man Assumed to himself by habit of will (κατὰ σχέσιν τῆς γνώμης)[108] or by favour (κατ' εὐδοκίαν), and though there remained two distinct natures, there was nevertheless one subject (*prosōpon*) to which all the actions of the Saviour could be referred, one Son because of the union (ἕνωσις).

(iii) Theodore meant a great deal more by this union κατ' εὐδοκίαν than might appear at first sight – more indeed than Nemesius seems to have appreciated. Since God is everywhere, unlimited and uncircumscribed, it is a specific act of favour (εὐδοκία) for him to be specially or particularly present. Thus he is present in a special way in the apostles and in the elect, as a particular act of grace. When he chooses to dwell in the Man Assumed, he does this ὡς ἐν υἱῷ (as in a son) uniting the whole of the Assumed to himself. This, for Theodore, is a unique case of his particular presence, produced by a deliberate act of divine will,[109] unique because he operated completely in him.[110]

(iv) The unity of *prosōpon* meant more than a unity of appearance; for when Theodore speaks of a unity of subject in his scriptural exegesis he uses the word *prosōpon*. Furthermore, it has been shown[111] that Theodore placed great weight on the notion of 'participation', in both his christology and his soteriology. His theology has its roots in the sacrament of Baptism; baptism and the gift of the Spirit effected a sharing in the divine immutability, an anticipation of the life of the age to come. The Saviour was one in whom that participation was uniquely realized in all its fullness so that there was effected a unity of *prosōpon* defined in terms of his sharing the honour, the worship, the lordship of the God-Logos. For Theodore 'participation' was a way of uniting two distinct natures without either being compromised.

(v) Although Theodore occasionally uses unguarded expressions which suggest that a perfect man was adopted by the divine Logos as his special dwelling-place, this is not really the drift of his meaning. For Theodore, Jesus was no 'mere man'; at no point was the Logos separated from the Man he assumed. Their perfect union was never destroyed, otherwise a 'mere man' he would indeed have been. If Theodore stresses the duality, it is because for him the unity is obvious. In analysis of scriptural texts, he often notes that the unity is assumed, while carefully balanced phrases ensure that the truth about the two natures is not obscured. In speaking of the 'economy of his humanity', or of the divine condescension, Theodore constantly affirms the basic unity of the dual saving action, and asserts the priority of the divine initiative.[112]

3. A rounded view of Christianity

In the context of controversy, the temptation to exaggerate particular points against the opposition is easy. For this reason, the positive outline of Christianity according to Theodore which we now possess in his *Catechetical Lectures* is likely to present a truer picture of Theodore's theology than pointed quotations from works like that against Apollinarius, if only because it will be a more rounded one. The *Catechetical Lectures* consist of ten homilies on the creed, and a further six homilies explaining the Lord's Prayer and the liturgies of baptism and eucharist. Though tending to seem repetitive, a feature further exaggerated by the peculiarities of Syriac idiom, this set of discourses contains a remarkable conspectus of the heart of what Theodore believed. A sense of wonder and mystery, of awe and thanksgiving pervades much of what he has to say. We have already met his opening proclamation of new creation in Christ, of the kingdom to come in which Christians begin already to participate through the mysteries of the sacraments. To share in these mysteries, Christians must keep the faith handed down to them. So Theodore begins his exposition of the credal profession to be made at baptism. From time to time, he gives the conventional warnings against Jews and polytheists, against heretics and schismatics, but he concentrates upon a positive outline of what the Fathers meant, illustrating the clauses of the creed with passages from scripture carefully expounded. Patiently the precise distinctions of Christian theology are elucidated. If in the homilies concerned with christology Theodore labours the distinction between the natures, this is set in the overall context of an exposition of Christian teaching on the doctrine of God, of salvation, of the Christian life and sacraments. It is thus no mere controversial theory but an integral part of the whole presentation, and balanced by the wider perspective of the one central act of the divine initiative taken on man's behalf. Thus the dogmatic sections are framed in the proclamation of Theodore's faith, which is moulded at the deepest level by his response to Paul's eschatological perspectives, the present gift of the Spirit and the future hope anticipated in the sacraments.

Entry to the future kingdom depends upon adoption as sons of God. Adoption is an important theme in Theodore's thinking about salvation and one that has not so far been mentioned. For Theodore, the Logos was genuinely Son of God; the Man Assumed was adopted and united with that sonship, and the Man Assumed paved the way for all men. When he raised the body he assumed, he raised us and made us sit with him in heaven so that we might be glorified in him.[113] Theodore's theological presuppositions meant that he could not countenance θεοποίησις (divinization), but he rejoiced in υἰοποίησις (filiation). In the homilies on the sacraments, Theodore was able to work this theme out in highly dramatic terms. Needless to say, the details of the liturgy to which he refers are of immense value to liturgiologists, but it is his interpretation of the liturgical acts which is so forceful. Both baptism and eucharist perform sacramentally the events that took place in connection with Christ our Lord, in the belief that what happened to him will happen to us. Passion and resurrection are re-enacted so that the believer can participate in the action. The elements represent Christ lying stretched out on the altar as a sacrifice, but by the invocation of the Holy Spirit, these elements are transformed so as to become immortal, invisible, incorruptible, impassible and immutable, just as the body of Christ was made immortal by the resurrection. When we partake of the body and blood, we expect to be changed into an immortal and incorruptible nature. Through the sacrament we will be united to Christ our Lord whose body we believe ourselves to be. He was the first to receive this change; and 'we believe that through these symbols, as through unspeakable signs, we possess sometime beforehand the realities themselves.'[114] As the newborn baby is weak, so the newly baptized possesses only potentially the faculties of his immortal nature, but that possession is the ground of his future hope. Newborn babes need suitable food, and the sacramental food of the eucharist is nourishment suitable to our present state, though really a symbol which will cease in the age to come.

Theodore frequently speaks of the sacraments as 'mysteries', but what he seems to mean by this is 'signs' or 'symbols'; for he was not really interested in mystical theology, but rather in practical Christian action. As newborn babes, Christians cannot expect to be perfect, but they should endeavour to live in a manner worthy of their heavenly citizenship. Human weakness should not deter the believer from the sacrament, for 'if we do good works . . . and truly repent . . . undoubtedly we will obtain the gift of remission of sins in our reception of the holy sacrament.'[115] The Lord's Prayer indicates that we can have confidence in forgiveness if we forgive others. Theodore's exposition of the Lord's Prayer in fact highlights his interest in action rather than contemplation: 'Thy will be done on earth as it is in heaven' means that we must strive to imitate the life we will live in heaven, for heaven contains nothing contrary to God. True prayer, says Theodore in his introduction, does not consist in words, but in good works, love and zeal for duty.[116] It would be interesting if some of his writings on the ascetic life had survived and we could see more clearly how he applied his understanding of Christian salvation to its practical outworking in life. The only bit of information we have is that in his work *On Perfection*,

> he taught, admonished and warned the solitaries to be assiduous in solitude, and confirmed his words by testimonies from the books of the prophets, from the gospels and from the Pauline epistles. Anyone who reads with care this book on the perfection of solitaries will easily learn the things said by the Interpreter about solitude and how much he rebukes and reproves the solitaries who are distracted by worldly works outside it.[117]

Such expressions might suggest contemplative leanings in Theodore's asceticism, and likewise he tells his catechumens to avoid 'the commerce of this world'. Yet we can be pretty sure that when it came to working out the practical implications, scripture provided Theodore with the supreme guide for shaping a Christian life-style and making the ethical decisions so central to his understanding of human rationality. Obedience to God's law was fundamental, though set in the context of the gracious activity of a God who creates and re-creates.

Thus Theodore and Chrysostom, the two pupils of Diodore, shared a common outlook, and their mutual regard was lifelong, for Theodore was one of those to whom Chrysostom wrote from exile. It is a strange twist of fate that Chrysostom, having suffered in his lifetime, rapidly became one of the most honoured saints of the church, whereas Theodore was posthumously anathematized even though honoured and respected all his days. Little did Theodoret foresee his fate when he made the divine Theodore's death the culmination of his *Ecclesiastical History*.

IV. Polemical Correspondence and a Pamphlet War

The very year that Theodore died, Nestorius was consecrated bishop of Constantinople. Within a few months disturbances were beginning to surface. The story of the Nestorian controversy has been often told; the course of its history, of synod and counter-synod, of compromise and breakdown, can easily be read else-where.[118] Suffice it here to highlight the character of the controversy and the issues at stake by surveying the correspondence between Cyril and Nestorius, and the literary history of the notorious Twelve Anathemas.

The documents which concern us are to be found in the *Conciliar Acts*. For although most literature from the hands of those branded as heretics met destruction, from the time of the Council of Ephesus on, collections were made of documents relating to the controversial issues discussed at the oecumenical councils, and these were preserved together with the Conciliar minutes; so the *Acta Conciliorum Oecumenicorum*[119] become an important literary source from this date onwards. For the council of Ephesus (431), there are a number of different collections, some in Greek, some in Latin, with partly but not entirely overlapping material. The most important is the *Collectio Vaticana*, in which most of the material now to be discussed is to be found.[120] Here, then, we can read the correspondence of the principal actors in this doctrino-political battle, and in the process notice not only the explicit issues but hints of the 'hidden agenda' in the conflict.

Cyril began the correspondence by writing to Nestorius. His opening address has the conventional form of polite patriarchal diplomacy: 'To Nestorius most reverent and pious fellow-servant, greetings in the Lord'; and personal reference throughout is to 'your Piety' rather than 'you'. This respectful, but hardly sincere, formality is maintained throughout the correspondence, even as it becomes more barbed.

Cyril proceeds to explain the occasion for writing. He has had reports from Constantinople that Nestorius is getting upset. On enquiry he discovered that the cause of Nestorius' annoyance was a letter that he, Cyril, had written to the holy monks, a copy of which had found its way to the capital. Here then are hints of the activities of the spies and counter-spies employed by the patriarchs to keep a watch on each other's activities. The letter which caused Nestorius' distress is also to be found in the *Acta Conciliorum*. That Cyril had written it suggests that he may well have been preparing to use tactics against Nestorius similar to those employed by his uncle Theophilus against Chrysostom. The monks had long been the shock-troops used by the Alexandrian patriarchs to further their political aims; the alliance had been forged by Athanasius and was consolidated by his successors. Now Cyril had made sure of the monks' support by circulating a pastoral letter which raised a number of controversial christological points in a manner designed to arouse the emotions of the faithful while not seeming unreasonable or contentious himself. The Nicene Creed, he had written, established the divinity of Christ and so the virgin must be *Theotokos* – Mother of God. The title *Theotokos* is implied, if not always used, by scripture, the Fathers, the great Athanasius and Nicaea. It was the Word of God himself who became flesh, and that Logos of God who was made flesh, suffered, died and rose, we name the one Lord Jesus Christ. He was no 'mere man like us'. He was God even if he became flesh. You cannot sever the one Lord Jesus Christ into two, separating what was from the Holy Virgin from what was from God. The Logos emptied himself, fulfilling the economy of his manhood, and when he became man he was born of woman. Emmanuel is no mere 'God-bearing man', nor a mere instrument of the divine. If Christ is not truly Son nor God by nature, but a mere man like us, a mere instrument of the divinity, how can our salvation be from God? The target was clearly Nestorius' christological position. That Nestorius was upset is hardly surprising. Cyril was obviously informed of the stock phrases and arguments of the Antiochene theology, and capable of damning them by implication.

In his letter to Nestorius, however, Cyril expresses surprise that Nestorius had not considered his own position. Uproar had arisen prior to his own letter to the monks. Was it not Nestorius' own statements which had started it all? Cyril had been labouring to straighten out distorted propositions found in certain papers and sermons. Some had nearly reached the point of holding back from confessing that Christ was God and proposing instead that he was an instrument or tool of the divinity, a 'God-bearing man' and such like. How could anyone keep silent when the faith was being injured and such ideas being bandied about? If he did he would have to answer for his silence before Christ's judgment seat. Besides Celestine, bishop of Rome, together with his local bishops, had expressed concern, and wanted to know whether these papers really originated from Nestorius or not. Clearly when they wrote they were deeply offended. (In fact, though Cyril does not mention it here, he had himself alerted Celestine to the dangers of Nestorius' preaching, and Cyril was now writing to Nestorius at Celestine's instigation. The letters of Celestine provide clear evidence of the Rome-Alexandria axis carefully fostered by Cyril.) So, continued Cyril, there was upset and uproar all over the place. Nestorius had better explain himself, and stop the world-wide scandal. If there was to be peace, he had better call the Holy Virgin *Theotokos*, because everyone else was prepared to suffer for their faith in Christ.

For all Cyril's diplomatic address, this was clearly a declaration of war. Nestorius tried to play it cool. He only answered the letter because of the strong pressure exerted by Cyril's representative, upon whose praiseworthy qualities he chiefly dwelt, suggesting almost incidentally that Cyril's letter, to speak plainly, was not written in brotherly love, yet he would bear it patiently.

So Cyril had not got very far. The affair rumbled on, and a few months later Cyril wrote again. This was the famous *Second Letter to Nestorius* which was adopted as a standard of orthodoxy alongside Leo's *Tome* at the Council of Chalcedon.[121] It deals much more explicitly with the specific christological issues.

Cyril's opening paragraph is further evidence of behind-the-scenes activity. Cyril states that he has been informed that 'certain persons are gossiping to your Piety to the detriment of my character'. No doubt they expected 'to delight your ears', as he puts it, suggesting that the overt hostility between the two sees was ripe for exploitation by fugitives from justice, the ambitious, or the plain malicious. Cyril insists that Nestorius' informants were all condemned criminals whose appeal to Constantinople was quite unjustified. Clearly it was becoming more difficult to keep the correspondence polite, but Cyril continues to address Nestorius as a 'brother in Christ', and tries still to win Nestorius round by appealing to him as a pastor and teacher with responsibility to the church.

As in the letter to the monks, Cyril takes as his standard of orthodoxy the creed of Nicaea. When a lot of people have been offended, he suggests, it is necessary to remove the offence and establish healthy doctrine. The proper way of proceeding is to hold the Nicene creed in high esteem and allow it to determine the shape of one's doctrine. He then states what he thinks the Nicene Fathers meant. They said that it was the only-begotten Son himself who was incarnate, lived as man, suffered, rose and ascended; without actually stating it in so many words, he was trying to insist that the Logos was the subject of the incarnate experiences. This, he continued, is the line all must follow, while recognizing what is meant by being incarnate: "For we do not say that the Nature of the Word was *changed* and became flesh, nor that he was *transformed* into a complete human being, I mean one of soul and body; but this rather, that the Word having united to himself in his own *hypostasis*, in an ineffable and inconceivable manner, flesh animated with a rational soul, became man.' Cyril thus acknowledges the propriety of the Antiochene concern to preserve God's immutability and repudiates the suggestion that his own christology involves the Logos in change. He also affirms the full humanity of

Christ, excluding Apollinarianism by his formula 'flesh animated by a rational soul'. However, it is quite plain that he cannot say how the incarnation is to be conceived. Several times in the letter he refers to its 'ineffable and inconceivable' character. The one point he keeps reiterating is that, whatever the difficulties, it must be affirmed that it was the Logos who was incarnate, and there is only one Lord and Christ and Son. He admits that two Natures are involved, but their union, he says, is hypostatic, because the Logos united Manhood to himself 'in his own *hypostasis*'.

In expounding this position further Cyril deals with a number of difficulties which had already arisen in the debate. He asserts that it is possible to say that the Logos had his γέννησις from the Father, and also that he had a γέννησις κατὰ σάρκα from a woman. (Again we are faced with the problem that English does not have a single word covering both 'generation' and 'birth'.) This he had asserted in his letter to the monks, and the following words suggest that he had laid himself open to misinterpretation. (It was after all an Apollinarian idea.)[122] He denies that this means either that the Divine Nature began its existence in the Holy Virgin, or that the eternal Logos lacked something or had need of a second beginning of existence. He is simply said to have been born according to the flesh on the occasion when he united humanity to himself hypostatically for our sakes and our salvation, he explains.

But Cyril refuses to go on the defensive. This was no ordinary man who was born of the Holy Virgin; it was the Word himself who made his own the birth of his own flesh. The Word himself suffered and died – not that he suffered in his own proper nature, for the Divine is impassible because it is incorporeal. But when his own body suffered, he is said to have suffered for us himself, for the Impassible was in the suffering body. In other words, Cyril is trying to say that the incorporeal had accepted a corporeal, and therefore passible, state.

So, continues Cyril, we acknowledge one Christ and Lord, not worshipping a man alongside the Word and allowing division to creep in. If we reject this hypostatic union, we end up saying 'two Sons'. A unity of *prosōpa* just does not meet the case. 'For the scripture has not declared that the Word united to himself a man's person, but that he became flesh.' Accordingly there is no objection to calling the Holy Virgin *Theotokos*.

Cyril had made a serious attempt in this letter to expound his position, and had given attention to some of the problems involved. He concluded by saying that he had written 'out of the love which I have in Christ', and beseeching Nestorius 'thus to think and teach with us that the peace of the churches may be preserved and the bond of unanimity and love between the priests of God remain unbroken'. We should trust his motives sufficiently to realize that Cyril did fear deeply for the truth of the incarnation, and here at any rate he avoided extremist statements in the interest of achieving peace. No doubt he relished the prospect of forcing the bishop of Constantinople to knuckle under Alexandrian ascendency, but for the moment he avoided dictating and demanding.

Nestorius, however, was not the type to give way to anyone, least of all his greatest ecclesiastical rival. He was a determined and intolerant character with little tact, if Socrates' assessment is to be believed;[123] and at the moment he had the advantage that he was in favour with the court. So this time Nestorius replied to Cyril with some force, giving not an inch, but replying directly to Cyril's points. He begins by explicitly ignoring the insults at the start of Cyril's letter and coming straight to the theological points. He quotes Cyril's remarks about Nicaea and points out that the holy Fathers did *not* say that the consubstantial Godhead was passible or that the one co-eternal with the Father was γεννητής. In the phrase 'the one Lord Jesus Christ, his only-begotten Son', the Fathers carefully laid alongside each other the names belonging to each nature so that the one Lord is not divided, while at the same time the natures are not in danger of confusion because of the singleness of sonship. Paul taught the same thing in Philippians 2.5f. (a passage discussed by Cyril in the letter to the monks, and one that constantly reappears in the debate): since he was about to speak of passion, in order to avoid the implication that the divine Logos was παθητός, he used the name 'Christ', so indicating the single *prosōpon* of passible and impassible nature; for Christ can be called ἀπαθής and παθητός without any danger – for he is ἀπαθής in his Godhead and παθητος in his body.

Nestorius indicates that he could make many other observations on this, but in the interests of brevity he will proceed to Cyril's next point. He claims that the division of the natures is perfectly orthodox and the Fathers never spoke of a second γέννησις from woman. Cyril's pernickety account he finds inconsistent: he began by stressing that the Logos was ἀπαθής and unable to accept a second γέννησις, and then somehow he introduced the idea that he was παθητός and newly-created.

Scripture, claims Nestorius, attributes the economy, the birth (γέννησις) and the suffering (πάθος), not the Godhead but to the Manhood. Therefore the Holy Virgin is *Christotokos*, not *Theotokos*. He proceeds to quote long scriptural proofs. The body was the temple of the Godhead; the Godhead made it its own by an exact and divine συνάφεια (one of the words used for union or conjunction). This is the view that fits with the gospel tradition. To attribute birth and suffering and death to the Logos is to fall into pagan thinking and follow the heresies of Apollinarius and Arius.

Nestorius sympathizes with Cyril's desire to avoid conflict, quoting Paul's condemnation of the contentious, and he signs off with expressions of brotherliness and respect.

Reasoned debate, however, was becoming impossible. Cyril's *Third Letter to Nestorius* was not a personal reply to Nestorius' arguments, some of which were acute and valid, but a demand for submission from a synod of Egyptian bishops. The 'anti-Nestorius' campaign had acquired more and more momentum. When Cyril informed Celestine that he had had no success in getting Nestorius to recant, the pope held a synod in Rome (August 430), and in the *Acta Conciliorum* there appear several letters from Celestine announcing the verdict of this synod to interested parties in the East, to the clergy and people of Constantinople, Cyril, John of Antioch, and of course Nestorius himself. The verdict was an ultimatum: if Nestorius did not recant and confess the same faith as Rome and Alexandria within ten days of receiving the letter, he would be excommunicated. Cyril's synod in November confirmed the Roman synod and despatched the third letter, but the ultimatum was forestalled by an imperial summons to a General Council the following year. More water was to flow under the bridge before that council, however, and by the time it was held, the controversy was no longer merely a question of Nestorius' orthodoxy. The Eastern Church had been split into two hostile theological camps. The third letter was instrumental in thus deepening the conflict.

The tone of Cyril's third letter to Nestorius is no longer charitable and persuasive. The letter is a categorical demand for submission. The faith is being wronged; the law of affection must be abjured. Silence can be maintained no longer. The Egyptian synod is acting in harmony with the synod at Rome in counselling Nestorius to desist from his mischievous and perverse doctrines or he will be excommunicated. The disturbance of the churches and the scandalizing of the laity can no longer be tolerated. Nestorius has already been warned by Celestine's own letter.

The letter continues by saying that it is not sufficient for Nestorius simply to affirm the Nicene faith because the whole problem centres on the fact that he has interpreted it wrongly. What he has to do is to anathematize his own foul doctrines and promise to teach what is taught by all bishops, teachers and leaders of the churches throughout West and East. This is contained in the letters Nestorius has already received from Celestine and Cyril himself, but, to be sure there is no misunderstanding, the teaching is again stated in this letter.

There is no need to rehearse in detail the contents of the ensuing exposition, since much the same series of positive arguments and formulae are advanced as in the second letter. One addition, however, is sufficiently important to be mentioned, namely Cyril's appeal to the eucharist: we do not receive 'common flesh' or 'the flesh of a man sanctified', he says, but the flesh of the Word himself, which is life-giving only because it is the flesh of the Word who as God is himself Life. Apart from this new line of argument, the major difference between the two letters is the greater extent to which there appears explicit rejection of many typically Antiochene christological formulae. 'Indwelling' is not a strong enough account of the union; the Logos did not 'inhabit' the body, dwelling in it by grace in the same way as he indwells the saints. There is one Christ and Son and Lord, not a man conjoined with God in a unity of dignity and authority. Conjunction (συνάφεια) is not enough to describe the union since it suggests mere juxtaposition rather than a union of nature or hypostatic union. It is false exegesis to divide up scriptural texts between the natures as Nestorius does; human sayings and divine were spoken by one person. It is equally false to ascribe his titles and saving actions to the two different natures; and Cyril proceeds to discuss certain titles and texts which had become notorious in the course of the controversy. This more negative approach is crowned by Cyril's final demand that Nestorius anathematize twelve statements which are appended to the letter.

The Twelve Anathemas

Of all Cyril's acts, the drawing up of the Twelve Anathemas was the most tactless and divisive; for they themselves became the focus of controversy and aroused the deep suspicions of all the Antiochene party. They are bald hostile statements asserted without the necessary niceties and safeguards which Cyril had taken the trouble to include in his more discursive explanations. To the Antiochenes they were not merely provocative but blasphemous and doctrinally dangerous. As the controversy developed it became more important to them to ensure the withdrawal of the Twelve Anathemas than to defend Nestorius. Antiochene tracts attacked them; Cyril defended them in a series of apologies and counter-attacks. The pamphlet war was born.

The Antiochene party took the offensive. When Nestorius informed John, the bishop of Antioch, of the contents of Cyril's latest letter, almost immediately two critical treatises were produced, one by Andrew of Samosata representing the 'Orientals' (as the Antiochene bishops were called), and the other by Theodoret of Cyrus, the greatest of the Antiochene scholars. These survive through their extensive quotation in Cyril's replies, his *Apology against the Orientals* and his *Apology against Theodoret*. Cyril produced a further *Explanation of the Anathemas* during the course of the council of Ephesus, realizing the extent to which they were one of the biggest contributory factors in the breakdown of communications between the two parties. Somehow they had to be justified to the outside world, and especially the imperial court. The Antiochenes were convinced that they were Apollinarian, and were not afraid of broadcasting this view. Theodoret was not alone in hardly being able to believe that they were the work of Cyril, or of any real pastor in the church, because of their Apollinarian and blasphemous character. Someone even produced a series of counter-anathemas, which were attributed to Nestorius and survive in a Latin translation; but since they do not appear to be authentic and were not part of the immediate debate, they will be ignored in the discussion here.

The first anathema was directed against those denying that Emmanuel was truly God and refusing the title *Theotokos* to the Holy Virgin; in explanation of this demand it is asserted that the Word which originated from God (ὁ ἐκ Θεοῦ Λόγος) was born in a fleshly manner when he became flesh.

The Orientals fastened first on the explanatory clause and asked how anyone could agree that he was born 'in a fleshly manner' – that would imply a denial of the virgin birth. Was his birth 'fleshly' or 'divine' (θεοπρεπής)? But the Antiochene criticisms centred on the main problem – how can the divine admit change? His 'becoming flesh' cannot be any more literal than his becoming sin or a curse; it means his dwelling (σκήνωσις) in flesh. Theodoret concentrates on this point. Change cannot be attributed to the deity; God 'took' flesh according to Philippians 2.7. Theodoret is prepared to accept the title *Theotokos*, but only with careful explanations: what she bore was the temple (ναός) of the divine in which all the fullness of the divine dwelt bodily.

How then did Cyril meet the attack? To the Orientals he began by asserting that John 1.14 is a statement of the mystery of the incarnation; and Nicaea said that the Word which originated from God was incarnate and made man. Of course this union must have happened without change or mixture (ἀτρέπτως and ἀσυγχύτως), for the Logos is unchangeable (ἀναλλοίωτος) by nature. Secondly he suggested that if they insisted on his birth being θεοπρεπής, there was no reason why they should not call the virgin *Theotokos*; does an ordinary man have a divine birth? Furthermore it was ridiculous to suggest that he became flesh in the same way as he became sin or a curse; since he was sinless, the corollary of that argument is that he was not really incarnate at all. He was truly made flesh and made man without change or confusion; the manner of the Economy is ineffable. Cyril appends patristic citations to support his case.

Much the same kind of reply he gives to Theodoret: We do not speak of mixture or change when we say that the Logos became flesh, but of his indescribable and ineffable union with a holy body having a rational soul. The language of 'indwelling a temple' is not sufficient to describe this union, because that language can also be used of God's presence in the saints, and he quotes I Corinthians 3.16–17.

In his *Explanation* Cyril reiterates his main point that according to the Nicene creed, the Logos submits himself to the incarnate experiences, as well as being consubstantial with the Father. The Logos remained God, and was incarnate without change; the manner of the incarnation is simply beyond our conception or speech.

The second anathema is directed against those who deny that the Word which originated from God the Father was united hypostatically with the flesh.

Now the notion of hypostatic union was precisely the problem for the Antiochenes. They wished to affirm a unity, but to call it 'hypostatic' had all the wrong connotations for them, implying Apollinarianism, implying a mixture and confusion of natures, implying a 'natural union', that is, one brought about by something inherent in the nature of things and so by necessity, rather than one voluntarily undertaken by the gracious will of God. For Cyril it was the only way of speaking of a 'real' union. There seems to have been a genuine difference in use of terminology. To suggest, as some have,[124] that Theodoret should have realized what Cyril meant, since *hypostasis* had been given a specific meaning in the Trinitarian formula 'One *ousia* and three *hypostaseis*', is not quite fair. It was used there to distinguish a single individuality, and to affirm a single individuality in Jesus Christ could well imply a mixture or confusion if the phrase were approached from the christological stand-point of the Antiochenes. The explanation produced by Cyril probably did not reassure Theodoret. Besides, it seems likely that the formula καθ' ὑπόστασιν (hypostatically) was invented by Cyril and introduced an entirely novel terminology into the christological debate.[125] It is noticeable that years later when Nestorius wrote *The Bazaar of Heraclides*, he was still perplexed by the term.[126]

Discussion of this anathema does not appear at all in Cyril's *Apology to the Orientals*. Theodoret, however, insists that the Antiochenes, persuaded by the scriptures, do agree that there was a real union; but they reject the description *hypostatic* as being foreign to the scriptures and to the Fathers who interpreted them. If by describing the union as hypostatic a mixture of flesh and divinity is intended, then they oppose the term with zeal and condemn it as blasphemy. Mixture implies confusion; confusion undermines the peculiar character of each nature. By the text 'Destroy this temple and in three days I will raise it again', the Lord indicated the two natures – the destroyed temple and the raising God. ἕνωσις – union – is quite enough; it safeguards the distinction of natures and the one Christ.

Cyril retorts by stating what he means by καθ' ὑπόστασιν: it is the very nature and hypostasis of the Logos which was united to human nature, by some means other than confusion, as he has often stated before. Theodoret, he suggests, is really saying the same thing. In his *Explanation* Cyril again insists that it is the Logos which was incarnate – granted, without change in his own nature – and it is not legitimate to divide the one Christ into Man on his own (ἰδικῶς) and God on his own (ἰδικῶς) or we think in terms of two Sons and undermine the whole idea of incarnation.

The third anathema is directed against those who divide the natures after the union, and describe the union as an association (συνάφεια), in dignity, authority or power, rather than a conjunction (σύνοδος) by natural union (φύσει, that is, by *physis* = nature).

The issue here is much the same as in the previous anathema, but it introduces terminology which remained contentious; the Monophysites rejected Chalcedon because it spoke of '*in* two natures' rather than '*out of* two natures', that is, because it implied the continuing presence of two separate natures after the union. Here the Orientals pointed out that Cyril himself had spoken of two natures in his letter to the monks; had he now forgotten himself in confusing the two natures into one hypostasis and calling it a 'natural union'? Who could accept a physical union which excludes the action of grace? This must be an Apollinarian idea. In reply Cyril restates his familiar ground: the same Son and

Lord before the incarnation and after the incarnation – no division into two Sons. He quotes passages from Nestorius and proceeds to confute them. Nestorius consistently divides the natures, uniting them merely in a common worship, authority and a union of dignity alone. He quotes and defends his own statements concerning the two natures, insisting that the natures are not divisible after the union. He explains that by φύσει he means κατ' ἀλήθειαν – a real or true union – not a confusion; and he repudiates the teaching of Apollinarius.

Theodoret regarded the subtle distinction between συνάφεια and σύνοδος as unintelligible, and also drew attention to the necessity implied in a natural union. 'Naturally' we drink, sleep, breathe – that is, they are natural necessities, not acts of will. If the union was natural it was inevitable; it was not a voluntary act of God's love towards men. A union by intention and will is surely superior to a natural union. If Paul can speak of an 'outer man' and an 'inner man', what is wrong with speaking of two natures after the union? To Theodoret, Cyril spells out his meaning. What he denies is the view that two independent natures were joined σχετικῶς – by habit, or simply in dignity, authority or by having the common title 'Son'. The anathema opposes such empty language and affirms a 'natural union', that is, one not by habit, but in truth, and one that is indivisible. To think it means confusion or necessity is to misunderstand. The Logos could not be compelled to become man and suffer unwillingly, since in his own nature he is not susceptible to suffering and necessity. You cannot simply identify 'by nature' and 'by necessity'. All that the natural union means is a *real* union.

Cyril's *Explanation* of this anathema simply reiterates his basic objections to a dualistic christology.

The fourth anathema pursues the point by condemning those who differentiate scripture texts, assigning them to each appropriate nature. This was of course an important exegetical procedure among the Antiochenes, but what Cyril momentarily disregards was that it had been an important element in the great Athanasius' polemic against Arius. In the Formulary of Reunion, Cyril was obliged to climb down. In his *Explanation* Cyril justified the anathema by appeal to Philippians 2. Everything, divine and human, is ascribed here to the same subject. So all scripture texts should be applied to the one *prosōpon* (subject), since we believe Jesus Christ to be the one Son, that is the Word of God incarnate. The danger of ascribing texts to two subjects (*prosōpa*) is that it easily suggests two Sons. While giving nodding recognition to a distinction between 'divine' and 'human', he insists that the latter are to be referred to the incarnate state of the Logos, and is silent about his rejection of an important tradition.

In reply to the Antiochenes, however, he had been forced to admit the propriety of distinctions. Theodoret had suggested that Cyril might as well be Arius or Eunomius, and explicitly raised the question of the texts referring to the hunger, thirst, tiredness, sleep, ignorance, fear and loneliness of Jesus, texts which had long figured in orthodox polemic against Arianism. If they are applied to the God-Word, how can Wisdom be ignorant? he asks. Both he and the Orientals accuse Cyril yet again of 'mixture' and 'confusion'. Cyril repudiates that accusation, and insists that even though some things are said of Jesus Christ 'humanly' and others 'divinely', all apply to the one person of the incarnate Logos.

The fifth anathema was directed against those who say that Christ is a God-bearing man (θεόφορος ἄνθρωπος) not the Word made flesh, and *the seventh* was against those who say that Jesus was a man energized by the Word. Here the typically Antiochene vocabulary is singled out for condemnation, as it is also in *the eighth anathema*, which rules out any suggestion of an independent man assumed by the Logos and so co-worshipped and co-glorified. Also to be anathematized is the suggestion that Christ was empowered to do his mighty acts by the Spirit, as if the Spirit were foreign to himself and not his own (*anathema 9*), and the statement that a man born of woman was made high priest and apostle (*anathema 10*). The underlying accusation is one of adoptionism. How then do the Antiochenes defend such terms?

The Orientals firmly repudiate the idea that their formulae imply that he was energized simply like a man, like a prophet or an apostle or a righteous individual. They assert the scriptural basis for language like 'energizing' and doing signs by the power of the Spirit, and explain that his uniqueness consists in the fact that he was energized 'as a Son'. By co-worship is meant the single worship we offer to the one Son. As for *the tenth anathema*, they insist that God cannot be the subject of many texts in the Epistle to the Hebrews: how can God offer prayers and supplications with many tears, how can God learn obedience through suffering? In fact, they made a plausible case on the basis of realistic scriptural exegesis, though they did not meet Cyril's real difficulties: how is this Man Assumed different from a saint or a prophet? How can this be described as an incarnation of the Logos?

Theodoret covers several of the same points. We do offer one worship to the one Christ who is both God and Man; but we must insist that the Word did not change into flesh, nor the Man change into God. Scripture speaks of Christ's anointing with the Holy Spirit (and he produces a battery of texts); and it must be the manhood, not the Godhead, that was anointed. Is Cyril going to anathematize the prophets, the apostles and even Gabriel? The Epistle to the Hebrews makes quite plain the weakness of the assumed nature. The unchangeable nature did not change into flesh and learn obedience by experience. The Logos is not a creature; rather the one who is of David's seed was made high priest and victim and offered himself to God as a sacrifice. Compared with the Orientals, however, Theodoret insists rather more on the unity of person while defending the characteristic Antiochene expressions: When the Son of David made his sacrifice, he did it 'having the Logos united to him and inseparably conjoined.' There is no suggestion that θεόφορος ἄνθρωπος implies that he had just some particular divine grace; rather it means he was wholly united with the Godhead of the Son.

Was Cyril satisfied with these explanations? Hardly. In his later *Explanation* he feels no difficulty in making the same charges against the Antiochene position as he had done all along. The discussion has made no difference. Whatever Theodoret or the Orientals said, a God-bearing man still meant to him an ordinary saint; *we* are temples of the Holy Spirit, he replied. It is just not the same thing to say 'the Word became man' and 'God dwelt in a man'. Paul said, 'In him the whole fullness of the Godhead was pleased to dwell *bodily* – σωματικῶς, not σχετικῶς – by habit. The saints are energized by the Spirit; Jesus was different, for the energy and the spirit were his own. Unless the same one is God and Man, the claim to offer a single worship is false. As for the Epistle to the Hebrews, the contentious texts refer, of course, to the incarnate state, but the subject of all the experiences and activities is nevertheless the Logos, not a second subject – the Man Assumed. Furthermore, any idea that the man progresses to union with the Logos must be repudiated.

The remaining three anathemas condemn those who do not subscribe to certain Alexandrian Christological statements. *The sixth anathema* produced little discussion: it anathematized anyone who said that the Logos was the God or Lord of Christ, and did not agree that the same one is God and Man, the Word having become flesh. Theodoret hardly disputes Cyril's words; we do agree, he says, that 'the form of a servant' is God because of the union. Did he miss the point? Cyril's discussions confirm the suspicion that what he really had in mind was the affirmation that the Logos was the immediate subject of the incarnate experiences, though he never clearly states this in so many words. If they had realized what was at stake, the Antiochenes would certainly have qualified this statement, but as it stands it was perfectly consistent with Theodoret's christological position.

The eleventh anathema raises the question of the eucharist. Anyone suggesting that the flesh is not the Logos' very own flesh, and therefore life-giving, is anathematized. Needless to say the Antiochenes promptly accuse Cyril of Apollinarianism. Cyril has failed to say that the flesh was *ours*. We have to be very careful about speaking of the Logos' own flesh or we introduce confusion of the natures. Theodoret points out that Cyril keeps talking about the *flesh* like Apollinarius, and neither mentions that it was 'intelligent,' nor agrees that what was assumed was perfect Manhood. The flesh is life-giving because it is united with the Logos, and there is no escaping the two natures implied by such a statement. Cyril is obliged to defend himself from these charges. He explains that his language was merely intended to exclude the Nestorian suggestion that the flesh belonged to a separate human person. Of course 'flesh' means 'man in his completeness'; of course he took flesh from the virgin; of course the union is without confusion and the Logos remains unchanged.

The final anathema was the most provocative of all: Let anyone be anathema who does not confess that the Logos which originated from God suffered in the flesh, was crucified in the flesh, tasted death in the flesh. . . . Without qualification, suffering and death were predicated of the Logos. In the epistles Cyril had been more guarded. Was he just careless in framing the anathema? But anathemas were to be taken seriously. So did he wish to force the issue? If he did, he succeeded, but he also laid himself open to severe criticism. It was blasphemous to suggest that God was passible. If the Son was παθητός while being ὁμοούσιος τῷ Πατρί, then the Father was passible. The logical outcome of Cyril's statement was either Patripassianism or Arianism. Is it any wonder that the Antiochenes were sufficiently scandalized to condemn Cyril and his anathemas at the rival session of the council of Ephesus? This final anathema confirmed all their suspicions of the basic intent of the rest.

In his attack Theodoret declared that the ἀπαθής is above πάθη; only the παθητός can suffer. The 'form of a servant' suffered, the 'form of God' being with it, assenting to its suffering for the salvation of men and making the suffering its own through the union. When forced to explain, Cyril too spoke of the Logos making the sufferings of the flesh his own, while remaining ἀπαθής in his own nature. At this crucial point it seems as though the two sides were really not far apart in wrestling with the paradox; and yet it was here that each gave the deepest offence to the other. For the essential difference remains: the Antiochenes could not make the Logos directly the subject of incarnation, passion and death, whereas that was precisely what Cyril was trying to do.

With passions aroused on both sides, the bishops proceeded to Ephesus. Is it any wonder that communications broke down? Both saw the issues in terms of another serious heresy-hunt, each accusing the other. The fact that a Formulary of Reunion was reached two years later is really more remarkable than their reciprocal excommunication in 431. A few years later Cyril and Theodoret were engaged in a new exchange, Theodoret defending Diodore and Theodore from their Alexandrian critic. (Unfortunately these treatises exist only in fragmentary form, but they had an important place in the discussion which led to the eventual condemnation of the great Antiochene teachers, the 'Fathers of Nestorianism'.) The two sides remained suspicious of one another, and surely we should pay both Cyril and his opponents the compliment of attending to their views on the subject of their quarrel. There has been a tendency to argue that there was no real difference between the two contenders,[127] that their theologies were in reality very close and if only they could have talked out the issues calmly and sorted out their terminology in the peace and quiet of a seminar room, all discrepancies could have been ironed out. Politics got mixed up with theology and the condemnation of Nestorius was all a horrible mistake. But the actors thought they were fighting for truth. Nestorius cared only, in the end, that truth should prevail.[128] Of course, no serious human dispute is carried on in isolation from political, social or personal factors, but that does not mean that these exhaust everything there is to say about the issues. Of course, many arguments proceed because of emotion, prejudice and failure to listen to the other side, and these factors are particularly strong when people feel their faith under attack. But surely there were real issues: How could *God* be the subject of incarnate experiences? How could Christ be genuinely *man* if identified with God incarnate? The Antiochenes gave serious attention to the difficulties, and aroused the suspicions of the faithful by refusing to allow a direct identification; Cyril insisted on that direct identification and waved aside the difficulties, thinking that the reiteration of certain provisos met the problem sufficiently well. Controversy meant the exaggeration of each position, and many of the side-issues and mutual misunderstandings tended to obscure the point at which the real difference lay.

But a real difference there was, and neither position was really satisfactory.

But it is time to put this controversy into perspective. How much did it dominate the lives and literature of the three main figures we have found involved? Cyril and Theodoret had long episcopates and were by no means monopolized by this issue. But first let us turn to Nestorius whose life was inevitably coloured by his tragic role in the confrontation between two christological traditions.

V. Nestorius

It is my earnest desire that even by anathematizing me they may escape from blaspheming God [and that those who so escape may confess God, holy, almighty and immortal, and not change the image of the incorruptible God for the image of corruptible man, and mingle heathenism with Christianity . . . but that Christ may be confessed to be in truth and in nature God and Man, being by nature immortal and impassible as God, and mortal and passible by nature as Man – not God in both natures, nor again Man in both natures. The goal of my earnest wish is that God may be blessed on earth as in heaven]; but as for Nestorius, let him be anathema; only let men speak of God as I pray for them that they may speak. For I am with those who are for God, and not with those who are against God, who with an outward show of religion reproach God and cause him to cease from being God.[129]

It was a great Christian who wrote those words. There have been many who were prepared to die as martyrs for what they believed to be the truth, but Nestorius was prepared to live cursed and consigned to oblivion, as long as God was not dishonoured. The saving of God's honour, the exclusion of blasphemy and pagan mythology from the language of religious devotion, was what had motivated him all along; and we now know that he not only lived to see his theology vindicated, but even rejoiced to see it even though it meant no reprieve or recognition for him and his followers. As long as truth prevailed, he was prepared to suffer, to efface himself, rather than arouse renewed conflict, prejudice and misunderstanding. In tribulation he showed a greater generosity of spirit than many who have received the name saint rather than heretic.

Was Nestorius orthodox? Was Nestorius a 'Nestorian'? These questions have been repeatedly debated in the twentieth century, and there is a real sense in which the terms of the debate make the discussion fruitless and uninteresting. Each investigator tends to presuppose a different standard of 'orthodoxy'; do we measure by Chalcedon or by subsequent christological developments? If by Chalcedon, then Nestorius himself affirms that he could have accepted its main tenets; for he welcomed Leo's *Tome* to Flavian as a summary of his own theology.[130] Then, what is meant by Nestorianism? If we mean the traditional thumb-nail sketch of this heresy – teaching two Sons, dividing the Christ or treating him as a mere man, reintroducing Adoptionism and the false views of Paul of Samosata – then it is quite clear that Nestorius repeatedly repudiated the views attributed to him. If we mean the theology of the 'Nestorian church', the church 'established' in Persia and throughout the Orient for many centuries though out of communion with the West, then in the light of Chalcedon it is by no means clear that the Nestorians were heretical – though certainly they became so by standards later developed and undoubtedly they harboured extremist Dyophysites who found their home over the border. There are those for whom the definition of orthodoxy and heresy remains ecclesiastically vital, but for those interested in the workings of theological argument, it seems much more important to try and understand Nestorius against the background of his own time, the situation in the church and the theological questions at issue. In that situation, did Nestorius have an interesting contribution to make?

1. The sources

The upsurge of interest in Nestorius in the twentieth century was caused by the fact that just as Loofs was publishing a collected edition of his surviving fragments,[131] news was gradually percolating through that there existed a Syriac manuscript of his lost apology, the *Book of Heraclides*. South of Armenia and West of the Caspian sea is a mountainous area that falls within Iran (Persia). Here, in the late nineteenth century, some American missionaries heard of a manuscript in the possession of the Nestorian Patriarch which contained this lost work of Nestorius. Eventually copies reached Europe and the work of publication and translation slowly began.[132] Meanwhile, though the *Book of Heraclides* was still unpublished, Bethune-Baker was able to use it together with Loofs' fragments to produce his vindication of Nestorius in 1908,[133] quoting long sections in English translation. Careful literary analysis of the

Book of Heraclides had to wait for another half century,[134] but reconsideration of Nestorius' position was initiated. The *Book of Heraclides* provided a wider perspective against which the fragments could be more fairly judged. A fair assessment, however, depends upon giving due consideration to chronology and literary-critical problems; for Nestorius' stance in his later apology may not necessarily be simply equated with his position during the crisis – memory is affected by hindsight, after all – and the *Book of Heraclides* has to be used with care, for it seems to have been interpolated and may well be composite. What sources do we have, then, what is their chronology, and what is their character?

Nestorius, like most leading churchmen of the time, is said to have composed many treatises on various questions; but virtually nothing survived Theodosius' decree that all his works should be burned. Like John Chrysostom, Nestorius became bishop of Constantinople on the strength of his reputation for preaching; so at one time there were doubtless numerous sermons in circulation, but most of what has survived did so because its contents were regarded as damaging to Nestorius' position. Extracts from his sermons were quoted against him at the council and in Cyril's controversial writings. Some complete sermons were included in the *Conciliar Acts*, though these are in Latin translation, as is the material preserved by Marius Mercator, an African writer resident in Constantinople at the time of the controversy; but Greek fragments of the notorious sermons on *Theotokos* confirm parts of the text. Some fragments have established the Nestorian authorship of a sermon attributed to John Chrysostom, thus giving us at least one complete Greek homily which is undisputed. Various others have been attributed to Nestorius by certain modern scholars, but general agreement about their authenticity has so far not been reached.[135] In addition to these homiletic materials, we have a number of letters dating from the controversy, not just those to Cyril already examined, but also Latin versions of his letters to Celestine in Rome, and various other relevant letters, to the emperor, to John of Antioch, and to certain other contacts. Of course, all this material derives from hostile sources and may therefore give a distorted picture; brief quotations lack a context, and the selection of passages was no doubt determined by the desire to incriminate Nestorius. But the more complete examples of letters and sermons probably convey a reasonably accurate impression of Nestorius' stance during the controversy.[136]

After Ephesus Nestorius asked permission to return to his monastery near Antioch, and for a short period he was allowed to do that. Imperial decrees of 435, however, not only ensured the destruction of his books but banished him to Oasis in Upper Egypt; perhaps after the Formulary of Reunion his proximity had become an embarassment to John of Antioch, who had essentially sacrificed Nestorius for the sake of the peace of the churches. During the years of retreat and exile Nestorius turned to literary activity. Probably during the period in his monastery he composed an apology called *Tragedy* which gave his side of the case; and at some point he wrote a dialogue refuting Cyril called *Theopaschites*. Fragments of each of these are to be found in Loofs' collection. But by far the most significant of his extant works is the rediscovered *Book of Heraclides*, sometimes called *The Bazaar*.

It was the Syriac title which suggested the translation 'Bazaar', but the word was probably a rendering of the Greek πραγματεἶα; the translation should therefore be the less enigmatic 'treatise'. But why Heraclides? It seems as though the author was attempting to prevent immediate destruction of the book by adopting a pseudonym, but there is no attempt in the body of the book to conceal the identity of its author. Anyone who looked further than the title page was not going to be deceived. It is apparently a work of apology and explanation composed by Nestorius himself. The book is not quite complete and the contents are not homogeneous. The first part is in dialogue form, Nestorius discussing various different christological proposals with one Sophronius, rejecting docetism and 'mixture', and eventually proposing a christology which both preserves the two natures intact and affirms a unity of *prosōpon*. But the dialogue form is eventually abandoned and Nestorius in his own person gives an account of the events which doomed him, quoting letters and documents at length, discussing the theological and terminological points at issue, arguing with Cyril, accusing him of a serious miscarriage of justice, claiming that proper enquiry would have shown that he was orthodox and innocent of the charges brought against him, and that the great fathers, Gregory, Ambrose, and Athanasius taught his doctrine. Nestorius was out to prove that Cyril was deeply hostile and the whole affair turned on personal animosity; really he and Cyril were not far apart, and where they differed, Cyril was confused or wrong. The first major literary analysis suggested that the treatise as it stands is a compilation of two different works, and the opening dialogue is not in fact the authentic work of Nestorius;[137] this view has not met with universal acceptance[138] – though the literary case is quite strong, stronger than the theological differences observed.[139]

The work is frustrating to read, as Anastos points out:[140]

> It must be admitted that his style is often turgid and confusing. The repetitiousness of his great theological treatise, the *Bazaar of Heraclides*, is frustrating, wearisome and painful. It would have been vastly more effective if some expert rhetorician had pruned it of tautology, eliminated contradictions, added the necessary logical definitions which Nestorius unhappily eschewed, and reduced its length by a half or three quarters. Still, even in a morass of verbiage, the *Bazaar* is a document that merits careful consideration.

From the historian's point of view this is undoubtedly true, but we have yet to consider whether Anastos is right in thinking that in spite of its defects we find here 'the subtlest and most penetrating study of the mystery of the incarnation in the whole of patristic literature'. Its diffuse and chaotic form makes it a highly difficult work to comprehend and assess, and the fact that it is a constructive work of theology going deeper than the general Antiochene treatment of the subject is by no means immediately obvious.

2. Nestorius' position in the controversy

A number of interesting problems are posed by these literary remains of Nestorius. In the first place there is the question of consistency: does Nestorius give a fair account of the controversy in his apology, or did he as bishop of Constantinople act with greater provocation than he was later prepared to admit? Did he modify his position and refine it with qualifications in the years of reflection? Then there is the question of significance: were Nestorius' reflections really the product of subtle metaphysical analysis or was he simply confused and inconsistent? Finally there is the question of personality: what was Nestorius really like? How do we reconcile the self-effacing monk in exile with the headstrong bishop in Constantinople? Did character contribute to his tragedy as it did in the somewhat parallel case of Chrysostom? Clearly these questions need to be reviewed not only in the light of Nestorius' own statements, but also set against the impression he made on his contemporaries, one of whom was the church historian Socrates.

Socrates[141] explains Nestorius' downfall as the result of his own contentious spirit. Immediately after his consecration he said in public: 'Give me, my prince, the earth purged of heretics, and I will give you heaven as a recompense. Assist me in destroying heretics, and I will assist you in vanquishing the Persians.' He then set in motion a vicious persecution of heretics in the capital and in Asia Minor, earning the nickname 'Firebrand' after an Arian chapel had gone up in smoke. Socrates' estimate was that his own expulsion was no more than he deserved: as the proverb says, 'Drunkards never want wine, nor the contentious strife.'

As far as Socrates was concerned, the doctrinal charges brought against Nestorius had no substance:

> Having myself perused the writings of Nestorius, I have found him an unlearned man and shall candidly express the conviction of my mind concerning him . . . I cannot concede that he was either a follower of Paul of Samosata or of Photinus, or that he denied the divinity of Christ; but he seemed scared at the term *Theotokos* as though it were some terrible 'bugbear'. The fact is, the causeless alarm he manifested on this subject just exposed his extreme ignorance; for being a man of natural fluency as a speaker, he was considered well-educated, but in reality he was disgracefully illiterate.

This judgment Socrates bases upon the fact that he had not bothered to check up biblical and patristic authorities for using the title *Theotokos* of Mary; if he had, he would have found it in the works of Origen as well as others, Socrates states. However, 'puffed up with his ease of expression, he did not give his attention to the ancients, but thought himself the greatest of all'.

That Nestorius tended to act in haste and that he was over-sure of his own position can hardly be doubted. The high-handed way he addressed the bishop of Rome in the extant letters, his total want of tact in paying attention to some Western adherents of Pelagius who had been condemned at Rome some years before, all this suggests that he set himself up as the sole judge of heresy and was not disposed to accept advice or meddling from his fellow-patriarchs. He was determined and impetuous in dispute and liable to make strong statements open to misunderstanding; he himself admits that he had made some remark about not calling God an infant two or three months old.[142] Simple believers reacted to such comments as they did to his refusal to call Mary *Theotokos*, and it was of course that 'bugbear' around which the whole controversy revolved. There are different accounts of how the question of using that title for Mary set off the conflict. Socrates states that Nestorius took a strong line against *Theotokos* in support of a presbyter,

Anastasius, one of those who had come from Antioch in his entourage. Nestorius' strongly worded sermons against *Theotokos* are consistent with this account. Nestorius himself, however, claims[143] that he did not start the trouble but was drawn into it by an appeal from mutually hostile groups in Constantinople. The Apollinarian controversy lay behind the whole business: some gave the name 'Mother of God' to Mary, others 'Mother of Man', and each attached heretical labels to the other, Manichaeans or Apollinarians on the one side, Photinians or followers of Paul of Samosata on the other. Nestorius questioned each group and found that the first did not deny the humanity and the others did not deny the divinity; so he went for compromise – both titles were acceptable with certain reservations, but it would be better to avoid difficulties by using *Christotokos*. The groups went away happy and reconciled, he claims. Only the interference of outsiders like Cyril prolonged the question. Hints in his first sermon suggest that a debate had recently taken place in Nestorius' presence concerning the question whether Mary should be called *Theotokos* or *Anthrōpotokos*;[144] so his story finds some confirmation in sources from the time of the dispute. However, it does not seem altogether consistent with the fact that his sermons appear to exclude the title *Theotokos* entirely. Besides, that is what everyone apparently took him to mean at the time. So Nestorius must have been a determined critic of the term, whatever he said later. Yet there are several hints that even during the controversy he was prepared to allow it, if it were accompanied with proper safeguards: to the Pope he admitted that the term might be tolerated,[145] and to Cyril he confessed that he had nothing against it – 'only do not make the virgin a goddess'.[146] What worried Nestorius was not so much the term itself as the theological implications of careless usage; it too easily carried with it so many unacceptable corollaries. Only with great care and subtlety could one speak of God being born, God suffering, God dying. The unguarded language of faith could lead into all kinds of heretical snares. With characteristic resolution Nestorius waded into the attack, though he may be quite right in saying that he was not responsible for starting it all.

Years later, writing the *Bazaar*, Nestorius was still sure he was right. He insists that he has not changed.[147] He rejoices that God has raised up others to defend the truth.[148] We can surely accept that his self-effacement for the sake of truth is consistent with his earlier brusque activity on truth's behalf. In both cases he was trying to ensure that God was not blasphemed but given his due honour; and when he wrote the *Bazaar*, he still thought he was fighting Arians and Apollinarians in the unguarded statements of Cyril.

These considerations point towards answers to some of our enquiries, though more detailed examination of the sources could undoubtedly produce a more rounded assessment. But how consistent and intelligent is his doctrine? Socrates seems to have dismissed it as all froth and no substance. Are we to accept his judgment?

3. His own doctrinal position

The persistent criticism brought against the Antiochene theology has been that, dominated by the need to distinguish the two natures, it failed to give any account of the unity of the Christ. Most recent studies have been at pains to show how much Nestorius was concerned with Christ's unity of person,[149] and some have gone so far as to suggest[150] that Nestorius' 'prosopic union' was a serious attempt to give a metaphysically sound basis to the often-repeated Antiochene claim that they accepted one Son and one worship, without abandoning any of the hard-won principles of Antiochene theology in the process. Nestorius, it is said, worked with three basic metaphysical terms, *ousia* (substance), *physis* (nature) and *prosōpon* (person). A thing's *ousia* is what it is in itself; its *physis* is its totality of qualities, what gives it its distinctive characteristics; its *prosōpon* is its concrete manifestation, its external presentation. Divine *ousia* and human *ousia* being 'alien to one another' or mutually exclusive, could not be identified or united, so the union did not take place at that level. A union of *physis* could not mean anything but confusion – either an Apollinarian mixture producing a *tertium quid* or the complete absorption of one nature by the other.[151] So the only possible level at which the union could take place was that of *prosōpon*. The concrete manifestation is the one Son, our Lord Jesus Christ, who cannot be divided or separated into two; but underlying the common *prosōpon* are two natures and two *ousiai*, the divine and the human. What of the term *hypostasis*? Nestorius usually seems to have identified this with *ousia*;[152] in the trinitarian context he preferred to speak of three *prosōpa* rather than three *hypostaseis*, and in christology he speaks of each nature having its own *hypostasis*. But he recognises that the term is ambiguous, even stating that Cyril's phrase 'hypostatic union' could be acceptable if it meant not a union of *ousia* or *physis* but a union of *prosōpon*[153] (after all *hypostasis* and *prosōpon* were interchangeable in the trinitarian formula).

The 'prosopic union' thus becomes Nestorius' attempt to provide a metaphysical account of Christ's unity of person which did not involve the difficulties of a 'natural' or 'substantial' union, and Nestorius meant it to convey a 'real union'. The one Christ has 'two grounds of being', he is 'in two natures', as Chalcedon was later to affirm. God the Word and the Man in whom he came to be are not numerically two.[154] Christ is indivisible in his being Christ, but he is twofold in his being God and his being Man.[155] In other words the unity and the duality belong to different metaphysical levels.

The claim that Nestorius had begun to work out such a sophisticated account of the union even at the time of the controversy deserves some attention. It seems clear that whereas the Antiochenes in general tended to distinguish two classes of scriptural titles and sayings, those referring to the God-Logos and those referring to the Man, Nestorius chose to use three categories. Certain terms like Logos are specific references to his divine nature, and certain others specifically indicate his human nature; but the majority of titles refer neither to one nature alone nor the other, but to the common *prosōpon*, the Lord Jesus Christ. Hence his recommendation of *Christotokos* as a solution to the difficulties of using either *Theotokos* or *Anthrōpotokos* exclusively. God in his own essential nature was not born. The Trinity did not enter the virgin's womb. But Christ who was both God and Man, was born. Christ was not mere man, nor was he identical with God. To speak of the Logos becoming twofold in his nature, as Cyril did, was impossible for Nestorius. The Logos could not be the *prosōpon* of union; the two natures were not two states of the Logos' being, but the two 'grounds of being' of the one Christ. Of course, this implies a typically Antiochene 'symmetry', equal emphasis on the Godhead and the manhood; and the typically Antiochene safeguards for each nature are rigidly maintained. But whereas Theodore had tended to envisage each nature in very concrete terms, each being almost a separate person acting independently, Nestorius was anxious to present an account of one concrete individual with two distinguishable metaphysical bases.

However, if this was what Nestorius had in mind, he was certainly not very adept at making the point clearly. He inherited the Antiochene terminology and he was not altogether able to discard their very concrete ways of thinking. Thus he found it impossible to reserve the term *prosōpon* for the union; he could not avoid talk of a human *prosōpon* and a divine *prosōpon*. Thus each nature had its own *prosōpon* and the two natures remain personalized to the extent that his opponents were not altogether unfair in accusing him of teaching a 'double Christ', two persons acting independently. Nestorius himself speaks of them as 'self-sustaining',[156] and it is doubtful if he would have accepted the idea that the Two Natures were distinguishable merely in thought. Thus he was not sufficiently strict in his terminology to avoid misunderstanding. This is also true of his alleged distinction between *ousia* and *physis*. He often seems to identify the two and be very unclear about their specific application.[157] We may well ask whether he was not really rather confused by this metaphysical terminology, especially when we recall his difficulties with *hypostasis*. Socrates did not after all find his logical capabilities very impressive.

So what did Nestorius' 'prosopic union' mean? Was it one *prosōpon* with two underlying 'grounds of being'? Or was it two *prosōpa* uniting into a third? – in which case he faced the same difficulties about mixture as his opponents. Or was the word *prosōpon* used in two different senses, as Anastos suggests? Nestorius may have become dimly aware of these puzzles, for in the *Bazaar* we find a way of speaking not in evidence elsewhere, either in Nestorius' fragments or the other Antiochenes. Nestorius introduces the idea of an exchange of *prosōpa*, or a mutual reciprocity of *prosōpa*. He speaks of the divinity making use of the *prosōpon* of the humanity, and the humanity of that of the divinity.[158] In other words, the two *prosōpa* do not constitute a third by combination, but rather it is at the level of the *prosōpon* that two complete beings can interpenetrate without damage to the essential nature of either. On the basis of this idea it can be argued that Nestorius came to admit a *communicatio idiomatum*, though he remained well aware of the way in which this tradition could be misused by the unwary. (*Communicatio idiomatum* describes the doctrine that because of the union of natures in Christ, properties which are properly divine may be predicated of the human nature and properties properly human may be predicated of the divine.)

Nestorius does seem to be searching for a substantial basis for the union of two natures in Christ. The fact that this was his aim is most clearly indicated by his willingness to draw parallels between christological and trinitarian concepts:[159] 'As in the Trinity there is one *ousia* of three *prosōpa*, but three *prosōpa* of one *ousia*, here there is one *prosōpon* of two *ousiai* and two *ousiai* of one *prosōpon*.' 'Confess then the Assumer and the Assumed, each being one and in another, one not two, after the same manner as the manner of the Trinity.' Nestorius was attempting to provide a way of conceiving a real unity. But how successful he was is another question. One is tempted to think he was the victim of his own lack of definition, though part of the problem was that he did not have suitable metaphysical tools; but besides that, his thought was still over-shadowed by the legacy of the Arian and Apollinarian controversies. The sharp division between the divine and the human, the Creator and the created, was an axiomatic principle to be defended at all costs, and this in itself made his task well-nigh impossible. Chalcedon itself made no attempt to resolve the problem, content simply to affirm two in one and one in two without separation or mixture. It was precisely that confession that Nestorius was trying to establish.

So Nestorius was wrestling with the problems of the Antiochene theology he had inherited. In reaction to Arianism and Apollinarianism, it had produced an over-concrete picture of the man Jesus struggling against temptation, while the Logos remained transcendent and unconfined to the human temple he had fashioned for himself. Nestorius strove to put back into the centre the one Lord Jesus Christ, while refusing to compromise the 'Godness of God' or the 'Manness of Man'. In this endeavour he seems to have been remarkably consistent, and we should probably take his word for it that he did not change or seriously modify his christological position over the years. He carried the can for all the faults and difficulties of the Antiochene position while actually seeking ways to resolve them. That he was thoroughly misrepresented by his enemies cannot be doubted, though he may have asked for it by making manifestly provocative statements. When Theodoret was finally forced to anathematize Nestorius together with anyone who did not say the holy Mary was *Theotokos* and divided the one only-begotten Son, he must have known that he was associating Nestorius' name with a thoroughly misleading caricature of his actual teaching. It is hardly surprising that he conscientiously refused to desert Nestorius and his friends throughout twenty years of attack. With his own rather different approach, he was attempting to perform the same task as Nestorius – namely find a way of maintaining the traditional Antiochene insights while rediscovering the one Saviour, the one Lord Jesus Christ.

Nestorius was the victim. He has become the symbol of one type of christological position taken to extremes. And for that he suffered. He could legitimately complain that his condemnation had been unfair: Cyril had plotted his downfall; Cyril chaired the synod; Cyril was his accuser and his judge; Cyril represented Pope and Emperor. 'Cyril was everything!'[160] Nestorius had no chance of a hearing. There can be few who would defend the proceedings at Ephesus. Then his friends deserted him, and he went into exile in Egypt. There he was captured by invading barbarians, and on his escape surrendered himself to the Roman governor 'lest all future generations should be told the tragic story that it was better to be captured by barbarians than to take refuge with the Roman empire'.[161] The governor, however, kept him on the move, transferring him from place to place, while he lived in constant pain from injuries. But Nestorius was a monk, schooled to patience and endurance. There is no better testimony to the depth of his commitment than his refusal to appeal to Leo even though it was evident that Leo's *Tome* was a vindication of what he had himself stood for. He did not want the truth to suffer by association with his blackened name.[162] Did he live to hear of Chalcedon? In a recently published collection of Nestorian texts, it is stated that he lived twenty-two years after Ephesus,[163] which implies that he did; but the *Liber Heraclidis* provides no unambiguous evidence, though it certainly indicates that he saw the death of Theodosius and looked forward to a new council with assurance that truth would prevail. But 'as for me,' he concludes,

> I regard the sufferings of my life and all that has befallen me in this world as the suffering of a single day; and I have not changed all these years. Now my death approaches and every day I pray to God to dismiss me – me whose eyes have seen the salvation of God. Rejoice with me, Desert, thou my friend, my nurse, my home; and thou exile, my mother, who after my death will keep my body until the resurrection by the grace of God.   Amen.

VI. Cyril of Alexandria

1. His reputation

Cyril has provoked extreme reactions in both ancient and modern times. For some he has been the great Doctor of the Incarnation. His letters were given canonical status at Chalcedon and proved a foundation on which later thinkers would build. Chalcedonians and Monophysites agreed that Cyril was to be regarded as the prime authority on this question; and some modern studies have hailed Cyril as the one great fifth-century thinker to perceive the essentials for an incarnational theology and to seek ways of upholding them in a philosophical atmosphere which made his task formidable. True he was a bit hasty, they say, but an extract from a letter penned by him in the early phases of the controversy throws light on an aspect of his character of which few are aware:

> I love peace; there is nothing that I detest more than quarrels and disputes. I love everybody, and if I could heal one of the

brethren by losing all my possessions and goods, I am willing to do so joyfully; because it is concord that I value most ... But there is question of the faith and of a scandal which concerns all the churches of the Roman Empire ... The sacred doctrine is entrusted to us ... How can we remedy these evils? ... I am ready to endure with tranquillity all blame, all humiliations, all injuries provided that the faith is not endangered. I am filled with love for Nestorius; nobody loves him more than I do ... If, in accordance with Christ's commandment, we must love our very enemies themselves, is it not natural that we should be united in special affection to those who are our friends and brethren in the priesthood? But when the faith is attacked, we must not hesitate to sacrifice our life itself. And if we fear to preach the truth because that causes us some inconvenience, how, in our gatherings, can we chant the combats and triumphs of our holy martyrs?[164]

To some then, Cyril has been a saint, primarily concerned with the defence of Christian truth. To others, Cyril has appeared as an unscrupulous political operator, a true successor to his uncle Theophilus who contrived the downfall of John Chrysostom, a nasty piece of work out to achieve maximum power for the Alexandrian see by whatever possible means.[165] And recent emphasis on the part played by politics and personality receives some support from contemporaries. Isidore of Pelusium was a good friend of Cyril's, so much so that he could afford to offer him a rebuke for his conduct at Ephesus, implying that animosity had blinkered his judgment: 'Sympathy does not see distinctly; but antipathy does not see at all. If then you would be clear of both sorts of poor-sightedness, do not indulge in violent negations, but submit any charges made against you to a just judgment.'[166] His following remarks are revealing:

Many of those who were assembled at Ephesus speak satirically of you as a man bent on pursuing his private animosities, not as one who seeks in correct belief the things of Jesus Christ. 'He is sister's son to Theophilus,' they say, 'and in disposition takes after him. Just as the uncle openly expended his fury against the inspired and beloved John, so also the nephew seeks to set himself up in his turn, although there is considerable difference between the things at stake.'

Socrates[167] certainly disliked Cyril and most of the information he gives about him is designed to bring discredit on his early years as bishop – indeed, by comparison his behaviour in the Nestorian controversy appears restrained, for in Socrates' eyes, the chief blame for that affair rested on Nestorius' tactlessness and ignorance. Clearly Cyril made enemies easily, and it is hardly surprising that in a letter quoted as Theodoret's[168] amongst the Acts of Chalcedon, we find expressed heartfelt relief at Cyril's death and the suggestion that a large, heavy stone be placed on his tomb lest he provoke the dead so much that they send him back!

So Cyril poses the age-old problem: how can a man apparently be both saint and sinner – or in his case perhaps we should say, great theologian and moral blackguard? The extreme reactions on both sides are surely exaggerated; yet Cyril must have been a strong character with the ability to attract and repel. If we are to judge him as a scheming politician with little interest in anything but success, we have systematically to distrust his own protestations; but then he may have had little self-knowledge. What is most likely is that he had a strong-principled and iron personality with little ability to give in or be argued out of a position once he had taken it up. Like many other figures of history, he identified his standpoint with Truth, and was prepared to stop at nothing to ensure its triumph. This made it impossible for him to listen to others with sympathy, so that he can be convicted of misunderstanding and unfairness from his own writings.

What then do we know of his life and work prior to the great controversy? Do the first fifteen or so years of his episcopate throw any light on his motivations?

The first recorded fact about his life is that he accompanied his uncle to the Synod of the Oak which deposed John Chrysostom; and that prejudice lasted – long after the rest of the church had restored the name of John to the diptychs (i.e. the roll of those whose names should be included in the prayers of the liturgy), Cyril refused to follow suit. Once a decision was made, Cyril was not one to see any reason for going back on it. Nor can his uncle's political tactics have escaped his notice. There is undoubtedly a certain parallel between John's deposition and that of Nestorius thirty years later.

2. Earlier years

When his uncle died in 412, Cyril was not elected his successor unopposed, but he soon asserted himself in the city of Alexandria. His first act was the suppression of the Novatianist sect and the seizure of their ecclesiastical property. He rapidly came into conflict with the prefect, Orestes, and Socrates suggests that his major fault was meddling in secular affairs.[169] The real problem is to assess the degree of Cyril's responsibility for the dreadful events Socrates proceeds to relate. Alexandria was in any case a cosmopolitan city given to tumult and riot, with inter-racial feuds of an endemic nature. The 'third race' – the Christian populace – stood flanked by pagans and Jews, still strong in influence and numbers. Did Cyril stir up trouble? Or did a series of coincidences trigger the conflicts, as so often happens when a closely packed urban population is divided by race or religion?

The first outbreak of violence came when a great devotee of Cyril – the leader of applause when Cyril was preaching – was caught eavesdropping on an occasion when the prefect was issuing regulations for Jewish theatricals on the Sabbath. Orestes was already annoyed at Cyril's meddling in the city administration and, according to Socrates, arrested his supposed spy, and there and then publicly tortured him. Cyril complained to the Jewish leaders, who promptly plotted against the Christians. At night they raised an outcry that a certain church was on fire, and then slaughtered all the Christians who turned out to save it. Cyril promptly led a great army of Christians to the synagogues and drove all Jews out of the city, permitting the crowd to loot their property.

Alexandria was no stranger to anti-Semitic riots:[170] it had all happened before, even as long ago as the reign of Claudius, before Christian influence was appreciable. As then, reports and appeals went to the emperor. Orestes was particularly annoyed at the damage done to the city, no doubt economic damage in particular, by the loss of so large a section of the population. However, popular feeling could no longer stand the power conflict between civil and ecclesiastical authorities and in response to demand, Cyril made peaceful overtures to Orestes, only to have them rejected.

Subsequent events did nothing to help. About five hundred monks came to the city from the Nitrian desert to defend their Patriarch, and caught Orestes out in his chariot. It is clear that the monks saw Orestes as a representative of paganism, in spite of his protestations that he had been baptized by the bishop of Constantinople. They started abusing him and one threw a stone which struck Orestes on the head. The city population now rushed to the rescue and the monk who had injured the prefect was tortured so severely that he died. Cyril again sent a report to the emperor and, much to everyone's disgust, treated the victim as a martyr for the cause of Christ.

Worse was to follow. The most distinguished pagan of the time was a woman, Hypatia, a Neoplatonist philosopher who could hold her own in any academic circle. Orestes was clearly impressed by her and they were frequently in each other's company. The Christian mob decided it was she who was influencing Orestes against Cyril – the pagan connection again! They waylaid her, took her into a church, there lynched her and then burnt her mangled remains at a place called Cinaron. As Socrates states, 'Surely nothing can be further from the spirit of Christianity than to tolerate massacres, fights and such doings.' The reputation of the Alexandrian church was tarnished. But while this event was particularly horrible because of the personal nature of the atrocity, Alexandria was no stranger to anti-pagan riots. The suppression of paganism had been the subject of imperial edicts, but the authorities had often acted weakly or not at all, and it was fanatical monks who set fire to temples; twenty-five years earlier, Alexandria had witnessed the destruction of the Mithraeum and the Serapeum under the direction of Cyril's uncle, Theophilus.

It is hard to decide how far Cyril was responsible for instigating the events described (Socrates may have been reporting hostile rumours circulating in Constantinople); but it is clear that he gave more than tacit support to any who acted for Christianity against its two powerful religious rivals, sometimes indeed to the point of serious misjudgment. These events occurred in the first four years of his episcopate, and it is interesting to see that his literary activity, some of it in fact from a much later period, reflects the continuing struggle with non-Christians. His work against Julian was praised by Theodoret, and its very composition proves that the Nestorian controversy did not monopolize Cyril's interests even as late as the 430s. Paganism was still a prime issue. And the Jewish question has been described as 'the backdrop to Cyril's exegesis' in an interesting study by Robert Wilken:[171] Cyril needed to prove that the Old Testament belonged, not to the Jews, but to the Christians, and this issue has a predominant place, particularly in the Old Testament commentaries which seem to have been his earliest literary output.

From the very beginning, then, Cyril stood for the Christian cause, and was unbending in his determination. He had one aim in view, namely the establishment of Christian truth, and his single-mindedness blinded him to the doubtful morality of the means whereby his ends were achieved. In every age and situation the ethical corollaries of the Christian faith have been perceived differently. It took an Erasmus to see that tolerance and peace were truer to the spirit of Christ than war and fanaticism – though he was anticipated by occasional comments from such as the humane historian, Socrates. If the triumph of truth was at stake, Cyril was not one to attempt passive resistance rather than positive, if violent, action. And he had the traditions of his see to encourage him – the unflinching boldness of Athanasius, the determination of Theophilus, and the long-standing alliance between the Patriarch and the monks, the shock-troops of orthodoxy. Precedent was of particular importance to Cyril – he it was, after all, who developed the 'patristic argument' in theology, the appeal to statements of the Fathers alongside scripture as a means of ascertaining the proper tradition of interpretation. So, like his predecessors, Cyril was not afraid to take an uncompromising stand against all opposition, against heresy, paganism and the Jews, and with principle and precedent behind him, he had little reason to question that he was in the right. Just occasionally he seems to have been persuaded that his unbending attitudes had carried him a bit too far and, if he did not retract, at least he allowed things to drop. Silence about the anathemas permitted his reconciliation with John of Antioch, and it was not the first time that discretion had rescued his reputation: for Socrates reports that he allowed the memory of his pseudo-martyr to be gradually obliterated by silence. It was not Cyril after all who so overstepped the mark that Alexandrian ascendency was shattered and its theological legacy compromised, but his less worthy successor, Dioscorus. Cyril, though, had himself set such an unfortunate precedent, had so unleashed popular passions and so encouraged the shouting of over-simplified theological formulae, that he cannot wholly be exonerated from blame for the eventual schism. The Second Council of Ephesus, the 'Robber-Synod', was not out of line with the First, either in character or intention; it was just a yet more extreme case of the same type. Yet it is surely true to say that the trouble with Cyril was not outright wickedness so much as an inability to entertain the possibility that he might be in the wrong, before serious damage had been done.

Cyril's early years, then, do afford us some insight into the kind of man he was when the controversy with Nestorius broke out; and the works he wrote prior to the controversy also provide significant pointers for understanding the position he took up. The dating of Cyril's early works (that is, those written before 428 and the start of the christological conflict) is highly conjectural,[172] but the bulk of his output was exegesis of scripture, though at some point he also turned to anti-Arian polemics. Such was the training-ground in which his theological skills were refined, and in both areas he was wedded to Alexandrian traditions. His anti-Arian writings re-stated the ideas and arguments of Athanasius; his exegesis, avowedly a digest of the work of predecessors (though who they were he does not say),[173] takes up in the main the spiritualizing heritage that descended from Philo, through Clement and Origen, to Didymus. To understand the Nestorian controversy it is important to recognize that in his christology likewise, Cyril espoused an essential conservatism, and that his characteristic stance was a straightforward appeal to tradition. Originality, then generally regarded as dangerous innovation, was remote from Cyril's ambitions. It is this background which enables us to appreciate the sheer dynamic of his campaign. As far as his party was concerned, Cyril was not relaying the foundations or even building on them; he was simply doing a bit of repointing to the brickwork.

3. Old Testament exegesis

Yet Cyril was not simply a literary parrot like the later Byzantine scholastics.[174] His profound dependence on the past was married to a brilliant judgment of contemporary needs and an ability appropriately to recycle the traditional inheritance. His so-called 'exegetical' works are not all by any means formal commentaries. Cyril seems to have been drawn to the dialogue form, which is first evidenced in a series of dialogues between himself and a certain Palladius *On Worship in Spirit and Truth*.[175] Often treated as if it were a commentary on passages from the Pentateuch, this is really an exploration of the proper Christian attitude to the Law.

Cyril's approach is fundamentally conventional: righteousness comes not through the Law but through Christ. Moses is unable to free man from the tyranny of the devil, for Moses' Master is Christ. New Testament references provide Cyril with the starting-point for showing that the Mosaic covenant is a type and shadow, that Christian righteousness must exceed that of the scribes and Pharisees. The prophetic condemnation of Jewish sacrifices points forward to the pure sacrifice to be offered under the new covenant (an age-old Christian apologetic argument here re-furbished). The law was written $\delta\iota'$ $\dot{\eta}\mu\tilde{\alpha}\varsigma$ (for us), and its prescriptions operate at two levels, at the literal, practical level for the historical Israelites, but also as an image and type for the spiritual law of the church. All manner of legal prescriptions (e.g. those in Exod. 22 concerning restitution for theft) can be turned into meaningful spiritual commands, especially injunctions to goodness and loving one another. The law is holy, especially if its double significance is properly appreciated. Indeed, the whole law is summed up in loving God and one's neighbour (a claim based on

Matthew 22.40, Paul in Romans 13 and I John 4.20); this provides
the model for understanding the continuing relevance of the
decalogue to Christians.

Besides this, however, Cyril has perceived that the true meaning
of the law is to be expounded in terms of the drama of fall and
redemption. The pattern of exile and spiritual famine, followed by
repentance and return to a better life, is traced in various biblical
narratives: Abraham's migration and the exodus are taken as
paradigms of God's grace bringing conversion.

This, then, is no conventional commentary on selected Pentateuchal passages, as some accounts almost suggest. What we
have here is a thematic treatment aimed at presenting what might
be called a 'biblical theology', worked out in relation to the five
books of the law. The aim is to expose man's predicament and its
solution in Christ, showing how the Christian use of the Jewish
scriptures is an integral part of the whole theological construction.

Nearly everything here can be found in pre-Cyrilline writings.
Cyril does not introduce new types or new ideas. But somehow the
impact of this work is a magnificent justification of a whole
method of approach which often seems arbitrary and unacceptable;
instead of being dissipated in verse by verse allegory, it is concentrated in an impressive coherence, remarkable for its total grasp of
the distinctive Christian claim. Allegory naturally plays a large
part, but it is integrated into an overall setting which gives it a less
alien, non-biblical feel than is often the case. The two Testaments
are shown to cohere with one another through a systematic
theological presentation into which each link fits. Doubtless this is
done by using exegetical methods of questionable validity, but for
Cyril's time, for the contemporary battle with the Jews, it must
have provided powerful ammunition of a kind far more worthwhile
than the stones and looting of the street battles.

Cyril's other effort on the Pentateuch, possibly composed con-
currently since each work refers to the other, is of a quite different
character – indeed, the approach in the *Glaphyra* is much closer to a
systematic effort at a commentary.[176] But once again Cyril makes
no attempt to go through it verse by verse; in some sections he does
quote the text for detailed exegesis, but this is by no means always
the case: the Genesis narrative of Adam, for example, is never
quoted – the story is treated entirely in the light of its
ἀνακεφαλαίωσις (recapitulation) in Christ and what biblical quotations there are come almost exclusively from the New Testament.
So, keeping to the Pentateuchal order but not tied to every detail of
its text, Cyril presents a selection of narratives or themes from

which he can obtain maximum Christian capital. Thus, like most great theologians, he operates a 'canon within the canon', concentrating on prize passages which have stimulated his particular theological emphases, or can provide a vehicle for their expression. Interestingly enough, the creation story is given no attention at all; cosmogony preoccupied Basil and many others, but Cyril shows no interest in the subject outside his apologetic treatise against Julian. In his Old Testament exegesis he is preoccupied with the Christian claim to have the true key to its meaning.[177] Thus in his introduction he states that everything in Moses' writings signifies the mystery of Christ in riddles, and his tendency throughout is to choose narratives or themes with ancient typological meanings so as to bring out the spiritual sense of the Old Testament. This being the case it is perhaps not surprising to find that one book each suffices for Leviticus, Numbers and Deuteronomy, whereas Exodus takes three and Genesis predominates with seven.

Cyril's works on the Pentateuch have a particular interest since their very selectivity is indicative of the primary theological concerns with which he was exercised at the time of writing. While there can be little doubt that Wilken is right in seeing conflict with the Jews as the setting against which these works were produced, they also provide considerable insight into Cyril's basic understanding of man, sin, redemption, Christ and the essentials of Christian practice. As Wilken has also noted, the superiority of Christ to Moses and the Adam-Christ typology stand out as soteriological themes of great importance for Cyril's christology.[178] Christ's uniqueness lay in his role as the one who restored the lost image of God to man – the old 'recapitulation' theme is Cyril's link with the past and his presupposition for the future. It was because Nestorius threatened his basic Christian perceptions that Cyril's opposition was aroused.

Cyril's work on the prophets takes a more conventional commentary form and provides a clearer overall picture of his exegetical methods. Extant in their entirety are his commentaries on the Minor Prophets and on Isaiah, though many further fragments are traceable in the Catenae (authenticity is as usual a problem with this material, and the collections in Migne need to be examined with care). It is particularly interesting that his Commentary on the Minor Prophets[179] exists in full and can therefore be compared in detail with that of Theodore of Mopsuestia, the radical Antiochene. Needless to say, unlike Theodore, Cyril gives plenty of attention to prophetic and spiritual meanings, often teased out of the text by elaborate allegorical devices. More unexpected are the extensive explanations of historical background, and the attention he pays to the literal reference of the text. His introductory outlines, together with his interest in the prophet's intention, are features which bear comparison with the work of the Antiochenes, though often differing in detail.[180] The reality of the text's historical dimension and of its original message to the Israelites is fully admitted, even though it is by no means given the primacy accorded to it by Theodore. Kerrigan has argued that Cyril's exegesis is extremely eclectic, and that Jerome in particular exercised a considerable influence on him, drawing him away from exclusive dependence on the Alexandrian tradition. Certainly the excesses of Origenism have been abandoned, partially no doubt because the Origenist controversy had tempered current exegetical practice. But there may be other factors operating too: the prophet's denunciations provided fuel for Cyril's attacks on the Jews, the exile was an important indication of God's judgment upon them, and for Cyril their rejection of the prophets, who had after all heralded the coming transformation of Judaism through the Christ, was symptomatic of their continuing religious blindness. The two levels of meaning were equally important to Cyril where the prophetic books were concerned – for both pointed to the superiority of Christianity.

The two levels of meaning were also essential because they had a metaphysical basis of fundamental theological importance, and it is here that Cyril reveals his real kinship with the Alexandrian tradition. Cyril's conception of reality distinguished in Platonic manner between τὰ αἰσθητά (realities perceived by the senses) and τὰ νόητα (realities perceived by the mind) – the latter he regarded as the true realities (τὰ ἀληθινά), the spiritual realm (τὰ πνευμάτικα) discovered only through contemplation (θεωρία). These two realities coexisted in parallel, the former representing the latter in parables, signs and symbols (his words for this include: τύποι, παραδείγματα, σκιαί, αἰνίγματα and εἰκόνες).[181] Thus the sensible and intelligible worlds are distinct yet intimately related. God is transcendent (Cyril will have nothing to do with the Anthropomorphites), but the harmony of the created order is a symbol or sign of God's wisdom,[182] and man was intended to incarnate the image of God in the sensible world. There is a real sense in which Cyril's christology is grounded in this metaphysical theory, the Word Incarnate fulfilling the rôle that Adam failed to play, and guaranteeing the cohesion of the two distinct realms of reality. For Cyril the text of scripture likewise belonged to both worlds; the literal meaning referred to the objects of the sensible world, the

spiritual sense to spiritual realities. Closely parallel to his treatment of the Old Testament is Cyril's approach to the parables, as
evidenced in his *Commentary on Luke*.[183] The parables are images
of things not seen, of realities belonging to the intelligible and
spiritual world. They illustrate theological truths or point to
aspects of Christian conduct. The obvious outer sense of the
parable requires no explanation; but the object of the exposition is
to explore its inward, secret, unseen meaning. At times, perhaps
more particularly in his earlier works, Cyril denigrates the literal
meaning of scripture, and often he stresses that it is something to be
surpassed; but his regard for the literal meaning, elsewhere
expressed, parallels a refusal to admit to docetism. The sensible
world is not an illusion, but rather the vehicle of truth. This is the
core of Cyril's spirituality and this is why it is misleading to attach
party labels to his exegesis, suggesting that he combines features of
the Antiochene approach with the Alexandrian tradition. His
method of composition was eclectic, but his theory was a development of Alexandrian Platonism.

4. Dogmatic theology

Cyril's biblical interests were not confined to the Old Testament,
but his New Testament exegesis on the whole seems to date from a
later period. The two works which survive pretty extensively are
commentaries on the gospels of Luke and John, though sizable
fragments of other commentaries are also extant. Pusey's three-
volume edition of the *Commentary on John* adds the most
important of these, though as usual material drawn from the
Catenae needs to be treated with caution. The *Commentary on
John* must have been composed before the Nestorian controversy,
since its christological discussions never explicitly take up the
characteristic issues of the controversy, whereas the *Commentary
on Luke* does, and clearly belongs later. However, dogmatic issues
had begun to exercise Cyril at the time of the John commentary, a
work closely associated with his anti-Arian writings. Jouassard has
plausibly argued that it was in the mid-420s that these questions
began to claim Cyril's attention, since his paschal letters show no
anxiety about heresy prior to the encyclical of 424.[184]

The *Commentary on John* seems to have been preceded by the
Thesaurus de sancta Trinitate,[185] and some of its features are more
readily understood if we consider the latter work first. Liébaert[186]
has shown that this work is almost entirely based on Athanasius'
work *Contra Arianos* (Book III in particular) and a lost work *Contra
Eunomium*, which was probably the work of Didymus. Yet for all

its dependence on past material, it is a striking example of Cyril's ability to systematize and re-present the well-worn arguments. The work consists of thirty-five chapters, each of which presents a thesis (*logos*) which is then defended on the basis of a series of listed arguments or a compilation of scriptural testimonies. The sixth *logos*, for example, is 'that the Father begat the Son of himself without division or outflow'. This is followed by a number of Eunomian objections, each answered by a series of counter-arguments. The thirty-second *logos* is 'that the Son is God by nature, and if this, not something made or created'; and this is established on the basis of some 170 scriptural testimonies and arguments. Athanasius' work is never copied word for word – even his quotations from the writings of Arius are paraphrased. Athanasius' ideas are used but they are reordered and given totally new expression so as to present a more rigorous form of argument. Cyril has really sorted the subject out and provided a treatise which highlights the essential elements in the debate, clarifies the points one by one, and affords much more ready access to patristic theological method than the diffuse polemics of earlier writers. This matter of form is important for the John commentary; for here he indulges in dogmatic excursuses similarly ordered, with points marshalled into neat lists – theological mini-treatises of a form similar to that adopted for the whole of the *Thesaurus*.

There has been some debate about the sources of this work, many scholars affirming that Cyril had access to the works of Epiphanius and the Cappadocians. Liébaert convincingly maintains that his information is exclusively Alexandrian, and that there is no direct link with, for example, the works against Eunomius written by Basil or Gregory of Nyssa. This is an important conclusion, for it suggests that up to the Nestorian controversy, Cyril's theological awareness was very much bound by the Alexandrian situation and inheritance, and confirms the view that he had little contact with the directions that theology and exegesis were taking in Antioch and elsewhere. Unlike the Antiochenes, he shows little concern about post-Arian developments like Apollinarianism.[187] The Arian controversy remains for him the great dogmatic issue, and the Nicene faith is the answer to it. This is another significant pointer to Cyril's position at the outbreak of the christological battle.

So closely associated with the *Thesaurus* are the seven *Dialogues on the Trinity*[188] that we can hardly overlook them at this point. Having set out the anti-Arian argumentation in a methodical form, Cyril proceeded to give the case a more literary presentation. This is a more personal, polemical work, not so rigorous, freer in style;

but as Liébaert[189] notes, it follows the same outline scheme of subjects and is closely parallel to the first work. Cyril dedicated the work to the same Nemesinos as the *Thesaurus* and explains in the prologue that he proposes to treat the issue by presenting a debate between himself and Hermias, the *dramatis personae* being identified in the text by the use of A and B respectively; question and answer will facilitate the organization and effectiveness of the attack when a matter of such subtlety is at issue. So in the dialogues, B fulfils the role of reporting heretical theses, and A replies in arguments analogous to the *Thesaurus*. We have already noticed Cyril's liking for this particular form of literature. That he regarded these dialogues on the Trinity as a particularly effective work is shown by the fact that later he wrote an additional dialogue with Hermias on the questions raised by the Nestorian controversy. It has generally been assumed that to do this he rewrote the material used in his *De recta fide*, following the text so closely that Pusey found it convenient to print the two works on facing pages.[190] Recently, however, the priority of the *De recta fide* has been questioned.[191]

The seven dialogues, then, treat the central issues in the debate with Arius: that the Son is co-eternal and consubstantial with the Father; that the Son is begotten of him κατὰ φύσιν (by nature); that he is true God, just like the Father; that the Son is not a κτίσμα or ποίημα (something created or made); that all things proper to the Godhead, including its glory, belong φυσικῶς (naturally) to the Son, just as they do to the Father. Then, before adding a final dialogue on the divinity of the Holy Spirit, Cyril spends the sixth dialogue discussing how human attributes are properly ascribed to the Son, insisting that they do not belong to the nature of the Logos inasmuch as he is conceived to be and is God, but rather are attributed to him τῇ μετὰ σαρκὸς οἰκονομίᾳ (by the economy with flesh). This dialogue is particularly interesting for several reasons. (i) It alerts us to the fact that sanctification is at the heart of Cyril's soteriology – the Logos did not need to be sanctified, but the sanctification of his humanity by the coming of the Spirit meant the sanctification of human nature in him. This was basically Cyril's understanding of θεοποίησις (deification). (ii) The emphasis on the Logos' κένωσις (literally 'emptying') or ταπείνωσις (humiliation) is already to be found as a constituent motif in Cyril's thinking; he limited himself to the human condition and that is why human attributes are applicable to him. (iii) At this point, Cyril is prepared to speak of the Logos raising 'his own temple' (using John 2.9) – a form of speech which, coming from the

Antiochenes, he was later to attack mercilessly. This is not the only case of inconsistency perpetrated by Cyril in the heat of the battle; he had also used the phrase 'assuming the woman-born man or shrine like a robe' in the *Thesaurus*, and later vehemently attacked such expressions.[192]

Generally speaking, then, we find here in the *Dialogues* the same situation as in the *Thesaurus*. Cyril has taken over the language and theology of Athanasius, making few modifications. He tends to be more concerned with man's sinfulness than Athanasius;[193] he tends to speak of 'humanity' rather than 'flesh'; he also gives a little more stress to the 'psychological' weaknesses of human nature, like fear and dread. Yet at this stage, he does not seem to have noticed that positive affirmation of a human soul in the Christ could resolve some of the difficulties in confuting the Arians.[194] In the Alexandrian tradition, that affirmation was to be found only in the works of the notorious Origenist, Didymus, and Cyril inherited his uncle's anti-Origenism. Nor was he yet alive to the necessity of refuting Apollinarius.

The *Commentary on John*[195] sums up all that we have so far learned of Cyril, and highlights the basic theological stance from which his campaign against Nestorius was launched. The twelve books of the Commentary exist in their entirety apart from Books VII and VIII; for these, Pusey pieces together extensive fragments from the Catenae and some Syriac sources, but doubts have been expressed about the reliability of this material. The form of the work is a verse by verse commentary, and Cyril's interest in the two levels of interpretation remains an important element in his exegesis. He is not too concerned about historical discrepancies between John and the other gospels, even though he assumes that the literal sense is accurate and has some natural explanation. Far more interesting to him, however, are possible symbolic explanations. His interest in the spiritual sense of the gospel enables him to plumb the depths of Johannine symbolism in the signs and discourse material, particularly where it points to one of his favourite themes, the superiority of Christianity to Judaism, and the transference of the gospel from the Jews to the Gentiles.[196] It also stimulates allegorical interpretations of a less convincing kind.

But Cyril, in this commentary, is avowedly looking for a δογματικώτερα ἐξήγησις (a more dogmatic exegesis) and it is his new interest in propounding orthodox rather than heretical interpretation which gives this commentary its chief characteristics. Indeed, so prominent is this that thesis-type chapter headings have been supplied for much of the commentary, outlining the main purport of the dogmatic argument in each section. This dogmatic purpose leads to a concentration on controversial texts with christological implications, though christology and the anti-Arian argument are not the only interest: Book I.9 provides a lengthy refutation of the idea of the pre-existence of souls, in the same argumentative format as is found in other dogmatic excursuses. Inevitably in a work of commentary, the text of the Johannine gospel suggests the themes pursued, and since the gospel is primarily concerned with the person of Christ, it is not surprising that this theme predominates. This was after all Cyril's main concern at this stage – at least in so far as the Arian debate posed the problem.

The approach of Athanasius is still Cyril's model. To counter the Arian argument, Cyril points out that certain things were said by Jesus as a man, or even as a Jew, and insists that from such texts no ultimate conclusions about the nature of the Logos can be deduced. Really he is the transcendent Logos, *homoousios* with the Father; but the features of his earthly life are the outcome of his voluntary ταπείνωσις (humiliation) of which Philippians 2.5–11 is the classic expression. He remained what he was, and yet became man, subjecting himself to human limitations.[197] Like Athanasius, Cyril himself distinguished between divine and human attributes in the context of the anti-Arian argument, but it is noticeable that already he is insisting on the subjection of the Logos to human conditions in the incarnation, and occasionally criticizing the tendency to divide the Christ, though he does not yet explicitly attack characteristic Antiochene terminology.[198] As in the case of Athanasius, his statements occasionally have a docetic ring: 'he trembles and feigns (πλάττεται) confusion'; 'to suffer the appearance (σχῆμα) of confusion'; 'he seems to submit to death'.[199] Cyril does not merely speak of Jesus acting ὡς θεός (as God) or ὡς ἄνθρωπος (as man) in parallel; but he uses the phrase ὡς ἄνθρωπος σχηματίζεται, which 'could easily suggest that the whole human life of Jesus was a pretence'.[200] Yet Cyril's underlying thought is that the humanity is genuine enough as the external manifestation of the one Christ, the aspect of Christ which belongs to the world of the sensible.[201] The human feebleness is real, but belongs to the surface of the life of Christ. The gospel for him is all about the self-limitation of the Logos to the conditions of the created order. Once more we see Cyril grasping and developing a point which was to become central to his argument with Nestorius.

It is clear that for Cyril, biblical exegesis was his major theological activity. Though distracted into pamphleteering and controversy soon after composing the *Commentary on John,* his interpretative work did not cease. Exegetical treatises fill seven out of ten volumes of Migne's edition of Cyril's work; yet sizable portions of his biblical work have disappeared. Indeed, the other major surviving work, the *Commentary on Luke,* we mostly have not in the original but in a Syriac translation.

The *Commentary on Luke* in fact shows Cyril in a new light, for it is not really a formal commentary at all, but a series of homilies. Three complete homilies are actually extant in Greek; but a Syriac version of a great deal more was discovered in the last century and published by Payne Smith.[202] Further fragments have since appeared, and a new edition of the whole text has started to appear in the CSCO series.[203] It is often said that the Syriac version comprises 156 homilies, but some sections are so brief that they must clearly be extracts rather than complete texts. Nevertheless it has proved a significant find.

Cyril's interests in these homilies are primarily practical. He focuses on the gospel themes and places a great deal of emphasis upon ethical teaching, exhortation and above all, imitation of Christ through obedience and humility. Christ is the 'type' to be imitated, the example to be followed, through baptism, through temptation in the wilderness, through suffering and death. The Christian is to be united with Christ in living a life like his. The kingdom of God is a spiritual kingdom, found when one forsakes all for love of Christ; and as we have seen, the parables, like the Old Testament, point beyond themselves to spiritual realities, to God's grace and man's obedience. The needs of the congregation, then, are uppermost in his mind. Occasionally, however, those needs include warnings about dangerous interpretations. Thus the Nestorian controversy clearly lies behind his comments on Christ's baptism. True the Logos of God did not need to be baptized, but that is no reason for separating off the 'seed of David'; the baptism of Christ is justified as part of the 'economy', his acceptance of man's condition for the salvation of men.

5. The Nestorian controversy

Even though biblical exegesis largely occupied Cyril, there is no doubt that the christological controversy came to dominate his literary activity as well as his politics for a few important years. The first indication of his alarm at Nestorius' teaching is to be found in his seventeenth *Paschal Letter,* the one for 429. Cyril's letters announcing the date of Easter, misleadingly entitled *Homiliae Paschales,*[204] cover the years 414–442 (twenty-nine in all), and as already noticed, they probably provide some indication of the Patriarch's interests at various points in his career. They are predominantly of a practical character, exhorting the congregations to fasting and prayer, to celebration of the festival, to love and almsgiving; but they also reveal Cyril's polemical zeal against Jews and pagans, and particularly those Christians who tried to have it both ways, combining their Christian profession with participation in the festivities of other religions. These themes, together with exposition of the spiritual significance of the Old Testament as a shadow and type of the New, keep recurring over the years. The letter for 424, however, introduces discussion of the Trinity and the ἀγέννητος nature of the Son; and the letter for 429, though not mentioning Nestorius by name or even using the term *theotokos*, launches into a discussion of the incarnation, insisting that the child born of Mary is indissolubly Son of God and therefore Mary should be called 'Mother of God'. Cyril had already used a Paschal Letter to discuss the incarnation some years before (the eighth *Letter*, for 420); but here the object of his attack is obvious.

The second indication of Cyril's dawning concern is the *Letter to the Monks*. Cyril's efforts in the controversy were at first largely concentrated in correspondence – letters to the Roman Pope Celestine, to Nestorius himself, and to many other influential figures. Some of the more important epistles have already been discussed. Those letters directly concerned with the controversy are found in the *Acta Conciliorum*, but much of the rest of his surviving correspondence bears on the matter. None of it is personal; all of it is diplomatic. A collected, critical edition of Cyril's correspondence would be of enormous value; there is the collection in Migne, but it includes a number of spurious epistles, and for the most significant letters it has been superseded by the work of Schwartz on the *Acta Conciliorum*; besides, various new discoveries are scattered about in a variety of publications.[205]

Cyril also turned quite smartly to polemical treatises.[206] Five volumes *Adversus Nestorii blasphemias* were circulated in 430. Here Cyril subjects to searching criticism the sermons of Nestorius which had become so notorious, quoting sections, some of them particularly damning out of context, and pulling them apart. In the same year he submitted three papers to the imperial court *De recta fide*, one addressed to the Emperor Theodosius, another to Arcadia and Marina, his younger sisters, and the other to his wife Eudocia and his elder sister, Pulcheria. These were widely circulated as propaganda documents, although at the time they were not successful in turning imperial favour from Nestorius. Rabbula, bishop of Edessa, switching his support to Cyril, made a translation of the first in order to promulgate Cyril's theology in the Syriac-speaking areas of the Eastern Empire. As previously noted, the same work was probably readapted by Cyril himself as an eighth *Dialogue* with Hermias, known as the *Dialogus de incarnatione Unigeniti*. (If, as Durand has suggested, this *Dialogue* was prior to the *De recta fide*, then Cyril's christological development will need reconsideration.)

Cyril's pamphleteering, however, could not remain purely offensive. He soon had to defend his own position. We have already surveyed his three treatises written in defence of the Anathemas; he also wrote an *Apology to the Emperor* on his return from Ephesus, justifying his somewhat dubious carryings-on at the council.

After the Formulary of Reunion had been negotiated, the flood of christological treatises came to an end; but Cyril's interest did not entirely subside. He later summarized his christological position in two works which received wide distribution and were highly valued especially by the churches of the East: though in Greek surviving only in fragments, his *Scholia de incarnatione unigeniti* exists in Latin, Syriac and Armenian translations, an indication of its widespread appeal; and the *Quod unus sit Christus* is regarded as the mature culmination of all Cyril's christological work. As so often before, he here chose the dialogue form to give his views definitive literary expression.

The only other major work in this area was his treatise *Contra Diodorum et Theodorum*,[207] which gave such offence to Theodoret and nearly ruptured the delicate union which had been achieved. Quotations from Cyril's treatise are our chief source for the christological fragments of Diodore and Theodore; for Cyril's work provided the material on the basis of which they were eventually condemned, and it was used and quoted by such important controversialists as Severus of Antioch. Cyril does not seem to have read the works of the great Antiochene theologians for himself, but apparently based his work on hostile florilegia, collections of quotations from their works supplied by extreme anti-dualists, possibly Apollinarians;[208] for there is evidence that he was confused about the correct authorship of some of the series of statements he attacked.

Such were Cyril's christological writings; what then do they reveal of his christological thinking? A perusal of these works gives an overriding sense of repetitiveness. Certain phrases and arguments keep on recurring: the appeal to the title 'Emmanuel' – God with us; to the Nicene Creed; to Paul's account of the incarnation in Philippians 2. Mary must be called *Theotokos*, since she gave birth to 'God made man and enfleshed' (θεὸν ἐνανθρωπήσαντα καὶ σαρκώθεντα). There is one Son, one Lord Jesus Christ, both before and after the 'enfleshment' (σάρκωσις). There is not one Son who is the Logos of God the Father and another who is from the holy virgin. . . . The Logos who is before the ages (προαιώνιος) *is said* to be born from her *according to the flesh*. The flesh is *his own* (ἴδια), just as each one of us has his own body. Cyril insists on an 'exact union' (ἕνωσις ἀκριβής). These phrases come from the *First Letter to Succensus*,[209] where Cyril is answering queries about his theology from his correspondent, the bishop of Diocaesarea; but they could be paralleled from almost anywhere else in his christological work. Anticipating the usual criticisms, he goes on to say in this letter that this doctrine does not imply σύγχυσις (confusion) or σύγκρασις (mixture) of the Word, nor transformation of the body into the nature of the Godhead; what he intends to say is that 'inconceivably and in a way that is inexpressible, he united to himself a body ensouled with a rational soul' (σῶμα ἐψυχωμένον ψυχῇ νοερᾷ). He bore the likeness of a servant, while remaining what he was. This letter provides an excellent summary in brief of Cyril's recurring themes.

6. Cyril, Athanasius and Apollinarius

Yet for all the repetitiveness, it seems certain that Cyril's christology did not remain static over the years, but he responded to the demands of the controversy, introducing new elements into his christology to oppose the exaggerated dualism of Nestorius. Liébaert[210] took the line that it is necessary to study the pre-Nestorian writings to get an exact idea of Cyril's basic christological position. We have already observed the fact that fundamentally Cyril's early christology was theologically conservative, even unadventurous; he was mostly interested in clarifying the anti-Arian tenets of his great master, Athanasius. This in fact gave him a number of abiding principles which stood him in good stead against Nestorius. Cyril would have opposed a dualist christology anyway, as the *Commentary on John* shows, as well as the much earlier eighth *Paschal Letter*.[211] Here he had insisted that the Son of God was one and the same before and after his σάρκωσις (enfleshment); and on the authority of Athanasius, spoke of a σύνοδος (conjunction) of two things, Godhead and manhood. 'The God-Logos dwelt in his own temple, the body assumed from woman, having a rational soul', he stated, using language he later rejected to emphasize the christological union. Cyril's early christology, then, gave him the launch-pad from which he fired his attack on Nestorius. In an important article, Liébaert[212] has demonstrated that his first two attacks on Nestorius, the *Paschal Letter* and the *Letter to the Monks*, are entirely based on his previous, essentially Athanasian position, apart from a few fresh themes which are specific reactions to points raised by Nestorius himself in the sermons and papers to which Cyril had access. Interestingly enough, these new ideas include his appeal to the body-soul analogy as a model for understanding unity in Christ. Nevertheless, as the controversy progressed, some phrases which he had once been happy to use himself became suspect, and new elements and new vocabulary undoubtedly entered his anti-Nestorian writings. Where did Cyril get these new slogans from? He was the last person to develop a new theological direction and his whole stance was based on his conservatism – his conservation of the tradition.

Surprisingly enough that very conservatism is the key to Cyril's innovations. The new and specifically anti-dualist formulae which he adopted and made his own, came from what he believed to be important patristic sources. About the time of the controversy someone must have brought to his notice a work of Athanasius which spoke of the 'one enfleshed nature of the Logos'; a work of Gregory Thaumaturgus entitled *Kata meros pistis*, which affirmed a single worship and condemned dual worships, one divine and one human; a couple of works of Pope Julius, including a treatise *De Unione*, which affirmed not two beings, the Word and a man, or two hypostases, but one hypostasis of the incarnate Word; and a letter apparently connected with Dionysius, bishop of Corinth. These were the authoritative authors to which Cyril appealed and the authoritative documents on the basis of which he composed his anti-Nestorian writings. The precise, detailed correspondence between Cyril's works and these documents is set out clearly in an important article by P. Galtier;[213] particularly striking is the dependence of the Anathemas on these works. So Cyril thought he was appealing to the authority of respected figures of the past; little did he realise that he had been duped by the Apollinarians. Everyone of these treatises came from Apollinarius himself or members of his circle.[214] Thus Cyril inherited the particular slant of his opposition to dualism from Apollinarius, along with his insistence on the one nature and hypostasis of the Logos enfleshed; he used the very phrases and arguments that Apollinarius had used to assert the composite unity of Christ's person. Is it any wonder then that Cyril was accused of being an Apollinarian himself?

Given this documentary evidence of Cyril's unsuspecting dependence on Apollinarius, the question how far his theology is of an

Apollinarian tendency becomes all the more fascinating. It is commonly accepted that Cyril's position belongs to the Word-Flesh tradition of Alexandria, and that he never really makes the soul of Christ a 'theological factor' in his christology. Alerted to the condemnation of Apollinarius, he consistently explained *sarx* as meaning a man with a soul and a mind; but does it really make any difference to his basic theology? Many would say no; Cyril is incapable of doing real justice to the humanity of Christ, and his rejection of Apollinarianism is merely superficial.

Grillmeier,[215] on the other hand, drawing heavily on the *Second Letter to Succensus* where Cyril answers charges of Apollinarianism, has argued strongly that Cyril, though using Apollinarian formulae, nevertheless gave these phrases an essentially non-Apollinarian interpretation. Others have stressed the incompatibility of Cyril's various assertions, suggesting that he never reached a satisfactory synthesis of views which arose out of his reactions to the controversial situation. The most helpful insight into Cyril's position is probably that offered by R. A. Norris.[216] He believes that the problems of assessment and interpretation arise from the fact that the discussion is too much confined to the Word-Flesh, Word-Man models, neither of which adequately accounts for what Cyril was trying to confess. The fifth-century debate was conducted in terms of the conjunction of two natures, the union of Godhead and manhood in the Christ, and these were the parameters within which Cyril had to operate; but Cyril basically approached the problem from a quite different perspective. His primary mode of christological thinking was in terms of a 'narrative' concerning the Logos, who though being in the form of God, took upon himself the form of a servant. Philippians 2 and the Nicene creed he repeatedly appealed to, because he wanted to affirm that it was the pre-existent Logos who was incarnate. He was feeling after a theology of 'predication' which made the Logos the subject of both divine and human attributes, rather than a 'physical theory' of 'natures in union'. The problem, which he clumsily resolved by using undetected Apollinarian formulae, was to express his own approach in the current terminology. 'One nature' formulae were bound to prove more conducive to his purposes. But, as was inevitable, his use of these formulae has been constantly misunderstood, even though he consistently explained them, at any rate whenever explanation seemed necessary, not in terms of 'mixture', but in terms of the Logos' self-limitation to the conditions of human existence. Cyril was himself quite clear that this self-limitation included his submission to psychological as well as physical restraints; and on those grounds vociferously reiterated his rejection of Apollinarianism. Thus the clue to Cyril's thinking lies in his view of *kenōsis*, a theme already prominent in the pre-Nestorian writings, and his constant refrain thereafter. The Word 'made man and enfleshed' is Cyril's most frequent form of words, and supplied the meaning of his most notorious slogan: μία φύσις τοῦ θεοῦ Λόγου σεσαρκωμένη or σεσαρκωμένου (*mia physis tou theou Logou* – one nature of the God-Logos *sesarkōmene*, or interchangeably, *sesarkomenou* – enfleshed, agreeing either with 'nature' or with 'Logos'). The Word 'abased himself by submitting . . . to the limitations of the human condition', says Cyril in the *Quod unus sit Christus*.[217] The Logos did not cease to be himself in entering upon human existence; but on the other hand his human existence is entirely genuine. What Cyril could not admit was a potentially independent man assumed by the Logos-ἄνθρωπος θεόφορος (a God-bearing man). The Logos had to be the only subject, his (impersonal) humanity having no independent existence, but merely being the way of stating the conditions of existence to which the Logos subjected himself. The Logos is for Cyril the only *hypostasis*, and that was what he intended to convey by his formula 'hypostatic union'. That is also what he meant by 'one nature', not the result of a compounding of two independent natures, though his use of the phrase 'out of two natures' came near to suggesting that it did.

This basic picture explains the apparent docetism so often detected in the Cyrilline position, as well as other frequently discussed difficulties, like the paradoxical phrase ἀπαθῶς ἔπαθεν (he suffered without suffering) and his appeal to the soul-body analogy.[218] The Logos could not really undergo temptation or progress; yet as man he was tempted and learned by experience, while already having the perfection and knowledge proper to divinity.[219] Docetism? Not so for Cyril; both conditions were real, however inconceivable their concurrence in one individual. Cyril admitted that in his own nature the Logos was impassible and immortal, but whatever the difficulties he was determined to maintain the ancient tradition that the Son of God himself suffered and died on the cross. The soul-body analogy was some help here, since many then regarded the soul as by nature impassible on the grounds that it was incorporeal, though subject to passions by its association with the body. Cyril insisted that in the same way the Logos suffered through his own flesh, while remaining in his essential nature impassible. Basically, however, Cyril regarded the whole matter as beyond human explanation and yet still true; paradox is the best way of stating such truths. Analogies also may prove to be the only way of expressing things beyond human comprehension, and Cyril knew perfectly well that the inseparable union of body and soul in a human being was no more than an analogy for what happened in the incarnation, like the many other analogies employed: light and eye, word and voice, thought and mind, scent and flowers. Furthermore, he insisted that the flesh assumed by the Logos was an entire man complete with a soul and mind, thus excluding a literalist application of the analogy.

> He makes his own all that belongs, as to his own body, so to the soul, for he had to be shown to be like us through every circumstance both physical and mental, and we consist of rational soul and body; and as there are times when in the incarnation he permitted his own flesh to experience its proper affections, so again he permitted the soul to experience its proper affections, and he observed the scale of the χένωσις in every respect.[220]

So what happened to Cyril's christology was that he adopted monophysite formulae to counter the dyophysite position he thought he faced; and became more and more insistent that his description of the Logos' humanity included the human soul and mind as well as the flesh. Apollinarianism lies behind both moves; its contribution was undetected, its error repudiated. Cyril had an important contribution to make, however – a basic appeal to Christian tradition that it was the Son of God himself who was incarnate, suffered, died and was raised. That basic popular appeal was the secret of what success he had. The unfortunate thing was that he failed to give consistent and satisfactory expression to it in the intellectual conditions of his time. Translation into 'physical' terms, the language of *physis* and *hypostasis*, required the adoption of formulae which became slogans not merely open to misinterpretation, but actually deriving from a highly suspect source. Safeguards were not always carefully propounded, and this was especially so in the case of the Anathemas; but the slogans are not the real indicators of Cyril's thinking. Cyril spoke for the many faithful who received the eucharist as the flesh of the incarnate Logos and trusted that in this way they were assured resurrection by participating in the new humanity sanctified by the presence of the Logos himself.[221] The union of the spiritual and material worlds in the incarnation was at the heart of Cyril's metaphysical assumptions. He was wedded to the Alexandrian tradition of θεοποίησις, of deification realized by the saving initiative of God himself. So for him there was no point in winning the battle against Arius at the price of divorcing the Logos from mankind. The opposition to Nestorius was the natural corollary of Cyril's Athanasian heritage. It is really no wonder that Cyril's characteristic argument was an appeal to tradition, to scripture and the Fathers, whereas Nestorius appeared weak in patristic argument, appealing rather to *a priori* theological assumptions. Cyril was more prepared to sacrifice logic to his championship of what he saw as the saving realities and the truth passed down by tradition; in this he expressed the fundamental instincts of popular Christianity.

For all that, Cyril did proceed in an overbearing manner, and certainly deserved the rebuke of his mentor, Isidore. That he recognized the mistake of alienating the entire section of the church under the influence of the Antiochene Patriarchate, is clear from his positive and conciliatory reaction to the negotiations which produced the Formulary of Reunion, a peace treaty which he then had some difficulty in justifying to his more extreme followers. For the moment, however, Cyril was prepared to let the battle subside, and he tried to cultivate easier diplomatic relations with the see of Antioch, politely sending to bishop John his work *Against Julian*,[222] a fact which indicates that it must have been written at some point between 433 (the year of reunion) and 441 (the date of John's death). John's close friend and supporter, Theodoret of Cyrrhus, actually wrote congratulating Cyril on his excellent effort on behalf of the truth of Christianity.[223] There has been a suggestion that Cyril wrote the work deliberately to supersede that of Theodore of Mopsuestia, whose heretical views he objected to; but its reception by the Antiochenes suggests that no trace of such a motive was apparent to them.

7. *Against Julian*

The Emperor Julian the Apostate had written a blistering attack *Against the Galileans*, all the more damaging because he knew the sect from inside, was familiar with its apologetics and could quote its scriptures. Cyril dedicated his reply to the Christian Emperor Theodosius, and justified his work, written eighty to ninety years after Julian's, on the grounds that many believers had been shaken by Julian's arguments. Paganism was still very much alive in Alexandria and Julian's work gave encouragement to it. In the first book, Cyril, quoting extensively from a wide range of the classics, seeks to show that the scriptures are more ancient and more full of truth than the authorities of Greek literature and philosophy. The work against Julian has been regarded as our major evidence of Cyril's classical learning; for elsewhere he appears as a thoroughly ecclesiastical figure, and without this work of apology, his education in the traditional *paideia* appeared open to question, especially in view of his lack of a polished rhetorical style. Now R. M. Grant[224] has shown that Cyril's knowledge of pagan literature comes from independent researches, undertaken for the purpose of refuting Julian, by following up references in Eusebius' *Praeparatio Evangelica* and the works of other Christian predecessors. So his knowledge of the classics is distinctly limited, and his classical education is far from assured. From the second book on, Cyril quotes passages from Julian's work and sets about refuting them, rather as Origen had done in his reply to Celsus. On the basis of these quotations, some of them being quite extensive, a reconstruction of the first book of Julian's treatise has been possible,[225] though it is to some extent tentative since Cyril states that he rearranged Julian's material in order to avoid repetitions and bring similar subjects together. Furthermore Cyril was careful to omit invectives against Christ and other matter which might contaminate the minds of Christians. Ten books of Cyril's work are extant, and they cover only the first book of Julian's three-volume attack. Fragments of later books have been found in Greek and Syriac.

The arguments on both sides, pagan and Christian,[226] are not fundamentally different from the earlier exchanges between Celsus and Origen. Julian regards Plato as better than Moses, and attacks the Genesis accounts of creation and the fall. This he can do to some effect since he knew the scriptures first-hand. Moses did not teach *creatio ex nihilo*, for the 'deep', the 'darkness' and the 'waters' were apparently there already; and there is no account of the God of the Jews creating anything incorporeal – he just reordered pre-existent matter. The serpent was actually man's benefactor, because the ability to distinguish good and evil constitutes human wisdom. The story is detrimental to God who appears jealous of his own rights and powers; and in any case it is all just as much myth as the myths of the Greeks – what about the talking serpent? Julian objects to the favouritism of a God who is only concerned with a small tribe recently settled in Palestine, and attacks the scriptural accounts of his anger and resentment as anthropomorphic. The philosophers taught a God who is the Creator and universal Father of all, and bade men imitate the gods who are free from all passion and emotion. The Christians are not faithful to the teachings of the apostles; for Paul, Matthew, Luke and Mark did not call Jesus God – that was only introduced by John. The claim to fulfilment of prophecy is based on fabrications, and not even good ones at that – for Matthew and Luke disagree about the genealogy of Jesus. Julian also reiterates the ancient claim to Hellenic superiority in culture, learning, war and politics; in any case, if scripture is sufficient, why do Christians dabble in the learning of the Hellenes?

Cyril's reply has all the faults of partisanship. He attacks the myths of the Greeks without seeing the force of the pagan criticism of the scriptures. He defends the scriptures by appealing to the spiritual meanings discovered by allegory, and by proving thus that the Old Testament, contrary to Julian's argument, does in fact contain the doctrines of the church, Trinity and all. The Jews misunderstood their own writings. But apart from the first book, Cyril's reply is entirely piecemeal, concentrating on individual points and not attempting any synthesis or integrated response to the overall case Julian had mustered. Once again he shows himself wedded to the traditions of the past, this time the age-old apologetic arguments of the Fathers, while capable of adapting them to the immediate need before him. So, for all its faults, his treatise was welcomed and admired as a necessary contribution to the continuing battle against paganism; and it did something to paper over the cracks that still existed between the Patriarchates of Antioch and Alexandria.

It was the attack on Diodore and Theodore which revealed Cyril's continuing suspicions and once again exposed the nerves of such as Theodoret. No wonder his death was greeted with relief. Sadly Cyril, though hasty and intransigent, proved more tractable than his successor. Theodoret's position deteriorated rather than improved. It is time to examine the life and works of Cyril's most distinguished opponent.

VII. Theodoret of Cyrrhus

Theodoret we have already met several times in this book. That he alone should appear in more than one place is indicative of his wide-ranging interests and his major contribution to the life of the church in the fifth century. He has already appeared as a consciously 'orthodox' ecclesiastical historian, as a cultured apologist, and as a rather pious hagiographer. He was also a fine theologian and exegete of the Antiochene school, who found himself deeply involved in the controversies which led up to Chalcedon; his attack on Cyril's Anathemas has already been described and his defence of Diodore and Theodore has been mentioned. It is time to pull the threads together and get a clearer picture of Theodoret's life, personality and wide-ranging literary accomplishments.

1. Life

Theodoret turns out to be a highly attractive individual. We know him and his life quite intimately because of a wealth of his correspondence has been preserved. Like Paul, when under attack he was reluctantly drawn into surveying his life and his achievements, 'boasting' in self-justification, and thus passing on some fascinating information about his activities.[227] But these were the outbursts, not of a proud self-assertive man, but of a highly sensitive and conscientious servant of the church who was unable to accept that all he had done was to be written off by people he seriously regarded as dangerous heretics.[228] The mood passed. He returned to his monastery, found renewed calm and tranquillity, and then responded to dawning hopes of truth's vindication with a forgiving and thankful spirit.[229]

But this is to begin at the end. The date of Theodoret's birth, like that of most figures of antiquity, is very uncertain — probably 393 is all we can say. The circumstances of his birth, however, he reveals himself in his writings — they were after all rather exceptional. He was the child of a prosperous Antiochene couple who had been childless for many years. Encouraged by the fact that his rather flashy socialite mother had been cured of a serious eye complaint and converted to a sober life by Peter the Galatian, an ascetic living in an unoccupied tomb in the locality (a character described in Theodoret's *Historia religiosa* 9, from which we get this information), Theodoret's parents sought further help from the famous local holy men in her barrenness. For years their hopes were fed but not fulfilled, until Macedonius the Barley-Eater (Theodoret's *Historia religiosa* 13 is now the source) promised that a son would be born to her, provided that like Hannah she devoted him from birth to the service of God. So it is that in *Epistle* 81 Theodoret can describe himself as consecrated to God before his conception, and given an appropriate education.

What then was that education? The actual information Theodoret gives suggests that his education was exclusively religious. He paid weekly visits to Peter, was instructed by Macedonius and other ascetics, and at an early age became a lector. He speaks of Diodore of Tarsus and Theodore of Mopsuestia as his teachers, though certainly the former and probably the latter he can only have known through books. Undoubtedly it was their theological tradition in which Theodore was brought up.

But Theodoret was the child of prosperous parents in a city which had long been a centre of secular learning and culture. There

Libanius the pagan sophist had taught Chrysostom and Theodore. It would be surprising if Theodoret had not followed the classical *paideia* – and for all his silence, it is quite plain that he did. His correspondents included the sophists Aerius and Isokasius, with whom he was quite capable of exchanging pleasant nothings of a traditional rhetorical kind, complimenting them on the Attic purity of their language. In his letters he quotes from Homer, Sophocles, Euripides, Aristophanes, Demosthenes and Thucydides; he uses the ancient proverbs of Pittacus and Cleobulus, μηδὲν ἀγάν and μέτρον ἄριστον ('Nothing to excess' and 'Due measure is best').[230] There can be no doubt that he shared the common literary culture of the sophisticated urban upper classes, and that this was one reason for the fine quality of his apologetic work.[231] Yet he was also deeply imbued with the native Syrian culture; he spoke the vernacular and shared the simple piety of the Syrian peasants and ascetics. Indeed, Canivet has suggested that his first language was Syriac, and the very purity of his Greek proves that it was to him an acquired literary language.[232] He was a bridge between cultural extremes in the society of the late Roman empire, and this no doubt was the result of the 'dual education' ensured by the peculiar circumstances of his birth.

In his early twenties Theodoret inherited his parents' wealth, but it is hardly surprising, given his background, that he immediately gave it all up and distributed it to the poor. After his condemnation he was to write that he had nothing, no house, no land, no money, no tomb;[233] true to his principles he had not used his episcopate to enrich himself.

So Theodoret became a monk, apparently leaving Antioch to enter a monastery near Apamea – for when later deprived of his see, he begs permission to return there, explaining that it is 75 miles from Antioch and 20 miles from his episcopal city.[234] There he lived for about seven years, and then only left because he had been elected bishop of Cyrrhus, a small city deep in the Syriac-speaking countryside, not all that far from the Euphrates. His bishopric he always regarded as a charge entrusted to him by God, frequently saying in his letters that he preferred the withdrawal and peace of an ascetic's life. He made nothing for himself out of his position and contributed much in terms of energy, influence and finance to the local community for which he was responsible. With ecclesiastical revenues he put up public buildings, built two bridges and ensured a water supply by constructing an aqueduct. Thus he provided employment and improved the facilities of the little backwater over which he had been given charge. He clearly realized how desperate the social and economic position was. Peasant-farmers were being forced off the land by their inability to produce enough to meet their taxes and still have a livelihood. So we find a considerable number of letters in the collections which were written to officials or people with influence in the capital trying to get a reduction in dues and to encourage better administration.[235] Though still a young man when elected, Theodoret must rapidly have shown the powers of leadership and devotion to the community which lasted and developed in his thirty odd years as a bishop, and when he was under attack he could take pride in the fact that there had been no cause of complaint against him, no whisper of bribery or corruption, and neither he nor his clergy had ever been involved in any kind of lawsuit with anyone. It is a sad comment on the state of the church in this period that such a clean sheet was noteworthy.

The other achievement of which Theodoret boasted was his complete eradication of heresy in the 800 parishes of his diocese. He claims to have delivered 1000 souls from Marcion and whole villages from Arius and Eunomius. He had many battles with heretics, pagans and Jews.[236] Yet his letters have no tone of rancour or hard intolerance. Here we see a man who was sure he knew what was right and true, sincerely carrying out what he believed to be his duty in love for the souls lost in error and falsehood. All the more devastating to such a man was the judgment of a church council against him. Even then he was sure he was right, and subsequent events did vindicate him.

Something of Theodoret's involvement in the wider church struggle we have already observed. He must have been in his late thirties when he was drawn into battle against Cyril and wrote his *Refutation of the Twelve Anathemas*. He was present at Ephesus, stood out against Cyril's determination to open the council before John and the other Orientals arrived, and then led the delegation from the Antiochene splinter-group when the two sides were summoned to the capital. His uncompromising campaign against Cyril and the Anathemas may have contributed to the Antiochene loss of favour at court.[237] Theodoret knew his own mind.

Theodoret did indeed know his own mind. John of Antioch had some difficulty in persuading him to accept the Formulary of Reunion two years later. He doggedly refused to condemn Nestorius; as far as he was concerned Nestorius' views were not what the opposition suggested and were perfectly orthodox. Theodoret maintained a close friendship with Nestorius' fellow-exile, Count Irenaeus. One of the earliest letters we possess Theodoret wrote to

Irenaeus, wondering why he had not come to visit him.[238] He had been told Irenaeus was coming soon, and the letter describes how he kept dreaming of his arrival, expecting and hoping, and how he could not understand his disappointment. This must have been written before Irenaeus' sentence of exile was confirmed in 434. Later Irenaeus became bishop of Tyre, and we find more letters passing between him and Theodoret.[239] Theodoret's support for Irenaeus, who as bishop soon became the target of the opposition, and his long-standing refusal to condemn Nestorius, meant that when controversy broke out again in the late 440s, he was inevitably tarred with the same doctrinal brush.

However, for ten years or so the conflict remained quiescent. Though Theodoret reacted strongly against Cyril's attack on Diodore and Theodore, the peace was not seriously disrupted again until after Cyril's death. By then Antioch had a new patriarch, John's nephew, Domnus, who leaned very heavily upon Theodoret, the veteran theologian of the Antiochene party. Cyril's death was greeted with relief[240] and the new patriarch of Alexandria received from Theodoret a remarkably friendly and welcoming letter, praising his moderation and asking for his prayers.[241] The writer can hardly have known what Dioscorus was really like. They were soon to be the chief antagonists in a renewed doctrinal struggle. Theodoret's next letter to Dioscorus[242] was a statement of his theological position, drawn up in reply to a written complaint addressed by Dioscorus to Domnus about the tenor of Theodoret's preaching. Theodoret appeals to the myriads of listeners who can testify to the orthodoxy of his preaching in Antioch during six years under Theodotus, thirteen years under John, who himself joined in standing ovations during Theodoret's sermons, and a further seven years under Domnus. This letter, with its defensive outline of Theodoret's christological position, became very important in later discussions of Theodoret's orthodoxy, and appears among letters preserved with the *Acta Conciliorum*.

It appears then that Theodoret had been a regular preacher in Antioch; as we have seen, it is likely that his *Ten Discourses on Providence* were given on one of his preaching tours to the metropolitan centre. Under Domnus his visits there seem to have been prolongèd. The removal of Theodoret was clearly to be an important step in the campaign to weaken Antioch, especially since his theological reputation, or notoriety, had been further enhanced, by the publication of the *Eranistes*, of which more later. Sure enough in 448 an imperial decree confined Theodoret to his own see on the pretext that he had been summoning too many synods and disturbing the ecclesiastical peace. A number of letters[243] express Theodoret's dismay and annoyance at the arbitrariness of this ban. He had no objection to returning to his pastorate. He liked peace and his duty was to his people. He had never left except after repeated, pressing invitations. But if heretics of all kinds were allowed freedom of movement, why should he be excluded from all major cities? He had done nothing blameworthy. He had simply tried to uphold the faith. He was the victim of calumny. He proceeded to justify his life and his doctrine. Could not Anatolius or Nomus (both of whom held high office in the state) bring some influence to bear on his behalf? In his own personal difficulties, Theodoret addressed letters to those contacts at court which he had already approached on behalf of others.

But the Emperor, Theodosius, allowed Dioscorus to make all the running. The Second Council of Ephesus met in 449. Christened the 'Robber Synod' by Pope Leo, it not only condemned all the 'Nestorians', including Theodoret (who was not permitted to attend and was therefore unable to defend himself), but it even gave full approval to all the acts of the earlier Council of Ephesus under Cyril, including the acceptance of the notorious Twelve Anathemas. At this Theodoret's letters reached a new pitch of urgency and dismay. He wrote an appeal to Leo, bishop of Rome – *Epistle* 113, from which we get so much information about Theodoret's career. He wrote again to Anatolius,[244] seeking imperial permission to go to the West to plead his case, or else to retire to his monastery. He sorted out some last-minute affairs in his diocese, but he could not take his position lying down – as he explained to the bishop of Emesa, Uranius,[245] virtue includes courage and opposition to injustice; silence or resignation is inappropriate. Yet monastic life soon calmed him, and the death of Theodosius brought renewed hope. Almost the last new letter we possess is a request to Anatolius that he should press for a new council to set everything straight. And that, as we know, is exactly what happened – Chalcedon. Theodoret attended the Council of Chalcedon, and his orthodoxy was vindicated. All that was required of him was to condemn Nestorius, which he finally agreed to do.

Thereafter Theodoret's life is lost to view. It used to be assumed that he died only a few years later, but it has now been shown that he lived until 466.[246]

Theodoret's *Epistles*[247] have survived in two collections which hardly overlap, giving a total of 232 letters; some others have been preserved elsewhere, for example in the *Acta*. The correspondence is clearly of enormous interest from a biographical point of view, but there are other reasons why it is significant. As examples of the early Byzantine letter form, his epistles cannot be bettered.[248] There are patronage letters and letters of consolation; these follow rhetorical conventions, but that does not mean they are artificial – we too have conventional letter-writing styles, and Theodoret's letters have an attractive personal touch. There are many letters of Easter greeting, expressing the joy of the festival. There are invitations to feasts and dedications: To the Archōn Theodotus, the bishop writes (I paraphrase),

> Children are scared of Bony [μορμώ – the current bugbear used by nurses to keep their charges in order], students are scared of their tutors and teachers, men are scared of judges and officials, and lack of experience doubles their terror. So come and join in our festival so that everyone can see you are human.[249]

Through these letters the life of the fifth century becomes vivid. So does the life of a bishop, consulted on matters of faith and order by his colleagues, exercising pastoral care of individuals, especially those in distress or bereavement. It is clear that, however out of the way Cyrrhus appears, Theodoret did not live in isolation from the wider world: he wrote to two bishops in Persian Armenia where the church was suffering persecution from the state, offering sympathy, encouragement and guidance on the question of readmitting to communion those who had succumbed under pressure.[250] And he wrote many letters on behalf of African refugees, particularly a Christian senator and a bishop who had lost everything when the Vandals swept into Carthage and Libya.[251] There are also, as we have noted, a number of letters of particular interest from the doctrinal point of view, and it is to Theodoret's doctrinal work that we will now turn our attention.

2. His theological position

Was Theodoret a Nestorian? This question has been repeatedly discussed during his lifetime and since. He was vindicated at Chalcedon, but his anti-Cyrilline writings were condemned along with his master, Theodore of Mopsuestia, in the later Three Chapters controversy in 553. Many modern scholars have discussed the question, and there is considerable agreement that Theodoret began as a Nestorian but changed his position in the course of time, some dating the change at Chalcedon, others considerably earlier.[252] It seems doubtful, however, whether the question is worth pursuing along these lines – after all, Nestorius himself has been vindicated in the eyes of many scholars by the discovery of the *Bazaar of Heraclides*. The interesting question is whether Theodoret's basic christological position did change or advance during the course of the controversy; and to answer that question it may be more important to observe his basic theological concerns than to focus attention merely on his formulae.

But first, the evidence: what doctrinal works do we possess from the hand of Theodoret? There are a number of letters, as we have noticed already, all dating from the period between Ephesus (431) and Chalcedon (451); most of those of doctrinal interest belong to the latter part of that period when renewed controversy necessitated self-justification and the building of alliances. Also from this later period comes the *Eranistes*, a work of great importance which will be described in more detail shortly. From the time of the Council of Ephesus, we have the fragmentary remains preserved in the *Acta*: Theodoret's *Refutation of the Anathemas* (embedded in Cyril's defence), some sermons, some letters, some conciliar statements which seem to have been drafted by Theodoret's pen. Various other fragments and descriptions of works that he composed have come down to us; more important, however, are several works which survived among the works of other writers but have now been restored to Theodoret through the researches of modern scholarship. In the last century A. Ehrhard [253] showed that *On the Holy and Vivifying Trinity* and *On the Incarnation of the Lord*, two works ascribed to Cyril, in fact present the doctrinal views of Theodoret, and some fragments, quotations cited under Theodoret's name, prove that these treatises did indeed originate not from Cyril but from his opponent. Theodoret himself refers to both these works in his letters,[254] and they evidently share the standpoint of Theodoret's *Refutation of the Anathemas*. Another work with a similar history is the *Expositio rectae fidei*,[255] preserved among the writings of Justin Martyr, though clearly belonging to a much later period. Quite independently, two scholars[256] recognized it as the work of Theodoret, and there can be little doubt that this restoration is correct. In spite of the fact that one researcher, R. V. Sellers, assigned it to the same period as the *Eranistes*, the arguments for dating it early are much more compelling[257] – indeed, it seems likely that it pre-dates the outbreak of the christological controversies. If this is the case, then we have an excellent chance of plotting the shifts and continuities in Theodoret's thinking.

Between Ephesus and Chalcedon, a shift in emphasis certainly appears to have occurred. We have already reviewed Theodoret's debate with Cyril over the Anathemas. It is interesting to contrast Theodoret's attitude there with that found in his *Epistle* 83 to Dioscorus. Here many of his affirmations are distinctly reminiscent of Cyril's:

> One Saviour Jesus Christ, only-begotten Son of God, begotten of the Father before all ages, incarnated and made man . . . born of the Virgin Mary according to the flesh, who therefore is called 'Theotokos'. . . . He exists eternally as God, and is born of the Virgin Mary as Man . . . Only one Son exists, the God-Word made man.

Theodoret is concerned to defend himself from misrepresentation, asserting that he does not preach two Sons, supporting his statements from scripture, and from the Fathers, Alexander and Athanasius, Basil and Gregory, even acknowledging a debt to the writings of Theophilus and Cyril. He still insists that there must be no confusion between the flesh and the divine: 'We teach clearly the distinction of two natures, proclaiming the immutability of the divine nature.' But he is prepared to call the flesh of the Saviour divine inasmuch as it has become the flesh of the God-Word, as long as the idea that it is transformed into the divine is rejected as impious. Theodoret claims here that he had a friendly correspondence with Cyril (nothing of which has survived) and admired his work against Julian the Apostate. He begs Dioscorus to turn away from those who speak falsely, to consider the peace of the church, to make every effort to cure those who dare to alter true doctrines or else drive them out. He insists that if anyone says the virgin is not *Theotokos*, or that our Saviour Jesus Christ is only man, or divides the only-begotten and first-born of all creatures into two Sons, he should be cast from the Christian hope with the acclamation of all Christian people. This, he says, is what he really believes; it is no sail-trimming. This is Theodoret in very different mood from when faced with Cyril's Anathemas; he is conciliatory and it certainly seems as if he had recognized that the basic stance of the Alexandrians was an attempt to preserve an essential aspect of the tradition which, provided certain safeguards were included, he was not averse to adopting himself. The Logos he too regarded as the one incarnated – the subject of the saving action. Is this the result of a significant shift in his thinking?

One of the most influential studies of the subtle modifications which took place in Theodoret's christological formulae is that of M. Richard.[258] His main point is that Theodoret's later works use only abstract expressions for the humanity of Christ (ἡ ἀνθρωπίνη φύσις – human nature, τὸ ἀναληφθέν – the assumed, ἡ ἀνθρωπότης – humanity, etc.), whereas his early works do not hesitate to speak of 'the man', or 'the perfect man' (ὁ τέλειος ἄνθρωπος), treating him as a concrete individual. Following this hint, a corresponding shift in his soteriological language has been discovered:[259] in the *De Incarnatione* he is prepared to use graphic language of the man assumed being justified 'by his own toils' and prevailing over the devil 'by human φιλοσοφία, not by the power of divinity'; whereas later he gives little positive role to the human soul, and emphasizes the saving activity of the Logos who used the assumed humanity as an instrument. Again, in the *Refutation of the Anathemas*, the manhood, as priest and victim, offered the sacrifice to the divinity; later, in his exegesis of Hebrews, this dichotomy between the natures is played down, the subject of the sacrificial action being the incarnate God-Word. Many have been convinced that this represents a remarkable change in Theodoret's position; few theologians involved in controversy have had the humility to listen to the other side and concede that the opposition has a point; Theodoret had the grace to do so. Cyril had convinced him that there were dangers in treating the humanity as a concrete individual alongside the God-Word, that such expressions could lead to unacceptable division and imply a two Sons doctrine.

But has Theodoret's essential theological stance been modified? A number of reasons have been advanced for thinking that the contrast, though present, seems to have been overpressed. Concrete language for the manhood of Christ was common to all traditions in the previous century, and Cyril himself seems to have made a similar shift in his linguistic habits.[260] As for Theodoret's own position, on the one hand his basically 'symmetrical' christology remains the same:[261] he still balances divine and human expressions, giving both equal weight and failing to recognize the 'metaphysical dependence of the human on the divine'; and besides, in his later works, he still finds it difficult to attribute suffering to the Logos, so failing to make full allowance for the *communicatio idiomatum*. Thus his theology remains fundamentally dualistic. On the other hand,[262] he had always been concerned with the unity of Christ. Even in the works written prior to the controversy, this concern can be detected. In speaking of the union, he uses precisely the same vocabulary as he uses for the unity of the Trinity (ἑνόω, συνάπτω, μετέχω, κοινωνέω, and related nouns). He speaks of the Son or Christ existing *as God* and *as Man*. The majority of references to the human nature are already of the abstract, impersonal kind. Furthermore there are many sentences where the Logos is both the initiator and the subject of the saving action, the Logos even being the one who justifies the human nature 'by its own toils'. In these early works, his primary emphasis was directed against Arian and Apollinarian misinterpretations of the incarnation, and it was his conviction that the anathemas were Apollinarian which gave rise to his strong language in the *Refutation*. In this kind of controversial situation, he was bound to uphold hard-won truths about the distinction of natures; yet even here we noticed that Theodoret did not bother to contradict the Sixth Anathema because he accepted the point that there is one Lord Jesus Christ who is both God and Man.

So from somewhat contrasting angles it looks as though the essential features of Theodoret's christology were not fundamentally modified, and if we concentrate on the inner motivation of his christology, namely his soteriology,[263] this becomes even more apparent. Theodoret's ideal for man was the ἀπάθεια (passionlessness) and ἀτρεπτότης (changelessness) of the perfect monk who had overcome sin and fallibility. This was the ideal depicted in his *Historia religiosa*. In the *Eranistes*, however, he argues that God alone is truly ἀπαθής and ἄτρεπτος. Is he consistent here? It is his christology which redeems his consistency. Christ being the true mediator, the God-Man, united the two natures and so clothed man with ἀπάθεια, with the character of God himself. For Theodoret salvation did not mean the transformation of man into God (θεοποίησις), nor the realization of a natural kinship between the human and the divine, but rather the union of man with God by participation, neither God nor man sacrificing their integrity, but man becoming the image of God by being made like him. Such a soteriology Theodoret maintained throughout his life, and it remained fundamental to the structure and character of his christology.

We may observe Theodoret's position further by examining two doctrinal works from very different dates.

3. The *Expositio recta fidei*

The *Expositio* is a neat little treatise expounding the essentials of the Christian faith. Theodoret seems to regard it as the culmination of a series of works: having refuted the Jews and Greeks, he will now expound the healthy doctrine of faith. The work is catechetical or apologetic in flavour rather than controversial. The first half is concerned with the doctrine of the Trinity: one God, known in Father, Son and Holy Spirit. He explains with beautiful clarity the difference between *ousia* and *hypostasis*, and how the epithets ἀγέννητος, γεννητός and ἐκπόρευτος describe not a difference in *ousia* but in τρόποι ὑπάρξεως – manner of existing. This is one of the briefest and most lucid statements of trinitarian orthodoxy to be found in patristic literature. Theodoret goes on to speak of the great divide between Creator and created, and offers proofs that all three divine Persons belong to the superior category (thus refuting Arianism); they are united in a single activity and energy, both in the operation of grace and in creation. The mind of man, he continues, is incapable of grasping the divine (thus excluding the views of Eunomius); we know in part and through a glass darkly. Through θεωρία man may attach himself to God, and analogies give us some glimpse of what he is like, but God is ἀκατάληπτος (incomprehensible) and ἄρρητος (ineffable), both in himself and in his οἰκονομία (economy – his providential plan and outreach).

Theodoret now turns to expounding the οἰκονομία – by which he means the incarnation. Seeing the mess man was in as a result of Adam's fault, the Logos 'without leaving the heavens, came down to us' – in other words, his descent was not a physical act, but a voluntary act of the divine energy. He made a 'temple' for himself – a perfect man – and by a perfect union clothing himself with it, fulfilled the saving action on our behalf. As man he lived blamelessly, and through death paid what was owed; as God he raised up the destroyed and completely overcame death. There was one Son who as man was destroyed, and as God rose; but with respect to this one Son, it is necessary to divide the natures, assigning divine attributes or activities to the divine nature, and human to the human nature. As to the manner of the union, Theodoret is not afraid to confess ignorance – in fact, he is prepared to boast about it, for he believes in things which are simply not expressible. No one should expect complete clarification. But he is prepared to discuss certain analogies and he proceeds to explore the union of body and soul in the human being – another example of two natures in one person. There are certain qualifications to be made – the soul, for example, is involved in the passions of the body; indeed, it often suffers before the body does – but we cannot think that of the divinity of Christ. This analogy being only partially applicable, he explores another: the embodiment of light in the sun. After dealing with various difficulties and questions, Theodoret eventually confronts those who object to the division into two natures, accusing them of introducing confusion, mixture and change; they agree that he remained God while becoming flesh, so their refusal to accept two natures just produces nonsense. The idea that the body was divinized after the union, Theodoret also demolishes.

The basic distinction between the natures must hold. Yet in the end all arguments and questions lead to ἀπορία – perplexity. When I reach that point, says Theodoret, I cry out with wonder at the Christian mystery, that our faith is beyond mental grasp, beyond words, beyond understanding. The only suitable response in the end is praise.

Was this treatise written early, before the Nestorian controversy broke out? It seems very likely that it was. The emphasis is not exclusively christological; the controversial passages are explicable in the light of the Arian and Apollinarian controversies; and although there are interesting parallels with arguments that appear later, the work lacks discussion of some of the most contentious issues of the later controversy. Furthermore, later on Theodoret seems less inclined than here to fall back on agnosticism to avoid explaining the union – perhaps because he had learned that Cyril could also play that game. But if this is an early work then it is extremely significant; for here the bare bones of Theodoret's position are expressed, to some extent in terms which are elsewhere submerged, and this shows that whatever happened to Theodoret's formulae in the course of controversy, his position was not basically altered. The features to which I refer are (i) the basic distinction between Creator and created; (ii) the insistence that the Logos remains what he is in spite of the incarnation; and (iii) the assumption that the Logos is the subject of the act of incarnation, even though incarnate experiences are attributed to the manhood.

Theodoret does share Theodore's concern that it should be man in his completeness who should be saved, and accepts his view that only a genuine reversal of his moral failure will accomplish this. But the emphasis of Theodoret's work is much more pointedly and consistently directed towards the preservation of God's 'Godness'. This appears in what has been said about the *Expositio*; and it is reinforced not only by the emphasis of his arguments in the *Refutation of the Anathemas*, but also by the very titles he gives to the three dialogues that make up the *Eranistes*: ἄτρεπτος (unchangeable), ἀσύγχυτος (unconfused), ἀπαθής (impassible). Theodoret was determined to keep a hold on the hard-won ground taken from the Arians and Apollinarians. The Logos belonged to uncreated Being, man belonged to the created order. There is no mean between. The uncreated *ousia* cannot be mixed, changed or affected by anything external to itself. Only by an act of divine favour or will can God approach his creatures. The Alexandrian talk of the Word *becoming* flesh, of the flesh being *divinized*, of the *one nature* after the union, to Theodoret compromised all his basic theological instincts, and that remained true throughout his life and explains his dogged resistance first to Cyril, then to Eutyches. He seems to have recognized towards the end that he had misjudged Cyril's meaning; but then he thought that the Alexandrians seriously misjudged him and his Antiochene associates. Theodoret's basic position did not, I think, undergo any serious modification.

4. The *Eranistes*

Like the *Expositio*, this work beautifully illustrates the clarity and conciseness of Theodoret's style. It is a refreshing change from so much patristic literature. It also illustrates, as did the apologetic work described earlier (*The Cure of Pagan Maladies*), the brilliant way in which Theodoret could take over conventional forms and material from other sources, and yet produce a work which is no mere slavish copying, but a genuinely original creation within the constraints of the tradition.

The *Eranistes* consists of three dialogues between 'Collector' and 'Orthodoxus'. The characters are named to indicate their roles – for, as he explains in his prologue, Theodoret sees his opponents as picking up various ideas from heretical sources and producing doctrine which is neither traditional nor coherent. The dialogue form has enabled his argument to proceed through question and answer, propositions, elucidations, antitheses, and other dialectical procedures, but the form, he explains, he has modified by putting the name of the character speaking at the head of each statement made, rather than adopting a kind of narrative of the discourse with the names embedded in the text. (In other words, unlike Plato's dialogues, Theodoret's appear in the form in which a modern play is set out.) Each dialogue culminates in the production of a florilegium of patristic citations supporting the position for which Orthodoxus has argued – a device which on each occasion finally forces Eranistes to accept that Orthodoxus is right, especially as Orthodoxus has rounded off each collection with quotations from Apollinarius, in order to show that Eranistes' Monophysite position is even more extreme than that of that notorious heretic. As a consequence these florilegia have preserved some important fragments from the writings of Apollinarius, as well as others like Eustathius of Antioch.

Use of florilegia as a method of theological argument seems to have developed during the christological controversies. Lists of patristic quotations had been used extensively by Cyril, and Theodoret retaliated in kind. Both sides felt the need to appeal to the authority of scripture and the tradition of the Fathers, particularly as set out at Nicaea; thus to produce quotations from such generally revered teachers as Athanasius, the Cappadocians and John Chrysostom was an excellent method of procedure. At the very beginning of the First Dialogue, Eranistes and Orthodoxus agree that the question at issue is how to follow in the footsteps of the apostles, prophets and holy men – they are not indulging in a speculative exercise. The florilegia fit this intention exactly. It is likely that in the *Eranistes* Theodoret drew on earlier florilegia and there are a number of collections, for example in Leo's *Tome* and in the Chalcedonian *Acta*, which are related to those found here. However, Theodoret's originality has once again been recognized, in this case by Ettlinger,[264] who argues that his primary source was his own earlier work, the lost *Pentalogus* written against Cyril in 432. The passages from Leo's *Tome* were added later by a post-Chalcedonian copyist; and the Chalcedonian florilegium was dependent on Theodoret. In other respects Theodoret left his mark – he appealed to the works of ante-Nicene Fathers providing the link right back to the apostles, he deliberately avoided appealing to his own great authorities, Diodore and Theodore, on the grounds that they carried no weight with the opposition, and he chose instead to quote from Theophilus and Cyril of Alexandria – not to mention Apollinarius. Heretics were usually cited to prove their heresy – only here do we find heretical citations used to support the case being presented. Theodoret never stuck merely to convention!

The fourth part of the *Eranistes* often appears in manuscripts independently under the Latin title *Demonstratio per syllogismos*; but it is quite clear that it originally belonged with the dialogues and provided a concise restatement of the principal arguments covered.

In the first of the dialogues, Orthodoxus seems to make all the running. He gets Eranistes to agree that unchangeability is a divine characteristic which belongs to the whole Trinity, and then demands to know how the gospel can say 'The Word became flesh', attaching change to the unchangeable nature. Eranistes confesses ignorance as to how ('only he knows'), but he is prepared to assert the truth of the gospel willy-nilly. 'I do not know what this change into flesh is,' he says, 'but I have read "The Word became flesh".' Orthodoxus accepts that one should not enquire into hidden things, but asserts that one should not display ignorance of what is perfectly plain, either. The change into flesh cannot be literally true, no matter how much Eranistes protests that 'taking flesh' or 'dwelling in flesh' is different from 'becoming flesh'. Orthodoxus gets him to agree that God's unchangeability is scriptural, that scripture uses certain phrases symbolically, and so gradually leads him on to admitting the possibility that this text has to be interpreted in the light of others, like Hebrews 10.5, Philippians 2.6f. and the second half of the same verse, John 1.14; that is, he 'became flesh' by 'taking flesh' and 'dwelling among us' as in a temple. Eranistes enquires how the ancient teachers of the church understood this text, and so a preliminary florilegium is introduced into the dialogue, dealing simply with the exegesis of John 1.14. The main florilegium on the incarnation shortly follows, and the dialogue ends with Eranistes forced to accept that the God-Word is ἄτρεπτος, that he was not changed into flesh but took flesh. Certainly in this dialogue the characterization of Eranistes is weak compared with that of his opponent. Apart from a few spirited replies he appears as a rather dogged, unthinking fundamentalist taking refuge in the limits of human understanding, appealing to scripture texts in a rather literal-minded way, or reiterating that he became flesh without change, whatever that may mean. Orthodoxus on the other hand agrees on the necessity of sticking to scripture and tradition, but clearly believes that their meaning requires elucidation.

In the second dialogue, Eranistes is a more active participant. He is presented as offering for consideration and defending a number of the christological formulae which were to remain sacrosanct to the Monophysite party. The subject is now ἀσύγχυτος (unconfused), which means that the dialogue ranges over the whole question of whether two distinct natures are to be confessed. In the opening discussion, the debaters agree on the dismissal of Apollinarius' views and the completeness of Christ's human nature; but then Eranistes enquires whether it is right to call Jesus God or Man. Orthodoxus makes a very traditional statement about the Logos being incarnate, from which Eranistes deduces that he is to be called God, and adds that since they have agreed he was made man without change – indeed, remaining what he was – one must call him what he was, namely God. Orthodoxus replies that it is necessary to speak both of the assumer and the assumed; as scripture sometimes refers to man as soul and sometimes as body or flesh, so Christ must be confessed in two natures, as God and Man. But God, says Eranistes, fits him better, because God is the name of his nature, and Man is merely the name of the οἰκονομία (= incarnation). Orthodoxus protests that the οἰκονομία was real, and therefore the name Man is equally appropriate. Eranistes eventually accepts the idea of two natures, but says there were two only before the union; after the union there was just one. At that, Orthodoxus is easily able to demonstrate the inappropriateness of speaking of both natures pre-existing: the humanity did not exist before the union, only the Logos. Two natures after the union, yes; but not two natures before. Eranistes retorts *'out of* two natures not two natures', and pressed to explain, speaks of the union as ineffable and incomprehensible. Orthodoxus agrees but insists that each nature must remain pure and unmixed after the union, each having its own properties. Eranistes agrees to be persuaded by scripture, but sticks to his slogan: one nature after the union. He counteracts Orthodoxus' appeal to various texts by attributing them all to the incarnate Logos. All texts, he states, refer to the one enfleshed nature of the Logos. At that Orthodoxus refers back to their previous discussion: how can you talk of enfleshed God without attributing change to the Godhead or confusing the natures? Eranistes replies that two natures implies two Sons, and for a while takes over the initiative in the discussion. He gets Orthodoxus to admit that divine and human attributes are alike to be attributed to the one Christ. Orthodoxus, however, adds that both mixture and division have to be avoided, for to attribute confusion or mixture to the Godhead is blasphemous. He returns to the attack: how can Eranistes meet the challenge of Arius or Apollinarius? The ensuing discussion produces considerable agreement on the kind of christology needed to counter various heresies, but Eranistes is not yet satisfied that two natures does not imply two sons. Orthodoxus produces various arguments, showing, for example, that union without confusion is possible in the physical world, and that the humanity of Jesus was not swallowed up in his divinity. Eranistes eventually tries to clinch his case by adducing the eucharistic parallel, with which Orthodoxus both agrees and differs – for the bodily form, he points out, remains the same. When Eranistes protests that he sticks by the teachings of the church whatever arguments Orthodoxus may produce, the second florilegium is introduced, this time to establish that the flesh remains after the ascension, and that two natures without confusion are to be recognized in our Lord Jesus Christ.

Considering that Orthodoxus represents the author's view, one feels that in this dialogue Eranistes has been given quite a good chance to present his position. Theodoret had listened to the slogans and arguments of the opposition and was able to compose a fairly realistic and sympathetic picture of a typical Monophysite debater. He no longer misrepresents his opponent as an Apollinarian. He recognizes that there is a good deal of common ground, and he has the skill to use the dialogue form effectively to present both sides of the case, even though the total impact is of course a vindication of his own orthodox position. That position does not appear to be fundamentally different from that outlined in the *Expositio Rectae Fidei*. Theodoret may have been betrayed into more extreme statements by Cyril's provocative tactics over Nestorius, but his basic christological understanding was not transformed during the course of the controversy.

The third dialogue gives much the same impression. This dialogue tackles the heart of the problem – the Passion. In essence many of the arguments are not dissimilar from those that have gone before, but the debate is nearer the bone. Once again Eranistes is allowed to take the initiative in the discussion, and he is not often merely a foil for Orthodoxus' arguments. He has an important case to contribute and he does not let it go by default.

Orthodoxus states that they have agreed that the God-Word is ἄτρεπτος, that he was incarnate without change, that he took perfect manhood; scripture and the teachers of the church agree that after the union he remained what he was – unmixed, impassible, unchangeable, uncircumscribed, and so on. So the question of the passion remains. Eranistes opens: 'Who suffered?' 'Our Lord Jesus Christ', says Orthodoxus. 'So a man provided our salvation? Define what you believe Christ is.' When Orthodoxus offers the definition, 'The Son of the living God made man,' Eranistes states, 'God underwent suffering.' Orthodoxus, of course, cannot accept such a bald statement undermining the impassible with passion. As the discussion proceeds each side produces qualifications. Eranistes states that of course his divine nature is impassible, but he suffered in the flesh – that was why he became incarnate. Orthodoxus speaks of the body suffering, but this is no 'mere man', since it is the body of the God-Word and they were joined in an indivisible union. Both of them struggle with the paradox of the immortal dying and the impassible suffering, one dissolving it by attributing suffering and death to the body, the other asserting it on the basis of scripture. One accuses the other of blasphemy for suggesting that the ἀπαθής nature can be subject to πάθος; the other counters with the charge that anything else implies division of the one Lord Jesus Christ. They have an interesting discussion about what God can or cannot do, Orthodoxus suggesting that suffering is as alien to his nature as sin; the good cannot do evil, truth cannot be false, so all things are not possible to God. They discuss salvation, Orthodoxus emphasizing that sin is the greater problem, Eranistes tending to emphasize death; so for Eranistes the saving action of God is of primary importance, but Orthodoxus eventually brings convincing arguments from scripture that the suffering, death and ressurection were of the *body*, and that is why his resurrection can also be ours. He presses this point later by drawing attention to the fact that it is his flesh which is given for the life of the world; and that at the Last Supper he said 'This is my Body given for you.' Scripture never connects suffering with God himself, he asserts, even though he accepts the many texts adduced by Eranistes to prove that the Lord Jesus Christ suffered. Orthodoxus ought perhaps to have admitted that he was outmanoeuvred on this when Eranistes produced the text 'They crucified the Lord of glory'; but typically he gets round it by accepting that, on the basis of the *communicatio idiomatum*, the name of either nature can be applied to the one Christ. Basically the discussion revolves around the fact that Orthodoxus is prepared to say of the one Christ that as God he is immortal, impassible, unchangeable, etc., and as man he is mortal, passible, etc.; whereas Eranistes wishes to make a stronger statement designating the Logos as the subject of the incarnate experiences: by nature he is impassible, etc., but by being incarnate he took on a state in which he could in some real sense experience suffering and death. When Eranistes comes up with the Monophysite slogan ἀπαθῶς ἔπαθεν (he suffered without suffering), Orthodoxus laughs him to scorn; and yet sometimes they really do not seem all that far apart. Both agree that the Nicene creed states that the one *homoousios* with the Father was also the one who suffered and was crucified, each being prepared to admit that it is not straightforwardly true and certain qualifications have to be made.

Once more the concluding florilegium gives Orthodoxus an apparent victory over Eranistes, but the discussion has not been unfairly presented. If the other side had been able to read Theodoret's work with an open mind, there is little doubt that accommodation could have been reached. In a sense it was reached at Chalcedon, if only the Monophysites had not objected to the omission from the Definition of certain favourite slogans, the weakness of which Theodoret had here effectively demonstrated. They did after all disown Eutyches, just as the Antiochenes had come to disown Nestorius. Perhaps the purpose of the *Eranistes* was to try and convince the less extreme Alexandrians that they should abandon Eutyches and recognize how much common ground they had with the moderate Antiochenes.

In any case, it seems clear that Theodoret still stood by the basic theological principles outlined in his earlier work – the distinction between Creator and created is maintained, together with its implication, namely the recognition of two natures in Christ; but so is the acknowledgment that the Logos is the subject of the act of incarnation, even though incarnate experiences are properly attributed to the assumed nature and not to the Logos in his essential Being. What has changed is not so much his thought as his attitude and his emphases, to some extent also his terminology – the christological formulae which he had come to adopt through twenty years of debate.

5. Biblical exegesis

Theodoret belonged to the Antiochene tradition in his doctrine. He also belonged to the Antiochene tradition in his exegesis. Apart from everything else, Theodoret wrote an enormous number of biblical studies, some treatises in the form of question and answer concerning problem passages, others more straightforward commentaries. Between them, these works cover the Pentateuch with Joshua, Judges and Ruth; the books of Kings and Chronicles; the Psalms, the Song of Songs, Daniel, Ezekiel, Isaiah and Jeremiah; and the fourteen Epistles of St Paul.[265] The *Quaestiones*, covering the Old Testament books from Genesis to Chronicles, were written late in his life, after Chalcedon; the commentaries on the prophets and the apostle all seem to have been compiled during the period 433–438. These are not extended works of scholarship, nor are they homilies, but they have a devotional dimension and traces of oral delivery, features which suggest that like the *Discourses on Providence* they may well have been originally produced as lectures in Antioch.[266] All of this exegetical work survives (only his writings against Cyril were proscribed), and it provides us with our most extensive access to the Antiochene methods and exegetical achievement.

Indeed, that was once regarded as their only importance. Theodoret was thought to have reproduced Theodore to such an extent that his commentaries could supply gaps in what was known of Theodore's work.[267] If his commentaries had no other value, at least he had helped to preserve the Interpreter's work from oblivion. All the more interesting therefore has been the work of Godfrey Ashby and Paul Parvis, who have clearly established Theodoret's independence.[268] Even though he loyally leapt to the defence of Theodore when his master was attacked by Cyril, Theodoret did himself pass critical judgments on the exegetical work of his predecessors, amongst whom Theodore can be clearly identified. Comparisons between their commentaries where they overlap reveals the very considerable extent to which Theodoret departed from Theodore, while also highlighting Theodore's all-pervasive influence.

In the mechanics of exegesis (the dividing up of sentences, the definition of words, background explanations, tracing the connections of thought, elucidating the historical circumstances, and so on), Theodoret follows very closely the methods of Theodore. There are, however, few verbal parallels, and it certainly appears that, even though he was saturated in Theodore's work, Theodoret did not in fact refer to his commentaries when composing his own. Theodoret often approaches a particular passage rather differently, asking quite different questions. There are a number of occasions where he definitely disagrees with Theodore: Theodoret makes a great deal of the fact that Paul visited Colossae and knew the Colossians when he wrote his epistle; Theodore had asserted the opposite. The debate between them over this rumbles on through Theodoret's commentary. In other words, this was no slavish copying, and the suggestion that Theodoret duplicates Theodore[269] does not prove true on examination.

If the commentaries of Theodore and Theodoret have a similarity in method, they are marked by a difference in flavour. Lying behind this is not merely the difference in style (Theodore tends to write repetitive and cumbersome Greek, Theodoret's language is clear and concise). There is also a fundamental shift in perspective. For Theodore, as we have seen, there was a radical distinction between the old order and the new, a strong eschatological outlook which favoured discontinuity between the two Testaments. This perspective, so characteristic of Theodore, led him to deny the christological character of many Old Testament texts, to refuse to see any indications of the trinitarian nature of God in the Old Testament writings, and to reduce to a bare minimum direct prophecies of the New Age: a few types were permitted with rigidly defined safeguards and rules, a few predictions were acknowledged where hyperbolic expressions made certain statements inappropriate to the old order. The abandonment of this radical Two Ages dichotomy enabled Theodoret to develop a more explicitly Christian view of the Old Testament. As he tells us in the *Preface to the Psalms*,

I have consulted various commentaries, of which some fell into allegory, whilst others adapted the prophecies themselves to the history of the past, so that their interpretation applied more to Jews than to Christians. I have felt it my duty to avoid equally the two extremes. All that is relevant to ancient history ought to be recognized. But predictions concerning Christ our Saviour, the church of the Gentiles, the expansion of the gospel, the preaching of the apostles, ought not to be diverted from their proper sense and applied to other things as if they had been fulfilled by the Jews.

It must be Theodore he has in mind.

Theodoret, without sacrificing the historical content of the original works, is prepared to see the Christian dispensation foreshadowed and predicted in the Old Testament. So, unlike Theodore, Theodoret can relate Old and New Testament texts, using them to interpret each other. Much more than Theodore, Theodoret perceives a unity in the whole of scripture. The Old Testament does contain reference to the Trinity, and indeed points to the two natures of Christ. For Theodoret allows also a great deal of θεωρία – spiritual meanings. A text need no longer have one σκοπός: it can have both a historical reference and a predictive role, pointing to the messianic fulfilment. This makes an enormous difference to the *Commentary on the Psalms*: the LXX title εἰς τὸ τέλος (to the End/fulfilment) provided Theodoret with a clue, embedded in the scriptural text, to the messianic reference of any Psalm to which it is attached. (It actually represents the obscure Hebrew word translated by the RSV as 'To the Choirmaster'.) Some Psalms belonged to the context of David's life, some referred to the great saving events of Israel's history, but many Psalms were allowed a specifically christological reference, and many more were regarded as having a double, or even triple level of meaning. Similarly the prophets, while belonging to their own time and speaking to their contemporaries, nevertheless made predictions, and these were more often than not predictions of Christ. Theodoret emphatically rejects views which clearly came from Theodore, like the idea that Micah 4.1–3 refers to the return from Babylon to Jerusalem, insisting that its fulfilment is seen in the gathering of the Gentiles to the church. Whereas Theodore had suggested that the Song of Songs was just Solomon's love-poem, Theodoret indignantly repudiates 'those who slander the Song of Songs and believe the book is not spiritual'. It does describe a marriage, but it is the marriage of Christ and the church – and Theodoret is clearly dependent upon Origen for much of his exegesis. It is particularly interesting that Theodoret could adopt such an independent line in what was almost certainly his first commentary. Consciously rejecting allegory and asserting the principles of historical interpretation like other Antiochenes, Theodoret is yet able to give full weight to the church's traditions of spiritual exegesis. Not that every Old Testament verse can produce *theoria* – but certain basic biblical themes are to be interpreted in relation to their Christian fulfilment. Threefold invocations, mention of the Spirit, insistence on God's uniqueness – such texts show that the God of the Old Testament was the triune God of the Christians. Man, the creation of God but lost in sinfulness, finds his redemption and fulfilment in Christ. Christian salvation is prefigured in the great saving events of the Old Testament. Many images have their fulfilment in Christian baptism and eucharist. Theodoret reverts to the traditional types and messianic prophecies, many of which were enshrined in the liturgy, while still grasping the priority of historical interpretation.

When it comes to the New Testament, the contrast is perhaps less marked. There is less scope for θεωρία and Theodoret's comments are largely confined to explanatory notes. But there is still a contrast. Theodore's eschatological hope is reduced and the emphasis is placed on the present, the moral life of the believer or the sacramental life of the church. Theodoret's more guarded christological language and his tendency to make the Logos the subject of the saving actions gives a different slant to his exegesis of key Pauline texts. Theodoret is briefer and less heavily theological than Theodore, indeed, 'paradoxically Theodoret is probably closer to Theodore in content and to John (Chrysostom) in spirit'.[270] Practical issues submerge vague eschatological tensions. Like Chrysostom, Theodoret identified himself with the 'mainstream' church which had to find a practical mode of life and faith in the fifth-century world. It is ironic that one so solidly orthodox in intention should have had such a stormy career.

6. Other works

One of the last things Theodoret did was to compile an encyclopaedia of heresies: the *Compendium Haereticorum Fabularum* or *Epitome of Heretical Myths*. Theodoret had to prove himself in yet another field of ecclesiastical literature. The strange thing is that he does not seem to have used the work of Epiphanius – he mentions those he has consulted, including Justin, Irenaeus, Clement, Origen, Eusebius, Diodore and various others, but not Epiphanius. In contrast to Epiphanius, Theodoret attempted a logical rather than genealogical arrangement. His first book covers those who make another Creator and hold a docetic view of Christ:

this covers all the Gnostic movements from Simon Magus to Mani. The second book deals with the opposite type – those who acknowledge one God but treat Christ as a mere man: amongst these Theodoret includes Ebion, Theodotus, Paul of Samosata, Sabellius and Marcellus. Book III takes in various other heresies which fall between the two extremes – the Montanists, Novatians, Quartodecimans, and others who in many ways were very close to the orthodox. New heresies, by which is meant the post-Nicene crop of deviations, fill the fourth book: Arius, Eunomius, Apollinarius and others are accompanied by the Donatists and Meletians. In this book there appears a section on Eutyches, and more surprisingly, one on Nestorius. Probably the idea that this was an interpolation has to be rejected; Theodoret was writing after Chalcedon and might have feared reprisals if Nestorius had been conspicuous by his absence. The fifth book is almost a Theodoretan *De principiis*, giving an account of orthodox teaching, beginning at the ἀρχή – the first principle, and passing through the doctrine of God, creation, angels, demons, men, providence, the Saviour's οἰκονομία, christological questions, baptism, judgment, the End, and various ethical matters.

In his self-justificatory letters, Theodoret gives three slightly different lists of his earlier writings,[271] specifying that they were written some twenty years, others eighteen, fifteen or twelve years previously. His purpose was to show that he had always been orthodox, but these references are useful because many of the works can be identified with surviving treatises and so some approximation can be made of the date of each writing.[272] A little conflation of the lists indicates the range of his literary achievement: he had written against heretics – Arius, Eunomius, Apollinarius, Marcion and others; against Jews and Gentiles and the Persian Magi; on Providence, Theology and the Incarnation; a mystical book and the lives of saints; commentaries on the prophets and the apostle Paul. We know that he also wrote an *Ecclesiastical History* and at a later date his encyclopaedia of heresies and the *Quaestiones* on the Old Testament historical books – not to mention his letters and various controversial tracts. It is an impressive range, and it would not be surprising if he had produced a whole lot of imitative and plagiarized materials.

This was once the standard estimate of Theodoret's achievement – a mere imitator and epitomizer, drawing upon the previous work of historians, apologists and exegetes. The interesting thing about recent work is that over and over again a closer look at Theodoret's work has shown that he did make an original contribution to each of the tasks he undertook, that he did not merely copy slavishly but undertook independent researches, adapted the material to his own ends, modified what he had inherited and gave everything a shape and a clarity which increased its appeal to his readership.

Of course, Theodoret had no ambition to be original. All he wanted to do was to preserve the tradition of the scriptures and the fathers who interpreted them. But he seems to have realized that mere repetition was no way to fulfil that function, that there was a proper place for enquiry, for restatement, for reformulation, as new problems and circumstances arose. Each generation in promulgating the orthodox teaching of the church faced the task of assimilating the tradition and giving it application in its own situation. Theodoret was loyal to his friends, but he retreated from the extremes of Antiochene theology and exegesis in the interest of preserving the integrity and unity of the Christian tradition. His rather belligerent orthodoxy in the *Ecclesiastical History*, his unhappy role in the doctrinal controversies, should not be allowed to obscure his fundamentally Christian personality; ascetic and pastor, he typified fifth-century tendencies, acted as a bridge between different cultural levels and between pagan and Christian society, and proved to be a literary churchman of remarkably wide-ranging interests and abilities.

Notes

1. The Birth of Church History and its Sequel

1. Controversy has raged over the implications of this. Since Photius, some have understood it to mean 'slave of' or 'freedman of' Pamphilus; but the form is probably to be understood as a patronymic, with the implication that Pamphilus adopted Eusebius as his son and heir. He apparently inherited the library. See E. H. Gifford's edition, *Eusebii Pamphili Evangelicae Praeparationis Libri XV*, Vol. III.1, Oxford and New York 1903, vi-xi, for discussion. It remains possible that Eusebius took his name after his death as a token of respect. Their joint *Apologia pro Origene* exists only in Rufinus' Latin version.

2. Eusebius, *Vita Constantini* iv.36, GCS I, ed. I. A. Heikel, 1902.

3. Ibid. iii.61.

4. Eusebius, *Historia Ecclesiastica*, GCS II.1–2, ed. E. Schwartz, 1903–9; GCS V and VII also cover available versions of the *Chronicle*.

5. E.g. D. S. Wallace-Hadrill, *Eusebius of Caesarea*, London 1960.

6. R. M. Grant, *Eusebius as Church Historian*, Oxford and New York 1980; unfortunately this work reached me too late for much account to be taken of it in this chapter. It is recommended to the reader.

7. There is some dispute about the character of Julius Africanus' lost *Chronography*.

8. *HE* I.i.2.

9. D. S. Wallace-Hadrill, 'The Eusebian Chronicle. The Extent and Date of Composition of its Early Editions', *JTS* NS 6, 1955, 248–53.

10. J. Stevenson, *A New Eusebius*, London and New York 1957.

11. H. J. Lawlor reckoned that half the quotations in the *HE* would be otherwise unknown to us; see Eusebius, *Ecclesiastical History*, trans. with introd. and notes by H. J. Lawlor and J. E. L. Oulton, London and New York 1927, vol. II, 19.

12. P. Nautin, *Lettres et écrivains chrétiens des IIe and IIIe siècles*, Paris 1961.

13. Lawlor estimated that over 50 non-biblical quotations are mutilated, though this he attributed to incompetent copyists employed by Eusebius to transcribe passages. See Lawlor and Oulton, op. cit., 20–25. For numerous examples of exclusions, distortions and falsifications, see R. M. Grant, 'Eusebius and Church History', in *Understanding the Sacred Text*. Festschrift for M. S. Enslin, Valley Forge 1972, 233–47; and 'The Case against Eusebius, or Did the Father of Church History Write History?' *StudPatr* 12, 1975, 413–21.

14. H. J. Lawlor, *Eusebiana*, New York 1912; and the debate in the *Classical Quarterly* 19, 1924–5, by N. H. Baynes, H. J. Lawlor and G. W. Richardson.

15. See R. M. Grant, op. cit., for this and the following points.

16. A. Momigliano, 'Pagan and Christian Historiography', in *The Conflict between Paganism and Christianity in the Fourth Century*, ed. Momigliano, Oxford and New York 1963, 79–99; amplified by R. A. Markus, 'Church History and the Early Church Historians' in *The Materials, Sources and Methods of Ecclesiastical History*, ed. D. A. Baker (Studies in Church History 11), Oxford 1975, 1–17.

17. G. Bardy in his Introduction to his edition of the *Ecclesiastical History*, vol. IV (SC 73), reprinted 1971, 79.

18. Glenn F. Chesnut, *The First Christian Histories*, Paris 1977, chs. I and II.

19. *HE* i.1.2.

20. *Demonstratio Evangelica* iv.16; viii.1; text in GCS VI, ed. I. A. Heikel, 1913; text of *Praeparatio Evangelica*, GCS VIII.1–2, ed. K. Mras, 1954–6.

21. Texts: *Prophetic Eclogues* in PG 22; *Theophania*: Greek fragments ed. H. Gressmann in GCS III.2, 1904. Full text only in Syriac.

22. Gifford, op. cit., lists the fragments for which we are indebted to Eusebius; it is a very remarkable collection, including all we know of Numenius the Pythagorean, and the Neoplatonist Atticus, not to mention the extracts from Philo Judaeus and Porphyry.

23. *Praep. Evang.* vii; *Dem. Evang.* i.

24. For discussion of Eusebius' historical ideas, I am much indebted to J. Sirinelli, *Les vues historiques d'Eusèbe de Césarée durant la periode prénicéenne*, Dakar 1961. See also the similar account in Glenn F. Chesnut, op. cit. ch.IV.

25. Plagiarism: *Praep. Evang.* x; Moses' priority; ibid. xi–xiii (cf. *Theophania* ii.44 f.); fate and astrology: ibid. vi; anti-philosophers: ibid. xv; oracles: ibid iv–v; prophecy: *Dem. passim.*

26. This is stated as the purpose of the two works in the opening prefaces to the *Praeparatio* and the *Demonstratio.*

27. *Dem. Evang.* i.7; iii.2.

28. Ibid. iv.15.

29. Ibid. i.3.

30. Ibid., introd. to Book v.

31. *HE* ii.3.

32. *Dem Evang.* iii.

33. *Theophania* iii.2, and frequently.

34. *HE* viii.1.

35. Ibid. viii.13–16.

36. Ibid. ix.8.

37. *Laus Constantini* i–iii.

38. N. H. Baynes, 'Eusebius and the Christian Empire', in *Mélanges Bidez*, Paris 1934.

39. K. M. Setton, *The Christian Attitude to the Emperor in the Fourth Century*, New York and London 1941. See also Glenn F. Chesnut, op. cit. ch. VI.

40. Philosopher-king, etc.: *Laus* v; *Vita* iv. 48. Teacher: *Vita* iv. 29. Sun: *Laus* iii. Feast of the Kingdom: *Vita* iii.15.

41. H. A. Drake, *In Praise of Constantine: A Historical Study and New Translation of Eusebius' Tricennial Orations*, Berkeley 1976. A rather

different interpretation is found in T. D. Barnes, *Constantine and Euseb-ius*, Cambridge, Mass. 1981, but this has reached me too late for proper account to be taken of his criticisms of Drake.

42. Texts of the *Vita Constantini* and the *Laus Constantini*: GCS I, ed. I. A. Heikel, 1902.

43. *Vita* i.10.

44. Ibid. i.11.

45. H. A. Drake, op. cit., has a useful discussion of the critical problems, as well as providing an excellent historical study of the relationship between Eusebius and the emperor in terms of theology and religious policy.

46. N. H. Baynes, 'Constantine the Great and the Christian Church', *Proc. of British Academy*, 1929, discusses all the objections and argues for their authenticity in the very full footnotes.

47. A. H. M. Jones, 'Notes on the genuineness of the Constantinian documents in Eusebius' *Life of Constantine*', *JEH* 5, 1954, 196–200.

48. See H. A. Drake, op. cit., and R. H. Storch, 'The Eusebian Constan-tine', *Church History* 40, 1971, 145–55.

49. *Dem. Evang.* iv.2.

50. *Dem. Evang.* iv.3, 13. See below pp. 74 f.

51. *Praep. Evang.* iv.10, 17, 21.

52. Ibid. vii.15.

53. *HE* i.2.

54. E. Des Places, 'Numenius et Eusèbe de Césarée', *StudPatr* 12, 1975, 19–28.

55. F. Ricken, 'Die Logoslehre des Eusebios von Caesarea und der Mittelplatonismus', *Theologie und Philosophie* 42, 1967, 341–58. C. Luibheid, *Eusebius of Caesarea and the Arian Crisis*, Dublin 1978, does not take Eusebius' Platonist and Origenist background seriously enough.

56. *HE* i.2.

57. *Praep. Evang.* ii.4; *Dem. Evang.* iii.4.

58. H. von Campenhausen, *The Fathers of the Greek Church*, ET New York 1959, London 1963, ch. V.

59. *Dem. Evang.* iv.14. For Athanasius' use of the concept see below pp. 72 f.

60. *Dem. Evang.* iv.12.

61. See below p. 69.

62. A. Weber, *APXH. Ein Beitrag zur Christologie des Eusebius von Caesarea*, Rome 1965, suggests that Eusebius' position is pre-Nicene and entirely in line with tradition. Athanasius and Marcellus were the innovators.

63. Preserved by Athanasius in his *De decretis Nicaenae Synodi*; ET in *The Trinitarian Controversy*, ed. W. G. Rusch (Sources of Early Christian Thought), Philadelphia 1980.

64. J. N. D. Kelly, *Early Christian Creeds*, London and Toronto 1950, 217 ff.

65. For the following discussion I am indebted to G. C. Stead, 'Eusebius and the Council of Nicaea', *JTS* NS 24, 1973, 85 ff.

66. *Dem. Evang.* iv.3; v.1.

67. Athanasius, *De Decretis Nic. Syn.* 3; Socrates, *HE* i.23.

68. Text of *Contra Marcellum* and other doctrinal works, ed. E. Klostermann, in GCS IV, 1906.

69. A. Möhle reported the find of the *Commentary on Isaiah* in *ZNW* 33, 1934, 87–9. Text: GCS IX, ed. J. Ziegler. See also J. M. van Cangh, 'Nouveaux Fragments Hexaplaires. Commentaire sur Isaïe d'Eusébe de Césarée', *Revue Biblique* 78, 1971, 384–90; 79, 1972, 76.

70. *Dem. Evang.* vii.1.

71. Text of the *Onomasticon* ed. E. Klostermann in GCS III. 1, 1904. For a detailed account see C. V. Wolf, 'Eusebius of Caesarea and the Onomasticon', *The Biblical Archaeologist* 27, 1964, 66–96.

72. Epitome and fragments of the *Quaestiones Evangelicae* in PG 22.

73. The *Christian History* of Philip of Side, published in the 430s, is perhaps an exception, but it was apparently more like an encyclopaedia than a history. Socrates (*HE* vii.27) describes it as a collection of 'very heterogeneous materials', containing a 'medley of geometrical theorems, astronomical speculations, arithmetical calculations and musical principles' with geographical details and other irrelevant material. It was an attempt to cover the whole of history from the creation, according to Photius (*Bibl. Cod.* 35). All is lost apart from a few fragments.

74. Glenn F. Chesnut, *The First Christian Histories*, 168 f.

75. Socrates, *HE* i.1; text in PG 67.

76. For Socrates' theological and philosophical position, see Chesnut, op. cit. ch. VII, to whom I am indebted for the following comments.

77. Socrates, *HE* i.18.

78. Imperial tolerance: ibid. v.20; vii.41–2. Novatians: frequently, but cf. vii.46. Arians: vii.6.

79. Attitude to heresy: ibid. v.20 ff. Refusal to examine disputes: i.22. Disorder, etc.: ii.1.

80. Ibid. v. introd.; i.24.

81. Ibid. vi. introd.; the rest of Book vi deals with the Chrysostom affair. Chrysostom's relics were reburied in Constantinople in 438 by Theodosius II, i.e. shortly before Socrates wrote the history. That incident is described in vii.45.

82. Ibid. vi.20; on Nestorius, see vii.32.

83. Glenn F. Chesnut, 'Kairos and Cosmic Sympathy in the Church Historian Socrates Scholasticus', *Church History* 44, 1975, 69–75; and op. cit. 186 ff.

84. Socrates, *HE* v. introd. On the emperor's role see G. Downey, 'The Perspective of the Early Church Historians', *Greek, Roman and Byzantine Studies* 6, 1965, 57–70.

85. Socrates, *HE* vii.20.

86. Ibid. vii.32.

87. Ibid. vi. introd.; for suppression and distortion, see i.10.

88. E.g. Ibid. i.12, 15; ii.1.

89. Ibid. i.8; ii.15, 17.

90. Ibid. i.23. Cf. ii.21, where Socrates devotes a whole chapter to defending the orthodoxy of Eusebius with long quotations to prove his point from the *Contra Marcellum*.

91. Philostorgius, *HE* ii.11. Text in GCS, ed. J. Bidez, 2nd ed. rev. F. Winckelmann, 1972.

92. Illness, ibid. vii.10; earthquakes, xii.9; signs in heaven, x.9; for the other examples in this paragraph see xi.7, xii.8, 9.

93. Ibid. x.6.

94. Ibid. iii.11; for Constantinople, see ii.9; for the rivers, see iii.7–10.

95. Ibid. iii.26, x.9, xii.8; vii.14; x.11, iii.11 provide examples of the phenomena mentioned.

96. Ibid. viii.10.

97. Ibid. ii.17; for missions, see ii.5, iii.4–6; for Julian vii.4.

98. Note esp. viii.2–4, where describing the Eunomians' period of prosperity

99. Ibid. x.3.

100. Ibid. i.2; for Arius, see ii.3, x.2.

101. Socrates, *HE* i.21; iv.23.

102. Sozomen, *HE* vi.27; for Athanasius, see ii.17. Text in GCS, ed. J. Bidez and G. C. Hansen, 1960.

103. Ibid. vii.19.

104. Ibid iii.18.

105. The various suggestions are discussed by Glenn F. Chesnut, *The First Christian Histories*, p. 195 n. 20.

106. See chapter 5 below.

107. Theodoret, *HE* v.34. Text in GCS, ed. L. Parmentier; 2nd ed. rev. F. Scheidweiler, 1954.

108. Socrates, *HE* i.6; compare Theodoret, *HE* i.2–3.

109. Compare Theodoret, *HE* i.14–16 with Socrates, *HE* i.9.

110. Theodoret, *HE* i.1.

111. For the following paragraphs I am indebted to the works of P. Canivet, *Histoire d'une entreprise apologétique de Ve siecle*, Paris 1958; and his edition of the text: *Théodoret de Cyr, Thérapeutique des Maladies Helléniques*, 2 vols., SC 57, 1958.

112. Text in Y. Azéma, *Théodoret de Cyr. Discours sur la providence* (Budé), Paris 1954.

113. Theodoret, *Epp.* 113, 116, 145.

114. P. Canivet, op. cit.

115. For further details, see F. L. Cross, *The Early Christian Fathers*, London 1960, 192 ff.

116. E. E. Malone, *The Monk and the Martyr*, Washington 1950.

117. *Historia Monachorum*: text edited by A. J. Festugière (Subsidia Hagiographica 34), Brussels 1961; earlier edition in E. Preuschen, *Palladius und Rufinus*, Giessen 1897. Preuschen argued for Rufinus' priority; but see A. J. Festugière, 'Le problème littéraire de l'*Historia Monachorum*', *Hermes* 83 1955, 257–84. A French translation of the *Historia Monachorum* will be found in Festugière's *Les Moines d'Orient*, vol. IV.1, Paris 1965.

118. Dom Cuthbert Butler's discussion and text of the the *Lausiac History* is to be found in *Texts and Studies* 6, Cambridge 1904. There is an English translation by R. T. Meyer (ACW 34), 1965.

119. R. Draguet, 'Un nouveau témoin du texte G de l'Histoire Lausiaque (MS. Athènes 281)', *Analecta Bollandiana* 67, 1949, 300–8; and 'Butler et sa Lausiac History face à un ms. de l'edition I Wake 67', *Le Muséon* 63, 1950, 203–30. D. J. Chitty defended Butler in 'Dom Cuthbert Butler and the

Lausiac History', *JTS* NS 6, 1955 239–58. Draguet replied in 'Butleriana: Une mauvaise cause et son malchanceux avocat', *Le Muséon* 68, 1955, 239–58.

120. Socrates, *HE* iv.23.

121. It was suggested first by Reitzenstein, and pursued by Bousset in 'Komposition und Charakter der Historia Lausiaca', *Nachricten von der königlichen Gesellschaft der Wissenschaften zu Göttingen, Phil.-hist. Klasse*, 1917, 173–217; his further argument appeared in 'Zur Komposition der Historia Lausiaca', *ZNW* 21, 1922, 81–98. Nau's material had appeared in *Patrologia Orientalis* 4, 1908, 425–503.

122. P. Peeters, 'Une vie copte de S. Jean de Lycopolis', *Analecta Bollandiana*, 54, 1936, 359–83. His arguments are summarized in English by W. Telfer, 'The Trustworthiness of Palladius', *JTS* 38, 1937, 379–83.

123. R. Draguet, 'Le chapitre de l'Histoire Lausiaque sur les Tabénnesiotes', *Le Muséon* 57, 1944, 53–146; 58, 1945, 15–96. Also 'Une nouvelle source Copte de Pallade: le chapitre viii (Amoun)', *Le Muséon* 60, 1947, 227–55.

124. F. Halkin, 'L'Histoire Lausiaque et les vies grecques de S. Pachome', *Analecta Bollandiana* 48, 1930, 257–301. For his work on the Greek lives, see 'Les vies grecques de S. Pachome', *Analecta Bollandiana* 47, 1929, 376–83; and his edition *S. Pachomii Vitae graecae* (Subsidia hagiographica 19), Brussels 1932.

125. E.g. D. F. Buck, 'The Structure of the *Lausiac History*', *Byzantion* 46, 1976, 292–307.

126. D. Chitty, *The Desert a City*, Oxford 1966, 51 f.

127. Eusebius, *HE* vi.5.

128. Buck, art. cit.

129. E. D. Hunt, 'Palladius of Helenopolis: A Party and its Supporters in the Church of the late Fourth Century', *JTS* NS 24, 1973, 456–80.

130. The translations in this paragraph mostly follow R. T. Meyer; quotations are from the prologue and chs. 38 and 18.

131. R. Draguet, 'L'Histoire Lausiaque, une oeuvre écrite dans l'esprit d'Évagre', *Revue d'Histoire Ecclésiastique* 41, 1946, 321–64; 42, 1947, 5–49. Also R. T. Meyer, 'Palladius and Early Christian Spirituality', *StudPatr* 10, 1970, 379–90.

132. E. D. Hunt, art. cit., studies this relationship in detail. For further material on the Origenist controversy, see Chapter 4 below.

133. Socrates, *HE* vii.36.

134. P. R. Coleman-Norton, 'The Authorship of the *Epistola de Indicis gentibus et de Bragmanibus*', *Classical Philology* 21, 1926, 154–60.

135. Editions are listed in Bibliography B.

136. W. Bousset, *Apophthegmata*, Tübingen 1923, §19.

137. Derwas Chitty, 'Abba Isaiah', *JTS* NS 22, 1971, 47–72. See also his article 'The Books of the Old Men', *Eastern Churches Review* 6, 1974, 15–21. He had already dropped hints in *The Desert a City* (n. 126 above), 74 and 80 n. 117, and found confirmation when the Syriac was published by R. Draguet, *Les cinq recensions de l'Ascéticon syriaque d'abba Isaïe*, CSCO 294 (Scriptores Syriaci 123), Louvain 1968. Translation: *Abbé Isaïe: Recueil ascétique*. Introduction et traduction française par les moines des Solesmes, Begrolles 1970.

138. For details see Bibliography B.

139. The work is known as the *Verba Seniorum*; text in PL 73. 851–988, translation in Helen Waddell, *The Desert Fathers*, London and New York 1936 (selections only). (Quotations from the *Verba Seniorum* are normally from this translation, though I have made occasional modifications).

140. See J. C. Guy, *Recherches sur la tradition grèque des Apophthegmata Patrum* (Subsidia Hagiographica 36), Brussels 1962.

141. Alphabeticon: text in PG 65. Translation, Benedicta Ward, *The Sayings of the Desert Fathers*, London 1975. (Quotations from the Alphabeticon are from this translation.)

142. Codex Coislinianus, ed. F. Nau and published in instalments in the *Revue de l'Orient Chrétien* 12–14, 1907–9 and 17–18, 1912–13. Translation, Benedicta Ward, *The Wisdom of the Desert Fathers*, Oxford 1975.

143. J. C. Guy, op. cit., where he publishes some additional material.

144. Bousset, *Apophthegmata*.

145. Chitty, 'The Books of the Old Men'.

146. J. C. Guy, 'Remarques sur le texte des Apophthegmata Patrum', *RSR* 43, 1955, 252–8.

147. J. C. Guy, 'Educational innovation in the Desert Fathers', *Eastern Churches Review* 6, 1974, 44–51.

148. Alphabeticon: *Poemen* 174.

149. *Verba Seniorum* vii.33 // Codex Coislinianus 126. 201.

150. Alphabeticon: *John the Dwarf* 17 // *Verba Seniorum* xvii.7.

151. *Verba Seniorum* ii.2 // Alphabeticon: *Antony* 11.

152. *Verba Seniorum* x.111 // Codex Coislinianus 126.244.

153. Alphabeticon: *Arsenius* 6 // *Verba Seniorum* xv.7.

154. Alphabeticon: *Evagrius* 7 // *Verba Seniorum* xvi.2.

155. Alphabeticon: *Arsenius* 36.

156. Alphabeticon: *Poemen* 184.

157. Alphabeticon: *Moses* 3 // *Verba Seniorum* xvi.7.

158. Theodoret, *Historia religiosa*, ed. P. Canivet and A. Leroy-Molinghen, SC 234, 257, 1977.

159. For further details see A. Vööbus, *A History of Asceticism in the Syrian Orient*, 2 vols., Louvain 1960. An excellent summary article by Robert Murray, 'The Features of the Earliest Christian Asceticism', will be found in *Christian Spirituality* (Essays in honour of Gordon Rupp), ed. Peter Brooks, London 1975, 63–77. Also S. P. Brock, 'Early Syrian Asceticism', *Numen* 20, 1973, 1–19.

160. *Vitae Patrum* x.44 // Alphabeticon: *Poemen* 31.

161. P. Peeters, 'S. Syméon Stylite et ses premiers biographes', *Analecta Bollandiana* 61, 1943, 29–71; republished in *Le tréfonds oriental de l'hagiographie byzantine* ch.V (Subsidia Hagiographica 26), Brussels 1950.

162. M. Richard, 'Theodoret, Jean d'Antioche et les moines d'Orient' *Mélanges de Science Religieuse* 3, 1946, 148–61; republished in *Opera Minora* vol. II.

163. P. Canivet, *Le monachisme Syrien selon Théodoret de Cyr*, Paris 1977, 77 ff. My discussion in this entire section owes much to Canivet's work, here and in his edition of the *Historia religiosa*.

164. This is generally acknowledged in all discussions of this material. A full critical account of the manuscript tradition will be found in A. Leroy-

Molinghen, 'A propos de la Vie de Syméon Stylite', *Byzantion* 34, 1964, 375–84. The signs are that a new edition was produced by a later hand.
165. Canivet, op. cit., ch. V.
166. H. Delahaye, *Les Saints Stylites*, Brussels 1923, p.ix.
167. A. J. Festugière, *Antioche paienne et chrétienne*, Paris 1959, 346–87.
168. The following discussion owes much to Canivet, op. cit., ch. X.
169. Peter Brown, 'The Rise and Function of the Holy Man in Late Antiquity', *JRS* 61, 1971, 80–101.
170. Peter Brown, *The World of Late Antiquity*, London and New York 1971, 98.
171. A. J. Festugière, *Les Moines d'Orient* I, ch. 1, explores this theme fully.

2. *Athanasius and some Fellow-Alexandrians of the Fourth Century*

1. I am grateful to Donald Winslow (Episcopal Theological Seminary, Cambridge, Mass.) for some constructive criticisms of the first draft of this chapter; and to J. Steenson (Christ Church, Oxford) for some perceptive comments on a later draft, observations which stimulated a certain shift in perspective.
2. E. Schwartz suggested 323; for discussion of the date see articles by W. Telfer and N. H. Baynes in *JTS* 47–50, 1946–49. The most recent comprehensive study adopts the date 322: E. Boulerand, *L'Herésie d'Arius et la Foi de Nicée*, 2 vols., Paris 1972.
3. Sozomen, *HE* i.15.
4. Socrates, *HE* i.5.
5. Rufinus, *HE* i.1.
6. Sozomen, *HE* i.15.
7. Philostorgius, *HE* ii.2.
8. W. Telfer, 'Arius Takes Refuge at Nicomedia', *JTS* 37, 1936, 60–63, throws doubt on the story of Arius' visits to bishops in Palestine and Asia Minor.
9. Epiphanius, *Panarion* 69.4.
10. Epiphanius, *Panarion* 69.6; also in Theodoret, *HE* i.5. = No. 1 in H. G. Opitz, *Urkunden zur Geschichte des arianischen Streites* vol.III.1 of the projected Berlin Academy edition of Athanasius' works, Berlin 1934–41 (hereafter referred to as Opitz).
11. Epiphanius, *Panarion* 69.7; also in Athanasius, *De Synodis* 16.= Opitz no. 6.
12. But see Telfer, op. cit., who argues that Arius wrote this letter in Egypt and never toured the East at all.
13. The additional ν(n) is placed in brackets to indicate the ambiguity inherent in the word which made Arius' argument possible. It was Athanasius who clearly distinguished between ἀγένητος *(agenētos)* from γίνομαι *(ginomai* = I come into being) meaning 'unoriginate' or 'uncreated', and ἀγέννητος *(agennētos)* from γεννάω *(gennāo* = I beget) meaning 'unbegotten'. See further G. L. Prestige, *God in Patristic Thought*, London 1936, chs. II and VII; 'ΑΓΕΝ[Ν]ΗΤΟΣ and cognate words in Athanasius', *JTS* 34, 1933, 258–65.

14. Socrates, *HE* i.6. = Opitz no. 4b. This appears also in some mss of Athanasius' works, headed *Deposition of Arius and his associates*, with a covering letter requesting the clergy of Egypt to sign it.

15. Theodoret, *HE* i.4. = Opitz no. 14.

16. Appended to some mss. of Athanasius' *De Decretis* (33); quoted in Socrates, *HE* i.8 and Theodoret, *HE* i.12. = Opitz no. 22. ET in NPNF II.IV.

17. Socrates, *HE* i.26 and Sozomen, *HE* ii.27. =Opitz no. 30.

18. B. Altaner, *Patrology*, ET New York 1960, p. 310.

19. *C. Arianos* i.2,4, PG 26.16,20.

20. For a detailed discussion, see G. Bardy, 'La Thalie d'Arius', *Revue de Philologie* 53 (3rd series 1), 1927, 211–33 (reproduced in *Recherches sur Lucien d'Antioche*, Paris 1936, 246–74). Bardy publishes here the text of the fragments. See, however, the recent article by G. C. Stead, 'The *Thalia* of Arius and the Testimony of Athanasius', *JTS* NS 29, 1978, 20–52.

21. *De Synodis* 15. Opitz, *Die Apologien* (Vol. II.1 of the projected Berlin Academy edition of Athanasius' works, 1935–41), p. 242. But see the discussion by C. Kannengiesser, 'Ou et quand Arius composa-t-il sa Thalie?', in *Kyriakon*. Festschrift J. Quasten, Münster 1970, I,346–51.

22. Socrates, *HE* i.5; Sozomen, *HE* i.15.

23. T. E. Pollard, 'The Origins of Arianism', *JTS* NS 9, 1958, 104.

24. Maurice Wiles, 'In Defence of Arius', *JTS* NS 13, 1962, 339–47.

25. Robert Gregg and Dennis Groh, 'The Centrality of Soteriology in Early Arianism', *Anglican Theological Review* 59, 1977, 260–78. See further their *Early Arianism: a View of Salvation*, London and Philadelphia 1981.

26. Gregg and Groh, art. cit., 272.

27. J. N. D. Kelly, *Early Christian Creeds*, London and Toronto 1950, e.g. 213,235,253; cf. Athanasius, *De Decretis* 18–21.

28. E. Boulerand, op. cit. (n. 2 above), ch. IV *passim*.

29. L. W. Barnard, 'The Antecedents of Arius', *VC* 24, 1970, 172–88; 'What was Arius' Philosophy?' *Theologische Zeitschrift* 28, 1972, 110–17.

30. G. C. Stead, 'The Platonism of Arius', *JTS* NS 15, 1964,30.

31. Barnard, 'Antecedents', 180.

32. G. Bardy, *Recherches sur S. Lucien d'Antioche* (n. 20 above), is an exhaustive study of the evidence we possess concerning Lucian and his pupils. T. E. Pollard, art. cit., argues in support of Alexander's evidence, against the views of Bardy et al. For a comprehensive survey of the suggested possibilities see Boulerand, op. cit., ch. V.

33. L. W. Barnard, 'Antecedents'. The following remarks are based upon the work of Barnard and Stead, especially Stead's article on the *Thalia* (n. 20 above), and his 'Rhetorical Method in Athanasius', *VC* 30, 1976 121–37.

34. See above p. 18.

35. Gregory Nazianzen, *Oration* 21.14, PG 35.1096.

36. For the following points I am indebted to several essays in *Politique et Théologie chez Athanase d'Alexandrie*, ed. C. Kannengiesser, Paris 1974: chiefly, W. G. Rusch, 'A la recherche de l'Athanase historique', 161–80, but also Annik Martin, 'Athanase et les Meletiens (325–335)', 31–62, and L. W. Barnard, 'Athanase et les empereurs Constantin et Constance, 127–44. On the Meletians, see also L. W. Barnard, 'Athanasius

and the Meletian Schism in Egypt', *Journal of Egyptian Archaeology* 59, 1975, 183–89.

37. J. M. Leroux, 'Athanase et la seconde phase de la crise arienne (345–373)', *Politique et théologie*, 145–56.

38. W. H. C. Frend, 'Athanasius as an Egyptian Church Leader in the Fourth Century', in *Religion Popular and Unpopular in the Early Christian Centuries*, London 1976.

39. C. Kannengiesser, 'Le témoinage des Lettres Festales de S. Athanase sur la date de l'apologie *Contre les paiens, Sur l'incarnation du Verbe*', *RSR* 52, 1964, 91–100.

40. F. L. Cross, *The Study of St Athanasius*, Oxford 1945; E. P. Meijering, *Orthodoxy and Platonism in Athanasius*, Leiden 1968, also regards the work as the theological essay of a young man.

For detailed discussions of the crucial textual problem, namely the relationship between the Short and Long Recensions, see the survey and further research of C. Kannengiesser, 'Le texte court du *De Incarnatione Athanasien*', *RSR* 52, 1964, 589–96; 53, 1965, 77–111; also 'Les différentes recensions du traite *De Incarnatione Verbi* de S. Athanase', *StudPatr* 7, 1966, 221–29. The existence of the Short Recension was first noticed by J. Lebon, and was studied in detail by R. P. Casey: see G. J. Ryan and R. P. Casey, *The De Incarnatione of Athanasius* (Studies and Documents 14), London 1945/6, Part I, The Long Recension, by G. J. Ryan, Part II, The Short Recension, by R. P. Casey. The commonly accepted view that the Short Recension was Athanasius' own revision has been challenged by Kannengiesser, but he agrees (against H. G. Opitz in *Untersuchungen zur Überlieferung der Schriften des Athanasius*, Berlin 1935) that no doctrinal motivations can be detected in the redactional process; Casey described the shorter version as a secondary literary revision. It now seems generally accepted that the Long Recension is the original.

41. Recent reconsideration of the date was initiated by H. Nordberg in 1961. See 'A reconsideration of the date of Athanasius' *Contra Gentes* and *De Incarnatione*', *StudPatr* 3, 1961, 262–6, and *Athanasius' Tractates Contra Gentes and De Incarnatione. An attempt at Redating*, Helsinki 1961. Nordberg dated the work(s) as late as the reign of Julian the Apostate on the grounds that this provided an occasion for such an apologetic undertaking. But see the discussion by C. Kannengiesser in 'La date de l'Apologie d'Athanase "Contre les Paiens" et "Sur l'incarnation du Verbe"', *RSR* 58, 1970, 383–428. The date he suggests, namely the exile at Trier, is accepted by J. Roldanus in *Le Christ et l'homme dans la théologie d'Athanase d'Alexandrie*, Leiden 1968, following Kannengiesser's earlier article (n. 39 above). A number of scholars have expressed the fact that they are not convinced; see e.g. J. C. M. van Winden, 'On the Date of Athanasius' Apologetical Treatises', *VC* 29, 1975, 291–5. The relationship between the work of Athanasius and that of Eusebius seems to be almost decisive, however.

42. A. van Haarlem, *Incarnatie en verlossing bij Athanasius*, Wageningen 1961. F. L. Cross, op. cit., suggested that Athanasius was influenced as a theological student by Eusebius' visit to Alexandria in 311, but that is pure speculation.

43. M. J. Rondeau, 'Une nouvelle preuve de l'influence littéraire d'Eusèbe de Césarée sur Athanase: l'interpretation des psaumes', *RSR* 56, 1968, 385–434.

44. *Contra gentes* 46; the case is presented by Roldanus, op. cit., Appendix; see p. 375 n. 5 for further examples. See also E. Mühlenberg, 'Verité et Bonté de Dieu' in *Politique et Théologie*, 215–230.

45. Text and translation of the *Contra gentes* and *De Incarnatione*, ed. R. W. Thomson, Oxford Early Christian Texts, Oxford 1971.

46. It appears as a chapter-heading in the English translation by a religious of CSMV, *The Incarnation of the Word of God*, London 1953.

47. E.g. van Haarlem, op. cit.

48. *De incarnatione* 7.

49. Ibid. 4.

50. Ibid. 54. Note the difficulty of conveying Athanasius' thought in English. He did not mean that we become God in the sense that God is God; but he did mean something more than 'divine'. See discussion below pp. 73 f.

51. *Orationes contra Arianos*: text, PG 26; Kannengiesser is preparing a new edition for Sources Chrétiennes. Translation in NPNF II.IV.

52. J. Liébaert, *La doctrine christologique de S. Cyrille d'Alexandrie*, Lille 1951. See below pp. 250 f.

53. These remarks are based upon Kannengiesser's lecture delivered at the Eighth International Conference on Patristic Studies, Oxford 1979.

54. *C. Arianos* ii.67.

55. *C. Arianos* ii.47.

56. Detailed references for Athanasius' recurrent ideas are too numerous to record here. This applies to most of the material in the present paragraph.

57. *C. Arianos* iii.19–21.

58. *C. Arianos* i.9 ff. and frequently.

59. van Haarlem, op. cit. (n. 42 above); English summary ch. 5. L. Bouyer, *L'Incarnation et l'Église-Corps du Christ dans la théologie de S. Athanase*, Paris 1943, ch. 3. J. N. D. Kelly, *Early Christian Doctrines*, London 1958, New York 1959, 378.

60. *C. Arianos* iii.54–7.

61. *C. Arianos* iii.57. See the classic article by M. Richard, 'S. Athanase et la psychologie du Christ, selon les Ariens' *Mélanges de Science Religieuse* 4 (1947) 5–54; republished in *Opera Minora* II (Leuven 1977).

62. See below ch. 5.II.

63. For further discussion see my article, 'A Reconsideration of Alexandrian Christology', *JEH* 22, 1971, 103–14.

64. See further J. Roldanus, *Le Christ et l'homme dans la théologie d'Athanase d'Alexandrie* (n. 41 above); also A. Louth, 'Athanasius' understanding of the humanity of Christ' to be published in *Studia Patristica*. C. Kannengiesser also makes some interesting comments on Athanasius' interest in the νοῦς (mind) rather than the soul; the νοῦς of man should be fixed on God, the νοῦς is κατ᾽ εἰκόνα θεοῦ (according to God's image). The true image of God is the Logos; the incarnation made possible direct encounter with the image of God become Man, the 'Logos-in-body'. See his 'Athanasius of Alexandria and the Foundation of Traditional Christology', *Theological Studies* 34, 1973, 103–13; cf. 'Λόγος et νοῦς chez Athanase d'Alexandrie', *StudPatr* 11, 1972, 199–202.

302   *Notes to pages 75–82*

65. Roldanus also dates the work as early as 339 (op. cit.).
66. Texts in H. G. Opitz, *Die Apologien* (vol. II.1 of projected Berlin Academy edition of Athanasius' works, Berlin 1935–41). Translations will be found in NPNF.
67. Four *Letters to Serapion*: text, PG 26.525 ff; emended version by J. Lebon (SC 15), 1947. Translation by C. R. B. Shapland, *The Letters of St Athanasius concerning the Holy Spirit*, London 1951. See the comprehensive article by T. C. Campbell, 'The Doctrine of the Holy Spirit in the Theology of Athanasius' *SJT* 27, 1974, 408–40.
68. *Letters to Epictetus, Adelphius and Maximus*: text, PG 26.1049 ff. A more recent edition of the *Letter to Epictetus* was produced by G. Ludwig, Iena 1911. Translations in NPNF.
69. M. Richard, art. cit.; for the opposing view, see P. Galtier, 'S. Athanase et l'âme humaine du Christ', *Gregorianum* 36, 1955, 552–89.
70. *Tomus ad Antiochenos* 7; text in PG 26.796 ff; translation in NPNF.
71. J. N. D. Kelly, *Early Christian Doctrines*, 288 f. That Apollinarius himself interpreted the *Tome* in this way is clear; see below pp. 186 and 191 and P. Galtier, op. cit.
72. J. N. D. Kelly, *Early Christian Creeds*, London and Toronto 1950, 257 ff.
73. J. M. Leroux, art. cit. (n. 37 above).
74. C. B. Armstrong, 'The Synod of Alexandria and the schism of Antioch in AD 362', *JTS* 22, 1921, 206–21, 347–55.
75. Martin Tetz, 'Über Nikäische Orthodoxie. Der sog. Tomus ad Antiochenos des Athanasios von Alexandrien', *ZNW* 66, 1975, 194–222.
76. For details of the spurious works, consult the Patrologies and the *Clavis Patrum*.
77. J. Lebon, *Le Monophysisme Sévérien*, Louvain 1909, 227, 232. See below pp. 183 and 258 f.
78. W. Cureton, *The Festal Letters of Athanasius*, London 1848, Syriac text. Translation in NPNF. Cureton discovered a catalogue of all the letters, which has proved invaluable for reconstructing the chronology of Athanasius' life; in addition to the Syriac find, others have turned up in Coptic. For details consult the Patrologies and the *Clavis Patrum*.
79. Jerome, *De viris illustribus* 87.
80. For details and bibliography, consult the Patrologies and the *Clavis Patrum*.
81. Gregory Nazianzen, *Orat.* 21.5; Chrysostom, *Hom. in Matt.* 8.5; Augustine, *Confessions* 8.16; Jerome, loc. cit.
82. *Vita Antonii*: text in PG 26. 837 ff.; translation in NPNF.
83. The date has been recently discussed by L. W. Barnard, 'The date of Athanasius' *Vita Antonii*', *VC* 28, 1974, 169–75; a reply by B. R. Brennan, 'Dating Athanasius' *Vita Antonii*', appeared in *VC* 30, 1976, 52–4. The following remarks are derived from this exchange. For the question of historicity, see Hermann Dörries, 'Die Vita Antonii als Geschichtsquelle', in his *Wort und Stunde* I, Göttingen 1966, 145–224.
84. *Vita Antonii* 67–9, 82, 91.
85. Ibid. 14, 20 f., 67, 74.
86. Ibid. 72.
87. Ibid. 7; cf. 22–28, 38, 78, 84.

88. Ibid. 14, 74.

89. W. H. C. Frend, *The Early Church*, London 1965, Philadelphia 1966, 157.

90. Gregory Nazianzen, *Orat.* 21.

91. *De incarnatione* 54.

92. Palladius, *Lausiac History* 4.

93. Rufinus, *Apologia in Hieronymum* (Defence against Jerome) ii.12.

94. Jerome, *Adversus Rufinum* iii.28.

95. Ibid., ii.11; G. Bardy, *Didyme l'Aveugle*, Paris 1910, 33.

96. Jerome, *In epist. ad Gal.; In Matt.; In Osee proph.; In Isaiam; In Danielem*, etc.

97. Jerome, *In epist. ad Ephes.*, prolog.; *Ep.* 84.

98. Jerome, *In Zech.*, prolog.; *De viris illistribus* 109.

99. Rufinus, *Apol. in Hier.* ii.8, 12, 23, 25, etc.

100. Rufinus, *HE* ii.7; Socrates, *HE* iv.25 f.; Theodoret, *HE* iv.26.

101. Sozomen, *HE* iii.15.

102. Rufinus, *HE* ii.7.

103. For detailed discussion, see Bardy, op. cit., 218 ff.

104. Rufinus, *HE* ii.7; Socrates, *HE* iv.25; cf. Sozomen, *HE* iii.15.

105. Socrates, *HE* iv.26.

106. Rufinus, *HE* ii.7.

107. Philip Sidetes lists Didymus among the heads of the Catechetical School. W. J. Gauche, *Didymus the Blind, an Educator of the Fourth Century*, Washington 1934, claims to reconstruct the syllabus of the University and treats Didymus as Origen's successor in a formal sense.

108. G. Bardy, 'Aux origenes de l'école d'Alexandrie', *RSR* 27, 1937, 65–90; 'Pour l'histoire de l'école d'Alexandrie', *Vivre et Penser* (the wartime *Revue Biblique*) 2, 1942, 80–109. This view is followed by F. L. Cross, *The Early Christian Fathers*, London 1960, 118.

109. Rufinus, *Apol. in Hier.* ii.12.

110. Jerome acknowledges his debt to many commentaries; even before he made his translation of Didymus' *De Spiritu Sancto*, Ambrose drew heavily from it for his own treatise on the subject, and his *De mysteriis* was probably influenced by Didymus' *De Trinitate*. Augustine came under his influence. See Bardy, op. cit., 241–9.

111. L. Doutreleau questioned the attribution, 'Le De Trinitate est-il l'oeuvre de Didyme l'Aveugle?', *RSR* 45, 1957, 514–57; L. Béranger has shown that none of Mingarelli's arguments are conclusive, and that the attribution has to be demonstrated, if it can be, on other grounds, 'Sur deux énigmes du De Trinitate de Didyme l'Aveugle', *RSR* 51, 1963, 255–67.

112. There is general agreement that *Contra Eunomium* IV and V do not belong to Basil's treatise, and were not written by Basil; but discussion about whether they should be restored to Didymus continues. Two papers were delivered at the Oxford Patristic Conference 1979, one arguing that they were the work of Didymus (W. M. Hayes, 'Didymus the Blind *is* the author of *Adversus Eunomium* IV–V'), the other reviving the suggestion that the author might have been Apollinarius (R. Hübner, 'Der Autor von Ps.-Basilius, *Adversus Eunomium* IV and V – Apollinarius von Laodicea?'). Details of the earlier discussion will be found in the Patrologies; Funk suggested it, was followed by Bardy, but objections were raised by Leipoldt.

Lebon's treatment seemed conclusive: 'Le Pseudo-Basile (*Adv. Eunom.* IV–V) est bien Didyme d'Alexandrie', *Le Muséon* 50, 1937, 61–83. More recently the subject was taken up by B. Pruche, 'Didyme l'Aveugle est-il bien l'auteur des livres *Contre Eunome* IV et V attribués à Saint Basile de Césarée?', *StudPatr* 10, 1970, 151–5.

113. K. Holl, *Gesammelte Aufsätze* II, Tübingen 1928, 298–309, reprints the article in which he argued that Didymus was the author, but he did not convince Bardy (op. cit.).

114. For details, see Bibliography B. L. Doutreleau surveyed the find in two articles, L. Doutreleau and J. Aucagne, 'Que savons-nous aujourd'hui des papyrus de Toura?', *RSR* 43, 1955, 161–93; and L. Doutreleau and L. Koenen, 'Nouvel inventaire des Papyrus de Toura', *RSR* 55, 1967, 547–64. He also produced the edition of the *Commentary on Zechariah* for Sources Chrétiennes (3 vols., SC 82–5, 1962).

115. L. Doutreleau, 'Ce que l'on trouvera dans l'*In Zachariam* de Didyme l'Aveugle', *StudPatr* 3, 1961, 183–95.

116. *De Trinitate* i.18, PG 39.341.

117. For fuller discussion, see Doutreleau's Introduction to the *Commentary on Zechariah*, SC I, 55–64. A similar account of Didymus' exegetical methods will be found in A. Gesché, *La christologie du 'Commentaire sur les Psaumes' découvert à Toura*, Gembloux 1962.

118. *In Zech.*1.17–19, SC I, 198 ff.

119. Ibid. i.21 f., SC I, 200 ff.

120. Ibid. i.9, 15, 56–8, etc.

121. See W. A. Beinart, *'Allegoria' und 'Anagōgē' bei Didymos dem Blinden von Alexandria*, Papyrologische Texte und Abhandlungen 13, Berlin 1972.

122. J. H. Tigcheler, *Didyme l'Aveugle et l'exégèse allégorique, son commentaire sur Zacharie* (Nijmegen 1977). I am indebted to this work for the observations in this paragraph.

123. Jerome, *Adv. Ruf.* i.6; ii.16.

124. There is a useful summary of the situation in Quasten's *Patrology* III.99.

125. Didymus, *De Trin.* iii.1 (PG 39.773–6).

126. See above pp. 85 f. and note 112.

127. For a detailed discussion of Didymus' Trinitarianism, see Bardy, op. cit. (n. 95 above), ch. 3. This is, of course, largely based on the *De Trinitate*.

128. Bardy, op. cit., ch.3; Doutreleau, *Zech.*, Introd., I, p. 88. See also A. Gesché, op. cit. (n. 117 above).

129. *De Trin.* iii.21 (PG 39.904).

130. *De Trin.* iii.21 (PG 39.900); cf. iii.30.

131. *De Trin.* iii.2 (PG 39.797).

132. *De Trin.* iii.21 (PG 39.900–16).

133. Note esp. A. Gesché, 'L'âme humaine de Jesus dans la Christologie du IVᵉ Siècle. Le témoinage du commentaire sur les Psaumes découvert à Toura', *Revue d'Histoire Ecclésiastique* 54, 1959, 385; also M. F. Wiles, 'The Nature of the Early Debate about Christ's Human Soul', *JEH* 16, 1965, 139–51.

134. See my article, 'A Reconsideration of Alexandrian Christology', *JEH* 22, 1971, 103–14.

135. Socrates, *HE* iv.25.
136. See Bardy, op. cit., 222 ff.
137. Mingarelli's introduction and notes to the *De Trinitate* are reproduced in PG 39 with the text. W. J. Gauche, op. cit., 96 ff., discusses Didymus' teaching methods on the basis of this theory, and mentions the work of de Regnon who referred to *De Trin.* iii.4 'as an orderly and well-planned lecture of a capable teacher' (T. de Regnon, *Etudes de theologie positive sur la Sainte Trinité*, 4 vols., Paris 1892–8, III, 118–20). Gesché, op. cit. (n. 117 above), 38, speaks of the commentary as 'un cours professoral'.
138. *De Spiritu Sancto* 63 (PG 39.1086).
139. Note esp. his own justification of his style in *De Trin.* iii.1 (PG 39.781–4).
140. See *De Trin.* iii.2 – a summary of all the arguments used in the earlier books, giving a total of fifty-five brief points.
141. Doutreleau, *Zech.* Introd., 136.

3. The Cappadocians

1. The most important sources are the writings of the Cappadocians themselves, particularly Gregory Nazianzen, *Orat.* 43 on Basil and *Carmen de vita sua*; Gregory Nyssen, *Vita Macrinae*, and the collections of their correspondence. For details of texts see notes below.
2. Gregory Nazianzen, *Ep.* 1.
3. Gregory Nyss., *Vita Macrinae*.
4. Basil, *Ep.* 14; Gregory, *Epp.* 4, 5, 6. See Rosemary Ruether, *Gregory Nazianzen, Rhetor and Philosopher*, Oxford 1969.
5. In *Ep.* 2, Basil outlines the essentials of his monastic ideals to Gregory. On Basil's ascetic works see further below p. 106. The conventional view is that the *Philocalia* was compiled at this stage, but this view is purely conjectural. For an alternative see E. Junod, 'Remarques sur la composition de la *Philocalia* d'Origène par Basile de Césarée et Grégoire de Nazianze', *Revue d'histoire et de philosophie religieuse* 52, 1972, 149–56.
6. Gregory Naz., *Orat.* 1 and 2.
7. See Sozomen, *HE* vi.15, and Gregory Naz., *Orat.* 43. Basil's subsequent confrontation with Valens is a curious episode which poses some problems for the historian.
8. Gregory Nyss., *Ep.* 13 (if genuine) addressed to Libanius; but he also calls Basil his teacher in his *Hexaemeron* and the *De Opificio Hominis*.
9. Gregory Naz., *Ep.* 11.
10. Gregory Nyss., *De Virginitate* 3; Gregory Naz., *Ep.* 95.
11. Suggested by Basil, *Ep.* 14 to Gregory Naz.
12. The account of Gregory's dream is found in his homily *In 40 martyris*. See H. F. Cherniss, *The Platonism of Gregory of Nyssa*, New York 1930.
13. Gregory Naz., *Epp.* 40–46.
14. Gregory Naz., *Epp.* 47–49; *Carmen de vita sua*.
15. Basil, *Epp.* 58–60, 100. See J. Daniélou, 'Grégoire de Nysse à travers les lettres de saint Basile et de saint Grégoire de Nazianze', *VC* 19, 1965, 31–41.

16. The panegyric by Gregory Naz., *Orat.* 43, provides a glowing summary.

17. *Orat.* 7, 8 and 18.

18. *Orat.* 33; *Carmen de vita sua* 592 ff.

19. *Orat.* 27–31; see further below, pp. 113 f.

20. D. Balas, 'The Unity of Human Nature in Basil's and Gregory of Nyssa's Polemics against Eunomius', *StudPatr* 14, 1976, 275–81, discusses an interesting example of this. For the chronology of Gregory's works, see J. Daniélou, 'La chronologie des oeuvres de Grégoire de Nysse', *StudPatr* 7, 1966, 159–69.

21. W. Jaeger (ed. H. Dörries), *Gregor von Nyssa's Lehre vom Heiligen Geist*, Leiden 1966. See further, J. Daniélou, art. cit., and G. May, 'Gregor von Nyssa in der Kirchenpolitik seiner Zeit', *Jahrbuch der österreichischen Byzantinistischen Gesellschaft* 15, 1966, 105–32.

22. Texts of the letters: Basil: *Lettres*, ed. Y. Courtonne, 3 vols., Budé, Paris 1957, 1961, 1966: *The Letters*, ed. with ET R. Deferrari, 4 vols., LCL 1926ff., repr. 1950; ET also in NPNF. Gregory Nazianzen: three editions, all by P. Gallay, *Lettres*, 2 vols., Budé, Paris 1964, 1967; *Briefe*, GCS 1969; *Lettres théologiques*, SC 208, 1974; also ET of selection in NPNF. Gregory Nyssen: *Epistulae*, ed. G. Pasquali, *Opera* VIII.2, Jaeger ed., Berlin 1925/Leiden 1959; also ET of selection in NPNF.

23. J. Quasten, *Patrology* III.247.

24. Gregory Naz., *Epp.* 51–4.

25. The *Carmen de vita sua* (Book II.i, no. 11, PG 37.1029–1166) is of particular importance in this regard. The text of the *Poems* is in PG 37–38, though some are spurious or doubtful. Book I.ii, no. 8, has been edited separately by H. M. Werhahn, *Gregorii Nazianzeni Σύγκρισις βίων*, Wiesbaden 1953.

26. Rosemary Ruether, op. cit. (n. 4 above).

27. Gregory Naz., *Orat.* 2.

28. D. Amand, *L'Ascèse monastique de S. Basile*, Paris 1949.

29. *Orat.* 43.

30. *Carmen de vita sua* 530 ff; *Epp.* 17,50.

31. Gregory Naz., *Orat.* 2; Gregory Nyss., *In Ps.7*, *De Vita Moysis*. See T. Spidlik, *Grégoire de Nazianze: Introduction à l'étude de sa doctrine spirituelle*, Rome 1971, though he is probably over-optimistic in integrating the conflicting elements in Gregory's thought and temperament.

32. But see J. Gribomont, 'L'Origénisme de S.Basile', in *L'Homme devant Dieu. Mélanges H.Lubac* I Paris 1963, 281–94; he explores Basil's ambivalence towards his Origenist heritage.

33. All three made strong statements of this kind, particularly in anti-heretical works. For discussion of Gregory Nazianzen, see E. Fleury, *Hellénisme et Christianisme. S.Grégoire de Nazianze et son temps*, Paris 1930; and for Gregory Nyssen, H. F. Cherniss, op. cit. (n. 12 above). A. Meredith ascribes some of Gregory's statements to traditional anti-heretical motifs: see 'Traditional Apologetic in the *Contra Eunomium* of Gregory of Nyssa' *StudPatr* 14, 1976, 315–19.

34. Basil, *Ep.* 223; also the correspondence with Libanius (if genuine, which is disputed).

35. Basil, *An Address to Young Men on How They Might Derive Benefit*

from Greek Literature: text: *Aux Jeunes Gens*, ed. F. Boulanger (Budé), Paris 1935; text with ET in *The Letters*, LCL IV. More recent edition, *St Basil on the Value of Greek Literature*, ed. N. G. Wilson, London 1975. For an interesting discussion of the occasion of this address, see A. Moffatt, 'The Occasion of Basil's Address to Young Men', *Antichthon* 6, 1972, 74–86.

36. Basil, *Homilies on the Hexaemeron*: text, ed. S. Giet, SC 26, 1949; ET in NPNF. Y. Courtonne, *S. Basile et l'Hellenisme*, Paris 1934, is a detailed study of the *Hexaemeron* and its sources.

37. See further E. Amand de Mendieta, 'The Official Attitude of Basil of Caesarea as a Christian Bishop towards Greek Philosophy and Science', in *The Orthodox Churches and the West*, Studies in Church History 13, ed. D. Baker, Oxford 1976, 25–49.

38. M. Orphanos, *Creation and Salvation according to Basil of Caesarea*, Athens 1975, 42.

39. J. Gribomont, 'Les lemmes de citation de S.Basile indice de niveau littéraire', *Augustinianum* 14, 1975, 513–26.

40. Robert C. Gregg, *Consolation Philosophy: Greek and Christian 'Paideia' in Basil and the Two Gregories*, Patristic Monograph Series 3, Philadelphia 1975.

41. Gregory Naz., *Orat.* 4–5.

42. E. Fleury, op. cit., 99.

43. *Orat.* 7, 21, 43.

44. *Orat.* 25; on this see J. Coman, 'Hellénisme et Christianisme dans le 25e discourse de saint Grégoire de Nazianze', *StudPatr* 14, 1976, 290–301.

45. E.g. allusions to passages in Homer, Hesiod, Theognis, Solon, Simonides, Pindar, the tragedians, Aristophanes, Callimachus, Herodotus, Thucydides, Plutarch, Demosthenes, Lysias, Isocrates, Plato, Aristotle, Plotinus, and many others have been traced. See D. Amand, *Fatalisme et liberté dans l'antiquité grèque*, Louvain 1945; E. Fleury, op. cit., Y. Courtonne, op. cit.; H. F. Cherniss, op. cit., etc.

46. The text of Gregory's *Orations* will be found in PG 35–36. More recent editions are only those of F. Boulenger, *Grégoire de Nazianze Discours Funèbres en l'honneur de son frère Césaire et de Basile de Césarée* [*Orations* 7 and 43], Paris 1908 and A. J. Mason, *Five Theological Orations* (see n. 76 below. ET of select orations in NPNF.

47. For another estimate, see D. A. Sykes, 'The *Poemata Arcana* of St Gregory Nazianzen', *JTS* 21, 1970, 32–42; he is concerned simply with the dogmatic poems, and treats them as belonging to a flourishing genre of didactic verse.

48. The works of Gregory of Nyssa will be found in PG 44–46. A selection is translated in NPNF. Of the 'Jaeger' edition (see n. 64 below) all except vols. III.2, IV, VII.2 and X have been published. See Bibliography B.

49. F. Mann, 'Gregor, Rhetor et Pastor. Interpretation des Proömiums der Schrift Gregors von Nyssa, *De Infantibus praemature abreptis*', *VC* 31, 1977, 126–47. Cf. J. Daniélou, 'Le traité "Sur les enfants morts prematurement" de Grégoire de Nysse', *VC* 20, 1966, 159–82. The new edition of works mentioned in this paragraph is not yet available. Text in PG 46.

50. A. Meredith, 'Traditional Apologetic in the *Contra Eunomium* of Gregory of Nyssa', *StudPatr* 14, 1976, 315–19.

51. J. Daniélou, 'Grégoire de Nysse et le néoplatonisme de l'École

d'Athènes', *Revue des Etudes Grecques* 80, 1967, 395–401. For the more general points, see J. Daniélou, 'Orientations actuelles de la recherche sur Grégoire de Nysse', in *Écriture et culture philosophique dans la pensée de Grégoire de Nysse* (Actes du colloque de Chevetogne), ed. M. Harl, Leiden 1971: a useful review article which indicates the more specialized studies on which these statements are based.

52. H. F. Cherniss, op. cit.

53. Cf. Basil, *Ep.* 22. The discussion of Basil's ascetic teaching in this section is much indebted to D. Amand, *L'Ascèse monastique de S.Basile*, Paris 1949. Texts in PG 31; ET: W. K. L. Clarke, *The Ascetic Works of St Basil*, London and New York 1925.

54. J. Gribomont, *Histoire du texte des ascétiques de S. Basile*, Louvain 1953; S. Y. Rudberg, *Études sur la tradition manuscrite de S.Basile*, Uppsala 1953.

55. L. Lèbe, 'S.Basile et ses Règles morales', *Revue Benédictine* 75, 1965, 193–200.

56. J. Gribomont, 'Les Règles Morales de S.Basile et le Nouveau Testament', *StudPatr* 2, 1957, 416–26.

57. A useful summary in English will be found in F. X. Murphy, 'Moral and Ascetical Doctrine in St Basil', *StudPatr* 14, 1976, 320–26.

58. See above pp. 85 f. and n. 112. Text of the *Contra Eunomium*, PG 29. See W. M. Hayes, *The Greek Mss Tradition of (Ps.–) Basil's Adversus Eunomium*, Leiden 1972.

59. Text: B. Pruche, *Basile de Césarée. Traité du Saint-Esprit*, SC 77, 2nd ed. 1968. ET in NPNF.

60. Gregory Naz., *Theological Oration* 5 (*Orat.* 31). 24 ff.

61. R. P. C. Hanson, 'Basil's doctrine of tradition in relation to the Holy Spirit', *VC* 22, 1968, 241–55.

62. E. Amand de Mendieta, 'The Pair κήρυγμα and δόγμα in the Theological Thought of St Basil of Caesarea', *JTS* NS 16, 1965, 129–45; and *The Unwritten and Secret Apostolic Traditions in the Theological Thought of St Basil of Caesarea*, *SJT* Occasional Papers no. 13, Edinburgh 1965. Also B. Pruche, 'Δόγμα et κήρυγμα dans le traité *Sur le Saint-Esprit* de Saint Basile de Césarée en Cappadoce', *StudPatr* 9, 1966, 257–62.

63. J. Coman, 'La démonstration dans le traité *Sur le Saint Esprit* de Saint Basile le Grand. Préliminaires', *StudPatr* 9, 1966, 172–209.

64. For details see Bibliography B. In the following notes the new edition is consistently referred to as 'Jaeger', even though not all volumes were his work. ET in NPNF, but based on earlier editions and therefore differently ordered and entitled.

65. Gregory Nyss., *Refutatio Confessionis Eunomii* 33 (Jaeger, vol. II, 325; formerly known as *Contra Eunomium* II).

66. A. Meredith argues that the debate reflects current arguments within the philosophical schools, and that Eunomius, so far from being an Aristotelian, was closer to the mainstream Platonic tradition than his eclectic orthodox opponents: 'Orthodoxy, Heresy and Philosophy in the Later Half of the Fourth Century', *Heythrop Journal* 16, 1975, 5–21.

67. Gregory Nyss., *Contra Eunomium III.* 164 (Jaeger, vol. II, 106; formerly known as *Contra Eunomium IV*).

68. *Refutatio* 6–7 (Jaeger, vol. II, 315). See the following sections of the *Refutatio* for the unacknowledged arguments summarized in this paragraph.

69. *Contra Eunomium I.* 202 (Jaeger, vol. I, 85) and *Quod non sint tres dii* 117 (Jaeger vol. III, 38).

70. *Refutatio* 59 ff. (Jaeger, vol. II, 336).

71. *Catechetical Oration* 3, ed. J. H. Srawley, Cambridge 1903; ET, J. H. Srawley, London 1917.

72. See below Chapter 5, p. 183.

73. The discussion figures most prominently in *Contra Eunomium II* (Jaeger, vol. I, 226–409; formerly known as *Contra Eunomium XIIB* or *Antirrheticus against Eunomius' Second Book*). For discussion in detail, see pp. 66–71 of my paper, 'The God of the Greeks and the Nature of Religious Language', in *Early Christian Literature and the Classical Intellectual Tradition* in honorem Robert M. Grant, ed. W. R. Schoedel and R. L. Wilken, Paris 1979.

74. *Contra Eunomium III.*127–41 (Jaeger, vol. II,46 ff.).

75. *Contra Eunomium III.* 110 (Jaeger, vol. II, 41).

76. Text: *The Five Theological Orations of Gregory of Nazianzus*, ed. A. J. Mason, Cambridge Patristic Texts 1, Cambridge 1899.

77. Greg. Naz., *Ep.* 58 and *Orat.* 43.

78. For further discussion of many of the points in this section, see J. Plagnieux, *S. Grégoire de Nazianze, théologien*, Paris 1951.

79. *Theological Orations* 2 and 3 (*Orat.* 28 and 29); *Orat.* 45.

80. *Orat.* 16.

81. *Orat.* 1.

82. *Orat.* 45.22.

83. J. Daniélou, *Platonisme et théologie mystique*, Paris 1954. Cf. H. von Balthasar, *Présence et pensée*, Paris 1942. See Bibliography B for numerous subsequent studies bearing on this matter; also *Écriture et culture philosophique*, ed. M. Harl (see n. 51 above).

84. See the discussion in H. Dörrie, M. Altenburger, A. Schramm, *Gregor von Nyssa und die Philosophie.* Zweites internationales Kolloquium über Gregor von Nyssa, Freckenhorst bei Münster 1972 (Leiden 1976); especially G. C. Stead, 'Ontology and terminology in Gregory of Nyssa', 107–27, but also J. Daniélou, 'Grégoire de Nysse et la philosophie', 3–18.

85. R. E. Heine, *Perfection in the Virtuous Life*, Patristic Monograph Series 2, Philadelphia 1975; and E. Mühlenberg, *Die Unendlichkeit Gottes bei Gregor von Nyssa*, Göttingen 1966. But cf. C. W. Macleod, 'Allegory and Mysticism in Origen and Gregory of Nyssa' *JTS* NS 22, 1971, 362–79; and 'ΑΝΑΛΥΣΙΣ: A Study in Ancient Mysticism', Ibid. 21, 1970, 43–55.

86. T. P. Verghese, 'Διάστημα and Διάστασις in Gregory of Nyssa. Introduction to a concept and the posing of a problem', in Dörrie, Altenburger, Schramm, 243–60.

87. J. M. Rist, *Plotinus. The Road to Reality*, Cambridge and New York 1967, 185.

88. H. F. Cherniss, op. cit. (n. 12 above).

89. J. Daniélou, 'Le symbole de la caverne chez Grégoire de Nysse', in *Mullus.* Festschrift für T. Klauser, Münster 1964, 43–51.

90. E. Ferguson, 'Progress in perfection: Gregory of Nyssa's *Vita Moysis*',

StudPatr 14, 1976, 307–14; 'God's Infinity and Man's Immutability – Perpetual Progress according to Gregory of Nyssa', *Greek Orthodox Theological Review* 18, 1973, 59–78. Cf. J. Daniélou, *Platonisme*, and his Introduction to *From Glory to Glory: Texts from Gregory of Nyssa's Mystical Writings*, ed. and trs. H. Musurillo, New York 1961, London 1962.

91. E. Mühlenberg, op. cit. But see the criticisms of R. S. Brightman, 'Apophatic Theology and Divine Infinity in St Gregory of Nyssa', *Greek Orthodox Theological Review* 18, 1973, 404–23.

92. J. M. Rist, op. cit.

93. E.g. by Daniélou, *Platonisme*; G. Bebis, 'Gregory of Nyssa's *De Vita Moysis*: a philosophical and theological analysis', *Greek Orthodox Theological Review* 12, 1967, 369–93, etc.

94. For discussion of the interpretation of Plotinus, see A. H. Armstrong, ed., *Cambridge History of Later Greek and Early Medieval Philosophy*, Cambridge 1967; J. M. Rist, op. cit.

95. See further Mariette Canévet, 'La perception de la présence de Dieu. A propos d'une expression de la XIe homélie sur le Cantique des cantiques', *Epektasis*. Mélanges patristiques offerts au Cardinal J. Daniélou, ed. J. Fontaine and C. Kannengiesser, Paris 1972, 443–54, *pace* M. von Stritzky, *Zum Problem der Erkenntnis bei Gregor von Nyssa*, Münster 1973 who argues (subsequent to the work of Mühlenberg) that the mystical interpretation is dangerous because there is always a distinction between God and man and no mystical union as such.

96. Though see H. A. Wolfson, 'The identification of Ex Nihilo with Emanation in Gregory of Nyssa', *Harvard Theological Review* 63, 1970, 53–60.

97. Gregory Nazianzen, *Orat.* 43.

98. B. Bobrinskoy, 'Liturgie et ecclésiologie trinitaire de S. Basile', *Verbum Caro* 89, 1969, 1–32, compares the liturgy with Basil's *De Spiritu Sancto* and *Letters*, showing that the amplifications made to an older version are in line with Basil's theology. For the more archaic form, see J. Doresse and E. Lanne, *Un témoin archaïque de la liturgie copte de S. Basile*, Louvain 1960; also discussion by E. Capelle, 'Les liturgies "basiliennes" et S. Basile', in the same volume.

99. *Orat.* 2.

100. *Orat.* 16.

101. Basil, *Homiliae diversae*: text in PG 31. See also the *Homélies sur la richesse*, ed. Y. Courtonne, Paris 1935, and an edition of one homily by S. Y. Rudberg listed in Bibliography B.

102 Gregory Nyssen, *Explicatio apologetica in Hexaemeron* and *De opificio*: text in PG 44; the new edition of these works is not yet available.

103. W. Jaeger, *Two Rediscovered Works of Ancient Christian Literature: Gregory of Nyssa and Macarius*, Leiden 1954. Jaeger's view that 'Macarius' was dependent on Gregory initiated a major scholarly debate, involving not only the critical question but also the relationship between Gregory's ascetic teaching and that of the Messalians. For details see Bibliography B.

104. Gregory Nyssen, *Oratio catachetica*: new edition not yet available. For edition and translation by J. H. Srawley, see n. 7 above.

4. The Temper of the Times: Some Contrasting Characters of the Late Fourth Century

1. *St Cyril of Jerusalem's Lectures on the Christian Sacraments*, ed. F. L. Cross (Texts for Students), London 1951, contains the *Procatechesis* and the *Mystagogical Catecheses* (i.e. nos. 19–23), text and translation with a useful introduction. See also *Cyril of Jerusalem and Nemesius of Emesa*, introduction and translation of selections by W. Telfer (Library of Christian Classics IV), London and Philadelphia 1955. Full text in PG 33, though the critical edition by W. K. Reischl and J. Rupp, Munich 1848–60, reissued Hildesheim 1967, is to be preferred. Complete ET in NPNF. New critical text of the *Mystagogical Catecheses*, ed. A. Piédagnel, trs. P. Paris, SC 126, 1966.

2. E.g., even the names of those who replaced Cyril during his exiles are incompatible.

3. Jerome, *Chronicle* for 348, in GCS Eusebius VII, *Die Chronik des Hieronymus* (no. 47 of whole series), 1956, 237. 2–14.

4. Rufinus, *HE* i.23.

5. Theodoret, *HE* v.9, quotes the Council's letter.

6. Socrates, *HE* vii.7, followed by Sozomen, *HE* v.3.

7. A. A. Stephenson, 'St Cyril of Jerusalem's Trinitarian Theology', *StudPatr* 11, 1972, 234–41; and I. Berten, 'Cyrille de Jérusalem, Eusèbe d'Emèse et la théologie semi-arienne', *Revue des Sciences Philosophiques et Théologiques*, 52, 1968, 38–75.

8. J. Lebon, 'La position de S. Cyrille de Jérusalem dans les luttes provoquées par l'Arianisme', in *Revue d'Histoire Écclesiastique* 20, 1924, 181–210, 357–86.

9. Sozomen, *HE* iv.25.

10. According to Epiphanius (*Haer.* 73.37), Cyril had taken the step of consecrating a new bishop of Caesarea during Acacius' discomfiture. This no doubt exacerbated Acacius' hostility. Constantius soon came to favour Acacius and his party, and then, according to Theodoret (*HE* ii.23), Acacius informed the emperor that one of the things sold by Cyril was a 'holy robe' dedicated by Constantine himself. It is never easy to sort out truth and slander in the controversies of this period.

11. Cyril, *Cat. Orat.* vi.12 ff.; elsewhere others are sometimes mentioned, e.g. the Marcionites and Sabellius in xvi.4.

12. Ibid. xv. 27.

13. Ibid. xi.13.

14. Ibid. xvi.

15. Ibid. iv.9 (after Telfer's translation).

16. Ibid. iv.22–29.

17. Ibid., viii.6–8.

18. Ibid. ix.

19. The close parallels between this reconstructed Jerusalem creed and the creed of Constantinople (381) gave rise to the theory that Cyril had produced his creed at the Council and it was generally accepted by the

assembled bishops. This theory is now generally rejected; see J. N. D. Kelly, *Early Christian Creeds*, London and Toronto 1950, 311 ff.

20. Telfer, op. cit., 35 ff.

21. The full case is assembled in the important article by W. J. Swaans, 'A propos des "Catéchèses Mystagogiques" attribués à S.Cyrille de Jérusalem', *Le Muséon* 55, 1942, 1–43.

22. A. Piédagnel, *'Les Catéchèses Mystagogiques* de S.Cyrille de Jerusalem. Inventaire de la tradition manuscrite grecque', *StudPatr* 10, 1970, 141–5; see also his discussion of the authorship question in the introduction to the SC edition of the *Mystagogical Catecheses*.

23. Cross, op. cit., xxxix.

24. For one thing, Cyril gets worried in the last few lectures about running out of time. Did this happen year after year? In *Orat.* 14 he refers to 'yesterday's sermon'. Some details of this kind can be used to pin-point the date of the lectures: see Telfer, op. cit., 37 ff.

25. C. Beukers, '"For our Emperors, Soldiers and Allies". An attempt at dating the 23rd Catechesis by Cyrillus of Jerusalem' *VC* 15, 1961, 177–84.

26. E. Yarnold, 'The Authorship of the *Mystagogic Catecheses* attributed to Cyril of Jerusalem', *Heythrop Journal* 19, 1978, 143–61. In earlier articles (see Bibliography B), Yarnold demonstrated the probability of Ambrose's dependence on the *Mystagogical Catecheses*, which increases the likelihood of Cyril's authorship.

27. *Peregrinatio Etheriae*: text, Corpus Christianorum. Series Latina 175, Turnhout 1967, 37–90; ET, *Egeria: Diary of a Pilgrimage*, by G. E. Gingrans, ACW 38, New York 1970. On the problems of relating this text to the evidence of the *Catechetical Lectures* see Yarnold, art. cit., and A. A. Stephenson, 'The Lenten Catechetical Syllabus in Fourth-century Jerusalem', *Theological Studies* 15, 1954, 103–14.

28. Yarnold, art. cit.

29. Cyril's importance as an innovator is particularly stressed by G.Dix, *The Shape of the Liturgy*, London 1945, 329, 348–51.

30. For discussion, and especially comparison with the Liturgy of St James, see Dix, op. cit., 187 ff. Liturgical questions are also discussed by Swaans, art. cit., and G. Kretschmar, 'Die fruhe Geschichte der Jerusalemer Liturgie', *Jahrbuch für Liturgik und Hymnologie*, 1956, 22–46.

31. Dix, op. cit., 350.

32. Dix greatly underplays the evidence for 'partaking' in Cyril's lectures. It is true that in *Myst. Cat.* 5 sacrifice predominates, but that is not so in *Myst. Cat.* 4. See further P. Th. Camelot, 'Note sur la théologie baptismale des Catéchèses attribuées à S.Cyrille de Jérusalem', *Kyriakon.* Festschrift J. Quasten, ed. P. Granfield and J. A. Jungmann, Münster 1970, II.724–9.

33. Critical text: E. Bihain, 'L'épître de Cyrille de Jérusalem à Constantine sur la vision de la croix (BHG3 413)', *Byzantion* 43, 1973, 264–96. ET in Telfer, op. cit.

34. The story also appears in Sozomen, *HE* iv.5. Sozomen associates it with Cyril's consecration, but the letter gives no support to this dating.

35 Socrates, *HE* iii.20; Rufinus, *HE* i.57.

36. *Cat. Orat.* xv.15, where prophecies from Daniel and Matthew are used to indicate what to expect before the coming of Antichrist.

37. Text in *PG* 33, and the edition by Reischl and Rupp (see n. 1 above).

38. A. A. Stephenson, 'St Cyril of Jerusalem and the Alexandrian heritage', *Theological Studies* 15, 1954, 573–93; 'St Cyril of Jerusalem and the Alexandrian Christian Gnosis', *StudPatr* 1, 1957, 142–56.

39. Epiphanius, *Ancoratus* 9.

40. Ibid. 18.

41. Ibid. 63.

42. Ibid. 19.

43. Ibid. 9.

44. Text of *Ancoratus* and *Panarion*, ed. K. Holl, 3 vols., GCS, 1915, 1922, 1933. For rev. ed., see Bibliography B.

45. K. Holl. op. cit., Introduction, p. vii. Older scholars treated Epiphanius' language as degenerate; and the MS. tradition has a tendency to Atticize the text; see K. Holl, *Die handschriftliche Überlieferung des Epiphanius*, TU 36.2, 1910.

46. See J. N. D. Kelly, *Early Christian Creeds*, London and Toronto 1950, especially 318 ff. Also V. Palachkovsky, 'Une interpolation dans l'Ancoratus de S. Epiphane', *StudPatr* 7, 1966, 265–73. It looks as though the Nicene Creed originally stood in the text, and the Creed of Constantinople replaced it through the work of a later scribe or editor.

47. *Ancoratus* 19. The Greek of this and the following extract is quoted, so that those with the language can appreciate the credal flavour more strikingly: αὐτὸς ὁ ἅγιος Λόγος. . . . [here follow approximately 25 titles, epithets and prophetic descriptions of Christ drawn from scripture and tradition]. . . . ὁ ἄνθρωπος ἐν ἀληθείᾳ γεγονὼς καὶ θεὸς ἐν ἀληθείᾳ ὑπάρχων, μὴ τραπεὶς τὴν φύσιν, μὴ ἀλλοιώσας τὴν θεότητα, ὁ γεννηθεὶς ἐν σαρκὶ, ὁ σαρκωθεὶς λόγος, ὁ λόγος σὰρξ γενόμενος. . . .

48. *Ancoratus* 81:
ὁ μονογενὴς, ὁ τέλειος, ὁ ἄκτιστος, ὁ ἄτρεπτος, ὁ ἀναλλοίωτος, ὁ ἀπερινόητος, ὁ ἀόρατος, ἐνανθρωπήσας ἐν ἡμῖν. . . . ὁ δι᾽ ἡμᾶς πτωχεύσας πλούσιος ὤν. . . . κύριος εἷς, βασιλεὺς, Χριστὸς, ὁ υἱὸς τοῦ Θεοῦ, ἐν οὐρανῷ καθεσθεὶς ἐν δεξιᾷ τοῦ πατρός . . .

49. *Letter to Acacius and Paul* 3.

50. There has been some discussion about Epiphanius' understanding of heresy. Pétau (who edited the *Panarion* in 1622 and whose text is reproduced in PG 41–2) commented that Epiphanius does not use the word αἵρεσις in the usual theological sense, and Fraenkel, 'Histoire sainte et hérésie chez S. Epiphane de Salamine', *Revue de Théologie et Philosophie* 12, 1963, 175–91, draws attention to the 'neutrality of the terminology' he uses, describing it as striking in the work of a 'successor to Irenaeus and Tertullian who had used the words as technical terms for denouncing error'. However, the word was in fact the classical designation for different philosophical schools, and simply means 'division'. Besides, if R. A. Lipsius is right (*Zur Quellenkritik des Epiphanius*, Vienna 1865), Epiphanius' source included the pre-Christian sects: Dositheans, Sadducees, Pharisees, Herodians. Epiphanius' understanding of heresy is not entirely consistent: see E. Moutsoulas, 'Der Begriff "Häresie" bei Epiphanius von Salamis', *StudPatr* 7, 1966, 362–71, and F. M. Young, 'Did Epiphanius know what he meant by heresy?' to be published in a forthcoming volume of *Studia Patristica*.

51. *Panarion* i.5 (PG 41.181–4)=2.4–7 (GCS I, 174.21–175.13).
52. Ibid. i.8 (PG 41.189)=4.1.2 (GCS I, 179. 13–15).
53. The *Anakephalaiōsis* follows and partially distorts the order of the prefatory letter. It is in any case irrelevant since it is unlikely to be the work of Epiphanius himself.
54. Fraenkel's valiant attempt to schematize Epiphanius' underlying ideas surely must not be allowed to obscure the inconsistency of Epiphanius' treatment. Fraenkel argues (art. cit., 181 f.) that Epiphanius regarded Samaritanism as syncretistic, and therefore places it and its sects between Hellenism and Judaism in the text; and that this means that it is only in a secondary sense one of the basic divisions of mankind, but can still be regarded as one of the 'mothers of heresy'.
55. Lipsius, op. cit. The same order is found in Pseudo-Tertullian and Philastrius; it is likely they all got it from Hippolytus.
56. F. L. Horton, Jr., *The Melchizedek Tradition*, Cambridge and New York 1976, 90 ff.
57. Lipsius, op. cit. and further Hippolytus, *Contre les hérésies*, ed. P. Nautin, Paris 1949.
58. However, Epiphanius' accuracy has been defended by S. Benko, 'The Libertine Sect of the Phibionites according to Epiphanius', *VC* 21, 1967, 103–19.
59. Jerome, *Adversus Rufinum* 3.6.
60. *Epiphanius' Treatise on Weights and Measures*, text and translation by J. E. Dean, Chicago and Cambridge 1935.
61. Epiphanius, *De gemmis*. The Old Georgian Version and the Fragments of the Armenian Version ed. and trs. R. P. Blake and the Coptic-Sahidic Fragments ed. with Latin translation by H. de Vis (Studies and Documents 2), London 1934.
62. Karl Holl, 'Die Schriften des Epiphanius gegen die Bilderverehrung', in *Gesammelte Aufsätze zur Kirchengeschichte* II, Tübingen 1928, 351–87.
63. On the Origenist controversy, see Karl Holl, 'Die Zeitfolge des ersten origenistischen Streits', ibid., 310–50; and M. Villain, 'Rufin d'Aquilée. La querelle autour Origène', *RSR* 27, 1937, 5–18. A recent account in English will be found in J. N. D. Kelly's biography of Jerome, London 1975; summary accounts will be found in any standard early church history.
64. It is now generally accepted that Palladius of Helenopolis, the author of the *Lausiac History* (see above pp. 38 f.), was also the author of the *Dialogue*, though the ascription is not absolutely certain. The title of the only complete ms. describes it as 'An Historical Dialogue of Palladius, Bishop of Helenopolis, with Theodore, Deacon of Rome, concerning the Life and Conversation of the Blessed John Chrysostom, Bishop of Constantinople'. This identifies Palladius with the main character in the *Dialogue* itself, the anonymous bishop who tells the story. In fact, this identification is impossible; not only do the facts of the bishop's life fail to correspond with what is known of Palladius' movements, but also he refers to Palladius in the third person. The most likely explanation of the title is that the bishop is a fictional character and the title preserves a tradition of the *Dialogue's* authorship. Stylistic comparisons with the *Lausiac History* on the whole confirm this attribution. Its value as a source for Chrysostom's

life is not in any case dependent upon the authorship question. Text ed.
P. R. Coleman-Norton, Cambridge 1928, translation by Herbert Moore,
London 1921.

65. Other evidence, notably from the unpublished *Life of Martyrius* and
Photius' summary of the Acts of the Synod of the Oak, has recently been
exploited by F. van Ommerslaeghe. His article, 'Que vaut le témoinage de
Pallade sur la procès de S. Jean Chrysostom?', *Analecta Bollandiana* 95,
1977, 389 ff., should be consulted. See also his 'Jean Chrysostome en conflit
avec l'impératrice Eudoxie', ibid., 97, 1979, 131–59.

66. This point was convincingly argued by D. L. Powell in an unpublished paper entitled 'John Chrysostom and the Synod of the Oak' read at
the Oxford Patristic Congress, September 1975; I am grateful to him for
supplying a copy.

67. Sozomen, *HE* viii.2.

68. L. Meyer, *S. Jean Chrysostome. Maître de perfection chrétienne*,
Paris 1933; cf. the excellent articles by J. M. Leroux, 'Monachisme et
communauté chrétienne d'après saint Jean Chrysostome', in *Théologie de
la vie monastique. Études sur la tradition patristique*, Paris 1961, 143–90,
and 'Saint Jean Chrysostome et le monachisme', in *Jean Chrysostome et
Augustin*, ed. C. Kannengiesser, Paris 1975; also F. X. Murphy, 'The Moral
Doctrine of St John Chrysostom', *StudPatr* 11, 1972, 52–7.

69. These include the letters to Theodore, probably but not certainly of
Mopsuestia, on his relapsing from the monastic life (see R. E. Carter,
'Chrysostom's *Ad Theodorum Lapsum* and the early chronology of
Theodore of Mopsuestia', *VC* 16, 1962, 87–101): text ed. J. Dumortier,
SC 117, 1966; ET in NPNF, series I, vol. IX; an appeal to opponents of
monasticism, *Adversus oppugnatores vitae monasticae*, and a couple of
works on remorse, *De Compunctione*: texts in PG 47. The rhetorical
exercise comparing the king and the monk, on the model of Plato's contrast
between the tyrant and the philosopher in *Republic* ix, is now regarded as
spurious (J. A. Aldama, *Repertorium pseudo-Chrysostomicum*, Paris 1965
n. 327, and R. E. Carter, 'The Future of Chrysostom Studies', *StudPatr* 10,
1970, 20).

70. *Adversus oppugnatores vitae monasticae*, PG 47.372.

71. Besides the *De virginitate* (text in SC 125, ed. H. Musurillo and
B. Grillet, 1966), Chrysostom wrote some small works on widowhood,
against second marriages, etc. Texts in SC 138, ed. G. H. Ettlinger and
B. Grillet, 1968.

72. *De virginitate* viii–x.

73. *Adversus oppugnatores vitae monasticae*, PG 47.373–4.

74. Chrysostom, *De sacerdote*, ed. J. A. Nairn, Cambridge Patristic
Texts, 1906; ET in NPNF series I, vol. IX; by T. A. Moxon, London 1907;
and by G. Neville, London 1964.

75. The friend Basil whom Chrysostom deceived was identified by
Socrates (HE vi.3) as Basil of Caesarea; but this can hardly be correct. Basil
appears nowhere else in Chrysostom's works, not even his correspondence,
which is rather surprising in view of the intimacy indicated in the dialogue.
Perhaps Basil was a literary fiction, or at least a fictitious name; there are
signs that Chrysostom was influenced by Gregory Nazianzen's *De fuga*,
and Basil *was* Gregory's friend.

76. In two pastoral letters, *Adversus eos qui apud see habent virgines subintroductas*: text ed. J. Dumortier (Budé), Paris 1955. But see E. A. Clark, 'John Chrysostom and the *Subintroductae*', *Church History* 46, 1977, 171–85.

77. On *Vainglory and the Education of Children*: Haidachers's introduction and German translation was followed by critical editions of the text by F. Schulte in 1914 and B. K. Exarchos in 1955. The most recent and reliable work is the edition by A. M. Malingrey, SC 188, 1972. English translation in M. C. W. Laistner's *Christianity and Pagan Culture*, New York 1951.

78. The abrupt change in topic and some stylistic differences have been stressed, but do not seem sufficiently serious to suggest that this is a composite work.

79. Though earlier he had advocated sending boys to monasteries for moral education: *Adversus oppugnatores vitae monasticae*, PG 47.319–86. For a detailed study of Chrysostom's views on education see A. K. Danassis, *Johannes Chrysostomos. Pädagogisch-psychologische Ideen in seinem Werk*, Bonn 1971.

80. *De statuis* i.4, PG 49.22.

81. *De statuis* ii.8, PG 49.43.

82. *Hom. in Jn.* lxi.3, PG 59.340.

83. Socrates, *HE* vi.21.

84. R. Brändle, 'Jean Chrysostome: l'importance de Matt. 25:31–46 pour son éthique', *VC* 31, 1977, 47–52; O. Plassmann, *Das Almosen bei Johannes Chrysostomus*, Münster 1961; Bruno H. Vandenberghe, *S. Jean Chrysostome et la parole de Dieu*, Paris 1961, ch.VII. For more general treatments of almsgiving, see F. Quère-Jaulmes, 'L'aumone chez Grégoire de Nysse et Gregoire de Nazianze', *StudPatr* 8, 1966, 449–55; B. Constantelos, *Byzantine Philosophy and Social Welfare*, New Brunswick 1968; F. M. Young, 'Christian Attitudes to Finance in the First Four Centuries', *Epworth Review* 4, 1977, 78–86.

85. *De statuis* ii.5, PG 49.40.

86. *De Statuis* ii.7, PG 49.43.

87. *Hom. in ep. Heb.* xxxii.3, PG 63.223.

88. *Hom. in ep. Heb.* xiii.5, PG 63.110.

89. *Hom. in ep. Heb.* xxxiv.2, PG 63.234.

90. See C. Baur, *S. Jean Chrysostome et ses oeuvres dans l'histoire littéraire*, Paris 1907, 6 f.; F.-J. Thonnard, 'S. Jean Chrysostome et S. Augustine dans la controverse pélagienne', *Revue des Études Byzantines* 25, 1967, 189–218.

91. *Pace* H. von Campenhausen, *The Fathers of the Greek Church*, ET New York 1959, London 1963, 144. Cf. J. Coman, 'Le rapport de la justification et de la charité dans les homélies de S. Jean Chrysostome à l'Epitre aux Romains', *Studia Evangelica* 5 (TU 103), 1968, 248–71.

92. *Hom. in Rom* ii.6, PG 60.409.

93. *Hom. in Heb.* ix.4, PG 63.80 f.

94. Cf. W. C. van Unnik, 'παρρησία in the "Catechetical Homilies" of Theodore of Mopsuestia', in *Mélanges offerts à Mlle Christine Mohrmann*, Utrecht 1963, 12–22.

95. There is a confusing number of sermons against the Anomoeans, whose grouping in the manuscripts is also confused; for details see A. M.

Malingrey, 'La tradition manuscrite des homélies de Jean Chrysostome *De Incomprehensibili*', StudPatr 10, 1970, 22–28. There seem to have been basically two sets, one preached in Antioch, the other in Constantinople. The first group of five has been edited by A. M. Malingrey, *Jean Chrysostome. Sur l'incomprehensibilité de Dieu*, SC 28; 2nd ed., 1970; the second group is being prepared for publication, and meanwhile can be found in Migne, PG 48.

96. See below, ch. 5.II.

97. *Hom. in Heb.* xiii.3, PG 63.106.

98. *Hom. in Phil.* vii.2, 3, PG 62.231f.

99. *Hom. in Jn.* xxvi.1, PG 59.154.

100. *Hom. in Jn.* xi.2, PG 59.89.

101. *Baptismal Instructions*, trs. P. W. Harkins, ACW 31, 1963.

102. Jean Chrysostome, *Huit catéchèses baptismales*, ed. A. Wenger, SC 50, 1957.

103. *Instruction* IX.21–2: Montfaucon-Migne 1=Papadopoulos-Kerameus 1 (Harkins p. 138).

104. *Instruction* III.12: Stavronikita 3=Papadopoulos-Kerameus 4 (Harkins p. 60).

105. *Hom. in Heb.* xvii.3, PG 63.131.

106. E.g. A. J. Festugière, *Antioche paienne et chrétienne*, Paris 1959.

107. C. Baur, *St Chrysostom and His Time* (German original 1929; ET by M. Gonzaga, Westminster, Maryland, and London 1959) is regarded as the standard biography.

108. Baur, op. cit., 217.

109. *Hom. in Matt.* lxxxviii.3, PG, 58.779.

110. *Hom in Jn.* xxiii.1, PG, 59.137 f.

111. Translations of Chrysostom's exegetical homilies on the New Testament are to be found in *The Library of the Fathers*, Oxford 1840 ff.; texts in PG 57, 59, 60, 61, 62, 63, or F. Field, *Ioannis Chrysostomi interpretatio omnium epistularum Paulinarum*, Oxford 1845–62. For discussion of Chrysostom's exegesis, see F. H. Chase, *Chrysostom. A Study in the History of Biblical Interpretation*, Cambridge 1887.

112. *Hom. in Heb.* i.2, PG 63.15 f.

113. *Hom. in Phil.* vi. 1, PG 62.218.

114. Of recent years, there has been a considerable upsurge in Chrysostom studies, a great deal concentrated on cataloguing manuscripts, determining the authentic, producing critical texts and generally sorting out the critical problems. See especially: (i) M. Aubineau, *Codices Chrysostomici Graeci* I, Paris 1968, R. E. Carter, ibid., II and III, Paris 1968, 1970. This major catalogue, which covers manuscripts in the British Isles, Western Europe and America, is eventually to be extended to cover those in Eastern Europe and Greece. (ii) J. A. Aldama, *Repertorium pseudo-Chrysostomicum*, Paris 1965, is a catalogue of all those parts of the Chrysostom corpus (PG 47–64) which are now regarded as spurious. This is an essential reference book for serious study. (iii) The Patriarchal Institute for Patristic Studies in Thessaloniki is co-ordinating work on Chrysostom, compiling a comprehensive Chrysostom Bibliography, establishing a Chrysostom library and collecting microfilms of Chrysostom manuscripts. (iv) Sources Chrétiennes has been producing new critical texts: for texts

available and projected in 1973, see A. M. Malingrey, 'L'édition critique de Jean Chrysostome. Actualité de son oeuvre. Volumes parus. Projets', in P. C. Christou, *Symposion*. *Studies on Saint John Chrysostom* (*ΑΝΑΛΕΚΤΑ ΒΛΑΤΑΔΩΝ* 18), Thessaloniki 1973, 77–90. (v) For further work on Chrysostom, see the articles by R. E. Carter, 'The Future of Chrysostom Studies', *StudPatr* 10, 1970, 14–21, and 'The Future of Chrysostom Studies: Theology and *Nachleben'*, in Christou, op. cit. 129–36; for critical articles and texts available, see Bibliography B.

115. *Clavis Patrum Graecorum II*, Corpus Christianorum, ed. M. Geerard, Brepols-Turnhout 1974.

116. Text: *Lettres á Olympias*, ed. A. M. Malingrey (SC 13), 1947. An excellent study of the theme of suffering, though not confined to these letters, is E. Nowak, *Le chrétien devant la souffrance. Étude sur la pensée de Jean Chrysostome*, Paris 1972.

117. For Chrysostom's style and language, see A. Ameringer, *The Stylistic Influence of the Second Sophistic on the Panegyrical Sermons of St John Chrysostom*, Washington 1921, and C. Fabricius, *Zu den Jugendschriften des Johannes Chrysostomos: Untersuchungen zum Klassizismus des vierten Jahrhunderts*, Lund 1962.

118. W. W. Jaeger, *Nemesios von Emesa. Quellenforschungen zum Neuplatonismus und seinen anfängen bei Posidonios*, Berlin 1914. English readers may observe the effect of Jaeger's work on W. Telfer, the editor of *Cyril of Jerusalem and Nemesius of Emesa* (Library of Christian Classics, vol. IV), London and Philadelphia 1955.

119. Chiefly on the basis of the careful critical work of L. Edelstein in identifying the fragments of Posidonius. See L. Edelstein and I. G. Kidd, *Posidonius* Vol. I: *The Fragments*, Cambridge 1972. For further discussion see J. Dillon, *The Middle Platonists*, London 1976, New York 1977, 106 ff.

120. As suggested by K. Reinhardt, 'Poseidonios von Apamea', article in Pauly-Wissowa-Kroll, *Real-Encyclopädie der klassischen Altertumswissenschaft* 22, Stuttgart 1953, col. 773.

121. See the important articles by E. Skard, 'Nemesiosstudien' *Symbolae Osloenses* 15, 1936, 23–43; 17, 1937, 9–25; 18, 1938, 31–41; 19, 1939, 46–56; 22, 1942, 40–48.

122. Gregory Naz., *Epp.* 198–201, ed. P. Gallay (Budé), vol. 2, Paris 1967; and *Poem.* II.ii.7, PG 37.1551–77.

123. This identification was proposed by Tillemont. For discussion, see Telfer, op. cit., 209.

124. See the first of Skard's articles listed above.

125. Gregory Nazianzen, *Orat.* vii.10.

126. Telfer has provided a translation and commentary; so it is easily accessible to the English reader.

127. PG 40.733; Telfer, p. 393. For the translations, I am largely though not wholly quoting Telfer's version.

128. PG 40.708; Telfer, p. 372.

129. PG 40.709; Telfer, pp. 375 f.

130. PG 40.573–6; Telfer, pp. 282–5.

131. PG 40.596–7, 600; Telfer, pp. 295–9.

132. PG 40.708; Telfer, p. 373.

133. Only in the passage in the introductory chapter: PG 40.521–4; Telfer, pp. 244, 246. See discussion below pp. 167 f.

134. PG 40.512; Telfer, p. 236.

135. PG 40.525 ff., 532 ff. Telfer, pp. 248 ff., 254 ff.

136. PG 40.673; Telfer, p. 348.

137. PG 40.676 f.; Telfer, p. 351.

138. PG 40.729; Telfer, p. 390.

139. PG 40.688; Telfer, p. 359.

140. Ibid.; cf. PG 40.776 f.; Telfer, p. 419.

141. PG 40.805; Telfer, p. 443.

142. PG 40.685; Telfer, p. 358.

143. PG 40.513; Telfer, p. 236.

144. PG 40.676; Telfer, p. 379.

145. PG 40.677–80; Telfer, pp. 352 ff.

146. PG 40.685; Telfer, p. 357.

147. PG 40.776 f.; Telfer, pp. 418 f.

148. PG 40.779 f.; Telfer, pp. 420 f.

149. PG 40.533; Telfer, p. 254. Cf. PG 40.713–7, and Telfer's comments, pp. 379–82.

150. PG 40.508; Telfer, p. 229.

151. PG 40.512 f.; Telfer, op. cit. 235 f.

152. Reinhardt, art. cit. (n. 120 above).

153. PG 40.805; Telfer, p. 443.

154. PG 40.521 ff.; Telfer, pp. 244 ff.

155. PG 40.513 ff.; Telfer, op. cit. pp. 238 ff.

156. For the following discussion see Ch. III, 'On the Union of Soul and Body', *passim* (PG 40.592–609; Telfer, pp. 293–304).

157. H. von Campenhausen also recognized this, and included Synesius among *The Fathers of the Greek Church*, ET New York 1959, London 1963.

158. E.g. R. Volkmann, *Synesius von Cyrene*, Berlin 1869; W. S. Crawford, *Synesius the Hellene*, London 1901; G. Grützmacher, *Synesius von Kyrene*, Leipzig 1913.

159. Text of Synesius' treatises and hymns: *Hymni et opuscula*, ed. N. Terzaghi, 2 vols., Rome 1944; also in PG 66. New critical text of the hymns by A. dell'Era, Συνεσίου Κυρηναίου ὕμνοι ἔμμετροι, Rome 1968. ET, *Essays and Hymns of Synesius*, by A. Fitzgerald, 2 vols., Oxford and New York 1930. Text of the letters in *Epistolographi Graeci*, ed. R. Hercher, Paris 1873; also in PG 66 (with slightly different numbering). ET, *Letters of Synesius*, by A. Fitzgerald, Oxford and New York 1926 (following Hercher's numbering).

160. Socrates, *HE* vii.15.

161. Synesius refers to himself as old in a couple of letters (116 and 123); but in *Ep.* 72, he is younger than his suffragans, and in *Hymn* 8 (probably though not certainly written after 405), he refers to his youth. When he wrote his *Encomium on Baldness*, he was certainly bald; but that must have been well before his consecration and suggests that he lost his hair prematurely. The question cannot be finally settled.

162. W. S. Crawford, op. cit., put it two years earlier, but the later date, established by O. Seeck, 'Studien zu Synesios', *Philologus* 52, 1894, 442–83, has been generally accepted; see C. Lacombrade, *Synésios de Cyrène. Héllène et chrétien*, Paris 1951.

163. For this incident, see *Ep.* 57 (which is a public address erroneously placed among the letters), and *Epp.* 72, 79 and 89.

164. *Epp.* 105 and 57.

165. A glance at the footnotes of Terzaghi's edition is instructive in this regard. Many details will also be found in A. Fitzgerald's notes to his translations. W. S. Crawford, op. cit., tabulates a large collection of parallels in Appendix D.

166. According to *Ep.* 154 (no. 153 in PG), Synesius wrote a book on the chase, *Cynegetica.* In *Ep.* 105, he regrets having to give up a fondness for dogs and horses which he has had since childhood. In *Ep.* 40, he sends a horse to a friend with an account of its qualities. His needs in the way of horses, arrows and other military equipment are mentioned in *Epp.* 132 and 133 (131 and 132 in PG). Hunting analogies are frequent in his works.

167. *Ep.* 107. *De regno* 14 recommends a citizen-army. Other references to Synesius' leading military operations will be found in *Epp.* 89, 104, 108, 113, 132, 133, etc.

168. A. Fitzgerald's Introduction to the *Essays and Hymns* perhaps over-romanticizes Synesius' attachment to classical ideals of patriotism, but there is certainly an element of truth in his descriptions. In an age of diminishing social responsibility, Synesius was a bit of an anachronism. For a different slant on all this, see W. N. Bayless, 'Synesius of Cyrene: A Study of the Roles of the Bishop in Temporal Affairs', *Byzantine Studies: Études Byzantines* 4, 1977, 147–56.

169. *Ep.* 136 (135 in PG).

170. *Ep.* 105: his wife was a possible obstacle to his consecration, and Synesius refused to part from a perfectly legal and proper marital position simply for ecclesiastical advancement.

171. Socrates, *HE* vii.12, 37.

172. The exact date of the letter is disputed. See the most recent discussion, D. Roques, 'Le Lettre 4 de Synésios de Cyrène', *Revue des Études Grecques* 90, 1977, 263–95.

173. R. Pack, 'Folklore and Superstitions in the Writings of Synesius', *Classical Weekly* 43, 1949, 51–6.

174. *Epp.* 10, 16, 81.

175. *Ep.* 154 (153 in PG; the letters are not collected in chronological order).

176. C. Lacombrade, op. cit. (n. 162 above), dates the *Encomium on Baldness* before the trip to Constantinople; this masterly biography presents a plausible reconstruction of Synesius' life and the sequence of his works, but much of the dating must still be regarded as tentative. Lacombrade himself revises the date of the hymns in 'Perspectives nouvelles sur les hymnes de Synésios', *Revue des Études Grecques* 74, 1961, 439–49.

177. The *Constitutio* and *Catastasis.*

178. *Ep.* 133 (132 in PG).

179. C. Lacombrade, *Le Discours sur la Royauté de Synésios de Cyrène à l'empereur Arcadios*, Paris 1951.

180. Dio Chrysostom, *Orations* I–IV and LXII.

181. E.g. Fitzgerald, *Essays and Hymns* I, 227.

182. Charles Kingsley, *Hypatia*, Everyman edition, London 1907, re-issued 1968, p. 287 (the chapter on 'The Squire Bishop'). For an interesting

attempt to write a historical novel set in this period and based on a good many original sources and some genuine historical characters, this work is to be recommended.

183. *De regno;* cf. *Epp.* 101, 103; *Ad Paeonium de dono astrolabii.*

184. *Ep.* 57, 62.

185. *Calvitii Encomium* 20.

186. *Hymns* 3, 5 and 6 provide the examples.

187. Kingsley, *Hypatia,* p. 116.

188. The dating of Synesius' *Hymns* has been seen as the clue to his so-called conversion. However, Lacombrade has argued that they all date from approximately the same period. In *Synésios de Cyrène,* ch. 14, he dated them to 405–9, and detected a shift towards more explicitly Christian language, suggesting that it was the language of a sympathizer rather than a theologian. In a more recent article, 'Perspectives nouvelles sur les hymnes de Synésios', *Revue des Études Grecques* 74, 1961, 439–49, he dates them even earlier, 402–4.

189. *Ep.* 5 and *Catastasis.*

190. *Ep.* 105.

191. J. Bregman, 'Synesius of Cyrene: Early Life and Conversion to Philosophy', *California Studies in Classical Antiquity* 7, 1974, 55–88.

5. The Literature of Christological Controversy

1. See above pp. 17 f.

2. See above p. 74.

3. For a clear and forceful presentation of this distinction, see the work of F. A. Sullivan, *The Christology of Theodore of Mopsuestia,* Rome 1956.

4. See further R. V. Sellers, *Eustathius of Antioch,* Cambridge and New York 1928.

5. F. Loofs, *Nestorius and His Place in the History of Christian Doctrine,* Cambridge and New York 1914, and *Paulus von Samosata,* Leipzig 1924. R. V. Sellers, op. cit., develops this line of approach. See also his *Two Ancient Christologies,* London and New York 1940.

6. M. Spanneut, *Recherches sur les écrits d'Eustathe d'Antioche avec une édition nouvelle des fragments dogmatiques et exégétiques,* Lille 1948; and 'La position théologique d'Eustathe d'Antioche', *JTS* NS 5, 1954, 220–24.

7. *Fr.* 15, ed. Spanneut.

8. *Fr.* 41, ed. Spanneut.

9. C. E. Raven, *Apollinarianism,* Cambridge and New York 1923, 105, quoting fragments 159–61 from H. Lietzmann's collection in *Apollinaris und seine Schule,* Tübingen 1904, pp. 253 f. (cited henceforth as L 253 f., etc.).

10. Apollinarius, *Letter to Jovian* (L 250 ff.).

11. Apollinarius, *Letter to the Bishops of Diocaesarea* 1, L 255.

12. *Kata meros pistis* 3, L 168.

13. Ibid. 6 (L 169).

14. Ibid. 11 (L 171).

15. Ibid. 30 (L 178).

16. *De unione* 4 (L 186).

17. *Letter to Dionysius* (L 256 ff.).

18. E. Mühlenberg, *Apollinaris von Laodicea*, Göttingen 1969; but see the review articles: C. Kannengiesser, 'Une nouvelle interpretation de la christologie d'Apollinaire', *RSR* 59, 1971, 27–36; and R. Hübner, 'Gottes-erkenntnis durch die Inkarnation Gottes. Zu einer neue Interpretation der Christologie des Apollinaris von Laodicea,' *Kleronomia* 4, 1972, 131–61.

19. E.g. *De fide et incarnation* 4 (L 195).

20. *Fr.* 38 (L 213).

21. *Fr.* 150 (L 247).

22. *Fr.* 151 (L 248).

23. *Fr.* 76 (L 222).

24. See above p. 78.

25. *Letter to the Bishops of Dioceasarea* 2 (L 256).

26. Rufinus, *HE* ii.20; cf. Socrates, *HE* ii.46.

27. *Eranistes* II, ed. G. H. Ettlinger, Oxford 1975, 112 f. (the opening discussion of Book II).

28. E.g. *Fr.* 69 (L 220); *Tomus Synodalis*, L 263.

29. Quotations from *Frs.* 72, 29, 25, 89 (L 221, 211, 210, 227); and see especially *Frs.* 69 ff. (L 220 ff.).

30. *Fr.* 51 (L 216); and *Fr.* 70 (L 220).

31. Raven, op. cit.; G. L. Prestige, *Fathers and Heretics*, London and New York 1940.

32. *De fide et inc.* 3 (L 194).

33. *Fr.* 32 (L 211).

34. *Fr.* 50 (L 216).

35. *First Letter to Dionysius* 7 (L 259).

36. *Frs.* 113 (L 234) and 19 (L 209).

37. *Fr.* 10 (L 207).

38. *Fr.* 11 (L 207); *De unione* 5 (L 187); *De fide et inc.* 7 (L 199). See H. de Riedmatten, 'Some Neglected Aspects of Apollinarist Christology', *Dominican Studies* 1, 1948 239–60; and 'La Christologie d'Apollinaire de Laodicee', *StudPatr* 2, 1957, 208–34.

39. *Fr.* 36 (L 212); *Fr.* 116 (L 235).

40. *Fr.* 121 (L 237).

41. W. A. Wigram, *The Separation of the Monophysites* (London 1923).

42. *Metaphrasis in Psalmos*, ed. A. Ludwich (Teubner), Leipzig 1912. See J. Golega, *Der Homerische Psalter; Studien über die dem Apollinarios von Laodikeia zugeschreibene Psalmenparaphrase*, Ettal 1960.

43. G. L. Prestige, *St Basil the Great and Apollinarius of Laodicea*, London 1956; H. de Riedmatten, 'La correspondence entre Basile de Césarée et Apollinaire de Laodicée' *JTS* NS 7, 1956, 199–210, NS 8, 1957, 53–70.

44. *Kata meros pistis* 27 (L 176).

45. Ibid. 18–19 (L 173).

46. See further Prestige, loc. cit., n. 43 above.

47. Julian, *Epistle* 55 (fragments from a letter to Photinus preserved by Facundus), in *Works* III, LCL 1923.

48. Jerome, *De viris illustribus* 119.

49. R. Abramowski, 'Untersuchungen zu Diodor von Tarsus', *ZNW* 30, 1931, 234–62.

50. Sozomen, *HE* vi.25 for Apollinarius; Theodoret, *HE* ii.19 for Diodore.

51. Jerome, *De vir. ill.* 104, on Apollinarius' exegetical work. Exegetical fragments can be found in K. Staab, *Pauluskommentare aus der griechischen Kirche*, Munster 1933, and in E. Mühlenberg. *Psalmenkommentare aus der katenenüberlieferung*, Berlin 1975, vol. I, Apollinarius and Didymus. On Diodore's exegesis, see E. Schweizer, 'Diodor von Tarsus als Exeget', *ZNW* 40, 1941, 33–75.

52. M. Richard, 'Les traités de Cyrille d'Alexandrie contre Diodore et Theodore et les fragments dogmatiques de Diodore de Tarse', *Mélanges F. Grat* I, Paris 1946, 99–116; republished in M. Richard, *Opera Minora* vol. II, Louvain 1977.

53. A. Grillmeier, *Christ in Christian Tradition*, ET, London and New York 1965, 270 (2nd ed., 1975, 360) n. 34; a considerable discussion of the question of authenticity will be found in F. A. Sullivan, *The Christology of Theodore of Mopsuestia*, Rome 1956.

54. M. Brière, 'Fragments syriaques de Diodore de Tarse réédités et traduits pour la première fois', *Revue de l'Orient Chrétien* 10, 1946, 231–83, publishes the fragments from British Museum Codex 12156. R. Abramowski, 'Der Theologische Nachlass der Diodor von Tarsus', *ZNW* 42, 1949, 19–69 includes also Greek, Latin and Syriac fragments from elsewhere.

55. Schwartz, *ACO* I.i.6, 151 f., quoted in Abramowski, 'Nachlass', p. 62.

56. Originally advanced by Grillmeier in *Das Konzil von Chalkedon I*, Würzburg 1951; ET with revisions *Christ in Christian Tradition*, London 1965; with further revisions in 2nd ed., vol. I, 1975. (Vol. I of the 2nd ed. covers the same ground as the 1st ed; later volumes have not yet appeared.)

57. F. A. Sullivan, op. cit.; R. A. Greer, 'The Antiochene Christology of Diodore of Tarsus', *JTS* NS 17, 1966, 327–41.

58. Cyril of Alexandria, *Fragments*, in *Cyrilli Archiep. Alex. in S. Joannis Evangelium*, ed. P. E. Pusey, Oxford 1872, III.494. Abramowski, 'Nachlass', does not give the full quotation.

59. See above pp. 89 f.

60. E.g. *Frs.* 15, 17, 19 (Brière and Abramowski; henceforth cited as B. & Ab.).

61. These statements are found in *Frs.* 22, 28, 19, 20 (B. & Ab.); 35 (Ab. only).

62. These statements are drawn from *Frs.* 14, 12, 4 (B. & Ab.); cf. 44 (Ab. only).

63. *Frs.* 46–49 (Ab. only).

64. *Fr.* 27 (B. & Ab.).

65. *Fr.* 42 (Ab. only); cf. *Fr.* 30 (B. & Ab.).

66. The two fragments concerned are 2 and 26 (B. & Ab.); for discussion see M. Richard, 'L'Introduction du mot "hypostase" dans la théologie de l'incarnation', *Mélanges de Science Religieuse* 2, 1945, 5–32, 243–70, republished in *Opera Minora II*. See esp. R. A. Greer, op. cit. Both these passages are misinterpreted by R. Abramowski, 'Untersuchungen'.

67. *Frs.* 19, 20, (B. & Ab.); 31 (Ab. only).

68. These statements are drawn from *Frs.* 30 (B. & Ab., and cf. also 27); 31, 34 (AB. only); and 38 (Ab. only).

69. *Frs.* 46–49 (Ab. only).

70. *Fr.* 36 (Ab. only).

71. Abramowski, 'Untersuchungen', comments on the parallels, though he probably overestimates them by his misinterpretation of *Frs.* 2 and 26.

72. Theodore, *Catechetical Homilies* i, ed. A. Mingana, Woodbrooke Studies v (see n. 78 below), text 118 f., ET 19 f.

73. E.g. L. Patterson, *Theodore of Mopsuestia and Modern Thought*, London and New York 1926.

74. Socrates, *HE* vi.3; Sozomen, *HE* viii.2.

75. Chrysostom to Theodore, PG 47.277–316; the second letter is personal, the first more like a treatise and not entirely applicable to Theodore's situation. See R. E. Carter, 'Chrysostom's *Ad Theodorum lapsum* and the Early Chronology of Theodore of Mopsuestia', *VC* 16, 1962, 87–101.

76. John of Antioch, quoted by Facundus, *Defence of the Three Chapters* ii.2.

77. Theodore, *Controverse avec les Macédoniens*, ed. and trs. F. Nau, Patrologia Orientalis 9, Paris 1913, 637–67.

78. Theodore, *Catechetical Homilies*: Syriac text and ET, *Commentary of Theodore of Mopsuestia on the Nicene Creed* (= *Hom. cat.* i–x) and *Commentary . . . on the Lord's Prayer and the Sacraments of Baptism and the Eucharist* (= *Hom. cat.* xi–xvi), ed. A. Mingana, Woodbrooke Studies (cited henceforth as WS) v and vi, Cambridge 1932–3; also *Les Homélies Catéchétiques de Théodore de Mopsueste*, ed. with French trs. by R. Tonneau (Studi e Testi 145), Rome 1949.

79. *Theodori Mopsuesteni Commentarius in Evangelium Iohannis Apostoli*, ed. with Latin trs. by J.-M. Vosté, CSCO 115–16 (Syriac: series IV no. 3), Louvain 1940.

80. *Theodori Episcopi Mopsuesteni in epistolas B. Pauli commentarii*, ed. H. B. Swete, 2 vols., Cambridge 1880–2, reprinted Farnborough 1969 (Latin version with Greek fragments).

81. R. Devreesse, *Essai sur Théodore de Mopsueste* (Studi e Testi 141), Rome 1948; *Le Commentaire de Théodore de Mopsueste sur les Psaumes* (Studi e Testi 93), Rome 1939, etc. Relevant articles can be traced in the Patrologies.

82. M. Richard, 'Les traités de Cyrille d'Alexandrie contre Diodore et Théodore et les fragments dogmatiques de Diodore de Tarse', *Mélanges Felix Grat* I, Paris 1946, 99–116; 'La tradition des fragments du traité περὶ τῆς ἐνανθρωπήσεως de Théodore de Mopsueste', *Le Muséon* 56, 1943, 55–75 (both reprinted in *Opera Minora* II, Louvain 1977); Devreesse, *Essai*.

83. F. A. Sullivan, *The Christology of Theodore of Mopsuestia*, Rome 1956.

84. J. L. McKenzie, 'Annotations on the Christology of Theodore of Mopsuestia', *Theological Studies* 19, 1958, 345–73; cf. F. A. Sullivan, 'Further Notes on Theodore of Mopsuestia. A Reply to Fr. McKenzie' ibid. 20, 1959, 264–79.

85. J. L. McKenzie, 'The Commentary of Theodore of Mopsuestia on Jn. 1.46–51', *Theological Studies* 14, 1953, 73–84.

86. E.g. L. Pirot, *L'Oeuvre exégétique de Théodore de Mopsueste*, Rome 1913.

87. In a fragment quoted by Facundus, *Defence* iii.6.

88. The hyperbole shows that its reference goes beyond the immediate situation and its full meaning is to be found in Christ. See comment by M. F. Wiles in his article in *The Cambridge History of the Bible*, I, 501 (see n. 93 below).

89. Theodore discusses this point in the Introduction to his commentary on Jonah, PG 66.317–28.

90. *Commentary on . . . Paul*, Swete I, 73 ff.

91. *Comm. in Jn.*, ed. Vosté, 4 f. (Latin 2).

92. Ibid. 314 (Latin 224).

93. On the above points see further M. F. Wiles, *The Spiritual Gospel*, Cambridge 1960, and *The Divine Apostle*, Cambridge 1967; and the excellent summary article, 'Theodore of Mopsuestia as Representative of the Antiochene School', in *The Cambridge History of the Bible* I, Cambridge and New York 1970, 489–510. Also Rowan Greer, *Theodore of Mopsuestia: Exegete and Theologian*, London 1961.

94. Greer, op. cit. ch. 1.

95. R. A. Norris, *Manhood and Christ*, Oxford and New York 1963.

96. *Commentary on . . . Paul*, Swete, I, 128–31.

97. R. A. Norris, op. cit.

98. Gennadius, *De vir. ill.* 12.

99. A fragment from *De Inc.* ii, in Swete, II, 291 ff. (see n. 80 above).

100. *Hom. cat.* iv, WS v, 152, ET 45 (see n. 78 above).

101. *Hom. cat.* v, WS v, 161, ET 52.

102. *De Inc.* ix.1, Swete, II, 300.

103. Ibid.; see also *Comm. in Jn.*1.14, Vosté 33 f. (Latin 23).

104. *Hom. cat.* viii, WS v, 207, ET 90.

105. Sullivan, op. cit., especially 219 ff.

106. R. A. Norris, op. cit.

107. See above pp. 168 f.

108. *De Inc.* vii, Swete, II, 310.

109. Ibid. 294 ff.

110. Joanne Dewart, 'The Notion of "Person" underlying the Christology of Theodore of Mopsuestia', *StudPatr* 12, 1975, 199–207.

111. Luise Abramowski, 'Zur Theologie Theodors von Mopsuestia', *Zeitschrift für Kirchengeschichte* 72, 1961, 263–93.

112. *Hom. cat.* viii *passim* and often elsewhere.

113. Fragment from Theodore's *On Priesthood*, in A. Mingana, *Early Christian Mystics*, WS vii, 95 f. Cf. *Comm. in Jn.*, Vosté, 315 (Latin 225).

114. *Hom. cat.* xvi, WS vi, 256, ET 115; cf. *Hom. cat.* xii–xvi, *passim*.

115. *Hom. cat.* xvi, WS vi, 259, ET 118.

116. *Hom. cat.* xi, WS vi, 126, ET 3.

117. Quoted in *Early Christian Mystics*, WS vii, 109 f.

118. Apart from the standard church histories, see R. V. Sellers, *The Council of Chalcedon*, London 1953.

119. *Sacrorum Conciliorum nova et amplissima collectio*, ed. J. D. Mansi, 31 vols., Florence 1757–98; reprint and continuation by L. Petit and J. B. Martin, 53 vols., Paris and Leipzig 1901–27. New edition, *Acta Conciliorum Oecumenicorum*, ed. E. Schwartz, Berlin 1914–40, referred to as *ACO*.

120. The *Collectio Vaticana* (*ACO* I.i.1–6) contains all except Cyril's

Apology against the Orientals, which is to be found in the *Collectio Atheniensis* (ACO I.i.7); this contains some 58 items not found in other Greek collections.

121. These documents are available with notes and translations in T. H. Bindley and F. W. Green, *The Oecumenical Documents of the Faith,* London and New York 1955.

122. See above p. 183.

123. Socrates, *HE* vii.29; see below pp. 233 f.

124. E.g. Sellers, op. cit., 10.

125. M. Richard, 'L'introduction du mot "Hypostase" dans la théologie de l'incarnation', republished in *Opera Minora* II, Louvain 1977. See also the comments of H. Chadwick in 'Eucharist and Christology in the Nestorian Controversy', *JTS* NS 2, 1951, 145–64.

126. See below pp. 230 f. and 236.

127. E.g. Sellers, op. cit., and *Two Ancient Christologies,* London and New York 1940; G. L. Prestige, *Fathers and Heretics,* London and New York 1940; also Milton V. Anastos, 'Nestorius was Orthodox', *Dumbarton Oaks Papers* 16, 1962, 119–40.

128. See below p. 229.

129. *Le Livre d'Héraclide de Damas,* French. trs. with Introduction and notes by F. Nau, Paris 1910 (henceforth cited as N), 323; Nestorius, *The Bazaar of Heraclides,* ed. and trs. G. R. Driver and L. Hodgson, Oxford and New York 1925 (henceforth cited as DH), 370. According to L. Abramowski, *Untersuchungen zum Liber Heraclidis des Nestorius,* CSCO 242 (Subsidia 22), Louvain 1963, the section in brackets bears the marks of the interpolator; however the same attitude is found in the surrounding sentences, so the main point is not affected by that literary-critical hypothesis.

130. N 298/DH 340.

131. F. Loofs, *Nestoriana,* Halle 1905.

132. Nestorius, *The Book of Heraclides*: Syriac text, R. P. Bedjan, Paris 1910. For translations see n. 129 above.

133. J. F. Bethune-Baker, *Nestorius and his Teaching,* Cambridge and New York 1908.

134. L. Abramowski, op. cit.

135. The additional material published by Nau appended to his translations of the *Liber Heraclidis* is generally accepted. For other suggestions, consult the Patrologies.

136. The material described in this paragraph will be found collected together in Loofs, *Nestoriana.*

137. Abramowski, op. cit.

138. E.g. L. I. Scipioni, *Nestorio e il concilio di Epheso* (Studia Patristica Mediolanensia), Milan 1975. See also Roberta C. Chesnut, 'The Two Prosopa in Nestorius' *Bazaar of Heraclides', JTS* NS 29, 1978, 392–409.

139. H. E. W. Turner, 'Nestorius Reconsidered', *StudPatr* 13, 1975, 306–21.

140. Milton V. Anastos, 'Nestorius was Orthodox', *Dumbarton Oaks Papers* 16, 1962, 123.

141. Socrates, *HE* vii.29, 31–2.

142. N 120 f./DH 136 f. Socrates reports a similar remark as having given scandal.

143. N 91 f./DH 99 f. Cf. Loofs, *Nestoriana*, 185 and 203, for parallel accounts in a letter to John and a fragment of the *Tragedy*.

144. *Nestoriana*, 251 f.

145. Ibid. 167.

146. Ibid. 353.

147. N 88/DH 95; N 330/DH 378.

148. N 327/DH 374 f.

149. Bethune-Baker, op. cit.; E. Amann, art. 'Nestorius' in *Dictionnaire de Théologie Catholique* XI, 76–157; etc. Survey in H. E. W. Turner, art. cit.

150. Anastos, art. cit. Cf. L. Hodgson, 'The Metaphysic of Nestorius', *JTS* 19, 1918, 46–55 (republished as Appendix IV in DH).

151. E.g. N 263 f./DH 298 f. Various other sections revolve around the question of definition, e.g. N 127–63/DH 143–85. The alternatives are discussed at length in the dialogue (esp. N 18 f./DH 20 f.), which Hodgson and Anastos took to be authentic Nestorius. There seems little reason to doubt that it represents with slightly more clarity what Nestorius himself attempts to say elsewhere.

152. DH 156 n. 2, cf. A. R. Vine, *An Approach to Christology*, London 1948, 113 ff. Abramowski, op. cit., 213 ff., notes that the word is not used in christological contexts until well into the controversy. This confirms Richard's view that Cyril introduced it, and it was by no means a natural term for the Antiochenes. See above pp. 222 f.

153. N 138 f./DH 156 f.

154. *Nestoriana*, 224.

155. *Nestoriana*, 280.

156. N 265/DH 300 f.

157. H. E. W. Turner, art. cit. (n. 139 above).

158. E.g. N 140 f./DH 159, and often, esp. N 183/DH 207 and N 212 f./DH 240 f.: the humanity making use of the *prosōpon* of the divinity and the divinity of the *prosōpon* of the humanity. For an interesting discussion of this, see R. C. Chesnut, art. cit. (n. 138 above).

159. Grillmeier, *Christ in Christian Tradition*, ET, 1965, 439 ff. (2nd ed., 1975, 508 ff.), quoting N 219/DH 247; 448 (2nd ed. 516), quoting N 183/DH 207 (altered).

160. N 117/DH 132.

161. *Nestoriana*, 199.

162. N 330/DH 378.

163. L. Abramowski and A. E. Goodman, *A Nestorian Collection of Christological Texts*, Cambridge and New York 1972, vol. II, 24.

164. Extract from A. Kerrigan, *St Cyril of Alexandria. Interpreter of the Old Testament* (Analecta Biblica 2), Rome 1952, 7, quoting Schwartz, *ACO* I.i.1, 108 f. Kerrigan here follows very closely the material and judgments of H. du Manoir, *Dogme et Spiritualité chez S. Cyrille d'Alexandrie*, Paris 1944.

165. See e.g. H. von Campenhausen, *The Fathers of the Greek Church*, ch.12; the discussion in H. Chadwick, 'Eucharist and Christology in the Nestorian Controversy', *JTS* NS 2, 1951, 145–64; and the assessments in many of the major histories of the early church.

166. As quoted in J. Stevenson, *Creeds, Councils and Controversies*, London and New York 1966, 300 (translation slightly altered).

167. Socrates, *HE* vii.13 ff.

168. Theodoret, *Ep.* 180.
169. Socrates, *HE* vii.15.
170. H. I. Bell, 'Anti-semitism in Alexandria', *JRS* 31, 1941, 1–18; and *Jews and Christians in Egypt*, London 1924.
171. Robert L. Wilken, *Judaism and the Early Christian Mind. A Study of Cyril of Alexandria's Exegesis and Theology*, New Haven, Conn. 1971.
172. J. Liébaert, *La Doctrine Christologique de S.Cyrille d'Alexandrie avant la querelle Nestorienne*, Lille 1951; but see the article by G. Jouassard, 'L'activité littéraire de S.Cyrille d'Alexandrie jusqu'à 428', *Mélanges E.Podechard*, Lyons 1945, 159–75. Liébaert does not accept Jouassard's argument. For Joussard's reply see 'La date des écrits antiariens de S. Cyrille d'Alexandrie', *Revue Bénédictine* 87, 1977, 172–8.
173. Kerrigan, op. cit., 246 ff.
174. The difference in method is explained by Liébaert, op. cit., 38.
175. Cyril, *De adoratione in Spiritu et veritate*: text, PG 68.
176. Cyril, *Glaphyra in Pentateuchum*: text, PG 69.
177. This observation is made by Wilken, op. cit; see esp. ch. 4.
178. Wilken, op. cit., also his 'Exegesis and the History of Theology: Reflections on the Adam-Christ Typology in Cyril of Alexandria', *Church History* 35, 1966, 139–56.
179. *Cyrilli Archiepiscopi Alexandrini in XII Prophetas*, ed. P. E. Pusey, 2 vols., Oxford 1868.
180. Kerrigan, op. cit., 96 ff., tabulates comparable passages.
181. Cyril's exegetical terminology is studied in detail by Kerrigan, op. cit., 35 ff., 112 ff., and is related to his metaphysical assumptions, 42 ff., 126 ff.
182. H. du Manoir, op. cit. (n. 164 above), ch. 2.
183. Kerrigan, op. cit., 198, 394 ff.
184. G. Jouassard, art. cit. (n. 172 above).
185. Cyril, *Thesaurus de sancta Trinitate*: text, PG 75.
186. Liébaert, op. cit., passim, especially chs. 1 and 2.
187. Liébaert, op. cit., 154 ff., followed by A. Grillmeier, *Christ in Christian Tradition*, ET London 1965, 330; this point of view may be a little exaggerated in view of the contents of *Paschal Letter* viii, but it is plausible to suggest that Cyril merely adopts current formulae and has no real appreciation of the post-Arian developments in Antioch.
188. Cyril, *Dialogues sur la Trinité*, ed. G. M. de Durand (SC 231, 237, 246), 1976–8.
189. Liébaert, op. cit., ch. 3.
190. *S. Cyrilli Alexandrini De Recta Fide ad Imperatorem etc.*, ed. P. E. Pusey, Oxford 1877.
191. *Deux dialogues christologiques*, ed. G. M. de Durand (SC 97), 1964; see Introduction.
192. G. L. Prestige, *Fathers and Heretics*, London and New York 1940, develops this point on p. 156.
193. W. J. Burghardt, *The Image of God in Man according to Cyril of Alexandria*, Washington 1957, develops a number of points of difference between Cyril and his great predecessor.
194. Liébaert, op. cit., 117, 172 ff., 179.

195. S. *Cyrilli Alexandrini in Joannem commentaria,* ed. P. E. Pusey, 3 vols., Oxford 1872.

196. See M. F. Wiles, *The Spiritual Gospel,* for further development of this and the following points, especially 32 ff.

197. The opening of Book II.5 contains this particular explanation. Cyril is discussing the story of the Samaritan woman.

198. Liébaert, op. cit.

199. On John 11.33; 13.21; 6.38 (Pusey II.280, II.363, I.487).

200. M. F. Wiles, op. cit., p. 138.

201. Du Manoir, art. cit. (n. 164 above), 155 ff.

202. S. *Cyrilli Alexandriae archiepiscopi Commentarii in Lucae evangelium quae supersunt syriace e manuscriptis apud Museum Britannicum,* ed. R. Payne Smith, Oxford 1858; ET, *A Commentary upon the Gospel according to St Luke by St Cyril, Patriarch of Alexandria,* 2 vols., Oxford 1859. Greek homilies in PG 77.

203. S. *Cyrilli Alexandrini commentarii in Lucam* I, ed. J. B. Chabot, CSCO 140 (Syriac 70), Paris and Leipzig 1912; reprinted with Latin trs. by R. M. Tonneau, 2 vols., Louvain 1953–4.

204. *Homiliae paschales:* text, PG 77.

205. For details, consult the Patrologies and the *Clavis Patrum.*

206. The text of the most important of these is found in S. *Cyrilli Alexandrini epistolae tres oecumenicae,* Oxford 1875, and S. *Cyrilli Alexandrini de recta fide, etc.* Oxford 1877, both ed. P. E. Pusey. The most recent and best text for the majority of them is to be found in Schwartz, *ACO.* See also *Deux dialogues christologiques* (n. 191 above).

207. Fragments in *In Ioannem Commentaria,* ed. Pusey, vol. III.

208. M. Richard, 'Les traités de Cyrille d'Alexandrie contre Diodore et Théodore et les fragments dogmatiques de Diodore de Tarse', *Mélanges F. Grat I,* Paris 1946, 99–116; republished in M. Richard, *Opera Minora* II, Louvain 1977.

209. For the text of the *Letters to Succensus* see Schwartz, *ACO* I.i.6, 151–62.

210. Liébaert, op. cit., 78.

211. H. Chadwick, 'Eucharist and Christology in the Nestorian Controversy', *JTS* NS 2, 1951, 145–64, attributes Cyril's opposition to dualism in his early writings to an already existing tradition in Alexandria.

212. J. Liébaert, 'L'évolution de la christologie de S. Cyrille d'Alexandrie à partir de la controverse nestorienne. La lettre paschale XVII et la lettre aux Moines (428–9)', *Mélanges de Science Religieuse* 27, 1970, 27–48.

213. P. Galtier, 'Saint Cyrille et Apollinaire', *Gregorianum* 37, 1956, 584–609.

214. The texts will be found in H. Lietzmann, *Apollinaris von Laodicea und seine Schule,* Tübingen 1904.

215. A. Grillmeier, *Christ in Christian Tradition,* ET 1965, 400 ff. (2nd ed., 1975, 473 ff.).

216. R. A. Norris, 'Christological Models in Cyril of Alexandria', *StudPatr* 13, 1975, 255–68.

217. Cyril, *Quod unus sit Christus, Deux dialogues christologiques* (SC 97), 396.

218. Further discussion of the problems of Cyril's christology will be

found in H. Chadwick, art. cit. section III; and my article, 'A Reconsideration of Alexandrian Christology', *JEH* 22, 1971, 103–14.

219. This kind of statement is particularly common in Cyril's exegesis of the Epistle to the Hebrews, of which extensive fragments survive; see my article, 'Christological Ideas in the Greek Commentaries on the Epistle to the Hebrews', *JTS* NS 20, 1969, 150–63.

220. Cyril, *De recta fide ad Augustas* II.55 (PG 76.1413).

221. H. Chadwick, art. cit.

222. Cyril, *Against Julian*: text in PG 76.

223. Theodoret, *Ep.* 83.

224. R. M. Grant, 'Greek Literature in the Treatise *De Trinitate* and Cyril *Contra Iulianum*', *JTS* NS 15, 1964, 265–79.

225. Julian, *Against the Galilaeans*: text and translation of this reconstruction are conveniently available in the Loeb Classical Library, Julian, *Works* III, 1923.

226. These are surveyed in the recent book by William J. Malley, *Hellenism and Christianity* (Analecta Gregoriana 210), Rome 1979.

227. E.g. Theodoret, *Epp.* 81, 113, 116, 119 in SC II and III (see n. 247 below); also in PG 83 and NPNF.

228. *Epp.* 121, 122, 125.

229. *Epp.* 133–5, 138–41.

230. *Ep.* XLIII (SC I; the Roman numerals indicate those Epistles belonging to the shorter collection discovered by Sakkelion and published by him in 1885).

231. See above pp. 35 f.

232. P. Canivet, *Histoire d'une entreprise apologétique de Ve siècle*, Paris 1958, 25, n. 3.

233. *Ep.* 113; cf. 81.

234. *Ep.* 119.

235. See especially *Epp.* 42–47, but there are a number of others scattered about in the collections.

236. *Ep.* 113, to Pope Leo.

237. R. V. Sellers, *The Council of Chalcedon*, London 1953, 14 f. Some vehement denunciations of Cyril immediately after the council have been preserved in the *Acta*.

238. *Ep.* XIV.

239. *Epp.* 3, 12, 16.

240. *Ep.* 180.

241. *Ep.* 60.

242. *Ep.* 83.

243. *Epp.* 79–82.

244. *Ep.* 119.

245. *Ep.* 122.

246. E. Honigmann, 'Theodoret of Cyrrhus and Basil of Seleucia. The Time of Their Death', *Patristic Studies* (Studi e Testi 173), Rome 1953, 174–84.

247. Theodoret, *Correspondence*, ed. Y. Azéma, 3 vols. (SC 40, 98, 111), 1955, 1964–5.

248. M. M. Wagner, 'A Chapter in Byzantine Epistolography', *Dumbarton Oaks Papers* 4, 1948, 119–81.

249. *Ep.* XXXVI.

250. *Epp.* 77–78.

251. *Epp.* XXIII, 29–35, 52, 53.

252. The range of views is summarized by M. Mandac, 'L'Union christologique dans les oeuvres de Théodoret anterieures au concile d'Ephèse', *Ephemerides Theologicae Lovanienses* 47, 1971, 64–96.

253. *Die Cyrill von Alexandrien zugeschriebene Schrift περὶ τῆς τοῦ κυρίου ἐνανθρωπήσεως; ein Werk Theodorets von Cyrus*, ed. A. Ehrhard, Tübingen 1888. See J. Lebon, 'Restitutions a Théodoret de Cyr', *Revue d'Histoire Ecclésiastique* 26, 1930, 524–50. The text of these works will be found in PG 75 (i.e., attributed to Cyril).

254. *Ep.* 133 and Schwartz, *ACO* I.4, p. 85.

255. *Expositio rectae fidei*, text in J. T. C. Otto, *Corpus Apologetarum Christianorum saeculi secundi*, vol. 4, Jena 1880.

256. Lebon, art. cit.; R. V. Sellers, 'Pseudo-Justin's *Expositio Rectae Fidei*, a Work of Theodoret' *JTS* 46, 1945, 145–60.

257. M. Richard, 'L'activité litteraire de Théodoret avant le concile d'Ephèse', *Revue des Sciences Philosophiques et Théologiques* 24, 1935, 83–106; republished in *Opera Minora* II, Louvain 1977. M. F. A. Brok, 'The Date of Theodoret's *Expositio Rectae Fidei*', *JTS* NS 2, 1951, 178–83.

258. M. Richard, 'Notes sur l'évolution doctrinale de Théodoret', ibid., 25, 1936, 459–81; republished in *Opera Minora* II.

259. P. M. Parvis, *Theodoret's Commentary on the Epistles of St Paul*, Oxford University D.Phil. thesis, 1975, unpublished; he explores this question on pp. 293–307.

260. A. Gesché, *La christologie du 'Commentaire sur les Psaumes' découvert à Toura*, Gembloux 1962, 67 ff.; and G. M. de Durand's Introduction to Cyril's *Deux dialogues christologiques* (SC 97), 1964.

261. K. McNamara, 'Theodoret of Cyrus and the Unity of Person in Christ', *Irish Theological Quarterly* 22, 1955, 313–28.

262. M. Mandac, art, cit.

263. For Theodoret's soteriology, and its relationship to his christology, see G. Koch, *Strukturen und Geschichte des Heils in der Theologie des Theodoret von Kyros*, Frankfurt 1974.

264. For the critical details in this paragraph, I am indebted to G. H. Ettlinger's Introduction to his edition of the *Eranistes*, Oxford 1975.

265. The text of Theodoret's biblical works will be found in PG 80–82. The only recent edition is A. Möhle, *Theodoret von Kyros. Kommentar zu Jesaia*, Berlin 1932.

266. See above p. 37. On the date and form of Theodoret's commentaries I follow P. M. Parvis's Oxford thesis (n. 259 above). I am most grateful for the loan of this excellent study.

267. H. B. Swete, *Theodori Episcopi Mopsuesteni in epistolas B. Pauli commentarii*, Cambridge 1880–82, assumes that gaps in Theodore's work can be filled by referring to Theodoret.

268. G. W. Ashby, *Theodoret of Cyrrhus as Exegete of the Old Testament*, Grahamstown 1972; P. M. Parvis, op. cit. I am indebted to these studies for the following paragraphs.

269. Rowan A. Greer, *The Captain of our Salvation*, Tübingen 1973, 296.

270. P. M. Parvis, op. cit., 204.

271. *Epp.* 82, 113, 116.

272. There has been considerable discussion as to how rigidly these indications of date can be interpreted, and what precisely they indicate in terms of the relative dating of Theodoret's works; see Richard, 'L'activité litteraire . . .' (see n. 257 above), Canivet, op. cit. (n. 232 above), and articles in Patrologies and Encyclopedias, e.g. Bardy's article on Theodoret in the *Dictionnaire de Théologie Catholique*, and most recently G. F. Chesnut, 'The Date of Composition of Theodoret's Church History', *VC* 35, 1981, 245–52.

Bibliographies

Introductory Note
A conventional *Patrology* is a reference book, whose value lies substantially in its capacity to act as a bibliographical source. The following pages embrace that role. However, the fact that there are a number of conventional Patrologies now available in English, notably J. Quasten's three-volume work, has been taken into account in drawing up the following lists, whose aim is to supplement rather than supplant. Thus no attempt has been made to give complete bibliographies, but two partially overlapping lists with quite different purposes have been compiled.

Bibliography A assembles relevant material which is available in *English*, and is intended to aid those students who cannot cope with literature in a foreign tongue, and therefore find the conventional Patrology somewhat daunting.

Bibliography B is intended for the more specialized student, and assembles material published since 1960, thus updating Quasten for those subjects covered in this volume. The lists include critical texts in the original languages, publications in English, French and German, and an occasional work in some other European language where it seemed indispensable, or contained a useful English summary.

For the most part, the listing of general works has not been undertaken. There are, of course, many books and articles which concentrate on topics and in the process range over substantial ground in terms of source-material. A selection of such works is offered in the Bibliography for Chapter 5, particularly works relating to doctrine, christology and biblical exegesis. No attempt has been made to provide a complete list, but the student will be alerted to some important or interesting contributions.

The user of **Bibliography B** should also be alerted to other important bibliographical sources and reference works. The most important is the *Clavis Patrum Graecorum* being prepared for the *Corpus Christianorum Series Graeca* by M. Geerard. Volumes II and III (Turnhout 1974, 1979), which list the works of all those subjects treated in this book and many more besides, are already available. This is indispensable for locating critical texts and distinguishing the authentic material from the spurious. Additional bibliographical sources for relevant secondary literature include *Bibliographia Patristica*, ed. W. Schneemelcher, (Leiden 1959 ff): this is extremely comprehensive, but constantly behind the times – for example, Band 16–17 which covered the years 1971–2 appeared in 1978; more immediately up-to-date are the bibliographies published regularly in the *Revue d'Histoire Ecclésiastique*. Other useful reference books include the *Dictionnaire de Théologie Catholique*, the *Dictionnaire d'Archéologie Chrétienne et de Liturgie*, the *Dictionnaire d'Histoire et de Géographie Ecclésiastique* and the *Dictionnaire de Spiritualité*, not to mention Pauly-Wissowa, *Realencyclopädie der klassischen Altertumswissenschaft*, and the *Reallexikon für Antike und Christentum*. To this list, there should now be added the sizable encyclopedia in process of publication under the title, *Aufsteig und Niedergang der Römischen Welt*, Berlin 1972 ff. Teil II Bd. 16–28 will cover religion under the Empire. Volumes so far published are Bd. 16: Heidentum: Römische Religion, Allgemeines, 1978; Bd. 17: Heidentum: Römische Götterkulte, Orientalische Kulte in de römischen Welt, 1981; Bd. 19: Judentum: Allgemeines; Palästinischen Judentum, 1979; Bd. 23: Vorkonstantinisches Christentum: Verhältnis zu römischem Staat und heidnischer Religion, 1979–80.

The critical texts listed in Bibliography B frequently belong to series which contain other material published pre-1960. Occasionally these have been listed for reasons of completeness (e.g. in the case of the Jaeger edition of Gregory of Nyssa); but the student is reminded that earlier volumes of series (e.g. pre-1960 publications in GCS – *Die griechischen christlichen Schriftsteller* (Leipzig and Berlin 1897 ff.) can be traced in the older Patrologies like Quasten. The student interested in textual matters may indeed like to consult J. Irmscher and K. Treu, *Das Korpus der griechischen christlichen Schriftsteller. Historie, Gegenwart, Zukunft* (Berlin 1977). This series, and others like the *Corpus Christianorum* and *Sources Chrétiennes*, are constantly expanding, and a supplementary list is appended to the Bibliography alerting the reader to new critical texts already promised, which may indeed be published by the time this volume reaches his hands. For an up-to-date survey of patristic research, see 'Literature of Christian Antiquity 1975–79' by W. J. Burghardt in *Theological Studies* 41 (1980) 151–80.

Within each section of each Bibliography, items are listed in order of publication. Daggered items (†) are references derived from second-hand sources which I have not succeeded in obtaining and checking myself.

BIBLIOGRAPHY A

Works in English only. The list is somewhat selective, and a few more recent specialist items not mentioned here can be traced in Bibliography B.

CHAPTER 1

1. *General Books*

F. J. Foakes-Jackson, *A History of Church History*, Cambridge 1939.

K. M. Setton, *Christian Attitude towards the Emperor in the Fourth Century*, New York and London 1941.

A. H. M. Jones, *Constantine and the Conversion of Europe*, London 1948, New York 1949.

J. N. D. Kelly, *Early Christian Creeds*, London and Toronto 1950.

R. L. P. Milburn, *Early Christian Interpretations of History*, London and New York 1954.

Peter Brown, *The World of Late Antiquity*, London and New York 1971.

G. F. Chesnut, *The First Christian Histories*, Paris 1977.

Books on Monasticism

W. H. McKean, *Christian Monasticism in Egypt*, London and New York 1920.

E. E. Malone, *The Monk and the Martyr*, Washington 1950.

A. Vööbus, *A History of Asceticism in the Syrian Orient*, 2 vols., Louvain 1960.

E. R. Hardy, *Christian Egypt*, Oxford 1962.

Derwas Chitty, *The Desert a City*, Oxford 1966.

A. Louth, *The Origins of the Christian Mystical Tradition*, Oxford and New York 1981.

General Articles

N. H. Baynes, 'Constantine the Great and the Christian Church' *Proceedings of the British Academy* 15, 1929, 341–442.

A. Momigliano, 'Pagan and Christian Historiography in the Fourth Century AD', in *The Conflict of Paganism and Christianity in the Fourth Century*, ed. Momigliano, Oxford and New York 1963, 79–99, reprinted in his *Essays in Ancient and Modern Historiography*, Oxford and Middletown, Conn. 1977, 107–26.

G. Downey, 'The Perspective of the Early Church Historians', *Greek, Roman and Byzantine Studies* 6, 1965, 57–70.

R. A. Markus, 'Church History and the Early Church Historians', in *The Materials, Sources and Methods of Ecclesiastical History*, ed. D. A. Baker (Studies in Church History 11), Oxford 1975, 1–17.

Peter Brown, 'The Rise and Function of the Holy Man in Late Antiquity', *JRS* 61, 1971, 80–101.

Robert Murray, 'The Features of the Earliest Christian Asceticism', in *Christian Spirituality*, Essays in honour of Gordon Rupp, ed. Peter Brooks, London 1975, 63–77.

2. Eusebius of Caesarea

Translations

On the Theophaneia, trs. S. Lee, Cambridge 1843.

Eusebii Pamphili Evangelicae Praeparationis Libri XV, ed. and trs. E. H. Gifford, 4 vols. in 5, Oxford 1903.

Contra Hieroclem is contained in Philostratus, *Life of Apollonius of Tyana*, trs. F. C. Conybeare, LCL 1912.

The Proof of the Gospel (Demonstratio Evangelica), trs. W. J. Ferrer, 2 vols., London and New York 1920.

Ecclesiastical History, trs. K. Lake (with Greek text), 2 vols., LCL 1926, 1932.

Ecclesiastical History and Martyrs of Palestine, trs., introd. and notes by H. J. Lawlor and J. E. L. Oulton, 2 vols., London and New York 1927–8.

The History of the Church from Christ to Constantine, trs. G. Williamson (Pelican), Harmondsworth 1965, New York 1966.

In Praise of Constantine: A Historical Study and New Translation of Eusebius' Tricennial Orations by H. A. Drake, Berkeley 1976.

Church History, Life of Constantine and *Oration in Praise of Constantine*, NPNF II.I, reprinted 1979.

Books

H. J. Lawlor, *Eusebiana*. Essays on the *Ecclesiastical History* of Eusebius, New York 1912.

J. Stevenson, *Studies in Eusebius*, Cambridge and New York 1929.

F. J. Foakes-Jackson, *Eusebius Pamphili. Bishop of Caesarea and First Christian Historian. A Study of the Man and his Writings*, Cambridge 1933.

K. M. Setton, *Christian Attitude towards the Emperor in the Fourth Century*, New York and London 1941.

D. S. Wallace-Hadrill, *Eusebius of Caesarea*, London 1960.

H. von Campenhausen, *The Fathers of the Greek Church*, ET, New York 1959, London 1963, ch. V.

H. A. Drake, op. cit. (a good study as well as translation of the *Laus*).

C. Luibheid, *Eusebius of Caesarea and the Arian Crisis*, Dublin 1978.

A. A. Mosshammer, *The Chronicle of Eusebius and Greek Chronographic Tradition*, Lewisburg, Pa. 1979.

R. M. Grant, *Eusebius as Church Historian*, Oxford and New York 1980.

T. D. Barnes, *Constantine and Eusebius*, Cambridge, Mass. 1981.

Alistair Kee, *Constantine versus Christ*, London 1982.

Articles

H. J. Lawlor, 'The Chronology of Eusebius', *Classical Quarterly* 19, 1925, 94–101.

N. H. Baynes, 'Eusebius and the Christian Empire' in *Mélanges Bidez*, Brussels 1934, 13–18.

W. Seston, 'Constantine as Bishop', *JRS* 37, 1947, 127–31.

F. E. Cranz, 'Kingdom and Polity in Eusebius of Caesarea', *Harvard Theological Review* 45, 1952, 47–66.

A. H. M. Jones, 'Notes on the Genuineness of the Constantinian Documents in Eusebius' *Life of Constantine*', *JEH* 5, 1954, 196–200.

M. Miller, 'Archaic Literary Chronography', *Journal of Hellenic Studies* 75, 1955, 54–8.

D. S. Wallace-Hadrill, 'The Eusebian Chronicle. The Extent and Date of Composition of its Early Editions', *JTS* NS 6, 1955, 248–53.

W. Telfer, 'The Author's Purpose in the *Vita Constantini*', *StudPatr* 1, 1957, 157–67.

B. Gustafsson, 'Eusebius' Principles in Handling his Sources, as found in his *Church History* Books I–VIII' *StudPatr* 4, 1961, 429–41.

C. U. Wolf, 'Eusebius of Caesarea and the *Onomasticon*', *The Biblical Archaeologist* 27, 1964, 66–96.

R. H. Storch, 'The "Eusebian Constantine",' *Church History* 40, 1971, 145–55.

G. C. Stead, 'Eusebius and the Council of Nicaea', *JTS* NS 24, 1973, 85–100.

R. M. Grant, 'The Case against Eusebius, or Did the Father of Church History write history?', *StudPatr* 12, 1975, 413–21.

J. E. Bruns, 'The "Agreement of Moses and Jesus" in the *Demonstratio Evangelica* of Eusebius', *VC* 31, 1977, 117–25.

L. W. Barnard, 'Bede and Eusebius as Church Historians', in *Studies in Church History and Patristics* (*ΑΝΑΛΕΚΤΑ ΒΛΑΤΑΔΩΝ* 26), Thessaloniki 1978, 354–72.

S. Gero, 'The True Image of Christ: Eusebius' Letter to Constantia Reconsidered', *JTS* NS 32, 1981, 460–70.

3. **Socrates and Sozomen**

Translation

Ecclesiastical History, NPNF II.II, reprinted 1976.

4. **Theodoret**

See chapter 5.

5. **The Monastic Literature**

Translations

The Desert Fathers, ET with introd. by Helen Waddell, London and New York 1936.

Palladius, *The Lausiac History,* trs. R. T. Meyer (ACW 34), 1965.

The Wisdom of the Desert: Sayings from the Desert Fathers of the Fourth Century, sel. and trs. by T. Merton, Norfolk, Conn. 1960, London 1961.

The Sayings of the Desert Fathers, trs. Benedicta Ward, London 1975.

The Wisdom of the Desert Fathers, trs. Benedicta Ward, Oxford 1975.

Articles

C. Butler, Introd. and notes to Palladius, *The Lausiac History* (Texts and Studies 6), Cambridge 1904.

— 'Palladiana', *JTS* 22, 1921, 21–35, 138–55, 222–38.

P. R. Coleman-Norton, 'The Authorship of the *Epistola de Indicis gentibus et de Bragmanibus*', *Classical Philology* 21, 1926, 154–60.

W. Telfer, 'The Trustworthiness of Palladius', *JTS* 38, 1937, 379–83.

D. Chitty, 'Dom Cuthbert Butler and the Lausiac History', *JTS* NS 6, 1955, 239–58.

R. T. Meyer, 'Proverbs and Puns in Palladius' *Historia Lausiaca*', *StudPatr* 8, 1966, 420–23.

— 'Palladius and Early Christian Spirituality', *StudPatr* 10, 1970, 379–90.

— 'Lectio Divina in Palladius' in *Kyriakon*: Festschrift J. Quasten, Münster 1970, vol. I, 380–4.

E. D. Hunt, 'Palladius of Helenopolis: A Party and its Supporters in the Church of the Late Fourth Century', *JTS* NS 24, 1973, 456–80.

R. T. Meyer, 'Palladius and the Study of Scripture', *StudPatr* 13, 1975, 487–90.

D. F. Buck, 'The Structure of the *Lausiac History*', *Byzantion* 46, 1976, 292–307.

D. J. Chitty, 'The Books of the Old Men', *Eastern Churches Review* 6, 1974, 15–21.

L. Regnault, 'The Beatitudes in the Apophthegmata Patrum', ibid., 22–43.

J. C. Guy, 'Educational Innovation in the Desert Fathers', ibid., 44–51 (and other articles in that volume).

L. W. Barnard, 'Early Syriac Christianity', *VC* 22, 1968, 161–75.

S. P. Brock, 'Early Syrian Asceticism', *Numen* 20, 1973, 1–19.

R. Murray, 'The Features of the Earliest Christian Asceticism', in *Christian Spirituality*, Essays in Honour of Gordon Rupp, ed. Peter Brooks, London 1975, 63–77.

CHAPTER 2

1. Arius

Translation

The Trinitarian Controversy, ed. and trs. W. G. Rusch (Sources of Early Christian Thought), Philadelphia 1980.

Books

H. Gwatkin, *Studies of Arianism*, Cambridge 1890.

R. Gregg and D. Groh, *Early Arianism: a View of Salvation*, London and Philadelphia 1981.

Articles

W. E. Barnes, 'Arius and Arianism', *Expository Times* 46, 1934, 18–24.

W. Telfer, 'Arius takes refuge at Nicomedia', *JTS* 37, 1936, 60–63.

— 'When did the Arian Controversy begin?' *JTS* 47, 1946, 129–42.

N. H. Baynes, 'Sozomen, *Ecclesiastica Historia* I.15' *JTS* 49, 1948, 165–8.

W. Telfer, 'Sozomen I.15. A Reply', *JTS* 50, 1949, 187–91.

T. E. Pollard, 'The Origins of Arianism', *JTS* NS 9, 1958, 103–11.

H. A. Wolfson, 'Philosophical Implications of Arianism and Apollinarianism', *Dumbarton Oaks Papers* 12, 1958, 3–28.

W. P. Haugaard, 'Arius: Twice a heretic?', *Church History* 29, 1960, 251–63.

M. F. Wiles, 'In Defence of Arius', *JTS* NS 13, 1962, 339–47, republished in *Working Papers in Doctrine*, London 1976, 28–37.

G. C. Stead, 'The Platonism of Arius', *JTS* NS 15, 1964, 16–31.

L. W. Barnard, 'The Antecedents of Arius', *VC* 24, 1970, 172–88, republished in *Studies in Church History and Patristics* (*ANAΛEKTA BΛATAΔΩN* 26), Thessaloniki 1978, 295–311.

— 'What was Arius' Philosophy?', *Theologische Zeitschrift* 28, 1972, 110–17, republished ibid., 289–95.

R. C. Gregg and D. E. Groh, 'The Centrality of Soteriology in Early Arianism', *Anglican Theological Review* 59, 1977, 260–78.

C. Luibheid, 'Finding Arius', *Irish Theological Quarterly* 45, 1978, 81–100.

G. C. Stead, 'The *Thalia* of Arius and the Testimony of Athanasius', *JTS* NS 29, 1978, 20–52.

2. Athanasius

Translations

All the works discussed here are in NPNF II.IV, reprinted 1978, except the four *Letters to Serapion*, for which see *The Letters of St Athanasius concerning the Holy Spirit*, trs. C. R. B. Shapland, London and New York 1951.

More recent translations include:

The Life of Antony, trs. R. W. Meyer (ACW 10), 1950.
The Incarnation of the Word of God (*De incarnatione*) trs. by a religious of CSMV, London 1953.
Contra gentes and *De incarnatione*, ed. and trs. R. W. Thompson (Oxford Early Christian Texts), Oxford 1971.

Books

G. L. Prestige, *Fathers and Heretics*, London and New York 1940, ch. IV.
K. M. Setton, *Christian Attitude towards the Emperor in the Fourth Century*, New York and London 1941, ch. IV.
F. L. Cross, *The Study of St Athanasius*, Oxford 1945.
E. E. Malone, *The Monk and the Martyr*, Washington 1950, ch. III.
J. Pelikan, *The Light of the World*, New York 1962.
H. von Campenhausen, *The Fathers of the Greek Church*, ET New York 1959, London 1963, ch. VI.
E. P. Meijering, *Orthodoxy and Platonism in Athanasius*, Leiden 1968.
A. Louth, *The Origins of the Christian Mystical Tradition*, Oxford and New York 1981, ch. V.

Articles

N. H. Baynes, 'St Antony and the Demons', *Journal of Egyptian Archaeology* 40, 1954, 7–10.
T. E. Pollard, 'Logos and Son in Origen, Arius and Athanasius', *StudPatr* 2, 1957, 282–7.
H. Nordberg, 'A Reconsideration of the Date of Athanasius' *Contra Gentes* and *De Incarnatione*', *StudPatr* 3, 1961, 262–6.
R. Weijenborg, 'Apollinaristic Interpolations in the *Tomus ad Antiochenos* of 362', *StudPatr* 3, 1961, 324–30.
G. Florovsky, 'The Concept of Creation in St Athanasius', *StudPatr* 6, 1962, 36–57.
T. F. Torrance, 'Spiritus Creator. A Consideration of the Teaching of St Athanasius and St Basil', in his *Theology in Reconstruction* , London 1965, 209–28.
A. Louth, 'Reason and Revelation in St Athanasius', *SJT* 23, 1970, 385–96.
J. A. B. Holland, 'Athanasius versus Arius : What now?', *Reformed Theological Review* 28, 1969, 16–27.
— 'Athanasius and Arius II: Why the Impulse to Reduce?', ibid. 30, 1971, 33–47.
— 'III. The Solution of Athanasius', ibid. 30, 1971, 69–78.
— 'The Implications of Athansius for Us', ibid. 31, 1972, 1–9.
F. M. Young, 'A Reconsideration of Alexandrian Christology', *JEH* 22, 1971, 103–14.
J. Breckenridge, 'Julian and Athanasius; Two Approaches to Creation and Salvation', *Theology* 76, 1973, 73–81.

C. Kannengiesser, 'Athanasius of Alexandria and the Foundation of Traditional Christology', *Theological Studies* 34, 1973, 103–13.

L. W. Barnard, 'The Date of Athanasius' *Vita Antonii'*, VC 28, 1974, 169–75.

T. C. Campbell, 'The Doctrine of the Holy Spirit in the Theology of Athanasius', *SJT* 27, 1974, 408–40.

W. H. C. Frend, 'Athanasius as an Egyptian Christian Leader in the Fourth Century', in his collected studies, *Religion Popular and Unpopular in the early Christian Centuries*, London 1976.

L. W. Barnard, 'Athanasius and the Meletian schism in Egypt', *Journal of Egyptian Archaeology* 59, 1975, 183–9.

A. Louth, 'The Concept of the Soul in Athanasius' *Contra Gentiles – De Incarnatione'*, StudPatr 13, 1975, 227–31.

T. F. Torrance, 'Athanasius. A Study in the Foundations of Classical Theology', in his *Theology in Reconciliation*, London and Grand Rapids, Mich. 1975, 215–66.

J. C. M. van Winden, 'On the Date of Athanasius' Apologetical Treatises', *VC* 29, 1975, 291–5.

B. R. Brennan, 'Dating Athanasius' *Vita Antonii' VC* 30, 1976, 52–4.

G. C. Stead, 'Rhetorical Method in Athanasius', *VC* 30, 1976, 121–37.

F. S. Clarke, 'Lost and Found: Athanasius' Doctrine of Predestination', *SJT* 29, 1976, 435–50.

J. D. McCoy, 'Philosophical Influences on the Doctrine of the Incarnation in Athanasius and Cyril of Alexandria', *Encounter* (Indianapolis) 38, 1977, 362–91.

L. W. Barnard, 'Athanasius and the Roman State', *Latomus* 36, 1977, 422–37; republished in *Studies in Church History and Patristics* (*ANAΛEKTA BΛATAΔΩN* 26), Thessaloniki 1978, 312–28.

3. Didymus the Blind

Unfortunately none of the works of Didymus are available in English, and hardly any studies.

W. J. Gauche, *Didymus the Blind, an Educator of the Fourth Century*, Washington 1934.

Articles bearing on Didymus' christology:

M. F. Wiles, 'The Nature of the Early Debate about Christ's Human Soul', *JEH* 16, 1965, 139–51.

F. M. Young, 'A Reconsideration of Alexandrian Christology', *JEH* 22, 1971, 103–14.

CHAPTER 3

General article

Brooks Otis, 'Cappadocian Thought as a Coherent System', *Dumbarton Oaks Papers* 12, 1958, 95–124.

1. **Basil of Caesarea**

Translations

Ascetical Works, trs. W. K. L. Clarke, London 1925.

Letters, trs. R. J. Deferrari, 4 vols., LCL 1926–39 (vol. IV includes the *Address to Young Men on how they might Derive Benefit from Greek Literature.*

Ascetical Works, trs. M. M. Wagner (Fathers of the Church), Washington 1950.

Letters, trs. A. C. Way, 2 vols. (Fathers of the Church), Washington 1951–5.

Letters exchanged between Basil and Apollinarius, trs. G. L. Prestige, in his *St Basil the Great and Apollinarius of Laodicea*, ed. H. Chadwick, London 1956.

Exegetic Homilies, trs, A. C. Way (Fathers of the Church), Washington 1963.

On the Spirit, Hexaemeron, and *Letters*, NPNF II. VIII, reprinted 1978.

Books

E. F. Morison, *St Basil and his Rule*, Oxford and New York 1912.

W. K. L. Clarke, *St Basil the Great. A Study in Monasticism*, Cambridge 1913, New York 1914.

L. V. Jacks, *St Basil and Greek Literature*, Washington 1922.

M. Murphy, *St Basil and Monasticism*, Washington 1930.

M. M. Fox, *The Life and Times of St Basil the Great as Revealed in his Works*, Washington 1939.

H. von Campenhausen, *The Fathers of the Greek Church*, ET New York 1959, London 1963, ch.VII.

E. Amand de Mendieta, *The Unwritten and Secret Apostolic Tradition in the Theological Thought of St Basil of Caesarea* (SJT Occasional Papers 13), Edinburgh 1965.

M. Orphanos, *Creation and Salvation according to St Basil of Caesarea*, Athens 1975.

P. J. Fedwick, *The Church and the Charisma of Leadership in Basil of Caesarea*, Toronto 1979.

Eric Osborn, *Ethical Patterns in Early Christian Thought*, Cambridge and New York 1976, ch.3.

T. A. Kopecek, *A History of Neo-Arianism*, 2 vols. (Patristic Monograph Series 8), Cambridge, Mass. 1979.

Articles

J. F. Callahan, 'Greek Philosophy and the Cappadocian Cosmology', *Dumbarton Oaks Papers* 12, 1958, 29–57.

E. Amand de Mendieta, 'The Pair $K\acute{\eta}\rho\upsilon\gamma\mu\alpha$ and $\Delta\acute{o}\gamma\mu\alpha$ in the Theological Thought of St Basil of Caesarea' *JTS* NS 16, 1965, 129–42.

T. F. Torrance, 'Spiritus Creator. A Consideration of the Teaching of St.

Athanasius and St Basil', in his *Theology in Reconstruction*, London 1965, Grand Rapids, Mich. 1966, 209–28.

R. P. C. Hanson, 'Basil's Doctrine of Tradition in Relation to the Holy Spirit', *VC* 22, 1968, 241–55.

A. Moffatt, 'The Occasion of Basil's Address to Young Men', *Antichthon* 6, 1972, 74–86.

M. Aghiorgoussis, 'Image as "sign" (semeion) of God: Knowledge of God through the Images According to St Basil' (trans. N. Pissare) *Greek Orthodox Theological Review* 21, 1976, 19–54.

—'Applications of the Theme "Eikon Theou" (Image of God) According to St Basil', ibid. 265–88.

E. Amand de Mendieta, 'The official attitude of Basil of Caesarea as a Christian Bishop towards Greek Philosophy and Science' in *The Orthodox Churches and the West*, ed. D. A. Baker (Studies in Church History 13), Oxford 1976, 25–50.

F. X. Murphy, 'Moral and Ascetical Doctrine in St Basil', *StudPatr* 14, 1976, 320–36.

Charles A. Frazee, 'Anatolian Asceticism in the Fourth Century: Eustathius of Sebasteia and Basil of Caesarea', *Catholic Historical Review* 66, 1980, 16–33.

D. J. Geanakoplos, 'St Basil, "Christian Humanist" of the "Three Hierarchs" and Patron Saint of Greek Letters', *Greek Orthodox Theological Review* 25, 1980, 94–102.

J. T. Lienhard, 'St Basil's *Asceticon Parva* and the *Regula Benedicti*', *Studia Monastica* 22, 1980, 231–42.

D. J. Constantelos, 'Basil the Great's Social Thought and Involvement', *Greek Orthodox Theological Review* 26, 1981, 81–6.

Sherman Garnett, 'The Christian Young and the Secular World: St Basil on Pagan Literature', *Greek Orthodox Theological Review* 26, 1981, 211–23.

L. J. Swift, 'Basil and Ambrose on the Six Days of Creation', *Augustinianum* 21, 1981, 317–28.

2. Gregory of Nazianzus

Translations

5 *Theological Orations* and 3 *Letters on Apollinarianism* in *The Christology of the Later Fathers*, ed. E. R. Hardy (Library of Christian Classics 3), London and Philadelphia 1954 (reprinted from NPNF).

Selected Orations and *Letters*, NPNF II.VII, reprinted 1978.

Books

H. von Campenhausen, *The Fathers of the Greek Church*, ET New York 1959, London 1963, ch. VIII.

R. Ruether, *Gregory of Nazianzus: Rhetor and Philosopher*, Oxford 1969.

D. F. Winslow, *The Dynamics of Salvation*, Cambridge, Mass. 1979.

Articles

B. Otis, 'The Throne and the Mountain: An Essay on St Gregory Nazianzus', *Classical Journal* 56, 1961, 146–65.
A. Musurillo, 'The Poetry of Gregory of Nazianzus', *Thought* 45, 1970, 45–55.
D. A. Sykes, 'The *Poemata Arcana* of St Gregory Nazianzen', *JTS* NS 21, 1970, 32–42.
E. P. Meijering, 'The Doctrine of the Will and of the Trinity in the Orations of Gregory of Nazianzus', in his *God Being History*, Amsterdam 1975, 103–13.
J. Egan, 'Gregory of Nazianzus and the Logos Doctrine', in *Word and Spirit*, ed. J. Plevnik, Willowdale, Ont. 1975, 281–322.
D. A. Sykes, 'The *Poemata Arcana* of St Gregory Nazianzen: Some Literary Questions', *Byzantinische Zeitschrift* 72, 1979, 6–15.

3. Gregory of Nyssa

Translations

Catechetical Oration, trs. J. H. Srawley, London 1917.
Catechetical Oration and *On Not Three Gods*, trs. C. C. Richardson in *The Christology of the Later Fathers*, ed. E. R. Hardy (Library of Christian Classics 3) London and Philadelphia 1954.
On the Lord's Prayer. On the Beatitudes, trs. H. C. Graef (ACW 18), 1954.
From Glory to Glory. Texts from Gregory of Nyssa's mystical writings, selected with introd. by J. Daniélou, trs. H. Musurillo, New York 1961, London 1962.
Ascetical Works, trs. V. W. Callahan (Fathers of the Church), Washington 1967.
The Life of Moses, trs. E. Ferguson and A. J. Malherbe (Classics of Western Spirituality), New York 1978.
Many of Gregory's works are translated in NPNF II.V, reprinted 1979.

Books

H. F. Cherniss, *The Platonism of Gregory of Nyssa*, Berkeley 1930.
T. A. Goggin, *The Times of St Gregory of Nyssa as Reflected in his Letters and the Contra Eunomium*, Washington 1947.
W. Jaeger, *Two Rediscovered Works of Ancient Christian Literature. Gregory of Nyssa and Macarius*, Leiden 1954.
H. von Campenhausen, *The Fathers of the Greek Church*, ET New York 1959, London 1963, ch. IX.
A. E. Dunstone, *The Atonement in Gregory of Nyssa*, London 1964.
D. Balas, *ΜΕΤΟΥΣΙΑ ΘΕΟΥ: Man's Participation in God's Perfections according to St Gregory of Nyssa*, Rome 1966.
R. Heine, *Perfection in the Virtuous Life*. A Study of the relationship

between edification and polemical theology in Gregory of Nyssa's *De Vita Moysis* (Patristic Monograph Series 2), Cambridge, Mass. 1975.

A. Louth, *The Origins of the Christian Mystical Tradition*, Oxford and New York 1981.

Articles

J. H. Srawley, 'St Gregory of Nyssa on the Sinlessness of Christ', *JTS* 7, 1906, 434–41.

J. T. Muckle, 'The Doctrine of Gregory of Nyssa on Man as the Image of God', *Mediaeval Studies* 7, 1945, 55–84.

A. H. Armstrong, 'Platonic Elements in St Gregory of Nyssa's Doctrine of Man', *Dominican Studies* 1, 1948, 113–26.

E. V. McClear, 'The Fall of Man and Original Sin in the Theology of Gregory of Nyssa', *Theological Studies* 9, 1948, 175–212.

M. M. Wagner, 'A Chapter in Byzantine Epistolography', *Dumbarton Oaks Papers* 4, 1948, 129–40.

M. E. Keenan, '*De Professione Christiana* and *De Perfectione*. A Study of the Ascetical Doctrine of St Gregory of Nyssa', ibid. 5, 1950, 167–207.

J. P. Cavernos, 'Gregory of Nyssa on the Nature of the Soul', *Greek Orthodox Theological Review* 1, 1955, 133–41.

G. B. Ladner, 'The Philosophical Anthropology of St Gregory of Nyssa', *Dumbarton Oaks Papers* 12, 1958, 59–94.

A. E. Dunstone, 'The Meaning of Grace in the Writings of Gregory of Nyssa', *SJT* 15, 1962, 235–44.

W. Telfer, 'The Birth of Christian Anthropology', *JTS* NS 13, 1962, 347–54.

J. E. Pfister, 'A Biographical Note: The Brothers and Sisters of St Gregory of Nyssa', *VC* 18, 1964, 108–13.

A. Philippou, 'The Doctrine of Evil in St Gregory of Nyssa', *StudPatr* 9, 1966, 251–6.

G. S. Bebis, 'Gregory Nyssen's "*De Vita Moysis*": A Philosophical and Theological Analysis', *Greek Orthodox Theological Review* 12, 1967, 369–93.

C. W. Macleod, '*ΑΝΑΛΥΣΙΣ*: A study in Ancient Mysticism', *JTS* NS 21, 1970, 43–55.

H. A. Wolfson, 'The Identification of Ex Nihilo with Emanation in Gregory of Nyssa', *Harvard Theological Review* 63, 1970, 53–60.

C. W. Macleod, 'Allegory and Mysticism in Origen and Gregory of Nyssa', *JTS* NS 22, 1971, 362–79.

R. S. Brightman, 'Apophatic Theology and Divine Infinity in St Gregory of Nyssa', *Greek Orthodox Theological Review* 18, 1973, 97–114.

E. Ferguson, 'God's Infinity and Man's Mutability: Perpetual Progress According to Gregory of Nyssa', ibid., 59–78.

— 'Progress in Perfection: Gregory of Nyssa's *Vita Moysis*', *StudPatr* 14, 1976, 307–14.

A. Meredith, 'Traditional Apologetic in the *Contra Eunomium* of Gregory of Nyssa', *StudPatr* 14, 1976, 315–19.

B. Otis, 'Gregory of Nyssa and the Cappadocian Conception of Time', *StudPatr* 14, 1976, 327–57.

E. Mühlenberg, 'Synergism in Gregory of Nyssa', *ZNW* 68, 1977, 93–122.

D. Balas, 'Plenitudo Humanitatis: The Unity of Human Nature in the Theology of Gregory of Nyssa', in *Disciplina Nostra* – Essays in memory of R. F. Evans, ed. D. F. Winslow (Patristic Monograph Series 6), Cambridge, Mass. 1979.

General Studies of the Cappadocians

H. Musurillo, 'History and Symbol. A Study of Form in Early Christian Literature', *Theological Studies* 18, 1957, 357–86.

J. F. Callahan, 'Greek Philosophy and the Cappadocian Cosmology', *Dumbarton Oaks Papers* 12, 1958, 31–57.

J. F. Mitchell, 'Consolatory Letters in Basil and Gregory of Nazianzus', *Hermes* 96, 1968, 299–318.

D. F. Winslow, 'Christology and Exegesis in the Cappadocians', *Church History* 40, 1971, 389–96.

T. A. Kopecek, 'The Social Class of the Cappadocian Fathers', ibid. 42, 1973, 453–66.

— 'The Cappadocian Fathers and Civic Patriotism', ibid. 43, 1974, 293–303.

R. C. Gregg, *Consolation Philosophy: Greek and Christian Paideia in Basil and the Two Gregories* (Patristic Monograph Series 3), Cambridge, Mass. 1975.

A. Meredith, 'Orthodoxy, Heresy and Philosophy in the Latter Half of the Fourth Century', *Heythrop Journal* 16, 1975, 5–21.

— 'Asceticism Christian and Greek', *JTS* 27, 1976, 313–32.

D. Balas, 'The Unity of Human Nature in Basil's and Gregory of Nyssa's Polemics against Eunomius', *StudPatr* 14, 1976, 275–81.

F. M. Young, 'The God of the Greeks and the Nature of Religious Language', in *Early Christian Literature and the Classical Intellectual Tradition* In honorem R. M. Grant, ed. W. R. Schoedel and R. L. Wilken, Paris 1979.

CHAPTER 4

1. Cyril of Jerusalem

Translations

Lectures on the Christian Sacraments (*Procatechesis* and 5 *Mystical Catecheses*), text ed. F. L. Cross, trs. R. W. Church (Texts for Students 51), London 1951.

Selections from the *Catechetical Lectures*, in *Cyril of Jerusalem and Nemesius of Emesa*, ed. W. Telfer (Library of Christian Classics 4), London and Philadelphia 1955.

Procatechesis and Catecheses 1–12, trs. L. P. McCauley and A. A. Stephenson (Fathers of the Church), Washington 1968.

Catecheses 13–18. Mystagogical Lectures. Sermon on the Paralytic. Letter to Constantine trs. L. P. McCauley and A. A. Stephenson (Fathers of the Church), Washington 1970.

Book

H. M. Riley, *Christian Initiation*. A comparative study of the interpretation of the baptismal liturgy in the mystagogical writings of Cyril of Jerusalem, John Chrysostom, Theodore of Mopsuestia and Ambrose of Milan, Washington 1974.

Articles

A. A. Stephenson, 'The Lenten Catechetical Syllabus in Fourth Century Jerusalem', *Theological Studies* 15, 1954, 103–14.

— 'St Cyril of Jerusalem and the Alexandrian Heritage', *Theological Studies* 15, 1954, 573–93.

— 'St Cyril of Jerusalem and the Alexandrian Christian Gnosis', *StudPatr* 1, 1957, 142–56.

C. Beukers, '"For our Emperors, Soldiers and Allies." An attempt at dating the 23rd Catechesis by Cyrillus of Jerusalem', *VC* 15, 1961, 177–84.

A. A. Stephenson, 'St Cyril of Jerusalem's Trinitarian Theology', *StudPatr* 11, 1972, 234–41.

E. J. Yarnold, '"Ideo et Romae fideles dicuntur qui baptizati sunt": a note on De Sacramentis 1.1', *JTS* NS 24, 1973, 202–7.

— 'Did Ambrose know the Mystagogical Catecheses of St Cyril of Jerusalem?', *StudPatr* 12, 1975, 184–9.

— 'The Authorship of the Mystagogical Catecheses attributed to Cyril of Jerusalem?', *Heythrop Journal* 19, 1978, 143–61.

2. Epiphanius of Salamis

Translations

De Gemmis, ed and trs. R. P. Blake and H. de Vis (Studies and Documents 2), London 1934.

Treatise on Weights and Measures, ed. and trs. J. E. Dean, Chicago and Cambridge 1935.

Article

S. Benko, 'The libertine Gnostic sect of the Phibionites according to Epiphanius', *VC* 21, 1967, 103–19.

3. John Chrysostom

Translations

Address on Vainglory and the Right Way for Parents to Bring Up Their Children, appended to M. L. W. Laistner, *Christianity and Pagan Culture in the Later Roman Empire*, New York and Oxford 1951.

Commentary on St John, trs. T. A. Goggin, 2 vols. (Fathers of the Church), New York 1957–60.

Chrysostom and his Message (selections from his sermons), trs. S. Neill, London 1962, New York 1963.

Baptismal Instructions, trs. P. W. Harkins (ACW 31), 1963.

Works, NPNF I.IX–XIV, reprinted 1975–79.

Discourses against Judaizing Christians, trs. P. W. Harkins (Fathers of the Church), Washington 1979.

Books

F. H. Chase, *Chrysostom. A Study in the History of Biblical Interpretation*, London 1887.

T. E. Ameringer, *The Stylistic Influence of the Second Sophistic on the Panegyrical Sermons of St John Chrysostom*, Washington 1921.

M. A. Burns, *Saint John Chrysostom's Homilies on the Statues*, Washington 1930.

K. M. Setton, *Christian Attitude towards the Emperor in the Fourth Century*, New York and London 1941.

D. Attwater, *St John Chrysostom*, London and Toronto 1959.

C. Baur, *John Chrysostom and his Time*, 2 vols., ET Westminster, Maryland and London 1959–60.

H. von Campenhausen, *The Fathers of the Greek Church*, ET New York 1959, London 1963, ch. XI.

H. M. Riley, *Christian Initiation*. A comparative study of the interpretation of the baptismal liturgy in the mystagogical writings of Cyril of Jerusalem, John Chrysostom, Theodore of Mopsuestia and Ambrose of Milan, Washington 1974.

Eric Osborn, *Ethical Patterns in Early Christian Thought*, Cambridge and New York 1976, ch. 4.

Articles

H. M. Hubbel, 'Chrysostom and Rhetoric', *Classical Philology* 19, 1924, 261–76.

P. R. Coleman-Norton, 'Saint John Chrysostom and the Greek Philosophers', *Classical Philology* 25, 1930, 305–17.

A. H. M. Jones, 'St John Chrysostom's Parentage and Education', *Harvard Theological Review* 46, 1953, 171–3.

G. M. Ettlinger, 'Some Historical Evidence for the Date of St John Chrysostom's Birth in the Treatise "Ad viduam iuniorem"', *Traditio* 16, 1960, 373–80.

A. Kenny, 'Was Chrysostom a Semi-Pelagian?', *Irish Theological Quarterly* 27, 1960, 16–29.

R. E. Carter, 'The Chronology of Saint John Chrysostom's Early Life', *Traditio* 18, 1962, 357–64.

P. W. Harkins, 'Pre-baptismal Rites in Chrysostom's Baptismal Catecheses', *StudPatr* 8, 1966, 219–38.

R. Hill, 'St. John Chrysostom's Teaching on Inspiration in "Six Homilies on Isaiah"', *VC* 22, 1968, 19–37.

R. E. Carter, 'The Future of Chrysostom Studies', *StudPatr* 10, 1970, 14–21.

P. W. Harkins, 'Chrysostom the Apologist. On the Divinity of Christ' in *Kyriakon*. Festschrift J. Quasten, ed. P. Granfield and J. A. Jungmann, Münster 1970, I, 441–51.

F. X. Murphy, 'The Moral Doctrine of St John Chrysostom', *StudPatr* 11, 1972, 52–7.

E. A. Clark, 'John Chrysostom and the *Subintroductae*', *Church History* 46, 1977, 171–85.

E. A. Clark, 'Sexual Politics in the Writings of John Chrysostom', *Anglican Theological Review* 59, 1977, 3–20.

4. Nemesius of Emesa

Translation

On the Nature of Man, selections in *Cyril of Jerusalem and Nemesius of Emesa*, ed. W. Telfer (Library of Christian Classics 4), London and Philadelphia 1955.

Articles

N.B. the useful introduction and commentary in Telfer, op. cit.

W. Telfer, 'The Birth of Christian Anthropology', *JTS* NS 13, 1962, 347–54.

L. W. Barnard, 'Father of Christian Anthropology', *ZNW* 63, 1972, 254–70.

5. Synesius of Cyrene

Translations

Letters, trs. A. Fitzgerald, London and New York 1926.

Essays and Hymns, trs. A. Fitzgerald, 2 vols., London and New York 1930.

Books

A. Gardner, *Synesius of Cyrene. Philosopher and Bishop*, London 1886.

W. S. Crawford, *Synesius the Hellene*, London 1901.

J. C. Pando, *The Life and Times of Synesius of Cyrene as revealed in his works*, Washington 1940.

K. M. Setton, *Christian Attitude towards the Emperor in the Fourth Century*, New York and London 1941.

H. von Campenhausen, *The Fathers of the Greek Church*, ET New York 1959, London 1963, ch. X.

Articles

C. H. Coster, 'Synesius. A Curialis of the time of Arcadius', *Byzantion* 15, 1940–41, 10–38.

R. Pack, 'Folklore and Superstitions in the Writings of Synesius', *Classical Weekly* 43, 1949, 51–6.

C. H. Coster, 'Christianity and the Invasions. Synesius of Cyrene', *Classical Journal* 55, 1960, 290–312.

H.-I. Marrou, 'Synesius of Cyrene and Alexandrian Neoplatonism', in *The Conflict between Paganism and Christianity in the Fourth Century*, ed. A. Momigliano, Oxford 1963, 126–50.

J. Bregman, 'Synesius of Cyrene: Early Life and Conversion to Philosophy', *California Studies in Classical Antiquity* 7, 1974, 55–88.

W. N. Bayless, 'Synesius of Cyrene: a study of the Role of the Bishop in Temporal Affairs', *Byzantine Studies/Études Byzantines* 4, 1977, 147–56.

CHAPTER 5

General: a selection of works on doctrine, christology and exegesis

(Other relevant material will be found in the Bibliographies for chapters 2 and 3)

Translations

T. H. Bindley and F. W. Green, *The Oecumenical Documents of the Faith*, London and New York 1955.

H. Bettenson, *The Early Christian Fathers*, Oxford and New York 1956.

— *Documents of the Christian Church*, Oxford and New York 1963.

J. Stevenson, *Creeds, Councils and Controversies*, London and New York 1966.

H. Bettenson, *The Later Christian Fathers*, Oxford and New York 1970.

M. Wiles and M. Santer, *Documents in Early Christian Thought*, Cambridge and New York 1975.

The Seven Ecumenical Councils of the Undivided Church, NPNF II. XIV, reprinted 1977.

The Christological Controversy, trs. R. A. Norris (Sources of Early Christian Thought), Philadelphia 1980.

Books

G. L. Prestige, *Fathers and Heretics*, London and New York 1940.

R. V. Sellers, *Two Ancient Christologies*, London and New York 1940.
— *The Council of Chalcedon*, London 1953.
J. N. D. Kelly, *Early Christian Doctrines*, London and New York 1958.
H. von Campenhausen, *The Fathers of the Greek Church*, ET New York 1959, London 1963.
A. Grillmeier, *Christ in Christian Tradition*, ET London and New York 1965, enlarged and revised 1975.
T. E. Pollard, *Johannine Christology and the Early Church*, Cambridge and New York 1970.
Jaroslav Pelikan, *The Christian Tradition*. A History of the Development of Doctrine:
Vol. 1: The Emergence of the Catholic Tradition (100–600). Chicago and London 1971.
Vol. 2: The Spirit of Eastern Christendom (600–1700), Chicago 1974.
R. P. C. Hanson, *The Attractiveness of God*, London and Atlanta Ga. 1973.
H. Cunliffe-Jones, *A History of Christian Doctrine*, Edinburgh 1978.
D. S. Wallace-Hadrill, *Christian Antioch*, Cambridge 1982.

W. A. Wigram, *The Separation of the Monophysites*, London 1923.
A. S. Atiya, *A History of Eastern Christianity*, London 1968.
W. H. C. Frend, *The Rise of the Monophysite Movement*, Cambridge and New York 1972.

The Cambridge History of the Bible, vol. 1: *From the Beginnings to Jerome*, ed. P. R. Ackroyd and C. F. Evans, Cambridge and New York 1970.
M. F. Wiles, *The Spiritual Gospel*, Cambridge and New York 1960.
— *The Divine Apostle*, Cambridge and New York 1967.

Articles

R. L. Wilken, 'Tradition, Exegesis and the Christological controversy', *Church History* 34, 1965, 123–42.
R. A. Norris, 'Towards a Contemporary Interpretation of the Chalcedonian Definition', in *Lux in Lumine*. Essays to honor W. N. Pittenger, ed. R. A. Norris, New York 1966, 62–79.
F. M. Young, 'Christological Ideas in the Greek Commentaries on the Epistle to the Hebrews', *JTS* NS 20, 1969, 150–63.
— 'A Reconsideration of Alexandrian Christology', *JEH* 22, 1971, 103–14.

1. Eustathius, Apollinarius, Diodore

Books

C. E. Raven, *Apollinarianism*, Cambridge and New York 1923.
R. V. Sellers, *Eustathius of Antioch*, Cambridge and New York 1928.
G. L. Prestige, *St Basil the Great and Apollinarius of Laodicea*, London 1956.

Articles

H. de Riedmatten, 'Some Neglected Aspects of Apollinarist Christology', *Dominican Studies* 1, 1948, 239–60.

H. A. Wolfson, 'Philosophical Implications of Arianism and Apollinarianism', *Dumbarton Oaks Papers* 12, 1958, 3–28.

T. F. Torrance, 'The Mind of Christ in Worship: The Problem of Apollinarianism in the Liturgy', in his *Theology in Reconciliation*, London 1975, Grand Rapids, Mich. 1976, 139–215.

R. A. Greer, 'The Antiochene Christology of Diodore of Tarsus', *JTS* NS 17, 1966, 327–41.

2. **Theodore of Mopsuestia**

Translations

Catechetical Homilies in *The Commentary on the Nicene Creed* and *The Commentary on the Lord's Prayer and the Sacraments of Baptism and Eucharist*, ed. and trs. A. Mingana, Woodbrooke Studies v and vi, Cambridge 1932–3.

Books

L. Patterson, *Theodore of Mopsuestia and Modern Thought*, London and New York 1926.

F. J. Reine, *The Eucharistic Doctrine of the Mystagogical Catecheses of Theodore of Mopsuestia*, Washington 1942.

F. A. Sullivan, *The Christology of Theodore of Mopsuestia*, Rome 1956.

Rowan Greer, *Theodore of Mopsuestia. Exegete and Theologian*, London 1961.

R. A. Norris, *Manhood and Christ*, Oxford and New York 1963.

H. M. Riley, *Christian Initiation* (see p. 347).

H. B. Swete, Introduction to *Theodori Episcopi Mopsuesteni in epistolas B. Pauli commentarii*, I, Cambridge 1880, reprinted Farnborough 1969.

Articles

J. L. McKenzie, 'A New Study of Theodore of Mopsuestia', *Theological Studies* 10, 1949, 394–408.

K. McNamara, 'Theodore of Mopsuestia and the Nestorian Heresy', *Irish Theological Quarterly* 19, 1952, 254–78; 20, 1953, 172–91.

J. L. McKenzie, 'The Commentary of Theodore of Mopsuestia on John 1.46–51', *Theological Studies* 14, 1953, 73–84.

— 'Annotations on the Christology of Theodore of Mopsuestia', *Theological Studies* 19, 1958, 345–73.

F. A. Sullivan, 'Further notes on Theodore of Mopsuestia: a reply to Fr. McKenzie', *Theological Studies* 20, 1959, 264–79.

R. E. Carter, 'Chrysostom's *Ad Theodorum Lapsum* and the Early Chronology of Theodore of Mopsuestia', *VC* 16, 1962, 87–101.

M. F. Wiles, 'Theodore of Mopsuestia as Representative of the Antiochene School', in *Cambridge History of the Bible* 1, 1970, 489–510.

Joanne Dewart, 'The Notion of "Person" underlying the Christology of Theodore of Mopsuestia', *StudPatr* 12, 1975, 199–207.

3. Nestorius

Translation

The Bazaar of Heraclides, ed. and trs. G. R. Driver and L. Hodgson, Oxford and New York 1925.

Books

J. F. Bethune-Baker, *Nestorius and his Teaching*, Cambridge and New York 1908.

F. Loofs, *Nestorius and his place in the history of Christian Doctrine*, Cambridge and New York 1914.

A. R. Vine, *An Approach to Christology*, London 1948.

Articles

L. Hodgson, 'The Metaphysic of Nestorius', *JTS* 19, 1918, 46–55; republished as an appendix in Driver and Hodgson, op. cit.

H. Chadwick, 'Eucharist and Christology in the Nestorian Controversy', *JTS* NS 2, 1951, 145–64.

Milton V. Anastos, 'Nestorius was Orthodox', *Dumbarton Oaks Papers* 16, 1962, 119–40.

Carl E. Braaten, 'Modern Interpretations of Nestorius', *Church History* 32, 1963, 251–67.

R. A. Greer, 'The Image of God and the Prosopic Union in Nestorius' *Bazaar of Heraclides*', in *Lux in Lumine*. Essays to honor W. N. Pittenger, ed. R. A. Norris, New York 1966, 46–61.

G. S. Bebis, 'The Apology of Nestorius: A New Evaluation', *StudPatr* 11, 1972, 107–12.

H. E. W. Turner, 'Nestorius Reconsidered', *StudPatr* 13, 1975, 306–21.

R. C. Chesnut, 'The two *prosopa* in Nestorius' *Bazaar of Heraclides*', *JTS* NS 29, 1978, 392–409.

4. Cyril of Alexandria

Books

A. Kerrigan, *St Cyril of Alexandria. Interpreter of the Old Testament* (Analecta Biblica 2), Rome 1952.

W. J. Burghardt, *The Image of God in Man according to Cyril of Alexandria*, Washington 1957.

H. von Campenhausen, *The Fathers of the Greek Church*, ET New York 1959, London 1963, ch. XII.

C. Dratsellas, *Man in his Original State and in the State of Sin according to St Cyril of Alexandria*, Athens 1971.

R. L. Wilken, *Judaism and the Early Christian Mind. A Study of Cyril of Alexandria's Exegesis and Theology*, New Haven, Conn. 1971.

E. Gebremedhin, *Life-giving Blessing*, Uppsala 1977.

W. J. Malley, *Hellenism and Christianity*, Rome 1978.

Articles

J. S. Romanides, 'St Cyril's "One physis or hypostasis of God the Logos incarnate" and Chalcedon', *Greek Orthodox Theological Review* 10, 1964/5, 82–107.

R. L. Wilken, 'Exegesis and the History of Theology: Reflections on the Adam-Christ Typology in Cyril of Alexandria', *Church History* 35, 1966, 139–56.

E. P. Meijering, 'Cyril of Alexandria on the Platonists and the Trinity', and 'Some Reflections on Cyril of Alexandria's Rejection of Anthropomorphism', in his *God Being History*, Amsterdam 1975, 114–27, 128–32.

R. A. Norris, 'Christological Models in Cyril of Alexandria', *StudPatr* 13, 1975, 255–68.

J. D. McCoy, 'Philosophical Influences on the Doctrine of the Incarnation in Athanasius and Cyril of Alexandria', *Encounter* (Indianapolis) 38, 1977, 362–91.

5. Theodoret of Cyrrhus

Translation

Ecclesiastical History, Eranistes, Letters, NPNF II.III, repr. 1979.

Books

G. W. Ashby, *Theodoret of Cyrrhus as Exegete of the Old Testament*, Grahamstown 1972.

Articles

R. V. Sellers, 'Pseudo-Justin's *Expositio Rectae Fidei*. A Work of Theodoret', *JTS* 46, 1945, 145–60.

F. L. Cross, 'Pseudo-Justin's *Expositio Rectae Fidei*. A Further Note on the Ascription' *JTS* 47, 1946, 57 f.

M. M. Wagner, 'A Chapter in Byzantine Epistolography', *Dumbarton Oaks Papers* 4, 1948, 119–81.

M. F. A. Brok, 'The Date of Theodoret's *Expositio Rectae Fidei*' *JTS* NS 2, 1951, 178–83.

G. Ashby, 'Theodoret of Cyrrhus on Marriage', *Theology* 72, 1969, 482–91.

G. F. Chesnut, 'The Date of Composition of Theodoret's *Church History*', *VC* 35, 1981, 245–52.

BIBLIOGRAPHY B

Works published since 1960. See introductory note for reference works and other aids.

CHAPTER 1

1. General

Books

G. F. Chesnut, *The First Christian Histories*, Paris 1977.

Articles

A. Momigliano, 'Pagan and Christian Historiography in the Fourth Century AD' in *The Conflict between Paganism and Christianity in the Fourth Century*, ed. Momigliano, Oxford and New York 1963, 79–99; reprinted in his *Essays in Ancient and Modern Historiography*, Oxford and Middletown, Conn. 1977, 107–26.

G. Downey, 'The Perspective of the Early Church Historians', *Greek, Roman and Byzantine Studies* 6, 1965, 57–70.

R. A. Markus, 'Church History and the Early Church Historians', in *The Materials, Sources, Methods of Ecclesiastical History*, ed. D. A. Baker (Studies in Church History 11), Oxford 1975, 1–17.

2. Eusebius of Caesarea

Texts and translations

The History of the Church from Christ to Constantine, trs. G. Williamson (Pelican), Harmondsworth 1965, New York 1966.

Histoire ecclésiastique, ed. G. Bardy, 4 vols. (SC 31, 41, 55, 73), reprinted 1965–71.

The Essential Eusebius, selections trs. C. Luibheid, New York and London 1966.

† *Kirchengeschichte*, ed. H. Kraft, Munich 1967.

Gegen Marcell; Über die kirchliche Theologie; Die Fragmente Marcells, ed. E. Klostermann, 2nd ed., G. Hansen (GCS IV), 1972.

La préparation évangelique I, ed. J. Sirinelli and E. Des Places (SC 206), 1974;
II–III, ed. E. Des Places (SC 228), 1976;
IV–V.17, ed. O. Zink and E. Des Places (SC 262), 1980;
† V.18–VI, ed. E. Des Places (SC 266), 1980;
VII, ed. G. Schroeder and E. Des Places (SC 215), 1975.
Der Jesajakommentar, ed. J. Ziegler (GCS IX), 1975.
Über das Leben Constantins, etc., ed. I. A. Heikel, 2nd ed., F. Winkelmann (GCS I), 1975.
In Praise of Constantine: A Historical Study and New Translation of Eusebius' Tricennial Orations, H. A. Drake, Berkeley 1976.
Church History, Life of Constantine, In Praise of Constantine, NPNF II.I, reprinted 1979.

Books

D. S. Wallace-Hadrill, *Eusebius of Caesarea*, London 1960.
J. Sirinelli, *Les vues historiques d'Eusèbe de Césarée durant la periode prénicéenne*, Dakar 1961.
A. Dempf, *Der Platonismus des Eusebius, Victorinus und Pseudo-Dionysius*, Munich 1962.
F. Winckelmann, *Die Textbezeugung der 'Vita Constantini' des Eusebius von Caesarea* (TU 84), Berlin 1962.
A. Dempf, *Eusebius als Historiker*, Munich 1964.
A. Weber, *APXH. Ein Beitrag zur Christologie des Eusebius von Caesarea*, Rome 1965.
H. A. Drake, *In Praise of Constantine* (above, includes a historical study of some importance).
C. Luibheid, *Eusebius of Caesarea and the Arian Crisis*, Dublin 1978.
A. A. Mosshammer, *The Chronicle of Eusebius and Greek Chronographic Tradition*, Lewisburg, Pa. 1979.
R. M. Grant, *Eusebius as Church Historian*, Oxford and New York 1980.
T. D. Barnes, *Constantine and Eusebius*, Cambridge, Mass. 1981.
Alistair Kee, *Constantine versus Christ*, London 1982.

Articles

B. Gustafsson, 'Eusebius' Principles in Handling his Sources, as found in his *Church History* Books I–VII', *StudPatr* 4, 1961, 429–41.
E. Ferguson, 'Eusebius and Ordination', *JEH* 13, 1962, 139–44.
J. Sirinelli, 'Quelques allusions à Melchisédech dans l'oeuvre d'Eusèbe de Césarée', *StudPatr* 6, 1962, 233–47.
C. U. Wolf, 'Eusebius of Caesarea and the *Onomasticon*', *The Biblical Archaeologist* 27, 1964, 66–96.
R. E. Somerville, 'An Ordering Principle for Book VIII of Eusebius' *Ecclesiastical History*: A Suggestion', *VC* 20, 1966, 91–7.
J. Lassus, 'L'Empereur Constantin, Eusèbe et les lieux saints', *Revue de l'Histoire des Religions* 171, 1967, 135–44.

F. Ricken, 'Die Logoslehre des Eusebius von Caesarea und der Mittel-platonismus', *Theologie und Philosophie* 42, 1967, 341–58.

R. M. Grant, 'Eusebius HE VIII. Another Suggestion', *VC* 22, 1968, 16–18.

H. Kloft, 'Zur *Vita Constantini* I.14', *Historia* 19, 1970, 509–14.

S. Pieszczoch, 'Notices de la collégialité chez Eusèbe de Césarée (*Histoire Ecclésiastique*)', *StudPatr* 10, 1970, 302–5.

G. J. M. Bartelink, '"Maison de Prière" comme dénomination de l'église en tant qu'édifice, en particulier chez Eusèbe de Césarée', *Revue des Études Grecques* 84, 1971, 101–18.

J. van Cangh, 'Nouveaux Fragments Hexaplaires. *Commentaire sur Isaïe* d'Eusèbe de Césarée', *Revue Biblique* 78, 1971, 384–90; 79, 1972, 76.

R. M. Grant, 'Early Alexandrian Christianity', *Church History* 40, 1971, 133–44 [Eusebius not to be trusted!].

R. H. Storch, 'The "Eusebian Constantine"', *Church History* 40, 1971, 145–55.

R. M. Grant, 'Eusebius and Church History' in *Understanding the Sacred Text:* Essays in Honour of M. S. Enslin on the Hebrew Bible and Christian Beginnings, ed. J. Reumann, Valley Forge 1972, 233–47.

G. M. Lee, 'Eusebius *HE* 3.39.4', *Biblica* 53, 1972, 412.

C. Luibheid, 'Eusebius of Caesarea and the Nicene Creed', *Irish Theological Quarterly* 39, 1972, 299–305.

J. M. Sansterre, 'Eusèbe de Césarée et la naissance de la théorie "Césaropapiste"', *Byzantion* 42, 1972, 131–95, 532–94.

E. J. Yarnold, 'Baptism and Pagan Mysteries in the Fourth Century', *Heythrop Journal* 13, 1972, 247–67.

G. F. Chesnut, 'Fate, Fortune, Freewill and Nature in Eusebius of Caesarea', *Church History* 42, 1973, 165–82.

G. C. Stead, 'Eusebius and the Council of Nicaea', *JTS* NS 24, 1973, 85–100.

R. M. Grant, 'Papias in Eusebius' *Church History*', in *Mélanges d'Histoire des Religions offerts à H.-C. Puech*, Paris 1974, 209–13.

D. S. Wallace-Hadrill, 'Eusebius of Caesarea's "Commentary on Luke"; Its Origin and Early History', *Harvard Theological Review* 67, 1974, 55–63.

— 'Eusebius of Caesarea and the *Testimonium Flavianum* (Josephus, Antiquities XVIII.63 f.)', *Journal of Ecclesiastical History* 25, 1974, 353–62.

T. D. Barnes, 'The Composition of Eusebius' *Onomasticon*', *JTS* NS 26, 1975, 412–15.

R. M. Grant, 'The Case against Eusebius, or Did the Father of Church History Write History?', *StudPatr* 12, 1975, 413–21.

E. Des Places, 'Numénius et Eusèbe de Césarée', *StudPatr* 13, 1975, 19–28.

H. D. Saffrey, 'Les extraits du περὶ τ'ἀγαθοῦ du Numénius dans le livre xi de la *Préparation évangélique* d'Eusèbe de Césarée', *StudPatr* 13, 1975, 46–51.

H. von Campenhausen, 'Das Bekenntnis Eusebs von Caesarea (Nicaea 325)', *ZNW* 67, 1976, 123–39.

D. König-Ockenfels, 'Christliche Deutung der Weltgeschichte bei Euseb von Cäsarea', *Saeculum* 27, 1976, 348–65.

J. E. Bruns, 'The "Agreement of Moses and Jesus" in the *Demonstratio Evangelica* of Eusebius', *VC* 31, 1977, 117–25.

A. M. Denis, 'L' "Historien anonyme" d'Eusèbe (*Praep. Ev.* 9.17–18) et la crise des Macchabées', *Journal for the Study of Judaism* 8, 1977, 42–9.

L. W. Barnard, 'Bede and Eusebius as Church Historians', in *Studies in Church History and Patristics (ΑΝΑΛΕΚΤΑ ΒΛΑΤΑΔΩΝ* 26), Thessaloniki 1978, 354–72.

Jean-Paul Rey-Coquais, 'Le calendrier employé par Eusèbe de Césarée dans les *Martyres de Palestine*', *Analecta Bollandiana* 96, 1978, 55–64.

F. Ricken, 'Zur Rezeption der platonischen Ontologie bei Eusebios von Kaisareia, Areios und Athanasios', *Theologie und Philosophie* 53, 1978, 321–52.

M. Kertsch, 'Traditionelle Rhetorik und Philosophie in Eusebius' Antirrhetikos gegen Hierocles', *VC* 34, 1980, 145–71.

S. Gero, 'The True Image of Christ: Eusebius' Letter to Constantia Reconsidered', *JTS* NS 32, 1981, 460–70.

3(a). Socrates Scholasticus

Translation

Ecclesiastical History, NPNF II.II, reprinted 1976.

Articles

G. F. Chesnut, 'Kairos and Cosmic Sympathy in the Church Historian Socrates Scholasticus', *Church History* 44, 1975, 161–66.

P. Périchon, 'Pour une édition nouvelle de l'historien Socrate: les manuscrits et les versions', *RSR* 53, 1965, 112–20.

(b). Philostorgius

Kirchengeschichte mit dem Leben des Lucian von Antiochen und den Fragmenten eines arianischen Historiographen, ed. J. Bidez, 2nd ed., F. Winckelmann (GCS), 1972.

(c). Sozomen

Text and translation

Kirchengeschichte, ed. J. Bidez, 2nd ed., G. Hansen (GCS), 1960.
Ecclesiastical History, NPNF II.II, reprinted 1976.

(d). Theodoret

See Chapter 5.

4. The Monastic Literature

(The lists are restricted to those works discussed here; for other hagiographical material, consult recent numbers of *Analecta Bollandiana*.)

General works

E. R. Hardy, *Christian Egypt*, Oxford 1962.
A. J. Festugière, *Les Moines d'Orient*, 4 vols., Paris 1961–65. An introductory volume is followed by French translations of a number of primary sources, including the *Historia Monachorum*.
D. Chitty, *The Desert a City*, Oxford 1966.

Texts and translations

The History of Palladius on the Races of India and the Brahmans, ed. J. D. Derrett (Classica et Mediaevalia), Copenhagen 1960.
Historia Monachorum in Aegypto, ed. A. J. Festugière (Subsidia Hagiographica 34), Brussels 1961.
Palladius, *The Lausiac History*, trs. R. T. Meyer (ACW 34), 1965.
Les sentences des pères du désert I (Pelage et Jean), introd. L. Regnault, trs. J. Dion and G. Oury, Solesmes 1966.
Palladius, *De gentibus Indiae et Bragmanibus*, ed. W. Berghoff, Meisenheim 1967.
Les apophtegmes des pères du désert (série alphabétique), ed. J. C. Guy, Begrolles 1968.
Abbé Isaïe: Recueil ascétique, introd. and trs. the monks of Solesmes, Begrolles 1970.
Les sentences des pères du désert II and III (Coislin. 126+Greek, Syriac, Coptic, etc.; unpublished collections), ed. L. Regnault, trs. the monks of Solesmes, Solesmes 1970, 1976.
Les formes syriaques de la matière de l'Histoire Lausiaque, ed. R. Draguet, CSCO 399 (Scriptores Syri 174), Louvain 1978.
[For English translations, see Bibliography A; German translations are not listed. Recently published material in Syriac, Coptic, etc. (i.e. non-Greek versions) are not listed.]

Books

J. C. Guy, *Recherches sur la tradition grecque des Apophthegmata Patrum* (Subsidia Hagiographica 36), Brussels 1962.
M. Aubineau, *Sept Folios d'Apophtegmes, dans un Ms. d'Oxford: Bodl. Greek Theol.b.8.*, Athens 1974.

Articles

Hermann Dörries, 'Die Beichte im alten Mönchtum', *Wort und Stunde* I, Göttingen 1966, 225–50; 'Die Bibel im ältesten Mönchtum', ibid. 251–76.

R. T. Meyer, 'Proverbs and Puns in Palladius' *Historia Lausiaca*', *StudPatr* 8, 1966, 420–3.

P. Devos, 'La "Servante de Dieu" Poemenia d'après Pallade, la tradition copte et Jean Rufus', *Analecta Bollandiana* 87, 1969, 189–212.

R. T. Meyer, 'Palladius and Early Christian Spirituality', *StudPatr* 10, 1970, 379–90.

— 'Lectio Divina in Palladius', in *Kyriakon*. Festschrift J. Quasten, ed. P. Granfield and J. A. Jungmann, Munster 1970, I, 380–4.

A. de Vogüé, 'Points de contact du chapitre XXXIII de l'Histoire Lausiaque avec les écrits d'Horsièse', *Studia Monastica* 13, 1971, 291–4.

E. D. Hunt, 'Palladius of Helenopolis: a Party and its Supporters in the Church of the Late Fourth Century' *JTS* NS 24, 1973, 456–80.

B. Berg, 'The Letter of Palladius on India', *Byzantion* 44, 1974, 5–16.

P. Devos, 'Les nombres dans l'Historia monachorum in Aegypto', *Analecta Bollandiana* 92, 1974, 97–108.

R. T. Meyer, 'Palladius and the Study of Scripture', *StudPatr* 13, 1975, 487–90.

D. F. Buck, 'The Structure of the *Lausiac History*', *Byzantion* 46, 1976, 292–307.

J.-C. Guy, 'Les Apophthegmata Patrum', in *Théologie de la vie monastique. Etudes sur la tradition patristique*, Paris 1961, 73–84.

F. von Lilienfeld, 'Anthropos Pneumatikos – Pater Pneumatophoros: Neues Testament und *Apophthegmata Patrum*', *StudPatr* 5, 1962, 382–92.

— 'Jesus-Logion und Väterspruch. Die synoptischen Jesus-Reden in der Auslegung der Agroikoi der ägyptischen Wüste nach den *Apophthegmata Patrum*', in *Studia Byzantina*, ed. J. Irmscher, Halle-Wittenberg 1966, 169–83.

— 'Paulus-Zitate und paulinischen Gedanken in den *Apophthegmata Patrum*', *Studia Evangelica* 5 (TU 103), 1968, 286–95.

L. Leloir, 'La prière des pères du désert d'après les collections arméniennes des Apophtegmes', in *Mélanges liturgiques offerts au Dom B. Botte*, Louvain 1972, 311–26.

J. Geraldes Freire, 'Traductions latines des Apophthegmata Patrum', in *Mélanges C. Mohrmann*, Utrecht 1973, 164–71.

J. M. Sauget, 'La version sahidique des *Apophthegmata Patrum* et son modèle grec', *Orientalia Christiana Periodica* 39, 1973, 445–53.

D. J. Chitty, 'The Books of the Old Men', *Eastern Churches Review* 6, 1974, 15–21.

J. C. Guy, 'Educational Innovation in the Desert Fathers', ibid., 44–51.

L. Regnault, 'The Beatitudes in the Apophthegmata Patrum', ibid., 22–43.

C. Hannick, 'La version slave des Paterika', *Irenikon* 47, 1974, 355–60.

L. Regnault, 'La prière continuelle 'Monologistos' dans la littérature Apophtegmatique', ibid., 467–93.

L. Leloir, 'Les orientations essentielles de la spiritualité des Pères du desert d'après les "Paterica" arméniens', *Revue de Théologie et Philosophie* 24, 1974, 30–47.

M. van Esbroeck, 'Les apophtegmes dans les versions orientales', *Analecta Bollandiana* 93, 1975, 381–9.

A. Guillaumont, 'Le problème des deux Macaires dans les "Apophthegmata Patrum"', *Irenikon* 48, 1975, 41–59.

L. Regnault, 'Quelques apophtegmes arabes sur la "Prière de Jesus"', *Irenikon* 52, 1979, 344–55.

J. Gribomont, 'Le monachisme au sein de l'église en Syrie et en Cappadoce', *Studia Monastica* 7, 1965, 7–24.

S. P. Brock, 'Early Syrian Asceticism' *Numen* 20, 1973, 1–19.

Robert Murray, 'The Features of the Earliest Christian Asceticism', in *Christian Spirituality*. Essays in honour of Gordon Rupp, ed. Peter Brooks, London 1975, 63–77.

For further material on Syrian monasticism, see Theodoret Bibliography below (ch. 5).

CHAPTER 2

1. Arius

Books

M. Simonetti, *Studi sull' Arianesimo*, Rome 1965.

E. Boularand, *L'Hérésie d'Arius et la 'Foi' de Nicée*, 2 vols., Paris 1972.

M. Simonetti, *La crisi ariana nel IV secolo*, Rome 1975.

R. E. Person, *The Mode of Theological Decision at the Early Councils*. An enquiry into the function of scripture and tradition at the councils of Nicaea and Ephesus, Basel 1978.

R. Lorenz, *Arius Judaizans? Untersuchungen zur dogmengeschichtlichen Einordnung des Arius*, Göttingen 1979.

R. Gregg and D. Groh, *Early Arianism: A View of Salvation*, Philadelphia and London 1981.

Articles

W. P. Haugaard, 'Arius: Twice a Heretic?', *Church History* 29, 1960, 251–63.

A. Tuilier, 'Le sens du terme ὁμοούσιος dans le vocabulaire théologique d'Arius et de l'école d'Antioche', *StudPatr* 3, 1961, 421–30.

M. F. Wiles, 'In Defence of Arius', *JTS* NS 13, 1962, 339–47, reprinted in *Working Papers in Doctrine*, London and New York 1976, 28–37.

G. C. Stead, 'The Platonism of Arius', *JTS* NS 15, 1964, 16–31.

E. Boularand, 'Les débuts d'Arius', *Bulletin de Littérature ecclésiastique* 65, 1964, 175–203.

— 'Aux sources de la doctrine d'Arius', *Bulletin de Littérature ecclésiastique* 68, 1967, 3–19.

L. W. Barnard, 'The Antecedents of Arius', *VC* 24, 1970, 172–88, reprinted in *Studies in Church History and Patristics* (*ΑΝΑΛΕΚΤΑ ΒΛΑΤΑΔΩΝ* 26), Thessaloniki 1978, 295–311.

C. Kannengiesser, 'Ou et quand Arius composa-t-il la Thalie?', in *Kyriakon. Festschrift J. Quasten*, ed. P. Granfield and J. A. Jungmann, Münster 1970, I, 346–51.

L. W. Barnard, 'What was Arius' Philosophy?', *Theologische Zeitschrift* 28, 1972, 110–17, reprinted in *Studies in Church History and Patristics*, 289–95.

P. Nautin, 'La doctrine d'Arius', *Annuaire de l'École pratique des Hautes Études*, V\ue section: Sciences Religieuses 83, 1974–5, 231 f.

R. C. Gregg and D. E. Groh, 'The Centrality of Soteriology in Early Arianism', *Anglican Theological Review* 59, 1977, 260–78.

C. Luibheid, 'Finding Arius', *Irish Theological Quarterly* 45, 1978, 81–100.

G. C. Stead, 'The *Thalia* of Arius and the Testimony of Athanasius', *JTS*, NS 29, 1978, 20–52.

F. Ricken, 'Zur Rezeption der platonischen Ontologie bei Eusebios von Kaisareia, Areios und Athanasios', *Theologie und Philosophie* 53, 1978, 321–52.

2. Athanasius

Texts and Translations

Five Homilies; Expositio fidei; Sermo major, ed. H. Nordberg (Societas Scientarum Fennica. Commentationes Humanarum Litterarum 30.2), Helsinki 1962.

Sur l'incarnation du Verbe, ed. C. Kannengiesser (SC 199), 1973.

Contra gentes and *De incarnatione*, ed. and trs. R. W. Thomson (Oxford Early Christian Texts), Oxford 1971.

Discours contre les paiens, ed. P. T. Camelot (SC 18), 2nd ed. 1977.

Select Writings and Letters, NPNF II.IV, reprinted 1978.

Versions

H. Hoppenbrouwers, *La plus ancienne version latine de la Vie de S.Antoine par S. Athanase*, Nimègue 1960.

G. A. Egan, *The Armenian Version of the Letters of Athanasius to Bishop Serapion concerning the Holy Spirit* (Studies and Documents 37), Salt Lake City 1968.

R. W. Thomson, *Athanasiana Syriaca* I-IV (Syriac + translation),
CSCO 257–8 (Scriptores Syri 114–5), 1965; 272–3 (118–9), 1965;
324–5 (142–3), 1972; 386–7 (167–8), 1977.

Books

A. van Haarlem, *Incarnatie en verlossing bij Athanasius*, Wageningen
1961, with English summary.
H. Nordberg, *Athanasius' Tractates Contra Gentes and De In-
carnatione. An attempt at Redating* (Societas Scientarum Fennica.
Commentationes Humanarum Litterarum 28.3), Helsinki 1961.
J. Pelikan, *The Light of the World*, New York 1962.
H. Nordberg, *Athanasius and the Emperor* (Soc. Sc. Fen. Comm. Hum.
Litt. 30.3), Helsinki 1963.
D. Ritschl, *Athanasius. Versuch einer Interpretation*, Zurich 1964.
P. Merendino, *Paschale Sacramentum*. Eine Untersuchungen über die
Osterkatechese des hl. Athanasius von Alexandrien in ihrer Be-
ziehung zu den frühchristlichen exegetisch-theologischen Über-
lieferungen, Münster 1965.
B. Salleron, *Matière et corps du Christ chez saint Athanase d'Alexan-
drie*, Rome 1967.
E. P. Meijering, *Orthodoxy and Platonism in Athanasius. Synthesis or
Antithesis*, Leiden 1968; 2nd ed. 1974.
J. Roldanus, *Le Christ et l'homme dans la théologie d'Athanase
d'Alexandrie*. Étude de la conjunction de sa conception de l'homme
avec sa Christologie, Leiden 1968.
A. Laminski, *Der Heilige Geist als Geist Christi und Geist der
Glaübigen*. Der Beitrag des Athanasios von Alexandrien zur
Formulierung des trinitarischen Dogmas in vierten Jahrhundert,
Leipzig 1969.
C. Kannengiesser, ed., *Politique et Théologie chez Athanase d'Alexan-
drie*, Actes du Colloque de Chantilly, Paris 1974.
K. M. Girardet, *Kaisergericht und Bishofsgericht*. Studien zu den
Anfängen des Donatistenstreites (313–15) und zum Prozess des
Athanasios von Alexandrien (328–46), Bonn 1975.
G. Larentzakis, *Einheit der Menschheit, Einheit der Kirche bei
Athanasius. Vor- und nachchristliche Soteriologie und Ek-
klesiologie bei Athanasius von Alexandrien*, Graz 1978.
A. Louth, *The Origins of the Christian Mystical Tradition*, Oxford and
New York 1981.

Articles

H. Nordberg, 'A Reconsideration of the Date of Athanasius' *Contra
Gentes* and *De Incarnatione*', *StudPatr* 3, 1961, 262–6.
R. W. Thomson, 'A Syriac Corpus of Athanasiana', *StudPatr* 3, 1961,
142–5.
R. Weijenborg, 'Apollinaristic Interpolations in the *Tomus ad*

Antiochenus of 362', *StudPatr* 3, 1961, 324–30.

G. Florovsky, 'The Concept of Creation in St Athanasius', *StudPatr* 6, 1962, 36–57.

R. W. Thompson, 'The Text of the Syriac Athanasian Corpus', in *Biblical and Patristic Studies for R. P. Casey*, ed. J. N. Birdsall and R. W. Thomson, Freiburg 1963, 250–64.

— 'Some Remarks on the Syriac Version of Athanasius' *De Incarnatione*,' *Le Muséon* 77, 1964, 17–28.

C. Kannengiesser, 'Le témoinage des *Lettres Festales* de S.Athanase sur la date de l'apologie *Contre les paiens, Sur l'incarnation du Verbe*', *RSR* 52, 1964, 91–100.

— 'Le texte court du *De Incarnatione* Athanasien', *RSR* 52, 1964, 589–96; 53, 1965, 77–111.

R. W. Thomson, 'The Transformation of Athanasius in Armenian Theology', *Le Muséon* 78, 1965, 747–69.

T. F. Torrance, 'Spiritus Creator. A Consideration of the Teaching of St Athanasius and St Basil', in his *Theology in Reconstruction* London 1965, 209–28.

Herman Dörries, 'Die *Vita Antonii* als Geschichtsquelle', in *Wort und Stunde* I, Göttingen 1966, 145–224.

C. Kannengiesser, 'Les différentes recensions du traité *De incarnatione Verbi* de S. Athanase', *StudPatr* 7, 1966, 221—29.

G. Egan, 'A Treatise attributed to Athanasius', *Le Muséon* 80, 1967, 139–51.

M. J. Rondeau, 'L'Épître à Marcellinus sur les Psaumes', *VC* 22, 1968, 176–97.

— 'Une nouvelle preuve de l'influence littéraire d'Eusèbe de Césarée sur Athanase: l'interpretation des psaumes', *RSR* 56, 1968, 385–434.

J. A. Holland, 'Athanasius versus Arius: what now?', *Reformed Theological Review* 28, 1969, 16–27.

C. Kannengiesser, 'La date de l'Apologie d'Athanase "Contre les Paiens" et "Sur l'incarnation du Verbe"', *RSR* 58, 1970, 383–428.

A. Louth, 'Reason and Revelation in St Athanasius', *SJT* 23, 1970, 385–96.

F. M. Young, 'A Reconsideration of Alexandrian Christology', *JEH* 22, 1971, 103–14.

G. Bartelink, 'Observations de critique textuelle sur le plus ancienne version latine de la *Vie de S.Antoine* par S.Athanase', *Revue Bénédictine* 81, 1971, 92–5.

J. A. Holland, 'Athanasius and Arius II: Why the Impulse to Reduce?', *Reformed Theological Review* 30, 1971, 33–47.

— 'III. The Solution of Athanasius', ibid., 30, 1971, 69–78.

— 'The Implications of Athansius for us', ibid., 31, 1972, 1–9.

R. Y. Ebied and L. R. Wickham, 'A Note on the Syriac Version of Athanasius *Ad Epictetum* in Ms BM Add.14557', *JTS* NS 23, 1972, 144–54.

C. Kannengiesser, 'Λόγος et νοῦς chez Athanase d'Alexandrie', *StudPatr* 11, 1972, 199–202.

C. Kannengiesser, 'Le recourse au Livre de Jérémie chez Athanase d'Alexandrie' in *Epektasis*. Mélanges patristiques offerts au Cardinal Daniélou, ed. J. Fontaine and C. Kannengiesser, Paris 1972, 317–25.

H. Saake, 'Das Präskript zum ersten Serapionbrief des Athanasios von Alexandria als pneumatologisches Programm', *VC* 26, 1972, 188–99.

M. Aubineau, 'Une homélie pascale attribuée à S. Athanase d'Alexandrie dans le Sinaiticus gr. 492' in *Zetesis*. Album amicorum Prof. Dr. E. de Strycker, Utrecht 1973, 668–78.

I. Backes, 'Das trinitarische Glaubensverständnis beim hl. Athanasius der Grosse', *Trierer Theologische Zeitschrift* 82, 1973, 129–40.

C. Kannengiesser, 'Athanasios von Alexandrien. Seine Beziehungen zu Trier und Seine Rolle in der Geschichte der christlichen Theologie', ibid. 141–53.

J. Breckenridge, 'Julian and Athanasius; Two Approaches to Creation and Salvation', *Theology* 76, 1973, 73–81.

P. Christou, 'Uncreated and created, unbegotten and begotten in the theology of Athanasius of Alexandria', *Augustinianum* 13, 1973, 399–409.

C. Kannengiesser, 'Athanasius of Alexandria and the Foundation of Traditional Christology', *Theological Studies* 34, 1973, 103–13.

H.-J. Sieben, 'Athanasius über den Psalter. Analyse seines Briefes an Marcellinus', *Theologie und Philosophie* 48, 1973, 157–73.

M. Tetz, 'Markellianer und Athanasios von Alexandrien. Die markellianische Expositio fidei ad Athanasium des Diakons Eugenios von Ankyra', *ZNW* 64, 1973, 75–121.

L. W. Barnard, 'The Date of Athanasius' *Vita Antonii*', *VC* 28, 1974, 169–75.

T. C. Campbell, 'The Doctrine of the Holy Spirit in the Theology of Athanasius', *SJT* 27, 1974, 408–40.

W. H. C. Frend, 'Athanasius as an Egyptian Christian Leader in the Fourth Century', *New College Bulletin* 8, Edinburgh 1974, 20–37; reprinted in his *Religion Popular and Unpopular in the Early Christian Centuries*, London 1976, ch. 16.

E. P. Meijering, 'Athanasius on the Father as the Origin of the Son', *Nederlands Archief voor Kerchgescheidenis* 55, 1974, 1–14, reprinted in his *God Being History*, Amsterdam 1975.

— 'ΗΝ ΠΟΤΕ ΟΤΕ ΟΥΚ ΗΝ Ο ΥΙΟΣ. A Discussion of Time and Eternity', *VC* 28, 1974, 161–8, reprinted ibid.

A. Heron, 'Zur Theologie der "Tropici" in den Serapionbriefen des Athanasius', *Kyrios* 14, 1974, 3–24.

D. Staniloae, 'Die Erlosungslehre des hl. Athanasius des Grossen', ibid. 25–42.

P. M. Strohm, 'Die Trinitätslehre des hl. Athanasius und ihr Missverstehen im Abendland', ibid. 43–60.

D. Dimitrijevic, 'Die Christologie des hl. Athanasius und ihre Bedeutung fur die Auffassung der Eucharistie', ibid. 61–84.

E. Theodorou, 'Die Diakonie der Kirche nach dem hl. Athanasius', ibid. 85–96.

P. Meinhold, 'Die gesamtchristliche Bedeutung des hl. Athanasius', ibid. 97–114.

C. D. G. Müller, 'Athanasius von Alexandrien als koptischer Schriftsteller', ibid. 195–204.

W. Schneemelcher, 'Die Epistula Encyclica des Athanasius', in *Gesammelte Aufsätze*, Thessalonica 1974, 290–337.

L. W. Barnard, 'Athanasius and the Meletian Schism in Egypt', *Journal of Egyptian Archaeology* 59, 1975, 183–89.

— 'Some Liturgical Elements in Athanasius' Festal Epistles', *StudPatr* 13, 1975, 337–42.

— 'Two Notes on Athanasius', *Orientalia Christiana Periodica* 41, 1975, 344–56, reprinted in *Studies in Church History and Patristics (ANAΛEKTA BΛATAΔΩN* 26) (Thessaloniki 1978, 329–40.

A. Louth, 'The Concept of the Soul in Athanasius' *Contra Gentiles – De Incarnatione*', *StudPatr* 13, 1975, 227–31.

C. Kannengiesser, 'Le mystere pascal du Christ selon Athanase d'Alexandrie', *RSR* 63, 1975, 407–42.

M. Tetz, 'Über nikäische Orthodoxie. Der sog. tomus ad Antiochenos des Athanasios von Alexandrien', *ZNW* 66, 1975, 194–222.

T. F. Torrance, 'Athanasius. A Study in the Foundations of Classical Theology', in his *Theology in Reconciliation*, London 1975, 215–66.

J. C. M. van Winden, 'On the Date of Athanasius' Apologetical Treatises', *VC* 29, 1975, 291–5.

B. R. Brennan, 'Dating Athanasius' *Vita Antonii*', *VC* 30, 1976, 52–4.

F. S. Clarke, 'Lost and Found: Athanasius' Doctrine of Predestination', *SJT* 29, 1976, 435–50.

G. C. Stead, 'Rhetorical Method in Athanasius', *VC* 30, 1976, 121–37.

L. W. Barnard, 'Athanasius and the Roman State', *Latomus* 36, 1977, 422–37, reprinted in *Studies in Church History and Patristics (ANAΛEKTA BΛATAΔΩN* 26) Thessaloniki 1978, 312–28.

J. D. McCoy, 'Philosophical Influences on the Doctrine of the Incarnation in Athanasius and Cyril of Alexandria', *Encounter* (Indianapolis) 38, 1977, 362–91.

S. Brock, 'A Baptismal Address attributed to Athanasius', *Oriens Christianus* 61, 1977, 92–102.

F. Ricken, 'Zur Rezeption der platonischen Ontologie bei Eusebios von Kaisareia, Areios und Athanasios', *Theologie und Philosophie* 53, 1978, 321–52.

A. Vööbus, 'Entdeckung einer unbekannten Biographie des Athanasios von Alexandrien', *Byzantinische Zeitschrift* 71, 1978, 36–40.

George Dragas, 'Holy Spirit and Tradition: The Writings of St Athanasius', *Sobornost* (inc. *Eastern Churches Review*) 1.1, 1979, 51–72.

M. Tetz, 'Zur Biographie des Athanasius von Alexandrien', *Zeitschrift für Kirchengeschichte* 90, 1979, 304–38.

A. Hamilton, 'Athanasius and the Simile of the Mirror', *VC* 34, 1980, 14–18.

G. C. Stead, 'Athanasius' *De Incarnatione*: An Edition Reviewed', *JTS* NS 31, 1980, 378–90.

3. Didymus the Blind

Texts and translations

Sur Zacharie, ed. L. Doutreleau (SC 83, 84, 85), 1962.

Kommentar zum Ecclesiastes I, ed. G. Binder and L. Liesenborghs (Papyrologische Texte und Abhandlungen), Bonn 1965.

Kommentar zu Hiob, ed. A. Henrichs, 3 vols. (Pap. Texte und Abh.), Bonn 1968.

Psalmenkommentar I, ed. L. Doutreleau *et al.* (Pap. Texte und Abh.), Bonn 1969.

Psalmenkommentar II–V, ed. M. Grönewald (Pap. Texte und Abh.), Bonn 1968–70.

Kommentar zum Ecclesiastes I–VI, ed. G. Binder, L. Liesenborghs, J. Kramer, B. Krebber and M. Grönewald (Pap. Texte und Abh.), Bonn 1969–79.

De Trinitate I, ed. J. Hönscheid, Meisenheim 1975.

De Trinitate II.1–7, ed. I. Seiler, Meisenheim 1975.

Sur la Genèse, ed. P. Nautin and L. Doutreleau (SC 233, 244), 1976, 1978.

Books

L. Béranger, *Études sur la Christologie du De Trinitate attribué à Didyme l'Aveugle*, Lyons 1960.

A. Gesché, *La Christologie du 'Commentaire sur les Psaumes' découvert à Toura*, Gembloux 1962.

W. A. Bienert, *'Allegoria' und 'Anagoge' bei Didymos der Blinden von Alexandria* (Patristische Texte und Studien 13), Berlin 1972.

J. H. Tigcheler, *Didyme l'Aveugle et l'exégèse allégorique, son commentaire sur Zacharie*, Nijmegen 1977.

Articles

L. Doutreleau, 'Ce que l'on trouvera dans l'*In Zachariam* de Didyme l'Aveugle', *StudPatr* 3, 1961, 183–95.

L. Béranger, 'Sur deux énigmes du *De Trinitate* de Didyme l'Aveugle', *RSR* 51, 1963, 255–67.

M. Bogaert, 'Fragment inédit de Didyme l'Aveugle en traduction latine ancienne', *Revue Bénédictine* 73, 1963, 9–16.

L. Doutreleau, 'Le *De Spiritu Sancto* de Didyme et ses éditeurs', *RSR* 51, 1963, 383–406.

R. Merkelbach, 'Konjecturen und Erlauterungen zum Psalmenkommentar des Didymos', *VC* 20, 1966, 214–26.

L. Doutreleau and L. Koenen, 'Nouvel inventaire des Papyrus de Toura', *RSR* 55, 1967, 547–64.

A. Henrichs, 'Didymos in koptischer Übersetzung', *Zeitschrift für Papyrologie und Epigraphie* 4, 1969, 219–22.

L. Doutreleau, 'Étude d'une tradition manuscrite: le *De Spiritu Sancto* de Didyme', in *Kyriakon. Festchrift* J. Quasten, Münster 1970, I, 352–89.

B. Pruche, 'Didyme l'Aveugle est-il bien l'auteur des livres *Contre Eunome* IV et V attribués à Saint Basile de Césarée?', *StudPatr* 10, 1970, 151–5.

S. Brock, 'Didymus the Blind on Bardaisan', *JTS* NS 22, 1971, 530.

J. C. M. van Winden, 'Didyme l'Aveugle sur la Genèse I.10. A propos d'une première édition', *VC* 32, 1978, 60–65.

CHAPTER 3

The Cappadocians in general

Text

Origène, *Philocalie 21–27 (Sur le libre arbitre)* ed. E. Junod (SC 226), 1976.

Books

J. Bernardi, *La prédication des Pères cappadociens*. Le prédicateur et son auditoire, Marseille 1968.

R. C. Gregg, *Consolation Philosophy: Greek and Christian Paideia in Basil and the Two Gregories* (Patristic Monographs 3), Cambridge, Mass. 1975.

T. A. Kopecek, *A History of Neo-Arianism*, 2 vols. (Patristic Monographs 8), Cambridge, Mass. 1979.

Articles

J. Gribomont, 'Le monachisme au sein de l'église en Syrie et en Cappadoce', *Studia Monastica* 7, 1965, 7–24.

F. Quere-Jaulmes, 'L'aumône chez Grégoire de Nysse et Grégoire de Nazianze', *StudPatr* 8, 1966, 449–55.

M. Harl, 'Les trois quarantaines de la vie de Moïse, schéma idéal de la vie du moine-évêque chez les Pères cappadociens', *Revue des Études Grecques* 80, 1967, 407–12.

J. F. Mitchell, 'Consolatory Letters in Basil and Gregory of Nazianzus', *Hermes* 96, 1968, 299–318.

M. van Parys, 'Exégèse et théologie trinitaire: Prov. 8.22 chez les Pères cappadociens', *Irenikon* 43, 1971, 493–514.

D. F. Winslow, 'Christology and Exegesis in the Cappadocians', *Church History* 40, 1971, 389–96.

E. Junod, 'Remarques sur la composition de la *Philocalia* d'Origène par Basile de Césarée et Grégoire de Nazianze', *Revue d'histoire et de philosophie religieuses* 52, 1972, 149–56.

T. A. Kopecek, 'The Social Class of the Cappadocian Fathers', *Church History* 42, 1973, 453–66.

— 'The Cappadocian Fathers and Civic Patriotism', ibid. 43, 1974, 293–303.

E. Amand de Mendieta, 'Les deux homélies sur la création de l'homme que les manuscrits attribuent à Basile de Césarée ou à Grégoire de Nysse', in *Zetesis*. Album amicorum Prof. Dr E. de Strycker, Utrecht 1973, 695–716.

A. Meredith, 'Proverbes viii. 22 chez Origène, Athanase, Basile et Grégoire de Nysse' in *Politique et Théologie chez Athanase d'Alexandrie*, ed. C. Kannengiesser, Paris 1974, 349–58.

— 'Orthodoxy, Heresy and Philosophy in the Latter Half of the Fourth Century', *Heythrop Journal* 16, 1975, 5–21.

— 'Asceticism Christian and Greek', *JTS* NS 27, 1976, 313–32.

D. Balas, 'The Unity of Human Nature in Basil's and Gregory of Nyssa's Polemics against Eunomius', *StudPatr* 14, 1976, 275–81.

F. M. Young, 'The God of the Greeks and the Nature of Religious Language', in *Early Christian Literature and the Classical Intellectual Tradition*. In honorem R. M. Grant, ed. W. R. Schoedel and R. L. Wilken, Paris 1979, 47–74.

P. Maraval, 'Encore les frères et soeurs de Grégoire de Nysse', *Revue d'histoire et de philosophe religieuses* 60, 1980, 161–6.

1. Basil of Caesarea

Texts and translations

Lettres, ed. Y. Courtonne, 2 vols. (Budé), Paris 1961, 1966.

L'homélie de Basile de Césarée sur le mot 'Observe-toi toi-même', ed. S. Y.Rudberg, Stockholm 1962.

Exegetic Homilies, trs. A. C. Way (Fathers of the Church), Washington 1963.

Über den heiligen Geist, introd. and trs. M. Blum, Freiburg 1967.

Les règles monastiques, introd. and trs. L. Lèbe, Maredsous 1969.

Sur l'origine de l'homme (*Hexaemeron* X–XI), ed. A. Smets and M. van Esbroek (SC 160), 1970.

Briefe II, introd. and trs. W. D. Hauschild, Stuttgart 1973.

Saint Basil on the Value of Greek Literature, text and commentary by N. G. Wilson, London 1975.

On the Spirit, Hexaemeron, Letters, NPNF II.VIII, reprinted 1978.

Books

J. Doresse and E. Lanne, *Un témoin archaïque de la liturgie copte de S. Basile*, with appendix by E. Capelle, *Les liturgies 'basiliennes' et S. Basile*, Louvain 1960.

T. Spidlik, *La sophiologie de S. Basile*, Rome 1961.

H. Dehnhard, *Das Problem der Abhängigkeit des Basilius von Plotin* (Patristische Texte und Studien 3), Berlin 1964.

E. Amand de Mendieta, *The Unwritten and Secret Apostolic Tradition in the Theological Thought of St Basil of Caesarea* (*SJT* Occasional Papers 13), Edinburgh 1965.

W. M. Hayes, *The Greek Manuscript Tradition of (Ps.) Basil's Adversus Eunomium IV–V*, Leiden 1972.

Y. Courtonne, *Un témoin du IVe siècle oriental. Saint Basile et son temps d'après sa correspondence*, Paris 1973.

L. Schucan, *Das Nachleben von Basilius Magnus 'ad adolescentes'. Ein Beitrag zur Geschichte des christlichen Humanismus*, Geneva 1973.

M. Orphanos, *Creation and Salvation according to St Basil of Caesarea*, Athens 1975.

P. J. Fedwick, *The Church and the Charisma of Leadership in Basil of Caesarea*, Toronto 1979.

E. Amand de Mendieta and Stig Y. Rudberg, *Basile de Césarée: la tradition manuscrite directe des neuf homélies sur l'Hexaémeron, étude philologique* (TU 123), Berlin 1980.

P. Luislampe, *Spiritus vivificans. Grundzüge einer Theologie des heiligen Geistes nach Basilius von Caesarea*, Münster 1981.

Articles

E. Amand de Mendieta, 'The Critical Edition of St Basil's Homilies on the Hexaemeron', *StudPatr* 3, 1961, 38–43.

J. Bernardi, 'La date de l'Hexaémeron de saint Basile' *StudPatr* 3, 1961, 165–9.

J. Gribomont, 'Saint Basile' in *Théologie de la vie monastique: études sur la tradition patristique*, Paris 1961, 99–114.

W. E. Pitt, 'The Origin of the Anaphora of the Liturgy of St Basil', *Journal of Ecclesiastical History* 12, 1961, 1–13.

E. Rouillard, 'La tradition manuscrite des Homélies diverses de saint Basile', *StudPatr* 3, 1961, 116–23.

S. Rudberg, 'The Manuscript Tradition of the "Moral" Homilies of St Basil', *StudPatr* 3, 1961, 124–8.

G. J. M. Bartelink, 'Observations de saint Basile sur la langue biblique et théologique', *VC* 17, 1963, 85–104.

J. Gribomont, 'L'origénisme de S. Basile', in *L'homme devant Dieu. Mélanges H. Lubac I*, Paris 1963, 281–94.

M. Aubineau, 'Un témoin du *De Baptismo* attribué à S. Basile: le Codex Harleianus 5666', *JTS* NS 15, 1964, 75 f.

B. Pruche, 'Autour du traité sur le Saint-Esprit de S. Basile de Césarée', *RSR* 52, 1964, 204–32.

E. Amand de Mendieta, 'The Pair Κήρυγμα and Δόγμα in the Theological Thought of St Basil of Caesarea', *JTS* NS 16, 1965, 129–42.

H. Dörries, 'Basilius und das Dogma von Heiligen Geist', *Wort und Stunde* I, Göttingen 1965, 118–44.

S. Giet, 'Basile, était-il sénateur?', *Revue d'Histoire Ecclésiastique* 60, 1965, 429–44.

J. Gribomont, 'Le monasticisme au sein de l'église en Syrie et en Cappadoce', *Studia Monastica* 7, 1965, 21 f.

A. Heising, 'Der Heilige Geist und die Heiligung der Engel in der Pneumatologie des Basilius von Cäsarea', *Zeitschrift für katholische Theologie* 87, 1965, 257–308.

L. Lèbe, 'S. Basile et ses Règles Morales', *Revue Bénédictine* 75, 1965, 193–200.

T. F. Torrance, 'Spiritus Creator. A Consideration of the Teaching of St Athanasius and St Basil', in his *Theology in Reconstruction*, London 1965, Grand Rapids, Mich. 1966, 209–28.

E. Amand de Mendieta, 'L'édition critique des homélies de Basile de Césarée', *StudPatr* 7, 1966, 35–45.

L. Lèbe, 'Saint Basile. Note à propos les Règles monastiques', *Revue Bénédictine* 76, 1966, 116–19.

R. Cadiou, 'Le problème des relations scolaires entre S. Basile et Libanius', *Revue des Études Grecques* 79, 1966, 89–98.

J. Coman, 'La demonstration dans le traité *Sur le Saint Esprit* de Saint Basile le Grand', *StudPatr* 9, 1966, 172–209.

B. Pruche, 'Δόγμα et Κήρυγμα dans le traité *Sur le Saint-Esprit* de Saint Basile de Césarée en Cappadoce', *StudPatr* 9, 1966, 257–62.

E. Rouillard, 'Peut-on retrouver le texte authentique de la prédication de saint Basile?', *StudPatr* 7, 1966, 90–101.

K. Treu, 'Fragmente von vier Handschriften des der Basilius-Homilien in Moskau (Lenin-Bibliothek Gr.166, 7.19.20.26)', *StudPatr* 7, 1966, 102–5.

J. Blomqvist, 'Basilius der Grosse *De legendis libris gentilium* V.28–34 Boulenger (572C Migne)', *Eranos* 65, 1967, 169 f.

E. Rouillard, 'Recherches sur la tradition manuscrite des Homélies Diverses de S. Basile', *Revue Mabillon* 57, 1967, 1–16, 45–55.

U. Knorr, 'Der 43. Brief des Basilius der Grosse und die Nilus-Briefe', *ZNW* 58, 1967, 279–86.

J. E. Bamburger, 'Μνήμη-Διάθεσις. The Psychic Dynamisms in the Ascetical Theology of St Basil', *Orientalia Christiana Periodica* 34, 1968, 233–51.

R. P. C. Hanson, 'Basil's Doctrine of Tradition in Relation to the Holy Spirit', *VC* 22, 1968, 241–55.

B. Bobrinskoy, 'Liturgie et ecclésiologie trinitaire de saint Basile', *Verbum Caro* 89, 1969, 1–32.

J. M. Hornus, 'La divinité du saint-Esprit comme condition du salut personnel selon Basile', *Verbum Caro* 89, 1969, 33–62.

P. C. Christou, 'L'enseignement de saint Basile sur le saint-Esprit', *Verbum Caro* 89, 1969, 86–99.

N. Corneanu, 'Les efforts de saint Basile pour l'unité de l'église', *Verbum Caro* 90, 1969, 43–67.

U. Knorr, 'Einige Bemerkungen zu vier unechten Basilius-Briefe', *Zeitschrift für Kirchengeschichte* 80, 1969, 375–81.

E. Amand de Mendieta, 'L'authenticité de la lettre 45 de Basile de

Césarée', *StudPatr* 19, 1970, 44–53.

D. Savramis, 'Basilius der Grosse als Vermittler zwischen Himmel und Erde', *Kyrios* 10, 1970, 65–75.

A. Moffatt, 'The Occasion of Basil's Address to Young Men', *Antichthon* 6, 1972, 74–86.

F. van de Paverd, 'Die Quellen der kanonischen Brief Basilios des Grossen', *Orientalia Christiana Periodica* 38, 1972, 5–63.

E. Amand de Mendieta, 'Les deux homélies sur la création de l'homme que les manuscrits attribuent à Basile de Césarée ou à Grégoire de Nysse', in *Zetesis*. Album amicorum Prof. Dr. E. de Strycker, Utrecht 1973, 695–716.

G. May, 'Basilios der Grosse und die römische Staat', in *Bleibendes im Wandel der Kirchengeschichte* für H. von Campenhausen, ed. B. Moeller and G. Ruhbach, Tübingen 1973, 47–70.

J. Taylor, 'St Basil the Great and Pope St Damasus I', *Downside Review* 91, 1973, 186–203, 262–74.

J. Gribomont, 'Les lemmes de citation de S. Basile indice de niveau litteraire', *Augustinianum* 14, 1974, 513–26.

E. Oberg, ''Ως παρά. Wer schreib den sogenannten 150. Brief des Basileios?', *Zeitschrift für Kirchengeschichte* 85, 1974, 1–10.

M. Aghiorgoussis, 'Image as "Sign" (*semeion*) of God: Knowledge of God through the Images according to St Basil' (trans. N. Pissare), *Greek Orthodox Theological Review* 21, 1976, 19–54.

— 'Applications of the Theme '*Eikon Theou*' (Image of God) according to St Basil', ibid., 265–88.

E. Amand de Mendieta, 'La plus ancienne tradition manuscrite (ixe et xe siècles) des homélies de Basile de Césarée sur l'Hexaémeron', *StudPatr* 14, 1976, 253–74.

— 'The Official Attitude of Basil of Caesarea as a Christian Bishop towards Greek Philosophy and Science', in *The Orthodox Churches and the West*, ed. D. A. Baker (Studies in Church History 13), Oxford 1976, 25–50.

F. X. Murphy, 'Moral and Ascetical Doctrine in St Basil', *StudPatr* 14, 1976, 320–26.

E. F. Osborn, 'Basil the Great' in *Ethical Patterns in Early Christian Thought*, Cambridge 1976, ch. 3.

J. Verhees, 'Pneuma, Erfahrung und Erleuchtung in der Theologie des Basilius des Grossen', *Ostkirchlichen Studien* 25, 1976, 43–59.

J. Verhees, 'Die Bedeutung der Transzendenz des Pneuma bei Basilius', *Ostkirchlichen Studien* 25, 1976, 285–302.

J. Gribomont, 'Un aristocrate revolutionaire, évêque et moine: S. Basile', *Augustinianum* 17, 1977, 179–91.

J. Rippinger, 'The Concept of Obedience in the Monastic Writings of Basil and Cassian', *Studia Monastica* 19, 1977, 7–18.

E. Amand de Mendieta, 'Les neufs homélies de S. Basile de Césarée sur l'Hexaémeron', *Byzantion* 48, 1978, 337–68.

P. J. Fedwick, 'A Commentary of Gregory of Nyssa or the 38th Letter of Basil of Caesarea', *Orientalia Christiana Periodica* 44, 1978, 31–51.

M. B. von Stritzky, 'Das Theodizeeproblem in der Sicht des Basilius von Caesarea', in *Studien zur Religion und Kultur Kleinasiens für K. Dörner* II, Leiden 1978, 868–81.

J. Verhees, 'Mitteilbarkeit Gottes in der Dynamik von Sein und Wirken nach der Trinitätstheologie des Basilius des Grossen', *Ostkirchliche Studien* 27, 1978, 3–24.

G. Chantraine, 'Erasme et saint Basile', *Irenikon* 52, 1979, 451–90.

P. J. Fedwick, 'The Citations of Basil of Caesarea in the Florilegium of Pseudo-Antony Melissa', *Orientialia Christiana Periodica* 45, 1979, 32–44.

E. Lamberz, 'Zum Verständnis von Basileios' Schrift "Ad adolescentes"', *Zeitschrift für Kirchengeschichte* 90, 1979, 221–41.

J. Leroy, 'L'influence de saint Basile sur la reforme studite d'après les Catéchèses', *Irenikon* 52, 1979, 491–506.

John Wortley, 'An Unpublished Legend of an Unworthy Priest and St Basil the Great (BHG 1449)', *Analecta Bollandiana* 97, 1979, 363–72.

Charles A. Frazee, 'Anatolian Asceticism in the Fourth Century: Eustathius of Sebasteia and Basil of Caesarea', *Catholic Historical Review* 66, 1980, 16–33.

D. J. Geanakoplos, 'St Basil, "Christian humanist" of the "Three Hierarchs" and Patron Saint of Greek Letters', *Greek Orthodox Theological Review* 25, 1980, 94–102.

J. T. Leinhard, 'St Basil's *Asceticon Parva* and the *Regula Benedicti*', *Studia Monastica* 22, 1980, 231–42.

D. J. Constantelos, 'Basil the Great's Social Thought and Involvement', *Greek Orthodox Theological Review* 26, 1981, 81–6.

Sherman Garnett, 'The Christian Young and the Secular World: St Basil's Letter on Pagan Literature', *Greek Orthodox Theological Review* 26, 1981, 211–23.

L. J. Swift, 'Basil and Ambrose on the Six Days of Creation', *Augustinianum* 21, 1981, 317–28.

2. Gregory of Nazianzus

Texts and translations

Die fünf theologischen Reden, ed. and trs. J. Barbel, Düsseldorf 1963.

Lettres, ed. P. Gallay, 2 vols. (Budé), Paris 1964, 1967.

Briefe, ed. P. Gallay (GCS), 1969.

La Passion du Christ. Tragédie, ed. A. Tuilier (SC 149), 1969.

Adversus mulieres se adornantes. Gegen die Putzsucht des Frauen, ed. and trs. A. Knecht, Heidelberg 1972.

Lettres théologiques, ed. P. Gallay and M. Jourjon (SC 208), 1974.

De vita sua, ed. and trs. C. Jungck, Heidelberg 1974.

Discours 1–3, ed. J. Bernardi (SC 247), 1978.

Select Orations and Letters, NPNF II.VII, reprinted 1978.
Discours 27–31, ed. P. Gallay and M. Jourjon (SC 250), 1979.
Discours 20–23, ed. J. Mossay and G. Lafontaine (SC 270), 1980.

Books

M. Hauser-Meury, *Prosopographie zu den Schriften Gregors von Nazianz*, Bonn 1960.
B. Wyss, *Gregor von Nazianz. Ein griechisch-christlicher Dichter des 4. Jahrhunderts*, Darmstadt 1962.
J. Szymusiak, *Éléments de théologie de l'homme selon Grégoire de Nazianze*, Rome 1963.
J. Mossay, *La mort et l'au-delà dans S. Grégoire de Nazianze*, Louvain 1966.
R. Ruether, *Gregory of Nazianzus: Rhetor and Philosopher*, Oxford 1969.
T. Spidlik, *Grégoire de Nazianze: Introduction à l'étude de sa doctrine spirituelle*, Rome 1971.
H. Althaus, *Die Heilslehre des heiligen Gregor von Nazianz*, Münster 1973.
H. G. Beck, *Rede als Kunstwerk und Bekenntnis* (Bayerischen Akademie der Wissenschaften 1977.4), Munich 1977.
M. Kertsch, *Bildersprache bei Gregor von Nazianz. Ein Beitrag zur spätantiken Rhetorik und Popularphilosophie*, Graz 1978.
D. F. Winslow, *The Dynamics of Salvation*, Cambridge, Mass. 1979.

Articles

B. Otis, 'The Throne and the Mountain: An Essay on St Gregory Nazianzus', *Classical Journal* 56, 1961, 146–65.
P. Devos, 'S. Grégoire de Nazianze et Héllade de Césarée en Cappadoce', *Analecta Bollandiana* 79, 1961, 91–101.
Jean Plagnieux, 'Saint Grégoire de Nazianze', in *Théologie de la vie monastique. Études sur la tradition patristique*, Paris 1961, 115–30.
J. Mossay, 'La date de l'*Oratio II* de Grégoire de Nazianze et celle de son ordination', *Le Muséon* 77, 1964, 175–86.
J. T. Cummings, 'Towards a Critical Edition of the *Carmen de vita sua* of St Gregory Nazianzen', *StudPatr* 7, 1966, 52–9.
J. Szymusiak, 'Grégoire de Nazianze et le péché', *StudPatr* 9, 1966, 288–307.
— 'Pour une chronologie des discours de S. Grégoire de Nazianze', *VC* 20, 1966, 183–9.
H. M. Werhahn, 'Dubia und spuria unter den Gedichten Gregors von Nazianz', *StudPatr* 7, 1966, 337–47.
B. Delfgaauw, 'Gregor von Nazianz: Antikes und christliches Denken', *Eranos Jahrbuch* 36, 1967, 113–63.
P. Muraille, 'L'Église, peuple de l'oikumène d'après saint Grégoire de Nazianze', *Ephemerides Theologicae Lovanienses* 44, 1968, 154–78.
A. Cameron, 'Gregory of Nazianzus and Apollo', *JTS* NS 20, 1969, 240 f.

H. Dörrie, 'Die Epiphanias-Predigt des Gregor von Nazianz (hom 39) und ihre geistgeschichtliche Deutung', in *Kyriakon. Festschrift J. Quasten*, ed. P. Granfield and J. A. Jungmann, Münster 1970, I, 409–23.

J. Mossay, 'La prédication "liturgique" de Grégoire de Nazianze', *StudPatr* 10, 1970, 402–6.

A. Musurillo, 'The poetry of Gregory of Nazianzus', *Thought* 45, 1970, 45–55.

Stig Y. Rudberg, *'ΣΤΗΛΑΙ ΟΥΚ ΑΚΙΝΗΤΟΙ*. A Metaphor in Letter 154 of Gregory Nazianzen' in *Kyriakon. Festschrift J. Quasten*, ed. P. Granfield and J. A. Jungmann, Münster 1970, I, 424–6.

D. A. Sykes, 'The *Poemata Arcana* of St Gregory Nazianzen', *JTS* NS 21, 1970, 32–42.

F. Quere-Jaulmes, 'Les Pères sont-ils jansénistes? Remarques sur la traduction classique de Grégoire de Nazianze', *RSR* 45, 1971, 270–5.

C. Walter, 'Liturgy and the illustration of Gregory Nazianzen's Homilies. An Essay in Iconographical Methodology', *Revue des Études Byzantines* 29, 1971, 183–212.

J. Szymusiak, 'Les sites de Nazianze et Karbala', in *Epektasis*. Mélanges patristiques offerts au Cardinal J. Daniélou, ed. J. Fontaine et C. Kannengiesser, Paris 1972, 845–8.

J. Mossay, 'L'intervention "angélique" dans les funerailles de Constance IIe. Note sur Grégoire de Nazianze *Orat.* V.16' in *Mélanges B. Botte*, Louvain 1972, 379–99.

G. M. Lee, 'Gregor von Nazianz. Oratio XV. In Macchabaeorum Laudem 4', *ZNW* 64, 1973, 152 f.

E. P. Meijering, 'The Doctrine of the Will and of the Trinity in the Orations of Gregory of Nazianzus', *Nederlands Theologisch Tijdschrift* 27, 1973, 224–34, reprinted in his *God Being History*, Amsterdam 1975, 103–13.

C. Astruc, 'Remarques sur les signes marginaux de certains manuscrits de S. Grégoire de Nazianze', *Analecta Bollandiana* 92, 1974, 289–95.

M. Kertsch, 'Gregor von Nazianz' Stellung zu θεωρία und πρᾶξις aus der Sicht siner Reden', *Byzantion* 44, 1974, 282–9.

J. Szymusiak, 'Grégoire le Theologien, disciple d'Athanase' in *Politique et Théologie chez Athanase d'Alexandrie*, ed. C. Kannengiesser, Paris 1974, 359–63.

J. Egan, 'Gregory of Nazianzus and the Logos Doctrine', in *Word and Spirit*, ed. J. Plevnik, Willowdale, Ont. 1975, 281–322.

J. Mossay, 'Note sur Grégoire de Nazianze Oratio VIII.21–2', *StudPatr* 12, 1975, 113–18.

J. Whittaker, 'Proclus, Procopius. Psellus and the Scholia on Gregory Nazianzen', *VC* 29, 1975, 309–13.

J. Bernardi, 'Grégoire de Nazianze critique de Julien', *StudPatr* 14, 1976, 282–9.

J. Coman, 'Hellénisme et christianisme dans le 25e Discours de Saint Grégoire de Nazianze', *StudPatr* 14, 1976, 290–301.

M. Kertsch, 'Ein Bildhafter Vergleich bei Seneca, Themistios, Gregor von Nazianz und sein kynisch-stoischer Hintergrund', *VC* 30, 1976, 241–57; 31, 1977, 298–307.

F. van de Paverd, 'A Text of Gregory of Nazianzus Misinterpreted by F. E. Brightman' *Orientalia Christiana Periodica* 42, 1976, 197–206.

T. Spidlik, 'La *theoria* et la *praxis* chez Grégoire de Nazianze', *StudPatr* 14, 1976, 358–64.

L. R. Wickham and F. J. Williams, 'Some Notes on the Text of Gregory Nazianzen's *First Theological Oration*', *StudPatr* 14, 1976, 365–70.

D. F. Winslow, 'Orthodox Baptism – A Problem for Gregory Nazianzen', *StudPatr* 14, 1976, 371–4.

G. Lafontaine, 'La tradition manuscrite de la version arménienne des Discours de Grégoire de Nazianze', *Le Muséon* 90, 1977, 281–340.

J. Mossay, 'Grégoire de Nazianze. Travaux et projets récents. Chronique', *L'Antiquité Classique* 46, 1977, 594–602.

— 'Gregor von Nazianz in Konstantinopel (379–81 AD)', *Byzantion* 47, 1977, 223–38.

J. Noret, 'Les manuscrits sinaitiques de Grégoire de Nazianze', *Byzantion* 48, 1978, 146–207.

G. Lafontaine, 'Une homélie copte sur le diable et sur Michel, attribuée à Grégoire le Théologien', *Le Muséon* 92, 1979, 37–60.

B. Lorenz, 'Zur Seefahrt des Lebens in den Gedichten des Gregor von Nazianz', *VC* 33, 1979, 234–41.

J. Mossay, 'Le manuscrit grec de la Bibliothèque Historique de la Marine. Le Vincennensis S.H.1 (S. Grégoire de Nazianze)', *Le Muséon* 92, 1979, 288–98.

M. Sicherl, J. Mossay and G. Lafontaine, 'Travaux préparatoires pour une édition critique de Grégoire de Nazianze', *Revue d'Histoire Ecclésiastique* 74, 1979, 626–39.

D. A. Sykes, 'The *Poemata Arcana* of St Gregory Nazianzen: some literary questions', *Byzantinische Zeitschrift* 72, 1979, 6–15.

3. Gregory of Nyssa

Texts and Translations

Gregorii Nysseni Opera: the Jaeger Edition (all parts published are listed irrespective of date of publication: all in Leiden since 1952):

I–II *Contra Eunomium Libri*, ed. W. Jaeger and H. Langerbeck, Berlin 1921; 1960.

III.1 *Opera dogmatica minora*, ed. F. Müller, 1958.

V. *In Psalmorum Inscriptiones; In Sextum Psalmum; In Ecclesiasten Homiliae*, ed. J. Macdonough and P. Alexander, 1962.

VI. *In Canticum Canticorum commentarius*, ed. H. Langerbeck, 1960.

VII.1 *De Vita Moysis*, ed. H. Musurillo, 1964.

VIII.1 *Opera Ascetica*, ed. W. Jaeger, J. P. Cavernos, V. W. Callaghan, 1952.

VIII.2 *Epistulae*, ed. G. Pasquali, Berlin 1925, 1959.

IX. *Sermones*, ed. G. Heil, A. van Heck, E. Gebhardt, A. Spira, 1967 ff.

Supplementum: Auctorum Incertorum De creatione hominis vulgo Basilii vel Gregorii Nysseni Sermones; De Paradiso, ed. H. Hörner, 1972.

From Glory to Glory. Texts from Gregory of Nyssa's mystical writings, selected with introd. by J. Daniélou, trs. H. Musurillo, New York 1961, London 1962.

† *Die Aufstieg des Moses*, ed. M. Blum, Freiburg 1963.

De pauperibus amandis orationes duae, ed. A. van Heck, Leiden 1964 (text and Latin commentary).

Traité de la virginité, ed. M. Aubineau (SC 119), 1966.

† *Grégoire de Nysse. La colombe et la tenèbre.* Textes extraits des *Homélies sur le Cantique des Cantiques*, M. Canévet, Paris 1967.

Ascetical Works, trs. V. W. Callahan (Fathers of the Church), Washington 1967.

Vie de Moïse, ed. J. Daniélou (SC 1), 3rd ed. 1968.

Encomium in S. Stephanum protomartyrem, ed. O. Lendle, Leiden 1968.

Vie de Sainte Macrine, ed. P. Maraval (SC 178), 1971.

Die grosse katechetische Rede. Oratio catechetica magna, ed. J. Barbel, Stuttgart 1971.

De Christi natu. Die Weihnachtspredigt Gregors von Nyssa, Überlieferungsgeschichte und Texte, ed. F. Mann, Münster 1975.

† *Über das Wesen des christlichen Bekenntnisses; Über das Vollkommenheit; Über die Jungfraulichkeit*, ed. W. Blum, Stuttgart 1977.

The Life of Moses, trs. E. Ferguson and A. J. Malherbe (Classics of Western Spirituality), New York 1978.

Select Works and Letters, NPNF II.V, reprinted 1979.

Books

A. E. Dunstone, *The Atonement in Gregory of Nyssa*, London 1964.

D. Balas, *ΜΕΤΟΥΣΙΑ ΘΕΟΥ: Man's Participation in God's Perfections according to St Gregory of Nyssa*, Rome 1966.

E. Konstantinou, *Die Tugendlehre Gregors von Nyssa in Verhältnis zu der antik-philosophischen und jüdisch-christlichen Tradition*, Wurzburg 1966.

W. Jaeger (ed. H. Dörries), *Gregor von Nyssa's Lehre vom Heiligen Geist*, Leiden 1966.

E. Mühlenberg, *Die Unendlichkeit Gottes bei Gregor von Nyssa*, Göttingen 1966.

R. Staats, *Gregor von Nyssa und die Messalianer*. Die Frage der Priorität zweier altkirchlichen Schriften (PTS 8), Berlin 1968.

J. Daniélou, *L'être et le temps chez Grégoire de Nysse*, Leiden 1970. (A collection of articles from various sources not listed separately here.)

M. Harl, *Écriture et culture philosophique dans la pensée de Grégoire de Nysse*, Actes du colloque de Chevetogne, 1969, Leiden 1971.

378 *Bibliographies*

M. von Stritzky, *Zum Problem der Erkenntnis bei Gregor von Nyssa*, Münster 1973.

R. M. Hübner, *Die Einheit des Leibes Christi bei Gregor von Nyssa*, Leiden 1974.

R. Heine, *Perfection in the Virtuous Life*. A study of the relationship between edification and polemical theology in Gregory of Nyssa's *De Vita Moysis* (Patristic Monograph Series 2), Cambridge, Mass. 1975.

H. Dörrie, M. Altenburgher, A. Schramm, *Gregor von Nyssa und die Philosophie*. Zweites internationales Kolloquium über Gregor von Nyssa, 1972, Leiden 1976.

K. Bjerre-Aspegren, *Braütigam, Sonne und Mutter*. *Studien zu einigen Gottesmetaphern bei Gregor von Nyssa*, Lund 1977.

M. N. Esper, *Allegorie und Analogie bei Gregor von Nyssa*, Bonn 1979.

Articles

J. Daniélou, 'Grégoire de Nysse et le Messalianisme', *RSR* 48, 1960, 119–34.

— 'Saint Grégoire de Nysse dans l'histoire du monachisme' in *Théologie de la vie monastique. Études sur la tradition patristique*, Paris 1961, 131–42.

G. Gebhardt, 'Titel und Zeit der Rede Gregors von Nyssa "In Suam ordinationem"', *Hermes* 89, 1961, 503–7.

A. E. Dunstone, 'The Meaning of Grace in the Writings of Gregory of Nyssa', *SJT* 15, 1962, 235–44.

R. Gillet, 'L'homme divinisateur cosmique dans la pensée de saint Grégoire de Nysse', *StudPatr* 6, 1962, 62–83.

J. Gribomont, 'Le *De Instituto Christiano* et le Messalianisme de Grégoire de Nysse', *StudPatr* 5, 1962, 312–22.

B. Kötting, 'Gregor von Nyssa's Wallfahrtskritik', *StudPatr* 5, 1962, 360–7.

W. Telfer, 'The Birth of Christian Anthropology', *JTS* 13, 1962, 347–54.

J. Daniélou, 'Le symbolisme cosmique de la croix', *La Maison-Dieu* 75, 1963, 23–36.

A. Baker, 'The Great Letter of Ps.-Macarius and Gregory of Nyssa', *Studia Monastica* 6, 1964, 381–7.

J. E. Pfister, 'A Biographical Note: The Brothers and Sisters of St Gregory of Nyssa', *VC* 18, 1964, 108–13.

J. Daniélou, 'Grégoire de Nysse à travers les lettres de saint Basile et de saint Grégoire de Nazianze', *VC* 19, 1965, 31–41.

A. F. J. Klijn, 'Some Remarks on the Quotations of the Gospels in Gregory of Nyssa's "De Instituto Christiano" and Macarius' "Epistula Magna"', *VC* 19, 1965, 164–8.

O. Lendle, 'Zur Überlieferung der zweiten Predigt Gregors von Nyssa auf Stephanus', *Byzantinische Zeitschrift* 58, 1965, 320–6.

A. Baker, 'Pseudo-Macarius and Gregory of Nyssa', *VC* 20, 1966, 227–34.

J. Daniélou, 'Le traité "Sur les enfants morts prematurement" de

Grégoire de Nysse', *VC* 20, 1966, 159–82.

J. Daniélou, '*L'Adversus Arium et Sabellium* de Grégoire de Nysse et l'Origénisme Cappadocien', *RSR* 54, 1966, 61–6.

— 'La chronologie des oeuvres de Grégoire de Nysse,' *Stud Patr* 7, 1966, 159–69.

G. May, 'Gregor von Nyssa in der Kirchenpolitik seiner Zeit', *Jahrbuch der österreichischen Byzantinistischen Gesellschaft* 15, 1966, 105–32.

A. Philippou, 'The Doctrine of Evil in St Gregory of Nyssa', *StudPatr* 9, 1966, 251–6.

A. Spira, 'Rhetorik und Theologie in den Grabreden Gregors von Nyssa', *StudPatr* 9, 1966, 106–14.

G. S. Bebis, 'Gregory Nyssen's *De Vita Moysis*: A Philosophical and Theological Analysis', *Greek Orthodox Theological Review* 12, 1967, 369–93.

P. Courcelle, 'Grégoire de Nysse lecteur de Porphyre', *Revue des Études Grecques* 80, 1967, 402–6.

J. Daniélou, 'Grégoire de Nysse et le Neoplatonisme de l'École d'Athènes', *Revue des Études Grecques* 80, 1967, 395–401.

C. Kannengiesser, 'L'infinité divine chez Grégoire de Nysse', *RSR* 55, 1967, 55–65.

R. Staats, 'Die Asketen aus Mesopotamien in der Rede des Gregor von Nyssa', *VC* 21, 1967, 165–79.

J. Bouchet, 'La vision de l'économie du salut selon Grégoire de Nysse', *Rev. de Science Philosophiques et Théologiques* 52, 1968, 613–44.

J. F. Callahan, 'The Serpent and *H PAXIA* in Gregory of Nyssa', *Traditio* 24, 1968, 17–41.

M. Canévet, 'Nature du mal et économie du salut chez Grégoire de Nysse', *RSR* 56, 1968, 87–96.

J. Daniélou, 'Chrismation prébaptismale et divinité de l'Ésprit chez Grégoire de Nysse', *RSR* 56, 1968, 177–98.

A. M. Ritter, 'Gregor von Nyssa "In suam ordinationem". Eine Quelle für die Geschichte des Konzils von Konstantinopel 381?', *Zeitschrift für Kirchengeschichte* 79, 1968, 308–28.

J. C. M. van Winden, 'Grégoire de Nysse, *De Anima et Resurrectione*, PG 46, 17A', *VC* 22, 1968, 256.

M. Canévet, 'Le "De instituto christiano" est-il de Grégoire de Nysse?', *Revue des Études Grecques* 82, 1969, 404–23.

G. May, 'Die Datierung der Rede "In suam ordinationem" des Gregor von Nyssa und die Verhandlungen mit dem Pneumatomachen auf des Konzil von Konstantinopel 381', *VC* 23, 1969, 38–57.

M. van Parys, 'Un colloque sur Grégoire de Nysse', *Irenikon* 42, 1969, 540–5.

R. Staats, 'Die Datierung von "In suam ordinationem" des Gregor von Nyssa', *VC* 23, 1969, 58 f.

M. Alexandre, 'Le *De Mortuis* de Grégoire de Nysse', *StudPatr* 10, 1970, 35–43.

J. Daniélou, 'Salbung und Taufe bei Gregor von Nyssa', *Kyrios* 10, 1970, 1–7.

C. W. Macleod, '*ΑΝΑΛΥΣΙΣ*: A Study in Ancient Mysticism', *JTS* NS 21, 1970, 43–55.

H. A. Wolfson, 'The Identification of *Ex Nihilo* with Emanation in Gregory of Nyssa', *Harvard Theological Review*, 63, 1970, 53–60.

J. Daniélou, 'Grégoire de Nysse et l'origine de la fête de l'Ascension', in *Kyriakon. Festschrift J. Quasten*, ed. P. Granfield and J. A. Jungmann, Münster 1970, II, 663–6.

M. Harl, 'From Glory to Glory. L'interpretation de 2 Cor.3.18b par Grégoire de Nysse et la liturgie baptismale', ibid., II,730–5.

C. W. Macleod, 'Allegory and Mysticism in Origen and Gregory of Nyssa', *JTS* NS 22, 1971, 362–79.

J. Munitz, 'The Church at Prayer: Ecclesiological Aspects of Gregory of Nyssa's *In Canticum Canticorum*', *Eastern Churches Review* 3, 1971, 385–95.

J. Daniélou, 'La θεωρία chez Grégoire de Nysse', *StudPatr* 11, 1972, 130–45.

M. Alexandre, 'L'interpretation de Luc 16.19–31 chez Grégoire de Nysse', in *Epektasis. Mélanges patristiques offerts au Cardinal J. Daniélou*, ed. J. Fontaine and C. Kannengiesser, Paris 1972, 425–41.

M. Canévet, 'La perception de la présence de Dieu. A propos d'une expression de la XIe homélie sur le *Cantique des cantiques*', ibid. 443–54.

E. Corsini, 'L'harmonie du monde et l'homme microcosme dans le De hominis opificio', ibid. 455–62.

R. M. Hübner, 'Gregor von Nyssa als Verfasser der sog. Ep. 38 des Basilius', ibid., 463–90.

G. May, 'Einige Bemerkungen über das Verhältnis Gregors von Nyssa zu Basilius dem Grossen', ibid. 509–15.

H.-I. Marrou, 'Une théologie de la musique chez Grégoire de Nysse?' ibid., 501–8.

M.-J. Rondeau, 'Exégèse du psautier et anabase spirituelle chez Grégoire de Nysse', ibid. 517–31.

H.-D. Saffrey, 'Homo Bulla. Une image epicurienne chez Grégoire de Nysse', ibid. 533–44.

R. S. Brightman, 'Apophatic theology and divine infinity in St Gregory of Nyssa', *Greek Orthodox Theological Review* 18, 1973, 97–114.

E. Ferguson, 'God's Infinity and Man's Mutability: Perpetual Progress according to Gregory of Nyssa', ibid. 59–78.

E. Amand de Mendieta, 'Les deux homélies sur la création de l'homme que les manuscrits attribuent à Basile de Césarée ou à Grégoire de Nysse. Le problème de leur redaction', in *Zetesis*. Album amicorum Prof. Dr E. de Strycker, Utrecht 1973, 695–716.

P. Canart, 'Recentissimus, non deterrimus. Le texte de la Lettre II de Gregoire de Nysse dans la copie d'Alvise Lollino (Cod. Vaticanus Gr. 1759)', ibid. 717–731.

J. Daniélou, 'Metempsychosis in Gregory of Nyssa', in *The Heritage of the Early Church*: Essays in honour of G. V. Florovsky, ed. D. Nieman and M. Schatkin, Rome 1973, 227–43.

R. Staats, 'Gregor von Nyssa und das Bischofsamt', *Zeitschrift für Kirchengeschichte* 84, 1973, 149–73.

W. Blum, 'Eine Verbindung der zwei Hölengleichnisse; der heidnischen Antike bei Gregor von Nyssa', *VC* 28, 1974, 43–9.

D. F. Duclow, 'Gregory of Nyssa and Nicholas of Cusa: Infinity, Anthropology and the Via Negativa', *Downside Review* 92, 1974, 102–8.

M. von Stritzky, 'Beobachtungen zur Verbindung zwischen Gregor von Nyssa und Augustin', *VC* 28, 1974, 176–85.

A. Moutiana, 'La conception du salut universel selon Saint Grégoire de Nysse', in *Weg in die Zukunft*, ed. A. T. Khoury, Leiden 1975, 135–54.

P. J. Alexander, 'Gregory of Nyssa and the Simile of the Banquet of Life', *VC* 30, 1976, 55–62.

J. Daniélou, 'Onction et Baptême chez Grégoire de Nysse', *Ephemerides Liturgicae* 90, 1976, 440–45.

E. Ferguson, 'Progress in Perfection: Gregory of Nyssa's *Vita Moysis*', *StudPatr* 14, 1976, 307–14.

M. Mees, 'Mensch und Geschichte bei Gregor von Nyssa', *Augustinianum* 16, 1976, 317–36.

A. Meredith, 'Traditional Apologetic in the *Contra Eunomium* of Gregory of Nyssa', *StudPatr* 14, 1976, 315–19.

B. Otis, 'Gregory of Nyssa and the Cappadocian Concept of Time', *Stud Patr* 14, 1976, 327–57.

F. Mann, 'Gregor, rhetor et pastor. Interpretation des Proömiums der Schrift Gregors von Nyssa, *De Infantibus praemature abreptis*', *VC* 31, 1977, 126–47.

E. Mühlenberg, 'Synergism in Gregory of Nyssa', *ZNW* 68, 1977, 93–122.

P. J. Fedwick, 'A Commentary of Gregory of Nyssa or the 38th Letter of Basil of Caesarea', *Orientalia Christiana Periodica* 44, 1978, 31–51.

David Balas, '*Plenitudo Humanitatis*: the Unity of Human Nature in the Theology of Gregory of Nyssa', in *Disciplina Nostra* – Essays in memory of R. F. Evans, ed. D. F. Winslow (Patristic Monograph Series 6), Cambridge, Mass. 1979.

J. Verhees, '*ENEPΓEIAI* des Pneumas als Beweis für seine Transzendenz in der Argumentation des Gregor von Nyssa', *Orientalia Christiana Periodica* 45, 1979, 5–31.

J. C. M. van Winden, 'A Textual Problem in Gregory of Nyssa *Apologia in Hexaemeron* ch. 69', *VC* 33, 1979, 179.

P. Plass, 'Transcendent Time and Eternity in Gregory of Nyssa', *VC* 34, 1980, 180–92.

J. B. Cahill, 'The Date and Setting of Gregory of Nyssa's *Commentary on the Song of Songs*', *JTS* NS 32, 1981, 447–60.

CHAPTER 4

1. Cyril of Jerusalem

Texts and translations

Catéchèses baptismales et mystagogiques, trs. J. Bouvet, Namur 1962.
Catéchèses mystagogiques, ed. A. Piédagnel, trs. P. Paris (SC 126), 1966.
Procatechesis and Catecheses 1–12, trs. L. P. McCauley and A. A. Stephenson (Fathers of the Church), Washington 1968.
Catecheses 13–18. Mystagogical Lectures. Sermon on the Paralytic. Letter to Constantine, trs. L. P. McCauley and A. A. Stephenson (Fathers of the Church), Washington 1970.
'L'épître de Cyrille de Jérusalem à Constantine sur la vision de la croix (BHG³413)', ed. E. Bihain, *Byzantion* 43, 1973, 264–96.

Book

H. M. Riley, *Christian Initiation*. A comparative study of the interpretation of the baptismal liturgy in the mystagogical writings of Cyril of Jerusalem, John Chrysostom, Theodore of Mopsuestia, and Ambrose of Milan, Washington 1974.

Articles

C. Beukers, '"For our Emperors, Soldiers and Allies". An Attempt at Dating the 23rd Catechesis by Cyrillus of Jerusalem', *VC* 15, 1961, 177–84.
E. Bihain, 'La source d'une texte de Socrate (*HE* ii.38.2) relatif à Cyrille de Jérusalem', *Byzantion* 32, 1962, 81–91.
A. Piédagnel, 'A propos des *Catéchèses mystagogiques* de Cyrille de Jérusalem', *RSR* 55, 1967, 565.
I. Berten, 'Cyrille de Jérusalem, Eusèbe d'Émèse et la théologie semi-arienne', *Revue des Sciences Philosophiques et Théologiques* 52, 1968, 38–75.
P. Th. Camelot, 'Note sur la théologie baptismale des Catéchèses attribuées à S.Cyrille de Jérusalem', in *Kyriakon. Festschrift J. Quasten*, ed. P. Granfield and J. A. Jungmann, Münster 1970, II, 724–9.
A. Piédagnel, '*Les Catéchèses Mystagogiques* de Saint Cyrille de Jérusalem. Inventaire de la tradition manuscrite grecque', *StudPatr* 10, 1970, 141–5.
A. Renoux, 'Une version arménienne des catéchèses mystagogiques de Cyrille de Jérusalem', *Le Muséon* 85, 1972, 147–53.
A. A. Stephenson, 'St Cyril of Jerusalem's Trinitarian Theology', *StudPatr* 11, 1972, 234–41.
E. J. Yarnold, 'Baptism and Pagan Mysteries in the Fourth Century', *Heythrop Journal* 13, 1972, 247–67.

E. J. Yarnold, ' "Ideo et Romae fideles dicuntur qui baptizati sunt"': a note on *De Sacramentis* 1.1', *JTS* NS 24, 1973, 202–7.

— 'Did St Ambrose know the Mystagogical Catecheses of St Cyril of Jerusalem?', *StudPatr* 12, 1975, 184–9.

— 'The Authorship of the *Mystagogical Catecheses* attributed to Cyril of Jerusalem', *Heythrop Journal* 19, 1978, 143–61.

E. J. Cutrone, 'Cyril's *Mystagogical Catecheses* and the Evolution of the Jerusalem Anaphora', *Orientalia Christiana Periodica* 44 (1978) 52–64.

2. Epiphanius of Salamis

Texts

Epiphanio contro Mani (*haer.* LXVI), ed. C. Riggi, Rome 1967.

Panarion 34–64, ed. K. Holl, rev. ed. J. Dummer (GCS II), 1980.

Books

D. Fernandez, *De mariologia sancti Epiphanii*, Rome 1968.

L. A. Eldridge, *The Gospel Text of Epiphanius of Salamis*, Salt Lake City 1969.

Articles

P. Fraenkel, 'Histoire sainte et hérésie chez saint Epiphane de Salamine, d'après le tome I du Panarion', *Revue de Théologie et Philosophie* 12, 1963, 175–91.

E. Moutsoulas, 'Der Begriff "Häresie" bei Epiphanius von Salamis', *StudPatr* 7, 1966, 362–71.

V. Palachkovsky, 'Une interpolation dans l'*Ancoratus* de S. Epiphane', *StudPatr* 7, 1966, 265–73.

S. Benko, 'The Libertine Gnostic Sect of the Phibionites according to St Epiphanius', *VC* 21, 1967, 103–19.

P. Fraenkel, 'Une réédition du *Panarion* d'Epiphane', *Revue de Théologie et Philosophie* 19, 1969, 111–14.

B. Hemmerdinger, 'Saint Epiphane, iconoclaste', *StudPatr* 10, 1970, 118–20.

W. Lackner, 'Zum Zusatz zu Epiphanios' von Salamis *Panarion* Kap. 64', *VC* 27, 1973, 56–8.

E. Moutsoulas, 'L'oeuvre d'Epiphane de Salamine *De mensuris et ponderibus* et son unité litteraire', *StudPatr* 12, 1975, 119–22.

C. Riggi, 'Nouvelle lecture du *Panarion* LIX.4 (Epiphane et divorce)', *StudPatr* 12, 1975, 129–34.

P. Nautin, 'Epiphanios', *Annuaire de l'École pratique des Hautes Études*, V^e section: Sciences Religieuses 83, 1974–5, 232 f.

B. M. Weischer, 'Die Glaubenssymbole des Epiphanios von Salamis und des Gregorios Thaumaturgos im Qērellos', *Oriens Christianus* 61, 1977, 20–40.

B. M. Weischer, 'Die ursprungliche nikänische Form des ersten

Glaubenssymbols im Ankyrōtos des Epiphanios von Salamis', *Theologie und Philosophie* 53, 1978, 407–14.

R. M. Hübner, 'Die Hauptquelle des Epiphanios (*Panarion*, Haer.65) über Paulus von Samosata: Pseudo–Athanasius, *Contra Sabellianos*', *Zeitschrift für Kirchengeschichte* 90, 1979, 201–20.

B. M. Weischer, 'Ein arabisches und äthiopisches Fragment der Schrift "De XII Gemmis" des Epiphanios von Salamis', *Oriens Christianus* 63, 1979, 103–5.

M. Mees, 'Textformen und interpretation von Jn 6 bei Epiphanios', *Augustinianum* 21, 1981, 339–64.

3. John Chrysostom

Critical Aids

Codices Chrysostomici Graeci
  I . Britanniae et Hiberniae, ed. M. Aubineau, Paris 1968.
  II . Germaniae, ed. R. E. Carter, Paris 1968.
  III. Americae et Europae Occidentalis, ed. R. E. Carter, Paris 1970.
J. A. Aldama, *Repertorium pseudo-chrysostomicum*, Paris 1965.
Indices Chrysostomici, ed. A-M. Malingrey, vol. I: Ad Olympiadem, etc. avec M.-L. Guillaumin, Hildesheim 1978.

Texts and translations

Commentary on St John, trs. T. A. Goggin (Fathers of the Church), 2 vols. New York 1957, 1960.
Sur la providence de Dieu, ed. A.-M. Malingrey (SC 79), 1961.
'L'homélie de S. Jean Chrysostome "A son retour d'Asie"', ed. A. Wenger, *Revue des Études Byzantines* 19, 1961, 110–23.
Chrysostom and his Message (selections from his sermons), trs. S. Neill, London 1962, New York 1963.
Baptismal Instructions, trs. P. W. Harkins (ACW 31), 1963.
Lettre d'exil à Olympias et à tous les fidèles, ed. A.-M. Malingrey (SC 103), 1964.
Six Books on the Priesthood, trs. G. Neville, London 1964.
†*In Praise of St Paul*, trs. T. Halton, Boston 1964.
A Théodore, ed. J. Dumortier (SC 117), 1966.
La virginité, ed. H. Musurillo, trs. B. Grillet (SC 125), 1966.
A une jeune veuve et *Sur le mariage unique*, ed. G. Ettlinger, trs. B. Grillet (SC 138), 1968.
Lettres à Olympias, ed. A.-M. Malingrey (SC 13), 2nd ed. 1968.
†*De Sancta Babyla, Contra Iulianum et Gentiles*, ed. M. Schatkin, Ann Arbor, Michigan 1968.
Sur l'incompréhensibilité de Dieu, ed. A.-M. Malingrey (SC 28), 2nd ed. 1970.
'Une homélie inédite de Jean Chrysostome sur l'Epiphanie', ed. A. Wenger, *Revue des Etudes Byzantines* 29, 1971, 117–35.

Sur la vaine gloire et l'education des enfants, ed. A.-M. Malingrey (SC 188), 1972.

Works, NPNF I. IX–XIV, reprinted 1975–9.

Discourses against Judaizing Christians, trs. P. W. Harkins (Fathers of the Church), Washington 1979.

Sur le sacerdoce, ed. A.-M. Malingrey (SC 272), 1980.

Homélies sur Ozias, ed. J. Dumortier (SC 277), 1981.

Das Leben des heiligen Johannes Chrysostomus, trs. L. Schläpfer, Düsseldorf 1966 (German translation of Palladius' *Life*).

Douze récits byzantins sur Saint Jean Chrysostome, ed. F. Halkin (Subsidia Hagiographica 60), Brussels 1977.

Books

C. Baur, *John Chrysostom and his Time*, 2 vols., ET Westminster, Maryland 1959–60.

S. Verosta, *Johannes Chrysostomus. Staatsphilosoph und Geschichtstheologie*, Graz 1960.

O. Plassman, *Das Almosen bei Johannes Chrysostomus*, Münster 1961.

B. Vandenberghe, *Saint Jean Chrysostome et la parole de Dieu*, Paris 1961.

C. Fabricius, *Zu den Jugendschriften des Johannes Chrysostomos: Untersuchungen zum Klassizismus des vierten Jahrhunderts*, Lund 1962.

H. Tardif, *Jean Chrysostome*, Paris 1962.

J. Korbacher, *Ausserhalb der Kirche kein Heil? Ein dogmengeschichtliche Untersuchungen über Kirche und Kirchenzugehorigkeit bei Johannes Chrysostomus*, Munich 1963.

P. Stockmeier, *Theologie und Kult des Kreuzes bei Johannes Chrysostomus. Ein Beitrag zum Verstandnis des Kreuzes im 4 Jahrhundert*, Trier 1966.

T. M. Finn, *The Liturgy of Baptism in the Baptismal Instructions of St John Chrysostom*, Washington 1967.

† M. Fougias, *The Social Message of St John Chrysostom*, Athens 1968.

T. Nikolaou, *Der Neid bei Johannes Chrysostomus. Unter Berucksichtigung der griechischen Philosophie*, Bonn 1969.

F. van de Paverd, *Zur Geschichte der Messliturgie in Antiocheia und Konstantinopel gegen Ende des vierten Jahrhunderts: Analyse der Quellen bei Johannes Chrysostomos*, Rome 1970.

A. K. Danassis, *Johannes Chrysostomos. Pädagogisch-psychologische Ideen in seinem Werk*, Bonn 1971.

E. Nowak, *Le chrétien devant la souffrance. Étude sur la pensée de Jean Chrysostome*, Paris 1972.

A. M. Ritter, *Charisma im Verstandnis des Johannes Chrysostomos und seiner Zeit*, Göttingen 1972.

P. C. Christou, *Symposium. Studies on St John Chrysostom* (*ΑΝΑΛΕΚΤΑ ΒΛΑΤΑΔΩΝ* 18), Thessaloniki 1973.

R. Kaczynski, *Das Wort Gottes in Liturgie und Alltag der Gemeinden des Johannes Chrysostomos*, Freiburg 1974.

H. M. Riley, *Christian Initiation* (see p. 382), Washington 1974.

C. Kannengiesser, *Jean Chrysostome et Augustin*. Actes du colloque de Chantilly 1974, Paris 1975.

R. Brändle, *Matth. 25.31–46 im Werk des Johannes Chrysostomos*, Tübingen 1979.

B. Goodall, *The Homilies of John Chrysostom on the Letters of St Paul to Titus and Philemon* (California Classical Studies 20), Berkeley 1979.

Articles

G. J. M. Bartelink, '"Philosophie" et "Philosophe" dans quelques oeuvres de Jean Chrysostome', *Revue d'ascétique et de mystique*, 144, 1960, 486–92.

G. M. Ettlinger, 'Some Historical Evidence for the Date of St John Chrysostom's Birth in the Treatise "Ad viduam iuniorem"', *Traditio* 16, 1960, 373–80.

A. Kenny, 'Was St John Chrysostom a semi-Pelagian?', *Irish Theological Quarterly* 27, 1960, 16–29.

J. Dumortier, 'Les citations bibliques des lettres de S.Jean Chrysostome à Theodore (PG 47.277–316)', *StudPatr* 4, 1961, 78–83.

J-M. Leroux, 'Saint Jean Chrysostome: Les Homélies sur les Statues', *StudPatr* 3, 1961, 233–9.

— 'Monachisme et communauté chrétienne d'après S. Jean Chrysostome', in *Théologie de la vie monastique*, Paris 1961, 143–90.

A.-M. Malingrey, 'Vers une édition critique des oeuvres de Saint Jean Chrysostome', *StudPatr* 3, 1961, 81–4.

P. G. Racle, 'A la source d'un passage de la VIIe catéchèse baptismale de S. Jean Chrysostome?', *VC* 15, 1961, 46–53.

R. E. Carter, 'Chrysostom's *Ad Theodorum Lapsum* and the Early Chronology of Theodore of Mopsuestia', *VC* 16, 1962, 87–101.

— 'The Chronology of Saint John Chrysostom's Early Life', *Traditio* 18, 1962, 357–64.

H. Benedict Green, 'The Significance of the Pre-baptismal Seal in St John Chrysostom', *StudPatr* 6, 1962, 84–90.

A.-M. Malingrey, 'Étude sur les manuscrits d'un texte de Jean Chrysostome "De Providentia Dei" incipit Ἰατρῶν μὲν παῖδες', *Traditio* 18, 1962, 25–68.

T. P. Halton, 'Saint John Chrysostom "De Fato et Providentia"': A Study of its Authenticity', *Traditio* 20, 1964, 1–24.

F. J. Leroy, 'Les manuscrits de Montfaucon et l'édition de S. Jean Chrysostome', *Traditio* 20, 1964, 411–18.

A.-M. Malingrey, 'Études sur les manuscrits d'un texte de Jean Chrysostome: Lettre d'exil à Olympias et à tous les fidèles, incipit Οἶδα μὲν ὅτι τοῖς παχυτέροις', *Traditio* 20, 1964, 418–27.

— 'Études sur les manuscrits des lettres de Jean Chrysostome à Olympias', *Traditio* 21, 1965, 425–44.

E. Amand de Mendieta, 'L'amplification d'un thème socratique et stoicien dans l'avant-dernier traité de Jean Chrysostome', *Byzantion* 36, 1966, 353–81.

E. Bickersteth, 'Edition with translation of a Hypapante Homily ascribed to John Chrysostom', *Orientalia Christiania Periodica* 32, 1966, 53–77.

J. Dumortier, 'L'ancienne tradition latine de l'*Ad Theodorum*', *StudPatr* 7, 1966, 178–83.

P. W. Harkins, 'The Text Tradition of Chrysostom's Commentary on John', *StudPatr* 7, 1966, 210–20.

— 'Pre-baptismal Rites in Chrysostom's Baptismal Catecheses', *StudPatr* 8, 1966, 219–38.

A.-M. Malingrey, 'La tradition latine d'un texte de Jean Chrysostome (*Quod nemo laeditur*)', *StudPatr* 7, 1966, 248–54.

H. Sorlin, 'Un commentaire inédit sur Job, attribué à S. Jean Chrysostome', *StudPatr* 7, 1966, 543–8.

P. Krüger, 'Eine bisher unbekannte Homilie des hl. Johannes Chrysostomos in syrische Übersetzung', *Oriens Christianus* 51, 1967, 78–96.

A.-M. Malingrey, 'Role du Parisinus Gr. 657 dans l'établissement du texte des lettres de Jean Chrysostome à Olympias', *Traditio* 23, 1967, 439–41.

F.-J. Thonnard, 'S. Jean Chrysostome et S. Augustin dans la controverse pélagienne', *Revue des Études Byzantines* 25, 1967, 189–218.

M. Aubineau, 'Une enquète dans les manuscrits chrysostomiens: opportunité, difficultés, premier bilan', *Revue d'Histoire Ecclésiastique* 63, 1968, 5–26.

J. Coman, 'Le rapport de la justification et de la charité dans les homélies de Saint Jean Chrysostome à l'Épître aux Romains', *Studia Evangelica* 5 (TU 103), 1968, 248–71.

R. Hill, 'St John Chrysostom's Teaching on Inspiration in "Six Homilies on Isaiah"', *VC* 22, 1968, 19–37.

F. Leduc, 'La thème de la vaine gloire chez S. Jean Chrysostome', *Proche-Orient Chrétien* 19, 1969, 3–32.

— 'L'eschatologie, une préoccupation centrale de S. Jean Chrysostome', *Proche-Orient Chrétien* 19, 1969, 109–34.

A.-M. Malingrey, 'Un essai de classement dans la tradition manuscrite des Homélies de Jean Chrysostome "De Incomprehensibili"', *Traditio* 25, 1969, 339–53.

M.-J. Rondeau, 'Une pseudo-preface aux Psaumes de Saint Jean Chrysostome', *JTS* NS 20, 1969, 241–5.

R. E. Carter, 'The Future of Chrysostom Studies', *StudPatr* 10, 1970, 14–21.

F. T. Gignac, 'The Text of Acts in Chrysostom's Homilies', *Traditio* 26, 1970, 308–15.

P. W. Harkins, 'Chrysostom's *Sermo ad Neophytos*', *StudPatr* 10, 1970, 112–17.

A.-M. Malingrey, 'La tradition manuscrite des homélies de Jean Chrysostome *De Incomprehensibili*', *StudPatr* 10, 1970, 22–8.

P. W. Harkins, 'Chrysostom the Apologist. On the Divinity of Christ', in *Kyriakon*. Festschrift J. Quasten, ed. P. Granfield and J. A. Jungmann, Münster 1970, I, 441–51.

H. Musurillo, 'John Chrysostom's Homilies on Matthew and the version of Anianus', in *Kyriakon* I, 452–60.

M. Schatkin, 'The authenticity of St John Chrysostom's *De Sancto Babyla, Contra Iulianum et Gentiles*' in *Kyriakon* I, 474–89.

J. Streub, 'Divus Alexander-Divus Christus', in *Kyriakon* I, 461–73.

J.-P. Bouhot, 'Version inédite du sermon 'Ad neophytos' de S. Jean Chrysostome, utilisée par S. Augustin', *Revue des Études Augustiniennes* 17, 1971, 27–41.

J.-M. Leroux, 'Jean Chrysostome et la querelle origéniste', in *Epektasis*. Mélanges patristiques offerts au Cardinal J. Daniélou, ed. J. Fontaine and C. Kannengiesser, Paris 1972, 335–41.

F. Graffin and A.-M. Malingrey, 'La tradition syriaque des homélies de Jean Chrysostome sur l'incomprehensibilité de Dieu', in *Epektasis*, 603–10.

F. X. Murphy, 'The Moral Doctrine of St John Chrysostom', *StudPatr* 11, 1972, 52–7.

J. C. Sladden, 'Chrysostom and Confirmation', *StudPatr* 11, 1972, 229–33.

J. Lecuyer, 'Saint Jean Chrysostome et l'ordre du diaconat', in *Mélanges B.Botte*, Louvain 1973, 295–310.

H. Dörries, 'Erneuerung des kirchlichen Amts im vierten Jahrhundert. Die Schrift *De Sacerdotio* des Johannes Chrysostomos und ihre Vorlage, die *Oratio de fuga sua* des Gregor von Nazianz', in *Bleibendes im Wandel der Kirchengeschichte* für H. Campenhausen, ed. B. Moeller and G. Ruhbach, Tübingen 1973, 1–46.

A. M. Ritter, 'Erwägungen zum Antisemitismus in der alten Kirche. Johannes Chrysostomos, Acht Reden wider die Juden', in *Bleibendes im Wandel. . . . (cit. sup.)*, 71–91.

P. Harkins, 'Chrysostom's Post-baptismal Instructions', in *The Heritage of the Early Church* for G. V. Florovsky, ed. D. Niemann and M. Schatkin, Rome 1973, 151–65.

M. Schatkin, 'St John Chrysostom's Homily on the Protopaschites: Introduction and Translation' in *The Heritage of the Early Church*, 167–86.

M. Aubineau, 'Textes chrysostomiens dans les manuscrits athonites Dochariou 12 et Koutloumous 29, 30, 54, 55', *Kleronomia* 6, 1974, 97–104.

— 'Un nouveau "Panegyricon chrysostomien" pour les fêtes fixes de l'année liturgique, Athos Panteleimon 58', *Analecta Bollandiana* 92, 1974, 79–96.

— 'Soixant-six textes, attribués à Jean Chrysostome, découverts dans le codex Athos Iviron 255', *VC* 29, 1975, 55–64.

F. Halkin, 'L'éloge de S. Jean Chrysostome par Proclus de Constantinople', *Analecta Bollandiana* 93, 1975, 20.

J. L. Malkowski, 'The Element of ἄκαιρος in John Chrysostom's anti-Jewish Polemic', *StudPatr* 12, 1975, 222–31.

J. Noret, 'Un fragment exégétique de Chrysostome trouvé dans une reliure', *Analecta Bollandia* 93, 1975, 182.

F. van Ommeslaeghe, 'La valeur historique de la *Vie de S. Jean Chrysostome* attribuée à Martyrius d'Antioche (BHG 871)', *StudPatr* 12, 1975, 478–83.

A. Piédagnel, 'L'angoisse du salut des Juifs dans l'âme de l'Apôtre Paul d'après le *De Laudibus Pauli* de Jean Chrysostome', *StudPatr* 13, 1975, 269–72.

K. Treu, 'Ein Berliner Chrysostomos-Papyrus (P.6788A)', *StudPatr* 12, 1975, 71–5.

M. Zitnik, 'Θεὸς φιλάνθρωπος bei Johannes Chrysostomos', *Orientalia Christiana Periodica* 41, 1975, 76–118.

M. Aubineau, 'La vie inédite de Chrysostome par Martyrius. Un nouveau témoin: Athos Koutloumousiou 13', *Analecta Bollandiana* 94, 1976, 394.

F. Halkin, 'Un appendice inédot à la *Vie de S. Jean Chrysostome* par Symeon Métaphraste', *Analecta Bollandiana* 94, 1976, 19–21.

F. Leduc, 'Pèche et conversion chez Saint Jean Chrysostome', *Proche-Orient Chrétien* 26, 1976, 34–58; 27, 1977, 15–42.

A.-M. Malingrey, 'Pour une édition critique du "De Sacerdotio" de Jean Chrysostome', *Traditio* 32, 1976, 347–52.

F. van Ommeslaeghe, 'Une vie acéphale de saint Jean Chrysostome dans le Batopedinus 73', *Analecta Bollandiana* 94, 1976, 317–56.

M. Zitnik, 'Das Sein des Menschen zu Gott nach Johannes Chrysostomos', *Orientalia Christiana Periodica* 42, 1976, 368–401; 43, 1977, 18–40.

R. Brändle, 'Jean Chrysostome: L'Importance de Matth. 25.31–46 pour son éthique', *VC* 31, 1977, 47–52.

J-P. Bouhot, 'Une homélie de Jean Chrysostome citée par Julien de Tolède', *Revue des Études Augustiniennes* 23, 1977, 122 f.

E. A. Clark, 'John Chrysostom and the *Subintroductae*', *Church History* 46, 1977, 171–85.

— 'Sexual Politics in the writings of John Chrysostom', *Anglican Theological Review* 59, 1977, 3–20.

F. van Ommeslaeghe, 'Que vaut le témoinage de Pallade sur le procès de saint Jean Chrysostome?', *Analecta Bollandiana* 95, 1977, 389–414.

H. de Lubac, 'Le Dialogue sur le Sacerdoce de saint Jean Chrysostome', *Nouvelle Revue Théologique* 100, 1978, 822–31.

M. Aubineau 'Un extrait retrouvé chez Cosmas Indicopleustès d'un *Discours sur l'aumône* de saint Jean Chrysostome (PF 49.293)', *Bulletin de Littérature ecclésiastique* 80, 1979, 213–18.

F. van Ommeslaeghe, 'Jean Chrysostome en conflit avec l'impératrice

F. van Ommeslaeghe, 'Jean Chrysostome en conflit avec l'impératrice Eudoxie. Le dossier et les origines d'une légende', *Analecta Bollandiana* 97, 1979, 131–59.
E. Dekkers, 'Limites sociales et linguistiques de la pastorale liturgique de S. Jean Chrysostome', *Augustinianum* 20, 1980, 119–29.
F. van Ommeslaeghe, 'Jean Chrysostome et le peuple de Constantinople', *Analecta Bollandiana* 99, 1981, 329–49.

4. Nemesius of Emesa

Text

De Natura Hominis, ed. G. Verbeke and J. R. Moncho, Leiden 1975.

Book

A. Kallis, *Der Mensch im Kosmos, das Weltbild Nemesios' von Emesa*, Münster 1978.

Articles

W. Telfer, 'The Birth of Christian Anthropology', *JTS* NS 13, 1962, 347–54.
R. C. Dales, 'An Unnoticed Translation of the Chapter *De Elementis* from Nemesius' *De Natura Hominis*', *Mediaevalia et Humanistica* 17, 1966, 13–19.
E. Wyller, 'Die Anthropologie des Nemesios von Emesa und die Alkibiades I–tradition', *Symbolae Osloenses* 44, 1969, 126–45.
L. W. Barnard. 'Father of Christian Anthropology', *ZNW* 63, 1972, 254–70.

5. Synesius of Cyrene

Texts and translations

A. dell' Era, Συνεσίου Κυρηναίου ὕμνοι ἔμμετροι, Rome 1968.
Hymnes, ed. and trs. C. Lacombrade, vol. I (Coll. Universitaires de France), Paris 1978.
Epistolae, ed. A. Garzya (Scriptores Graeci et Latini), Rome 1979.

Articles

C. H. Coster, 'Christianity and the Invasions. Synesius of Cyrene', *Classical Journal* 55, 1960, 290–312.
C. Lacombrade, 'Perspectives nouvelles sur les hymnes de Synésios', *Revue des Études Grecques* 74, 1961, 439–49.
H.-I. Marrou, 'Synesius of Cyrene and Alexandrian Neoplatonism', in *The Conflict between Paganism and Christianity in the Fourth Century*, ed. A. Momigliano, Oxford and New York 1963, 126–50, reprinted in H.-I. Marrou, *Patristique et Humanisme*, Paris 1976.
H. Strohm, 'Zur Hymnendichtung des Synesios von Kyrene', *Hermes* 93, 1965, 47–54.

W. Lackner, 'Zu einer bislang ungeklärten Stelle im "Dion" des Synesios', *Byzantion* 39, 1969, 152–4.

J. Vogt, 'Synesios und Seefahrt', in *Kyriakon*. Festschrift J. Quasten, ed. P. Granfield and J. A. Jungmann, Münster 1970, I,400–8.

C. Lacombrade, 'Une nouvelle édition des hymnes de Synésios de Cyrène', *Revue des Études Grecques* 84, 1971, 151–7.

K. Smolak, 'Zur Himmelfahrt Christi bei Synesios von Kyrene (Hy.8.31–54)', *Jahrbuch der Österreichischen Byzantinischen Gesellschaft* 20, 1971, 7–30.

J. Vogt, 'Synesius im Glück der landlichen Einsamkeit', *Museum Helveticum* 28, 1971, 98–108.

J. Bregman, 'Synesius of Cyrene: Early Life and Conversion to Philosophy', *California Studies in Classical Antiquity* 7, 1974, 55–88.

E. Calvacanti, 'Y a-t-il des problèmes Eunomiens dans la pensée trinitaire de Synésius?', *StudPatr* 13, 1975, 138–44.

W. N. Bayliss, 'Synesius of Cyrene: A Study of the Role o the Bishop in Temporal Affairs', *Byzantine Studies: Études Byzantines* 4, 1977, 147–56.

W. Cramer, 'Zur Entwicklung der Zweigewaltenlehre. Ein unbeachteter Beitrag des Synesios von Kyrene', *Römische Quartalschrift* 72, 1977, 43–56.

D. Roques, 'Le lettre 4 de Synésios de Cyrène', *Revue des Études Grecques* 90, 1977, 263–95.

CHAPTER 5

General: a selection of works on doctrine, christology and exegesis

N.B. English works published since 1960 which appear in Bibliography A (pp. 350 f.) are not listed again here.

Texts and translations

Acta conciliorum oecumenicorum, ed. E. Schwartz, Berlin 1914–40, reprinted 1959–74.

† *Ephèse et Chalcédoine. Actes des conciles*, trs. A. J. Festugière, Paris.

† *Actes du Concile de Chalcédoine*. Sessions III–VI, trs. A. J. Festugiére, introd. H. Chadwick, Paris 1982.

Iohannes–Kommentare aus der griechischen Kirche, ed. J. Reuss (TU 89), Berlin 1966.

Les anciens commentateurs grecs des Psaumes, ed. R. Devreesse (Studi e Testi 264), Rome 1970.

Pauluskommèntare aus der Katenenüberlieferung, ed. E. Mühlenberg, Berlin 1975, 1977.

Books

P.-Th. Camelot, *Ephèse et Chalcédoine*, Histoire des conciles oecumeniques II, Paris 1962.

A. Luneau, *L'Histoire du salut chez les Pères de l'Église*, Paris 1964.

J. Liébaert, *L'Incarnation: I. Des Origines au Concile de Chalcédoine*, Histoire des Dogmes III, Paris 1966

P. Trummer, *Anastasis*. Beitrag zur Auslegung und Auslegungsgeschichte von I Kor. 15 in der griechischen Kirche bis Theodoret, Vienna 1970.

In Principio. Interpretations des premiers versets de la Genèse, Paris 1973.

R. A. Greer, *The Captain of our Salvation*, Tübingen 1973.

C. Schäublin, *Untersuchungen zur Methode und Herkunft der Antiochenischen Exegese*, Bonn 1974.

F. L. Horton, *The Melchizedek Tradition*, Cambridge and New York 1976.

Articles

J. C. M. van Winden, 'In the beginning. Some observations on Patristic interpretation of Gen.1.1', *VC* 17, 1963, 105–21.

†Camillus Hay, 'Antiochene Exegesis and Christology', *Australian Biblical Review* 12, 1964, 10–23.

Greek Orthodox Theological Review 10 (1964–5) is devoted to articles on Christology.

A. Louth, 'The Hermeneutical Question approached through the Fathers', *Sobornost* Series 7 No. 7, 1978, 541–9.

K. A. D. Smelik, 'The witch of Endor. I Sam. in Rabbinic and Christian exegesis till 800 AD', *VC* 33, 1979, 160–79.

1. Apollinarius of Laodicea

Books

J. Golega, *Der homerische Psalter; Studien über die dem Apollinarios von Laodikeia zugeschreibene Psalmenparaphrase* (Studia Patristica et Byzantina), Ettal 1960.

E. Mühlenberg, *Apollinarius von Laodicea*, Göttingen 1969.

Articles

R. Cadiou, 'Apollinaire et l'Isaïe de Qumran', *Revue de l'histoire des religions* 171, 1967 145–8.

—, 'Apollinaire Plotinien', *Bulletin de l'association Guillaume Budé* 25, 1966, 450–57.

R. Hübner, 'Gotteserkenntnis durch die Inkarnation Gottes. Zu einer neue Interpretation der Christologie des Apollinaris von Laodicaea', *Kleronomia* 4, 1972, 131–61.

C. Kannengiesser, 'Une nouvelle interprétation de la christologie d'Apollinaire', *RSR* 59, 1971, 27–36.

T. F. Torrance, 'The Mind of Christ in Worship: The Problem of Apollinarianism in the Liturgy', in his *Theology in Reconciliation*, London and Grand Rapids, Mich. 1975, 139–215.

J. Reuss, 'Ist Apollinaris von Laodicea Verfasser eines Lukas-Kommentars?', *Ostkirchliche Studien* 26, 1977, 28–34.

2. Diodore of Tarsus

Text

Commentarii in Psalmos, ed. J. M. Olivier (Corpus Christianorum. Series Graeca), Turnhout 1980.

Articles

L. Abramowski, 'La prétendue condamnation de Diodore de Tarse en 499', *Revue d'Histoire Ecclésiastique* 60, 1965, 64 f.

R. A. Greer, 'The Antiochene Christology of Diodore of Tarsus', *JTS* NS 17, 1966, 327–41.

M.-J. Rondeau, 'Le Commentaire des Psaumes de Diodore de Tarse et l'exégèse antique du Psaume 109/110', *Histoire des Religions* 176, 1969, 153–88; 177, 1970, 5–33.

C. Schaeublin, 'Diodor von Tarsus gegen Porphyrios', *Museum Helveticum* 27, 1970, 58–63.

3. Theodore of Mopsuestia

Texts

Bar Chadbschaba. *Geschichte der um der Wahrheit willen verfölgten Väter* I. *Theodor von Mopsuestia*, ed. S. Grill, Heiligenkreuz 1962.
Commentarius in XII Prophetas, ed. H. N. Sprenger, Wiesbaden 1977.
Expositio in Psalmos. Iuliano Aeclanensi interprete, ed. L. De Coninck (Corpus Christianorum. Series Latina 88A), Turnhout 1977.

Books

R. Greer, *Theodore of Mopsuestia: Exegete and Theologian*, London 1961.

E. Wang, *Théodore de Mopsueste et les origines du pélagianisme*, Paris 1961.

U. Wickert, *Studien zu den Pauluskommentaren Theodors von Mopsuestia*, Berlin 1962.

R. A. Norris, *Manhood and Christ: A Study in the Christology of Theodore of Mopsuestia*, Oxford and New York 1963.

G. Koch, *Die Heilsverwicklichung bei Theodor von Mopsuestia*, Munich 1965.

J. M. Dewart, *The Theology of Grace of Theodore of Mopsuestia*, Washington 1971.

H. M. Riley, *Christian Initiation* (see p. 382), Washington 1974.

Articles

L. Abramowski, 'Zur Theologie Theodors von Mopsuestia', *Zeitschrift für Kirchengeschichte* 72, 1961, 263–93.

R. E. Carter, 'Chrysostom's *Ad Theodorum Lapsum* and the Early Chronology of Theodore of Mopsuestia' *VC* 16, 1962, 87–101.

394 Bibliographies

T. Jansma, 'Théodore de Mopsueste. Interpretation du livre de la Genèse, fragments de la version syriaque (BM Add. 17189 fol. 17–21)', *Le Muséon* 75, 1962, 63–92.

U. Wickert, 'Die Personlichkeit des Paulus in der Pauluskommentaren Theodors von Mopsuestia', *ZNW* 53, 1962, 51–66.

W. C. van Unnik, 'παρρησία in the *Catechetical Homilies* of Theodore of Mopsuestia', in *Mélanges offert à Mlle C. Mohrmann*, Utrecht 1963, 12–22.

A. Vööbus, 'Regarding the Theological Anthropology of Theodore of Mopsuestia', *Church History* 33, 1964, 115–24.

W. F. Macomber, 'Newly Discovered Fragments of the Gospel Commentaries of Theodore of Mopsuestia', *Le Muséon* 81, 1968, 441–7.

M. Gibson, 'Theodore of Mopsuestia: A Fragment in the Bodleian Library' *JTS* NS 21, 1970, 104 f.

K. Schäferdick, 'Theodor von Mopsuestia als exeget des vierten Evangeliums', *StudPatr* 10, 1970, 242–6.

J. M. Dewart, 'The Notion of "Person" Underlying the Christology of Theodore of Mopsuestia', *StudPatr* 12, 1975, 199–207.

S. Khalil, 'Théodore de Mopsueste dans le 'Fihrist' d'Ibn An-Nadin, *Le Muséon* 90, 1977, 355–63.

4. Nestorius

Books

L. Abramowski, *Untersuchungen zum Liber Heraclidis des Nestorius* (CSCO 242, subsidia 22), Louvain 1963.

L. I. Scipioni, *Nestorio e il concilio de Epheso*, Milan 1974.

Articles

A. Grillmeier, 'Das Scandalum Oecumenicum des Nestorius in kirchlichdogmatischer und theologiegeschichtlicher Sicht', *Scholastik* 36, 1961, 321–56.

M. V. Anastos, 'Nestorius was Orthodox', *Dumbarton Oaks Papers* 16, 1962, 117–39.

L. I. Scipioni, 'Il Libro di Eraclide di Nestorio', *StudPatr* 6, 1962, 221–32.

C. Braaten, 'Modern Interpretations of Nestorius', *Church History* 32, 1963, 251–67

R. A. Greer, 'The Image of God and the Prosopic Union in Nestorius', *Bazaar of Heraclides*', in *Lux in Lumine*. Essays to honor W. N. Pittenger, ed. R. A. Norris, New York 1966, 46–61.

A. Grillmeier, 'Zum Stand der Nestorius-Forschung', *Revue de Théologie et Philosophie* 41, 1966, 401–10.

A. van Roey, 'Two New Documents of the Nestorian Controversy', *StudPatr* 7, 1966, 308–13.

G. S. Bebis, 'The Apology of Nestorius: A New Evaluation', *StudPatr* 11, 1972, 107–12.

A. Ziegenhaus, 'Die Genesis des Nestorianismus', *Münchener Theologische Zeitschrift* 23, 1972, 335–53.

A. van Roey, 'Le florilège nestorien dans le Traité contre Nestorius de Théodote d'Ancyre', *StudPatr* 12, 1975, 155–9.

H. E. W. Turner, 'Nestorius Reconsidered', *StudPatr* 13, 1975, 306–21.

H. J. Vöght, 'Papst Coelestin und Nestorius', in *Konzil und Papst* für H. Tüchle, Munich 1975, 85–102.

R. C. Chesnut, 'The two *prosopa* in Nestorius', *Bazaar of Heraclides*, *JTS* NS 29, 1978, 392–409.

G. Jouassard, 'Le cas de Nestorius', *Revue d'Histoire Ecclésiastique* 74, 1979, 346–8.

5. Cyril of Alexandria

Texts

Deux dialogues christologiques, ed. G. M. de Durand (SC 97), 1964.

'The Letter of Cyril of Alexandria to Tiberius the Deacon. Syriac Version', ed. R. Y. Ebied and L. R. Wickham, *Le Muséon* 83, 433–82.

'An Unknown Letter of Cyril of Alexandria in Syriac', ed. R. Y. Ebied and L. R. Wickham, *JTS* NS 22, 1971, 420–43.

A Collection of Unpublished Syriac Letters of Cyril of Alexandria, ed. R. Y. Ebied and L. R. Wickham (CSCO 359–60), Louvain 1975.

Dialogues sur la Trinité I, II, III, ed. G. M. de Durand (SC 231, 237, 246), 1976–78.

Homilien und Briefe zum Konzil von Ephesos, ed. B. M. Weischer, Wiesbaden 1979. (=Qerellos IV.1: Aethiopic version. Other volumes published can be traced from this text if required.)

Books

C. Dratsellas, *Man in his Original State and the State of Sin according to St Cyril of Alexandria*, Athens 1971.

R. L. Wilken, *Judaism and the Early Christian Mind. A study of Cyril of Alexandria's exegesis and theology*, New Haven, Conn. 1971.

A. Vööbus, *Discoveries of Great Import on the Commentary on Luke by Cyril of Alexandria*, Stockholm 1973.

E. Gebremedhin, *Life-giving Blessing*. An Inquiry into the Eucharistic Doctrine of Cyril of Alexandria, Uppsala 1977.

J. Malley, *Hellenism and Christianity*. The Conflict between Hellenic and Christian Wisdom in the *Contra Galilaeos* of Julian the Apostate and the *Contra Iulianum* of St Cyril of Alexandria, Rome 1978.

Articles

A. Dupré La Tour, 'La δόξα du Christ dans les oeuvres exégétiques de Saint Cyrille d'Alexandrie', *RSR* 48, 1960, 521–43.

J. Meyendorff, 'Εφ'' ᾧ (Rom.5.12) chez Cyrille d'Alexandrie et Théodoret', *StudPatr* 4, 1961, 157–61.

G. Jouassard, 'Saint Cyrille d'Alexandrie aux prises avec la "communi-cation des idiomes" avant 428 dans ses ouvrages anti-ariens', *StudPatr* 6, 1962, 112–21.

R. M. Grant, 'Greek Literature in the Treatise *De Trinitate* and Cyril *Contra Iulianum*', *JTS* NS 15, 1964, 265–99.

J. S. Romanides, 'St Cyril's "One physis or hypostasis of God the Logos incarnate" and Chalcedon', *Greek Orthodox Theological Review* 10, 1964/5, 82–107. (This issue of the review was devoted to a number of relevant articles of varying quality.)

M. Richard, 'Deux lettres perdues de Cyrille d'Alexandrie' *StudPatr* 7, 1966, 274–77.

R. L. Wilken, 'Exegesis and the History of Theology: Reflections on the Adam–Christ Typology in Cyril of Alexandria', *Church History* 35, 1966, 139–56.

B. M. Weischer, 'Der Dialog "Dass Christus Einer ist" des Cyrill von Alexandrien', *Oriens Christianus* 51, 1967, 130–85.

F. M. Young, 'Christological Ideas in the Greek Commentaries on the Epistle to the Hebrews', *JTS* NS 20, 1969, 150–63.

J. Liébaert, 'L'évolution de la christologie de S. Cyrille d'Alexandrie à partir de la controverse nestorienne. La lettre paschale XVII et la lettre aux Moines (428–9)', *Mélanges de Science Religieuse* 27, 1970, 27–48.

G. Langgärtner, 'Der Descensus ad inferos in den Osterbriefen des Cyrill von Alexandrien', in *Wegzeichen*. Festgabe H. M. Budermann, Würzburg 1971, 95–100.

M. Santer, ''Εκ πνεύματος ἁγίου καὶ Μαρίας τῆς παρθένου' *JTS* NS 22, 1971, 162–71.

F. M. Young, 'A Reconsideration of Alexandrian Christology', *JEH* 22, 1971, 103–14.

M. Aubineau, 'Deux homélies de Cyrille d'Alexandrie', *Analecta Bollandiana* 90, 1972, 100.

E. P. Meijering, 'Cyril of Alexandria on the Platonists and the Trinity', *Nederlands Theologisch Tijdschrift* 27, 1974, 16–29, reprinted in his *God Being History*, Amsterdam 1975, 114–27.

— 'Some Reflections on Cyril of Alexandria's Rejection of An-thropomorphism' *Nederlands Theologisch Tijdschrift* 28, 1974, 297–301, reprinted ibid., 128–32.

R. A. Norris, 'Christological Models in Cyril of Alexandria', *StudPatr* 13, 1975, 255–68.

P. M. Parvis, 'The *Commentary on Hebrews* and the *Contra Theodorum* of Cyril of Alexandria', *JTS* NS 26, 1975, 415–9.

M. Santer, 'The Authorship and Occasion of Cyril of Alexandria's Sermon on the Virgin (Hom. Div. IV)', *StudPatr* 12, 1975 144–50.

J. Reuss, 'Bemerkungen zu den Lukas-Homilien des Titus von Bostra', *Biblica* 57, 1976, 538–41.

T. F. Torrance, 'The Mind of Christ in Worship: The Problem of Apollinarianism in the Liturgy' in his *Theology in Reconstruction*, London 1975, 139–215.

G. Jouassard, 'La date des écrits anti-ariens de S.Cyrille d'Alexandrie', *Revue Bénédictine* 87, 1977, 172–8.

J. D. McCoy, 'Philosophical Influences on the Doctrine of the Incarnation in Athanasius and Cyril of Alexandria', *Encounter* (Indianapolis) 38, 1977, 362–91.

J. M. Labelle, 'Saint Cyrille d'Alexandrie', *Revue des Sciences Religieuses* 52, 1978, 135–58; 53, 1979, 23–42.

S. Gero, 'Cyril of Alexandria, Image Worship and the Vita of Rabban Hormizd', *Oriens Christianus* 62, 1978, 77–97.

A. de Halleux, 'Cyrille, Théodoret et le "Filioque"', *Revue d'Histoire Ecclésiastique* 74, 1979, 597–625.

B. de Margerie, 'L'exégèse christologique de saint Cyrille d'Alexandrie', *Nouvelle Revue Théologique* 102, 1980, 400–25.

6. Theodoret of Cyrrhus

Texts and translations

Correspondance, ed. Y. Azema, I-LII (SC 40), 1955; 1–95 (SC 98), 1964; 96–147 (SC 111), 1965.

Eranistes, ed. G. Ettlinger, Oxford 1975.

Theodoreti Cyrensis Quaestiones in Octateuchum, ed. W. F. Mardos and A. Saenz-Badillos, Madrid 1979.

Histoire des moines de Syrie, ed. P. Canivet and A. Leroy-Molinghen, 2 vols. (SC 234,257), 1977, 1979.

Ecclesiastical History, Eranistes, Letters, NPNF II.III reprinted 1979.

Commentaire sur Isaïe I, ed. J.-N. Guinot (SC 276), 1980.

J. Lebon, *Le moine Saint Marcien*: étude critique des sources; édition de ses écrits, Louvain 1968 (the sources include Theodoret).

Books

P. Canivet, *Théodoret et le monachisme syrien avant le concile de Chalcédoine*, Paris 1961.

P. Naaman, *Théodoret de Cyr et le monastère de saint Maroun; les origines des Maronites*, Beyrouth 1971.

G. W. Ashby, *Theodoret of Cyrrhus as exegete of the Old Testament*, Grahamstown 1972.

G. Koch, *Strukturen und Geschichte des Heils in der Theologie des Theodoret von Cyrus*, Frankfurt 1974.

P. Canivet, *Le monachisme syrien selon Théodoret de Cyr*, Paris 1977.

Articles

P. Canivet, 'Théodoret et le monachisme syrien avant le concile de Chalcédoine', in *Théologie de la vie monastique. Études sur la tradition patristique*, Paris 1961, 241–82.

— 'Théodoret et le Messalienisme', *Revue Mabillon* 51, 1961, 26–34.

A. Leroy-Molinghen, 'Les manuscrits de *l'Histoire Philothée* de Théodoret de Cyr', *Byzantion* 34, 1964, 27–47.

— 'A propos de la Vie de Syméon Stylite (Théodoret de Cyr, *Histoire*

Philothée 26)', *Byzantion* 34, 1964, 375–84.

— 'De quelques abrégés et recueils d'extraits de l'*Histoire Philothée*', *Byzantion* 35, 1965, 601–5.

P. Canivet, 'Le περὶ 'Αγάπης de Théodoret de Cyr postface de l'*Histoire Philothée*', *StudPatr* 7, 1966, 143–58.

A. Adnès and P. Canivet, 'Guérisons miraculeuses et exorcismes dans l'*Histoire Philothée* de Théodoret de Cyr', *Revue de l'Histoire des Religions* 171, 1967, 53–82, 149–79.

G. W. Ashby, 'Theodoret of Cyrrhus on Marriage', *Theology* 72, 1969, 482–91.

P. Canivet, 'Catégories sociales et titulaire laïque et ecclésiastique dans l'*Histoire Philothée* de Théodoret de Cyr', *Byzantion* 39, 1969, 209–50.

F. M. Young, 'Christological Ideas in the Greek Commentaries on the Epistle to the Hebrews', *JTS* NS 20, 1969, 150–63.

F. D. Gillard, 'Theodoretus, *Historia Ecclesiastica* 4.9.5', *Byzantinische Zeitschrift* 63, 1970, 283 f.

M. Mandac, 'L'union christologique dans les oeuvres de Théodoret antérieures au concile d'Ephèse', *Ephemerides Theologicae Lovanienses* 47, 1971, 64–96.

P. Canivet, 'L'Apôtre Pierre dans les écrits de Théodoret de Cyr', in *Epektasis*. Mélanges patristiques offerts au Cardinal J. Daniélou, ed. J. Fontaine and C. Kannengiesser, Paris 1972, 29–46.

A. Leroy-Molinghen, 'A propos du texte de "l'Histoire Philothée" de Theodoret de Cyr', in *Zetesis*. Album amicorum Prof. Dr. E. de Strycker, Utrecht 1973, 732–5.

G. Ettlinger, 'Some Problems Encountered in Editing Patristic Texts, with Special Reference to the *Eranistes* of Theodoret of Cyrus', *StudPatr* 12, 1975, 25–29.

P. Canivet, 'Contributions archéologiques à l'histoire des moines de Syrie (4e–5[e]sc.) A propos l'*Histoire Philothée* de Théodoret (444 env.)', *StudPatr* 13, 1975, 444–60.

Paul Devos, 'La structure de l'*Histoire Philothée* de Théodoret de Cyr. Le nombre de chapitres', *Analecta Bollandiana* 97, 1979, 319–36.

F. Petit, 'La tradition de Théodoret de Cyr dans les chaînes sur la Genèse', *Le Muséon* 92, 1979, 281–86.

G. F. Chesnut, 'The Date of Composition of Theodoret's *Church History*, *VC* 35, 1981, 245–52.

Supplementary list of texts and critical aids
announced as in press or in preparation

1. *Athanasius*
Commentary on the Psalms, G. M. Vian (Patristic Institute of Rome).
Lettres à Serapion (SC 15), 2nd ed.

2. *Didymus the Blind*
The publication of the Tura Papyri continues in *Papyrologische Texte und Abhandlungen* (Bonn).

3. *Basil the Great*

P. J. Fedwick, *Basil of Caesarea: A Comprehensive Guide to All the Manuscripts, Ancient Testimonia and Quotations, Editions, Translations and Studies of his Works*, Toronto: Pontifical Institute for Medieval Studies.
Homilien zum Hexaemeron, ed. E. Amand de Mendieta and S. Y. Rudberg (GCS).

4. *Gregory of Nazianzus*

Carmina, ed. M. Sicherl, *Corpus Christianorum. Series Graeca.*
Orationes, ed. J. Mossay (ibid.).
Discours 24–6, ed. J. Mossay (SC).

5. Gregory of Nyssa

Gregorii Nysseni Opera (the Jaeger edition): Vol. X.1 has been announced.
A Lexicon Gregorianum is planned as a conclusion to the series.
La création de l'homme (SC 6), 2nd edition.
Forthcoming: *Bibliographie zu Gregor von Nyssa*. Leiden: Brill.

6. *Epiphanius von Salamis*

GCS vol. III is being revised by J. Dummer.

7. *John Chrysostom*

De Sancta Babyla contra Iulianum et Gentiles, ed. M. Schatkin (SC).
De Laudibus Pauli, ed. A. Piédagnel (SC).
In Corpus Christianorum. Series Graeca:
   Commentarii in Proverbia, ed. M. Richard and H. Hennephof
   Commentarii in Actus Apostolorum, ed. F. Gignac.
Editions of the following are promised: *In Job*, ed. H. Sorlin; *Ad Stagiram*, ed. C. Fabricius; *De Incomprehensibili Hom. vii–xii*, ed. A-M.Malingrey; and *De Fato et Providentia*, ed. F. Bonnière.

8. *Cyril of Alexandria*

Commentarii in Iohannem, ed. A. Heitlinger (*Corpus Christianorum. Series Graeca*).
Anti-Nestorian Treatises; Letters (Fathers of the Church).

9. *Theodoret of Cyrrhus*

Eranistes (Fathers of the Church).

10. *Biblia Patristica*

Index des citations et allusions bibliques dans la littérature patristiques (published so far: Vols. I–II covering 1st–3rd centuries excluding Origen).

Index of Subjects

Select Index of Greek Words